Here's What the Experts
the *PowerBoat Guide...*

MW00604994

"The PowerBoat Guide is an invaluable source of layout and performance information and an absolute must for the boat buyer."
Dave Gilman, Gilman Yachts, Palm Beach, FL

"Congratulations on publishing the *PowerBoat Guide*. Our brokers feel this is a valuable tool. We consider it indispensable in our four West Coast offices."
David Fraser, David Fraser Yachts, Newport Beach, CA

"I find the *PowerBoat Guide* to be well researched, accurate and very informative. I'm happy to endorse this product without reservation and look forward to future editions."
Arthur DeFever, Naval Architect, San Diego, CA

"Our brokers always recommend the *PowerBoat Guide* to clients whenever they're uncertain about what they're looking for in a boat. It makes buyers a lot more knowledgeable about the different models and saves us all a lot of time."
Bill Thompson, The Marine Group, Palm Beach Gardens, FL

"The *PowerBoat Guide* has proven to be a valuable tool for the boat sales business. We use it daily to help us with customers as well as to prepare accurate specification sheets. The information regarding performance and layouts has been particularly useful."
Jeff Boger, Berry-Boger Yacht Sales, N. Myrtle Beach, SC

"As Chairman of the Society of Accredited Marine Surveyors (SAMS), I know surveyors well and they seldom agree on anything. Yet it seems that every one of them has a well-worn copy of the *PowerBoat Guide* and they all agree that it's an extremely valuable publication."
Mickey Strocchi, Chairman SAMS, Jacksonville, FL

"I just wanted to tell you how much we value the *PowerBoat Guide* here in Seattle. We have ten brokers and they each refer to it on a daily basis. It has been a wealth of information for us."
Jerry Schei, Western Yacht Sales, Seattle, WA

"Impressive. This is an absolutely first-rate piece of research. I am not surprised that the *PowerBoat Guide* has quickly become an industry standard."
John Slaven, John B. Slaven, Inc., Mt. Clemens, MI

"I've found the *PowerBoat Guide* especially helpful for clients who are unsure of exactly what they want in a boat. It's a great time-saver."
Bill Kimball, Rybovich Spencer Yacht Sales, West Palm Beach, FL

"I'm glad to see someone finally took the initiative to do this and I'm looking forward to the 3rd edition. The book is excellent and we use it all the time. Please keep us on your mailing list."
Whit Kirkland, Merrill-Stevens Yachts, Miami, FL

"This should be a very useful and informative book for yacht lovers, boat owners and prospective buyers everywhere."
Jack Hargrave, Naval Architect, West Palm Beach, FL

"We have several *PowerBoat Guides* in our office and they are in constant use by our brokers and their clients. It's an absolute must on every yacht broker's desk."
Frank Gordon, Frank Gordon Yacht Sales, Ft. Lauderdale, FL

"It's about time! For years I've searched brochures and magazines and gone through the entire paper chase. Now I have an accurate reference source which saves me time from the inevitable search for information."
Chuck Kotovic, Emerald Yacht & Ship Brokers, Milwaukee, WI

"All of our brokers are in agreement regarding the importance of the *PowerBoat Guide*. The profiles and layouts included for each boat give our clients the total picture of a particular model and narrows down the selection process. We look forward to seeing the next edition soon."
Jim Winch, Bradford International, Ft. Lauderdale, FL

"As a marine surveyor, I am always interested in background information on all makes and models of boats. The *PowerBoat Guide* has given me a comprehensive source of reference with an easy-to-use format. Thank you for your valuable contribution to the boating industry."
Gerald Slakoff, Marine Surveyor, Ft. Lauderdale, FL

"Thank you for publishing the *PowerBoat Guide*. It has been a very valuable tool in my brokerage office and we recommend it without hesitation to hundreds of our clients."
Norm Clavio, Class Sea Yachts, Barrington, IL

3rd Edition

POWERBOAT GUIDE

Mark Parker and Ed McKnew

International Marine
Camden, Maine

in cooperation with

American Marine Publishing

COVER PHOTO: Hatteras 67 Cockpit MY

PUBLISHED BY:
International Marine
A Division of McGraw-Hill, Inc.
Blue Ridge Summit, PA 17294
1-800-822-8158

In cooperation with:

American Marine Publishing, Inc.
P.O. Box 30577
Palm Beach Gardens, FL 33420-0577
1-800-832-0038

ISBN O-8774236-0-1

Printed in the United States of America

M 10 9 8 7 6 5 4 3

CONTENTS

CROSS REFERENCE INDEX

Before concluding that a specific model is not included in the PowerBoat Guide, be sure to consult this Cross Reference Index. This is particularly true with Taiwan boats — they are often imported under different names and identification can be difficult. Many other boats have had more than one name (or more than one builder) and a lot of Motor Yacht and Cockpit Motor Yacht models (basically the same boat) have been combined on a single page for brevity.

LOOKING FOR: **GO TO:**

INTRODUCTION

The PowerBoat Guide is written to satisfy the need of consumers and marine industry professionals for a dependable source of information on inboard powerboats. Over 850 of the most popular models are featured in these pages, including motor yachts, trawlers, convertibles, sportfishermen and express cruisers. In addition to factory photos and complete specifications, each page contains such hard-to-find data as model updates, performance figures and production history. Throughout, it has been the objective of the authors to provide a comprehensive and reliable reference guide of significant value to the user.

The book is divided by manufacturer into 42 chapters with the final Notable Designs section presenting the products of smaller builders or those who produce only a few inboard models. (Whenever we select five or more models from the same builder we create a separate chapter under the manufacturer's name.) A special effort has been made to include data on popular Asian boats as well as specialty designs aimed primarily at regional markets. It has not been the intention of the authors to include every inboard model ever built; rather, selections were made on the basis of relative popularity as judged by the authors. In general, if a production model is likely to be found on the nation's new or used boat markets an effort has been made on our part to include it in the appropriate chapter. The fact that a particular model is not included in these pages should not be construed in a negative context. In some cases the manufacturer or importer was unable (or sometimes unwilling) to provide the necessary information. In others — especially true with out-of-production designs or boats from manufacturers long out of business — the data required was simply unavailable to us.

We have added a new feature this year — Index Listings for yacht brokers and dealers, and a similar Index for surveyors. These companies are seeking your business and we hope you will contact them when you require their services.

The first-time reader will discover that the authors' opinions are sometimes freely expressed. Advertising hype notwithstanding, some boats are simply better than others and those that stand out at either extreme are occasionally noted. No attempt has been made to maliciously abuse a particular model, and the comments expressed reflect only the authors' opinions. As always, the services of a competent marine professional are strongly recommended in the sale or purchase of any boat.

The following details should be kept in mind when using the PowerBoat Guide:

❏ Whenever possible, performance figures have been obtained from the manufacturer or a reliable dealer or broker. When such information was unavailable (or when builders refused to provide it), the authors have relied upon their own research together with hands-on experience. The speeds are estimates and in most cases are based on boats with average cruising or fishing equipment.

❏ Where there are two floorplans, if one is later than another the more recent layout is on the bottom.

❑ Speeds are always given in knots, and distances are measured in nautical miles. To convert knots to miles per hour (or nautical miles to statute miles), multiply by 1.14.

❑ Unless otherwise noted, the cruising speed for gas-powered boats is calculated at 3000–3200 rpm.

❑ The cruising speed for diesel-powered boats is calculated as follows:
Detroit (2-stroke) Diesels — 200; 250 rpm below maximum rpm rating
Other (4-stroke) diesels — 300; 400 rpm below maximum rpm rating

❑ In the Specifications Box:
"LWL" is the length of the hull at the waterline.
"Clearance" refers to bridge clearance, or height above the waterline including an arch if the boat has one.
"Designer" refers to the designer of the hull only, and may or may not refer to the designer of the superstructure and/or interior.
"NA" means not available.

The contents of this third edition represent the culmination of over six years of intensive research, evaluation, lost income and writing. Nevertheless, the authors recognize that some inaccuracies are bound to occur in a publication of this size. Readers who detect errors — or who disagree with the opinions expressed — are invited to bring their comments to the attention of the authors. We genuinely welcome such criticisms and comments and we're always quick to make corrections and revisions when necessary.

Finally, the authors wish to thank the following individuals without whose help and generous assistance this book would not have been possible. They are largely responsible for the success this book enjoys today:

Floyd Appling, Jr
Bill Burgstiner
Steve & Delores Brown
Dave & Judy Calhoun
Top & Sandy Cornell
George & Helene Gereke
Edward & Betty Groth

USEFUL TERMS

Abaft - behind

Athwartships - at a right angle to the boat's length

Bulkhead - an upright partition separating compartments in a boat

Bulwark - a raised portion of the deck designed to serve as a barrier

Chine - the point at which the hullsides and the bottom of the boat come together

CID - referring to the cubic inch displacement of an engine

Coaming - vertical surface surrounding the cockpit

Cuddy - generally refers to the cabin of a small boat

Deadrise - the angle from the bottom of the hull (not the keel) to the chine

Deep-V Hull - a planing hull form with at least 18° of constant deadrise

Displacement Hull - a hull designed to go through the water and not capable of planing speed

Forefoot - the underwater shape of the hull at the bow

Freeboard - the height of the sides of the boat above the waterline

GPH - gallons per hour (of fuel consumption)

Gunwale - (also gunnel) the upper edge of the sheerline

Hull Speed - the maximum practical speed of a displacement hull. To calculate, take the square root of the LWL and multiply by 1.34.

Knot - one nautical mile per hour. To convert knots to statute mph, multiply by 1.14.

Modified-V Hull - a planing hull form with less than 17° of transom deadrise

Nautical Mile - measurement used in salt water. A nautical mile is 6,076 feet.

Planing Speed - the point at which an accelerating hull rises onto the top of the water. To calculate a hull's planing speed, multiply the square root of the waterline length by 2.

Semi-Displacement Hull - a hull designed to operate economically at low speeds while still able to attain efficient planing speed performance

Sheerline - the fore and aft line along the top edge of the hull

Sole - a nautical term for floor

Statute Mile - measurement used in fresh water. A statute mile equals 5,280 feet.

Tender - refers to (a) a dinghy, or (b) lack of stability

WOT - wide open throttle

YACHT BROKER & DEALER INDEX

ALABAMA

KV Yacht Brokerage
PO Box 292 (Zeke's Landing Marina)
Orange Beach, AL 36561
205-981-4300; Fax 205-981-4304
Brokerage, In-Water Display

Marine Group, Inc.
PO Box 650
Orange Beach, AL 36561
205-981-9200; Fax 205-981-9137
New Boats, Brokerage

A&M Yacht Sales
5004 Dauphin Island Pkwy.
Mobile, AL 36605
205-471-6949; Fax 205-479-4625
New Boats, Brokerage

Mobile Hatteras
5004 Dauphin Island Pkwy.
Mobile, AL 36605
205-471-6949; Fax 205-479-4625
New Boats

Bay Yacht Sales
4960 Dauphin Island Pkwy.
Mobile, AL 36605
205-476-8306; Fax 205-473-3802
New Boats, Brokerage

CALIFORNIA

Executive Yacht Management Inc.
646-A Venice Blvd.
Marina Del Rey, CA 90291
310-306-2555
Brokerage

California Yacht Sales
2020 Harbor Island Drive
San Diego, CA 92101
619-295-9669; Fax 619-295-9909
New Boats

DeFever Yacht & Ship Brokerage
2730 Shelter Island Dr.
San Diego, CA 92106
619-222-2414; Fax 619-225-0930
New Boats, Brokerage

Mikelson Yachts
2330 Shelter Island Dr., #202
San Diego, CA 92106
619-222-5007; Fax 619-223-1194
New Boats

R.D. Snyder Yacht Sales
1231 Shafter St.
San Diego, CA 92106
619-224-2464; Fax 619-224-7396
Brokerage

Fraser Yachts
3471 Via Lido #200
Newport Beach, CA 92263
714-673-5252; Fax 714-673-8795
New Boats, Brokerage

Ardell Yacht & Ship Brokers
2101 W. Coast Hwy
Newport Beach, CA 92663
714-642-5735; Fax 714-642-9884
Brokerage

Falmouth Yachts
510 31st St., Suite D
Newport Beach, CA 92663
714-723-4225; Fax 714-723-4093
New Boats

Executive Yacht & Ship Brokers
3205 S. Victoria
Oxnard, CA 93035
805-984-1004; Fax 805-985-4365
Brokerage

D'Anna Yacht Center
11 Embarcadero West, #100
Oakland, CA 94607
510-451-7000; Fax 510-451-7026
New Boats, Brokerage

CONNECTICUT

Randall Yacht Sales
145 S. Montowese St.
Branford, CT 06405
203-481-3866; Fax 203-481-8699
Brokerage

Essex Island Yachts, Ltd.
Foot of Ferry St., Essex Island Marina
Essex, CT 06426
203-767-8645; Fax 203-767-0075
Brokerage

Storm Haven Yachts
PO Box 85
Newtown, CT 06470-0085
203-426-0806
Brokerage

Don Zak's Shoreline Yacht Sales
54 Ferry Road
Old Saybrook, CT 06475
203-395-0866; Fax 203-395-0877
New Boats, Brokerage

FLORIDA

Offshore Yacht & Ship Brokers
256-B Riberia St.
St. Augustine, FL 32084
904-829-9224; Fax 904-825-4292
New Boats, Brokerage

First Coast Yacht Sales
103 Yacht Club Dr.
St. Augustine, FL 32095
904-824-7293; Fax 904-829-6779
Brokerage

Daytona Marina & Boatworks
645 South Beach St.
Daytona Beach, FL 32114
904-253-6266; Fax 904-253-8174
Brokerage

Yacht Brokerage USA
3948 S. Peninsula Dr.
Daytona Beach, FL 32127
904-760-9353
Brokerage

Ortega River Boat Yard
4451 Herschel St.
Jacksonville, FL 32210
904-387-5538; Fax 904-388-7476
Brokerage

Cape Yacht Brokerage
800 Scallop Dr.
Port Canaveral, FL 32920
407-799-4724; Fax 407-799-0096
Brokerage

Yacht Brokerage USA
613 Rockledge Dr.
Rockledge, FL 32955
407-636-3600; Fax 407-636-3606
Brokerage

HMY Yacht Sales
850 NE 3rd. St. (Harbour Towne Marina)
Dania, FL 33004
305-926-0400; Fax 305-921-2543
New Boats, Brokerage

ZK Marine
1000 NE 3rd St. (Harbour Towne Marina)
Dania, FL 33004
305-923-7441; Fax 305-923-7477
New Boats, Brokerage

Rhodes Yacht Brokers
2901 NE 28th Court
Lighthouse Point, FL 33064
305-941-2404; Fax 305-941-2507
Brokerage

Universal Yachts, Inc.
916 E. Sample Rd.
Pompano Beach, FL 33064
305-786-2911; Fax 305-786-1937
Brokerage

Hatteras in Miami
2550 S. Bayshore Dr.
Coconut Grove, FL 33133
305-854-1100; Fax 305-854-1186
New Boats, Brokerage

Merrill-Stevens Yacht Sales
2701 S. Bayshore Dr., #605
Miami, FL 33133
305-858-5911; Fax 305-858-5919
Brokerage

Florida Yacht Charters & Sales
1290 Fifth Street
Miami Beach, FL 33139
305-532-8600; Fax 305-672-2039
New Boats, Brokerage

Blake Davis Yacht Brokerage
7601 E. Treasure Dr.
North Bay Village, FL 33141
305-866-8329
Brokerage

Custom Brokerage Yacht Sales
11422 SW 87th Terrace
Miami, FL 33173
305-598-9875; Fax 305-598-2239
Brokerage

Northrop & Johnson
3575 NE 207th St., #B-16
Adventura, FL 33180
305-933-3344; Fax 305-933-3523
New Boats, Brokerage

Hatteras of Lauderdale
401 SW 1st Ave.
Ft. Lauderdale, FL 33301
305-462-5557; Fax 305-462-0029
New Boats, Brokerage

Yacht Brokerage USA
1700 E. Los Olas Blvd., Suite 101
Ft. Lauderdale, FL 33301
305-463-1255; Fax 305-463-7733
Brokerage

Four Points Yacht & Ship Brokers
915 Middle River Dr., #516
Ft. Lauderdale, FL 33304
305-568-2200; Fax 305-561-3192
New Boats, Brokerage

Sea Yachts, Inc.
837 NE 20th Ave.
Ft. Lauderdale, FL 33304
305-522-0993; Fax 305-768-9027
New Boats, Brokerage

Marine Unlimited, Inc.
232 Basin Dr.
Lauderdale-By-The-Sea, FL 33308
305-491-0430; Fax 305-771-6122
Brokerage

Oceanus Institute, Inc.
4332 E. Tradewinds Ave.
Lauderdale-By-The-Sea, FL 33308
305-772-5773
Brokerage

Tom Klein Yacht
5200 N. Federal Hwy., Suite 2
Ft. Lauderdale, FL 33308
305-772-7070; Fax 305-772-7086
Brokerage

Bradford International
3151 State Road 84
Ft. Lauderdale, FL 33312
305-791-2600; Fax 305-791-2655
New Boats, Brokerage

Castlemain, Inc.
300 SW 2nd Ave., Suite 4
Ft. Lauderdale, FL 33312
305-760-4730; Fax 305-760-4737
New Boats, Brokerage

Classic Yacht Sales
2945 State Rd. 84
Ft. Lauderdale, FL 33312
305-584-3440; Fax 305-583-3083
New Boats, Brokerage

Jackson Marine Sales
1915 SW 21st Ave.
Ft. Lauderdale, FL 33312
305-792-4900; Fax 305-587-8164
New Boats, Brokerage

Yacht Search - The Professional
Brokerage
2150 SE 17th St.
Ft. Lauderdale, FL 33315
305-524-1823; Fax 305-525-3074
Brokerage

Alexander Yachts, Inc.
2150 SE 17th St., Suite 201
Ft. Lauderdale, FL 33316
305-763-7676; Fax 305-763-7758
New Boats, Brokerage

American Trading Industries
500 SE 17th St., #220
Ft. Lauderdale, FL 33316
305-522-4254; Fax 305-522-4435
New Boats, Brokerage

Atlantic Pacific Sailing Yachts
2244 SE 17th St.
Ft. Lauderdale, FL 33316
305-463-7651; Fax 305-779-3316
New Boats, Brokerage

Bollman Yachts
2046 SE 17th St.
Ft. Lauderdale, FL 33316
305-761-1122; Fax 305-463-9878
Brokerage

Bruce A. Bales Yacht Sales
1635 S. Miami Rd., #2
Ft. Lauderdale, FL 33316
305-522-3760; Fax 305-522-4364
Brokerage

Dave D'Onofrio Yacht Sales, Inc.
1875 SE 17th St. (Marriott Marina)
Ft. Lauderdale, FL 33316
305-527-4848; Fax 305-462-6817
New Boats, Brokerage

Frank Gordon Yacht Sales
801 Seabreeze Blvd. (Bahia Mar Yachting
Ctr.)
Ft. Lauderdale, FL 33316
305-525-8476; 305-525-6024
Brokerage

Garcia Yacht Sales
1323 SE 17 St, #220
Ft Lauderdale, FL 33316
305-763-6152; Fax 305-763-6152
Brokerage

High-Tech Marine
1535 SE 17th St. Quay
Ft. Lauderdale, FL 33316
305-524-6911; Fax 305-524-7107
New Boats, Brokerage

Jet Sea Yacht Brokerage
1650 SE 17th St., #204
Ft. Lauderdale, FL 33316
305-766-2600; Fax 305-766-2611
New Boats, Brokerage

Merritt Yacht Brokers
2040 SE 17th St.
Ft. Lauderdale, FL 33316
305-761-1300; Fax 305-463-8617
Brokerage

Peter Kehoe & Associates
2150 SE 17th St., #107
Ft. Lauderdale, FL 33316
305-767-9880; Fax 305-767-9884
Brokerage

Royce Yacht & Ship Brokers
1600 SE 17th St., #418
Ft. Lauderdale, FL 33316
305-764-0100; Fax 305-764-0192
Brokerage

Trans-Coastal Yacht Brokerage
515 Seabreeze Blvd.
Ft. Lauderdale, FL 33316
305-767-8830; Fax 305-767-8942
Brokerage

Walsh Yachts Inc.
1900 S.E. 15th Street
Ft. Lauderdale, FL 33316
305-525-7447; Fax 305-525-7451
New Boats, Brokerage

Woods & Oviatt
Pier 66 Marina, 2301 SE 17th St.
Ft. Lauderdale, FL 33316
305-463-5606; Fax 305-522-5156
New Boats, Brokerage

Yacht & Ship Sales, Inc.
2501 S. Federal Hwy.
Ft. Lauderdale, FL 33316
305-779-7447; Fax 305-779-3735
Brokerage

J. Woods Marine Group
808 NE 20th Ave.
Ft. Lauderdale, FL 333304
305-764-8770; Fax 305-764-8771
Brokerage

Palm Beach Yacht Club Brokerage
800 N. Flagler Dr.
West Palm Beach, FL 33401
407-833-8633; Fax 407-833-8639
New Boats, Brokerage

Rybovich-Spencer Group
4200 N. Dixie
West Palm Beach, FL 33407
407-844-4331; Fax 407-844-8393
New Boats, Brokerage

Island Yacht Sales Of Palm Beach
1000 US Hwy 1
North Palm Beach, FL 33408
407-627-5001; Fax 407-627-0528
Brokerage

Hatteras in Palm Beach
2410 PGA Blvd., #155
Palm Beach Gardens, FL 33410
407-775-3531; Fax 407-775-8790
New Boats, Brokerage

The Marine Group
2401 PGA Blvd., Suite 104
Palm Beach Gardens, FL 33410
407-627-9500; Fax 407-627-9503
Brokerage

O'Brien Yacht Sales
3010 SW 14th Place
Boynton Beach, FL 33426
407-738-6676; Fax 407-738-1658
Brokerage

South Florida Marine Sales
3283 Harrington Dr.
Boca Raton, FL 33496
407-750-5155; Fax 407-750-8533
Brokerage

Capt. Jack's Yacht Brokerage
101 - 16th Ave. South
St. Petersburg, FL 33701
813-825-0757; Fax 813-822-6415
Brokerage

Great American Boat Yards
6810 Gulfport Blvd.
St. Petersburg, FL 33707
813-384-3428; Fax 813-381-1401
New Boats, Brokerage

Bob Anslow Yacht Sales, Inc.
4554 Central Ave. Suite M
St. Petersburg, FL 33711
813-327-1617; Fax 813-323-3042
Brokerage

West Florida Yachts
4880 - 37th St. South
St. Petersburg, FL 33711
813-864-0310; Fax 813-867-6860
Brokerage

Royal Yacht & Ship Brokers
3859 Central Ave.
St. Petersburg, FL 33713
813-327-0900; Fax 813-327-7797
New Boats, Brokerage

Yacht Brokerage USA
4401 Central Ave.
St. Petersburg, FL 33713-8232
813-328-1255; Fax 813-328-1796
Brokerage

Anchor Yachts International
1110 Pinellas Bayway Dr.
St. Petersburg, FL 33715
813-867-8027; Fax 813-864-1359
Brokerage

Great American Boat Yards
1310 Lee Street
Ft. Meyers, FL 33901
813-334-8622; Fax 813-334-0207
New Boats, Brokerage

Yacht Brokerage USA
1700 Medical Lane
Ft. Myers, FL 33907
813-936-5595; Fax 813-936-0544
Brokerage

Yacht-Eng, Inc.
13601 McGregor Blvd., #16
Ft. Myers, FL 33919
813-481-3511; Fax 813-481-3064
Brokerage

Bain Yacht Sales
1200 E. Retta Espanade
Punta Gorda, FL 33950
813-637-1335; Fax 813-637-8057
Brokerage

Yacht Perfection Inc.
1601 W. Marion Ave #203 D
Punta Gorda, FL 33950
813-637-8111; Fax 813-637-9918
Brokerage

Yacht Brokerage USA
4110 127th St. West
Cortez, FL 34215
813-792-9100; Fax 813-794-6922
Brokerage

Modern Classic Yachtworks, Inc.
1666 Main St.
Sarasota, FL 34236
813-955-7733; 813-957-3132
Brokerage

Yacht Registry
343 Causeway Blvd.
Dunedin, FL 34698
813-733-0334; Fax 813-733-6754
Brokerage

East-West Yachts
10 Avenue A, Ft. Pierce Yacht Ctr.
Ft. Pierce, FL 34950
407-466-1240; Fax 407-466-1242
Brokerage

East-West Yachts
1405 NE Indian River Dr.
Jensen Beach, FL 34957
407-287-9192; Fax 407-283-6629
Brokerage

Taber Yacht Sales
Pirates Cove Marina, Box 1687
Port Salerno, FL 34992
407-288-7466; 407-288-7476
New Boats, Brokerage

Stuart Hatteras
110 N. Federal Hwy
Stuart, FL 34994
407-692-1122; Fax 407-692-1341
New Boats, Brokerage

GEORGIA

Robert P. Minis
102 McIntosh Dr.
Savannah, GA 31406
912-354-6589
Brokerage

ILLINOIS

Class Sea Yachts
207 N. Hager
Barrington, IL 60010
708-382-2100; Fax 708-381-1265
Brokerage

INDIANA

H&M Yacht Brokerage
1 Newport Dr.
Michigan City, IN 46360
219-879-7152
Brokerage

LOUISIANA

A&M Yacht Sales/New Orleans Hatteras
126 South Roadway
New Orleans, LA 70124
504-282-6800
New Boats, Brokerage

Flagship Marine
6701C S. Shore Harbor Blvd.
New Orleans, LA 70126
504-242-9000; Fax 504-246-3908
New Boats, Brokerage

MAINE

Midcoast Yacht Sales
Kehail Point, Box 221
Westport, ME 04578
207-882-6445; Fax 207-882-4250
Brokerage

MARYLAND

Arnold C. Gay Yacht Sales
"C" Street, Box 538
Solomons, MD 20688
410-326-2011; Fax 410-326-2012
New Boats, Brokerage

Solomons Yacht Brokerage
PO Box 380, 255 "A" Street
Solomons, MD 20688
410-326-6748; Fax 410-326-2149
Brokerage

Anchor Bay Yacht Sales
202 Nanticoke Rd.
Essex, MD 21221
410-574-0777; Fax 410-574-8364
Brokerage

Yacht Net, Ltd.
1912 Forest Dr.
Annapolis, MD 21401
410-263-0993; Fax 410-267-7967
Brokerage

Gemini Marine Group Inc.
326 1st. Street, #32
Annapolis, MD 21403
410-267-0377; Fax 410-267-6127
New Boats, Brokerage

Interyacht, Inc.
318 Sixth Street
Annapolis, MD 21403
301-269-5200; Fax 301-269-0571
Brokerage

Martin Bird & Associates
326 First St.
Annapolis, MD 21403
301-268-1086; Fax 301-268-0942
Brokerage

Annapolis Motor Yachts
P.O. Box 2193
Annapolis, MD 21404
301-268-7171; Fax 301-268-6921
Brokerage

William Magness Yachts
207 Tackle Circle
Chester, MD 21619
301-643-8434; Fax 301-643-8437
Brokerage

Chesapeake Motoryacht Sales
Tilghman St. at Town Creek, Box 417
Oxford, MD 21654
410-226-0002; Fax 410-226-5699
New Boats, Brokerage

Maryland Yachts, Inc.
PO Box 216
Oxford, MD 21654
410-226-5571; Fax 410-226-5080
New Boats, Brokerage

Warehouse Creek Yacht Sales
301 Pier One Rd.
Stevenville, MD 21666
410-643-7878; Fax 410-643-7877
Brokerage

Jackson Marine Sales Inc.
PO Box 483, Hances Point
North East, MD 21901
410-287-9400; Fax 410-287-9043
New Boats, Brokerage

Nautilus Yacht Sales
PO Box 56
Georgetown, MD 21930
410-275-1100; Fax 410-275-1133
Brokerage

MASSACHUSETTS

Worldwide Yachts
350 Lincoln St., #105
Hingham, MA 02043
617-740-2628; Fax 617-740-1325
Brokerage

John G. Alden & Co.
89 Commercial Wharf
Boston, MA 02110
617-227-9480; Fax 617-523-5465
New Boats, Brokerage

Norwood Marine
R-24 Ericsson St.
Dorchester, MA 02122
617-288-1000; Fax 617-282-5728
New Boats, Brokerage

Nauset Marine, Inc.
Box 357, Route 6A
Orleans (Cape Cod), MA 02653
508-255-0777; Fax 508-255-0373
New Boats, Brokerage

MICHIGAN

Jefferson Beach Marina
41700 Conger Bay Dr.
Mt. Clemens, MI 48045
313-463-6126; Fax 313-463-8970
New Boats, Brokerage

John B. Slaven, Inc.
Box 864, 31300 N. River Rd.
Mt. Clemens, MI 48046
313-463-0000; Fax 313-463-4317
New Boats, Brokerage

Jefferson Beach Marina
24400 E. Jefferson
St. Clair Shores, MI 48080
313-778-7600; Fax 313-778-4766
New Boats, Brokerage

Barrett's Yacht & Boat Brokerage
821 W. Savidge St.
Spring Lake, MI 49456
616-842-1202; Fax 616-842-5735
Brokerage

Oselka Marina
514 Oselka Dr.
New Buffalo, MI 49117
616-469-2600; Fax 616-469-0988
New Boats, Brokerage

Grand Isle Marina
1 Grand Isle Dr.
Grand Haven, MI 49417
800-854-2628; Fax 616-842-8783
New Boats, Brokerage

Jarvis & Associates, Yacht Brokers
2056 Averills Circle
Traverse City, MI 49684
616-946-7979; Fax 616-946-7994
Brokerage

The Harbor Boat Shop
13240 W. Bayshore Dr.
Traverse City, MI 49684
616-922-3020
New Boats, Brokerage

Charlevoix Boat Shop
101 E. Mason (Harborside)
Charlevoix, MI 49720
616-547-2710; Fax 616-547-2444
Brokerage

MINNESOTA

Owens Yacht Sales
371 Canal Park Dr.
Duluth, MN 55802
218-722-9212; Fax 218-722-4730
Brokerage

NEW JERSEY

Catskill Classic Yachts
1 Cherry Lane
Ramsey, NJ 07446
201-327-5000; Fax 201-327-6848
New Boats, Brokerage

Comstock Yacht Sales
704 Princeton Ave.
Brick Town, NJ 08724
908-899-2500; Fax 908-892-3763
New Boats, Brokerage

Twin Lights/Bluewater Yachts
197 Princeton Ave.
Brick, NJ 08724
908-295-3500; Fax 908-295-0230
New Boats, Brokerage

Sportside Marine
201 Union St.
Brielle, NJ 08730
908-223-6677; Fax 908-223-1215
Brokerage

Bob Massey Yacht Sales
1668 Beaver Dam Rd.
Pt. Pleasant, NJ 08742
908-295-3700; Fax 908-892-0649
New Boats, Brokerage

Clarks Landing Marina
847 Arnold Ave.
Pt. Pleasant, NJ 08742
908-899-5559; Fax 908-899-5572
New Boats, Brokerage

NEW YORK

Sparkman & Stevens
79 Madison Avenue
New York, NY 10016
212-689-9292; Fax 212-689-3884
New Boats, Brokerage

City Island Yacht Sales
673 City Island Ave.
City Island, NY 10464
212-885-2300; Fax 212-885-2385
Brokerage

McMichael Yacht Brokers
447 E. Boston Post Rd.
Mamarneck, NY 10543
914-381-5900; Fax 914-381-5060
Brokerage

New York Yacht Corp.
102 Woodcleft Ave.
Freeport, NY 11520
516-546-3377; Fax 516-223-8393
Brokerage

Taber Yacht Sales
1410 Manhanset Ave.
Greenport, NY 11944
516-477-8938; Fax 516-477-8940
New Boats, Brokerage

Star Island Yacht Club & Marina
P.O. Box 2180
Montauk Point, NY 11954
516-668-5052; Fax 516-668-5503
New Boats, Brokerage

Bruce Taite Yacht Sales
PO Box 1928
Sag Harbor, NY 11963
516-725-4222; Fax 516-725-9886
Brokerage

NORTH CAROLINA

Nelson Yacht Sales
103 Hill St., Box 1129
Beaufort, NC 28516
919-728-3663; Fax 919-728-5333
New Boats, Brokerage

Spooners Creek Yacht Sales
Rt. 2, Lands End Rd.
Morehead City, NC 28557
919-726-8082; Fax 919-726-9806
New Boats, Brokerage

Quay & Associates, Inc.
PO Box 563
Oriental, NC 28571
919-249-1825; Fax 919-249-2240
Brokerage

RHODE ISLAND

Little Harbor Yacht Sales
One Little Harbor Landing
Portsmith, RI 02871
401-683-5600; Fax 401-683-3009
New Boats, Brokerage

SOUTH CAROLINA

Yacht Brokerage USA
22 Windemere Blvd, Suite C
Charleston, SC 29407
803-763-1224; Fax 803-763-4215
Brokerage

American Yacht Sales
1880 Andell Buffs Blvd.
Johns Island, SC 29455
800-234-8814; Fax 803-768-7300
New Boats, Brokerage

Berry-Boger Yacht Sales
Box 36, Harbour Place, #203
N. Myrtle Beach, SC 29597
803-249-6167; Fax 803-249-0105
New Boats, Brokerage

TENNESSEE

Nashville Yacht Brokers, Inc.
1 Vantage Way, Suite B-100
Nashville, TN 37228
615-259-9444; Fax 615-259-9481
Brokerage

TEXAS

Western Gulf Yacht Sales
513 Sixth St.
Kemah, TX 77565
713-334-7525; Fax 713-538-2233
New Boats, Brokerage

Ship And Sail
300 Admiralty Way
Kemah, TX 77565
713-334-0573; Fax 713-334-2697
New Boats, Brokerage

Gibson-Weaver, Inc.
2511B Nasa Road 1, Suite 100
Seabrook, TX 77586
713-326-1574; Fax 713-532-1173
New Boats, Brokerage

Ron's Yacht Brokerage
1101 Shipyard Dr., Box 621
Seabrook, TX 77586
713-474-5444; Fax 713-474-7024
Brokerage

Fox Yacht Sales
Box 772, Island Moorings Marina
Port Aransas, TX 78373
512-749-4870; Fax 713-538-2233
Brokerage

VIRGINIA

Commonwealth Yachts
PO Box 1070
Gloucester Point, VA 23062
804-642-2156; Fax 804-642-4766
Brokerage

WASHINGTON

Edmonds Yacht Sales
300 Admiral Way
Edmonds, WA 98020
206-774-8878; Fax 206-771-7277
New Boats, Brokerage

Yacht Doc
8031 NE 112th St.
Kirkland, WA 98034
206-820-9659; Fax 206-823-8913
Brokerage

Trans Coastal Yacht Brokerage
1800 Westlake Ave. N., #201
Seattle, WA 98109
206-284-4547; Fax 206-284-4337
Brokerage

Brigadoon Yacht Sales
1111 Fairview Ave. North
Seattle, WA 98109
206-282-6500; Fax 206-282-2410
New Boats, Brokerage

Elliott Bay Yachting Center
2601 West Marina Pl., #E
Seattle, WA 98199
206-285-9499; Fax 206-281-7636
Brokerage

Padden Creek Marine Inc.
Ninth & Harris
Bellingham, WA 98225
206-733-6248; Fax 206-733-6251
New Boats, Brokerage

LaConner Yacht Sales
Box 680
La Conner, WA 98257
206-466-3300; Fax 206-466-3533
Brokerage

WISCONSIN

Emerald Yacht Ship Mid America
759 N. Milwaukee Street
Milwaukee, WI 53202
414-271-2595; Fax 414-271-4743
Brokerage

Professional Yacht Brokerage
9501 W. Morgan Ave.
Milwaukee, WI 53228
414-321-8880; Fax 414-321-7411
Brokerage

Professional Yacht Sales
451 S. Second St.
Prescott, WI 54021
715-262-5762; Fax 715-262-5658
New Boats, Brokerage

Sturgeon Bay Yacht Harbor
306 Nautical Drive
Sturgeon Bay, WI 54235
414-743-3311; Fax 414-743-4298
New Boats, Brokerage

MARINE SURVEYOR INDEX

PROFESSIONAL SURVEYOR ASSOCIATIONS:

A.B.Y.C. (American Boat & Yacht Council)
A.I.M.S. (American Institute of Marine Surveyors)
A.S.A. (American Society of Appraisers)
M.S.P.G. (Marine Surveyors Professional Guild)
N.A.M.I. (National Association of Marine Investigators)
N.A.M.S. (National Association of Marine Surveyors)
N.F.P.A. (National Fire Protection Association)
S.A.M.S. (Society of Accredited Marine Surveyors)
S.N.A.M.E. (Society of Naval Architects & Marine Engineers)

ALABAMA

Donald Smith
Port City Marine Services
PO Box 190321
Mobile, AL 36619
205-661-5426
SAMS, ABYC

ARKANSAS

Angus Rankin
PO Box 264
Maynard, AR 72444
501-892-8300
SAMS

CALIFORNIA

Donald Brandmeyer
Brandmeyer International
2447 Sparta Dr.
Palos Verdes, CA 90274-6538
310-519-1979
NAMS

Clark Barthol
Clark Barthol Marine Surveyors
27 Buccaneer St.
Marina Del Rey, CA 90292
310-823-3350
NAMS

William Butler
PO Box 11914
Marina Del Rey, CA 90295
310-396-1791
SAMS

Thomas Bell
Thomas Bell & Associates
1323 Berkeley Street
Santa Monica, CA 90404
310-306-1895
SAMS, ABYC

Don Parish
4140 Oceanside Blvd., #159-320
Oceanside, CA 92056
619-721-9410
SAMS, ABYC

Marine Survey Group
1310 Rosecrans St., #K
San Diego, CA 92106
619-224-2944
SAMS, NAMS

Todd Schwede
A.N. Tillett & Associates
2390 Shelter Island Dr., #220
San Diego, CA 92106
619-226-1895
SAMS

Marvin Henderson
Marvin Henderson Marine Surveyors
2727 Shelter Island Dr., #C
San Diego, CA 92106
619-224-3164
NAMS

Charles Driscoll
Frank Wyatt Marine Surveyors
1967 Shaffer St.
San Diego, CA 92106
619-223-8167
NAMS

Bill Beck
444-A N. Newport Blvd.
Newport Beach, CA 92663
714-642-6673
SAMS

Robert Armstrong
American Marine Surveyors, Inc.
3639 E. Harbor Blvd., #203-B
Ventura, CA 93001
805-644-9330
NAMS

Skip Riley, A.M.S.
Maritime Surveyors
414 Fernando Drive
Ojai, CA 93023
805-646-1714
SAMS

Mike Pierce
Mike Pierce Industries
1811 Diego Way
Oxnard, CA 93030
805-657-9490
SAMS

Donald Young
Donru Surveyors & Adjusters
32 Cannery Row
Monterey, CA 93940
408-372-8604
SAMS, ABYC

Stanley Wild
Stan Wild & Associates
2316 Buena Vista
Alameda, CA 94501
510-521-8527
NAMS

John Kelly
Kelly & Associates
PO Box 10331
Napa, CA 94581
707-226-8155
SAMS, ABYC

Richard Christopher
Marine Surveyor & Consultant
14705 Watsonville
Morgan Hill, CA 95037
415-368-8711
SAMS, ABYC

Archibald Campbell
Campbell's Marine Survey
340 Countryside Drive
Santa Rosa, CA 95401
707-542-8812
SAMS, ABYC, ASME, SNAME

Rod Whitfield, A.M.S.
R.J. Whitfield & Associates, Inc.
PO Box 365
Isleton, CA 95641
800-344-1838
SAMS

CONNECTICUT

Albert Truslow
Truslow Marine Surveying
PO Box 9185
Forestville, CT 06011-9185
203-583-6503
SAMS

J. Mitchell DePalma
Connecticut Yacht Survey Corp.
PO Box 842
Branford, CT 06405
203-488-0265
SAMS, ABYC

William Robbins
New England Marine Surveyors
19 Commerce St., Box 533
Clinton, CT 06413
203-669-4018
SAMS

Welles Worthen
Marine Surveyors, Inc.
102 Milford Point Rd.
Milford, CT 06460
203-874-2445
SAMS

Thomas Greaves
Greaves Yacht Service
30 Toby Hill Road
Westbrook, CT 06498
203-399-6966
SAMS

Marine Surveyors Bureau
1440 Whalley Ave, #128
New Haven, CT 06515
203-323-0225
NAMS, ASA, NFPA, ABYC

William Stadel
1088 Shippan Ave.
Stamford, CT 06902
203-324-2610
SAMS

FLORIDA

Downing Nightingale, Jr.
North Florida Marine Services
3360 LakeShore Blvd.
Jacksonville, FL 32210-5348
904-384-4356
SAMS

Ted Willandt
Marine Network
2771-25 Monument Rd., Box 210
Jacksonville, FL 32225-3547
904-641-3334
SAMS, ABYC

Mickey Strocchi
Strocchi & Company
PO Box 16541
Jacksonville, FL 32245-6541
904-398-1862
SAMS

Eugene Briggs
Gene Briggs & Associates
505 Decatur Ave.
Pensacola, FL 32507
904-456-4968
SAMS

Richard Everett
PO Box 13512
Pensacola, FL 32591
904-435-9026
SAMS, ABYC, NFPA

Rollie Tallman
American Boat Brokerage
2548 Alton Rd.
Deltona, FL 32738
904-789-0971
SAMS

Russell Thomas
Thomas Marine Surveyors
737 Bywood Dr., NE
Palm Bay, FL 32905
800-352-6287
NAMS, SAMS, SNAME

Lawrence O'Pezio
Marine Safety Consultants, Inc.
677 George King Blvd., #112
Cape Canaveral, FL 32920
407-783-1771
NAMS, ABYC, NFPA

Channing Chapman
Clyde Eaton & Assoc., Inc.
PO Box 231862
Cocoa, FL 32923-1862
407-633-0860
ABYC, NFPA

A. Brough Treffer
2865 S. Tropical Trail
Merritt Island, FL 32952
407-453-6046
SAMS, NFPA, ABYC

Richard Fortin
Marine Surveyor & Consultant
1405 - 19th St., SW
Vero Beach, FL 32962
407-567-9286
ABYC, SNAME

James Macefield
Macefield Marine Services, Inc.
3389 Sheridan St., #178
Hollywood, FL 33021
305-784-9188
SAMS

Capt. Larry Dukehart
PO Box 1172
Islamorada, FL 33036-1172
305-664-9452
SAMS, ABYC, NFPA

Edwin Crusoe
Key West Marine Services
PO Box 4854
Key West, FL 33040
305-872-9073
NAMS

George Stuck
PO Box 5481
Key West, FL 33045
305-294-4959
SAMS

Dewey Acker, A.M.S.
Acker Marine Surveyors
551 61st St. Gulf
Marathon, FL 33050
305-743-3434
SAMS, ABYC

Mark Rhodes
Rhodes Marine Surveyors
3650 N. Federal Hwy., #212
Lighthouse Point, FL 33064
305-946-6671
SAMS, ABYC, NFPA

Anthony Pavlo
Alp's Marine Surveying, Inc.
281 NW 42nd Ave.
Coconut Creek, FL 33066
305-973-1135
SAMS

Ronald Silvera
R.E. Silvera & Associates
1904 SW 86th Ave.
North Lauderdale, FL 33068
305-720-8660
SAMS, SNAME, ABYC

Sidney Kaufman
American Nautical Services, Inc.
254 NE Fourth St.
Miami, FL 33132
305-358-1414
SAMS, ABYC

Brett Carlson
Marine Surveyor & Adjuster
1002 NE 105th St.
Miami Shores, FL 33138
305-891-0445
SAMS

Dave Alter
Dave Alter & Associates
PO Box 560-532
Miami, FL 33156
305-667-0326
SAMS

William Streeter
B&S Marine Inc.
PO Box 970752
Miami, FL 33197
305-253-3035
SAMS

Drew Kwederas
Global Adventure Marine Associates
4120 NE 26th Ave.
Ft. Lauderdale, FL 33308
305-566-4800
ABYC, NFPA, ASNE

Kurt Merolla
Merolla Marine Surveyors & Consultants
4761 NE 29th Ave.
Ft. Lauderdale, FL 33308
305-722-8090
NAMS, SAMS, SNAME, ABYC, NFPA

Gregory Newton
Marine Evaluation Service
1323 SE 17th St., #119
Ft. Lauderdale, FL 33316
305-763-9562
NAMS

Gerald Slakoff
Slakoff & Associates
1525 S. Andrews Ave.
Ft. Lauderdale, FL 33316
305-525-7930
SAMS

Norman Schreiber II
Transtech - Marine Division
PO Box 350247
Ft. Lauderdale, FL 33335
305-537-1423
NAMS, SNAME, ABYC, NFPA

John Reynolds
Jack Reynolds International
11172 NW 35th St., Box 450485
Ft. Lauderdale, FL 33345-0485
800-833-9698
SAMS

Capt. A.T. Kyle
Marine Consultants & Surveyors
6428 Heather Way
West Palm Beach, FL 33406
407-964-6189
SAMS

Robert Despres
Despres & Assoc., Marine Surveyors
332 Pine St.
West Palm Beach, FL 33407
407-820-9290
SAMS

Tom Drennan
Continental Marine Consultants, Inc.
700 North US Hwy. 1
North Palm Beach, FL 33408
305-844-6111
NAMS

Richard Thompson
Lakes/Coastal Marine Surveys
235 E. Tall Oaks Circle
Palm Beach Gardens, FL 33410
407-622-9283
SAMS

H. Jack MacDonald, Inc.
Marine Surveyors & Consultants
1257 Periwinkle Place
West Palm Beach, FL 33414
407-731-0471
SAMS, ABYC, NFPA

James Sanislo
C&J Marine Surveyors
4163 Frances Dr.
Delray Beach, FL 33445
407-495-4920
SAMS

Thomas Price
Price Marine Services, Inc.
9418 Sharon St. SE
Hobe Sound, FL 33455
407-546-0928
SAMS, ABYC, NFPA

William King
Atlantic Marine Survey
6201 SE Monticello Terrace
Hobe Sound, FL 33455-7383
407-545-0011
SAMS

Melvin Allen
Allen's Boat Surveying & Consulting
638 North U.S. Hwy 1, Suite 207
Tequesta, FL 33469-2397
407-747-2433
SAMS

Larry Hardin
Hardin Marine Survey
910 Dogwood Dr., Apt. 442
Delray Beach, FL 33483
407-265-2720
SAMS

Dick Williamson
Professional Marine Surveys, Inc.
7491-C5 N. Federal Hwy, #232
Boca Raton, FL 33487
407-272-1053
SAMS, ABYC, NFPA

Capt. E. Bay Hansen
Capt. E. Bay Hansen, Inc.
1302 N. 19th St., #101
Tampa, FL 33605
813-248-6897
NAMS

Henry Pickersgill
Henry W. Pickersgill & Co., Inc.
4118 W. Euclid Ave.
Tampa, FL 33629
800-348-8105
NAMS

Charles Harden
Harden Marine Associates, Inc.
P.O. Box 13256
Tampa, FL 33681-3256
813-254-4273
SAMS

L. Frank Hamlin
L.F. Hamlin, Inc.
14085 E. Parsley Dr.
Madeira Beach, FL 33708
813-393-1905
NAMS

Richard Koogle
5849 Millay Ct.
North Ft. Myers, FL 33903
813-997-5146
SAMS

Veronica Lawson
Veronica M. Lawson & Associates
PO Box 1201
Naples, FL 33939
813-434-6960
NAMS

Donald Walwer, A.M.S.
D&G Marine Company
58 Ocean Blvd.
Naples, FL 33942
813-643-0028
SAMS

Arthur Buchman, Jr.
12118 Chancellor Blvd.
Port Charlotte, FL 33953
813-743-2198
SAMS

Jeff Brown
8716 - 54th Ave. West
Bradenton, FL 34210
813-794-3998
SAMS

Ardian J. Volney & Co.
5806 Whistlewood Circle
Sarasota, FL 34232
813-371-8781
SAMS

Robert Buckles
R.C. Buckles Associates, Inc.
15 Crossroad, #250
Sarasota, FL 34239
813-924-3013
SAMS

Dean Greger
Coastal Marine Surveyors
23 Winston Dr.
Belleair, FL 34616
813-581-0914

Kermit Naylor
Southern Yacht Surveyors
2895 Del Rio Dr.
Belleair Bluffs, FL 34640
813-585-8949
NAMS

Elaine Miranda
9400 Mainlands Blvd. W.
Pinellas Park, FL 34666
813-577-4128
SAMS

Ted Stevens
Stevens & Stevens, Ltd.
3250 Candice Ave., #132
Jensen Beach, FL 34957
407-229-6394
SAMS

Tom Fexas
Tom Fexas Yacht Design
333 Tressler Dr., Suites B&C
Stuart, FL 34994
407-287-6558
NAMS

Marty Merolla
4300 SE St. Lucie Blvd., #128
Stuart, FL 34997
407-286-4880
NAMS

Douglas Newbigin
Stuart Yacht Design
450 SW Salerno Rd.
Stuart, FL 34997
407-283-1947
SAMS

HAWAII

Michael Doyle
Mike Doyle, Ltd.
606 Fort St., Room 300
Honolulu, HI 96813
808-521-9881
NAMS

E.H. "Chip" Gunther
All Ship & Cargo Surveys, Ltd.
965-A2 Nimitz Highway
Honolulu, HI 96817
808-538-3260
NAMS

John Mihlbauer
All Ship & Cargo Surveys, Ltd.
965-A2 Nimitz Highway
Honolulu, HI 96817
808-538-3260
NAMS

ILLINOIS

James Singer, A.M.S.
1854 York Lane
Highland Park, IL 60035
708-831-9157
SAMS, ABYC

John Boltz
Inland Surveyors, Inc.
307 N. Michigan Ave., #1008
Chicago, IL 60601
312-329-9881
NAMS
Lee H. Asbridge
480 N. McClurg Ct., #1002
Chicago, IL 60611
312-527-4860
SAMS

ILLINOIS

Tim Kleihege
Great Lakes Marine Surveying, Inc.
2831 Lakewood Trail
Porter Beach, IN 46304
312-663-2503
SAMS, ABYC
Robert Craig
323 West Main St.
Richmond, IN 47374-4161
317-966-9807
SAMS

KENTUCKY

Gregory Weeter
Riverlands Marine Surveyors
817 Huntington Rd.
Louisville, KY 40207
502-897-9900
NAMS

LOUISIANA

Pete Peters
Bachrach & Wood/Peters Assoc.
PO Box 7415
Metairie, LA 70010-7415
504-454-0001
SAMS

John Illg
Summit Design Services
6444 Jefferson Hwy.
Harahan, LA 70123
504-737-3267
NAMS

Sewell "Si" Williams
Arthur H. Terry & Co.
101 W. Robt. E. Lee Blvd., #200
New Orleans, LA 70124
504-283-1514
NAMS, SAMS, ASA, SNAME

J. Anthony Brown
A.B. Marine Consulting
1397 E. Stephensville Rd.
Morgan City, LA 70380
504-384-5184
SAMS

Hubert S. Gallagher
52246 Highway 90, Apt 2
Slidell, LA 70461
504-641-2921
SAMS

Michael Schiehl
M.J. Schiehl & Associates, Inc.
PO Box 146
Denham Springs, LA 70727-0146
504-664-2108
NAMS

MAINE

William Leavitt
Chase, Leavitt & Company
10 Dana St.
Portland, ME 04112
207-772-3751
NAMS

Bob Cartwright
North American Marine Surveying, Ltd.
PO Box 205
Boothbay, ME 04537
207-633-5062
NAMS, SNAME

MARYLAND

Ernie Leeger
2506 Buckingham Court
Abingdon, MD 21009
410-515-0155
ABYC

Pete Dawson, Jr.
Chesapeake Marine Surveys
PO Box 322
Mayo, MD 21106-0322
410-798-5077
NAMS, NFPA

C. Robert Skord, Jr.
Skord & Company
400 Forest Beach Rd.
Annapolis, MD 21401
410-757-7454
NAMS, SAMS

Frederick E. Hecklinger, Inc.
17 Hull Ave.
Annapolis, MD 21403
410-268-3018
NAMS

Terence Fitzsimmons
Kaufman Design, Inc.
222 Severn Ave., Box 4219
Annapolis, MD 21403
410-263-8900
NAMS

Michael Kaufman, III
Kaufman Design, Inc.
222 Severn Ave., Box 4219
Annapolis, MD 21403
410-263-8900
NAMS

Hartoft Marine Survey
PO, Box 3188
Annapolis, MD 21403
410-263-3609

Parricia Kearns
Marine Associates
PO Box 3441, 2 Leeward Ct.
Annapolis, MD 21403
410-263-2419
NAMS, SNAME

Clyde Eaton
Clyde Eaton & Assoc., Inc.
PO Box 4609
Annapolis, MD 21403
800-347-7331
ABYC, NFPA

Don Miller
Beacon Marine Surveys
2916 Cox Neck Rd. E.
Chester, MD 21619
410-643-4390
SAMS

Woodrow Loller
204 Washington Ave.
Chestertown, MD 21620
410-778-5357
NAMS, ABYC

Catherine C. McLaughlin
29142 Belchester Rd.
Kennedyville, MD 21645
410-348-5188
SAMS

William Thomte
Atlantic Marine Surveyors
PO Box 299
St. Michaels, MD 21663
410-745-3080
NAMS, SNAME

John Neal, Jr.
J.R. Neal & Associates
PO Box 2088
Ocean City, MD 21842-2088
301-524-7114
SAMS, ASA

John Griffiths
John R. Griffiths, Inc.
785 Knight Island Rd.
Earleville (Eastern Shore), MD 21919
410-275-8750
NAMS, ABYC

MASSACHUSETTS

Ralph Merrill
Certified Marine Surveyors
48 - 19th Street
Lowell, MA 01850
508-459-3082
SAMS, ABYC

Wayne Robinson
Admiralty Consulting & Surveying
50 Dunster Lane
Winchester, MA 01890
617-721-7307
SAMS

Capt. Norman Le Blanc
PO Box 185
Beverly, MA 01915
508-921-1151
SAMS

Tom Hill
Atlantic & Pacific Surveyors
27 Ferry St.
Gloucester, MA 01930
508-283-7006
SAMS, ABYC, NFPA

Capt. Guilford Full
Capt. G.W. Full & Associates
46 Cedar St.
Marblehead, MA 01945
617-631-4902
NAMS

Edwin Boice
Robert N. Kershaw, Inc.
PO Box 285
Braintree, MA 02184
617-843-4550
SAMS, NAMS

Raymond Gaffey
Robert N. Kershaw, Inc.
PO Box 285
Braintree, MA 02184
617-843-4550
SAMS, NAMS

Robert Kershaw
Robert N. Kershaw, Inc.
PO Box 285
Braintree, MA 02184
617-843-4550
NAMS, SAMS

Donald Pray
91 Blanchard Rd.
South Weymouth, MA 02190
617-335-3033
SAMS, ABYC, NFPA

Norman Schreiber II
Transtech - Marine Division
140 Wendward Way
Hyannis, MA 02601
508-776-1670
NAMS, SNAME, ABYC, NFPA

Donald Walwer, A.M.S.
D&G Marine Company
145 Wamisco Rd., Box 635
North Eastham, MA 02651
508-255-2406
SAMS

MICHIGAN

Melvin Wamsley
Accurate Marine Surveying
21829 Oakwood
East Detroit, MI 48021
313-775-6775
SAMS

Harry Canoles, A.M.S.
Marine Appraisal Survey Service, Inc.
3723 Bay Road
Erie. MI 48133
313-723-7404
SAMS

Capt. Ted Polgar
Marine Surveyor & Consultant
7588 Seneca Trail
Temperance, MI 48182
313-847-1087

Jim Cukrowicz
Personal Marine Services
52671 CR 388
Grand Junction, MI 49056
616-434-6396
SAMS

Capt. A. John Lobbezoo, A.M.S.
Great Lakes Marine Surveyors, Inc.
Box 466, 16100 Highland Dr.
Spring Lake, MI 49456-0466
616-842-9400
SAMS, ABYC, NFPA

Jeff Amesbury
213 Franklin St.
Boyne City, MI 49712
616-582-7329
SAMS

MINNESOTA

Paul Liedl
Croix Marine Consultants
531 Mariner Dr.
Bayport, MN 55003
612-439-7748
SAMS, ABYC

John Rantala, Jr.
Rantala Marine Surveys & Services
1671 10th Ave, #2
Newport, MN 55055
612-458-5842
SAMS

A. William Fredell
408 Quarry Lane
Stillwater, MN 55082
612-439-5795
SAMS

MISSOURI

Jim Hill, CMS
PO Box 390 C, Rte. 1
St. Charles, MO 63301
314-258-3306

MISSISSIPPI

Rush Andre', A.M.S.
Marine Surveyor & Consultant
414 McGuire Circle
Gulfport, MS 39507
601-863-5962
SAMS, ABYC, NFPA

Robert Payne
Marine Management, Inc.
PO Box 1803
Ocean Springs, MS 39564
601-872-2846
NAMS, ABYC

Clarence Hamilton
PO Box 378
Ocean Springs, MS 39564
601-875-5800
MSPG

NEW HAMPSHIRE

Gerald Poliskey
Independent Marine Services
194 Putnam St.
Manchester, NH 03102
603-644-4545
NAMS, SAMS

Capt. David Page, A.M.S.
2456 LaFayette Rd.
Portsmouth, NH 03801
603-433-1568
SAMS, ABYC, NAMI, NFPA

NEW JERSEY

John Klose
Bayview Associates
PO Box 368
Barnegat Light, NJ 08006
609-494-7450
SAMS

William Campbell
9 Gate Rd.
Tabernacle, NJ 08088
609-268-7476
NAMS, SNAME

Robert Gibble
25 Black Oak Dr.
Ocean View, NJ 08230
609-390-3708
NAMS, SAMS

NORTH CAROLINA

T. Fred Wright
M.B. Ward & Son, Inc.
PO Box 3632
Wilmington, NC 28406
919-392-1425
NAMS, ABYC

Ron Reeves
Atlantic Maritime Services
PO Box 344
Oriental, NC 28571
919-249-1830
SAMS

Bert Quay, A.M.S.
Quay Carolina Marine Surveys
PO Box 809
Oriental, NC 28571
919-249-2275
SAMS

NEW YORK

Gerald LaMarque
LaMarque Marine Services
6 Red Oak Dr.
Rye, NY 10580
914-967-7731
NAMS, ABYC, NFPA

Capt. Jim Dias
Marine Surveyors Bureau
221 Central Ave.
White Plains, NY 10606
914-684-9889
NAMS, SAMS, ABYC, NFPA

Marine Surveyors Bureau
30 S. Ocean Ave.
Freeport, NY 11520
516-683-1199
NAMS, ASA, NFPA, ABYC

John Robertson
Fire Traders, Inc.
One Washington Place
Amityville, NY 11701
516-598-2824
NAMS

David McClay
Quality Boat Carpentry
57 Maple Ave.
Northport, NY 11768
516-757-9415
SAMS

Paul Robinson
Marifax Marine Services
21 Swanview Dr.
Patchogue, NY 11772
516-654-3300
SAMS, ABYC

Capt. Henry Olsen
PO Box 283
Port Jefferson, NY 11777
516-928-0711
NAMS, SNAME

Joseph Gaigal
Suffolk Marine Surveying
RFD 1, Box 174G
St. James, NY 11780
516-584-6297
SAMS, ABYC, NFPA

Long Island Marine Surveyor, Inc.
PO Box 542
Sayville, NY 11782
516-589-6154
ABYC, NFPA

Chris Garvey
Garvey Marine Surveyors
143 West Montauk Highway
Hampton Bays, L. I., NY 11946
516-728-5429
SAMS

Edward Viola
Edward J. Viola Marine Surveying
PO Box 430
Mattituck, NY 11952
516-298-9518
NAMS

Kenneth Weinbrecht
Ocean Bay Marine Services, Inc.
241 Carleton Drive
East Yaphank, NY 11967
516-924-4362
SAMS

Stephen Maddock
Clyde Eaton & Assoc., Inc.
PO Box 2957
Southampton, NY 11969
800-424-2513
ABYC, NFPA

William Matthews
Admiralty Marine Surveyors & Adjusters
PO Box 183
Westhampton, NY 11977-0183
516-288-3263
NAMS, SNAME, ABYC

Thomas Crowley
Upstate Marine Consultants, Inc.
8840 New Country Dr.
Cicero, NY 13039
315-699-0024
ABYC, NFPA

Walter Lawrence
Lawrence Marine Services
PO Box 219
Alton, NY 14413
315-483-6680
SAMS

Shawn Bartnett
Bartnett Marine Services, Inc.
52 Ontario St.
Honeoye Falls, NY 14472
716-624-1380
NAMS, ABYC, NFPA, SNAME

OHIO

Capt. Darrell Walton
West Sister Marine Survey
12513 Lagoon Drive
Curtice, OH 43412
419-836-8264
SAMS

Ray McLeod, A.M.S.
Douglas & McLeod, Inc.
209 River St., Box 398
Grand River, OH 44045
216-352-6156
SAMS, ABYC

OREGON

Charles Thompson
450 W. Lexington Ave.
Astoria, OR 97103
503-325-4062
SAMS

PENNSYLVANIA

William Major, A.M.S
Bristol Yacht Services, Inc.
110 Mill St.
Bristol, PA 19007
215-788-0870
SAMS, ABYC

PUERTO RICO

Julian Ducat
Octagon Marine Services
PO Box 3209, Old San Juan Station
San Juan, PR 00902-3209
809-722-8785
SAMS

RHODE ISLAND

Charles Morvillo
Star Marine Surveyors
1700 Smith St.
North Providence, RI 02911
401-353-1960
SAMS

SOUTH CAROLINA

Carl Foxworth
Industrial Claims Service
515 Creekside Dr.
Murrells Inlet, SC 29576
803-651-2800/704-536-7511
SAMS, ABYC

TEXAS

Lee Pearson
Pearson Enterprises
PO Box 301169
Houston, TX 77030-1169
713-622-8802
SAMS, ABYC, SNAME

Fred Struben
The Dutchman Co.
604 Pebbleshire Dr.
Houston, TX 77062
713-480-7096
NAMS, SNAME, ASA

J.B. Oliveros
J.B. Oliveros, Inc.
127 Marlin St.
Galveston, TX 77550
409-763-3123
NAMS, ABYC

Drake Epple
Perry's Marine Survey Co.
1902 Bayport Blvd., #109
Seabrook, TX 77586
713-474-5273
ABYC

Richard Frenzel
Dixieland Marine, Inc.
PO Box 2408
Corpus Christi, TX 78403
512-946-5566
SAMS, ABYC

Peter Davidson
Peter Davidson & Associates
341 Melrose Ave.
Corpus Christi, TX 78404
512-884-7245
SAMS

Marc McAllister
McAllister Marine Surveying Co.
PO Box 6375
Corpus Christi, TX 78466-6375
512-855-2172
NAMS, ABYC, NFPA

VIRGINIA

Ralph Brown
11337 Orchard Lane
Reston, VA 22090-4431
703-435-1258
SAMS

George Zahn, Jr.
Ware River Associates
Route 3, Box 1050
Gloucester, VA 23061
804-693-4329
SAMS, SNAME. ABYC, NFPA

Steven Knox
Knox Marine Consultants
10 Crawford Pky, Tidewater Marina
Portsmouth, VA 23704
804-393-9788
NAMS, SAMS

WASHINGTON

Arnett & Berg Marine Surveyors
PO Box 70424
Seattle, WA 98107-0424
206-283-8884
SAMS, ABYC, NFPA

Robert McEwen
Reisner, McEwen & Associates
2500 Westlake Avenue North
Seattle, WA 98109
206-285-8194
NAMS, ABYC

Wm. Leiter Hockett, CMS
3415 NW 66th
Seattle, WA 98117
206-783-7617
NAMS

Carl Anderson
8048 9th Ave. NW
Seattle, WA 98117
206-789-2315
SAMS

Dennis Johnson
15734 Greenwood Ave. North
Seattle, WA 98133
206-365-6591

Matthew Harris
Reisen, McEwen & Harris, Inc.
1333 Lincoln St., #323
Bellingham, WA 98226
206-647-6966
NAMS, SAMS

Kenneth Rider
Rider Associates
338 E. Cascade Place
Oak Harbor, WA 98277
206-675-8475

WISCONSIN

Rice Adjustment Company
11422 N. Port Washington Rd.
Milwaukee, WI 53217-0529
414-241-6060
NAMS

CANADA
Ivan Herbert
Universal Marine Consultants, Ltd.
5 Carriageway Ct.
Bedford, Nova Scotia B4A 3V4
902-835-2283
NAMS

Kelvin Colbourne
Kelvin Colbourne & Associates
PO Box 24 FP
Washago, Ontario L0K 2B0
705-689-8820
SAMS, ABYC

Peter Larkins
Larkins Marine Surveyors
6570 - 68th St.
Delta, B.C. V4K 4E2
604-940-1221
SAMS

Chris Small
Chris Small Marine Surveyors
214 - 1650 Duranleau St.
Vancouver, B.C. V6H 3S4
604-681-8825
NAMS

Geoffrey Gould
Quality Marine Surveyors, Ltd.
PO Box 1105
Prince Ruppert, B.C. V8J 4H6
604-624-4138
SAMS

ABOUT THE AUTHORS

Ed McKnew has been a yacht broker and powerboat design enthusiast for many years. He holds a business degree from Oakland University in Rochester, Michigan, and worked for several years in the solid waste business before becoming a yacht broker in 1977. Moving to the Houston area in 1984, he operated a yacht brokerage office in Clear Lake, Texas, before leaving the business in 1987 to work on the manuscript for the original PowerBoat Guide. Ed currently divides his time between working as a yacht broker, writing, and pursuing his interest in Civil War history. He is single and lives in Palm Beach Gardens, Florida.

Mark Parker has been a powerboat enthusiast since before he can remember. A graduate of South West Texas State University with a business degree in marketing, Mark also holds a Master's license and has captained several large sportfishing boats. He is a native Texan and worked as a broker with the Bertram/Viking dealer in Houston for six years before moving to South Florida in 1989. Mark currently divides his time between operating a yacht brokerage firm and publishing the PowerBoat Guide. He and his wife, Sherri, live in Palm Beach Gardens, Florida.

ALBIN

Brief History

Albin Marine was originally a Swedish builder of marine diesel engines. In 1967 the company introduced their first production boat — the Albin 27 sloop — while the Albin 25 Double Cabin was the company's first powerboat model in 1969. The current management obtained the North American rights to the Albin name in the mid 1970s when the line was expanded with a series of trawler-style boats built in Taiwan. Recent years have seen the introduction of several smaller U.S.-built cruisers and sportfishermen.

Selected Albin Inboard Models

Albin 27 Cruiser   Albin 40 Sundeck

Albin 32 Sportfisher   Albin 43 Trawler

Albin 33 Trawler   Albin 43 Sundeck

Albin 34 Motor Yacht   Albin 48 Cutter

Albin 36 Trawler   Albin 49 Tri Cabin

Albin 40 Trawler

Main Office

Albin Marine, Inc., P.O. Box 228, 143 River Rd., Cos Cob, CT 06807
203-661-4341

ALBIN 27 DIESEL CRUISER

The Albin 27 Diesel Cruiser is a descendant of the well-known Swedish Albin 25, one of the best selling small craft ever built. Because of her salty appearance and sturdy construction, the Albin 27 has been popular for a number of years with family cruisers seeking an easily handled and economical boat with the privacy of an aft cabin layout. Hull construction is solid fiberglass and a full-length keel provides a full measure of protection for the prop in shallow waters. While the Albin's interior accommodations are necessarily basic they are nonetheless adequate for two undemanding couples. Perhaps the best feature of the Albin 27 is the center cockpit layout with inboard seating and protected helm. With the canvas and side screens deployed, she becomes a great overnight camper. Built in the U.S., the Albin 27 Cruiser is inexpensive to operate and requires very little maintenance. Several 4- and 6-cylinder diesel engines have been available over the years and all will provide an economical 2–3 gph at moderate cruising speeds of 10–12 knots. Note that bow thrusters and additional fuel are standard in newer models. ❏

SPECIFICATIONS

Length	26'9"
Length WL	24'4"
Beam	9'8"
Draft	2'6'
Weight	6,800#
Clearance	NA
Water	30 Gals.
Fuel	72/100 Gals.
Cockpit	NA
Hull Type	Semi-Disp.
Designer	Joe Puccia

Production
1983-Current

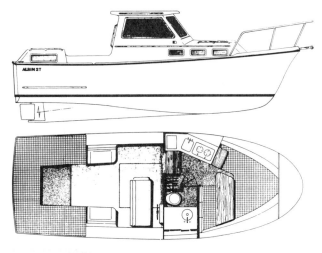

ALBIN

ALBIN 32 SPORTFISHER

The Albin nameplate is generally associated with trawler-style cruising yachts from Taiwan. The 32 Sportfisher represents a departure from that heritage — a serious attempt to crack the sportfishing market with a practical and fuel efficient trunk cabin express cruiser. Built in Rhode Island on a modified-V hull with a full-length keel and 14° of deadrise aft, the Albin 32 features a large fishing cockpit with livewell, bait rigging center, transom door, seawater washdown, and lockable rod storage as standard. The sidedecks are wide and high bulwarks provide secure footing in rough seas. Below, the U-shaped dinette will sleep two and a unique mid-cabin fitted beneath the bridgedeck has a double berth and a single berth to port. Headroom is excellent thanks to the raised foredeck and hatches in the cockpit sole provide good access to the engine and V-drive units. With the now-standard 300-hp Cummins diesel the Albin 32 Sportfisher will cruise around 18 knots with an outstanding 700 miles-plus range. Optional twin 250/300-hp Cummins will deliver cruising speeds to 26 knots. Note that a bow thruster is standard with single-screw installations. ❑

SPECIFICATIONS

Length	32'4"
Beam	12'3"
Draft	3'10"
Weight	13,500#
Clearance	8'10"
Water	96 Gals.
Fuel	280 Gals.
Cockpit	92 Sq. Ft.
Hull Type	Modified-V
Designer	T. Compton

Production
1989–Current

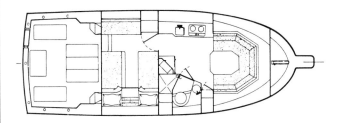

ALBIN 33 TRAWLER

Although she enjoyed only a brief production run (1979–80), Albin 33 Trawlers seem to show up regularly on the used boat markets. She's basically a scaled-down version of Albin's popular 36 Trawler — a traditional double cabin design with a deckhouse galley and two private heads. Notably, the profile of the 33 is pleasing in spite of her short LOA. She's built of fiberglass on a semi-displacement hull with a sharp entry and generous flare at the bow, hard aft chines, and a deep keel for directional stability and prop protection. The interior of the Albin 33 is finished with either teak or mahogany, and a good deal of craftsmanship is evident in the belowdecks joinery. A U-shaped dinette is abaft the lower helm, and there are two overhead grabrails in the salon. The galley is on the small side but still adequate for basic food prep short of gourmet meals. High bulwarks surround the teak walkaround deck and two sliding access doors provide easy access to the deck. A solid and efficient family cruiser, the Albin 33 Trawler burns only 2.5 gph at her 7-knot hull speed with a single Lehman diesel. ❑

SPECIFICATIONS

Length	32'6"
Length WL	NA
Beam	11'5"
Draft	3'7"
Weight	16,800#
Clearance	NA
Water	150 Gals.
Fuel	330 Gals.
Hull Type	Semi-Disp.
Designer	Albin

Production
1979–80

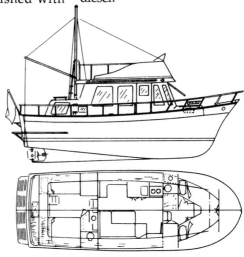

ALBIN

ALBIN 34 MOTOR YACHT

The Albin 34 Motor Yacht (it must be hard to keep a straight face when calling this a motor yacht) is an affordably priced family cruising boat with a distinctive trawler-like profile. Built in the U.S. and designed as the next step up from the Albin 27, the 34 is a curious boat. While the salon may appear to be large from the outside, it's more like a pilothouse inside with its lower helm station, port and starboard sliding deck doors and large wraparound cabin windows. The forward cabin includes the galley, head with stall shower, and a U-shaped dining settee that converts to a queen-size berth at night. A second head is aft in the small owner's stateroom. Getting down from the bridge to the salon in anything but calm water could be tricky. This boat evolved from the original Albin 34 Diesel Cruiser introduced in 1985. A single 250-hp Cummins diesel (standard power) will cruise the Albin 34 MY about 15–16 knots. Twin 157-hp Isuzu diesels are are optional and deliver an economical 18 knots cruise and 21 knots wide open. Note that a bow thruster is standard in the single-screw version. ❏

SPECIFICATIONS

Length	34'0"
Length WL	30'6"
Beam	11'6"
Draft	3'6"
Weight	14,000#
Clearance	NA
Water	70 Gals.
Fuel	200 Gals.
Hull Type	Modified-V
Designer	Albin

Production
1989–90

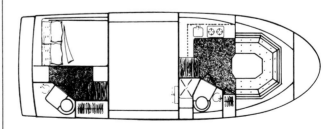

ALBIN 36 TRAWLER

The Albin 36 continues to be a popular boat among those who enjoy the look of a traditional, trawler-style yacht and the economy of single-screw power. A handsome design, she's built at the Kha Shing yard in Taiwan and features a conventional double cabin layout with a full teak interior. An in-line galley is located in the salon along with a lower helm station, deck access door, and an L-shaped convertible settee. Both fore and aft staterooms are comfortable and have access to a private head with a tub/shower located aft. Construction is solid fiberglass (although a few early models had glass–over–plywood superstructures) and a full-length skeg provides complete protection to the underwater running gear. Her flybridge will seat eight and is fitted with a mast and boom for a steadying sail. Finished with an abundance of exterior brightwork, the teak decks, rails, cabintop, doors, and hatches all add much to her appearance but require considerable maintenance. A standard 135-hp Lehman diesel will cruise the Albin 36 Trawler at 7.5 knots for 750–800 miles while burning only 3 gph. Newer models with the optional 210-hp Cummins will cruise around 10–11 knots. ❏

SPECIFICATIONS

Length	35'9"
Length WL	31'3"
Beam	13'2"
Draft	3'6"
Weight	18,500#
Clearance	12'4"
Water	220 Gals.
Fuel	350 Gals.
Hull Type	Semi-Disp.
Designer	Albin

Production
1978–Current

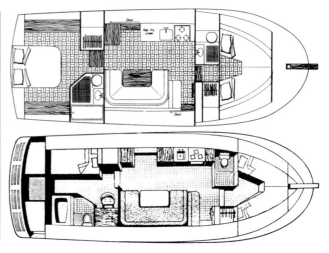

ALBIN

ALBIN 40 TRAWLER

The current Albin 40 Trawler (there was an earlier model during 1983–85) is a classic trawler-style double cabin with a simulated lapstrake hull and plenty of exterior teak trim. Construction is solid fiberglass on a conventional semi-displacement hull with moderate beam and hard chines aft. The keel is deep enough to protect the running gear in the event of a grounding. The galley-down floorplan of the Albin 40 has remained basically unchanged since she was introduced in 1987. There's a queen-size berth in the aft cabin along with a tub/shower in the head. The salon dimensions are about average for a 40-footer and the full teak interior is a model of quality woodworking. A lower helm is standard and there are port and starboard deck doors in the salon. The walkaround sidedecks are wide and protected by raised bulwarks all around. A dinghy can be carried on the trunk cabin (over the master stateroom) and the mast and boom are standard. The Albin 40 can be ordered with single or twin diesels — 135-hp Lehmans or 210-hp Cummins. At her 8-knot cruising speed she'll have an average range of about 700 miles. ❏

SPECIFICATIONS

Length	39'5"
Length WL	36'6"
Beam	13'2"
Draft	3'6"
Weight	23,500#
Clearance	NA
Water	220 Gals.
Fuel	400 Gals.
Hull Type	Semi-Disp.
Designer	Albin

Production
1987–Current

ALBIN 40 SUNDECK

The Albin 40 Sundeck is a traditional Taiwan-trawler design built on a conventional semi-displacement, hard chine hull with generous flare at the bow and an attractive sheerline. (Note that her sistership, the Albin 40 Trawler, is essentially the same boat but with a walkaround aft deck and smaller master stateroom dimensions). Both models share the same two-stateroom interior layout with the galley-down and heads fore and aft. The abundant teak woodwork yields a rather dark interior but one traditionalists will no doubt find to their liking. Joinerwork is very good throughout. The flybridge will accommodate six, and there's room on the full-width aft deck for several pieces of outdoor furniture. A single 135-hp Lehman diesel is standard but most Albin 40s have been sold with twin 135-hp Lehmans (10 knots cruise/13 knots top) or the more powerful 210-hp Cummins (12 knots cruise/15 top). Note that the props and rudders are well protected from grounding by the deep skeg. Moderately priced and inexpensive to operate, the Albin 40 is a competent family cruiser with a comfortable ride and good range. ❏

SPECIFICATIONS

Length......................39'5"
Length WL ....36'6"
Beam........................13'2"
Draft ....3'6"
Weight ....23,500#
Clearance ....NA
Water.................220 Gals.
Fuel ....400 Gals.
Hull Type ....Semi-Disp.
Designer ....Albin

Production
1987–Current

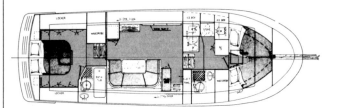

ALBIN 43 TRAWLER

Built of fiberglass in Taiwan, the Albin 43 is a comfortable and practical cruising yacht with a classic trawler profile. Her expansive twin-stateroom, galley-down layout is well suited to dockside entertaining or extended cruising for two couples. Storage, interior lighting, helm visibility, and deck access are all excellent. A single diesel engine is standard, but most Albin 43s have been delivered with twin 135-hp Lehman engines (8 knots cruise and 11 knots top) and newer models have been available with 210-hp Cummins for a 12–13 knot cruising speed. Average cruising range is an impressive 650–700 miles. Underway, the Albin 43 handles like the heavy displacement yacht that she is with a comfortable ride in most sea conditions. High bulwarks and generous bow flare insure a dry, secure ride offshore. The extensive use of interior and exterior teak is typical of Asian boats, and in the Albin 43 the joinerwork is very impressive indeed. The popular 43 Sundeck model with a raised aft deck has been offered since 1981. Traditional styling and rugged construction will insure the Albin 43's market appeal for some time. ❑

SPECIFICATIONS

Length	42'6"
Length WL	37'11"
Beam	14'6"
Draft	4'1"
Weight	30,000#
Clearance	NA
Water	300 Gals.
Fuel	500 Gals.
Hull Type	Semi-Disp.
Designer	C.S. Chung

Production
1979–Current

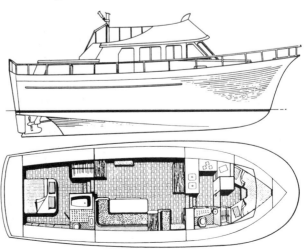

ALBIN

ALBIN 43 SUNDECK

The Albin 43 Sundeck is a handsome design based on the Albin 43 Trawler. Her full-width aft deck is larger than that on the 43 Trawler model, and the aft stateroom is more spacious as well. In other respects, the two boats are the same. The hull is constructed of solid fiberglass, and a deep keel provides grounding protection for the running gear. Albin offers a choice of three interior floorplans in the 43 Sundeck including a three-stateroom, deckhouse galley arrangement. Well-crafted teak interior paneling and cabinetry abound and large wraparound windows allow for plenty of natural salon lighting. Hatches in the salon sole provide good access to the engine room, but outboard space is limited due to the location of the fuel tanks. A lower helm is standard and deck access doors are port and starboard in the salon. Note the tub/shower in the aft head compartment. The 43 Sundeck (and the 43 Trawler) are offered with single or twin diesels. With twin 135-hp Lehmans, expect a cruising speed of 8–9 knots and a top speed of 11 knots. The 49 Cockpit model (same boat inside) was introduced in 1989. ❑

SPECIFICATIONS

Length	42'6"
Length WL	37'11"
Beam	14'6"
Draft	4'1"
Weight	30,000#
Clearance	NA
Water	300 Gals.
Fuel	500 Gals.
Hull Type	Semi-Disp.
Designer	C.S. Chung

Production
1981–Current

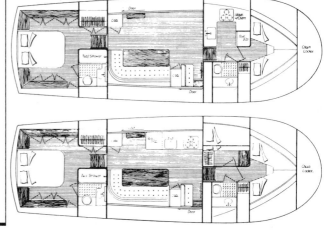

ALBIN 48 CUTTER

Originally called the Palm Beach 48 when she was introduced in 1983, the Albin 48 Cutter features an extremely deep-V (24° deadrise) Airex cored hull together with a relatively narrow beam — characteristics that generally result in good heavy weather performance. The 48 Cutter is built in Taiwan and comes with the full teak interior typical of most Asian boats. Two floorplans are offered. The three-stateroom version has stacked single berths in the guest cabin, V-berths forward, and the galley aft in the salon. The two-stateroom layout features a much larger salon with the galley-down and an offset double berth forward. In both, the owner's cabin has a queen-size berth with a tub/shower in the head. An entranceway opens from the aft stateroom to the cockpit with its transom door, swim platform, and hideaway shower. At only 31,000 lbs, the Albin 48 Cutter is a good performer. Volvo 307-hp diesels are standard (18 knots cruise/22 top) and Cat 375-hp diesels are optional (23 knots cruise/27 knots top). Albin hasn't built any 48 Cutters recently although the model is still available. ❏

SPECIFICATIONS

Length	47'9"
Length WL	43'0"
Beam	14'0"
Draft	4'0"
Weight	31,000#
Clearance	NA
Water	300 Gals.
Fuel	600 Gals.
Hull Type	Deep-V
Designer	Hunt Assoc.

Production
1983–Current

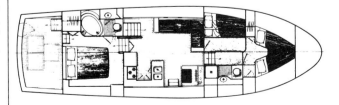

ALBIN 49 TRI CABIN

The Albin 49 Tri Cabin is a traditional Taiwan trawler with better–than–average lines and comfortable cruising accommodations for three couples. She's built on a semi-displacement hull with a fine bow entry and a relatively deep keel for stability and grounding protection. While the Albin 49 doesn't have the raised, full-width sundeck of most newer aft-cabin yachts, her full walkaround sidedecks and protective overhangs remain practical and attractive cruising features. The "Tri Cabin" refers to the staterooms in the Albin 49: there are three, each with a double berth (a slide-out affair in the forward stateroom). A convenient ladder leads directly from the lower helm area to the spacious flybridge. Notably, there are bathtubs in both heads. The interior is completely finished with teak paneling and cabinetry and the joinerwork is up to furniture-quality standards. Several engine options have been offered, but with the popular 120/135-hp Lehmans the Albin 49 Tri Cabin will cruise economically at 8–9 knots with a cruising range of around 800 miles. ❏

SPECIFICATIONS

Length	48'4"
Length WL	43'0"
Beam	15'1"
Draft	3'8"
Weight	39,050#
Clearance	13'6"
Water	320 Gals.
Fuel	620 Gals.
Hull Type	Semi-Disp.
Designer	George Stadel

Production
1979–Current

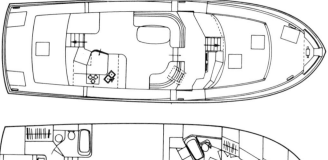

ALBIN

ATLANTIC

Brief History

Originally called the Atlantic Boat & Yacht Company, the first Atlantic model — the 44 Motor Yacht — came off the line in 1975. Financial difficulties forced the sale of the assets in 1975 to the newly formed St. Augustine Boat Works. In the early 1980s the company secured the molds to the Hargrave-designed Prairie trawlers, thus expanding their lineup to 47 feet. The name was changed to Atlantic Yacht Corp. in 1987.

Selected Atlantic Inboard Models

Atlantic 30 LRC   Atlantic 37 Double Cabin
Atlantic 34 Sportsman   Atlantic 44 Motor Yacht
Atlantic 34 Convertible   Atlantic 47 Motor Yacht

Main Office

Atlantic Yacht Corp., P.O. Box 1318, Palatka, FL 32178-1318
904-328-8348

13

ATLANTIC 30 LONG RANGE CRUISER

Introduced as the Prairie 29 Coastal Cruiser in 1978, Atlantic began producing this boat as the 30 Long Range Cruiser in 1982 when they acquired the tooling. She's built on a semi-displacement hull with a wide beam, hard chines, and a long keel. The jaunty lines and upright appearance of the Prairie 29/Atlantic 30 only hint at her spacious interior accommodations. Designed as a fuel-efficient trawler at a time when energy prices were high, she's also a comfortable cruiser with plenty of living room for one couple. Storage space is particularly good for such a small boat. There's a shower in the head, the deckhouse galley is well equipped, and the furnishings are basic and straightforward. Huge cabin windows make the small salon seem open and quite spacious. A lower helm was optional and the dinette can be rigged for a couple of guests. Several gas and diesel engine options (including twins) were offered. Most were powered with a single 85-hp Perkins and cruise economically at 6–7 knots. While Atlantic sold only a few 30 LRC models, there were over 50 Prairie 29s built. ❏

SPECIFICATIONS

Length	29'0"
Length WL	26'0"
Beam	12'0"
Draft	3'0"
Weight	12,000#
Clearance	12'7"
Water	100 Gals.
Fuel	100 Gals.
Hull Type	Semi-Disp.
Designer	Jack Hargrave

Production
1978–84

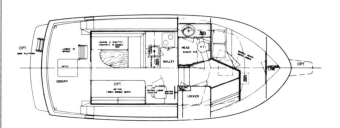

ATLANTIC 34 SPORTSMAN

Atlantic Yachts is best known for their quality trawler-style cruisers and motor yachts so it came as a surprise in 1988 to see their first new design in years fall into the sportfisherman category. Now Atlantic's best-selling boat, the 34 Sportsman is built on a solid fiberglass hull with a modified-V bottom and generous flare at the bow. Her large two-level cockpit is offered in several layouts for use as an express cruiser or sportfisherman. A centerline hatch in the bridgedeck exposes the engines and two outboard deck hatches can be unscrewed and removed for full access. The helm station and passenger seats are located on the raised deck where visibility is good in all directions. Below, the cabin accommodations are laid out in the conventional manner with V-berths forward, an enclosed head with shower, small galley, and a dinette seating area. Standard gas 454-cid Crusaders will cruise the Sportsman at 25 knots and reach a top speed of 31–32 knots with a tower and full tanks. Optional 300-hp GM 8.2 diesels cruise around 27 knots and reach 31 knots wide open. Note that the Atlantic 34 is available in hardtop, flybridge, and convertible models as well. ❏

SPECIFICATIONS

Length.....................34'0"
Beam......................12'0"
Draft ....3'0"
Weight ....13,500#
Clearance ....8'0"
Water..................40 Gals.
Fuel ....300 Gals.
Cockpit..............52 Sq. Ft.
Hull Type.........Modified-V
Designer ......Joe Scopinich

Production
1988–Current

ATLANTIC 34 CONVERTIBLE

The Atlantic 34 Convertible is built on the same hull as her sistership, the popular Atlantic 34 Sportsman. Introduced in 1989, she's built on a modified-V hull with 16° of transom deadrise and gererous flare at the bow. The conservative lines and small flybridge of the 34 Convertible result in a rather plain-Jane appearance at dockside. Basically, Atlantic engineers created the Convertible by adding a deckhouse and bridge to the existing 34 Sportsman. The resulting salon area is fully enclosed and serves as a comfortable indoor entertainment and lounge center. The layout forward of the salon is identical to the Sportsman. (Note that there is no stateroom privacy door.) While the interior of the Atlantic 34 Convertible is not notably spacious, the teak parquet sole, off-white laminates, and teak trim combine to present an attractive and low-maintenance decor. A good performer, standard gas 454-cid Crusaders will cruise around 22 knots and reach a top speed of 29-30 knots. Optional (and popular) 300-hp GM 8.2 diesels will cruise around 23 knots and reach 26 knots wide open. So far, this hasn't been a notably popular boat for Atlantic. ❑

SPECIFICATIONS

Length......................34'0"
Beam.......................12'0"
Draft ....3'2"
Weight ....16,000#
Clearance ....NA
Water..................40 Gals.
Fuel ....300 Gals.
Cockpit..............52 Sq. Ft.
Hull Type.........Modified-V
Designer......Joe Scopinich

Production
1989–Current

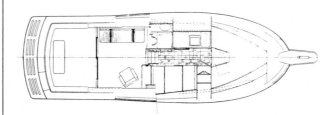

ATLANTIC 37 DOUBLE CABIN

Boating enthusiasts will recognize the Atlantic 37 Double Cabin as the old Prairie 36 Coastal Cruiser, an attractive Hargrave design built on a semi-displacement hull with soft chines and a full-length keel. Prairie produced the 36 model from 1979 until early 1982 when the company closed. Meanwhile, the 36 had been well received and she quickly gained a reputation as a good-quality, long-range family cruiser, albeit at a somewhat hefty price. Atlantic Yachts acquired the tooling and molds, and production resumed in 1982 as the Atlantic 37. The floorplan has been rearranged by moving the galley-down and adding a stall shower in the forward head, resulting in a large salon and comfortable accommodations for four. Note that Atlantic uses more interior teak and fewer laminates than in the previous Prairies. Those powered with twin 120/135-hp Lehman diesels will cruise at up to 10 knots, and the twin 250-hp Cummins (or GM) diesels cruise at 14 knots and reach a top speed of 18 knots. An absence of exterior teak reduces her maintenance requirements considerably. ❏

SPECIFICATIONS

Length	36'7"
Length WL	33'0"
Beam	13'9"
Draft	3'3"
Weight	22,000#
Clearance	14'0"
Water	200 Gals.
Fuel	350 Gals.
Hull Type	Semi-Disp.
Designer	Jack Hargrave

Production
1982–Current

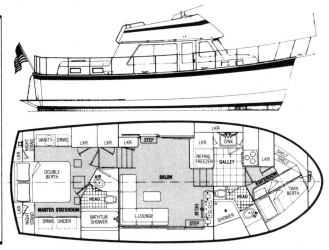

ATLANTIC 44 MOTOR YACHT

The Atlantic 44 Motor Yacht is a conservatively styled cruising yacht with one of the more attractive profiles in her class. She's been in production since 1977 — a long time for any design these days — and her appearance has changed very little over the years. Several two-stateroom floorplans have been offered. The current versions have the galley and dinette down a few steps from the salon with a choice of lower helm or entertainment center. The master stateroom is quite spacious and includes a walkaround queen berth. The interior is finished with teak paneling and cabinetry, and the overall effect is subdued and very pleasing. Outside, the raised afterdeck (a full 12' x 14') is notably large for a 44-foot yacht. Obviously designed with long-range cruising in mind, the Atlantic 44 has been offered with a variety of engines including the 135-hp Lehmans and the more powerful 375-hp Cats. At her 8.3-knot hull speed, the Atlantic 44 will cruise economically for 800–900 miles with optional fuel. Planing speeds of 19–20 knots are possible with the Caterpillar diesels. ❏

SPECIFICATIONS

Length	43'8"
Length WL	38'6"
Beam	14'0"
Draft	3'5"
Weight	30,000#
Clearance	13'8"
Water	240 Gals.
Fuel, Std	320 Gals.
Fuel, Opt	620 Gals.
Hull Type	Modified-V
Designer	Jack Hargrave

Production
1977–Current

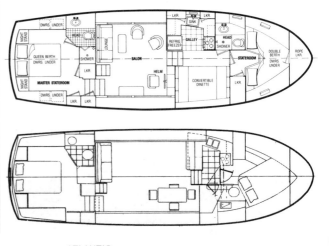

ATLANTIC

ATLANTIC 47 MOTOR YACHT

The Atlantic 47 Motor Yacht began life back in 1981 as the Prairie 46. Atlantic picked up Prairie's tooling for this (and other) models when Prairie went out of business in 1982. Thus was born the updated and revised Atlantic 47 Motor Yacht, a stylish and very traditional Hargrave-designed family cruising yacht with good sea-keeping characteristics and a fair turn of speed. The three-stateroom layout has excellent storage and includes a unique guest cabin — actually a den with a built-in desk and bookcases. Teak paneling and woodwork (good quality joinerwork) are used extensively throughout and a light oak interior has been optional in recent years. The optional afterdeck enclosure with wing doors transforms this area into a comfortable second salon complete with a wet bar and built-in TV. A cockpit version of the Atlantic 47 eliminates the guest stateroom/den and one head; in other respects the two layouts are very similar. The optional GM 6-71TI and 450-hp 6V92TA diesels cruise the Atlantic 47 MY at 17 knots and reach 20 knots top. The 550-hp 6V92TAs will reach a top speed of around 23 knots. ❑

SPECIFICATIONS

Length	46'9"
Length WL	42'6"
Beam	16'0"
Draft	3'9"
Weight	41,000#
Clearance	18'0"
Water	400 Gals.
Fuel, Std	400 Gals.
Fuel, Opt	800 Gals.
Hull Type	Modified-V
Designer	Jack Hargrave

Production
1982–Current

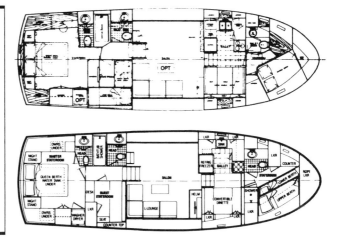

BAYLINER

Brief History

Bayliner was a tiny Arlington, Washington builder of runabouts when Orin Edson purchased the company in 1965. Under his leadership the company established the efficient assembly-line production standards that enabled Bayliner to offer its products at prices other manufacturers were unable to match. By the mid-1980s, Bayliner was recognized as the largest volume builder of pleasure boats in the world. The company was purchased by the Brunswick Corp. in late 1986.

Selected Bayliner Inboard Models

Bayliner 3288 Motor Yacht	Bayliner 3785 Avanti
Bayliner 3350 Montego	Bayliner 3888 Motor Yacht
Bayliner 3485 Avanti	Bayliner 4050 Bodega
Bayliner 3486 Convertible	Bayliner 4387 Aft Cabin
Bayliner 3550 Bristol	Bayliner 4388 Mid-cabin
Bayliner 3688 Motor Yacht	Bayliner 4588 Motor Yacht

Main Office

Bayliner Marine Corp., P.O. Box 24467, Seattle, WA 98124
206-435-5571

21

BAYLINER 3288 MOTOR YACHT

Bayliner calls their 3288 a "Motor Yacht" — a bit of advertising hype that might be considered a slight exaggeration in just a 32-foot boat. (For the record, she was called the 3270 Explorer when introduced in 1981.) Marketed as an affordable family cruiser, the Bayliner 3288 is a modern flybridge sedan with attractive lines and a comfortable interior layout that features a midships stateroom tucked below the salon dinette. Both the flybridge and cockpit are of average dimensions and are designed for enjoyable cruising. The 3288's hull is fully cored resulting in a lightweight and extremely fuel-efficient package. Propeller pockets allow the engines to be set well aft for maximum interior volume, and the keel provides protection for the running gear. Notably, the engine room is reached through large hatches in the cockpit. Twin 4-cylinder diesel engines were originally offered in the 3270, however in recent years the small 135-hp Hino diesels have become popular. While speeds are slow (16-knots cruise/17–18 top), the fuel economy is a very impressive 11–12 gph. ❏

SPECIFICATIONS

Length	32'1"
Length WL	28'10"
Beam	11'6"
Draft	2'11"
Weight	13,800#
Clearance	13'10"
Water	65 Gals.
Fuel	200 Gals.
Hull Type	Modified-V
Designer	D. Livingston

Production
1981–Current

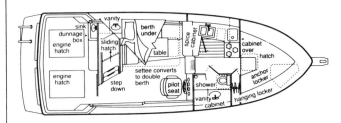

BAYLINER 3350 MONTEGO

During most of her years in production, the 3350 Montego was the largest boat in the Bayliner fleet. Thanks to the use of V-drives that allowed the engines to be moved well aft in the hull, the interior is exceptionally spacious even by today's standards. With the galley located in the salon, there is space for two private staterooms and a separate shower stall in the head. Her roomy 9'x10' salon is surrounded by large areas of safety glass, and the view from the lower helm is very good. The interior of each cabin is finished with high-pressure laminates, vinyl wall coverings, and teak trim. All of this interior space results in a rather small cockpit, but it should suffice for the needs of most cruisers. Two large hatches in the cockpit sole provide access to the engines and V-drive units. A pair of 250-hp gas engines were standard and provide a cruising speed of around 20 knots and a top speed of 28. Fuel economy is close to a mile per gallon, but the small fuel tanks limit range to less than 200 miles. With a deep 17° of transom deadrise, the 3350 Montego rides and handles well. ❑

SPECIFICATIONS

Length......................32'3"
Beam.........................11'5"
Draft ....3'0"
Weight ....12,500#
Clearance ....NA
Water....................70 Gals.
Fuel ....200 Gals.
Cockpit..............53 Sq. Ft.
Hull Type ....Modified-V
Designer ....Bayliner

Production
1974–78

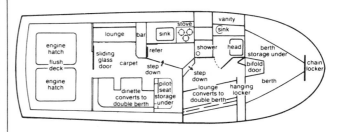

BAYLINER 3485 AVANTI SUNBRIDGE

An affordable price and sleek Mediterranean styling made the Bayliner 3485 Avanti a success among family sportboat enthusiasts until replaced with the newer 3785 Avanti in 1990. Like many other boats in her category, the 3485 (called the 3450 until the 1989 models) has plenty of sex appeal with her colorful hull graphics, Med-style bow rail, oval ports, and swept-back radar arch. The hull is fully cored to save weight and side exhausts serve to keep the noise down and gas fumes out of the cabin. With nearly 13' of beam, the 3485 Avanti is a roomy boat below with a spacious accommodation plan featuring a private aft stateroom in addition to the forward stateroom. The interior is tastefully finished with modern designer fabrics and oak trim. Cockpit seating is provided opposite the helm in the wraparound lounge/entertainment area. Access to the engines and V-drive units is via removable hatches in the cockpit sole. Standard 330-hp 454-cid gas engines will cruise the Bayliner 3485 Avanti around 20 knots and top out at 28 knots. Fuel consumption at cruising speed is approximately 22 gph. ❏

SPECIFICATIONS

Length	33'9"
Beam	12'10"
Draft	3'0"
Weight	12,000#
Clearance	9'6"
Water	50 Gals.
Fuel	205 Gals.
Hull Type	Modified-V
Designer	Bayliner

Production
1987–89

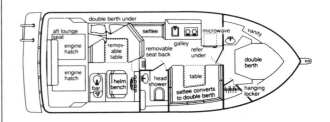

BAYLINER 3486 CONVERTIBLE

Introduced in 1987 as the 3460, the Bayliner 3486 Convertible is an inexpensive and versatile family cruiser with a distinct Mediterranean profile. While her dramatic lines and bold hull graphics will probably have limited appeal in the hard-core sportfishing community, the 3486 Convertible does have a fair-sized cockpit and features a standard bait station with an insulated livewell and sink, two in-deck fishboxes, raw water washdown, and a transom door. Inside, there's a compact mid-stateroom located beneath the salon sole in addition to the usual forward stateroom. The lower helm was standard (the instruments were updated for 1989) and the interior is a blend of white fiberglass surfaces, modern fabrics, and attractive teak paneling and trimwork. The wraparound cabin windows provide an uninterrupted 360° view of the outside world. Engine access (from the cockpit) is tight and so is the working space. A popular boat, twin 260-hp gas engines were standard and will cruise the Bayliner 3486 Convertible at around 20 knots. Top speed is 27–28 knots. ❏

SPECIFICATIONS

Length......................33'9"
Beam.....................12'10"
Draft ....3'0"
Weight ....13,900#
Clearance ....15'0"
Water..................65 Gals.
Fuel ....315 Gals.
Cockpit.......................NA
Hull Type........Modified-V
Designer ....Bayliner

Production
1987–89

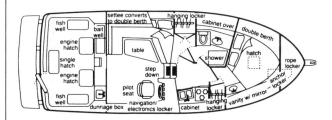

BAYLINER 3550 BRISTOL

Not ranked among the most successful of Bayliner designs, the 3550 Bristol was an inexpensive family cruiser with an attractive profile and several innovative design features. Beginning with an unusually large flybridge, the 3550 Bristol has a unique fold-down walkway with steps leading to the foredeck. The cockpit is somewhat small but the interior is surprisingly spacious as V-drives allow the engines to be moved aft to free up cabin space. Both staterooms are fitted with double berths, and the double-entry head compartment includes a separate stall shower. On the salon level, the large galley and serving counter are opposite the standard lower helm console. With the salon settee converted into a double berth at night, the Bayliner 3550 will sleep three couples with a minimum of privacy. An average performer, standard twin 330-hp gas engines will cruise the Bayliner 3550 Bristol at 18–19 knots and reach a top speed of around 27 knots. With her generous 400-gallon fuel capacity, the cruising range is an impressive 225–250 nautical miles. ❏

SPECIFICATIONS

Length	35'0"
Length WL	29'6"
Beam	13'1"
Draft	3'2"
Weight	16,000#
Clearance	11'6"
Water	150 Gals.
Fuel	400 Gals.
Cockpit	70 Sq. Ft.
Hull Type	Modified-V
Designer	Bayliner

Production
1978–81

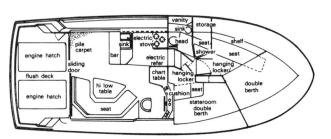

BAYLINER 3688 MOTOR YACHT

Built on a conventional modified-V hull with 14° of transom deadrise and prop pockets, the new Bayliner 3688 Motor Yacht (really a flybridge sedan) is an inexpensive and good-looking family cruiser with a very innovative interior floorplan similar to the Bayliner 32 and 38 MYs. There are V-berths in the forward stateroom — a cramped area for a 38' boat with only a draw curtain for privacy — and a double berth is fitted into the mid-cabin beneath the salon sole. In an unusual design configuration, portside steps just inside the salon door lead down to the mid-cabin where there's partial standing headroom and a built-in vanity. The result is a fairly compact salon almost consumed by the L-shaped settee and standard lower helm. Note the absence of a stall shower in the head. Additional features include a stylish integral swim platform with shower and transom door, wide sidedecks, and a comfortable flybridge with seating for six. Twin 200-hp US Marine diesels (with V-drives) are standard. No racehorse, the Bayliner 3688 MY will cruise economically at around 15 knots (at 1 mpg) and reach a top speed of 17–18 knots. ❏

SPECIFICATIONS

Length	36'1"
Length WL	NA
Beam	12'2"
Draft	2'11"
Weight	13,700#
Clearance	13'10"
Water	96 Gals.
Fuel	250 Gals.
Hull Type	Modified-V
Designer	Bayliner

Production
1992–Current

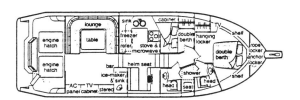

BAYLINER 3785 AVANTI SUNBRIDGE

The 3785 Avanti Sunbridge is the largest of Bayliner's Avanti express models and the only one offered with inboard engines. This is the same boat as the now-discontinued 3485 Avanti Sunbridge with the addition of a molded swim step. With nearly thirteen feet of beam, the 3785 is a roomy boat below with a large U-shaped dinette, hideaway galley, and a second stateroom located aft beneath the cockpit lounge. Overnight accommodations for up to six are provided when the dinette is converted. Note that the head is not equipped with a separate shower stall

— an unusual omission in a boat this large. The cockpit is particularly well arranged for entertaining with a huge lounge fitted just opposite the helm. The oversized, reinforced swim platform is designed to support the weight of a jet ski (or other personalized watercraft), and hatches in the cockpit sole provide access to the engines and V-drive units. With standard 330-hp gas inboards, the 3785 Avanti's cruising speed is around 21 knots and the top speed is 29–30 knots. A poor seller, production lasted only a year and the boat was discontinued in 1991. ❑

SPECIFICATIONS

Length	36'7"
Length WL	NA
Beam	12'10"
Draft	3'0"
Weight	13,150#
Clearance	9'6"
Water	50 Gals.
Fuel	205 Gals.
Cockpit	NA
Hull Type	Modified V
Designer	Bayliner

Production
1990–1991

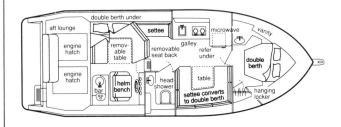

BAYLINER 3888 MOTOR YACHT

Bayliner has had a lot of success with the 3888 Motor Yacht since her introduction in 1983. (Until 1989, she was called the 3870 MY.) Although not a "motor yacht" in the accepted sense of the word, she is a roomy sedan with plenty of interior volume and cruising comforts that most families will love. The 3888 features an innovative two-stateroom layout with a mid-cabin below the salon sole and separate heads for each stateroom. Notable is the double-entry tub/shower stall with direct access from the master stateroom. Also unusual in a 38-foot boat is the cockpit access to the engine room. Early models were powered with twin 135-hp Mitsubishi 6-cylinder diesels, but these engines were dropped in 1986 in favor of U.S. Marine 175-hp diesels — an update that boosted the cruising speed from 14 to 18 knots and the top speed from 18 to 21 knots. Fuel consumption at cruising speeds (2750 rpm) is a startling 14 gallons per hour making the 38 an extremely fuel-efficient boat considering her size. With over 900 sold, the Bayliner 3888 has been a decidedly popular boat. ❏

SPECIFICATIONS

Length	38'2"
Beam	13'5"
Draft	3'2"
Weight	19,608#
Clearance	14'10"
Water	80 Gals.
Fuel	304 Gals.
Hull Type	Modified-V
Designer	Bayliner

Production
1983–Current

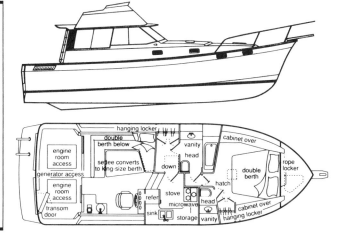

BAYLINER 4050 BODEGA

Although the somewhat boxy profile of the Bayliner 4050 Bodega has often been remarked upon, no one will dispute her generous living areas. Indeed, the interior accommodations of the Bodega rival those found in much larger boats. A total of three staterooms are provided (including a truly spacious master) together with a very large salon and galley area. Although the emphasis is clearly on interior comforts, the outdoor entertainment areas are equally large and include a raised aft deck and a huge 150 sq. ft. flybridge. A unique fold-down ladder leading from the bridge to the foredeck is a popular feature found in later models. The Bodega is a light boat for her size and the freeboard is quite high. With standard 330-hp 454-cid gas engines, she'll cruise at 14–15 knots while consuming about 28 gph. Top speed is 24 knots, and the range at cruising speed is approximately 200 miles. The solid fiberglass hull is designed with moderate bow flare, a shallow keel and 14° of deadrise at the transom. Production of the 4050 Bodega ended in 1983 with the introduction the following year of the Bayliner 45 Motor Yacht. ❏

SPECIFICATIONS

Length......................40'0"
Beam.......................14'0"
Draft ....3'8"
Weight ....23,000#
Clearance ....NA
Water................114 Gals.
Fuel ....400 Gals.
Hull Type.........Modified-V
Designer ....Bayliner

Production
1978–83

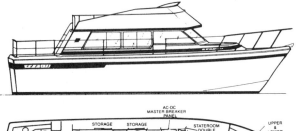

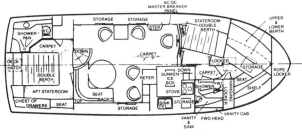

BAYLINER

BAYLINER 4387 AFT CABIN MY

Bridging the gap between Bayliner's popular 4588 MY and 3888 MY is the new 4387 MY, a modern aft cabin design showing a good deal of European styling influence. Her modified-V hull carries 14° of deadrise at the transom and at only 19,500 lbs., she's a light boat for her size. The design emphasis of this model is clearly on comfortable interior accommodations. Although the salon dimensions are not notably generous, the large 360° wraparound windows create a surprisingly spacious impression. A lower helm is standard and the galley and dinette are down from the salon

level. Both staterooms are fitted with double berths. Topside, the 4387 features a large flybridge with seating for six, a foredeck sun pad, and an integral transom platform with molded boarding steps. The sundeck is large enough for a few folding chairs and comes with a wet bar. Standard power for the Bayliner 4387 MY is 330-hp gas engines which will cruise around 17 knots with a top speed of 26 knots. Optional 220-hp U.S. Marine diesels cruise around 20 knots and reach 25 knots top. With only 300 gallons of fuel the cruising range is limited with the gas engines. ❑

SPECIFICATIONS

Length	43'1"
Length WL	NA
Beam	14'3"
Draft	3'0"
Weight	19,500#
Clearance	13'6"
Water	100 Gals.
Fuel	300 Gals.
Hull Type	Modified-V
Designer	Bayliner

Production
1990–Current

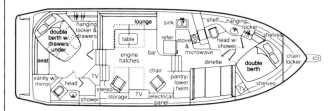

BAYLINER 4388 MID CABIN

Bayliners may not represent any landmarks for quality in the boating industry, but few would argue that their designs aren't innovative and practical from the family cruising point of view. The Bayliner 4388 Mid Cabin is a case in point. By moving the salon bulkhead well aft, the interior is unusually large for a sedan of this size, although the cockpit is definately on the small side. Included in the wide-open floorplan are two staterooms (each with a double berth), two heads with a common shower stall, lower helm, and a roomy salon which is open to the galley. Note that the double berth in the (compact) guest stateroom extends below the galley floor, and that the galley and lower helm are raised a couple of steps from the salon level. Outside, there's a shower and fold-down swim platform in the transom, and the flybridge is arranged with the helm console forward and guest seating aft. Engine access is via hatches in the cockpit sole. Standard 250-hp U.S. Marine diesels (with V-drives) will cruise the Bayliner 4300 at 22 knots and reach around 25–26 knots top. ❏

SPECIFICATIONS

Length	43'1"
Length WL	NA
Beam	14'3"
Draft	3'0"
Weight	19,000#
Clearance	13'6"
Water	100 Gals.
Fuel	300 Gals.
Hull Type	Modified-V
Designer	Bayliner

Production
1991–Current

4388 MID-CABIN MOTORYACHT

BAYLINER 4588 MOTOR YACHT

Flagship of today's Bayliner fleet, this handsome pilothouse yacht has become recognized as one of the best big-boat values in the industry. A careful blend of Pacific West Coast styling and comfortable interior accommodations result in a long-range motor yacht with instant eye appeal. Pilothouse yachts make excellent cruisers, and they offer obvious advantages in bad weather or cold climates. In the case of the Bayliner 4588, the raised wheelhouse is set well forward over the deck and visibility is excellent. While she can sleep three couples, this is really a two-couple boat with the third stateroom easily used as a den/study. Outside, the bridge overhang provides weather protection in the cockpit, and the flybridge will accommodate a Whaler. With standard 220-hp U.S. Marine diesels (240-hp since 1991), the Bayliner 4588 will cruise at 16–17 knots where the fuel economy is nearly 1 mpg — hard to believe in a 45-foot yacht. The hull is fully cored to reduce weight, and a sharp entry and 15" keel provide good seakeeping qualities. Already a big marketing success with over 350 built, the 4588 MY is a lot of boat considering her affordable price. ❑

SPECIFICATIONS

Length......................45'4"
Beam......................14'11"
Draft ....3'0"
Weight ....28,000#
Clearance ....15'6"
Water..................200 Gals.
Fuel ....500 Gals.
Hull Type.........Modified-V
Designer ....Bayliner

Production
1984–Current

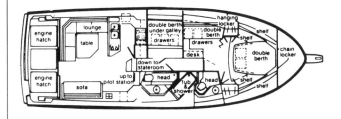

BERTRAM

Brief History

Bertram began building boats in 1961 with the introduction of the world-famous Bertram 31 with its then-radical deep-V hull design. The company pioneered in the use of fiberglass and is recognized today as a leader in the construction of high-quality and well-engineered tournament sportfishing boats. Bertram has been owned by several companies over the years including the Whittaker Corporation, and has recently been purchased by a group of Italian investors following bankruptcy.

Selected Bertram Inboard Models

Bertram 28 FB Cruiser
Bertram 28 Sport Fisherman
Bertram 28 Bahia Mar
Bertram 28 Moppie
Bertram 30 FB Cruiser
Bertram 31 FB Cruiser
Bertram 31 Sport Fisherman
Bertram 31 Bahia Mar
Bertram 33 FB Cruiser
Bertram 33 Sportfisherman
Bertram 35 Convertible
Bertram 37 Convertible
Bertram 38 Salon
Bertram 38 Convertible

Bertram 38 III Convertible
Bertram 38 Special
Bertram 42 Motor Yacht
Bertram 42 Convertible
Bertram 43 Convertible
Bertram 46 Convertible
Bertram 46 Motor Yacht
Bertram 50 Convertible
Bertram 54 Convertible
Bertram 58 Motor Yacht
Bertram 58 Convertible
Bertram 60 Convertible
Bertram 72 Convertible

Main Office

Bertram Yachts, 3663 NW 21st St., Miami, FL 33142
305-633-8011

BERTRAM 28 FLYBRIDGE CRUISER

The immensely popular Bertram 28 Flybridge Cruiser is the best-selling Bertram ever. Designed along the lines of the successful 31 Flybridge Cruiser, the 28 quickly earned a reputation as a capable offshore fisherman. An excellent sea boat with a wide beam and a large bi-level cockpit, she's built on a deep-V hull with a steep 23° of deadrise at the transom. Inside, her layout includes berths for four with a convertible dinette, an efficient galley area, and a spacious head with shower. The woodgrain mica interior was dropped in 1983 and replaced with a contemporary light oak woodwork. Updates in 1990 included a rearranged interior with a more open floorplan and an enlarged flybridge. An optional teak interior became available in 1991. Superior workmanship, constant engineering updates and product refinement have kept the 28 FBC at the forefront of small fishing boat designs. Twin 228/230-hp gas engines (21 knot cruise/30 knots top) were standard until 1986 when they were replaced with the current 260-hp MerCruisers (23 cruise/32 top). Updates in 1992 include optional 230-hp Volvo diesels (28-knot cruise). Fuel increases came in 1980 and 1986. ❏

SPECIFICATIONS

Length	28'6"
Length WL	23'4"
Beam	11'0"
Draft	2'8"
Weight	12,060#
Clearance	9'4"
Water	54 Gals.
Fuel	165/185/240
Cockpit	85 Sq. Ft.
Hull Type	Deep-V
Designer	Dave Napier

Production
1971–Current

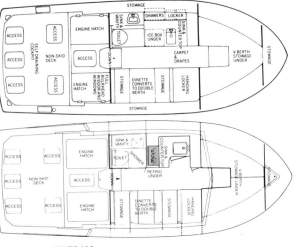

BERTRAM

BERTRAM 28 SPORT FISHERMAN

The Bertram 28 Sport Fisherman has the same deep-V hull (23° deadrise) and distinctive profile of the 28 Flybridge Cruiser, but with an open cabin for improved fishability. A galley and dinette were optional and the head is fitted below the forward berths in the cabin. Simple and easy to clean, this type of basic open-air layout is ideal in a serious sportfishing day boat. Few changes were made to the 28 Sport Fisherman during her long production run, and while she never attained the level of popularity enjoyed by the more versatile 28 Flybridge Cruiser, used models are still valued today by experienced offshore anglers. From the standpoint of construction and design, few production fishing boats in this size range can match the performance of the Bertram 28 SF in bad weather. Note the unique grabrails which serve to divide the cockpit and keep spectators away from the action. Most were powered with 230-hp MerCruiser engines which provide a cruising speed of around 21 knots and 30 knots at full throttle. A Bertram 28 Hardtop was also offered on the same hull. ❏

SPECIFICATIONS

Length	28'6"
Length WL	23'4"
Beam	11'0"
Draft	2'8"
Weight	11,320#
Clearance	9'4"
Water	27 Gals.
Fuel	185
Cockpit	85 Sq. Ft.
Hull Type	Deep-V
Designer	Dave Napier

Production
1971–83

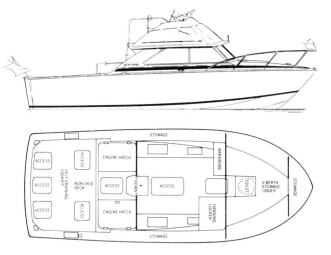

BERTRAM

BERTRAM 28 BAHIA MAR

The Bertram 28 Bahia Mar shares the same hull as the Bertram 28 FBC and SF models. Easily recognized in a crowd, her low-profile deckhouse and wraparound windshield reflect a distinctive European styling influence. The Bahia Mar is a superb sea boat, and her deep-V hull design and low center of gravity result in superior offshore performance and handling characteristics. A no-compromise fishing boat at heart, she features a large, unobstructed cockpit with low freeboard and a simple (but rather well finished) cabin arrangement offering basic accommo-dations for two. Visibility from the helm position is good and sightlines are excellent in all directions. The original raised engine boxes were eliminated in the 1986 models in favor of a flush deck; either way, service access to the motors is good. An impressive per-former, standard 260-hp MerCruiser gas engines will cruise the Bertram 28 Bahia Mar around 23 knots (21 gph) and reach a top speed of 32–33 knots. Updates for 1992 include 230-hp Volvo diesels (29+ knots cruise). Note that the fuel capacity was increased in 1986 to 240 gallons. ❏

SPECIFICATIONS

Length	28'6"
Length WL	23'4"
Beam	11'0"
Draft	2'8"
Weight	11,700#
Clearance	7'9"
Water	48 Gals.
Fuel	185/240 Gals.
Cockpit	85 Sq. Ft.
Hull Type	Deep-V
Designer	Dave Napier

Production
1985–Current

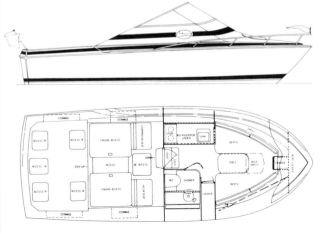

BERTRAM 28 MOPPIE

The latest in a long string of Bertram 28-footers, the Moppie is a stylish inboard runabout with the quality engineering and construction features expected of a Bertram product. Her sleek, Eurostyle profile is attractively accented with a painted windshield frame and bowrails, and the Moppie has the modern sportboat "look" popular with many of today's performance-boat buyers. She's built on the standard Bertram 28 deep-V hull with solid fiberglass construction and a steep 23° of deadrise at the transom. Aside from her superb offshore handling characteristics,

the Moppie's primary attraction is her expansive and versatile bi-level cockpit layout. The lower level has a full 85 sq. ft. of unobstructed fishing space with plenty of room for a mounted chair. In a practical design application, the galley is concealed in molded lockers abaft the helm and companion seats in the cockpit. The compact cabin accommodations are basic with a head and V-berths. A good performer with standard 260-hp gas engines, the 28 Moppie will cruise at 24 knots and reach a top speed of around 32 knots. Updates for 1992 include 230-hp diesels which cruise at 29 knots. ❑

SPECIFICATIONS

Length	28'6"
Length WL	23'4"
Beam	11'0"
Draft	2'7"
Weight	10,400#
Clearance	7'1"
Water	27 Gals.
Fuel	234 Gals.
Cockpit	85 Sq. Ft.
Hull Type	Deep-V
Designer	Dave Napier

Production
1987–Current

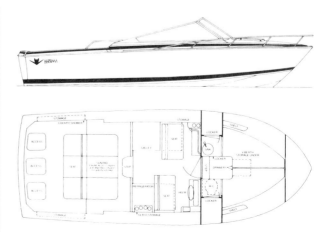

BERTRAM 30 FLYBRIDGE CRUISER

Bertram rarely misfires when it comes to new model introductions, so it's notable when one of their designs fails to catch on with the public. Such was the case with the Bertram 30 Flybridge Cruiser — a boat that some (including a lot of industry professionals) thought destined to replace the classic Bertram 31 in the hearts of serious anglers. She's exactly the same length as the Bertram 31, but with slightly smaller cockpit dimensions, less transom deadrise (18.5° vs. 23°), improved trolling stability, and a notably dryer ride. The improvements

carried into the interior as well, where the Bertram 30's stylish oak-paneled accommodations provide luxuries undreamed of in the old Bertram 31. Lasting only two years in production, the Bertram 30 Flybridge Cruiser proved too expensive for the market and she was withdrawn in 1985. With standard MerCruiser 340-hp gas engines, she'll cruise at 22 knots (29 gph) and reach a top speed of about 30 knots. Note that a handsome (but very traditional) 30-foot express model was also available with the same cabin layout. ❑

SPECIFICATIONS

Length	30'7"
Beam	11'4"
Draft	3'0"
Weight	16,500#
Clearance	8'5"
Water	61 Gals.
Fuel	220 Gals.
Cockpit	101 Sq. Ft.
Hull Type	Deep-V
Designer	Dave Napier

Production
1984–85

BERTRAM

BERTRAM 31 FLYBRIDGE CRUISER

Nothing in powerboating has equalled the continued worldwide popularity of the original deep-V boat — the Bertram 31. Nearly 2,000 were built over the years and used models are continually in demand regardless of age or condition. With her enclosed cabin, the Flybridge Cruiser proved to be the most popular of the Bertram 31 series. Unquestionably, the chief attribute of the Bertram 31 is her legendary deep-V hull design. In addition to her superb seakeeping characteristics (and well-known wet ride), the 31 FBC has a large and uncluttered fishing cockpit and a comfortable (if Spartan) cabin with overnight berths for four. Regular production ended in 1983, but 23 "Silver Anniversary" models were built in 1986 with oak interiors and custom hull striping. Twin 330-hp MerCruiser gas engines have powered the majority of the Bertram 31s, with GM, Caterpillar, or Cummins diesels offered as options. The Mercs cruise around 23 knots with a top speed of 32+ knots. Diesel-powered models have less speed but greatly improved range (300+ miles). Note that the fuel capacity increased in 1972 from 170 to 222 gallons. ❏

SPECIFICATIONS

Length	30'7"
Length WL	27'2"
Beam	11'2"
Draft	3'1"
Weight	10,600#
Clearance	11'0"
Water	18 Gals.
Fuel	170/222 Gals.
Cockpit	110 Sq. Ft.
Hull Type	Deep-V
Designer	Ray Hunt

Production
1961–83

BERTRAM

BERTRAM 31 SPORT FISHERMAN

The Bertram 31 Sport Fisherman is the quintessential American fishing machine — a genuine classic that gave birth to the deep-V hull design and (not incidentally) to the Bertram company as well. This is one of the few small boats that can compete in bluewater tournament events without being at all out of place. Performance in head and following seas is outstanding, and her open cabin layout and ease of maintenance quickly earned the 31 SF a loyal and dedicated following among serious anglers and charter boat operators. Over 500 changes were made in the Bertram 31 during her long production run (mainly cosmetic or hardware-related), but the only significant design modification consisted of widening the hull chines in the early days. Standard 330-hp MerCruiser gas engines will cruise around 23 knots (27 gph) and reach a top speed of 33 knots. The fuel capacity was increased in 1972 from the original 170 gallons to 222 gallons. A stable and highly maneuverable sportfisherman, used Bertram 31s are always in demand despite her reputation for being a wet boat in a chop. ❑

SPECIFICATIONS

Length	30'7"
Length WL	27'2"
Beam	11'2"
Draft	3'1"
Weight	10,600#
Clearance	11'0"
Water	18 Gals.
Fuel	170/222 Gals.
Cockpit	110 Sq. Ft.
Hull Type	Deep-V
Designer	Ray Hunt

Production
1961–82

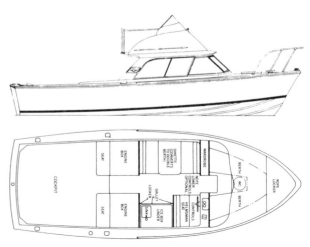

BERTRAM

BERTRAM 31 BAHIA MAR

Built on the legendary Bertram 31 deep-V hull with a steep 23° of deadrise at the transom, the 31 Bahia Mar is an open sportcruiser design with a large fishing cockpit and basic interior accommodations for two. Bahia Mars have attracted a remarkable following among serious anglers who have come to appreciate her numerous fishing attributes. Thanks to her low-profile and low center of gravity, the 31 Bahia Mar is a stable fishing platform and ranks with the best modern designs when it comes to overall fishability. Her completely open cockpit arrangement puts the helm close to the action, and the cockpit itself is much larger than in most other sportfishermen of her size and type. Visibility from the helm is another feature fisherman have come to admire in the Bahia Mar 31 — sightlines are excellent in all directions. The Bahia Mar is considered a superb all-round utility boat and many have seen years of operation in charter and dive-boat fleets. Engine options and performance data are about the same as in the Bertram 31 FB Cruiser and Sportfish models. ❑

SPECIFICATIONS

Length	30'7"
Length WL	27'2"
Beam	11'2"
Draft	2'9"
Weight	9,400#
Clearance	8'3"
Water	18 Gals.
Fuel	222 Gals.
Cockpit	147 Sq. Ft.
Hull Type	Deep-V
Designer	Ray Hunt

Production
1966–81

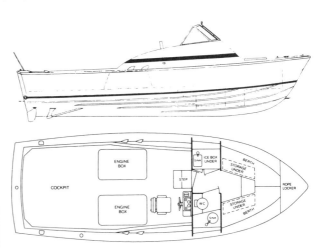

BERTRAM

BERTRAM 33 FLYBRIDGE CRUISER

The Bertram 33 FB Cruiser is a particularly flexible boat that can provide adequate service as a weekend fisherman while still offering excellent cruising accommodations. Built on a deep-V hull (17° deadrise), the high deckhouse profile of the 33 FBC makes her a somewhat tender boat offshore. She was originally offered with a single-stateroom layout until a more popular two-stateroom interior became standard in 1980. In 1981 a new tournament flybridge was added, and in 1984 a teak interior decor replaced the woodgrain mica cabinetry. The Bertram 33 II version was introduced in 1988 and features a restyled flybridge and an oak interior. Changes in 1990 included a revised layout with a stall shower in the head. In 1992 a varnished maple interior became standard (teak is optional). Twin 454-cid gas engines will cruise the Bertram 33 around 19 knots. Optional 270-hp Cats cruise at 23 knots and the newer 320-hp Cats cruise at 26-27 knots and reach 32 knots top. Note that the fuel capacity was increased for the gas models in 1980 although today's diesel-powered 33s are fitted with a 250-gal. tank. ❑

SPECIFICATIONS

Length	33'0"
Beam	12'6"
Draft	3'0"
Weight	22,800#
Clearance	12'6"
Fresh Water	70 Gals.
Fuel, Gas	250/315
Fuel, Dsl	255 Gals.
Cockpit	72 Sq. Ft.
Hull Type	Deep-V
Designer	Dave Napier

Production
1977–Current

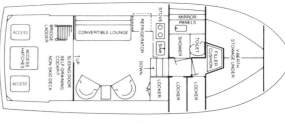

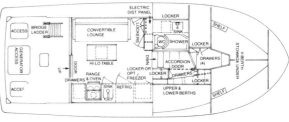

BERTRAM

BERTRAM 33 SPORT FISHERMAN

Built on the same deep-V hull as the 33 FB Cruiser, the Bertram 33 SF has a much larger cockpit than the 33 FBC, but no salon. Her aggressive low-profile lines, spacious flybridge, and top-quality engineering have made the 33 a favorite with deep-water fishermen. The interior accommodations were enlarged and rearranged in 1986 by moving the cabin bulkhead aft a few inches and replacing the dinette with a settee. The loss in cockpit space (122 to 116 sq. ft.) is negligible. An light oak interior was added in 1985, the fly-bridge was restyled in 1988 and a maple interior became standard in 1992. Engines are located under raised boxes in the cockpit for easy access. Twin 330-hp MerCruiser gas engines are standard (20 knot cruise/29 knots top), and 270-hp 3208T Cat diesels were optional (23 knots cruise/27 knots top). Beginning in 1992 optional 320-hp Cats cruise at 27 knots and reach 31 knots top. Note that the fuel capacity for gas models was increased to 310 gallons in 1980. The 33 SF is a big boat for her size with good styling, superior construction, and proven offshore performance. Resale values are generally very strong. ❏

SPECIFICATIONS

Length	33'0"
Beam	12'6"
Draft	3'0"
Weight	22,400#
Clearance	11'6"
Water	70 Gals.
Fuel, Gas	250/310 Gals.
Fuel, Dsl	250 Gals.
Cockpit	116 Sq. Ft.
Hull Type	Deep-V
Designer	Dave Napier

Production
1979–Current

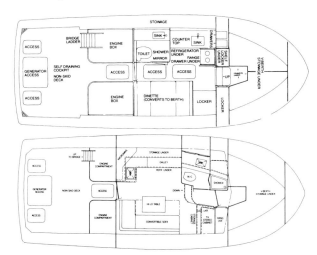

BERTRAM 35 CONVERTIBLE

Few boats can rival the 15-year production run enjoyed by the Bertram 35 Convertible. For many, 35 feet is the ideal size for a sportfisherman short of going into serious debt. Although the large interior is suitable for family cruising, the Bertram 35 is most at home as a fisherman where her large cockpit, precise handling, and terrific sea-keeping qualities are most appreciated. Twin 350-hp Crusader gas engines were standard (19–20 knots cruise/28 top), with Cummins V-555s (around 17 knots cruise/23 knots top) or 300-hp Cat 3208Ts (23 knots cruise/28 knots top) available as options. With these 300-hp turbo-Cats (1981–85 models), the Bertram 35 becomes a much-improved performer. A new Bertram 35 II model came out in 1981 with an updated tournament-style flybridge design, and in 1984 a long-overdue teak interior replaced the previous woodgrain mica decor. The vinyl cockpit sole was replaced with fiberglass in 1982 — a notable improvement. Used Bertram 35 Convertibles are always in demand and generally bring a premium price at resale. ❏

SPECIFICATIONS

Length	35'4"
Length WL	30'3"
Beam	13'3"
Draft	3'2"
Weight	22,500#
Clearance	12'6"
Water	50/75 Gals.
Fuel	285/273 Gals.
Cockpit	92 Sq. Ft.
Hull Type	Deep-V
Designer	Dave Napier

Production
1970–85

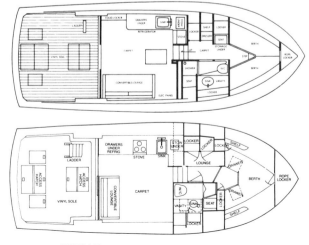

BERTRAM

BERTRAM 37 CONVERTIBLE

Modern construction and superb styling characterize the Bertram 37, an aggressive-looking sportfisherman designed for tournament-level activities. Using the latest in unidirectional fabrics and carbon fiber composites, the 37 is built on a deep-V hull (18° deadrise) cored from the waterline up. She's dry and stable offshore and able to run in seas that keep other boats her size tied up at the docks. Her two-stateroom layout is luxuriously furnished and includes overhead rod storage in the salon, over/under bunks in the small guest cabin, a walkaround island berth forward, and light oak cabinetry and woodwork throughout. In 1992 a varnished maple interior became standard. (Note that 1986 models had a grey lizzard-skin interior.) GM 450-hp 6V92s cruise at a brisk 28 knots (31 knots top), and for 1992 the optional 550-hp 6V92s will cruise at *over* 30 knots and reach a blistering 34+ knots wide open. Cat 375-hp diesels cruise around 23 knots and have a top speed of 27 knots. Considered by many to be the best in her class (and priced accordingly), the Bertram 37 receives high marks for her top-quality engineering and exceptional performance. ❏

SPECIFICATIONS

Length	37'9"
Length WL	32'9"
Beam	13'3"
Draft	3'9"
Weight	27,910#
Clearance	12'11"
Water	100 Gals.
Fuel	473 Gals.
Cockpit	93 Sq. Ft.
Hull Type	Deep-V
Designer	Dave Napier

Production
1986–Current

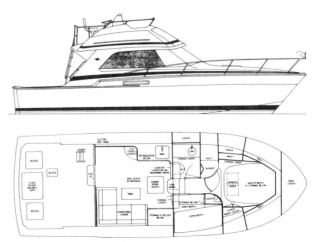

BERTRAM

BERTRAM 38 SALON

The Bertram 38 Salon was introduced in 1969 and for several years represented Bertram's only motor yacht model. She was based on the earlier 37 Salon (1967–69), an all-fiberglass double cabin design with a deep-V hull and a low-profile superstructure. With the 38 Salon, Bertram reworked the deckhouse and updated the interior to more contemporary standards. The galley-up, two-stateroom floorplan features twin berths in the aft stateroom, V-berths forward, and two head compartments with a stall shower aft. The interior is fully paneled with woodgrain mica. The galley is small, and hatches in the salon sole provide access to an average-sized engine room. Outside, the helm is protected with a wraparound windshield and hardtop. The aft deck, while not large by modern standards, is sufficient for a few folding deck chairs. Twin gas engines were standard with GM and Cummins diesels offered as options. With the gas engines, the Bertram 38 Salon will cruise at 16–17 knots and reach a top speed of around 25 knots. The 320-hp Cummins engines cruise around 18–19 knots. The 283-hp GM 8V53s cruise about 17–18 knots. ❏

SPECIFICATIONS

Length	38'6"
Length WL	NA
Beam	13'0"
Draft	3'6"
Weight	22,000#
Clearance	NA
Water	94 Gals.
Fuel	340 Gals.
Hull Type	Deep-V
Designer	Ray Hunt

Production
1969–75

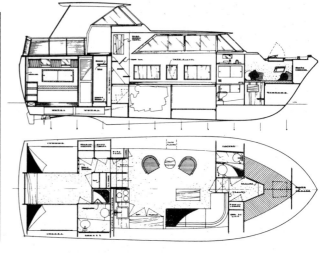

BERTRAM

BERTRAM 38 CONVERTIBLE

The Bertram 38 Convertible was the second of three 38-foot Bertram models built over the years, the first being a Hunt-designed flybridge cruiser produced for the family market back in the early 1960s. In the case of the 38 Convertible, the emphasis was on fishability, pure and simple. Her deep-V hull (22° deadrise aft) was designed along the lines of the original Bertram 31 and her extra-wide beam provides the stability often missing in a deep-V design. Long out of production but still popular with budget-minded anglers, her large and uncluttered fishing cockpit and practical cabin accommodations continue to appeal to anglers in spite of her age. The interior is efficiently arranged with the galley-up, V-berths in the forward stateroom, and over/under berths in the guest cabin. By any standard, the woodgrain mica interior of the Bertram 38 is plain but clean-up is easy. Twin 325-hp gas engines were standard (18 knot cruise/27 knots top), however most of the Bertram 38 Convertibles were delivered with the GM 8V53 or Cummins V903 diesels and cruise around 17–18 knots. ❏

SPECIFICATIONS

Length	37'8"
Length WL	32'11"
Beam	14'5"
Draft	3'6"
Weight	26,000#
Clearance	NA
Water	100 Gals.
Fuel	350 Gals.
Cockpit	109 Sq. Ft.
Hull Type	Deep-V
Designer	Ray Hunt

Production
1970–76

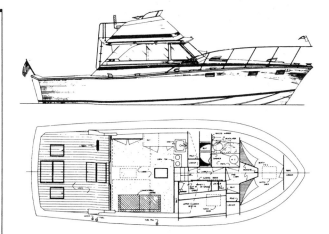

BERTRAM 38 III CONVERTIBLE

The Bertram 38 III is an entirely different boat from the earlier Bertram 38 Convertible (1970–76). She has a more graceful profile, less beam, a shallower "V" bottom (from 22° deadrise to a more moderate 17° at the transom), and improved handling and performance characteristics. Aimed at the sportfishing market, the 38 III's large cockpit and tournament-style flybridge make her extremely well suited for serious bluewater events. Inside, her two-stateroom layout is efficient and well organized. Updates in 1982 replaced the original Nautilex cockpit sole with a fiberglass deck, and a new teak interior became standard. A little wet at times, the 38 III is otherwise known as a capable sea boat with a good cruising range. Nearly all were diesel powered. The most popular options were Cat 300-hp diesels (19–20 knots cruise), and the Cat 355-hp and Cummins 380-hp VT903 engines — both of which cruise around 23–24 knots. Production ceased in 1987 with the introduction of the new Bertram 37. A total of 331 Bertram 38 IIIs were built making her one of the best-selling 38' sportfishing boats ever. ❑

SPECIFICATIONS

Length	38'5"
Length WL	33'0"
Beam	13'3"
Draft	4'2"
Weight	30,400#
Clearance	13'0"
Water	100 Gals.
Fuel	395 Gals.
Cockpit	100 Sq. Ft.
Hull Type	Deep-V
Designer	Dave Napier

Production
1978–86

BERTRAM 38 SPECIAL

The Bertram 38 Special is a high-quality, fast-action sportfisherman with a huge fishing cockpit for serious tournament-level pursuits. Her hull is the same as that used in the 38 III Convertible but with balsa coring placed in the hullsides forward of the engine bulkhead. The design philosophy behind the 38 Special was to give the bluewater angler a pure, no-nonsense fishing machine with good performance and plenty of range. Although the interior is limited in size, the rounded bulkheads and radiused corners make the most of the available space. Visibility from the raised helm position is very good. A small hatch provides routine access to the engines and the entire bridgedeck sole is removable for major work. Caterpillar 375-hp diesels were standard (25 knot cruise/29 knots wide open). GM 6V71TAs rated at 435-hp were optional and increased the cruising speed to about 27 knots and the top speed to 31 knots. Among the more expensive dayboats, the Bertram 38 Special enjoyed limited market success due to her high cost and production ended after just two years. ❏

SPECIFICATIONS

Length	38'5"
Beam	13'3"
Draft	4'2"
Weight	27,000#
Clearance	9'11"
Water	100 Gals.
Fuel	395 Gals.
Cockpit	97 Sq. Ft.
Hull Type	Deep-V
Designer	Bertram

Production
1986–87

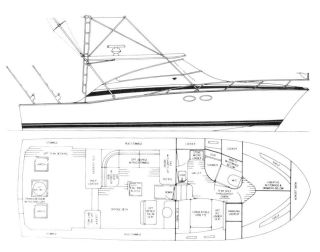

BERTRAM 42 MOTOR YACHT

A distinctive flush deck profile gives the Bertram 42 Motor Yacht the stately appearance still admired by many motor yacht traditionalists. Designed on a deep-V hull with 17° of deadrise aft, this is the same hull used in the production of the Bertram 42 Convertible. The interior layout is certainly the most notable feature of the 42 Motor Yacht. By placing the forward companionway to starboard, the galley space was enlarged and the salon took on impressive visual proportions. A new teak interior became available in 1983, and a queen berth in the master stateroom was standard beginning in 1986. No lightweight, the Bertram 42 MY can handle the kind of offshore sea conditions that keep other motor yachts her size in protected waters. The majority were powered with the 335-hp GM 6-71TI diesels. With these engines, the range is about 250 miles at a 19-knot cruising speed. Later models using the 375-hp 6V71TA diesels cruise around 22 knots while burning 35 gph. Figures for the standard 330-hp gas engines are 16 knots at cruise and 22–23 knots at full throttle. ❏

SPECIFICATIONS

Length......................42'6"
Beam.......................14'10"
Draft ....4'0"
Weight ....39,000#
Clearance...............17'11"
Water.................150 Gals.
Fuel ....406 Gals.
Hull Type ....Deep-V
Designer ....Bertram

Production
1973–87

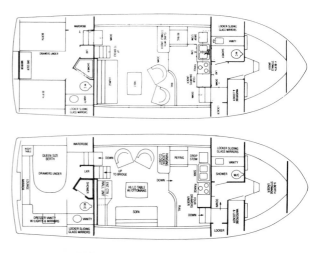

BERTRAM 42 CONVERTIBLE

One of Bertram's most successful boats, the 42 Convertible needs no introduction to experienced tournament-level sportfishermen. A total of 329 were built and her exceptional heavy-weather performance, superb fishability, good range, and top-quality construction have earned for the Bertram 42 a reputation as a classic design. Heavily built on a deep-V hull (17° deadrise), numerous changes were made during her long production run. In 1981 the twin sliding salon doors were replaced with a single door, and the flybridge helm position was moved from portside to the centerline. A new teak interior replaced the earlier wood-grain mica decor, and the vinyl cockpit sole was upgraded to fiberglass in 1982. The following year a queen bed became standard in the master stateroom. A restyled flybridge in 1986 added much to her rakish profile, and a new oak interior became available in 1987. Cummins 420-hp diesels (popular through 1979) and 435-hp GM 6V92TAs (1980–84 models) cruise around 24 knots, and the more recent 475-hp 6V92TAs cruise at 25+ knots. Resale values are consistently strong. ❑

SPECIFICATIONS

Length	42'6"
Beam	14'10"
Draft	4'0"
Weight	39,400#
Clearance	14'11"
Water	150 Gals.
Fuel	488 Gals.
Cockpit	108 Sq. Ft.
Hull Type	Deep-V
Designer	Bertram

Production
1975–87

BERTRAM

BERTRAM 43 CONVERTIBLE

The introduction of the Bertram 43 Convertible in 1988 was greeted with enthusiastic media reviews. Indeed, there is much to like about the Bertram 43 Convertible. She's the fourth in the series of "new breed" Bertram designs, beginning with the 54 Convertible in 1981 and leading to the 37 and 50 Convertibles in 1986–87. Built on the new Bertram hull design with balsa coring in the hullsides and 17.5° deadrise aft, the 43 Convertible handles and performs like the thoroughbred sportfisherman she is — agile, dry, and fast. Her elegant two-stateroom interior is luxuriously appointed and finished with light oak joinerwork. First offered with a galley-up layout and two heads, an alternate galley-down floorplan was introduced in 1989 (at the expense of one of the heads). The cockpit is a full 120 sq. ft., and an extended bridge overhang shades the bait and tackle stations. A well-designed raised electronics console at the helm eliminates the need for an overhead electronics cabinet. GM 550-hp 6V92TA diesels will cruise the Bertram 43 around 25 knots with a top speed of 28+. Range at a hard cruise is over 300 miles. ❏

SPECIFICATIONS

Length......................43'4"
Beam.....................14'11"
Draft ....4'4"
Weight ....41,890#
Clearance.................13'5"
Water.................160 Gals.
Fuel ....567 Gals.
Cockpit ....120 Sq. Ft.
Hull Type ....Deep-V
Designer ....Bertram

Production
1988–Current

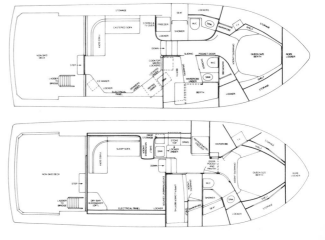

BERTRAM 46 CONVERTIBLE

With some 500 built before production ended in 1987, the Bertram 46 Convertible was for a number of years the standard by which other production sportfishing boats were measured. Her popularity has much to do with the seakeeping ability of Bertram's deep-V (19° deadrise) hull. Originally a two-stateroom boat with the galley-down, a three-stateroom model (the 46 II) was available during 1983–85. Significant design changes include a single sliding salon door (replacing double doors) in 1981, a fiberglass cockpit sole (replacing the Nautilex) plus a new teak interior in 1982, and a standard transom door in 1985. The 46 III model (1986–87) features an updated layout with oak woodwork and a centerline queen forward. Prior to 1981, the most popular engines were the GM 435-hp 8V71TIs which cruise around 20 knots and reach 23 knots top. In 1981, the 570-hp 8V92TIs became available (around 24 knots cruise), and the 600-hp versions (1985–87) added another knot of speed. Note that the fuel capacity was increased to 720 gallons in 1983. Resale values are excellent in all markets. ❏

SPECIFICATIONS

Length......................46'6"
Beam.......................16'0"
Draft ....4'6"
Weight ....44,900#
Clearance ....15'6"
Water ....230/246 Gals.
Fuel............620/720 Gals.
Cockpit ....117/130 Sq. Ft.
Hull Type ....Deep-V
Designer ....Bertram

Production
1971–87

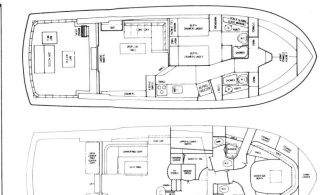

BERTRAM

BERTRAM 46 MOTOR YACHT

A cruising yacht with spacious interior accommodations and traditional flush deck styling, the Bertram 46 Motor Yacht was designed for those who place a premium on solid construction and unsurpassed engineering. She was built on the same deep-V (19° transom deadrise) hull as the 46 Convertible and is notable for her good offshore handling characteristics and comfortable ride. Her conventional interior layout includes a spacious salon with a mid-level galley and dinette and private staterooms fore and aft. A tub/shower is fitted in the aft head compartment.

Outside, the large aft deck area provides an excellent open-air entertainment platform. Design changes in the Bertram 46 MY were few — a stall shower was added to the forward head in 1977, an updated teak interior became standard in 1982, and a queen berth (previously optional) replaced twin single beds in the master stateroom in 1986. GM 8V71TI diesels will cruise the Bertram 46 Motor Yacht at 19–20 knots with a range of about 300 miles. Optional 570-hp 8V92s offered after 1980 will cruise around 22 knots and reach a top speed of 25 knots. ❑

SPECIFICATIONS	
Length	46'6"
Beam	16'0"
Draft	4'8"
Weight	45,600#
Clearance	18'8"
Water	230 Gals.
Fuel	615 Gals.
Hull Type	Deep-V
Designer	Bertram

Production
1973–87

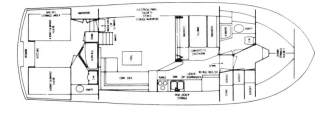

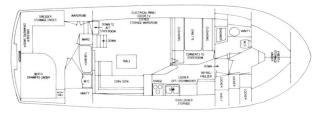

BERTRAM 50 CONVERTIBLE

It isn't how fast you go, it's how you go fast that counts. In the case of the Bertram 50 Convertible, that means big and beautiful and at no small expense. Introduced in 1987, the Bertram 50 follows in the high-tech footsteps of the Bertram 54 and 37 Convertibles. A well-styled boat with a truly aggressive profile, the Bertram 50 is considered by many to represent the state of the art in production sportfishermen of her size. Initially offered in a three-stateroom layout with the galley-up, a spacious two-stateroom galley-down interior with an enormous salon

became available in 1988. The cockpit is equipped with a transom door and tackle center, and a wraparound helm console eliminates the need for an overhead electronics box. A great-running boat, standard 735-hp GM 8V92TA diesels will cruise the Bertram 50 Convertible at 24-25 knots with a range of over 400 miles. Wide open, the speed is 29 knots. Twin 820-hp MAN diesels introduced in 1989 provide cruising speeds of 27+ knots (31 knots top). This has been a popular model for Bertram and resale values are strong. ❏

SPECIFICATIONS

Length	50'0"
Beam	16'0"
Draft	4'9"
Weight	56,531#
Clearance	15'9"
Water	175 Gals.
Fuel	1,046 Gals.
Cockpit	108 Sq. Ft.
Hull Type	Deep-V
Designer	Bertram

Production
1987–Current

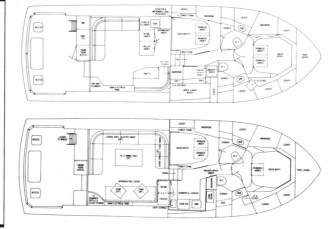

BERTRAM

BERTRAM 54 CONVERTIBLE

A proven tournament winner and sportfishing mega-yacht, the Bertram 54 Convertible is built on a modern deep-V hull with balsa-core construction above the waterline. She was the first of the "new generation" Bertrams, and with her seemingly perfect blend of design, engineering, and construction, she provides absolutely outstanding rough-water performance. Her luxurious three-stateroom/three-head interior offers good living and storage space, and the cockpit (with access to the engine room) is enormous. The generators were relocated from under the cockpit sole to the engine room in 1984. The front windshield was glassed-in for 1986, and updates in 1987 included a restyled flybridge, a queen berth forward, increased fuel capacity and a new oak interior. The 800-hp GM 12V71 diesels were a popular option (over the standard 675-hp units) and cruise at 25-26 knots (29 knots top). The 900-hp 12V71s (1985–86) cruise at a fast 27 knots (31 knots top), and the current 1080-hp 12V92s cruise the Bertram 54 Convertible an honest 30 knots and deliver 33 knots wide open. ❏

SPECIFICATIONS

Length......................54'0"
Beam.....................16'11"
Draft ....5'2"
Weight ....65,000#
Clearance ....16'8"
Water................250 Gals.
Fuel........1200/1419 Gals.
Cockpit............144 Sq. Ft.
Hull Type ....Deep-V
Designer........Dave Napier

Production
1981–Current

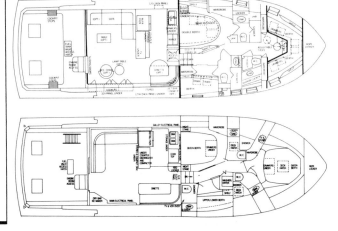

BERTRAM

BERTRAM 58 MOTOR YACHT

The largest of Bertram's production motor yachts, the 58 Motor Yacht incorporates the traditional flush deck styling of the smaller Bertram 42 and 46 models and features a lavish three-stateroom interior of spacious dimensions. With a low center of gravity and sharing the same hull as the 58 Convertible, the Bertram 58 MY enjoys a reputation for being a true offshore cruiser. Her flybridge is small by today's standards, but the sidedecks are wide and the covered aft deck features a protected lower helm and plenty of entertainment space. Inside, the main salon and cabins are a tasteful blend of luxury fabrics and grain-matched teak cabinetry and paneling. The huge owner's stateroom is particularly impressive and comes with a walka-round king-size bed and a tub/shower in the head. Several Bertram 58s have been fitted with a ten-foot cockpit extension adding great versatility while taking nothing away from her performance. GM 12V71 diesels (650-hp/675-hp) will cruise the Bertram 58 around 18 knots and reach a top speed of 21–22 knots. The cruising range is an excellent 350–400 miles. ❏

SPECIFICATIONS

Length	58'3"
Beam	17'11"
Draft	5'4"
Weight	87,500#
Clearance	18'0"
Water	275 Gals.
Fuel	1,250 Gals.
Hull Type	Modified-V
Designer	Bertram

Production
1976–86

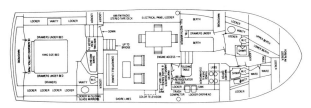

BERTRAM 58 CONVERTIBLE

The Bertram brochures hardly overstated the matter when they referred to the 58 Convertible as a "hugely elegant machine." Huge indeed — only the Hatteras 60 Convertible exceeded her in size among production sportfishing yachts of her era. The 58 Convertible's hull is solid fiberglass with a full keel and 15° of deadrise aft (the least amount of "V" in any Bertram hull). Notably, the decks and superstructure were built of aluminum. Among her attributes is a ride that many consider to be the best in this size range. Designed for serious tournament-level competition and comfortable offshore cruising, the Bertram 58's massive cockpit dimensions will accommodate two full-size fighting chairs. Her luxurious three-stateroom/three-head teak interior features a huge main salon with extravagant entertaining potential. The flybridge is arranged with two helm stations — one well forward and one aft to view the cockpit action. At 90,000 lbs., the Bertram 58 Convertible is no lightweight, but her performance with 675-hp 12V71 diesels is a respectable 18 knots at cruise and around 21 knots top. ❑

SPECIFICATIONS

Length	58'3"
Beam	17'11"
Draft	5'6"
Weight	90,000#
Clearance	19'5"
Water	300 Gals.
Fuel, Std	1,300 Gals.
Fuel, Opt	2,020 Gals.
Cockpit	168 Sq. Ft.
Hull Type	Modified-V
Designer	Bertram

Production
1977–83

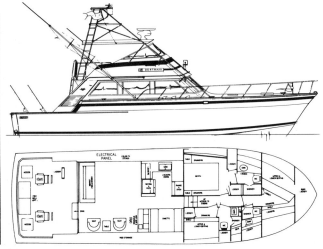

BERTRAM

BERTRAM 60 CONVERTIBLE

Introduced at the 1990 Miami Boat Show, the Bertram 60 Convertible projects the classic styling and aggressive good looks common to all modern Bertram designs. Credit for her striking profile goes to designer Dave Napier, who stretched and reworked the existing Bertram 54 hull to create what may be the finest 60' convertible yet seen from a production yard. She's built on a deep-V hull (17° deadrise) and is balsa-cored from the waterline up. Construction and engineering are state of the art. Priced at a cool $1 million-plus, the Bertram 60 features an opulent galley-up, three-stateroom layout similar to that found on the 54 with the extra length used to open up the salon and midships stateroom dimensions. A stall shower in the starboard guest head has been added, and the entire layout is finished with beautiful maple paneling. The cockpit comes complete with an oversized transom door, tackle center with freezer, and engine room access. The flybridge helm is simply a work of art. Powered with DDA 16V92TA diesels, the Bertram 60 Convertible will cruise at an honest 31+ knots and reach 34–35 knots wide open. ❑

SPECIFICATIONS

Length	60'0"
Beam	16'11"
Draft	5'4"
Weight	85,000#
Clearance	16'8"
Water	250 Gals.
Fuel	1,630 Gals.
Cockpit	144 Sq. Ft.
Hull Type	Deep-V
Designer	Dave Napier

Production
1990-Current

BERTRAM 72 CONVERTIBLE

The real story behind the new Bertram 72 Convertible is her high-tech construction. Designed to be one of the fastest yachts of her kind in the world, the 72 makes extensive use of balsa coring throughout the hull including the bottom — a first for any Bertram yacht. The all-new hull is a deep-V with 17° of deadrise and a sweeping sheer stepped just forward of the cockpit. The interior can be customized to an owner's specifications, however the three-stateroom, three-head layout with the galley-up should prove to be popular among sportfishermen. (Note the full-width master stateroom below the galley.) The bridge is enclosed and air conditioned, and a second outside helm overlooks the massive cockpit. A convenient day head is provided on a small deck abaft the salon bulkhead. Additional features include a huge walk-in engine room, a sea chest to eliminate thru-hulls, trolling valves and an optional bow thruster. The first hulls were fitted with 1,960-hp MTUs although 1,440-hp GM 16V92s are standard. Speeds with the MTUs are around 30 knots at cruise and 34 knots wide open. ❑

SPECIFICATIONS

Length......................72'6"
Beam.........................18'5"
Draft ....6'9"
Weight ....120,000#
Clearance ....19'10"
Water..................300 Gals.
Fuel................2,570 Gals.
Cockpit............193 Sq. Ft.
Hull Type ....Deep-V
Designer ....Bertram

Production
1990-Current

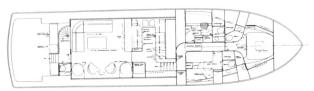

BLACKFIN

Brief History

Blackfin began production in 1973 with a popular 24-foot inboard center console fishing boat. Since then the company has slowly expanded their line of deep-V sportfishing boats and is today considered an industry leader in the upper end sportfisherman market. Still owned and operated by the founder, Blackfins tend to be expensive boats and they appeal primarily to experienced anglers.

Selected Blackfin Inboard Models

Blackfin 27 Combi

Blackfin 29 Combi

Blackfin 29 Flybridge

Blackfin 32 Sportfisherman

Blackfin 32 Combi

Blackfin 33 Flybridge

Blackfin 33 Sportfisherman

Blackfin 38 Combi

Blackfin 38 Convertible

Main Office

Blackfin Yacht Corp., P.O. Box 22982, Ft. Lauderdale, FL 33335
305-525-6314

BLACKFIN 27 COMBI

While the majority of 27 Combis have been powered with outboards, Blackfin offers an inboard version of this rugged dayboat for those who prefer the dependability and ease of maintenance of inboards and an unobstructed transom. Like all Blackfin models, the 27 is built on a solid fiberglass, deep-V hull (24° deadrise aft) with a very sharp entry, reverse outer chines, and plenty of bow flare. An inner liner is used to add stiffness to the hull, and the cockpit contains some 60 sq. ft. of usable space. Raised engine boxes provide excellent access to the motors while doubling as convenient seats for watching the baits. Forward, the nicely appointed V-berth cuddy features a marine head, sink, and standing headroom. Crusader 245-hp gas engines provide a cruising speed of 25 knots and a top speed of around 35 knots. Not an inexpensive boat, the soft ride and superb seakeeping characteristics of the Blackfin 27 have made her a desirable small fisherman in today's market. Note that a dual console Blackfin 27 Fisherman model is also available with an inboard. ❑

SPECIFICATIONS

Length	27'8"
Beam	10'0"
Draft	2'5"
Weight	8,780#
Clearance w/T-top	7'10"
Water	30 gals.
Fuel	230 Gals.
Cockpit	61 Sq. Ft.
Hull Type	Deep-V
Designer	C. Jannace

Production
1985–Current

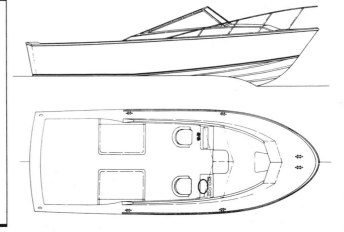

BLACKFIN

BLACKFIN 29 COMBI

A no-nonsense tournament sportfisherman, the Blackfin 29 Combi is built on the same deep-V (22° deadrise) hull as the Blackfin 29 flybridge model. A good-looking boat with unsurpassed performance in rough seas, her relatively wide beam and low center of gravity make the 29 Combi a stable offshore trolling platform. Below, the small and tastefully decorated cabin features a convertible dinette forward together with a mini-galley and a stand-up head with shower — good overnight accommodations for a couple of anglers but not designed with extended cruising in mind. Storage space is excellent and the cabin headroom is 6'2". Probably overbuilt by most current production standards, the 29 Combi's ride is remarkably soft and dry. Note the outboard rudders for precise steering and reduced shaft angles. The raised engine boxes provide excellent access to the motors, and on the 29 Combi they double as a seating area for watching the baits. Standard 454-cid gas engines cruise the Combi at 26–27 knots and the popular 300-hp Cummins cruise an economical (1.3 mpg) 28–29 knots. ❑

SPECIFICATIONS

Length	29'4"
Beam	10'6"
Draft	2'5"
Weight, Gas	10,025#
Weight, Dsl	12,120#
Water	30 Gals.
Fuel	250 Gals.
Cockpit	62 Sq. Ft.
Hull Type	Deep-V
Designer	C. Jannace

Production
1983–Current

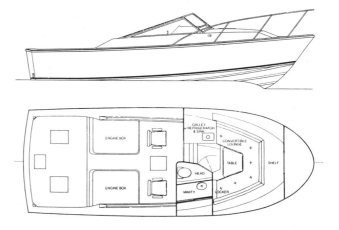

BLACKFIN 29 FLYBRIDGE SF

The Blackfin 29 Flybridge Sportfisherman is a great looking small convertible and one of the few under-30' boats of her type capable of running with the heavy hitters in offshore tournament events. She shares the same deep-V hull design (22° deadrise aft) as the 29 Combi with generous flare at the bow and outboard-mounted rudders. The Blackfin 29 is a superb fisherman with a clean, unobstructed cockpit and an easy-to-reach flybridge. The fact that she has a stylish and comfortable interior layout only adds to her appeal. Finished with white mica countertops and cabinetry and trimmed in teak, the Blackfin 29's cabin accommodations allow her to serve as a practical weekend family cruiser. Raised boxes in the cockpit provide excellent access to the engines and a generator — or an extra 39 gallons of fuel, but not both — is optional. Standard 454-cid Crusader gas engines will cruise the Blackfin 29 SF around 22–23 (30 gph) knots and turn a top speed of 32 knots. Optional 300-hp Cat 3116 diesels cruise at an economical 25–26 knots and reach about 29 knots wide open. ❑

SPECIFICATIONS

Length	29'4"
Beam	10'9"
Draft	2'6"
Weight, Gas	11,109#
Weight, Dsl	13,604#
Clearance	9'4"
Water	50 Gals.
Fuel	250 Gals.
Cockpit	56 Sq. Ft.
Hull Type	Deep-V
Designer	C. Jannace

Production
1986–Current

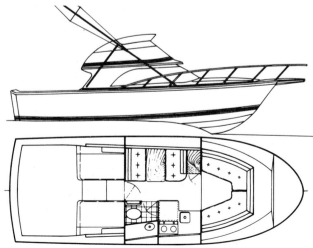

BLACKFIN 32 SPORTFISHERMAN

With her low and purposely aggressive profile, the Blackfin 32 SF has the unmistakable look of a serious bluewater tournament machine. Like all Blackfins, she was built on a rugged deep-V hull (21° deadrise) and her wide beam adds stability not often found in boats this size. Not surprisingly, the modern good looks of the Blackfin 32 are backed up by solid construction and superb offshore performance. The cabin is finely detailed with off-white mica laminates trimmed in teak and offers comfortable — if basic — overnight accommodations for four.

There's room in the cockpit for a full size tuna chair and the raised engine boxes provide cockpit seating as well as good access to the motors. Standard 454-cid gas engines will cruise the Blackfin 32 around 18 knots and reach 27 knots top. Several diesel options were offered over the years. The popular 300-hp Cat diesels cruise about 24 knots and the 375-hp versions can cruise at an honest 30 knots and turn 34–35 knots wide open. A proven sportfisherman with a large and devoted following, used models tend to have strong resale values. ❑

SPECIFICATIONS

Length	31'9"
Beam	11'11"
Draft, gas	2'5"
Draft, dsl	2'8"
Weight	17,800#
Clearance	NA
Water	60 Gals.
Fuel	304 Gals.
Cockpit	71 Sq. Ft.
Hull Type	Deep-V
Designer	C. Jannace

Production
1980–91

BLACKFIN

BLACKFIN 32 COMBI

The Blackfin marketing people once dubbed the 32 Combi the "944 Turbo of sportfishing boats." No doubt; she really is one helluva fishing boat for those who can afford her premium price. She's built on the already-proven deep-V hull of the Blackfin 32 Sportfisherman with extreme flare at the bow and a sharp 21° deadrise at the transom. The design of the Blackfin 32 Combi is similar to other Combi models introduced over the past decade. She's a low-profile, open sportfisherman with a large bi-level fishing cockpit — a capable offshore performer with comfortable and stylish cabin accommodations. There's full standing headroom under the foredeck and the white Formica surfaces and teak trim present a modern, tasteful appearance. The Combi's huge cockpit runs about half of the boat's length and provides seating for three passengers opposite the helm. Standard 454-cid Crusader gas engines will cruise the 32 Combi at 24 knots (31+ top), and the optional 300-hp Cat 3116 diesels will cruise economically at around 26 knots and reach 29–30 knots wide open. ❏

SPECIFICATIONS

Length	31'9"
Beam	11'11"
Draft	2'8"
Weight, Gas	15,081#
Weight, Dsl	17,788#
Clearance	NA
Water	50 Gals.
Fuel	304 Gals.
Cockpit	NA
Hull Type	Deep-V
Designer	C. Jannace

Production
1988–Current

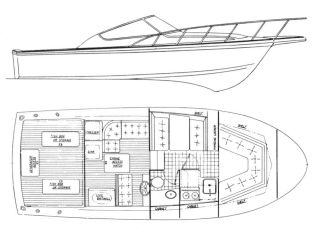

BLACKFIN 33 FLYBRIDGE

A beautiful and hot-running boat, the 33 Flybridge replaces the legendary Blackfin 32 — a fishboat classic dear to the hearts of many anglers. She's heavily built on a new hull design with plenty of beam and a steep 21° of transom deadrise. Blackfin still doesn't use coring materials in their hulls so there's nothing high tech here in the way of construction. Anyone who's fished a 32 will appreciate the 33's enlarged fishing cockpit with its two in-deck fish boxes and now-standard transom door. Engine boxes are retained in the 33's cockpit layout and both motors are easily accessed. Interior space has been dramatically increased in the new 33 FB thanks to the additional beam, and the crowned foredeck provides standing headroom forward. The white Formica cabinetry and stylish teak trim are appealing and the stall shower is a pleasant surprise. The flybridge is large for a 33-footer with bench seating forward of the helm and a large console for flush-mounting electronics. While 454-cid gas engines are standard, most owners will likely opt for the optional 375-hp Cats with their 26-knot cruising speed and 30-knot top end. ❏

SPECIFICATIONS

Length	32'11"
Beam	12'0"
Draft	2'11"
Weight	18,645#
Clearance	10'0"
Water	80 Gals.
Fuel	340 Gals.
Cockpit	80 Sq. Ft.
Hull Type	Deep-V
Designer	Blackfin

Production
1990–Current

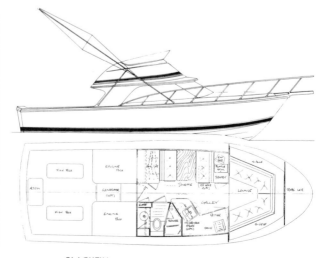

BLACKFIN

BLACKFIN 33 SPORTFISHERMAN

When Blackfin acquired the assets of Cary Marine back in the 1970s, included in the package was this 32'6" hull originally designed as an offshore racer. Long and slender with a drooped nose and low freeboard, Blackfin engineers took this hull, modified it for a sportfishing application, and in 1978 introduced the Blackfin 32 (later changed to 33) Sportfisherman. At the time, one writer referred to her as the Rolls Royce of open fishing boats. Serious anglers were impressed with the fishability of the Blackfin 33's large and unobstructed cockpit, and she soon became recognized as a rugged, hard-core sportfishing boat. She also has a reputation for truly awesome performance in nasty seas and there are many who consider her to be one of the best-handling boats available. Definitely a no-frills ride, the cuddy cabin consists only of two 7' berths and a marine toilet. Used Blackfin 33s are found today with a wide range of power, including outboards. The standard 454-cid gas engines cruise at a fast 26–27 knots and run at 36+ wide open. The optional 210-hp Cat diesels will cruise at 21–22 knots and reach 26 knots top. ❏

SPECIFICATIONS

Length	32'6"
Length WL	28'0"
Beam	9'9"
Draft	2'8"
Weight	10,470#
Clearance	10'8"
Water	30 Gals.
Fuel	225 Gals.
Cockpit	NA
Hull Type	Deep-V
Designer	John Bird

Production
1978–84

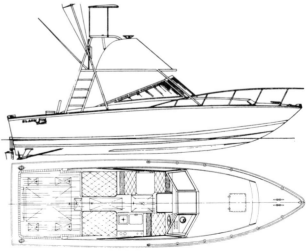

BLACKFIN

BLACKFIN 38 COMBI

The Blackfin 38 Combi is a hard-core express fisherman with the rugged good looks and built-in fishability one expects of a Blackfin product. Built on a solid fiberglass deep-V hull with 18° of transom deadrise, she's actually a stretched version of the earlier Blackfin 36 Combi (1987–88), the difference being the larger cockpit of the 38 model. The Combi makes a great first impression on those who enjoy the open helm and bi-level cockpit layout of an express-type fishing boat. There's a full 120 sq. ft. fishing platform on the lower level and L-shaped passenger seating opposite the helm on the raised deck. While the 38 Combi may have less living space below than other day boats her size, the cabin includes an island berth forward (or V-berths), convertible dinette, full galley, and stall shower in the head. A revised dinette floorplan with a double berth forward became standard in 1991. The stylish Formica surfaces and teak trim combine to add an upscale feel to the decor besides being easy to clean. A good-running boat, optional 485-hp GM 6-71 or 550-hp 6V92 diesels cruise around 29–30 knots and reach 33 knots wide open. ❑

SPECIFICATIONS

Length	38'3"
Beam	14'5"
Draft	3'9"
Weight	34,170#
Clearance	12'9"
Water	135 Gals.
Fuel	514 Gals.
Cockpit	135 Sq. Ft.
Hull Type	Deep-V
Designer	C. Jannace

Production
1989–Current

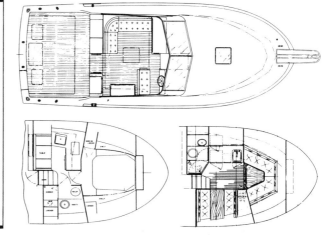

BLACKFIN 38 CONVERTIBLE

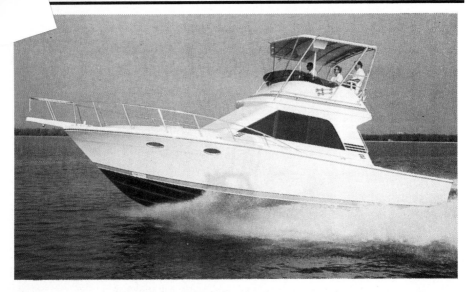

For those who can afford the cost of a top-quality flybridge sportfisherman, Blackfin's new 38 Convertible is worth a hard look. She's actually a stretched version of the Blackfin 36 Convertible (1987–88) which the 38 replaces in the Blackfin fleet. The extra two feet of LOA have gone into the cockpit bringing the total square footage to 120 vs. 91 in the 36' model — a big improvement. The transom deadrise (18°) remains the same. The original two-stateroom, galley-up layout (not shown below) was replaced for 1990 with a more open mid-level galley floorplan with the choice of a dinette or a second stateroom. Modern light ash cabinetry and durable fabrics make this an easy interior to clean. The cockpit is free of obstructions and includes a walk-thru transom door and in-deck fish boxes as standard equipment. A good performer, twin 425-hp Cats will cruise the Blackfin 38 Convertible around 23 knots and reach 27–28 knots top. The 485-hp GM 6-71s deliver a 28-knot cruising speed and 31+ at full throttle, and the 550-hp 6V92s will produce an honest 30-knot cruise and a top speed of 33 knots. ❑

SPECIFICATIONS

Length	38'3"
Beam	14' 5"
Draft	4'0"
Weight	35,970#
Clearance	13'0"
Water	135 Gals.
Fuel	514 Gals
Cockpit	122 Sq. Ft.
Hull Type	Deep-V
Designer	C. Jannace

Production
1989–Current

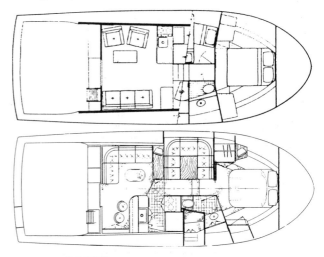

BLUEWATER

Brief History

Bluewater began building houseboats in the 1950s and branched into the motor yacht market in 1974. The company has since developed a series of moderately priced yachts with single-level interiors and condo-style accommodations. Bluewaters are known for their huge sundecks and shallow draft hulls. Always popular with inland and coastal cruisers, modern Bluewater designs have successfully shed the "houseboat" appearance of early production models.

Selected Inboard Models

Bluewater 44 Coastal Cruiser

Bluewater 45 Motor Yacht

Bluewater 47 Sedan Cruiser

Bluewater 48 Coastal Cruiser

Bluewater 51 Coastal Cruiser

Bluewater 53 Coastal Cruiser

Bluewater 55 Coastal Cruiser

Bluewater 55 Yacht

Bluewater 60 Yacht

Main Office

Bluewater Yachts, 811 E. Maple, Mora, MN 55051
612-679-3811

BLUEWATER 44 COASTAL CRUISER

The Bluewater 44 Coastal Cruiser is a comfortable cruising yacht ideally suited for inland and coastal waters. It's interesting to note that the 44 was built on the same 14' wide hull used in the construction of all Coastal Cruiser models to 55 feet in length. In the Bluewater 44, one can expect the following: an oversized interior layout, big wraparound cabin windows for a magnificent outside view, a completely outrageous party-sized sundeck, reasonable performance, and (thanks to her prop pockets) the unique ability to cruise in only two feet of water. For those who enjoy exploring islands and out-of-the-way inlets, the Bluewater 44 offers tremendous close-in flexibility. Actually, the 44 Coastal Cruiser is an enlarged and restyled version of the popular Bluewater 42 Coastal Cruiser (1984–89) featuring a molded swim step, sleeker foredeck lines, and more rake at the bow. The same floorplans were offered in both boats. Relatively small (for a boat this size) 270-hp Crusader gas engines will cruise the Bluewater 42 and 44 Coastal Cruisers at 14–15 knots with a top speed of around 22 knots. ❏

SPECIFICATIONS

Length	47'10"
Length WL	36'2"
Beam	14'0"
Draft	1'11"
Weight	24,000#
Clearance	11'7"
Water	116 Gals.
Fuel	240 Gals.
Hull Type	Modified-V
Designer	Bluewater

Production
1987–89

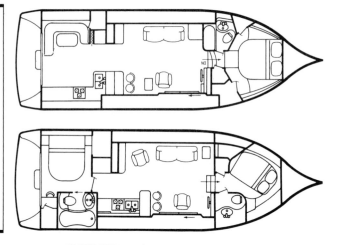

BLUEWATER

BLUEWATER 45 MOTOR YACHT

Smallest of the current Bluewater fleet, the 45 is built on the same 14' beam hull used in the production of all Bluewater yachts including the 60 MY. Where her bigger sisters are narrow, the beam of the new 45 seems about right and she comes off as a well-proportioned boat with a good deal of eye appeal. Construction is solid fiberglass and her modest keel and recessed prop pockets result in a draft of less than 2 feet — an important sales feature for those who cruise in shallow waters. Unlike most other Bluewater models, the floorplan is arranged with the master stateroom forward. Note that the galley is aft in the 45 which allows for a large salon. A lower helm and deck access door are standard and a sliding door aft opens to the integral swim deck. This is a particularly bright and inviting layout and the 45 MY contains more interior living and entertaining space than any other yacht in her class. And that's not even counting her bridge which is huge for a 45-footer. With standard 454-cid Crusader gas engines the Bluewater 45 will cruise at a sedate 14–15 knots and reach a top speed of about 20 knots. ❏

SPECIFICATIONS

Length	49'7"
Length WL	NA
Beam	14'0"
Draft	1'11"
Weight	26,000#
Clearance	14'4"
Water	116 Gals.
Fuel	375 Gals.
Hull Type	Modified-V
Designer	Bluewater

Production
1992–Current

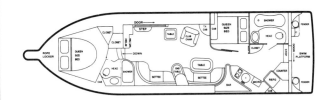

BLUEWATER 47 SEDAN CRUISER

While the entire *current* Bluewater fleet employs the company's shallow draft, prop-pocket hull design, there are several earlier Bluewater models that used more conventional semi-displacement or modified-V hulls. The Bluewater 47 Sedan (and her sistership, the 52 MY) was built on a lightweight semi-displacement hull designed for very economical cruising at displacement speeds (7–8 knots) while still being capable of modest planing speed performance — a "dual mode" hull popular with several builders some years ago when fuel costs had everyone worried. The layout of the Bluewater 47 includes only a single master stateroom leaving the rest of the floorplan available for the large raised salon forward, lower helm console, and a very spacious galley and dining area aft. The windows are huge in this boat and the outside view is excellent. Sliding doors open to the covered cockpit and there's flybridge seating for a crowd. While the detailing and workmanship found in the Bluewater 47 are less than impressive, her new-boat price was very attractive. Standard 454-cid gas engines cruise at a sedate 14–15 knots and deliver a top speed of around 19 knots. ❏

SPECIFICATIONS

Length	47'0"
Length WL	NA
Beam	15'0"
Draft	3'8"
Weight	30,000#
Clearance	13'5"
Water	130 Gals.
Fuel	370 Gals.
Hull Type	Semi-Disp.
Designer	Bluewater

Production
1981–85

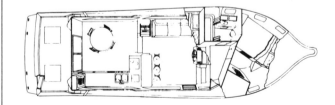

BLUEWATER 48 COASTAL CRUISER

The Bluewater 48 Coastal Cruiser features the attractive lines and sculptured, low-freeboard profile common to all of the newer Bluewater models. Having made the Coastal Cruiser name synonymous with waterborne entertainment, the 48 retains the vast bridgedeck and popular single-level interior layout that Bluewater enthusiasts have come to love. A shallow 2-foot draft allows close-in running and the props are protected in the (likely) event of a grounding. This ability to explore shallow waters and streams is unique in a motor yacht and Bluewater actually encourages owners to beach their boats rather than using a dinghy to get ashore. Two floorplans are offered — a two-stateroom layout or a more open single-stateroom arrangement with the dinette and galley aft in place of the guest cabin. The single-level, apartment-style interior is finished with attractive light oak woodwork, white laminates, and oversized cabin windows for plenty of natural lighting. With standard 454-cid Crusader gas engines, the Bluewater 48 Coastal Cruiser will cruise at a modest 14–15 knots and reach a top speed of around 20 knots. ❏

SPECIFICATIONS

Length	48'8"
Length WL	NA
Beam	14'0"
Draft	1'11"
Weight	25,000#
Clearance	11'2"
Water	116 Gals.
Fuel	375 Gals.
Hull Type	Modified-V
Designer	Bluewater

Production
1990–Current

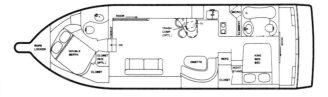

BLUEWATER 51 COASTAL CRUISER

The Bluewater 51 Coastal Cruiser is a light-displacement cruising yacht designed primarily for inland and coastal waters. She combines spacious houseboat-style accommodations with the versatile shallow draft hull found in all Bluewater Coastal Cruisers. With only 14 feet of beam, the 51 is a narrow boat, but the interior is expansive and completely open. Her standard floorplan is somewhat unconventional when compared with most other modern motor yachts. Rather than dividing the fore and aft cabins with companionways and bulkheads in the normal motor yacht fashion, the 51 has the living areas essentially on a single-level. Two- and three-stateroom accommodation plans were offered in the 51 Coastal Cruiser, together with a U.S. Coast Guard-certified "Party" version with zero staterooms, his and hers heads forward, and the rest of the boat turned over to entertainment for up to 49 guests. Not a fast boat, Crusader 454-cid gas engines will cruise at 13–14 knots and reach about 19 knots wide open. Note that Bluewater also offered a 51 Cockpit model based on this same hull. ❏

SPECIFICATIONS

Length	51'0"
Length WL	49'5"
Beam	14'0"
Draft	1'11"
Weight	26,000#
Clearance	11'7"
Water	130 Gals.
Fuel	320 Gals.
Hull Type	Modified-V
Designer	Bluewater

Production
1984–89

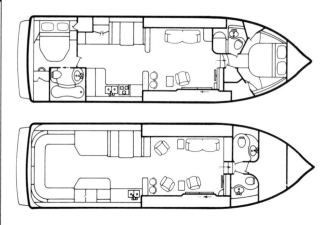

BLUEWATER 53 COASTAL CRUISER

Currently the newest member of the Bluewater family, the 53 Coastal Cruiser is built on the same narrow-beam hull as the rest of the fleet with a shallow keel and prop pockets aft. (Other manufacturers must sometimes envy the ease with which Bluewater uses this standard hull to produce so many models.) Like her sisterships, the 53 has a wide-open floorplan laid out on a single level from the stern all the way forward to the helm. Oversize windows, excellent headroom, and a modern decor add to the impression of spaciousness. Her three-stateroom interior is attrac-tively finished with teak trim and Formica cabinets and countertops. All of the appliances are house-size and there's more living area in the 53 than many larger boats. There's a new, wide inte-grated swim platform/deck accessed from the master stateroom *or* the fly-bridge via wide molded steps. The fly-bridge is huge and surrounded with built-in settees — a real party platform. Engine access is unique: one is under the berth in the midships stateroom and the other is beneath a swing-away galley counter. Standard 454-cid Crusader gas engines will cruise at 13–15 knots. ❑

SPECIFICATIONS

Length w/pulpit ......54'7"
Length WL....................NA
Beam........................14'0"
Draft ....1'11"
Weight ....26,000#
Clearance ....14'5"
Water.................116 Gals.
Fuel ....375 Gals.
Hull Type.........Modified-V
Designer ....Bluewater

Production
1991–Current

BLUEWATER 55 COASTAL CRUISER

The Bluewater 55 Coastal Cruiser is a restyled version of the popular Bluewater 51 with a more rakish profile and the versatility of an integral swim platform. If expansive interior dimensions and party-size sundecks are priorities, the 55 Coastal Cruiser is the only answer short of buying a true houseboat. Every inch of the 55's relatively narrow beam is used inside, and the living quarters from the forward stateroom aft are arranged on a single level. The visual effect is that of a much larger and more expensive yacht. The home-style interior decor is con-temporary, and the comfort level is high indeed. Note that the lower helm station was standard. The 55 Coastal Cruiser was available in either a two- or three-stateroom layout in addition to a zero-stateroom Coast Guard-certified "Party" version for commercial or charter service. As far as the vast upper level sundeck is concerned, it must be seen to appreciate fully its entertainment potential. With 454-cid Crusader gas engines, the Bluewater 55 Coastal Cruiser will cruise at 13–14 knots and run around 19 knots wide open. ❏

SPECIFICATIONS

Length	55'0"
Length WL	NA
Beam	14'0"
Draft	1'11"
Weight	29,000#
Clearance	14'9"
Water	140 Gals.
Fuel	375 Gals.
Hull Type	Modified-V
Designer	Bluewater

Production
1987–89

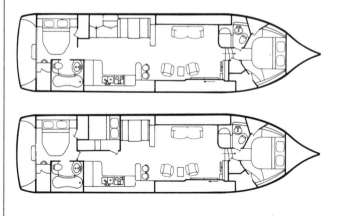

BLUEWATER 55 YACHT

The best-selling model for Bluewater, the new 55 Yacht is a modern, low-profile motor cruiser with stylish lines and an aggressive, rakish profile. Built on a narrow, shallow-draft hull with only 7° of deadrise aft, the 55 is basically a warmed-over version of the previous 55 Coastal Cruiser (1987–89) with a slightly modified interior and a sleeker profile. She's designed to be beached, and the bow is reinforced with a Kevlar strip incorporated in the laminate. The props are recessed into tunnels at the transom, and a long 10" keel provides grounding protection. It's true that the Bluewater 55 is meant for entertaining and relaxed cruising, but company officials claim that she's equally at home in off-shore waters. Her three-stateroom layout includes two full heads and a lower helm with a hideaway console. Port and starboard stairways lead to the huge full-width bridgedeck where guests can take advantage of more sun-deck space than anything short of an aircraft carrier. Standard 360-hp (502-cid) gas engines cruise the Bluewater 55 at 14–15 knots and deliver a top speed of around 19 knots. ❏

SPECIFICATIONS

Length	59'0"
Length WL	NA
Beam	14'0"
Draft	1'11"
Weight	29,000#
Clearance	11'6"
Water	140 Gals.
Fuel	600 Gals.
Hull Type	Modified-V
Designer	Bluewater

Production
1990–Current

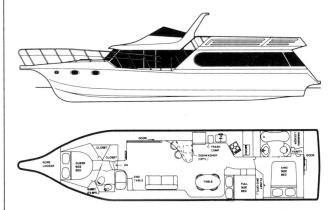

BLUEWATER 60 YACHT

The 60 Yacht is the flagship of the current Bluewater fleet. She's a good-looking design with a modern Eurostyle profile and a wide-open interior layout designed for cruising and entertaining. The 60 Yacht is on the same 14'-wide hull used in other Bluewater yachts and while she's certainly a roomy boat, her beam is quite narrow compared to other motor yachts in her size range. Like all current Bluewater models, her two-stateroom floorplan is arranged on a single level from the cockpit forward to the guest stateroom bulkhead. Oversize cabin windows and good headroom add to the impression of space inside, but the large and thoughtfully arranged cockpit and an enormous 240 sq. ft. flybridge (with retractable instrument panels) are the real focal points of the boat. One advantage of a narrow hull is less wetted surface (or drag) and less weight. Consequently, the 60 is able to use gas engines to deliver decent cruising speeds (13–14 knots) instead of diesels. Cummins 300-hp diesels are offered but rarely ordered. Overall, the Bluewater 60 is a low-cost family cruiser with great cruising and entertaining potential. ❏

SPECIFICATIONS

Length	64'0"
Length WL	NA
Beam	14'0"
Draft	1'11"
Weight	35,000#
Clearance	11'7"
Water	200 Gals.
Fuel	600 Gals.
Hull Type	Modified-V
Designer	Bluewater

Production
1990–Current

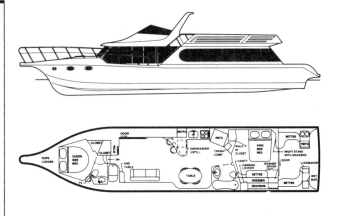

CALIFORNIAN

(MARSHALL BOAT CO.)

Brief History

The Marshall Boat Company introduced the first Californian models in 1972. By the early 1980s the company was producing several trawler-style yachts to 52 feet in length. Wellcraft purchased Californian in 1984 only to sell it back to the original owner in 1987. The company was again sold, this time to the Carver Boat Company who today builds the new-style Californians in North Carolina.

Selected Californian Models

Californian 34 Diesel Cruiser

Californian 35 Convertible

Californian 35 Motor Yacht

Californian 38 Convertible

Californian 38 LRC

Californian 38 Motor Yacht

Californian 42 LRC

Californian 43 Cockpit MY

Californian 50 Trawler

Main Office

The Marshall Boat Co. is no longer in business. Tooling for the most recent Californian models was acquired by Carver Yachts in 1987.

83

CALIFORNIAN 34 DIESEL CRUISER

Traditionally styled and showing a distinct trawler profile, the Californian 34 Sedan is an enjoyable family cruising boat with exceptional low-speed economy and (when equipped with the right engines) true planing-speed performance. The 34's modified-V hull has a fine entry forward and gradually levels out into nearly flat aftersections for stability and greater speed. While most trawler-style boats have been imported from Asia, the Californians were among the few to have been built in the U.S. Wide sidedecks give her a rather narrow salon although the two private staterooms below come as a surprise on such a small boat. Mahogany woodwork is applied throughout the interior. Outside, the aft deck area is large enough for a few deck chairs, and there's seating for everyone on the large flybridge. Cruising speed is about 7 knots (5 gph) with twin 85-hp Perkins diesels. Several other diesel options were offered in the Californian 34, including a pair of Perkins 200-hp turbo-diesels that will cruise around 18 knots (14 gph) and turn 22–23 knots wide open. ❏

SPECIFICATIONS

Length	34'6"
Beam	12'4"
Draft	3'2"
Weight	18,000#
Clearance	10'8"
Water	75 Gals.
Fuel	250 Gals.
Cockpit	70 Sq. Ft.
Hull Type	Modified-V
Designer	J. Marshall

Production
1979–82

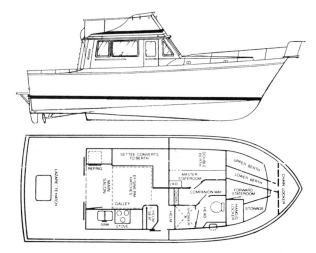

CALIFORNIAN

CALIFORNIAN 35 CONVERTIBLE

A stylish and good-looking boat, the Californian 35 Convertible was introduced during the time of Wellcraft's ownership of Californian Yachts. A sporty profile and a unique window treatment give the 35 a distinctive look and make her an easy boat to spot at a distance. This is the same hull as used in the 35 Motor Yacht and the short-lived Californian 34 MX Express Sportfisherman. Suitable as a family cruiser or weekend fisherman, the interior of the Californian 35 is quite spacious and the grain-matched teak cabinetry is very impressive. Berths for four are available (with the salon sofa converted) and a stall shower is fitted in the head. The relatively small cockpit of the Californian 35 can support some recreational fishing activities although the step along the cabin bulkhead restricts the installation of a mounted tackle center. Molded cockpit steps lead to wide sidedecks making foredeck access easy and secure. Gas engines were standard, but the economical 210-hp Cat diesels proved popular. At a cruising speed of 17 knots the fuel consumption is just 15 gph — or better than 1 mpg. ❏

SPECIFICATIONS

Length....................34'11"
Beam.......................12'4"
Draft ....3'2"
Weight ....18,000#
Clearance ....10'8"
Water....................75 Gals.
Fuel ....300 Gals.
Cockpit........................NA
Hull Type.........Modified-V
Designer.......Bruce Collier

Production
1985–87

CALIFORNIAN 35 MOTOR YACHT

Trying to build a double cabin yacht on a 35-foot hull is no easy trick (it's been tried before and since by several manufacturers) and the results are generally less than satisfactory from the standpoint of styling. In this, the Californian 35 Motor Yacht was more successful than most. Her profile is somehow less boxy and her appearance is surprisingly easy on the eye. Perhaps this is due to the arch or the window treatment, but in any case the Californian 35's profile is unusually attractive considering her small size. Notable features include an all-teak interior, a lower helm and dinette in the salon area, a tight but well-organized aft cabin, overnight berths for six, and (surprise) stall showers in both heads. This is a lot of interior for only 35 feet and the Californian makes the most of it with room for the entire family. The hardtop was a popular option, and the aft deck area is particularly large considering her length. Gas engines were standard but many Californian 35 Motor Yachts were sold with the optional 210-hp Caterpillar diesels for an easy 16-knot cruise (15 gph) and 20 knots at full throttle. ❏

SPECIFICATIONS

Length	34'11"
Length WL	NA
Beam	12'4"
Draft	3'2"
Weight	19,000#
Clearance	NA
Water	75 Gals.
Fuel	270 Gals.
Hull Type	Modified-V
Designer	Bruce Collier

Production
1985–87

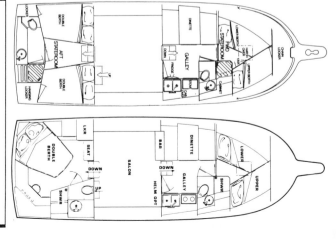

CALIFORNIAN 38 CONVERTIBLE

The first impression of the Californian 38 Convertible is that of a good-looking family cruiser with attractive styling and above-average finish work. Her lines are clean and uncluttered and considerable bow flare has been used to create what appears to be a broad, trawler-style foredeck. Like all Californian models, the sidedecks of the 38 Convertible are notably wide and secure with cockpit steps for easy access. Her roomy cockpit will easily handle a full-size tuna chair, and if fishing or diving is a priority the 38 is capable of heading offshore. Inside, the two-stateroom interior layout is fully paneled and trimmed with superb teak joinerwork. An in-line galley runs along the port side of the salon and wraparound cabin windows provide plenty of natural lighting. The tournament-style flybridge will seat five comfortably. Twin 210-hp Caterpillar diesels are often seen in Californian 38s and speeds are a modest (but efficient) 15 knots at cruise and around 19 knots top. The larger turbocharged Caterpillar 300-hp diesels will cruise about 20–21 knots and reach a top speed of about 23 knots. ❏

SPECIFICATIONS

Length	37'8"
Length WL	36'6"
Beam	13'3"
Draft	3'6'
Weight	25,000#
Clearance	14'6"
Water	100 Gals.
Fuel	400 Gals.
Cockpit	NA
Hull Type	Modified-V
Designer	Bruce Collier

Production
1984–87

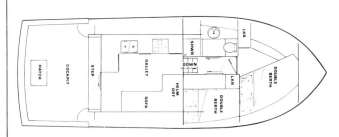

CALIFORNIAN 38 LRC

The California 38 Long Range Cruiser has the same trawler-like profile and modified-V hull form as the smaller Californian 34. Available with either a single or twin stateroom interior layout, the 38 LRC might best be described as a comfortable family cruiser with surprising, un-trawlerlike performance. Rich mahogany interiors are one of the nicer features seen in the early Californian models, and the woodwork in the 38 is carefully matched and well crafted. As a practical cruising boat, the LRC will disappoint no one with her comfortable salon, roomy cockpit, and wide, well-protected sidedecks. A lower helm was standard and the large, wraparound cabin windows provide an abundance of natural lighting. Twin sliding doors open into the cockpit with enough space for lounging or recreational fishing. Notably, exterior teak trim is kept to a minimum. The helm is set well forward on the bridge and seating is provided for as many as six. With a pair of 300-hp turbo-Cats, the Californian 38 LRC will cruise around 20 knots and reach a top speed of 24 knots. ❏

SPECIFICATIONS

Length	37'8"
Length WL	36'6"
Beam	13'0"
Draft	3'6"
Weight	28,000#
Clearance	14'6"
Water	100 Gals.
Fuel	400 Gals.
Cockpit	NA
Hull Type	Modified-V
Designer	J. Marshall

Production
1980–84

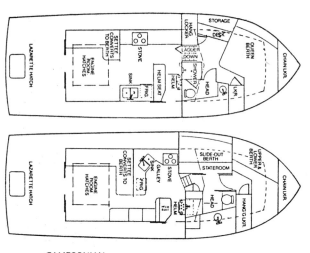

CALIFORNIAN 38 MOTOR YACHT

Built on a revised hull first used in the Californian 38 LRC, the 38 Motor Yacht is a much more modern boat with a double cabin layout and a raised aft deck with hardtop. An optional (but popular) radar arch gives her an impressive motor yacht "look" in spite of a relatively short LOA. Her solid fiberglass modified-V hull features a three-quarter length skeg for low speed handling and flat aftersections for efficient planing performance. The conventional aft cabin floorplan includes two spacious staterooms, each with its own head and stall shower.

Two variations of this layout were available — one with the galley-down and the other with the galley in the main salon. Hinged steps in the forward companionway provide access to a particularly well-designed engine room with good working space outboard of the motors. Standard engines for the Californian 38 Motor Yacht were 210-hp Caterpillar diesels which cruise around 14 knots and burn only 15 gph. (Turbo-Cats were also available.) Note that the Californian 43 Cockpit MY is basically the same boat with a 5' cockpit extension. ❏

SPECIFICATIONS

Length	37'8"
Length WL	36'6"
Beam	13'3"
Draft	3'6"
Weight	28,000#
Clearance	14'6"
Water	100 Gals.
Fuel	365 Gals.
Hull Type	Modified-V
Designer	J. Marshall

Production
1983–87

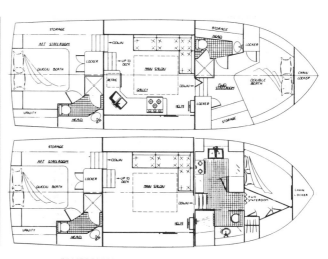

CALIFORNIAN

CALIFORNIAN 42 LRC

A popular boat, the Californian 42 LRC is a very traditional trawler-style design with a somewhat boxy appearance. For her length, she's not an especially roomy boat inside although the accommodations are certainly satisfactory. The 42's relatively narrow beam and wide sidedecks take their toll in the salon dimensions, but the layout is still comfortable and the mahogany woodwork is attractive. The forward stateroom configuration is somewhat unusual with stacked single berths to starboard just opposite the head — a seemingly practical layout for cruising but seldom seen. A stall shower is fitted in the forward head and a tub/shower is aft. Note that there are two sliding deck access doors in the salon as well as direct access to the cockpit from the aft stateroom. There were three separate salon layouts available, all with an integrated galley. As with most Californians, the engine room is very well arranged with good outboard engine access. Twin 210-hp Caterpillar diesels were standard. With a light load and trim tabs, it's possible to get the Californian 42 on plane and cruising at 12–13 knots. ❏

SPECIFICATIONS

Length......................41'8"
Length WL...................NA
Beam........................13'8"
Draft ....3'4"
Weight ....31,000#
Clearance ....NA
Water................175 Gals.
Fuel ....500 Gals.
Hull Type ....Semi-Disp.
Designer ....J. Marshall

Production
1979–84

CALIFORNIAN 43 COCKPIT MY

Take a perfectly acceptable 38' motor yacht and add a 5' cockpit and you end up with a more versatile and better-looking family cruiser. The Californian 43 Cockpit MY is easily one of the more desirable CMYs in her size range thanks to her attractive lines and roomy interior. While her profile shows a distinctive trawler-style bow, the 43 is built on a conventional modified-V hull with hard chines aft and a long skeg below. Her standard layout has the galley-up in the salon and a huge forward stateroom. The optional galley-down floorplan opens up the salon consider-ably at the expense of a smaller guest stateroom — probably the preferred arrangement. The rich walnut wood-work is impressive and a nice departure from teak. Because the master stateroom is very large, the afterdeck is spacious as well. Like all Californians, the sidedecks are wide and (in this case) well protected with raised bulwarks. A comfortable seaboat with an easy ride, Cat 210-hp diesels were standard in the 43 CMY. She'll cruise economically at 13–14 knots and reach 17 knots top. Larger Cats or GM diesels were optional.   ❏

SPECIFICATIONS

Length	43'8"
Length WL	NA
Beam	13'3"
Draft	3'6"
Weight	32,000#
Clearance	14'6"
Water	140 Gals.
Fuel	400 Gals.
Hull Type	Modified-V
Designer	J. Marshall

Production
1983–87

CALIFORNIAN 50 COCKPIT TRAWLER

Originally built by Marshall Marine in California, Wellcraft took over production of the Californian 50 Cockpit Trawler in 1983 when they acquired the Californian molds from Marshall. With just 14'2" of beam she's a narrow boat for her length and the interior dimensions are somewhat compact. Her profile is that of a traditional trawler but her bottom is a semi-displacement design with a short keel (not deep enough to protect the props) and flat aftersections. The Californian 50 was offered with a standard galley-down layout or with the galley-up on the salon level. Note the full-size tub in the master head. While the salon in either floorplan is indeed narrow (the sidedecks are wide on this boat) the large 360° cabin windows allow for plenty of outside natural lighting. The interior woodwork is mahogany throughout. The afterdeck is suitably large for a 50-footer with plenty of entertaining space and the engine room is huge with good access to the motors. Standard engines for the Californian 50 were 300-hp Cats. She'll cruise efficiently at 13 knots and reach about 16 knots wide open. GM 6V92s were optional. ❑

SPECIFICATIONS

Length	50'0"
Length WL	NA
Beam	14'2"
Draft	4'0"
Weight	39,000#
Clearance	18'6"
Water	275 Gals.
Fuel	600 Gals.
Hull Type	Semi-Disp.
Designer	J. Marshall

Production
1981–84

CARVER

Brief History

Carver began building wooden runabouts in the late 1950s, and by the mid-1970s the company was well into fiberglass construction. Always popular in northern markets, Carver has grown in recent years to become a major U.S. builder with a full line of moderately priced family cruisers, sport boats, and motor yachts, including (since 1987) the upscale Californian series of motor yachts. Carver was purchased in 1991 by Genmar which also owns Hatteras and Wellcraft.

Selected Carver Inboard Models

Carver 28 Mariner/Voyager

Carver 28 Riviera

Carver 28 Aft Cabin

Carver 28 Sedan

Carver 32 Aft Cabin

Carver 32 Convertible

Carver 32 Mariner

Carver 32 Montego

Carver 33 Mariner

Carver 33 Voyager

Carver 33 Aft Cabin

Carver 34 Voyager

Carver 538 Montego

Carver 638 Santego

Carver 36 Aft Cabin

Carver 36 Aft Cabin MY

Carver 36 Mariner

Carver 38 Aft Cabin

Carver 38 Santego

Carver 42 Motor Yacht

Carver 42 Cockpit MY

Carver 43 Cockpit MY

Californian 42 Convertible

Californian 44 Veneti

Californian 45 Motor Yacht

Californian 48 Motor Yacht

Californian 48 Convertible

Californian 48 Cockpit MY

Californian 52 Cockpit MY

Californian 55 Cockpit MY

Main Office

Carver Boat Co., Industrial Drive, Pulaski, WI 54162
414-822-3214

93

CARVER 28 MARINER/VOYAGER

Enjoying a long and successful production run, the Carver 28 is one of the most popular small family sedans to be found. She was available in a Voyager or Mariner model, the difference between the two being the choice of interior floorplans. The Mariner has the galley and head forward, and in the Voyager they're located aft (just inside the salon door) with a standard lower helm. Both layouts include an offset double berth in the stateroom and overnight berths for as many as six. Carvers have always been known for their spacious floorplans the 28 Mariner/Voyager is no exception. Seating accommodations for as many as eight people are provided in the cabin, there's room in the head to take a shower without being cramped, and the cockpit is large enough for a couple of anglers. The flybridge is huge (for a 28-footer) with built-in lounge seating and an adjustable table that converts into a full-width sun pad. A hard-riding boat in a chop, standard 220-hp Crusader gas engines (with V-drives) will cruise the 28 Mariner/Voyager at 18–19 knots (17 gph) and reach around 27 knots wide open.   ❏

SPECIFICATIONS

Length	28'0"
Beam	11'1"
Draft	2'10"
Weight	10,300#
Clearance	9'11"
Water	51 Gals.
Fuel	150 Gals.
Cockpit	NA
Hull Type	Modified-V
Designer	Carver

Production
1983–90

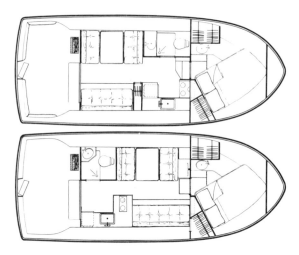

CARVER 28 RIVIERA

Building a true aft-cabin layout into a 28-foot hull is no easy trick. Space is at a premium and most past attempts at such designs have been only marginally successful. The Carver 28 Riviera proved an exception and she was a stable part of the Carver fleet for several years. Slightly boxy in appearance, the radar arch improves the Riviera's profile considerably. In the eyes of most owners the best part about the 28 Riviera is her open-air center cockpit with its wraparound windshield. Here, the driver has good helm visibility in all directions and there's seating for six around a dinette table and jump seat. When the weather turns sour, snap on the camper-style canvas enclosure panels and keep on driving. It's well that the cockpit is comfortable since the 28's interior is a tight fit. With the cockpit table converted, a total of six berths can be provided. Twin 220-hp gas engines are located below the cockpit sole, and routine access is difficult thanks to an unwieldy hatch cover. A wet boat with a decidedly hard ride in a chop, the cruising speed of the Carver 28 Riviera is 21 knots and the top speed is around 28 knots. ❑

SPECIFICATIONS

Length	28'0"
Length WL	NA
Beam	11'1"
Draft	2'10"
Weight	8,900#
Clearance	9'3"
Water	52 Gals.
Fuel	160 Gals.
Hull Type	Modified-V
Designer	Carver

Production
1983–89

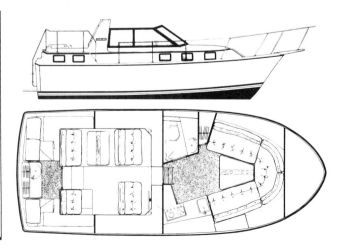

CARVER

CARVER 28 AFT CABIN

Exactly *why* anyone would want a 28-foot double cabin mini-motor yacht is hard to fathom but leave it to Carver to build one first and then develop the market. Smartly styled and built on a wide-beamed hull with 16° of transom deadrise, the 28 Aft Cabin is the smallest double cabin model in production. Her compact floorplan is arranged with the galley, convertible dinette, and head forward. There are berths for *three* in the small aft stateroom. In spite of her limited dimensions, the 28 Aft Cabin's salon manages to feature a full-length sleeper sofa as well as an optional lower helm. Lacking a private head, the aft cabin is thoughtfully equipped with a sink and vanity. (Note that the berths in the aft cabin extend slightly below the salon sole.) The large wraparound cabin windows make the interior of the Carver 28 seem larger than it actually is. Outside, the aft deck area has room for a couple of folding chairs and there's seating for three on the small flybridge. Crusader 350 cid gas engines are standard and cruise the 28 Aft Cabin at 17 knots with a top speed of around 25–26 knots. ❏

SPECIFICATIONS

Length	30'2"
Length WL	NA
Beam	11'10"
Draft	2'11"
Weight	11,700#
Clearance	11'6"
Water	51 Gals.
Fuel	162 Gals.
Hull Type	Modified-V
Designer	Carver

Production
1991–Current

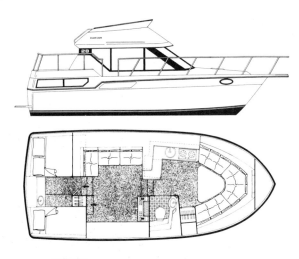

CARVER

CARVER 28 SEDAN

It's safe to say the Carver 28 is the largest 28' sedan in the business. (Her nearly 12' beam is about what you'd expect for the average 34-footer.) Sharing the same hull used for the Carver 28 Aft Cabin, construction is solid fiberglass and transom deadrise is 16°. A well-styled little cruiser designed for coastal and inland waters, the interior accommodations of the 28 Sedan are spacious indeed for a boat of this size. Two floorplans are available — one with a lower helm and the other without. Notably, there's a privacy door for the forward stateroom rather than just a curtain. Overnight berths are provided for up to six in either layout and the galley is quite large and well arranged. The spacious interior dimensions (including excellent headroom throughout) come at the expense of a very small cockpit. The flybridge, however, is huge with guest seating that converts into a sun lounge. Hatches in the cockpit sole provide access to the engines and the V-drives are reached through the salon sole. Optional 350 cid gas engines will cruise the Carver 28 Sedan at 17 knots and deliver a top speed of around 26–27 knots. ❏

SPECIFICATIONS

Length	30'6"
Beam	11'10"
Draft	2'11"
Weight	12,500#
Clearance	9'11"
Water	51 Gals.
Fuel	150 Gals.
Cockpit	NA
Hull Type	Modified-V
Designer	Carver

Production
1991–Current

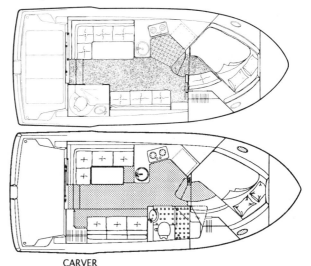

CARVER

CARVER 32 AFT CABIN

The fact that the Carver 32 Aft Cabin managed to remain in production for so many years says a lot about her popularity with the public. Her slightly boxy exterior appearance masks a roomy double-cabin interior with comfortable accommodations. Sharing the same hull as the 32 Convertible model, the appeal of the 32 Aft Cabin version lies in the private aft stateroom where two berths (one is a slide-out double) flank a small head compartment fitted snugly against the aft bulkhead. An aft cabin layout is seldom found in a 32-foot boat and in the Carver it works. Notable features include standing headroom throughout, adequate storage space, a stall shower in the forward head compartment, and a large galley with a full-size upright refrigerator. Outside, the raised aft deck can handle a few folding chairs and the bridge will seat five. Unlike the 32 Convertible, the engines in the Aft Cabin are located below the salon sole in a conventional straight-drive installation. The cruising speed with 270-hp Crusader gas engines is 16 knots and the top speed is 25–26 knots. ❏

SPECIFICATIONS

Length	32'0"
Length WL	28'1"
Beam	11'7"
Draft	2'10"
Weight	12,000#
Clearance	11'6"
Water	84 Gals.
Fuel	182 Gals.
Hull Type	Modified-V
Designer	Carver

Production
1983–90

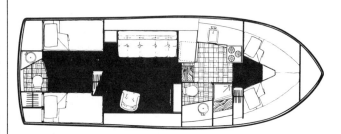

CARVER 32 CONVERTIBLE

Enough Carver 32 Convertibles have been sold since 1984 to make this a well-known model in most boating markets. Designed for comfortable family cruising, the 32's styling is admittedly conservative and somewhat plain but the belowdecks layout is very innovative. Interior volume is increased by using V-drives to locate the engines beneath the cockpit rather than below the salon sole. Hidden beneath the raised dinette, the Carver 32 features a unique mini-stateroom with limited standing headroom and a private access door from the galley. With that, the 32 Convertible is an honest two-stateroom boat — rare in any 32-footer. The compact galley is down four steps from the salon level and includes a full-size refrigerator. Note that the stall shower in the head is a convenience seldom found in a boat of this size. A sliding glass door leads into the cockpit where a transom door and swim platform were standard. Two lift-out hatches in the cockpit sole provide good service access to the engines and the entire deck can be removed when necessary. Twin 270-hp gas engines will cruise the Carver 32 Convertible around 17 knots and she'll reach 26–27 knots wide open. ❏

SPECIFICATIONS

Length	32'0"
Length WL	28'1"
Beam	11'7"
Draft	2'10"
Weight	12,600#
Clearance	11'6"
Water	84 Gals.
Fuel	220 Gals.
Cockpit	57 Sq. Ft.
Hull Type	Modified-V
Designer	Carver

Production
1984–91

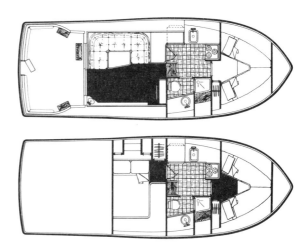

CARVER 32 MARINER

The Carver 32 Mariner was introduced in 1985 as a downsized version of the popular 36 Mariner. Her unorthodox appearance has drawn a lot of outright abuse in the past few years but Carver dealers laughed all the way to the bank since a lot of Mariner 32s were sold — over 650, which certainly qualifies her as a successful model by anyone's standard. Her primary appeal as a family cruiser is the huge single-level interior layout that successfully uses every possible square inch of space available in the hull. The result is a truly social boat with a king-size salon with room for a dinette as well as a sleeper sofa. A ladder in the salon provides a convenient second access to the expansive flybridge which is an open-air entertainment center in itself. Standard 270-hp gas engines (with V-drives) are located beneath the cockpit where access is convenient and fairly easy. A thirsty boat, the 32 Mariner burns around 21 gph at a modest cruising speed of 16 knots. The top speed is around 25–26 knots. Trim tabs are very useful in this model since both the engines and fuel tanks are located well aft. ❏

SPECIFICATIONS

Length	32'3"
Length WL	27'8"
Beam	12'4"
Draft	2'9"
Weight	12,000#
Clearance	10'10"
Water	92 Gals.
Fuel	192 Gals.
Cockpit	NA
Hull Type	Modified-V
Designer	Carver

Production
1985–91

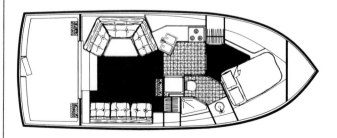

CARVER 32 MONTEGO

Carver's 32 Montego sport cruiser was built using the hull originally designed for the Carver 32 Mariner — a modified-V affair with a reasonably sharp entry, shallow keel, and a flat 6° of deadrise at the transom. While not known as an especially efficient hull, it does have the advantage of offering considerable beam with which to work. The Montego combines a sportboat profile with a comfortable interior layout and the result is a practical weekend family cruiser. Her full-width accommodation plan below is unusually spacious for a boat of this type and features a mini stateroom aft beneath the bridgedeck. The galley is forward in the salon, and a double-entry head with stall shower provides private access from the forward stateroom. The cabin is attractively decorated with textured wall coverings, Formica counters and cabinets, and stylish fabrics. Standard 270-hp gas engines (with V-drives) will cruise the Carver 32 Montego around 15–16 knots and the optional 350-hp Crusaders will cruise 21–22 knots and reach 30+ knots wide open. Note that in her final production year she was called the 534 Montego. ❏

SPECIFICATIONS

Length	32'3"
Length WL	27'2"
Beam	12'4"
Draft	2'9"
Weight	13,000#
Clearance	9'0"
Water	92 Gals.
Fuel	192 Gals.
Cockpit	NA
Hull Type	Modified-V
Designer	Carver

Production
1987–91

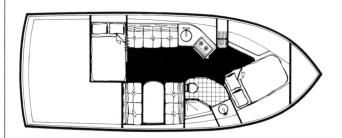

CARVER 33 MARINER

Long a popular boat, the Carver 33 Mariner sold well for a decade, and today they're a common sight in many of the nation's coastal waters and inland lakes. Known primarily for her huge interior layout and boxy appearance, the original 33 Mariner was built with a plywood superstructure (1975–76) while later models are all fiberglass in construction. Stepping down into the single-level floorplan, one is immediately impressed with the spacious dimensions of the combined salon and galley area. Obviously designed as a family cruiser, the 33 Mariner features a stall shower in the head and a unique bulkhead ladder in the salon for direct access to the bridge. (The cockpit ladder can also be used, but the interior passage is a more convenient and quicker route.) The Mariner's flybridge is massive and features an L-shaped lounge which can be converted into an outdoor double berth when the weather is right. Sidedecks are practically non-existent. Several engine options (with V-drives) were offered and most provide cruising speeds from 17–20 knots and top speeds to around 27 knots. ❑

SPECIFICATIONS

Length	32'6"
Beam	12'0"
Draft	2'6"
Weight	11,620#
Clearance	NA
Water	75 Gals.
Fuel	145 Gals.
Cockpit	NA
Hull Type	Modified-V
Designer	Carver

Production
1975–84

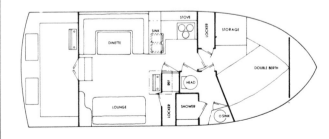

CARVER 33 VOYAGER

It's probably fair to assume that sex appeal was not one of the Carver 33 Voyager's prominent selling points. With her awkward lines and top-heavy profile, the Voyager has little to recommend from the standpoint of styling. Her best features are inside where her large and expansive interior still makes the Voyager a great weekend party cruiser for coastal and inland waters. While the floorplan dimensions aren't notably generous by today's maxi-beam standards, the Voyager was one of the earlier boats to use an angled bulkhead in the forward stateroom to permit a double berth rather than conventional V-berths. The lower helm was standard, and a shower stall is located in the head compartment. With the dinette and salon sofa converted, the 33 Voyager will provide overnight berths for six. The cockpit is large enough for a couple of folding deck chairs and there's bench seating on the flybridge for five. Several engine choices were offered in the Carver 33 Voyager — all with V-drives. The cruising speed with the 270-hp Crusaders is 16–17 knots and the top speed is around 24 knots. ❑

SPECIFICATIONS

Length	32'9"
Beam	12'0"
Draft	2'3"
Weight	13,000#
Clearance	11'9"
Water	70 Gals.
Fuel	200 Gals.
Cockpit	NA
Hull Type	Modified-V
Designer	Carver

Production
1977–81

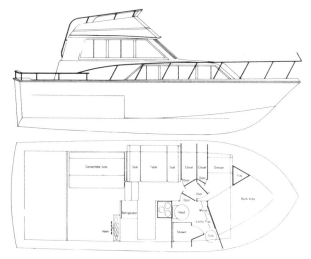

CARVER

CARVER 33 AFT CABIN

Designing an aft cabin yacht on just a 33' hull involves some compromises and one normally expects shortcomings on such a boat. In the case of the Carver 33 Aft Cabin, however, it's hard to find much to complain about. Her styling is reasonably attractive, the accommodations are comfortable, and her performance is certainly adequate for most weekend coastal cruisers. Built on a beamy, heavily constructed hull with a moderate 11° of transom deadrise, the Carver 33's galley-down floorplan is cleverly arranged to include two double berths, two heads, *and* a salon dinette — a practical cruising layout with large cabin windows adding to the impression of spaciousness. (Note that the angled berth in the forward stateroom is barely 6' long.) The salon dimensions are quite generous but both staterooms are compact. Additional features include flybridge seating for six, wide sidedecks, and good engine room access. Standard 454-cid gas engines will cruise the Carver 33 Aft Cabin at 18 knots (26–27 knots top) and optional 200-hp Volvo diesels cruise around 18 knots (22 knots top). ❏

SPECIFICATIONS

Length	36'0"
Length WL	NA
Beam	13'3"
Draft	2'7"
Weight	16,600#
Clearance	15'0"
Water	81 Gals.
Fuel	220 Gals.
Hull Type	Modified-V
Designer	Carver

Production
1991–Current

CARVER

CARVER 34 VOYAGER

New for 1992, the 34 Voyager is Carver's first raised pilothouse design. Billed as a long-range cruiser, she is in fact a reasonably stylish wide-beam sedan with a comfortable two-stateroom layout, a modern interior decor, and an affordable price tag. Pilothouse designs were once confined to northern markets where the value of an enclosed lower helm is obvious. Now their popularity is spreading south and the 34 Voyager will to appeal those who appreciate the versatility of a pilothouse layout — even a small one. With both galley and dinette on the bridgedeck level, the Voyager manages to have a roomy and comfortable salon and a decent cockpit. Notable features include a large flybridge with seating for six and a sun lounge, cockpit transom door, stall shower in the head, double berth in the guest stateroom, and excellent visibility from the lower helm. With the optional 340 gal. fuel capacity the Carver 34 has good range, especially when equipped with diesel engines. Standard 454-cid gas engines will provide a cruising speed of around 20 knots, and optional 225-hp Volvos will cruise economically (20 gph) at 20–21 knots. ❏

PRELIMINARY SPECS

Length	33'10"
Beam	13'3"
Draft	2'7"
Weight	14,000#
Clearance	NA
Cockpit	40 Sq. Ft.
Water	100 Gals.
Fuel, Std.	280 Gals.
Fuel, Opt.	340 Gals.
Hull Type	Modified-V
Designer	Carver

Production
1992–Current

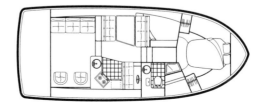

CARVER

CARVER 538 MONTEGO

Introduced in 1990 as the 35 Montego, the Carver 538 is a popular family cruiser with a comfortable mid-cabin layout and a modern sportboat profile. She's built on a solid fiberglass deep-V hull (19° deadrise aft) with a wide 13'2" beam. Not surprisingly, the 538 Montego is a roomy boat inside. The huge dinette/settee will seat six, a stall shower is fitted in the head, there's decent headroom in the mid-cabin, and both staterooms have privacy doors rather than curtains. The master stateroom is quite large and headroom throughout is very good thanks to the raised foredeck. The price for this wide-open and spacious interior layout (larger by far than most of her competitors) is seen in the cockpit where entertaining and moving-around space is at a premium. But the real downside to the Carver 538 is the unattractive bolt-on swim platform hanging like an afterthought off the transom — a cheap effort at modernizing a traditional hull. A good-running boat in a chop, 454-cid gas inboards with V-drives will cruise the Carver 538 Montego at 16–17 knots and reach a top speed of around 25 knots. ❑

SPECIFICATIONS

Length ....38'5"
Length WL....................NA
Beam.......................13'2"
Draft ....3'4"
Weight ....16,000#
Clearance..............15'11"
Water..................91 Gals.
Fuel ....250 Gals.
Hull Type ....Deep-V
Designer ....Carver

Production
1990–Current

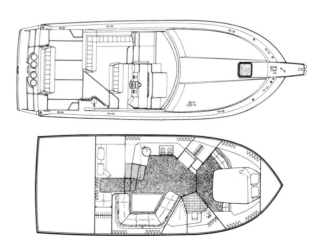

CARVER 638 SANTEGO

Introduced in 1989 as the 34 Santego, the Carver 638 is aimed squarely at the lucrative family cruiser market where Carver seems to thrive. If the Santego's profile is less than classic, her accommodations are near-perfect for entertaining and weekend activities. She combines a huge party-time flybridge with a mega-volume interior that is more than just a little impressive in a boat of this size. As wide-open and expansive as this interior is, however, the small cabin windows eliminate any outside natural lighting. The decidedly unattractive bolt-on swim platform fea-tures boarding steps port and starboard and molded storage racks for fenders. There's plenty of seating on the fly-bridge where a cutout forward of the helm folds down to reveal a centerline stairway to the foredeck. Additional features include a deep-V hull design with 19° deadrise aft, wraparound salon seating for eight, and a very large head compartment with stall shower. Access to the engines and V-drives is via hatch-es in the cockpit sole. With standard 454-cid gas engines the 638 Santego will cruise at 18 knots and reach 27 knots wide open. ❏

SPECIFICATIONS

Length	34'9"
Beam	13'2"
Draft	3'4"
Weight	16,000#
Clearance	15'0"
Water	101 Gals.
Fuel	200 Gals.
Cockpit	NA
Hull Type	Deep-V
Designer	Carver

Production
1989–Current

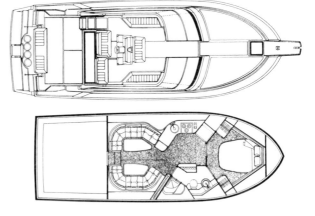

CARVER 36 AFT CABIN

When the Carver 36 Aft Cabin was introduced in 1982, she was the biggest boat ever built by the Carver Boat Corporation. Immediately successful (due in part to her affordable price), the 36 Aft Cabin was built on a "dual mode" trawler-style hull, meaning that she can run efficiently (and very economically) at slow 7–8 knot displacement speeds and still plane out when the throttles are fully applied. (The same hull was later used in the production of the 36 Mariner.) While the 36 isn't a fast boat, her interior accommodations are roomy and well suited to

the needs of family cruisers. A conventional double cabin floorplan features a large master stateroom aft with a tub/shower in the adjoining head compartment. A lower helm was standard, and the galley and dinette are both down from the salon level. Outside, the raised aft deck platform is large enough for a few folding chairs, and the bridge is only three steps removed with additional guest seating. Standard 350-hp Crusader gas engines will cruise the Carver 36 Aft Cabin around 16 knots and reach a top speed of approximately 26 knots. ❑

SPECIFICATIONS

Length	35'7"
Length WL	31'4"
Beam	12'6"
Draft	3'2"
Weight	18,500#
Clearance	11'9"
Water	109 Gals.
Fuel	240 Gals.
Hull Type	Modified-V
Designer	Carver

Production
1982–89

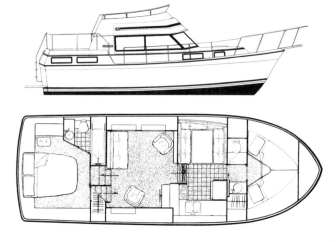

CARVER

CARVER 36 AFT CABIN MY

Introduced in 1990 as a replacement for the popular 36 Aft Cabin model, the new 36 Aft Cabin MY is a roomy and comfortable family cruising boat. Beginning with a balsa-cored hull with a steep 19° of transom deadrise, the 36 MY will do nothing to diminish Carver's reputation for packing a maximum of living space into a limited LOA. This is a much more open boat than the previous 36 Aft Cabin (thanks to a wider beam) and the interior is surprisingly spacious. The layout includes double berths in both staterooms, wraparound sofa in the salon, big U-shaped dinette, optional lower helm, full galley, and two heads. Carver has given the exterior lines of this new yacht a fairly attractive appearance in spite of a top-heavy look common to most of today's mini-motor yachts. While the aft deck is small and the sidedecks are narrow, the flybridge is very large with lounge seating for six. Standard power is a pair of 454-cid Crusader gas engines. Her 15 knot cruising speed (24 knots top) is somewhat disappointing but her performance in bad weather conditions is very good thanks to her nearly deep-V hull design. ❏

SPECIFICATIONS

Length	35'9"
Length WL	NA
Beam	13'10"
Draft	3'1"
Weight	18,500#
Clearance	15'0"
Water	80 Gals.
Fuel	240 Gals.
Hull Type	Modified-V
Designer	Carver

Production
1990–Current

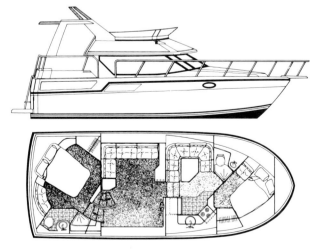

CARVER

CARVER 36 MARINER

It's no exaggeration to say that the huge interior of the Carver 36 Mariner comes as a surprise to most first-time observers. Her dockside profile is a little hard on the eye, but the splendid belowdecks accommodations and huge bridge are seldom matched in other boats her size. An outstanding design from the standpoint of space engineering, the 36 Mariner was a very successful model for Carver and led to the introduction in 1985 of the smaller and similarly styled 32 Mariner. She was built on the "dual mode" hull originally used for the Carver 36 Aft Cabin.

The two-stateroom interior arrangement is sure to appeal to entertainment-minded families and weekend cruisers. Bring your friends — the salon can seat eight and so can the flybridge. There's even a lounge on the foredeck for two sunbathers. The performance is not terribly impressive: 15–16 knots at cruise (at a thirsty 24 gph) and 25 knots top with the standard 350-hp Crusader gas engines. With both the motors and the fuel tanks located under the cockpit, trim tabs are useful to keep the Mariner's bow down at cruising speeds. ❏

SPECIFICATIONS

Length	35'7"
Length WL	31'4"
Beam	12'6"
Draft	3'2"
Weight	19,500#
Clearance	13'6"
Water	103 Gals.
Fuel	274 Gals.
Cockpit	NA
Hull Type	Modified-V
Designer	Carver

Production
1984–88

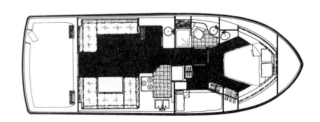

CARVER 38 AFT CABIN

A popular boat since her introduction in 1987, the Carver 38 Aft Cabin is an attractive double cabin design built on a modified-V hull with cored hullsides and a moderate 11° deadrise at the transom. Like most Carver models, the 38's exterior lines reflect her large interior volume. Indeed, for a 38' boat one can only marvel at Carver's expert utilization of space. Featuring an impressive designer-style decor with teak paneling and vinyl wallcoverings — and including double berths in both staterooms — the Carver 38's floorplan is comfortable and thoughtfully arranged.

Each head is fitted with a separate stall shower and a full-size dinette is opposite the galley a few steps down from the salon level. Outside, the raised aft deck is somewhat small owing to her large salon but still large enough for several deck chairs. The flybridge is arranged with a walkaround helm and bench seating for six guests. No racehorse, standard 454-cid Crusader gas engines will cruise the Carver 38 Aft Cabin at 14–15 knots with a top speed of around 24 knots. Optional 375-hp Cat diesels cruise at 22 knots and reach 25–26 knots wide open. ❑

SPECIFICATIONS

Length	37'6"
Length WL	32'7"
Beam	14'0"
Draft	3'4"
Weight	18,800#
Clearance	14'11"
Water	102 Gals.
Fuel	280 Gals.
Hull Type	Modified-V
Designer	Carver

Production
1987–Current

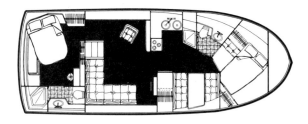

CARVER 38 SANTEGO

The Carver 38 Santego was designed for fun. The styling is contemporary and the accent is clearly on outdoor enjoyment. The Santego uses the same cored hull as Carver's 38 Aft Cabin model but that's where the similarities end. Where the Aft Cabin has the luxury accommodations of a motor yacht, the Santego is poised for daytime activities and has what must be the slickest family-style bridge layout imaginable. Seating surrounds the elevated helm console and a cutout in the bridge mold leads right out to the foredeck. Below, the Santego's single-level interior lay-out uses the full width of the hull to create a cavernous main salon with seating for a crowd. A two-stateroom floorplan (with a smaller galley) was introduced for 1990 as an alternative to the original single-stateroom layout. While the cockpit is fairly small, a unique swim platform provides convenient port and starboard boarding steps. For power, the Santego uses 454-cid Crusader gas engines located beneath the cockpit sole and driven through V-drives. Cruising speed is a lackluster 14–15 knots and the top speed is around 24 knots. ❏

SPECIFICATIONS

Length	37'6"
Length WL	32'7"
Beam	14'0"
Draft	3'5"
Weight	19,000#
Clearance	14'3"
Water	92 Gals.
Fuel	265 Gals.
Cockpit	NA
Hull Type	Modified-V
Designer	Carver

Production
1988–90

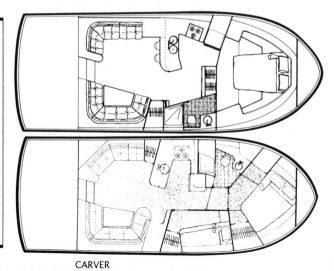

CARVER

CARVER 42 MOTOR YACHT

The introduction of the 42 Motor Yacht in 1985 marked Carver's entry into the luxury big-boat market. Perhaps it was the success of this model that encouraged Carver to acquire the Marshall Boat Co. with its line of 42'–55' Californian yachts. Always a popular boat for Carver, her conventional two-stateroom, galley-down floorplan is spacious and particularly well organized with the accent on comfortable furnishings and a stylish decor. When the dinette and salon sofa are converted, sleeping berths are available for eight persons. Most 42s have been delivered with the optional lower helm and hardtop. Twin 375-hp Caterpillar diesels have also proven a popular choice since they cruise the boat an honest 20 knots. Twin 454-cid gas engines (standard) cruise at about 13–14 knots and reach 23 knots wide open. The Carver 42 is built with a balsa-cored hull and aluminum flooring to save weight, and a grid-type stringer system is employed for additional hull strength. Attractively styled and affordably priced, the Carver 42 MY is often considered to be a lot of boat for the money. ❑

SPECIFICATIONS

Length......................42'0"
Length WL....................NA
Beam........................15'0"
Draft ....3'6"
Weight ....28,500#
Clearance ....20'0"
Water................170 Gals.
Fuel ....400 Gals.
Hull Type.........Modified-V
Designer ....Carver

Production
1985–Current

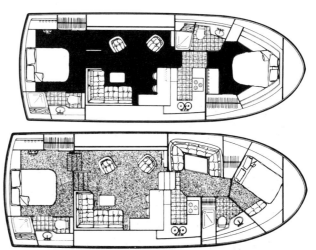

CARVER

CARVER 42 COCKPIT MY

The Carver 42 Cockpit Motor Yacht might just be the best-looking boat Carver ever built. Following by a year the successful introduction of the 42 Motor Yacht, she definitely has the edge on her sistership when it comes to styling. Unfortunately, the 42 Cockpit MY (an unusual designation since she has the appearance of a modern sedan) was a poor seller and was withdrawn from production after only three years. Her two-stateroom interior features a teak-paneled main salon with a built-in wet bar and entertainment center. The galley is down and a double berth was available in either (but not both) of the staterooms. Carver has been using very stylish decor packages in recent years, and both of the Carver 42 models are notable for their tasteful and well-decorated interiors. The steering wheel, sinks, and faucets were imported from Europe. Outside, the flybridge has a raised command console with an overhead electronics box built into the radar arch. Performance figures for the 42 Cockpit MY are the same as for the Carver 42 Motor Yacht. ❑

SPECIFICATIONS

Length	42'0"
Beam	15'0"
Draft	3'6"
Weight	23,150#
Clearance	16'6"
Water	170 Gals.
Fuel	400 Gals.
Cockpit	91 Sq. Ft.
Hull Type	Modified-V
Designer	Carver

Production
1986–88

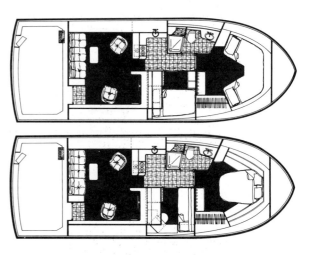

CARVER 43 COCKPIT MY

The Carver 43 Cockpit MY is basically a Carver 38 MY with a 5' cockpit extension. Built on a conventional modified-V hull with a moderate 11° of transom deadrise, the extra length provided by the cockpit addition makes the 43 a more versatile and (in the eyes of many) a better-looking boat than the original 38 MY. As usual, Carver packs a lot of living space into the interior with double berths in both staterooms, a full dinette, roomy salon, and separate stall showers in both heads. (A lower helm is optional.) With the convenience of the cockpit, this is an ideal floorplan for comfortable family cruising or weekend liveaboards. Note that a sliding door in the master stateroom provides direct access to the cockpit — a very practical feature. The foredeck is fitted with sun pads and wide sidedecks make getting around the deckhouse easy and safe. While the cockpit isn't large, there's room for a couple of deck chairs and a transom door and oversize swim platform are standard. Not a fast boat with standard 454-cid gas engines (14–15 knots cruise), optional 375-hp Cat diesels will cruise around 21 knots and reach a top speed of 24–25 knots.   ❑

SPECIFICATIONS

Length .... 44'3"
Beam .... 14'0"
Draft .... 3'4"
Weight .... 25,620#
Clearance .... 15'4"
Water .... 91 Gals.
Fuel .... 390 Gals.
Cockpit .... NA
Hull Type .... Modified-V
Designer .... Carver

Production
1991–Current

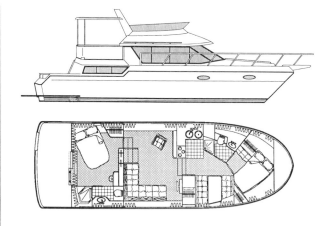

CALIFORNIAN 42 CONVERTIBLE

At 38,000 lbs., the Californian 42 Convertible is a relatively heavy boat for her size. She's built on a solid fiberglass hull with 15° of deadrise at the transom — the same hull used in the brief production run of the Californian 42 Motor Yacht. A comfortable boat inside, her two-stateroom interior is finished with teak paneling and woodwork (pre-1988 models had a walnut interior) and features a tapered double berth in the master stateroom and stacked single berths in the guest cabin. An earlier two-stateroom layout had the galley at mid-level and a second head with a stall

shower. Topside, the 42's tournament flybridge has the helm console aft with bench seating forward and good sight-lines to the cockpit. Additional features include wide sidedecks, inwale coaming, a transom door, and an 8 kw generator. Note that the cockpit engine room access is notable in an under-50' boat. Caterpillar 375-hp diesels deliver a cruising speed of 21–22 knots, and the 485-hp 6-71s will cruise the Californian 42 Convertible at 24 knots with a top speed of 27. The fuel capacity was increased in the 1989 models to 550 gallons. ❏

SPECIFICATIONS

Length......................42'5"
Length WL ....35'6"
Beam.......................15'2"
Draft ....4'4"
Weight ....38,000#
Clearance ....13'4"
Water.................190 Gals.
Fuel............400/550 Gals.
Cockpit.........................NA
Hull Type.........Modified-V
Designer.......Bruce Collier

Production
1986–89

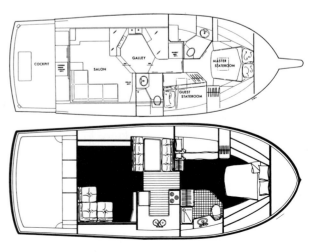

CALIFORNIAN 44 VENETI

The only express cruiser built in the Californian fleet, the 44 Veneti is a high-style sportboat with dramatic Mediterranean lines and luxurious big-boat accommodations. Constructed on a solid fiberglass hull with 15° of deadrise at the transom, her sleek profile and innovative features make the Veneti a practical and comfortable family cruiser. In her stock form, however, she lacks the colorful hull graphics and trim usually associated with today's big express cruisers. Her Eurostyle interior is a dramatic blend of white fiberglass and Formica surfaces and curved corners. Note that the Veneti offers two staterooms and two heads with stall showers — a unique floorplan in an express cruiser. A transom door opens to the integral swim platform and a wet bar and lounge were standard in the spacious bi-level cockpit. A pair of 375-hp Caterpillar diesels will cruise the Californian 44 Veneti at 19–20 knots and reach a top speed of approximately 24 knots. As good-looking as she is, the Veneti is no racehorse and her unimpressive performance stands in contrast to her sleek appearance. ❏

SPECIFICATIONS

Length	44'0"
Length WL	35'6"
Beam	15'2"
Draft	4'0"
Weight	25,000#
Clearance	10'0"
Water	190 Gals.
Fuel	400 Gals.
Cockpit	NA
Hull Type	Modified-V
Designer	Bruce Collier

Production
1988–89

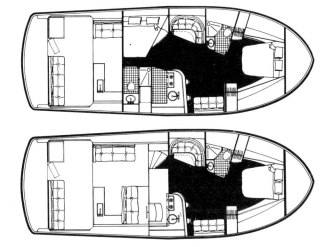

CARVER

CALIFORNIAN 45 MOTOR YACHT

The Carver Californian 45 MY is a good quality yacht with a handsome profile and comfortable cruising accommodations. She's built using the same seakindly modified-V hull as other boats in the Californian series with a 15'2" beam and 15° of deadrise at the transom. Her traditional two-stateroom interior layout has the galley and dinette down resulting in a spacious and very open main salon. The most recent layout features a centerline double berth in both staterooms and each head has a separate stall shower. Hand-rubbed teak cabinetry and woodwork are used extensively throughout and large cabin windows provide plenty of natural lighting in the salon and galley. The aft deck hardtop is standard. Her wide sidedecks allow secure passage fore and aft. No lightweight, the Californian 45 MY is generally recognized as a good performer in a chop. Powered with Caterpillar 375-hp diesels, she'll cruise at 16–17 knots and reach a top speed of about 21 knots. GM 485-hp 6-71s are optional. Note that the Californian 52 Cockpit MY is the same boat with a 7' cockpit extension. ❏

SPECIFICATIONS

Length	45'0"
Length WL	36'8"
Beam	15'2"
Draft	4'0"
Weight	40,000#
Clearance	17'3"
Water	190 Gals.
Fuel	400 Gals.
Hull Type	Modified-V
Designer	Bruce Collier

Production
1988–Current

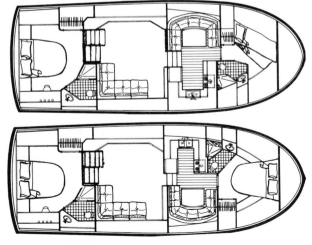

CALIFORNIAN 48 MOTOR YACHT

Originally built on a solid fiberglass hull, the Californian 48 Motor Yacht underwent significant changes in 1987 following Californian's purchase by Carver Boats. Foam coring is now used in the hullsides above the waterline and the resulting weight reduction is said to improve the 48's performance. With her clean and well-proportioned profile, the Californian 48 MY is a particularly handsome boat. Belowdecks, the interior is tastefully finished with teak cabinetry and woodwork (walnut in pre-'88 models) and attractive designer fabrics throughout.

Walkaround double berths are located in the fore and aft staterooms, and a slide-out settee in the small guest stateroom aft converts into a double. Notably, all three heads in the 48 MY are fitted with stall showers. A modest performer with the standard 375-hp Caterpillar diesels, she'll cruise at around 16 knots and reach a top speed of about 20 knots. The optional 485-hp 6-71s will cruise at 19–20 knots and turn 22+ knots wide open. Note that the stylish Californian 55 Cockpit MY (1988–current) is the same boat with a 7' cockpit. ❑

SPECIFICATIONS

Length	48'5"
Length WL	40'11"
Beam	15'2"
Draft	4'8"
Weight	43,000#
Clearance	17'3"
Water	210 Gals.
Fuel	560 Gals.
Hull Type	Modified-V
Designer	Bruce Collier

Production
1985–Current

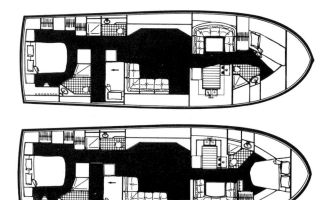

CALIFORNIAN 48 CONVERTIBLE

Built on the standard hull used for all of the current Californian models, the 48 was the largest convertible design in the Carver/Californian line-up. The styling is contemporary and accented by a modern glassed-in front windshield. Her attractive three-stateroom interior is visually impressive and finished throughout with well-crafted teak paneling (walnut in pre-1988 models). The salon dimensions are on the narrow side due to the wide sidedecks and relatively narrow beam of the 48's hull. Unlike many other floorplans in modern convertibles of her size, the Californian 48 has the master stateroom located to starboard of the companionway rather than forward in the bow — a practical arrangement. Standard features included stall showers in both heads, molded bow pulpit, and transom door and tackle center in the cockpit. Among several engine options, 550-hp 6V92s will cruise at 21 knots with a top speed of around 24 knots. The 650-hp 8V92s improve those speeds to 24 knots cruise and 27 knots top. Never a big seller, the 48 Convertible was withdrawn from production in 1989. ❑

SPECIFICATIONS

Length	48'5"
Length WL	40'11"
Beam	15'2"
Draft	4'8"
Weight	40,000#
Clearance	14'1"
Water	210 Gals.
Fuel	760 Gals.
Cockpit	NA
Hull Type	Modified-V
Designer	Bruce Collier

Production
1986–89

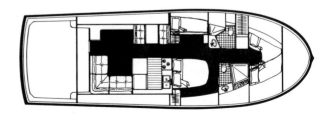

CALIFORNIAN 48 COCKPIT MY

Cockpit motor yachts have become increasingly popular in recent years and the Californian 48 CMY is one of the more stylish to be found in her size range. She was introduced in 1986 as a cockpit version of the existing Californian 42 Motor Yacht (1985–87) and shares the same hull used for the entire line of Californian models. A comfortable cruiser, the 48 has a conventional two-stateroom interior layout with the galley and dinette down from the salon level. Both staterooms have double berths and shower stalls are included in each head. One of the more appealing features of the Californian 48 is the attractive teak cabinetry and joinerwork. (Note that those built prior to 1988 have equally attractive dark walnut interiors.) A hardtop was standard as well as a bow pulpit, windlass, and swim platform. Although the cockpit is not adaptable to any serious fishing ambitions, it is equipped with a transom door for easy boarding access. A good-running boat offshore, standard 375-hp Cat diesels will cruise the Californian 48 Cockpit MY around 16–17 knots and reach a top speed of about 20 knots. ❑

SPECIFICATIONS

Length	48'5"
Length WL	40'11"
Beam	15'2"
Draft	4'8"
Weight	41,000#
Clearance	16'3"
Water	190 Gals.
Fuel	500 Gals.
Hull Type	Modified-V
Designer	Bruce Collier

Production
1986–89

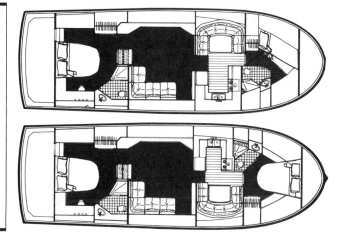

CALIFORNIAN 52 COCKPIT MY

The Californian 52 Cockpit MY evolved from the Californian 45 MY and they share the same deckhouse profile and two-stateroom floorplan. She's constructed on a notably efficient modified-V hull with cored hullsides, a shallow keel, and a solid fiberglass bottom. The transom deadrise is a fairly steep 15° and like all Californian hulls she's a seakindly boat offshore with good handling characteristics. With a generous 70 sq. ft., the cockpit is large enough for some light tackle fishing and a sliding glass door provides access from the master stateroom — a practical and convenient feature. Both staterooms include walkaround double berths and there's a stall shower in the forward head. The full teak interior is lush and the sensation of quality and craftsmanship is no illusion. The afterdeck (flush with the sidedecks, not raised) is big enough for a crowd and the flybridge is arranged with the helm forward and guest seating aft. A good-looking yacht with a modern profile, the Californian 52 Cockpit MY equipped with optional 425-hp Cats will cruise at 16–17 knots and reach 20 knots wide open. ❑

SPECIFICATIONS

Length	51'11"
Length WL	NA
Beam	15'2"
Draft	4'5"
Weight	43,500#
Clearance	12'10"
Water	185 Gals.
Fuel	740 Gals.
Hull Type	Modified-V
Designer	B. Collier

Production
1990–Current

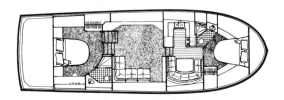

CARVER

CALIFORNIAN 55 COCKPIT MY

The Californian 55 CMY is easily among the best-looking mid-size cruising yachts on the market. Basically a Californian 48 MY with a big 7' cockpit, one of the most prominent features of the Californian 55 CMY is her enormous afterdeck — one of the largest to be found in any boat of this type. The flybridge is also quite large and the modern wraparound helm console provides space for flush-mounting electronics. Her standard three-stateroom floorplan (identical to the 48 MY) has the second guest stateroom *aft* of the salon and all three heads have separate stall showers. Teak paneling and cabinetry replaced the original dark walnut woodwork in 1989. The upscale interior is lavishly decorated with rich fabrics, contemporary furnishings, and top-quality hardware and appliances throughout. A popular boat (about 40 have been built), Caterpillar diesels are standard in the Californian 55 Cockpit MY but most have been equipped with the optional 485-hp 6-71s (around 20 knots cruise/23 knots top) or — better yet — 550-hp 6V92s which cruise at a fast 23 knots and top out around 25+ knots. ❑

SPECIFICATIONS

Length	54'6"
Length WL	NA
Beam	15'2"
Draft	4'3"
Weight	46,200#
Clearance	17'3"
Water	210 Gals.
Fuel	650 Gals.
Hull Type	Modified-V
Designer	B. Collier

Production
1988–Current

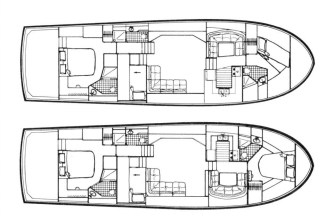

CHEOY LEE

Brief History

Cheoy Lee has been in the boatbuilding business for over a century although modern-day operations can be traced back to 1946 following the war. Cheoy Lee is the largest yacht builder in Asia with a product line that includes world-class sailing yachts, transoceanic trawlers, commercial vessels and custom mega-yachts. Family owned for four generations, Cheoy Lee is located in Hong Kong.

Selected Cheoy Lee Models

Cheoy Lee 32 Trawler

Cheoy Lee 35 Trawler

Cheoy Lee 40 LRC

Cheoy Lee 46 Trawler

Cheoy Lee 48 Sport Yacht

Cheoy Lee 48 Motor Yacht

Cheoy Lee 50 Trawler

Cheoy Lee 50 Sport Yacht

Cheoy Lee 52 Efficient MY

Cheoy Lee 55 Long Range MY

Cheoy Lee 58 Sport Yacht

Cheoy Lee 58 Motor Yacht

Cheoy Lee 66 Long Range MY

Cheoy Lee 66 Sport Yacht

Cheoy Lee 66 Fast MY

Cheoy Lee 83 Cockpit MY

Main Office

Cheoy Lee Shipyards, Ltd., 863-865 Lai Chi Kok Rd.,
Kowloon, Hong Kong
3-743-7710

125

CHEOY LEE 32 TRAWLER

After more than a decade in production, the Cheoy Lee 32 Trawler earned a reputation as a durable and economical cruiser with a large cockpit and fairly basic interior accommodations. Her solid fiberglass hull incorporates a deep forefoot and a full-length skeg for low-speed stability and prop protection. The cockpit, decks, and cabintop are teak-over-fiberglass, and the window frames, doors, and caprail are also teak. Wide sidedecks make passage around the Cheoy Lee 32's deckhouse especially easy. Inside, the salon is narrow but functional. Visibility from the lower helm is very good thanks to large deckhouse windows. (Note the curved corner windows up front.) Traditional teak paneling and cabinetry are found throughout the interior. Outside, a spacious cockpit area makes the Cheoy Lee 32 an excellent utility-type boat for fishing, diving, or coastal cruising. (Fresh water should never be in short supply with 200 gallons aboard.) A single Lehman 6-cylinder diesel provides economical 7-knot performance with a cruising range of nearly 1,000 miles. ❏

SPECIFICATIONS

Length	31'11"
Length WL	29'6"
Beam	12'0"
Draft	4'5"
Weight	19,000#
Clearance	NA
Water	200 Gals.
Fuel	360 Gals.
Cockpit	NA
Hull Type	Semi-Disp.
Designer	Cheoy Lee

Production
1977–86

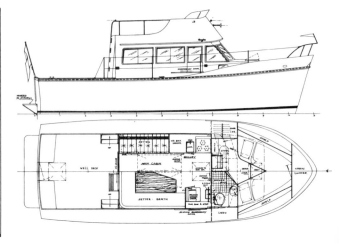

CHEOY LEE

CHEOY LEE 35 TRAWLER

Boasting an impressive cruising range of over 1,500 miles at 7.5 knots, the Cheoy Lee 35 Trawler will require only a single load of fuel annually to meet the cruising needs of the average family. Her traditional sedan profile is accented with teak trim and includes an extended hardtop for dingy storage and weather protection for the cockpit. At 21,000 lbs., the Cheoy Lee 35 is a heavy boat for her size and the ride is predictably soft and comfortable. The full-length skeg below protects the props and running gear in shallow water while making her a stable boat offshore. The hull construction is solid fiberglass with a teak overlay on the decks and cabintop. Wide walkways and sturdy rails on both sides of the house provide secure access to the foredeck. Inside, the cabin arrangements will accommodate four with the salon settee converted in the normal fashion. The forward stateroom is fitted with a double berth as well as a dressing table and settee. Visibility from the lower helm is good in nearly all directions and salon access to the single Lehman diesel is excellent. ❏

SPECIFICATIONS

Length	34'11"
Length WL	32'6"
Beam	12'0"
Draft	3'7"
Weight	21,000#
Clearance	NA
Water	210 Gals.
Fuel	650 Gals.
Cockpit	NA
Hull Type	Semi-Disp.
Designer	Cheoy Lee

Production
1979–86

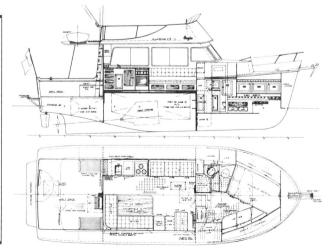

CHEOY LEE

CHEOY LEE 40 LONG RANGE CRUISER

The Cheoy Lee 40 Long Range Cruiser is a traditional flybridge trawler design of the type popular during the 1970s and early 1980s. She began life as the Cheoy Lee 40 Trawler in 1973, and the changes over the years were mostly minor. Hull construction is solid fiberglass, and a teak overlay is applied on the decks and cabintop. A deep, full-length keel protects the props and running gear and gives the owner a valuable margin of safety in shallow waters. Her all-teak interior originally had twin single berths in the aft stateroom, but later models were fitted with a double berth. Visibility from the lower helm station is very good. With the salon settee converted, overnight accommodations are provided for up to six. The great appeal of owning a trawler, of course, is the ability to cruise economically for hundreds of miles. With nearly a thousand nautical miles of range, the Cheoy Lee 40 Long Range Cruiser is easily capable of such long-distance cruising. Her reliable twin 6-cylinder Lehman diesels burn only 6 gph at a steady 8-knot displacement speed. Top speed is about 11–12 knots.   ❑

SPECIFICATIONS

Length	40'0"
Length WL	35'8"
Beam	14'6"
Draft	4'8"
Weight	38,000#
Clearance	NA
Water	250 Gals.
Fuel	650/710 Gals.
Hull Type	Semi-Disp.
Designer	Cheoy Lee

Production
1973–86

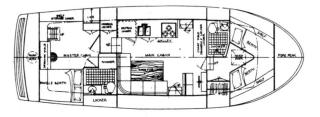

CHEOY LEE

CHEOY LEE 46 TRAWLER

The Cheoy Lee 46 Trawler has the distinction of being the smallest true double-deck production yacht ever built. A sturdy long-range cruiser with a salty profile and attractive sheer, she's constructed on a solid fiberglass displacement hull with a deep keel for protection of the running gear. Her floorplan is arranged with a deckhouse galley and three staterooms below. Because the beam is moderate and the sidedecks are wide, the salon dimensions are fairly compact for a 46-foot yacht. Aft in the salon is a staircase leading down to the private master stateroom with its centerline queen berth, built-in sofa, and direct access to the stand-up engine room. The large midships VIP stateroom is equal to the master stateroom in size and amenities but without an en-suite head. Other features include a full teak interior, day berth in the wheelhouse, foredeck seating, teak decks, and a roomy afterdeck with a bridge overhang for weather protection. The only engines offered in the Cheoy Lee 46 were the dependable Ford 120-hp Lehmans. She'll cruise economically at a 7–8 knots (burning about 6 gph) with a range of 800–850 miles. ❑

SPECIFICATIONS

Length	45'11"
Length WL	42'0"
Beam	14'8"
Draft	4'8"
Weight	49,200#
Clearance	NA
Water	510 Gals.
Fuel	820 Gals.
Hull Type	Disp.
Designer	Cheoy Lee

Production
1978–81

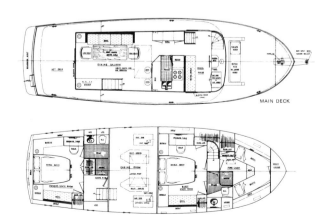

CHEOY LEE

CHEOY LEE 48 SPORT YACHT

The Cheoy Lee 48 Sport Yacht was the first modern production sportfishing boat ever offered by the Cheoy Lee yard. She's built on a unique hull form with 9° of deadrise aft and Airex coring in the hull and superstructure. Big and dramatic with a flat black mask running around the deckhouse and a Eurostyle arch on the bridge, her long foredeck and graceful sheer give the Cheoy Lee 48 Sport Yacht a distinctive appearance. Conceived as a serious sportfisherman with elegant interior comforts, the European decor (painted walls) found in early models was replaced with a more traditional teak interior. The innovative two-stateroom floorplan of the 48 Sport Yacht has the galley aft in the salon (adjacent to the entryway) and a unique curved corridor leads from the salon to the master stateroom. The cockpit, with a full 140 sq. ft. of space, is huge but the raised deck along the salon bulkhead restricts the installation of a full-size tackle center. A good performer with only 8V92TI diesels, the 48 Sport Yacht will cruise around 27 knots and reach a top speed of 30+ knots. ❑

SPECIFICATIONS

Length	48'0"
Length WL	43'0"
Beam	15'0"
Draft	4'0"
Weight	37,000#
Clearance	16'6"
Water	200 Gals.
Fuel	1,000 Gals.
Cockpit	140 Sq. Ft.
Hull Type	Modified-V
Designer	Tom Fexas

Production
1980–1986

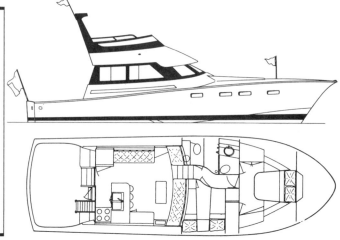

CHEOY LEE

CHEOY LEE 48 MOTOR YACHT

Introduced in 1981, the dramatic European styling and aggressive profile of the Cheoy Lee 48 Motor Yacht represented a bold departure from the conservative lines of most other production motor yachts. She's designed with two large staterooms (rather than three smaller cabins), both with a centerline queen berth and excellent storage capacity. An unusual feature of the 48 Motor Yacht's floorplan is the corridor leading from the salon forward to the galley and guest stateroom. The passageway steps are offset to the starboard side of the salon and then bend hard-left to the galley and dinette below. The main salon seems exceptionally spacious, although visual contact with the galley is completely eliminated. An unusual arrangement, but Tom Fexas doesn't design yachts for traditionalists. Outside, the huge flybridge (with sunpad) and a roomy aft deck area provide plenty of open-air lounging space. A good performer with GM 8V92TI diesels, the Cheoy Lee 48 Motor Yacht can cruise at a fast 27 knots and reach 30 knots wide open. Only six were built. ❑

SPECIFICATIONS

Length	48'0"
Length WL	43'0"
Beam	15'0"
Draft	4'0"
Weight	36,000#
Clearance	NA
Water	200 Gals.
Fuel	800 Gals.
Hull Type	Modified-V
Designer	Tom Fexas

Production
1981–86

CHEOY LEE 50 TRAWLER

The Cheoy Lee 50 Trawler is another in the series of long-range yachts that Cheoy Lee used to build for the American market. Originally a raised pilothouse sedan, in 1979 the Tri Cabin model (pictured above) featured an aft cabin below a raised main deck. Her slightly altered exterior still manages to retain a sedan-style profile. The 50 is an all-fiberglass boat built on a heavy displacement hull with a deep keel and protected props. The aft cabin floorplan used in the Tri Cabin model (1979–80) is a real surprise. Reached from a stairway in the salon, this roomy stateroom comes with a centerline double berth, private head and a writing desk. The sidedecks of the Cheoy Lee 50 are wide so the salon dimensions are somewhat confined. Note the bridge overhang around the decks and cockpit. Obviously made for those seeking tradition over glitz, the interior is fully finished with teak cabinetry and woodwork. There were several engine choices offered in the Cheoy Lee 50s including twin 120-hp Lehmans and 210-hp Cats. With 1,600 gallons of fuel her cruising range can exceed 2,000 miles at 7 knots. ❑

SPECIFICATIONS

Length w/Pulpit	51'6"
Length WL	NA
Beam	15'7"
Draft	5'7"
Weight	67,000#
Clearance	NA
Water	1200 Gals.
Fuel	1600 Gals.
Hull Type	Disp.
Designer	Cheoy Lee

Production
1974–80

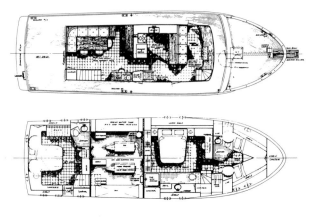

CHEOY LEE

CHEOY LEE 50 SPORT YACHT

Introduced in 1987 as a replacement for the 48 Sport Yacht, the Cheoy Lee 50 features greater beam, a third stateroom, and more conservative styling than her predecessor. Airex coring is used extensively in the construction of the hull, deck, and superstructure resulting in a strong, lightweight sportfisherman with a very good turn of speed. At only 36,000 lbs. — light indeed — the 50 Sport Yacht has the displacement of a much smaller boat. Her three-stateroom floorplan is efficiently arranged with the U-shaped galley forward and sep-arated from the salon by a serving counter. A walkaround double berth is fitted in the master stateroom, and both heads are equipped with separate stall showers. Outside, the sidedecks are wide and the uncluttered cockpit is designed for serious fishing activities. The tournament-style flybridge is large for a 50' convertible and features a built-in table and seating for eight. With standard 72-hp GM 8V92 diesels, the Cheoy Lee 50 Sport Yacht cruises at 25-26 knots and reaches a top speed of around 28 knots. ❑

SPECIFICATIONS

Length	50'8"
Beam	16'1"
Draft	3'2"
Weight	36,000#
Clearance	14'0"
Water	200 Gals.
Fuel	1000 Gals.
Cockpit	115 Sq. Ft.
Hull Type	Modified-V
Designer	Tom Fexas

Production
1987–Current

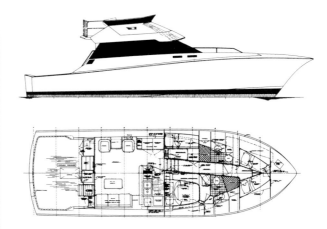

CHEOY LEE

CHEOY LEE 52 EFFICIENT MY

The Cheoy Lee 52 Efficient Motor Yacht is a distinctive boat with an upright and practical appearance to go with her economical operation. She's designed with the emphasis on interior living space and long-range cruising comfort. Featuring a spacious, wide-body salon and a deckhouse galley, the 52 EMY's teak-paneled, three-stateroom floorplan includes a huge master stateroom aft and two guest cabins forward. The current layout, featuring a full-beam midship guest cabin, was introduced in 1987. The salon is open to the galley, and a stairway from the wheelhouse leads to the flybridge. The covered aft deck area has space for a couple of deck chairs, and a door in the cockpit below provides direct access to the master stateroom. At her 9.3-knot hull speed, the Cheoy Lee 52 Efficient MY has a range of nearly 1,500 miles. Twin GM 8.2 diesels are standard and deliver cruising speeds in the neighborhood of 13–14 knots, and the optional 375-hp Cats will cruise around 18–19 knots. Note that the Cheoy Lee 47 Efficient MY is the same boat without the cockpit. ❑

SPECIFICATIONS

Length	51'11"
Length WL	47'6"
Beam	15'6"
Draft	3'10"
Weight	51,500#
Clearance	16'1"
Water	450 Gals.
Fuel	1,000 Gals.
Hull Type	Semi-Disp.
Designer	Cheoy Lee

Production
1984–Current

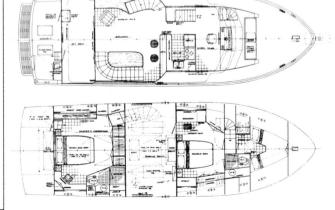

CHEOY LEE 55 LONG RANGE MY

It takes very little imagination to realize that the Cheoy Lee 55 Long Range Motor Yacht is a serious passagemaker. With 2,500 gallons of fuel, this is one motor yacht with genuine transatlantic capabilities. Her solid fiberglass hull has the same full displacement underbody as the earlier Cheoy Lee 55 Trawler, but an improved deck and superstructure profile have made the new 55 a more attractive boat. Two versions are available: The standard model came out in 1981 with a four-stateroom layout, and the 55 Wide Body model was introduced in 1987 with an enlarged salon (nearly 17' wide) and one less stateroom below. (Of the over forty Cheoy Lee 55s built so far, only two have been wide body models.) The lower deck living areas in both versions of the Cheoy Lee 55 are separated fore and aft by the walk-in engine room. Note that her sistership, Cheoy Lee 61 Cockpit MY, is the same boat with a 6-foot cockpit extension. Standard 210-hp Caterpillar diesels will cruise the Cheoy Lee 55 at 9.5 knots burning approximately 7 gph. ❏

SPECIFICATIONS

Length	54'10"
Length WL	50'0"
Beam	17'2"
Draft	5'4"
Weight	80,000#
Clearance	NA
Water	450 Gals.
Fuel	2,500 Gals.
Hull Type	Semi-Disp.
Designer	C. Wittholz

Production
1981–Current

CHEOY LEE

CHEOY LEE 58 SPORT YACHT

Distinctively styled and featuring a unique modified-V underwater profile, the Cheoy Lee 58 Sport Yacht is certainly one of the more dramatic boats to be found among the ranks of big offshore production sportfishermen. This yacht is meant to go fast — construction is high tech with lightweight Airex and Divinycell corings and unidirectional laminates throughout. The wide open cockpit includes direct engine room access, molded tackle centers, flush fishboxes and built-in storage. The flybridge is huge with the helm console set well aft and circular guest seating forward. Inside, the innovative salon of the Cheoy Lee 58 is arranged with two facing sectional sofas forward and the dinette and galley aft — a practical arrangement that eliminates a good deal of traffic through the boat. There are three staterooms on the lower level, two with walkaround double berths. In the Cheoy Lee fashion, the interior is completely paneled and finished with teak or ash woodwork. A fast boat with standard 870-hp 12V71 diesels, the Cheoy Lee 58 Sport Yacht will cruise fully loaded at 28 knots and reach a top speed of 30–31 knots. ❑

SPECIFICATIONS

Length	58'5"
Length WL	48'11"
Beam	17'10"
Draft	4'3"
Weight	58,500#
Clearance	15'10"
Water	150 Gal.
Fuel	1,000 Gals.
Cockpit	138 Sq. Ft.
Hull Type	Modified-V
Designer	Tom Fexas

Production
1986–Current

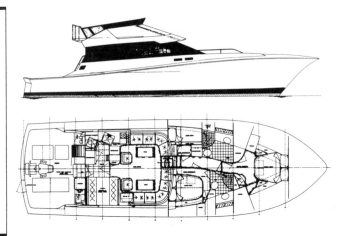

CHEOY LEE

CHEOY LEE 58 MOTOR YACHT

Sharing the same lightweight, high-tech hull used in the production of the 58 Sport Yacht, the Cheoy Lee 58 MY is a Fexas-style cruiser with a wide beam and a full-width deckhouse floorplan. Given the current popularity of galley-up layouts, it's notable that the 58 MY is arranged with the galley and dinette down. The helm is separate from the salon and three of the four staterooms have stall showers in the head. On the lower level, a corridor leading aft to the master stateroom divides the engine rooms and a full-size tub is fitted in the aft head compart-ment. Note that this standard floorplan can be customized and probably no two of these yachts will be the same. Additional features include port and starboard wheelhouse deck doors, a large aft deck with a protective bridge overhang, on-deck day head, Awlgrip finish, and a spacious salon with a choice of teak, ash, or oak woodwork. The truly social flybridge is arranged with a wet bar and wraparound lounge seating aft of the centerline helm console. A good performer with standard 735-hp 8-92s, the Cheoy Lee 58 MY will cruise at 23 knots and top out around 25–26 knots.❏

SPECIFICATIONS

Length ....58'5"
Beam.......................17'10"
Draft ....2'10"
Weight ....48,000#
Clearance ....25'0"
Water.................350 Gals.
Fuel ....1,000 Gals.
Cockpit.........................NA
Hull Type.........Modified-V
Designer..........Tom Fexas

Production
1990–Current

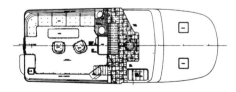

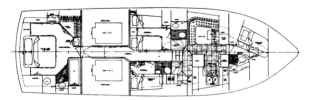

CHEOY LEE

CHEOY LEE 66 LONG RANGE MY

A popular and good-selling yacht, the Cheoy Lee 66 Long Range MY is an updated version of the earlier Cheoy Lee 66 Trawler first imported back in 1978. Restyled outside and updated with a fresh interior, the new model was introduced in 1983 and aimed at the high end of the luxury trawler market. The Cheoy Lee 66 will likely satisfy the most demanding owners with her sturdy appearance and extravagant cruising accommodations. The popular five-stateroom, galley-up layout provides overnight berths for up to twelve people. A four-stateroom, galley-down layout is also available. The sidedecks are very wide and protected by a bridge overhang, and the flybridge is immense. The Wide Body model, with a full-width salon and enlarged wheelhouse, was introduced in 1985 and currently accounts for about half of the Cheoy Lee 66 MY production. A comfortable offshore passagemaker, twin 350-hp GM 8V71N diesels cruise the Cheoy Lee 66 Long Range Motor Yacht at 10.5 knots with a top speed of 12–13 knots. The cruising range is approximately 2,000 nautical miles. ❏

SPECIFICATIONS

Length	65'6"
Length WL	59'0"
Beam	18'0"
Draft	5'3"
Weight	87,000#
Clearance	NA
Water	700 Gals.
Fuel	2,300 Gals.
Hull Type	Displacement
Designer	C. Wittholz

Production
1983–Current

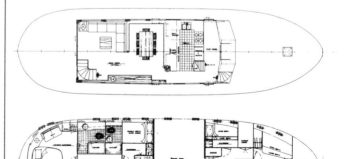

CHEOY LEE

CHEOY LEE 66 SPORT YACHT

The Cheoy Lee 66 Sport Yacht is more than a little different from most other production yachts of her size. Obviously dramatic in appearance, her high-tech construction and extensive coring materials have resulted in a lightweight hull with excellent performance. To gain needed interior volume, the engines have been located well aft by increasing shaft angles to the maximum allowable for proper running trim. One result of this increased space is a superb owner's stateroom just below the forward part of the salon complete with a tub in the adjoining head. Two guest staterooms and the crew quarters are located further forward. The Sport Yacht's plush salon is paneled with grain-matched teak woodwork, and the large deckhouse windows provide an abundance of natural lighting. The unique "observation deck" platform just aft of the salon bulkhead overlooks the spacious tournament-size cockpit where an engine room access door is located. With 870-hp GM 12V71TI diesels, the 66 Sport Yacht will cruise at a fast 26 knots. A 70' stretched version with a larger cockpit was built in 1989. ❏

SPECIFICATIONS

Length	66'0"
Length WL	57'0"
Beam	19'0"
Draft	4'6"
Weight	65,000#
Clearance	19'10"
Water	370 Gals.
Fuel	1,670 Gals.
Cockpit	176 Sq. Ft.
Hull Type	Modified-V
Designer	Tom Fexas

Production
1984–1987

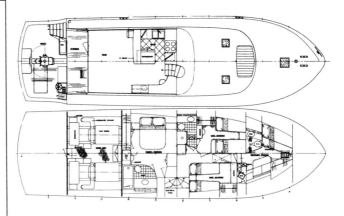

CHEOY LEE 66 FAST MOTOR YACHT

When she was introduced in 1984, the Fexas-designed 66 Fast Motor Yacht represented a radical departure from normal motor yacht standards. Even today her dramatic European profile, high-tech construction, and innovative floorplan continue to make this yacht the subject of interest among designers and boating enthusiasts. As production models go, the Cheoy Lee 66 Fast MY was not a notable sales success (only four were built). She's constructed on the same lightweight, Airex-cored hull used for her sistership, the Cheoy Lee 66 Sport Yacht. Note that the engines are moved aft by increasing shaft angles to the maximum allowable for proper running trim. The five-stateroom floorplan is unique: the owner's stateroom is located amidships, while the aft stateroom serves as guest quarters. The accommodations are very expansive, although the engine room is a tight fit. A superb performer for her size, standard 12V71TI diesels will cruise the Cheoy Lee 66 Fast Motor Yacht yacht at a surprising 22 knots and deliver a top speed of 25–26 knots. ❑

SPECIFICATIONS

Length	66'0"
Length WL	57'0"
Beam	19'0"
Draft	4'6"
Weight	83,500#
Clearance	19'10"
Water	370 Gals.
Fuel	1,670 Gals.
Hull Type	Modified-V
Designer	Tom Fexas

Production
1984–1987

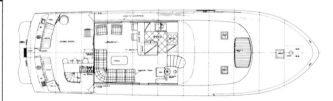

CHEOY LEE 83 COCKPIT MY

Just a few years ago the concept of a production 80' fiberglass motor yacht was just that — an idea whose time had not yet arrived. Today it's quite a different story and the Cheoy Lee 83 Cockpit MY is just one of several production mega-yachts affluent buyers can choose from. Among those, the Cheoy Lee 83 has been one of the most successful. She's another Tom Fexas design with the sleek profile and lightweight construction for which he and Cheoy Lee have become famous. The 83's hull and superstructure are fully cored and vacuum bagged. The lush interior features a truly spacious full-width salon with Burmese teak paneling throughout. A semi-custom yacht, her standard floorplan includes two huge master staterooms, two guest staterooms, and two more staterooms forward for the crew. There are separate engine rooms and pump rooms forward house the generators. A superb performer, 900-hp GM 12V71s will deliver an almost-unbelievable 21-knot cruising speed and a top speed of around 24 knots. At hull speed (11 knots) the Cheoy Lee 83 has a range of 2,500+ miles. Note that the Cheoy Lee 77 MY is the same boat without a cockpit.❏

SPECIFICATIONS

Length	82'11"
Length WL	72'10"
Beam	21'1"
Draft	5'4"
Weight	143,000#
Clearance	17'10"
Water	700 Gals.
Fuel	3,000 Gals.
Hull Type	Modified-V
Designer	Tom Fexas

Production
1987–Current

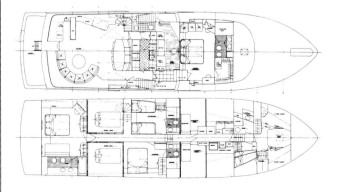

CHRIS CRAFT

Brief History

Chris Craft was founded in 1884 by Christopher Columbus Smith. Operating from a small shop in Michigan, the company grew to become the country's largest builder of pleasure boats during the 1960s and early 1970s. In recent years Chris Craft has had several owners and financial difficulties. The low point came in 1989 when the assets were sold at auction to industry giant OMC. Since then Chris Craft has reduced its fleet to mostly smaller boats.

Selected Inboard Models

Chris Craft 251 Catalina
Chris Craft 28 Catalina
Chris Craft 292 Sunbridge
Chris Craft 30 Tournament SF
Chris Craft 310 Catalina
Chris Craft 315 Commander
Chris Craft 320 Express Cruiser
Chris Craft 322 Catalina
Chris Craft 33 Corinthian
Chris Craft 33 Catalina
Chris Craft 332 Express
Chris Craft 333 Sedan
Chris Craft 336 Mid-cabin
Chris Craft 350 Catalina DC
Chris Craft 360 Sport Sedan
Chris Craft 360 Express
Chris Craft 372 Catalina DC
Chris Craft 38 Commander
Chris Craft 380 Corinthian DC
Chris Craft 381 Catalina DC

Chris Craft 392 Sport Sedan
Chris Craft 400 Express
Chris Craft 410 Motor Yacht
Chris Craft 42 Commander
Chris Craft 42 Sport Convertible
Chris Craft 422 Commander
Chris Craft 426/427 Catalina
Chris Craft 45 Commander SF
Chris Craft 45 Commander MY
Chris Craft 47 Commander MY
Chris Craft 480 Catalina DC
Chris Craft 482 Convertible
Chris Craft 500 Motor Yacht
Chris Craft 501 Motor Yacht
Chris Craft 502 Convertible
Chris Craft 55 Flush Deck MY
Roamer 60 Flush Deck MY
Roamer 60 Motor Yacht
Chris Craft 68 Enclosed FDMY

Main Office

Chris Craft, Inc., P.O. Box 25002, Bradenton, FL 34206
813-351-4900

CHRIS CRAFT 251 CATALINA

The 251 Catalina Express is surely one of the most popular and durable small family cruisers ever. She was built of molded fiberglass on a modified-V bottom, and her wide 9'9" beam gives the 251 a good deal of interior volume. Indeed, the roomy cabin accommodations are complete with V-berths, compact galley, stand-up head with sink, convertible dinette, and ample storage lockers and bins — a practical and efficient layout for a boat of this size and a big reason for the Catalina's enduring success over the years. Outside, the cockpit is large enough for light-tackle fishing or a few deck chairs, and a wraparound safety railing provides an added margin of security for guests. Fore and aft removable hatches in the cockpit sole provide good engine access. Visibility from the helm is excellent, and the sidedecks are wide enough to get safely forward. Nearly all of the 251 Catalinas were fitted with a single 225/230-hp gas engine. A rugged little boat, the cruising speed is 17–18 knots and the top speed is 25 knots. Note that models previous to 1980 carried only 50 gallons of fuel. ❑

SPECIFICATIONS

Length	25'4"
Beam	9'9"
Draft	2'3"
Weight	4,600#
Clearance	7'6"
Water	10 Gals.
Fuel	50/75 Gals.
Cockpit	NA
Hull Type	Modified-V
Designer	Chris Craft

Production
1974–86

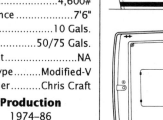

CHRIS CRAFT

CHRIS CRAFT 28 CATALINA

The 28 Catalina (along with the smaller 25 Catalina) formed the backbone of Chris Craft's presence in the small-size family cruiser market for many years. Sharing a similar profile and hull design, the 28 Catalina has a larger interior with overnight accommodations for six. While it's doubtful that six can actually cruise for any length of time in comfort, the layout is well suited to the needs of a small family. Primarily designed as a weekend cruiser, the roomy cockpit area can easily be used for casual fishing as well as swimming or diving activities. The hull of the 28 Catalina (a modified-V form with 15° of deadrise aft) is notable for its dry and comfortable ride. The "280" indicates a single engine, and the "281" designation denotes twin engines. Performance with a single 230-hp gas motor is 17–18 knots at cruise (10 gph) and 25 flat out. With twins, speeds increase to around 21 knots at cruise and 30 knots top. Twin engine models carry 125 gallons of fuel; single engine models carry 100 gallons. The Chris Craft 291 Catalina is basically the same boat as a 281 Catalina with the addition of a flybridge. ❏

SPECIFICATIONS

Length	28'11"
Length WL	24'5"
Beam	10'9"
Draft	2'5"
Weight	7,000#
Clearance	8'6"
Water	25 Gals.
Fuel	100/125 Gals.
Cockpit	65 Sq. Ft.
Hull Type	Modified-V
Designer	Chris Craft

Production
1978–85

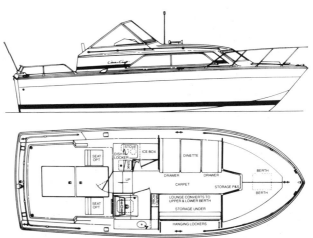

CHRIS CRAFT

CHRIS CRAFT 292 SUNBRIDGE

Introduced as a replacement for the aging 28 Catalina — and built on the 28 Catalina's hull — the Chris 292 Catalina Sunbridge Sedan is a versatile family boat with an attractive profile and an unusual amount of room for a 29' cruiser. The deckhouse is set well forward to allow space aft for a large cockpit suitable for fishing or casual entertaining. The interior layout of the Chris 292 Sunbridge is almost exactly the same as the older 28 Catalinas with overnight berths for up to six. The small galley will handle most basic food-prep necessities, and the stand-up head is equipped with a shower. Outside, the expansive flybridge has seating for the helmsman and up to four guests. Lift-out hatches in the cockpit sole provide good access to the twin 220-hp Crusader gas engines. An efficient performer, the Chris Craft 292 Catalina Sunbridge Sedan will cruise effortlessly at 19 knots at approximately 17 gallons per hour — excellent economy indeed. The top speed is about 28–29 knots depending upon the load. Like her sistership (the 28 Catalina), the 292 is a seaworthy design. ❏

SPECIFICATIONS

Length	28'11"
Beam	10'9"
Draft	2'3"
Weight	7,800#
Clearance	9'4"
Water	25 Gals.
Fuel	125 Gals.
Cockpit	NA
Hull Type	Modified-V
Designer	Chris Craft

Production
1986–89

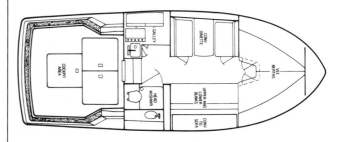

CHRIS CRAFT 30 TOURNAMENT SF

Sporting a handsome profile and a notably wide beam, the Chris 30 Tournament Fisherman has the distinction of being the only Chris Craft ever built on a deep-V, Hunt-designed offshore hull. With a steep 21° of deadrise at the transom and six lifting strakes, this boat is clearly built to run with the big boys when the weather gets nasty. Hull construction is solid fiberglass and the engines rest on inverted aluminum mounts — a very heavy-duty installation. Inside, the wide beam provides for a roomy cabin with berths for four and a stand-up head. A privacy curtain separates the V-berths from the salon and the woodwork is teak. Hinged engine boxes are forward in the cockpit, and with a full 120 sq. ft. of space, the cockpit is exceptionally large and easily fished. The flybridge is big, and the backrest on the aft bench seat folds down so the helmsman can get a view of the cockpit. Twin 250-hp gas engines will cruise the Chris 30 Tournament SF at 18 knots and reach a top speed of 25–26 knots. Trim tabs are required for proper running angle. ❑

SPECIFICATIONS

Length	30'2"
Length WL	25'10"
Beam	11'11"
Draft	2'6
Weight	13,500#
Clearance	11'8"
Water	45 Gals.
Fuel	184 Gals.
Cockpit	120 Sq. Ft.
Hull Type	Deep-V
Designer	Hunt Assoc.

Production
1975–77

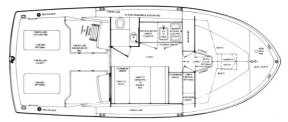

CHRIS CRAFT

CHRIS CRAFT 310 CATALINA

For a boat that remained in production for only three years, there seem to be a lot of Chris 310 Catalinas spread around the nation's marinas. Key to her popularity among owners is space — not only is the cockpit large enough for fishing, but the interior is surprisingly open for a 31-footer. The spacious accommodations of the Catalina are the result of moving the deckhouse well forward, thus trading the convenience of a foredeck for the benefits of interior and cockpit room. The lines suffer a little, but the versatile layout of the Catalina can't be denied.

Inside, the lack of a bulkhead separating the V-berth from the main cabin adds to the impression of volume. Visibility from the semi-enclosed lower helm is good and both seats fold away for access to the engines. The flybridge is small with limited guest seating. A pair of 250-hp gas engines give the Chris 310 Catalina a cruising speed of around 20 knots and a top speed of 26–27 knots. With just 150 gallons of fuel, range is limited. This hull, with only 5° of transom deadrise, was later used for the Chris Craft 315 Commander. ❑

SPECIFICATIONS

Length	30'10"
Beam	11'9"
Draft	2'3"
Weight	11,704#
Clearance	NA
Water	35 Gals.
Fuel	150 Gals.
Cockpit	90 Sq. Ft.
Hull Type	Modified-V
Designer	Chris Craft

Production
1979–81

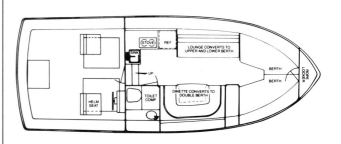

CHRIS CRAFT 315 COMMANDER

The primary design emphasis for the Chris Craft 315 Commander Sport Sedan was fishability — witness her large, unobstructed cockpit and low-profile appearance. The 315 was built on the same hull as the previous Chris 310 Catalina — a flat-bottom modified-V with 5° of deadrise at the transom and a shallow 10" keel for tracking. With her flat aftersections, the Chris 315 isn't too fond of a chop, but she is quick to plane and stable at trolling speeds. Her interior is rather cheery for a sportfishing boat with berths for four persons and room to store most of

the things that cruising families will need for a few days away from home. Updates in 1988 include raised engine boxes for improved engine access, a revised interior layout with the head aft, and a red oak interior decor. Standard features included teak covering boards in the cockpit, a spacious flybridge with bench seating in front of the helm console, and wide sidedecks for secure foredeck access. With the optional 330-hp gas engines, the 315 Sport Sedan will cruise around 22–23 knots and reach a top speed of 30+. ❏

SPECIFICATIONS

Length	30'10"
Beam	11'10"
Draft	2'4"
Weight	11,400#
Clearance	9'6"
Water	40 Gals.
Fuel	250 Gals.
Cockpit	NA
Hull Type	Modified-V
Designer	Chris Craft

Production
1983–90

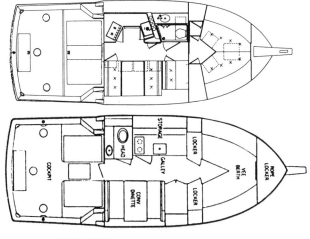

CHRIS CRAFT

CHRIS CRAFT 320 EXPRESS CRUISER

Introduced in 1987 as the 322 Amerosport, Chris Craft changed the model designation to the 320 EC (Express Cruiser) in 1990. An attractive design, the 320 gets the full sportboat treatment — hull graphics, arch, swept-back windshield, etc. — with overnight accommodations for as many as six. With her wide beam, the space below is well used to provide a practical and conventional interior. Modern designer fabrics and light-colored vinyls and laminates are combined to create an open and cheerful interior. The relatively large interior dimensions of the 32 EC are made possible through the use of V-drives that allow the engines to be moved aft under the cockpit. On deck, visibility from the raised command console is very good and the curved windshield is particularly handsome. With the optional bench seats installed at the transom the cockpit gets small in a hurry. Twin 270-hp Crusaders move the Chris 320 EC along at a respectable 19 knots while burning about 20 gph. Top speed is 29–30 knots. Larger 350-hp gas engines were optional and improve those speeds by 3–4 knots. ❏

SPECIFICATIONS

Length....................31'11"
Beam......................11'11"
Draft ....2'7"
Weight ....12,000#
Clearance ....10'9"
Water..................50 Gals.
Fuel ....200 Gals.
Cockpit.........................NA
Hull Type ....Deep-V
Designer..........Chris Craft

Production
1987–90

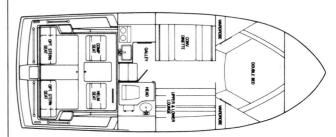

CHRIS CRAFT 322 CATALINA

Chris Craft originally introduced this boat in 1987 as the 320 Amerosport (the 322 Catalina designation was adopted for the 1990 model year). Built on a conventional modified-V hull of single-piece construction, the Catalina is a versatile family cruiser with modern, Eurostyle lines and an attractive profile. She features a large and tastefully decorated interior with a unique, almost hidden, second stateroom cleverly tucked away beneath the salon sole. The original teak interior trimwork was updated in 1989 to light oak. With the engines located aft and fitted with V-drives, the Catalina's interior dimensions are opened up considerably. On the downside, the spacious interior dimensions dictate a rather small cockpit which — together with the raised cockpit sole — precludes the 322 from any serious fishing ambitions. Note that the optional molded swim platform is not integral with the hull. With a pair of Crusader 270-hp gas engines, the Chris 322 Catalina will cruise about 19 knots (20 gph) and has a cruising range of 150–175 miles. ❑

SPECIFICATIONS

Length	31'11"
Beam	11'11"
Draft	2'8"
Weight	11,320#
Clearance	NA
Water	50 Gals.
Fuel	200 Gals.
Cockpit	NA
Hull Type	Deep-V
Designer	S. McGown

Production
1987–90

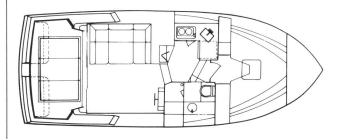

CHRIS CRAFT 33 CORINTHIAN

The Chris Craft 33 Corinthian began life in 1971 as the Chris 33 Coho, a gigantic six-sleeper topped with an oversized bridge 8' wide and 10' long. A popular boat, the Coho (which had a fiberglass hull and flybridge, vinyl-covered wooden decks and a wooden superstructure) lasted until 1976 when the interior was revised and she became the all-fiberglass Chris 33 Offshore. Finally, in 1978, the name was again changed to Corinthian — this time with no apparent interior or styling changes. All told, the boat remained in production for a decade, which is a testament to her enduring popularity among family cruisers. Thanks to her extended, single-level cabin layout, the Corinthian is surprisingly roomy below. The raised cockpit is also quite large (for a 33-foot boat) and hatches in the sole provide good access to the engines. A lower helm was standard, and the flybridge is one of the largest to be found on a boat of this size. A versatile family cruiser, twin 250-hp gas engines will cruise the Chris Craft 33 Corinthian at a respectable 19 knots with a top speed of 26–27 knots. ❑

SPECIFICATIONS

Length......................33'1"
Length WL ....28'9"
Beam.......................12'4"
Draft ....2'4"
Weight ....11,976#
Clearance ....10'6"
Water..................40 Gals.
Fuel ....230 Gals.
Cockpit..............81 Sq. Ft.
Hull Type.........Modified-V
Designer..........Chris Craft

Production
1971–80

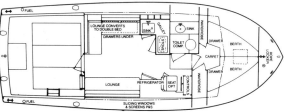

CHRIS CRAFT

CHRIS CRAFT 33 CATALINA

Originally introduced in 1974 as the 33 Sport Sedan, the Chris 33 Catalina has earned a good reputation over the years as a comfortable and durable mid-size family cruiser. Dated by today's standards, her distinctive profile makes the 33 an easy boat to recognize in a crowd. Overnight accommodations are available for as many as six persons. Interior features include a complete galley area, a convenient double-entry head compartment, and a fairly roomy salon with teak trim and a standard lower helm station. (Some of the earlier Sports Sedan models had a two-stateroom floorplan with the galley-up in the salon.) Wraparound cabin windows provide good ventilation and allow for excellent natural lighting inside. A sliding glass door opens to the cockpit where a ladder leads up to a very small flybridge. The hull is built of solid fiberglass with balsa coring in the decks and cabintop. Long out of production, used Chris Craft 33 Catalinas can still offer a lot of boat for a budget-minded family seeking a roomy cruiser. Twin 250-hp gas engines will cruise around 18 knots. ❑

SPECIFICATIONS

Length	33'1"
Beam	12'5"
Draft	2'4"
Weight	14,800#
Clearance	12'5"
Water	40 Gals.
Fuel	270 Gals.
Cockpit	NA
Hull Type	Modified-V
Designer	Chris Craft

Production
1974–80

CHRIS CRAFT

CHRIS CRAFT 332 EXPRESS

The Chris Craft 332 Express is built on a true deep-V hull with 18° of deadrise aft and balsa coring in the deck. Deep-Vs tend to be somewhat unstable in a beam sea (at slow speed) and they aren't usually noted for their fuel efficiency, but they do have superb handling qualities in heavy seas — a characteristic that quickly sets the 332 apart from many other family cruisers. Originally introduced in 1981 at the beginning of the trend toward Eurostyle sportboats, the 332 Express had a six-year production run during which she achieved a good deal of market success as an affordable family cruiser. During those years she underwent numerous updates including the addition of an arch in 1983 and, in 1986, a new interior floorplan plus a good-looking integral swim platform. Surprisingly, the Chris 332 Express has one of the larger cockpits to be found in a boat of her size and type. With big-block 454-cid gas engines she'll cruise comfortably around 21–22 knots and reach a top speed of 30+. In 1983, Chris Craft introduced a similarly styled mid-cabin model (the 336) with V-drives. ❏

SPECIFICATIONS

Length	33'0"
Beam	12'1"
Draft	2'9"
Weight	11,560#
Clearance	7'11"
Water	50 Gals.
Fuel	250 Gals.
Cockpit	NA
Hull Type	Deep-V
Designer	Chris Craft

Production
1981–86

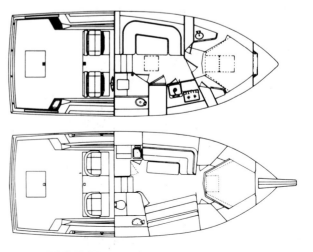

CHRIS CRAFT 333 SEDAN

Sharing the same deep-V, 18° deadrise hull design used in the production of the 332 Express model, the Chris Craft 333 Sedan is a reasonably stylish family cruiser with an unusually open interior layout. An expansive galley/dinette area is three steps down from the salon level and wraparound cabin windows above provide an abundance of natural lighting. While the salon itself isn't particularly large, it does include a lower helm station and room for an L-shaped convertible settee. In 1983, the 333 Sedan picked up a sleeker appearance thanks to the redesign of the cabin windows. (A queen-sized berth in the stateroom became standard that same year.) In 1986 — the last year of production — a redesigned and enlarged flybridge relocated the helm further aft and added bench seating forward of the console. Twin 454-cid gas engines cruise the Chris Craft 333 Sedan comfortably at around 20 knots while burning 26–28 gph. This boat is well behaved in bad weather and can take a chop better than most boats her size. In her final year of production she was marketed as the 333 Amerosport. ❏

SPECIFICATIONS

Length	33'0"
Length WL	NA
Beam	12'4"
Draft	2'9"
Weight	13,000#
Water	50 Gals.
Fuel	250 Gals.
Cockpit	NA
Hull Type	Deep-V
Designer	Chris Craft

Production
1981–87

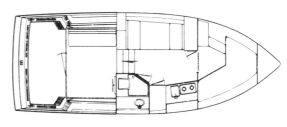

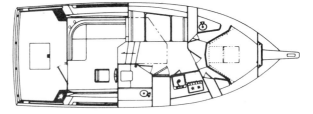

CHRIS CRAFT

CHRIS CRAFT 336 MID-CABIN

The growing popularity of mid-cabin family cruisers in the early 1980s prompted Chris Craft to rework the interior of the existing 332 Express to create the 336 Mid-cabin. Aside from the rugged deep-V hull used in the production of the 336, she features a very large cockpit with an elevated helm position and outdoor seating for up to eight. A portside companionway leads into a fairly confined interior with a private stateroom forward, galley (with upright refrigerator), convertible dinette, and a step-down mid-cabin. A bolt-on swim platform in 1986 improved the boat's profile (the interior decor was updated that year as well), but the layout remained essentially unchanged. Note the vanity in the forward stateroom and the privacy door (instead of a curtain) for the aft stateroom. The engines were moved aft in the 336 to accommodate the mid-cabin design and V-drives are used to deliver the power. Three removable hatches in the cockpit sole provide excellent engine access. Optional 340-hp Mer-Cruiser gas engines will cruise the Chris 336 at 21 knots and reach a top speed of around 30 knots. ❑

SPECIFICATIONS

Length	33'0"
Beam	12'1"
Draft	2'9"
Weight	12,360#
Clearance	7'11"
Water	50 Gals.
Fuel	250 Gals.
Cockpit	NA
Hull Type	Deep-V
Designer	Chris Craft

Production
1983–86

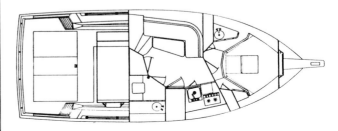

CHRIS CRAFT

CHRIS CRAFT 350 CATALINA DC

The Chris Craft 350 Catalina Double Cabin is one of the more popular family cruising boats produced in the last decade. Her profile may be less than inspiring but she has the interior accommodations and comfort of a much larger boat. The conventional double-cabin floorplan is well executed and features a surprisingly spacious master stateroom aft. Twin berths were standard in the aft stateroom in early models, although an optional double bed was available. There have been several floorplan and decor packages offered, the most recent (1986) featuring a contemporary blend of teak paneling and white Formica surfaces. The fuel capacity was increased to 250 gallons in 1983. Outside, the helm station is positioned just forward of the aft deck and wide sidedecks make passage around this boat very secure. Several power options were offered, but most were built with the twin 235-hp gas engines (14–15 knots cruise/24 top). Chris 350 Catalinas are regularly available in most markets. Note that she was built on the same hull used in the earlier 35 Sedan and 35 Commander Sport Cruiser models. ❏

SPECIFICATIONS

Length	35'1"
Length WL	NA
Beam	13'1"
Draft	2'10"
Weight	17,229#
Clearance	10'8"
Water	55/100 Gals.
Fuel	180/250 Gals.
Hull Type	Modified-V
Designer	Chris Craft

Production
1974–87

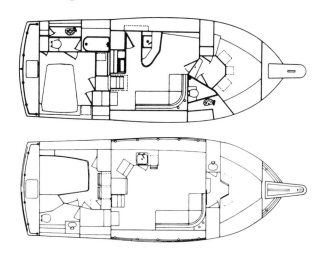

CHRIS CRAFT

CHRIS CRAFT 360 SPORT SEDAN

A continual favorite with those seeking an attractive and versatile family convertible, the Chris Craft 360 Commander Sport Sedan has been around for many years in one form or another. She began life in 1973 as a Tournament Fisherman model with two staterooms, became the Chris Craft 360 Commander in 1981, and went to a single-stateroom cabin layout in 1984. Exterior styling changes in 1985 (including a retooled flybridge and deckhouse) were the last significant updates before production ceased in 1986. The interior cabin dimensions are about average for a 36' convertible, and the cockpit is large enough for a mounted fighting chair and tackle center. The increased fuel capacity (to 400 gallons in 1983) improved the range of the Chris 360 considerably. Standard 454-cid gas engines will cruise at about 18 knots (27 gph) with a top speed of 27–28 knots. Among numerous diesel options, the 300-hp Caterpillar or 320-hp Cummins diesels bring the cruising speed of the Chris 360 Sport Sedan up to approximately 23 knots with a top speed of 26–27 knots. ❏

SPECIFICATIONS

Length	36'0"
Beam	13'0"
Draft	3'2"
Weight	22,600#
Clearance	11'11"
Water	75/100 Gals.
Fuel	300/400 Gals.
Cockpit	NA
Hull Type	Modified-V
Designer	Chris Craft

Production
1973–86

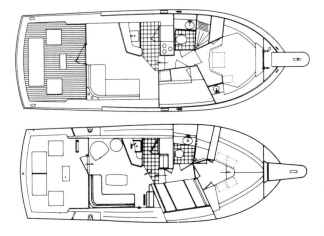

CHRIS CRAFT 360 EXPRESS CRUISER

Introduced in 1988 as the 370 Amerosport, the 360 EC (Express Cruiser) designation was added in 1990 when she received an all-new interior layout. Flagship of the current Chris Craft fleet, the 360 EC is constructed on a solid fiberglass deep-V hull (18° of deadrise at the transom) with a modern integral swim platform for swimming and diving activities. Styling is contemporary in the Euro-sportboat tradition with a modern sweptback windshield, high freeboard, arch, and plenty of cockpit seating. The original interior layout featured a salon dominated by facing curved sofas, V-berths forward, and a mid-cabin aft. The new floorplan has a wraparound lounge aft in addition to the mid-cabin stateroom — a very innovative and comfortable arrangement. Modular interior components and the lack of interior bulkheads result in a spacious cabin, although there's just a curtain for privacy in the forward stateroom. A good-running boat in a chop, standard 454-cid gas engines will cruise the Chris 360 Express Cruiser around 18 knots with a top speed of 26-27 knots. ❏

SPECIFICATIONS

Length	38'7"
Beam	13'0"
Draft	3'0"
Weight	15,000#
Clearance	NA
Water	50 Gals.
Fuel	300 Gals.
Cockpit	NA
Hull Type	Deep-V
Designer	D. Fletcher

Production
1988–Current

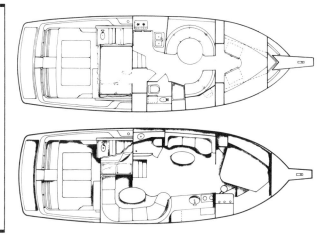

CHRIS CRAFT 372 CATALINA DC

Introduced in 1988 on an all-new modified-V hull design, the Chris Craft 372 Catalina Double Cabin is a practical aft cabin family cruiser with a surprisingly open interior layout. A comfortable boat, the bright mica counters and cabinets — plus her big wraparound cabin windows — make the salon and galley seem larger than they really are. (The original decor featured light ash paneling and trim.) Space aboard the 372 is efficiently used and Chris Craft's designers have managed to include two heads and a full dinette in an altogether practical layout. An optional hardtop is available for the aft deck, and molded-in steps lead to the flybridge with seating for four. The large aft deck provides a good outdoor entertainment platform. While the Chris 372 Catalina's profile suffers from the unavoidably boxy appearance shared by most double cabin designs under 40', she will appeal to families seeking a contemporary design at an affordable price. Twin 270-hp gas engines will cruise the 372 Catalina Double Cabin around 17–18 knots with a top speed of 27 knots. ❑

SPECIFICATIONS

Length	37'0"
Length WL	NA
Beam	13'10"
Draft	2'9"
Weight	15,800#
Clearance	NA
Water	100 Gals.
Fuel	250 Gals.
Hull Type	Modified-V
Designer	Chris Craft

Production
1988–90

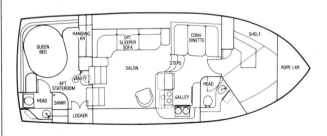

CHRIS CRAFT 38 COMMANDER

Introduced in 1964, the 38 Commander was the first fiberglass cruiser from Chris Craft. Her most talked-about feature was the unusual 3-piece hull (the bottom is one mold and the hullsides are two separate pieces) developed by Chris Craft engineers and later used in the production of several other all-fiberglass Chris Craft models. The trunk cabin design maintains a reasonably low profile although the small flybridge and raised cockpit sole are clearly from the past. Entering the salon, one steps down a few steps from the cockpit level. Accommodations are provided for six, and a sliding door offers some privacy in the forward stateroom. By today's standards, the cabin dimensions of the 38 are small but the semi-enclosed lower helm and large cockpit provide excellent outdoor space. There were two models of the 38 built — the Commander Sport Fish has a flybridge, and the Commander Sedan is a hardtop. Both share the same interior layout. In 1970, a revised Commander 38 Sedan came out with the same hull but a restyled deckhouse and updated interior. Note the small fuel capacity. ❑

SPECIFICATIONS

Length	38'0"
Beam	13'0"
Draft	3'0"
Weight	19,272#
Clearance	NA
Water	75 Gals.
Fuel	200 Gals.
Cockpit	NA
Hull Type	Modified-V
Designer	A. MacKerer

Production
1964–69

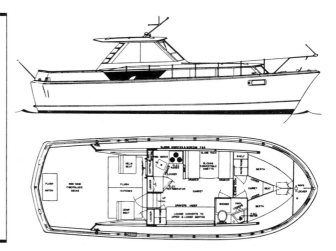

CHRIS CRAFT

CHRIS CRAFT 380 CORINTHIAN DC

The versatile Chris Craft 380 Corinthian Double Cabin has long been appreciated for her excellent indoor and outdoor cruising accommodations. Her primary attribute is an immense amount of deck space for entertaining. Originally developed as the Chris Craft Coho 38 (1973–75), the 380 Corinthian is clearly designed with family cruising in mind. Her open interior layout should easily satisfy those requiring comfortable family-style comfort and privacy. The Corinthian's original double cabin floorplan has undergone several design updates and modifications over the years. A queen berth in the master stateroom became standard in 1981, and in 1985 the galley was relocated aft and to starboard in a manner similar to earlier models. Outside, the Corinthian's cockpit is an extremely practical feature for any cruising boat, providing an easy boarding point while also serving as a swimming or diving platform. With standard 454-cid gas engines she'll cruise at 17 knots and has a top speed of 27. The Chris Craft 380 has been a very popular design with continuing appeal on the used boat market. ❏

SPECIFICATIONS

Length	38'0"
Length WL	33'6"
Beam	14'0"
Draft	3'0"
Weight	22,500#
Clearance	12'2"
Water	65 Gals.
Fuel	400 Gals.
Hull Type	Modified-V
Designer	Chris Craft

Production
1978–86

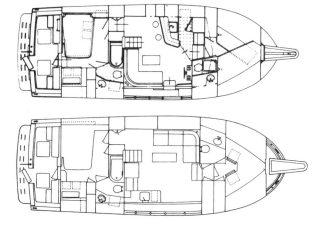

CHRIS CRAFT 381 CATALINA DC

The Chris Craft 381 Catalina Double Cabin is an enlarged version of the popular Chris 350 Catalina model introduced some years earlier. Built on the same hull as the 380 Corinthian, the 381 has an enormous interior — about as much as a 38' hull can handle. She may not be pretty on the outside, but the interior accommodations include very spacious main salon dimensions. Later model 381s feature a convenient breakfast bar separating the galley from the rest of the salon and two comfortable staterooms, each fitted with a double berth. Head-room is particularly good throughout, and while Chris Craft put out some gaudy interiors in the early 1980s, most 381 Catalina decors were stylish and quite comfortable. Outside, the glassed-in front windshield allows for bench seating on the foredeck. The sidedecks are wide and the helm position is conveniently located on the same level as the aft deck. With the standard 330-hp MerCruiser gas engines, the Chris Craft 381 Catalina Double Cabin will cruise at approximately 17 knots (28 gph) with a top speed of 26–27 knots. ❑

SPECIFICATIONS

Length	38'0"
Length WL	NA
Beam	14'0"
Draft	3'0"
Weight	21,600#
Clearance	11'7"
Water	65 Gals.
Fuel	410 Gals.
Hull Type	Modified-V
Designer	Chris Craft

Production
1980–89

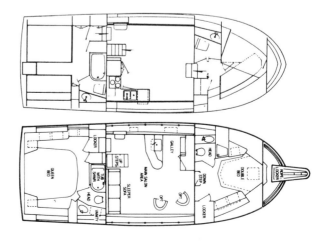

CHRIS CRAFT

CHRIS CRAFT 392 SPORT SEDAN

With her modern and aggressive profile, it's almost hard to believe that the Chris Craft 392 Commander Sport Sedan is actually the old Uniflite 38 Convertible dressed up in a modern package. Chris Craft first marketed this boat in 1985 as the 382 Commander Sport Sedan — basically the same model as the late Uniflite 38 Convertible. In 1986 a new deck and flybridge design resulted in a much improved profile, and in 1987 an updated interior and a glassed-in front windshield only added to her appeal. Several two-stateroom floorplans were offered, and in 1990 (her final year) a single-stateroom floorplan with a mid-level galley and oak paneling became standard (a two-stateroom layout was optional). Originally conceived as a sportfisherman, the Chris 392 is light-years ahead of the old Uniflite in appearance and decor. Retained, however, are the well-known offshore sea-keeping properties of the original hull design. Standard 454-cid gas engines will cruise at 17–18 knots and reach 27 knots at full throttle. The optional 375-hp Cats will cruise at 24 knots and turn a top speed of 28 knots. ❑

SPECIFICATIONS

Length	38'0"
Length WL	33'0"
Beam	13'11"
Draft	3'9"
Weight	28,000#
Clearance	12'0"
Water	100 Gals.
Fuel	350 Gals.
Cockpit	92 Sq. Ft.
Hull Type	Modified-V
Designer	Uniflite

Production
1985–90

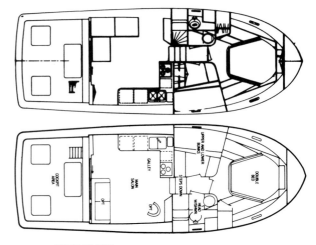

CHRIS CRAFT

CHRIS CRAFT 400 EXPRESS CRUISER

The 400 EC (called the 412 Amerosport from 1987–89) is a good-looking family sportboat with modern styling and plenty of sex appeal. The 400 model designation is confusing — she's actually 38'9" LOA without counting the bow pulpit and optional swim platform. This is a roomy boat with a full 14 feet of beam and generous accommodations inside and out. To date, the 400 EC is the largest of Chris Craft's express boat series. Her sweptback windshield and dramatic hull graphics give her a sleek, aggressive appearance and she's definitely an attention-getter at the dock. The 400 EC uses V-drives to move the engines beneath the cockpit and open up additional interior room. The result is a spacious floorplan with a small mid stateroom located aft beneath the bridgedeck. Outside, the helm position is set a bit low, but visibility is satisfactory and the console well arranged. The cockpit has U-shaped lounge seating for eight to ten passengers. Standard 454-cid gas engines will cruise the Chris 400 Express Cruiser at 17–18 knots and provide a top speed of close to 27 knots. ❑

SPECIFICATIONS

Length	38'9"
Beam	14'0"
Draft	3'2"
Weight	15,000#
Clearance	9'5"
Water	100 Gals.
Fuel	380 Gals.
Cockpit	80 Sq. Ft.
Hull Type	Modified-V
Designer	Richard Avery

Production
1987–90

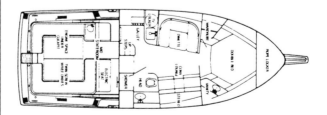

CHRIS CRAFT 410 MOTOR YACHT

It's a shame that Chris Craft never credits the designers of their boats in any company literature because whoever drew the plans for the original Chris Craft 41 Commander Motor Yacht had his finger right on the public pulse. This popular double cabin motor yacht had a production run of nearly 15 years. Affordably priced and offering a vast interior layout, the Chris 410's flush deck profile makes her appear larger than she actually is. While her lines are very conservative, the addition of a restyled and enlarged flybridge in 1980 enhanced her profile considerably.

Inside, the accommodations are comfortable and open, especially in the master stateroom where a queen berth (optional in earlier models) became standard in 1981. Various decor schemes have been used over the years, some good and others ...well, not so good. Big-block 454-cid gas engines were standard and provide a cruising speed of 15–16 knots and 24 knots top. With just 350 gallons of fuel, the 410's range is limited to approximately 200 miles. No longer in production, used Chris Craft 410 Motor Yachts are easily found in most markets. ❏

SPECIFICATIONS

Length	41'0"
Length WL	NA
Beam	14'0"
Draft	3'3"
Weight	26,565#
Clearance	15'10"
Water	100 Gals.
Fuel	350 Gals.
Hull Type	Modified-V
Designer	Chris Craft

Production
1972–86

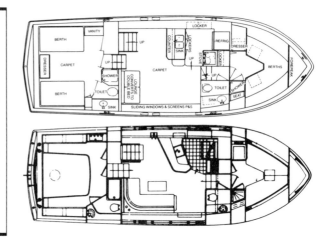

CHRIS CRAFT

CHRIS CRAFT 42 COMMANDER MY

Introduced in 1967, the 42 Commander Motor Yacht was at the time the largest all-fiberglass boat in the Chris Craft fleet. The distinction didn't last long; the 47 Commander MY came out in 1969, and during the early 1970s Chris Craft led the industry in the production of large motor yachts. The 42 is built using a unique three-piece hull — the bottom is one mold and the hullsides are two separate pieces. A molded sprayrail runs around the hull where the bottom is joined, and a long keel below adds stability. The two-stateroom, galley-down interior of the 42 Commander includes two private heads and features twin single berths in the aft stateroom and V-berths forward. The salon is small by today's standards but well arranged and easily updated. Wraparound cabin windows provide good natural lighting and a convenient sliding deck access door is to starboard. The original standard 300-hp gas engines will cruise the Chris Craft 42 Commander MY around 15 knots and reach about 26 knots wide open. GM 8V53N diesels were optional (17 knots cruise/20 knots top). ❏

SPECIFICATIONS

Length	42'0"
Length WL	NA
Beam	13'0"
Draft	3'2"
Weight	22,407#
Clearance	NA
Water	150 Gals.
Fuel	300 Gals.
Hull Type	Modified-V
Designer	A. MacKerer

Production
1967–72

CHRIS CRAFT 42 SPORTS CONVERTIBLE

When the 42 Commander Sports Convertible came out in 1968, she was aimed at the growing market for luxury sportfishermen/family cruisers. At the time, Chris Craft had developed a unique three-piece hull (the bottom is one mold and the hullsides are two separate pieces) used in several of their early fiberglass models. A molded sprayrail runs around the hull where the bottom is joined, and a long keel adds directional stability. The 42 Commander was one of the early fiberglass convertibles in her size range, although the cockpit sole is vinyl over teak planking. The two-stateroom layout originally had a mid-level galley, but that was later changed to a galley-up arrangement. All were fitted with a lower helm, and the interior is finished with simulated teak mica. Outside, the cockpit is large enough for fishing and the sidedecks are wide. The helm console is located forward on the bridge which severely limits cockpit visability. Standard 300-hp gas engines cruise the 42 Sports Convertible around 15 knots with a top speed of 24 knots. Note the old-fashioned foredeck mast and limited fuel capacity. ❏

SPECIFICATIONS

Length	42'0"
Beam	13'0"
Draft	3'2"
Weight	21,267#
Clearance	15'5"
Water	150 Gals.
Fuel	300 Gals.
Cockpit	NA
Hull Type	Modified-V
Designer	A. MacKerer

Production
1968–73

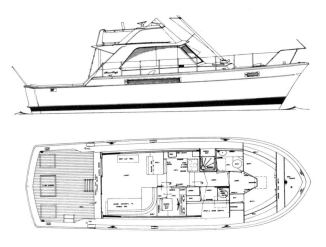

CHRIS CRAFT

CHRIS CRAFT 422 COMMANDER

Only a few production 42' sportfishermen have been around as long as the Chris 422 Commander. She was originally called the 42 Tournament Fisherman when introduced in 1974, and with a pair of GM 8V71TIs she was (and continued to be with 485-hp 6-71s) a reasonably fast boat for her size with a cruising speed of 24 knots and a top speed of 27 knots. Her modified-V hull proved to be extremely dry and stable in offshore conditions, and the classic convertible profile of the early Chris 42 is still handsome today. In 1983, an updated 421 model (with increased fuel) turned out badly and had a very disappointing interior layout and decor. The 422 was the final model. She made her debut in 1985 with a whole new deck and superstructure, a restyled flybridge, a glassed-in front windshield, and a teak interior. (An oak interior became standard in 1989.) Throughout all the model changes, the two-stateroom layout has been retained in one fashion or another. Retained too were the seakeeping qualities that have made the Chris Craft 42 Commander such a good performer over the years. ❑

SPECIFICATIONS

Length....................42'4"
Beam.......................14'0"
Draft ....3'11"
Weight ....33,000#
Clearance ....13'7"
Water.................125 Gals.
Fuel............400/525 Gals.
Cockpit............110 Sq. Ft.
Hull Type.........Modified-V
Designer..........Chris Craft

Production
1974–90

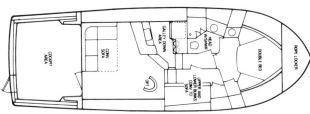

CHRIS CRAFT

CHRIS CRAFT 426/427 CATALINA DC

Perhaps most people won't recognize the Chris Craft 427 Catalina Double Cabin as a direct descendant of the old Uniflite 42 DC. Uniflite first introduced this design back in 1971 and production ran continuously until 1984, when the company closed down. At the time, Uniflite designers had just finished restyling the 42 with a more attractive profile and a fresh interior arrangement. When Chris Craft picked up the molds, they implemented the changes and resumed production of the boat in 1985 calling her the 425 Catalina. A newly designed deckhouse and bridge were added for 1986 in the 426 model, and in 1989 she was renamed the 427 Catalina. A good-riding boat, the Catalina has one of the better floorplan arrangements to be found in a double-cabin design. Both staterooms have centerline double berths and the large, U-shaped galley is down from the salon with a full dinette opposite. With standard 454-cid gas engines the cruising speed of the Chris 427 Catalina is 17–18 knots with about 27 knots at full throttle. The optional 375-hp Cat diesels will cruise at 21+ knots. ❏

SPECIFICATIONS

Length	42'0"
Length WL	37'7"
Beam	14'9"
Draft	3'6"
Weight	33,000#
Clearance	12'10"
Water	160 Gals.
Fuel	400 Gals.
Hull Type	Modified-V
Designer	A. Nordtvedt

Production
1985–90

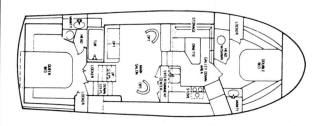

CHRIS CRAFT 45 COMMANDER SF

Although the Chris 45 Commander Sportfisherman was in production for nearly a decade, she never achieved the widespread popularity among hard-core anglers of the Hatteras 45 and 46 convertibles or the Bertram 46. The 45 Commander went into production in 1972 on a heavy, broad-beamed hull with a sharp entry and a nearly flat bottom at the transom. A conventional two-stateroom, galley-down interior was standard and a three-stateroom layout was also available (one of the first three-stateroom arrangements ever offered in a production boat of this size). Notable features include overhead rod storage in the salon, a big tournament-style flybridge, and good storage throughout. The large and well-organized cockpit includes two fish boxes, a livewell on the centerline, and a wide transom door. After playing around with the idea of gas turbines in early production models, a variety of optional diesel engines were offered over the years. Among them, the popular 425-hp GM 8V71s will cruise the Chris 45 Commander SF at a respectable 20 knots and reach 23 knots wide open.   ❏

SPECIFICATIONS

Length	45'6"
Beam	16'0"
Draft	3'11"
Weight	38,700#
Clearance	13'7"
Water	150 Gals.
Fuel	600 Gals.
Cockpit	NA
Hull Type	Modified-V
Designer	Chris Craft

Production
1972–81

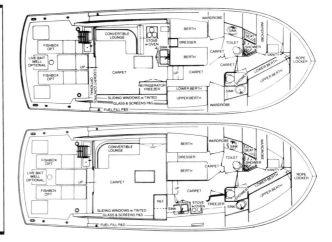

CHRIS CRAFT

CHRIS CRAFT 45 COMMANDER MY

The Chris Craft 45 Commander Motor Yacht is a traditional flush deck design with the classic Chris Craft motor yacht appearance. As a weekend retreat or coastal cruising yacht, the accommodations are more than adequate with a huge main salon dominating the floorplan. Early models were built with two-stateroom interior layouts and are remembered today for a unique, full-width forward stateroom with the head fitted in the forepeak. A popular three-stateroom arrangement with a deckhouse galley became available in 1977, and a more conventional two-stateroom interior with the galley-down followed the next year. Interestingly, a dinette was never offered in the 45 Commander MY. The flybridge proved a popular option, and most were so equipped. A comfortable yacht with a reputation for good handling characteristics, many 45 Commander Motor Yachts were powered with the popular 325-hp GM 8V71 diesels for an economical cruising speed of 16 knots and a top speed of about 19 knots. The cruising range is around 225–250 nautical miles. ❑

SPECIFICATIONS

Length......................45'0"
Length WL...................NA
Beam.......................15'0"
Draft ....4'2"
Weight ....39,400#
Clearance ....16'3"
Water................200 Gals.
Fuel ....500 Gals.
Hull Type.........Modified-V
Designer..........Chris Craft

Production
1972–81

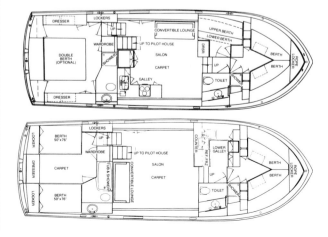

CHRIS CRAFT

CHRIS CRAFT 47 COMMANDER MY

The Chris Craft 47 Commander MY may be dated by today's standards, but many dealers and brokers have acquired from her a firsthand appreciation of the way Chris Craft used to build boats when that company's name stood foremost in the industry. The massive, solid fiberglass hull of the 47 Commander is probably bulletproof. The gelcoat is long-lasting, and all of the deck hardware was custom-crafted at the Chris Craft factory in Algonac, Michigan. A comfortable cruising yacht, the three-stateroom interior layout proved very popular and will be seen on nearly all used models. In 1973, the model designation was changed to Flush Deck, but no major changes were made in design. One common criticism is the small fuel and water tankage, which seriously limits her effective cruising range. Various diesel engine options were offered over the years with the GM 8V53s probably the most popular. They provide a very sedate cruising speed of 12–13 knots depending on load. With a somewhat narrow 15' beam, the handling and seakeeping qualities of the Chris Craft 47 Motor Yacht are very good. ❏

SPECIFICATIONS

Length	47'0"
Length WL	NA
Beam	15'0"
Draft	4'2"
Weight	41,500#
Clearance	13'0"
Water	80 Gals.
Fuel	350 Gals.
Hull Type	Modified-V
Designer	Chris Craft

Production
1966–76

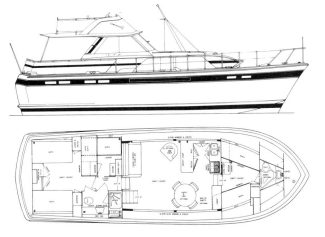

CHRIS CRAFT

CHRIS CRAFT 480 CATALINA DC

The Chris Craft 480 Catalina Double Cabin is another of the models Chris Craft acquired from Uniflite in 1985. Actually, the 480 Catalina is a 427 Catalina with a 6' cockpit addition. Uniflite had originally introduced this boat as the 48 Yacht Fisherman in 1980, and thanks to her good looks and sturdy construction she had already become a popular model. When Chris Craft put her back into production in 1985 it was soon apparent that they had a very appealing yacht with a proven reputation. Underway, the Chris 480 Catalina rides dry and comfortably on a modified-V hull with 13° of deadrise at the transom. Her two-stateroom interior accommodations are roomy and well decorated, and her raised aft deck has enough space for comfortable outdoor entertaining. The additional six feet of boat length of the Chris 480 DC does nothing to detract from her clean lines and brisk performance. A good-running boat, with 375-hp Cats the Chris 480 Catalina planes quickly and cruises at 21+ knots (30 gph) with a top speed of 25–26 knots. The range with the Cats is an impressive 350–400 miles. ❏

SPECIFICATIONS

Length	48'0"
Beam	14'9"
Draft	3'6"
Weight	34,000#
Clearance	12'10"
Water	160 Gals.
Fuel	590 Gals.
Cockpit	NA
Hull Type	Modified-V
Designer	A. Nordtvedt

Production
1985–89

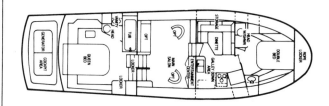

CHRIS CRAFT 482 CONVERTIBLE

Originally introduced in 1980 as the Uniflite 48 Convertible, the Chris Craft 482 Commander Convertible is built on a rugged modified-V hull with 14° of deadrise aft and balsa coring in the hullsides. Her long foredeck and huge cockpit immediately mark her as a tournament-style fisherman, although the luxurious interior of the 48 Commander is easily one of her more desirable features. Various floorplans were offered when she was built by Uniflite, but Chris Craft settled on the popular three-stateroom arrangement with a queen berth in the starboard master stateroom. Rich teak paneling and a modern decor highlight the spacious main salon. Chris Craft offered an optional glassed-in front windshield in later models in keeping with current design trends. At 48,000 lbs., the Chris 482 Commander is no lightweight, but with the standard GM 8V92TI diesels (600-hp) she can cruise at a steady 25–26 knots. With good offshore performance and 780 gallons of fuel, the Chris Craft 482 is a capable tournament contender. Note that the Chris Craft 502 Convertible (1989 only) was built on a stretched 482 hull. ❏

SPECIFICATIONS

Length	48'10"
Beam	15'9"
Draft	4'9"
Weight	48,000#
Clearance	13'9"
Water	200 Gals.
Fuel	780 Gals.
Cockpit	133 Sq. Ft.
Hull Type	Modified-V
Designer	A. Nordtvedt

Production
1985–1988

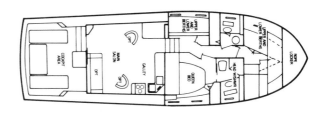

CHRIS CRAFT 500 MOTOR YACHT

This Chris Craft 500 has a fairly complex history. She was introduced in 1977 as the Pacemaker 46 MY — a classic David Martin design of extraordinary beauty — and production lasted until Pacemaker went out of business in 1980. Uniflite then acquired the tooling and production resumed in 1981 as the Uniflite 46 MY. By late 1983, Uniflite designers had stretched the mold four feet and the Uniflite 50 Motor Yacht was introduced. It was a short production run because Uniflite closed down shortly thereafter. Chris Craft then picked up the molds and produced both boats as the 460 and 500 Constellation models. (The 460 ended production in 1988.) For those who admire the traditional styling of a flush deck layout, the Chris 500 has much to offer. A tremendous amount of living space is available in her three-stateroom floorplan including a fully enclosed and paneled afterdeck that serves as a second salon. Below, a unique den/stateroom forward of the master stateroom includes a convertible settee with a desk and bookshelves. The Chris 500 MY has a cruising speed of 18 knots with standard 550-hp 6V92s and a top speed of 21 knots. ❏

SPECIFICATIONS

Length	50'6"
Length WL	NA
Beam	15'3"
Draft	4'4"
Weight	54,000#
Clearance	17'1"
Water	160 Gals.
Fuel	600 Gals.
Hull Type	Modified-V
Designer	David Martin

Production
1985–89

CHRIS CRAFT 501 MOTOR YACHT

The Chris Craft 501 MY (also called the 50 Constellation in her final year) is yet another refinement of the original Pacemaker 46 hull. A handsome and good-selling yacht, her extended deckhouse layout is aimed at those who prefer the increased entertainment capabilities of a full-width salon. While the 501 was built on a stretched mold, the deck and superstructure were new and designed by Chris Craft. By moving the pilothouse forward and relocating the engines further aft, the Constellation gains an expansive salon, genuine privacy in the aft cabin, and an engine room with standing headroom. A spiral staircase leads from the salon down to a truly impressive master stateroom where a tub is located in the adjoining head compartment. A new galley-up arrangement joined the original galley-down layout in 1990. Since the walka-round sidedecks are eliminated in this wide-body configuration, Chris Craft designers thoughtfully added a small aft deck suitable for line handling duties. Cruising speed of the Chris Craft 501 MY with 550-hp GM 6V92TA diesels is approximately 17 knots and the top speed is 18–19 knots. ❏

SPECIFICATIONS

Length	50'8"
Length WL	NA
Beam	15'5"
Draft	4'6"
Weight	49,000#
Clearance	NA
Water	260 Gals.
Fuel	778 Gals.
Hull Type	Modified-V
Designer	Chris Craft

Production
1987–90

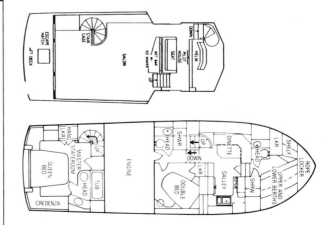

CHRIS CRAFT 502 CONVERTIBLE

To create the new Chris Craft 502 Commander, the hull of the 482 Convertible was stretched two feet and a new deck and superstructure were developed to give her the sleek and bold appearance of a modern sportfishing boat. Very narrow of beam (for a 50-footer), she rides on a proven modified-V hull design (inherited from the original Uniflite 48 Convertible) with cored hullsides and 12° of transom deadrise. The additional length has gone into the salon where the oak woodwork and light-colored fabrics create a completely modern decor. The 502 Commander has three staterooms and two full heads with a washer/dryer unit located in the forward cabin. The cockpit is fitted with an above-deck baitwell, freezer, transom door, direct engine room access, and molded-in steps to the sidedecks. The flybridge is very spacious with the helm console set aft for a good view of the cockpit. With her 735-hp 8V92s, the Chris 502 Convertible will cruise at 26–27 knots and reach 30 knots wide open. A poor-selling boat, only two were built during her one-year production run. ❏

SPECIFICATIONS

Length	50'10"
Length WL	45'0"
Beam	15'9"
Draft	4'9"
Weight	50,000#
Clearance	17'1"
Water	200 Gals.
Fuel	1,000 Gals.
Cockpit	NA
Hull Type	Modified-V
Designer	A. Nordtvedt

Production
1989 Only

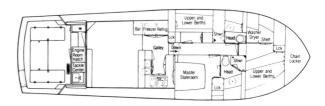

CHRIS CRAFT 55 FLUSH DECK MY

When the 55 Flush Deck was introduced in 1970, she was the largest fiberglass yacht in the Chris Craft fleet. Like many of the larger motor yachts of her era, the 55 was designed to be operated as a crewed vessel. She was built using a unique three-piece hull — the bottom is one mold and the hullsides are two separate pieces. A molded sprayrail runs around the hull where the bottom and sides are joined, and a long keel below adds directional stability. The first 55s were hardtop models with a covered afterdeck and semi-enclosed helm. In 1975, the Enclosed Flush Deck model turned the aft deck into a huge full-width main salon over 18' in length. While the flybridge was optional, most of the later 55s were so equipped. The accommodations include an expansive owner's stateroom and guest cabin aft, a mid-level dining salon and galley forward, and guest stateroom at the bow. Most of the 55 Flush Deck yachts were powered with 425-hp 8V71 diesels. Performance is about 15 knots at cruise and 18 knots wide open. Due to the boat's limited fuel capacity, the range at a hard cruise is less than 200 miles. ❑

SPECIFICATIONS

Length	55'0"
Length WL	NA
Beam	16'6"
Draft	4'0"
Weight	57,800#
Clearance	16'9"
Water	162 Gals.
Fuel	570 Gals.
Hull Type	Modified-V
Designer	Chris Craft

Production
1970–77

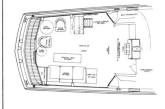

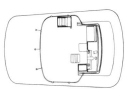

ROAMER 60 FLUSH DECK MY

The Chris Craft 60 Roamer Flush Deck is a traditional flybridge motor yacht with classic lines and a still-handsome profile. A descendant of the 58 Roamer (1969–72), the hull, deck, and superstructure of the 60 Roamer Flush Deck are of welded marine aluminum. While the 60 originally came with an open aft deck and semi-enclosed lower helm, many were built with the aft deck fully enclosed and turned into a full-width main salon. The galley and dinette are on the lower level forward of the formal dining room/salon and the three primary staterooms are aft. The bow stateroom can serve as an extra guest cabin or crew quarters. Early models offered the choice of a three- or four-stateroom layout (pictured below), and a revised three-stateroom floorplan with a full-width owner's suite became available in 1975. Several diesel options were offered in the 60 Roamer Flush Deck, but most were powered with the 12V71TIs. With those engines, she'll cruise at 17 knots and reach a top speed of around 20 knots. A popular yacht, a total of 26 were built during her production run. ❏

SPECIFICATIONS

Length	60'5"
Length WL	NA
Beam	17'3"
Draft	4'8"
Weight	68,500#
Clearance	17'0"
Water	300 Gals.
Fuel	1,260 Gals.
Hull Type	Modified-V
Designer	Chris Craft

Production
1972–76

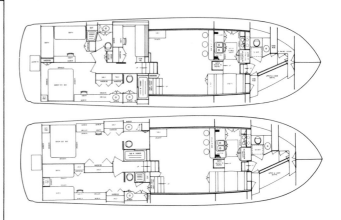

ROAMER 60 MOTOR YACHT

Although the last 60 Roamer was built in 1976, these luxurious and well-constructed motor yachts remain popular today in spite of their age. Built of aluminum, the 60 is a spacious yacht with a full-width deckhouse salon and a roomy aft deck for outdoor entertaining. The main galley (on the wheelhouse level) opens to the salon with a serving counter. All of the interior woodwork is teak. The three-stateroom lowerdeck layout of the 60 originally had the master suite to starboard and the two guest cabins to port. A more conventional three-stateroom floorplan in 1975–76 featured a full-width master stateroom with a king-size centerline berth and a bathtub in the head. A corridor between the engine rooms leads forward to the wheelhouse staircase. The separate crew quarters include a galley, dinette, full head, and upper and lower berths. Note the wraparound bulwark forward of the deckhouse. Clearly designed for elegant cruising, most 60 Roamers were powered with GM 12V71TI diesels. The cruising speed is 16–17 knots and the top speed is around 20 knots. A total of 20 were built. ❏

SPECIFICATIONS

Length	60'0"
Length WL	NA
Beam	17'2"
Draft	4'6"
Weight	70,000#
Clearance	19'3"
Water	300 Gals.
Fuel	1,260 Gals.
Hull Type	Modified-V
Designer	Chris Craft

Production
1974–76

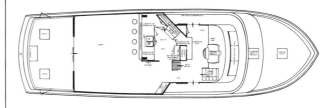

ROAMER 68 ENCLOSED FLUSH DECK

In the world of luxury motor yachts, the Chris 68 Roamer Enclosed Flush Deck is known for her distinctive appearance, practical layout, and rugged all-aluminum construction. This is a yacht dedicated to sophisticated entertaining and cruising on a grand scale. With the galley located on the forward lower level, the magnificent deckhouse salon is 20' long and includes a 5-seat bar abaft the enclosed wheelhouse — certainly one of the most expansive and elegant main salons found on any motor yacht of her size. The formal dining salon is forward of the wheelhouse and separated from the adjoining galley with its own dinette and day head. In the four-stateroom layout, the full-width owner's suite is opulent (note the "his" and "hers" bathrooms) and private from the twin guest staterooms. An optional three-stateroom arrangement provides for a small office just off the owner's cabin. The deckhouse and flybridge of the 68 Roamer were redesigned in 1975, but the floorplans remained the same. GM 12V71TIs will cruise this yacht at 16 knots and provide a top speed of 19 knots. ❏

SPECIFICATIONS

Length	68'4"
Length WL	NA
Beam	17'3"
Draft	4'10"
Weight	87,200#
Clearance	24'5"
Water	300 Gals.
Fuel	1,470 Gals.
Hull Type	Modified-V
Designer	Chris Craft

Production
1972–77

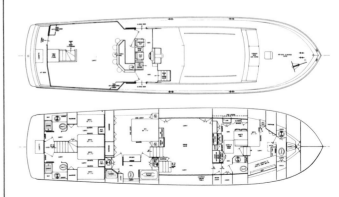

CRUISERS, INC.

Brief History

Cruisers, Inc. began operations in 1953 and became known for its series of wood lapstrake runabouts and cruisers. The company began the transition to fiberglass in 1965, and in 1972 Cruisers was purchased by Mirro Marine. In 1982 Cruisers was sold to private interests whose principals continue to operate the firm today. Cruisers expanded into the sportfish market with their purchase of Rampage Yachts in 1990.

Selected Cruisers Inboard Models

Cruisers Avanti Vee 296

Cruisers Esprit 2970

Cruisers Esprit 2980

Cruisers Sea Devil 3210

Cruisers Esprit 3260/3270

Cruisers Esprit 3360

Cruisers Esprit 3370

Cruisers Esprit 3380

Cruisers Esprit 3670/3675

Cruisers 3850 Aft Cabin

Cruisers 4280/4285 MY

Main Office

Cruisers, Inc., 804 Pecor St., Oconto, WI 54153
414-834-2211

183

CRUISERS AVANTI VEE 296

Introduced in 1984, the Avanti Vee 296 was a stylish and fairly popular family express cruiser for Cruisers, Inc. (Note that she was built on the prop-pocket hull of the original Villa Vee 288.) The compact cabin layout of the Avanti Vee 296 has the dinette placed aft in the salon beneath the raised helm position in the cockpit. An offset double berth is fitted into the stateroom forward, but there's only a curtain (no door) for privacy at night. The choice of fabrics and hardware was made with care and the boat has a good quality appearance throughout. Over-all, her interior layout is about average for a boat of this size and should satisfy the demands of most family cruisers. What sets the Avanti Vee 296 apart, however, is her positive foam flotation and superb glasswork. On deck, visibility from the helm is excellent, and the cockpit is large enough for five or six guests. Mid-size 350-cid gas engines (260/270 hp) provide a cruising speed of 19– 20 knots and a top speed of around 30 knots. Note that the Cruisers 291 Sea Devil (1984–85) is the same boat in sportfishing trim. ❑

SPECIFICATIONS

Length	28'8"
Length WL	24'11"
Beam	10'8"
Draft	2'9"
Weight	9,000#
Clearance	7'5"
Water	45 Gals.
Fuel	200/250 Gals.
Hull Type	Modified-V
Designer	Jim Wynne

Production
1984–87

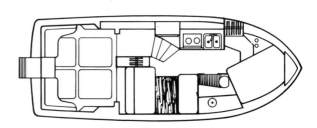

CRUISERS ESPRIT 2970

Introduced as the Cruisers Elegante 297, the Esprit 2970 has proven to be a very popular inboard express cruiser since her introduction in 1986. The Esprit has the same exterior profile as her sistership, the Avanti Vee 296, but with an enlarged mid-cabin floorplan able to sleep a total of six people. To achieve the greater interior volume, Cruisers engineers used V-drives to locate the engines aft beneath the cockpit sole thus freeing up the space necessary for the mid-cabin. The 2970 uses the same proven hull design (with prop pockets) as the original Villa Vee 288 model which came out in 1978. Below, the contemporary decor features teak paneling and good-quality hardware and appliances. Fabrics, wall coverings, fixtures, and systems are all first rate. Both fore and aft staterooms have draw curtains for sleeping privacy. The view from the elevated helm is good although trim tabs are occasionally required to keep the running angles down. The exterior gelcoat finish and deck hardware are above average. With standard 260/270-hp gas engines the Esprit 2970 cruises at around 20 knots and has a top speed of 29–30 knots. ❑

SPECIFICATIONS

Length	28'8"
Length WL	24'11"
Beam	10'8"
Draft	2'9"
Weight	9,000#
Clearance	7'5"
Water	45 Gals.
Fuel	200/250 Gals.
Hull Type	Modified-V
Designer	Jim Wynne

Production
1986–91

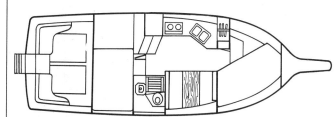

CRUISERS ESPRIT 2980

The Esprit 2980 was Cruisers' first inboard design in 1978 when she was introduced as the Villa Vee 288. A well-proportioned family cruiser with distinctive styling, her surprisingly spacious interior layout has a real salon (rare in such a small boat) with the galley on the lower level. Combined with her quality construction and practical layout, the 288 soon proved to be a popular family design. She was given the 298 designation in 1984, and since 1987 she's been called the Esprit 2980. Over the years numerous updates have been made (including a revised interior for 1989), but the basic design has remained essentially unchanged. From the beginning this boat has been noted for her large cockpit area, beamy interior floorplan, and prop-pocket hull design — a hull form later used in the production of most Cruisers inboard boats. A good performer, she'll cruise around 18 knots with the small 230-hp gas engines (26 knots top). With the 260-hp motors the Esprit 2980 will cruise about 20 knots and reach a top speed of 29–30 knots. ❑

SPECIFICATIONS

Length	28'8"
Length WL	24'11"
Beam	10'8"
Draft	2'9"
Weight	9,500#
Clearance	9'5"
Water	45 Gals.
Fuel	150/180 Gals.
Hull Type	Modified-V
Designer	Jim Wynne

Production
1978–90

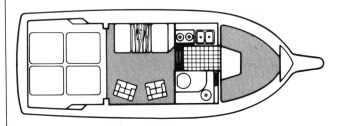

CRUISERS SEA DEVIL 3210

The Sea Devil 3210 proved to have a short production run for Cruisers. A good-looking boat, she's built on the same 31-foot hull as the Esprit 3260/3270 express cruisers. Aimed at the fisherman, the Sea Devil is a stylish design that should appeal to anglers who like their boats with a little sex appeal. A modern curved windshield and flush foredeck hatches are but two of the features that make the Sea Devil 3210 so attractive to the eye. The open cockpit is set up for serious fishing with rod holders, built-in livewells, and a large fish box all within easy reach. The transom door and integral platform are big pluses for anglers and divers. Visibility from the raised helm console is excellent and the Cruisers instrument panel is functional and well arranged. The interior layout is nearly identical to that in the Esprit 3260 — very upscale and fully equipped for comfortable family cruising. With 260-hp gas engines the Sea Devil 3210 will cruise at 19–20 knots with a top speed approaching 30 knots. The Sea Devil is no tournament monster but she certainly is easy on the eye. ❏

SPECIFICATIONS

Length	30'10"
Length WL	NA
Beam	10'10"
Draft	2'10"
Weight	9,500#
Clearance	7'0"
Water	45 Gals.
Fuel	250 Gals.
Hull Type	Modified-V
Designer	Jim Wynne

Production
1988–90

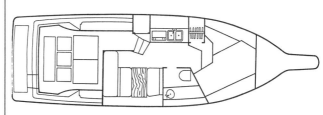

CRUISERS ESPRIT 3260/3270

The Cruisers 3260 and 3270 Esprit models are styled alike outside with the difference being the mid-cabin layout in the 3270 compared to the dinette arrangement in the 3260. The popularity of mid-cabins in today's express cruiser market has kept the 3270 in production while the 3260 was dropped from the Cruisers fleet in 1990. Power in the 3270 is delivered via V-drives, since the aft cabin extends into the area below the cockpit. The 3260, however, is a conventional straight drive installation. Both feature the upscale interior layout and quality detailing one expects in a Cruisers boat. With 250 gallons of fuel capacity, the 3260 has an additional 50 gallons over her sistership. Most people find the exterior lines of these family express cruisers to be extremely attractive with good glasswork and production detailing. Note the curved windshield, oval portlights, flush foredeck hatches, and stylish integral swim platform. With the standard 350-cid Crusader gas engines the Cruisers Esprit 3260/3270 models will cruise at 19–20 knots and reach a top speed of 30 knots. ❏

SPECS — 3270	
Length	30'10"
Length WL	NA
Beam	10'10"
Draft	2'10"
Weight	10,500#
Clearance	7'0"
Water	45 Gals.
Fuel	200/250 Gals.
Hull Type	Modified-V
Designer	Jim Wynne

Production
1988–Current

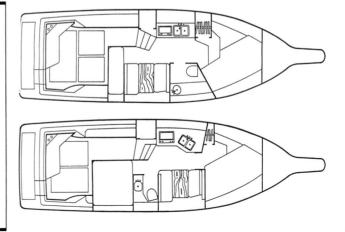

CRUISERS ESPRIT 3360

Introduced in 1983 as the Cruisers Ultra Vee 336, the Esprit 3360 is a roomy and comfortable family cruiser built to above-average production standards. She rides on a proven deep-V hull with recessed prop pockets allowing the engines to be set well aft to free up interior space. The Esprit 3360 is an especially attractive design in spite of her somewhat high deck profile. Inside, she features a unique mid-cabin (a "master stateroom," according to the Cruisers literature) with standing headroom, a privacy door, and direct access to the head — a very innovative and practical cabin arrangement. The guest stateroom is forward, and the portside settee converts into a double berth in the normal manner. In 1985, the 3360 received an additional 50 gallons of fuel capacity for increased range, and the original teak interior was revised with a more contemporary Eurostyle decor. Speeds are around 22 knots at cruise and 32 knots top with the standard 350-hp Crusader engines. Note that positive foam flotation placed throughout the hull makes the Cruisers Esprit 3360 unsinkable. ❏

SPECIFICATIONS

Length	32'10"
Length WL	NA
Beam	11'10"
Draft	2'9"
Weight	11,500#
Clearance	8'6"
Water	70 Gals.
Fuel	250/300 Gals.
Hull Type	Modified-V
Designer	Jim Wynne

Production
1983–88

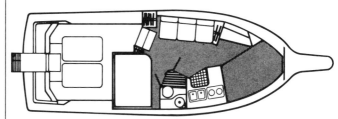

CRUISERS ESPRIT 3370

Built on the same hull as the Cruisers 3360 and having an identical appearance at dockside, the Cruisers Esprit 3370 replaces the private mid-cabin found in the 3360 with additional salon seating and a much more open interior layout. The difference is immediately apparent upon stepping below, where the 3370's expansive layout comes as a real surprise. The two matched L-shaped settees to starboard provide seating for up to eight people. This floorplan arrangement makes the Esprit 3370 a more versatile day boat than her sister-ship, and she'll still sleep six in privacy by converting the two salon sofas and closing the room divider. Headroom is a generous 6'5" in the cabin. The decor is luxurious and well crafted with quality fabrics and fixtures on display throughout. The hull of the Esprit is packed with sufficient flotation to keep her from sinking — a safety feature not found in any other production boat of her size outside of the Cruisers fleet. The Esprit 3370's cruising speed with optional 454-cid Crusader gas engines is about 21 knots with a top speed of 30 knots.   ❏

SPECIFICATIONS

Length	32'10"
Length WL	NA
Beam	11'10"
Draft	2'9"
Weight	11,500#
Clearance	8'6"
Water	70 Gals.
Fuel	300 Gals.
Hull Type	Modified-V
Designer	Jim Wynne

Production
1986–Current

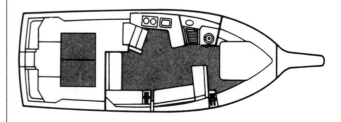

CRUISERS ESPRIT 3380

It's doubtful that many Esprit 3380s have been sold on the strength of sex appeal alone — she has a definite top-heavy appearance that just won't go away. Nevertheless, the 3380 (alias Chateau Vee 338 in 1987) has done well in the market for the past few years due to her practical family accommodations and quality construction. Like other Cruisers models, the 3380 Esprit uses prop pockets in the hull and features positive foam flotation for safety in the event of an accident. Below, the interior accommodations are particularly fashionable and well organized.

Note that the nearly hidden guest stateroom extends below the salon dinette, thus providing space for a double berth. Fortunately, the 3380 doesn't extend the salon's bulkhead so far aft as to eliminate a useful cockpit. Here there is room for a few chairs or space for casual fishing. The family-style flybridge is large enough for five and includes wraparound bench seating behind the helm. An average performer with 454-cid gas engines, the Cruisers Esprit 3380 will cruise at around 20 knots and reach 29–30 knots wide open. ❏

SPECIFICATIONS

Length	32'10"
Length WL	NA
Beam	11'10"
Draft	2'10"
Weight	13,000#
Clearance	11'6"
Water	70 Gals.
Fuel	300 Gals.
Hull Type	Modified-V
Designer	Jim Wynne

Production
1985–Current

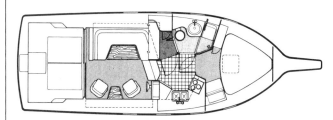

CRUISERS ESPRIT 3670/3675

The Cruisers Esprit 3670 and the more recent 3675 (introduced in 1991) are maxi-beam family boats with modern European styling and contemporary interior decors. Good-looking boats, the high foredeck profile is made necessary by their large interior volumes. The beautifully curved windshield, oval portlights, and integral swim platform are especially attractive, although the stainless steel radar arch is a matter of opinion. Inside, the accommodations are plush and completely luxurious. The 3675 is the more open design with more living space and a larger head but no dinette. The 3670, on the other hand, has a nicer forward stateroom with a walkaround island berth rather than the offset double found in the 3675. Both layouts have the head located within easy reach of the cockpit. Unlike other Cruisers express models, the 3670/3675 have the passenger seating forward and to port rather than aft behind the helmsman. Using V-drives to move the engines aft and free up interior space, both boats will cruise around 19 knots and reach a top speed of 29–30 knots with standard 454-cid gas engines. ❏

SPECIFICATIONS

Length	35'3"
Beam	13'0"
Draft	2'10"
Weight	17,500#
Clearance	9'7"
Water	110 Gals.
Fuel	300 Gals.
Cockpit	NA
Hull Type	Modified-V
Designer	Jim Ginter

Production
1989–Current

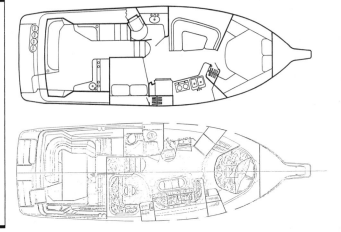

CRUISERS, INC.

CRUISERS 3850 AFT CABIN

The aggressive styling and slightly top-heavy profile of the Cruisers 3850 make her a distinctive boat in any marina. She's built on a modern fully cored hull with prop pockets and a fairly steep 16° of deadrise at the transom. The 3850 has a truly spacious interior with the accommodations of a much larger boat. Packed into this beamy hull are two staterooms with double berths, two full heads with a tub aft, a roomy U-shape galley with excellent storage *and* a washer/dryer, and a comfortable salon with curved companionway steps. Elegantly furnished and decorated, this is an impressive interior layout for just a 38-foot boat and one that cruising families will certainly enjoy. The raised aft deck is on the small side but the innovative reverse transom with it's molded boarding steps is a practical addition on a boat with this much freeboard. There's plenty of guest seating on the bridge, the sidedecks are decent, and a sun pad can be fitted on the foredeck. A thirsty boat with big-block 502-cid gas engines, the Cruisers 3850 Aft Cabin cruises at 15–16 knots (burning around 33 gph) and reaches a top speed of 25 knots. ❑

SPECIFICATIONS

Length	39'0"
Length WL	NA
Beam	14'0"
Draft	3'4"
Weight	20,000#
Clearance	17'3"
Water	100 Gals.
Fuel	400 Gals.
Hull Type	Modified-V
Designer	Cruisers

Production
1991–Current

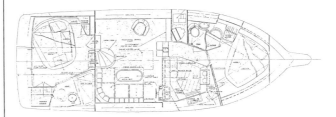

CRUISERS EXPRESS BRIDGE 4280/4285

For those who enjoy their socializing on a grand scale, the Express Bridge is loaded with design features not usually expected in a mid-size cruiser. Restyled on the outside for 1992, she's *still* an unattractive boat to us with a truly awkward profile. Inside, the expansive full-width interior is laid out on a single-level, providing remarkable living accommodations. The 4280 model has a two-stateroom layout (upgraded with two heads in 1992) with the galley in the salon. The 4285 (introduced in 1990) has only a single-stateroom but a much larger salon, a huge head, and a separate galley. While the upscale interiors of both models are impressive, it's the spacious flybridge to which guests will be attracted — there's seating for a crowd. Molded steps on both sides of the cockpit lead up to the bridge (no ladders to negotiate). Other features include cored hull construction, easy foredeck access, a reverse swim platform, and prop pockets below. Gas engines are standard (13 knots cruise/20 top). With optional 375-hp Cats or 400-hp 6V53s the Express Bridge will cruise at 20 knots and reach a top speed of around 24 knots. ❏

SPECIFICATIONS

Length	42'0"
Beam	14'6"
Draft	3'6"
Weight	27,000#
Clearance	13'3"
Water	160 Gals.
Fuel	400 Gals.
Cockpit	91 Sq. Ft.
Hull Type	Modified-V
Designer	Jim Wynne

Production
1988–Current

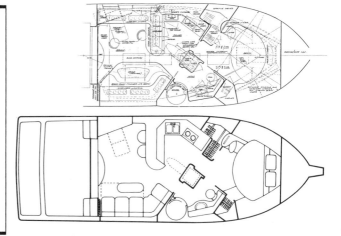

DEFEVER

Brief History

The models described in the following pages represent a cross section of some of the better known production DeFever designs. While different models have been built by several U.S. and Asian manufacturers over the years, the CTF yard in Taiwan is best known today for their series of DeFever trawlers and motor yachts up to 72 feet in length. DeFevers are well regarded as sturdy trawlers and offshore cruisers with traditional floorplans.

Selected DeFever Models

DeFever 34 Trawler

DeFever 40 Trawler

DeFever 40 Offshore

DeFever 41 Trawler

DeFever 43 Trawler

DeFever 44 Cruiser

DeFever 48 Cruiser

DeFever 49 Pilothouse

DeFever 52 Motor Yacht

DeFever 53 (POC) Motor Yacht

DeFever 60 Offshore Cruiser

Main Office

DeFever designs have been built by several U.S. and Asian Builders. For additional information, contact Arthur DeFever Yacht Sales, 2736 Shelter Island Dr., San Diego, CA 92106. (619)-222-2414

DEFEVER PASSAGEMAKER 34

The DeFever Passagemaker 34 is one of the few trawlers to have been built in America. Introduced by Jensen Marine in 1974, she preceded the flood of cheap Asian imports which eventually drove most U.S. builders out of the trawler market. The Passagemaker is constructed of fiberglass on a heavy, full-displacement hull with a long keel, rounded bilges, and a flared bow. Her appearance is that of a husky, seaworthy cruiser with genuine offshore capabilities. Inside, the accommodations are fairly modest and straightforward with berths for four and a linear galley aft of the helm. The interior is finished with teak woodwork and cabinetry, and 360° salon windows deliver plenty of natural lighting. Boarding the 34 is easy thanks to the transom door and teak platform, and the sidedecks are wide. A mast and boom were standard. A single Lehman 120-hp diesel will burn 2.5 gallons of fuel per hour at 7–8 knots for a cruising range of 1,000 miles. A few of these boats (slightly restyled) were sold under the Downeast name in 1980–81. Note that she's still built today in Mexico and marketed as the DeFever Baha 34. ❑

SPECIFICATIONS

Length	34'0"
Length WL	30'3"
Beam	12'3"
Draft	3'4"
Weight	19,300#
Clearance	NA
Water	100 Gals.
Fuel	360 Gals.
Hull Type	Displ.
Designer	A. DeFever

Production
1974–76

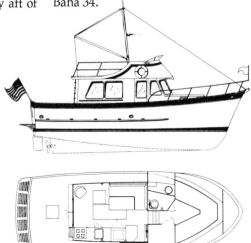

DEVEFER

DEFEVER 40 TRAWLER

Originally built in California and sold as the DeFever Passagemaker 40 Trawler, the new DeFever Baha 40 model (pictured above) is a direct descendent of the original design. Passagemaker built the all-fiberglass 40 from 1973–77. The molds were sold to Downeast Yachts, Inc. and production resumed (again in California) as the Downeast Trawler 40 in 1980. Downeast tooled up an inner liner pan which formed a new layout, but production lasted only through 1981 when Downeast went out of business. Production again began (now in Mexico) in 1989 as the DeFever Baha 40. Her salty profile, good sea-keeping qualities, wide sidedecks, and practical two-stateroom layout have made this a popular cruiser over the years. Although twin engines were offered in the past, most of the early models were powered with a single 130-hp Perkins diesel for a cruising speed of 7–8 knots at 3 gph. Twin 130-hp Perkins diesels are now standard. With 450 gallons of fuel and 300 gallons of water (200 gals. in the early Passagemaker models), the practical cruising range of the DeFever 40 is very good. ❑

SPECIFICATIONS

Length	39'0"
Length WL	34'7"
Beam	13'8"
Draft	4'0"
Weight	26,500#
Clearance	24'0"
Water	200/300 Gals.
Fuel	450 Gals.
Hull Type	Semi-Disp.
Designer	A. DeFever

Production
1973–81
1989–Current

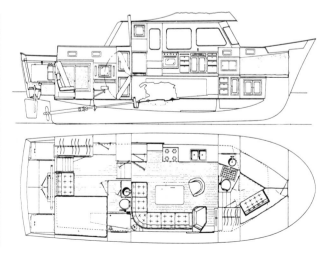

DEFEVER

DEFEVER 40 OFFSHORE CRUISER

The DeFever 40 is an unusual looking trunk cabin cruiser with a distinctive, almost-flat sheerline seldom seen in a trawler-style design. She's built by CTF in Taiwan on a solid glass hull with hard aft chines and a deep keel for prop protection. Her galley-up floorplan includes a large aft cabin, although that particular luxury comes at the expense of a rather compact salon. The U-shaped galley is aft in the salon which many consider an ideal location in a small cruiser. A lower helm is standard and there are port and starboard sliding deck doors in the salon. Teak paneling and cabinetry is used throughout the interior in the traditional Asian mode. Additional features of the DeFever 40 include full walkaround decks, a well arranged flybridge with plenty of guest seating around the helm, radar arch, and a decent engine room with fairly good access to the motors. Standard engines for the DeFever 40 have been the 240-hp Perkins diesels which deliver a comfortable 12–13 knot cruising speed. Optional 320-hp Cats will cruise around 15 knots and reach a top speed of 18 knots. ❑

SPECIFICATIONS

Length	40'0"
Length WL	35'6"
Beam	14'6"
Draft	3'10"
Weight	29,000#
Clearance	NA
Water	200 Gals.
Fuel	400 Gals.
Hull Type	Semi-Disp.
Designer	DeFever

Production
1985–Current

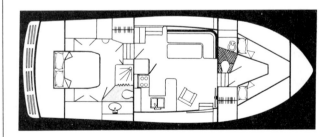

DEFEVER 41 TRAWLER

This traditional double cabin trawler was built in Taiwan by Bluewater Marine and enjoys a good deal of popularity on both East and West Coast markets. She's constructed on a solid fiberglass semi-displacement hull with a deep forefoot, flat aftersections, and a long keel which fully protects the running gear in the event of grounding. Her floorplan consists of a huge master stateroom with direct access to the aft deck, a fairly compact salon with the galley aft and deck doors port and starboard, and V-berths forward with a second head compartment. The varnished teak interior woodwork — and there's plenty of it — is quite impressive. The DeFever 41's house is set well forward on the deck and there's adequate space on the trunk cabin aft of the bridge for dinghy storage. Additional features include teak overlaid decks and cabin-top, wide sidedecks with raised bulwarks all around, and tub/shower in the aft head. With so much exterior teak, this boat is a maintenance nightmare. Most DeFever 41 Trawlers were fitted with single or twin 135-hp Lehman diesels. She'll cruise at a leisurely 7–8 knots while burning around 5 gph. ❏

SPECIFICATIONS

Length	40'7"
Length WL	34'7"
Beam	14'2"
Draft	4'0"
Weight	33,000#
Clearance	NA
Water	250 Gals.
Fuel	400/483 Gals.
Hull Type	Semi-Disp.
Designer	DeFever

Production
1983–88

DEFEVER 43 TRAWLER

A true displacement trawler with a distinctive flush deck profile, the DeFever 43 was built in Taiwan of solid fiberglass with a deep keel, protected props, and simulated lapstrake hullsides. Note the 40,000 lbs. displacement and tremendous fuel capacity of the 43—this is a serious deepwater cruiser with an honest 1,500-mile+ range. The unusual flush deck layout of the DeFever 43 Trawler results in a very large afterdeck while still permitting good headroom below in the master stateroom. It also provides for a spacious engine room with near-standing headroom and excellent engine access. Her two-stateroom floorplan is arranged with the U-shaped galley aft in the salon — an ideal layout in a cruising boat of this size. There are three deck access doors in the salon and the only stall shower is found in the aft head. Teak paneling and a teak parquet floors are used throughout the interior. Outside, the decks are teak and so are the swim platform, frames, handrails, and bow pulpit. The flybridge includes plenty of guest seating abaft the helm. Twin 120-hp Lehman diesels will cruise the DeFever 43 Trawler effortlessly at 7–8 knots. ❏

SPECIFICATIONS

Length	42'2"
Length WL	NA
Beam	14'0"
Draft	4'5"
Weight	40,836#
Clearance	NA
Water	500 Gals.
Fuel	1,072 Gals.
Hull	Displacement
Designer	DeFever

Production
1978–85

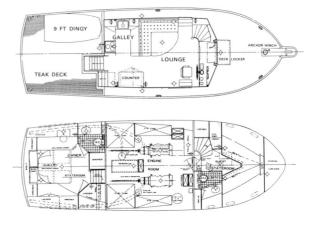

DEVEFER

DEFEVER 44 DIESEL CRUISER

The DeFever 44 is a heavy displacement long range cruiser built by the well-regarded CTF yard in Taiwan. Her attractive flush deck profile and trawler-style deckhouse suggest the comfortable and durable design that she is. Most will probably view the DeFever 44 as a trawler since the majority were sold with twin 120/135-hp Lehman diesels and the cruising speed is only 8–9 knots. Her lack of exterior teak trim continues to attract those who are seeking a trawler design without the usual maintenance headaches. Below, the interior is all teak. A notable (and very popular) feature of the DeFever 44 is her galley location — aft and to port in the salon and separated from the rest of the salon by a serving counter and overhead cabinetry. Both staterooms are served by a good-size head compartment (with a stall shower aft), and a walkaround double berth is located in the master stateroom. A door in the forward stateroom opens into the 44's huge engine room where outboard access is excellent. With her rugged and seakindly hull, the DeFever 44 is a serious cruising boat with better-than-average resale values. ❑

SPECIFICATIONS

Length	43'9"
Length WL	38'6"
Beam	14'9"
Draft	4'7"
Weight	44,000#
Clearance	NA
Water	364 Gals.
Fuel	900 Gals.
Hull Type	Semi-Disp.
Designer	A. DeFever

Production
1980–Current

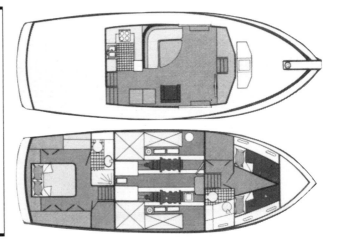

DEFEVER

DEFEVER 48 DIESEL CRUISER

A handsome design, the DeFever 48 is a heavy displacement long-range cruiser built by the CTF yard in Taiwan. She's constructed on a solid fiberglass semi-displacement hull with a moderately flared bow, a fine entry, and hard aft chines. Considered a trawler by most, the DeFever 48 is capable of planing speeds with engines larger than the standard twin 135-hp Lehman diesels. The Cat 375-hp diesels (found in some late models) provide a cruising speed of 14–15 knots. The DeFever 48 shares several design features with the smaller DeFever 44,

namely the galley arrangement (a U-shaped affair located aft in the salon) and the remarkably spacious engine room. Inside, the DeFever is finished with teak paneling and cabinetry throughout — all done to high Asian standards. The floorplan in the DeFever 48 includes three staterooms, two full heads, and a salon of average dimensions with a lower helm and sliding doors for deck access both port and starboard. A combination of good looks and sturdy very construction have earned the DeFever 48 a good reputation on the resale market. ❑

SPECIFICATIONS

Length	47'3"
Length WL	40'10"
Beam	15'0"
Draft	4'9"
Weight	50,000#
Clearance	NA
Water	500 Gals.
Fuel	950 Gals.
Hull Type	Semi-Disp.
Designer	A. DeFever

Production
1978–Current

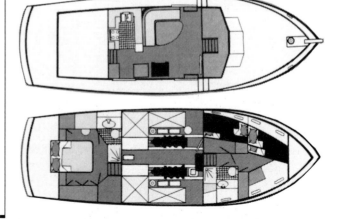

DEVEFER

DEFEVER 49 PILOTHOUSE

Arthur DeFever first designed a series of popular pilothouse trawlers for American Marine (Grand Banks) back in the late 1960s. Called Alaskans, these sturdy wooden passagemakers soon attracted a following of serious cruisers, and it was only a matter of time before similar designs became available in fiberglass. The DeFever 49 Pilothouse Trawler appeared in 1977. She was built by the Sen Koh and CTF yards in Taiwan on a solid fiberglass hull with teak decks, teak window frames, doors, rails, etc. A notably handsome boat with a go-any-

where appearance and enough bulk to deal with heavy seas, the DeFever 49's floorplan locates the master stateroom directly below the raised pilothouse with the guest stateroom forward. The interior is total teak. In recent years the DeFever 49 has been redesigned to eliminate some of the maintenance (in other words, less exterior teak), and the original soft-chined hull has been given flatter aft sections to reduce rolling. Powered with twin 135-hp Lehman diesels, the DeFever 49 is economical to operate and offers genuine long-range cruising potential. ❏

SPECIFICATIONS

Length	49'10"
Length WL	42'0"
Beam	15'0"
Draft	4'6"
Weight	50,000#
Clearance	17'0"
Water	400 Gals.
Fuel	800 Gals.
Hull Type	Semi-Disp.
Designer	A. DeFever

Production
1977–Current

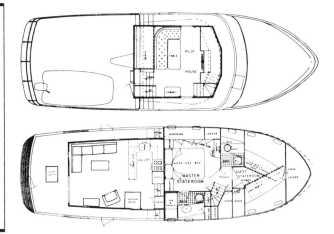

DEFEVER

DEFEVER 52 MOTOR YACHT

A popular yacht, the 52 Motor Yacht is a classic DeFever offshore design with a distinctive trawler-style profile and a superb cruising layout. She's built in Taiwan by C.T.F. on a solid glass displacement hull with a deep keel protecting the running gear. The standard double-deck layout has the galley open to the salon on the deckhouse level, a separate raised pilothouse (with bridge access), and three staterooms below — including a very generous midships VIP guest stateroom. Because this is a serious cruising yacht (and not a dockside condo), the DeFever 52 is designed with wide walkaround decks and a comfortable open-air afterdeck with wing doors. The interior is finished with plenty of teak paneling and woodwork throughout. Note the day head opposite the galley — very convenient. Additional features include a walk-in engine room, stall showers in each head, optional teak decks, and a large flybridge with seating for a crowd. Standard 210-hp Cat diesels cruise economically at 8–9 knots with a range of up to 2,000 miles. A Widebody version of the DeFever 52 is offered for those who desire a full-width salon. ❏

SPECIFICATIONS

Length	51'7"
Length WL	45'5"
Beam	16'8"
Draft	4'9"
Weight	77,000#
Clearance	NA
Water	500 Gals.
Fuel	1,500 Gals.
Hull	Displacement
Designer	DeFever

Production
1980–Current

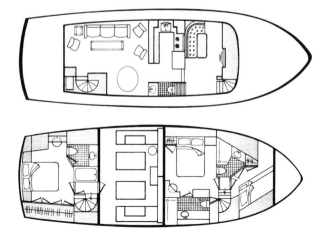

DEVEFER

DEFEVER 53 (POC) MOTOR YACHT

The DeFever 53 (also called the 53 POC for Performance Offshore Cruiser) is built in Taiwan by Sen Koh. Constructed with modern glass laminates and Divinycell foam coring in the hullsides, the first impression of the DeFever 53 is that of a much larger boat. The house is set well forward on the deck — a good indication of the spacious accommodations found below. The 53 is also distinguished by her wide and well-protected sidedecks (a disappearing feature in many modern motor yachts) which run completely around the house. (Note that a Widebody version is also available.) The all-teak interior is laid out on two levels with three staterooms and three full heads. The floorplan on the deckhouse level is fairly conventional with the pilothouse separated from the galley and main salon. The walk-in engine room is especially spacious and well designed. The popular 375-hp Caterpillar diesels will cruise the DeFever 53 at 13 knots and reach a top speed of 17 knots. A good-selling boat, over 70 have been delivered to date. Note that the DeFever POC 57 is a stretched and restyled version of the 53. ❑

SPECIFICATIONS

Length	52'7"
Length WL	NA
Beam	16'6"
Draft	4'8"
Weight	55,000#
Clearance	18'5"
Water	400 Gals.
Fuel	800 Gals.
Hull Type	Semi-Disp.
Designer	A. DeFever

Production
1986–Current

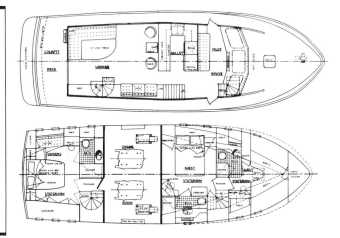

DEFEVER

DEFEVER 60 OFFSHORE CRUISER

De Fever 60

The DeFever 60 Offshore is a good-looking flush deck cruiser with a classic trawler profile and long-range capability. Built by CTF in Taiwan, the DeFever 60's hullsides are Airex-cored and a long, deep keel provides protection to the props and running gear. Her standard floorplan is arranged with four staterooms and three heads on the lower level with private salon access to the master suite. The galley is open to the salon and twin doors open to the large, protected afterdeck. While the salon dimensions aren't extravagant compared with other yachts her size, the spacious aft deck and walkaround decks are desirable characteristics of any serious cruising yacht. The interior of the DeFever 60 is teak in the traditional Asian mode. Additional features include a fake stack on the flybridge, covered sidedecks, port and starboard wheelhouse deck doors, wing doors, and a big engine room with access from the master stateroom. Standard 290-hp Cat 3306 diesels will cruise the DeFever 60 at 9–10 knots with about 2,000 miles of range. Note that the hull of this boat has been stretched to accommodate models up to 72 feet. ❑

SPECIFICATIONS

Length	59'3"
Length WL	NA
Beam	17'8"
Draft	5'6"
Weight	84,000#
Clearance	NA
Water	750 Gals.
Fuel	2,500 Gals.
Hull	Semi-Disp.
Designer	DeFever

Production
1978–Current

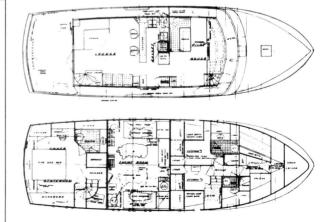

EGG HARBOR

Brief History

The Egg Harbor name goes back to 1946 when the company was founded by John Leek and Russel Post. Leek split off and began Pacemaker Yachts in the late 1940s, but the two companies merged in 1966 under the ownership of Fuqua Industries. In 1978 (at the height of the recession), Egg Harbor ceased production and was put up for sale. New owners took over in 1980 and today Egg Harbor is a private corporation. The company restyled its entire product line in 1990.

Selected Egg Harbor Models

Egg Harbor 33 Sedan	Egg Harbor 41 Sportfisherman
Egg Harbor 33 Convertible	Egg Harbor 42 Golden Egg
Egg Harbor 34 Golden Egg	Egg Harbor 43 Sportfisherman
Egg Harbor 36 Sedan	Egg Harbor 46 Sedan
Egg Harbor 37 Convertible	Egg Harbor 48 Sportfisherman
Egg Harbor 38 Golden Egg	Egg Harbor 54 Convertible
Egg Harbor 40 Sedan	Egg Harbor 58 Golden Egg
Egg Harbor 40 Motor Yacht	Egg Harbor 60 Convertible
Egg Harbor 41 Motor Yacht	

Main Office

Egg Harbor Yacht Co., P.O. Box 375, Egg Harbor, NJ 08215
609-965-2300

EGG HARBOR 33 SEDAN

The original Egg Harbor 33 Sedan was the first fiberglass hull ever built by the Egg Harbor Yacht Company. Designed primarily as a family cruiser, she was constructed with a mahogany deck and superstructure until 1978 when the switch was made to all-fiberglass construction. The standard floorplan arrangement has a two-stateroom layout with the galley in the salon. A galley-down version was offered in later models, and the head was also redesigned to accommodate a separate stall shower. Although the cockpit is small and the range is limited, the great appeal of the Egg Harbor 33 Sedan lies in her graceful profile, rich mahogany interior, and the extensive use of exterior teak, including teak covering boards and a solid teak cockpit sole. Her appearance improved dramatically when the fiberglass deck and house were introduced, and she remained in production until replaced in 1981 with the all-new Egg Harbor 33 Convertible. The popular 270-hp Crusader engines will cruise the Egg 33 Sedan at a modest 15–16 knots and she'll reach a top speed of about 23 knots. ❏

SPECIFICATIONS

Length	33'0"
Beam	13'2"
Draft	2'9"
Weight	13,000#
Clearance	NA
Water	50 Gals.
Fuel	216 Gals.
Cockpit	NA
Hull Type	Modified-V
Designer	Egg Harbor

Production
1971–81

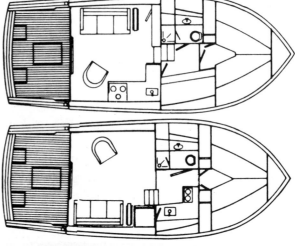

EGG HARBOR

EGG HARBOR 33 CONVERTIBLE

The Egg Harbor 33 Convertible Sedan was the first of the new-style Egg Harbor designs. She evolved from the Pacemaker 33 Sportfisherman, a good-looking flybridge sedan that went into production in 1979 and ended when Pacemaker closed down the following year. Egg Harbor picked up the tooling, revised the interior layout, and reintroduced her in 1982 as a replacement for the original 33 Sedan. In addition to the Convertible model, Egg Harbor also offered the 33 in an express fisherman version with no flybridge. Significantly, the fuel capacity of the newer Egg 33 is 320 gallons — a big improvement in range from the original 33 Sedan — and a teak interior replaced the original 33 Sedan's mahogany woodwork. From 1987 to 1989, a stretched version, the Egg Harbor 35 Sportfisherman, was built with a larger (102 sq. ft.) cockpit and 400 gallons of fuel. Upgrades on both eliminated the front windshield in later models. Always considered a great-looking boat for her size, standard 350-hp gas engines cruise the Egg Harbor 33s around 19 knots with top speed of 28–29 knots. ❑

SPECIFICATIONS

Length	33'0"
Beam	13'2"
Draft	2'5"
Weight	17,000#
Clearance	NA
Water	50 Gals.
Fuel	320 Gals.
Cockpit	70 Sq. Ft.
Hull Type	Modified-V
Designer	W. Nickerson

Production
1982–89

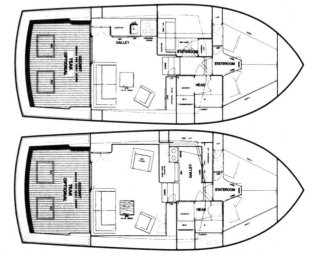

EGG HARBOR

EGG HARBOR 34 GOLDEN EGG

Smallest of the Egg Harbor lineup for 1990, the 34 Golden Egg employs the same hull used in the previous Egg Harbor 33 models but stretched to 34'6". The extra length has been used to give the 34 a larger cockpit area than the previous 33s, and the fuel capacity has been increased to 400 gallons — features that are sure to appeal to serious anglers. The most dramatic change, however, is in the crisp styling now incorporated throughout the Egg Harbor fleet. With her rakish profile and black-mask window treatment, the 34 is a handsome boat indeed. Two interior floorplans are offered: a two-stateroom, galley-up layout, and a single-stateroom version with a larger salon and the galley-down. A walkaround double berth is set on the centerline in the spacious forward stateroom, and the head compartment is fitted with a stall shower. Standard features include a generator, tackle center with sink and icebox, transom door, and teak covering boards. Twin 320-hp Crusader gas engines are standard (19 knots cruise/28 top) and Cummins 300-hp diesels are optional. ❑

SPECIFICATIONS

Length	34'6"
Beam	13'2"
Draft	3'2"
Weight	17,500#
Clearance	12'3"
Water	70 Gals.
Fuel	400 Gals.
Cockpit	113 Sq. Ft.
Hull Type	Modified-V
Designer	W. Nickerson

Production
1990-Current

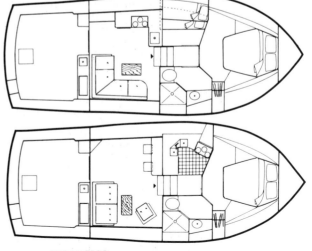

EGG HARBOR

EGG HARBOR 36 SEDAN

A good many fishermen find the 36' size range to be nearly ideal in a sportfishing boat. The cockpit is usually large enough for serious fishing, and a good design will retain the maneuverability of a much smaller hull. Such a boat is the Egg Harbor 36 Sedan. A good sea boat, she's built on a modified-V hull designed by Egg Harbor with a deep forefoot and flat aftersections for stability and quick planing. Early models were built with a glassed-over mahogany deckhouse, but in 1978 construction became all-fiberglass. The Egg 36 has the teak cockpit sole and teak covering boards that many fishermen find appealing in spite of the extra maintenance. The interior can accommodate up to six depending on the floorplan (there were a total of four). A Tournament Fisherman model in 1978 featured an improved bridge layout with bench seating forward of the helm and improved cockpit visibility. The standard 350-hp gas engines will cruise the Egg 36 at about 19 knots and reach 28 knots top. Note that a copy of the Egg Harbor 36 is now built in Taiwan and marketed as the Pace 36. ❏

SPECIFICATIONS

Length	36'0"
Beam	13'3"
Draft	2'9"
Weight	17,000#
Clearance	NA
Water	75 Gals.
Fuel	260/320 Gals.
Cockpit	NA
Hull Type	Modified-V
Designer	Egg Harbor

Production
1976-1985

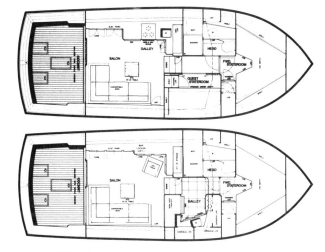

EGG HARBOR

EGG HARBOR 37 CONVERTIBLE

Built on a scaled-down version of the Egg 41 SF, the 37 Convertible is a modern family cruiser able to perform light-duty service as a weekend fisherman. The profile and appearance of the Egg Harbor 37 are not quite as graceful as those of the Egg 41, and the small size of her cockpit is immediately apparent. Nonetheless, the lush interior decor is every bit as impressive (and exactly the same size) as her bigger sister. One can only admire the beautiful teak joinerwork now common in all Egg Harbor models. The salon is clearly the centerpiece of the boat — a completely stylish and comfortable living area offered in a choice of two layouts. The 37's wide beam provides an interior volume seldom found on boats of her size. The hullsides are balsa cored, and the use of exterior teak trim is kept to a minimum. Twin 350-hp gas engines were standard in the Egg 37 for a cruising speed of 19–20 knots and a top speed of just under 30 knots. The 38 Double Cabin (1986–89) is essentially the same boat with an aft cabin replacing the 37's cockpit. The fuel was increased to 400 gallons in 1986 models. ❑

SPECIFICATIONS

Length	37'5"
Beam	14'5"
Draft	3'0"
Weight	24,000#
Clearance	NA
Water	80 Gals.
Fuel	340/400 Gals.
Cockpit	NA
Hull Type	Modified-V
Designer	W. Nickerson

Production
1985–89

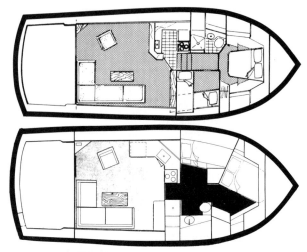

EGG HARBOR

EGG HARBOR 38 GOLDEN EGG

An all-new design, the 38 Golden Egg replaced the 37 Convertible in the Egg Harbor fleet in 1990. She's built on a modified-V hull form with a modest 8° of transom deadrise — the same basic hull used in the construction of earlier Egg Harbor models, only 5" wider. Like all of the current Egg Harbor designs, the 38 Golden Egg is a good-looking yacht with a rakish profile, wraparound black mask window treatment, and the long foredeck typical of many Jersey-style sportfishermen. A choice of two interior configurations is available (single-stateroom dinette version or two-stateroom layout), and both are arranged with the mid-level galley separated from the salon by a convenient serving counter. The full size cockpit is set up for serious fishing pursuits and includes a complete tackle center, livewell, transom door, fish box, and teak covering boards. Crusader 454-cid gas engines are standard but anglers are sure to favor the optional 375-hp Caterpillar or 400-hp 6V53 diesels, either of which will cruise the 38 Golden Egg around 22–23 knots and reach 25 knots wide open. ❑

SPECIFICATIONS

Length	38'6"
Beam	15'0"
Draft	3'10"
Weight	22,500#
Clearance	13'0"
Water	120 Gals.
Fuel, Gas	400 Gals.
Fuel, Dsl	500 Gals.
Cockpit	108 Sq. Ft.
Hull Type	Modified-V
Designer	W. Nickerson

Production
1990-Current

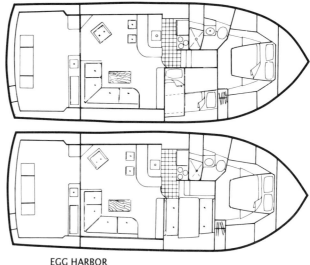

EGG HARBOR

EGG HARBOR 40 SEDAN

Introduced as a replacement for the Egg Harbor 38 Sedan in 1975, the principal difference between the Egg Harbor 40 Sedan and her predecessor is the 40's larger cockpit dimensions — something the Egg Harbor 38 sorely lacked. The original 38' hull was stretched to accommodate the 40-foot LOA, and the additional length adds much to the Egg Harbor 40's graceful profile. Her appearance was considerably enhanced when a new fiberglass deckhouse and flybridge replaced the wooden superstructure in 1978. Several interior floorplans were offered over the years with most of the recent models being two-stateroom layouts with a mid-level galley to port. In a significant production change, the original mahogany interiors were changed to teak in 1982. A large and unobstructed cockpit made the Egg Harbor 40 Sedan a popular and competent sportfisherman, and the teak sole and covering boards were standard. A Tournament Fisherman version introduced in 1978 moved the helm aft for better cockpit visibility. Optional 450-hp GM 6-71 diesels will cruise the Egg Harbor 40 Sedan around 25 knots and reach 28 knots wide open. ❏

SPECIFICATIONS

Length	40'0"
Beam	14'0"
Draft	2'9"
Weight	28,000#
Clearance	NA
Water	100 Gals.
Fuel	338 Gals.
Cockpit	95 Sq. Ft.
Hull Type	Modified-V
Designer	D. Martin

Production
1975–86

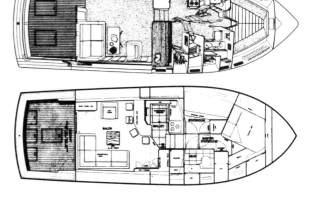

EGG HARBOR 40 MOTOR YACHT

The Egg Harbor 40 Motor Yacht was one of the last of the classic flush deck motor yacht designs introduced by any major U.S. manufacturer. Ending production in 1986, she was built on the reworked hull of the earlier Pacemaker 40 MY, whose molds and tooling Egg Harbor had acquired after Pacemaker closed down in 1980. A new superstructure and interior were added along with a traditional teak interior decor. A practical and straightforward cruising yacht, her conventional two-stateroom layout is centered around a salon that appears larger than her

dimensions might suggest. An enormous U-shaped galley is down from the salon level and only the aft head has a separate stall shower. Elsewhere, a built-in washer/dryer is fitted under the wet bar and the teak interior woodwork is all of furniture quality. The owner's aft stateroom is large for a 40-foot yacht and includes a home-size closet with real wardrobe space. A good-running boat, the optional 375-hp GM 6V53 diesels will cruise the Egg Harbor 40 Motor Yacht around 20 knots and reach a top speed of 22–23 knots. ❑

SPECIFICATIONS

Length	40'0"
Length WL	NA
Beam	14'1"
Draft	2'11"
Weight	30,000#
Clearance	16'2"
Water	100 Gals.
Fuel	300 Gals.
Hull Type	Modified-V
Designer	D. Martin

Production
1982–86

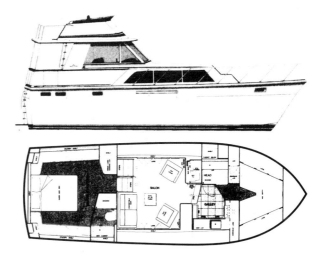

EGG HARBOR

EGG HARBOR 41 MOTOR YACHT

The Egg Harbor 41 Motor Yacht is a traditional flush deck design built on a fiberglass hull with a glassed-over mahogany superstructure. In terms of popularity, the 41 suffered from her wood construction during a period when most other builders had long since made the switch to all-fiberglass designs. Not unexpectedly, the production run was short-lived. Two interior floorplans were available (galley-up or galley-down versions), and an optional aft cabin queen berth was offered from the beginning. Varnished mahogany joinerwork is found in every cabin.

Topside, the 41 has an attractive mahogany control station and good helm visibility in all directions. The open aft deck is large enough for dockside entertaining with plenty of room for several furniture arrangements. The optional flybridge, while small by today's standards, greatly improves the resale value of used models. Those powered with the popular 310-hp J&T 6-71 diesels will cruise around 16–17 knots. On balance, the Egg Harbor 41 is a comfortable boat but somewhat dated design by modern motor yacht standards. ❏

SPECIFICATIONS

Length	40'7"
Length WL	NA
Beam	14'1"
Draft	2'11"
Weight	22,000#
Clearance	NA
Water	100 Gals.
Fuel	300 Gals.
Hull Type	Modified-V
Designer	Egg Harbor

Production
1975–77

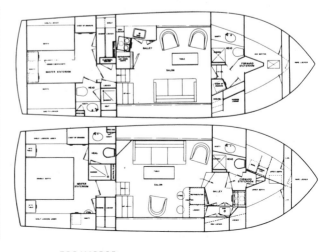

EGG HARBOR

EGG HARBOR 41 SPORTFISHERMAN

The Egg Harbor 41 Sportfisherman stands out among most mid-sized convertible models because of her huge cockpit and elegant interior accommodations. She's designed around a reworked Pacemaker 38 hull acquired by Egg Harbor when Pacemaker went out of business in 1980. A good-running boat with quick acceleration, the Egg 41 is built on a modified-V hull with a flat 8° of transom deadrise and balsa coring in the hullsides. She was introduced in 1984 in both a Sportfisherman and a Convertible Sedan version, the difference being the larger salon and smaller cockpit of the Convertible. The Sportfisherman is noted for a spacious and well-designed cockpit. The interiors of both boats are lush and furniture-quality teak cabinetry and paneling are everywhere. Outside, the exterior styling of the Egg Harbor 41 is clean and very graceful, and when fitted with a tower she has a decidedly serious appearance. Optional GM and Caterpillar diesels were the engines of choice for most. A pair of 375-hp Cats will cruise about 22 knots and the 6-71TIs cruise in the 26–27 knots range. ❏

SPECIFICATIONS

Length	40'10"
Beam	14'5"
Draft	3'0"
Weight	28,000#
Clearance	13'0"
Water	80 Gals.
Fuel	500 Gals.
Cockpit	NA
Hull Type	Modified-V
Designer	W. Nickerson

Production
1984–89

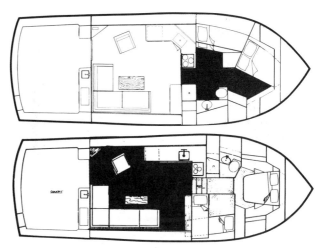

EGG HARBOR

EGG HARBOR 42 GOLDEN EGG

A new introduction for 1990, the 42 Golden Egg replaces both the 41 and 43 Convertibles in the revised Egg Harbor fleet. She's built on the same hull used in several other new Egg models with balsa coring from the waterline up and 8° of deadrise at the transom. The lines of the 42 are particularly graceful and a long foredeck complements her sleek sportfish profile. The interior choices are both two-stateroom affairs with the difference found in the salon layout. The very spacious interior is finished with teak woodwork and cabinetry with luxurious designer-style fabrics throughout. The cockpit is equipped with a tackle center, freezer, in-deck fish box, livewell, seawater washdown, transom door, and teak covering boards — all standard. Above, the tournament flybridge has the helm well aft for a good view of the cockpit action. Although gas engines are standard in the 42 Golden Egg, it's likely that most will be equipped with either 400-hp 6V53s (22-23 knots cruise/25 knots top) or the larger 485-hp 6-71 diesels (26 knots cruise/29 knots top). ❏

SPECIFICATIONS

Length	42'2"
Beam	15'0"
Draft	3'10"
Weight	27,000#
Clearance	13'0"
Water	120 Gals.
Fuel, Gas	500 Gals.
Fuel, Dsl	600 Gals.
Cockpit	120 Sq. Ft.
Hull Type	Modified-V
Designer	W. Nickerson

Production
1990-Current

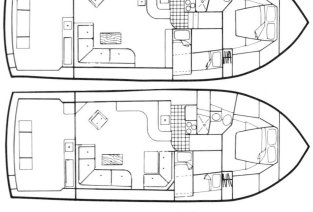

EGG HARBOR

EGG HARBOR 43 SPORTFISHERMAN

The Egg Harbor 43 Sportfisherman is easily one of the better-looking boats in her size class. She's built on a stretched version of the Egg 41 Sedan hull and carries an extra 100 gallons of fuel for improved range. Like many modern sportfishermen, the front windshield area is glassed in, and an aggressive, Eurostyle, flat black mask surrounds the deckhouse. The 43 Sportfisherman offers the spacious accommodations found in the Egg 41 Convertible along with the enormous cockpit found in the 41 Sportfisherman. The extra two feet of overall length has been used to enlarge the salon dimensions. Indeed, in the 43 Sportfisherman the interior appears to be that of a much larger boat. Teak cabinetry and paneling are used throughout and the craftsmanship is very good. The lush decor and spacious interior proportions make the Egg Harbor 43 an excellent boat for family cruising activities. The performance is about the same as the smaller 41 Sportfisherman. In 1987, the Egg Harbor 43 Double Cabin (1987–89) was introduced on the same hull with an aft stateroom in place of the cockpit. ❏

SPECIFICATIONS

Length	43'0"
Beam	14'5"
Draft	3'0"
Weight	32,000#
Clearance	NA
Water	80 Gals.
Fuel	600 Gals.
Cockpit	NA
Hull Type	Modified-V
Designer	W. Nickerson

Production
1986–89

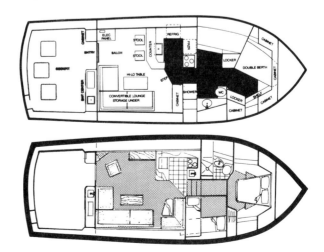

EGG HARBOR

EGG HARBOR 46 SEDAN

A handsome Jersey-style profile and good all-around accommodations made the Egg Harbor 46 Sedan a popular boat during her decade in production. Originally built with a fiberglass hull and mahogany deck and superstructure, Egg Harbor went to all-fiberglass construction in 1978, and the new tooling improved the appearance of the 46 dramatically. As a fisherman, she has the cockpit space and handling qualities generally demanded by serious bluewater anglers. As a family cruiser, several comfortable interior arrangements were available, including a three-stateroom version with a deckhouse galley. More popular, however, was the two-stateroom layout with the galley-down and a much more open salon area. As the Egg 46 matured she received the additional fuel capacity necessary for offshore work, and a new teak interior in 1982 replaced the original mahogany woodwork used in the earlier models. GM 8V71TIs will cruise the Egg Harbor 46 Sedan at around 20 knots and reach a top speed of 23. Note that this hull was stretched to create the well-regarded Golden Egg 48 in 1978. ❏

SPECIFICATIONS

Length	46'8"
Beam	15'0"
Draft	3'8"
Weight	38,000#
Clearance	NA
Water	100 Gals.
Fuel	500/628/788
Cockpit	NA
Hull Type	Modified-V
Designer	D. Martin

Production
1973–83

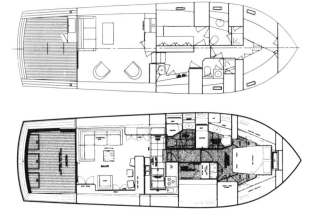

EGG HARBOR 48 SPORTFISHERMAN

Using the modified-V hull form of the Egg Harbor 46 Sedan (with a flat 2° deadrise at the transom), the Golden Egg 48 represented the last of the classic old-style Egg Harbor convertible designs. Aimed at the luxury end of the sportfishing market, she was originally offered in either a two- or three-stateroom layout with a large portside owner's stateroom. The floorplans were revised in 1982 when the galley became a permanent part of the salon and a new teak interior replaced the mahogany woodwork found in earlier models. Notably, the Egg Harbor 48 was one of the first production boats to have been equipped with the early 550-hp GM 8V92 diesels, resulting in a fast 25-knot cruising speed. Fast indeed for 1978, and only a few other production boats of her size could run with her. Additional features include a very spacious engine room with flooring all around the motors, teak cockpit sole and covering boards, spacious main salon with overhead grabrails, and large, wraparound cabin windows. (Note that late model Egg 48s have a solid front windshield.) ❑

SPECIFICATIONS

Length	48'2"
Beam	15'0"
Draft	4'4"
Weight	44,000#
Clearance	13'1"
Water	110/210 Gals.
Fuel	788 Gals.
Cockpit	NA
Hull Type	Modified-V
Designer	D. Martin

Production
1978–86

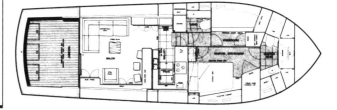

EGG HARBOR

EGG HARBOR 54 CONVERTIBLE

The Egg Harbor 54 Convertible can best be characterized as a scaled-down version of the company's 60 convertible introduced in 1986. Both share the same modified-V hull design with balsa coring in the hullsides and modern high-tech composites in the laminate. The cockpit in the Egg Harbor 54 is designed with serious tournament-level sportfishing in mind. With a wide 17'6" beam, her interior accommodations are expansive, and the three-stateroom belowdecks layout is unique. The owner's stateroom is to starboard of the companionway (rather than forward) and features a separate dressing room tucked beneath the salon sole and a tub/shower in the head. A second full head with shower serves the two guest staterooms. Note the utility room and washer/dryer area aft of the guest stateroom. On the deck-house level, the modern U-shaped galley is completely open to the salon. A door in the cockpit leads into the engine room where twin 750-hp 8V92s are standard. Good-running boats, the cruising speed of the Egg Harbor 54 is around 25 knots and the top speed is 28 knots. ❏

SPECIFICATIONS

Length	54'6"
Beam	17'6"
Draft	5'3"
Weight	64,000#
Clearance	15'10"
Water	220 Gals.
Fuel	1,000 Gals.
Cockpit	120 Sq. Ft.
Hull Type	Modified-V
Designer	D. Martin

Production
1988–Current

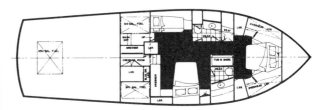

EGG HARBOR 58 GOLDEN EGG

The 58 Golden Egg replaced the 60 Sport Fisherman in the Egg Harbor fleet in 1990, although both boats are built on the same hull and share identical 59'6" LOAs. While the 58 retains the same high-tech construction of the earlier 60 SF, the deckhouse has been redesigned for an improved profile and the innovative interior configuration of the 60 has been reworked on the lower level. The most significant change is the elimination of the third private head in the forward guest stateroom. This opens up that cabin considerably and allows for the addi-tion of an enlarged walkaround center-line berth rather than the offset double berth in the earlier model. Now a three-stateroom, two-head layout, the huge master stateroom to starboard remains the same (including the very unique step-down dressing room below the salon floor), and the expansive galley and salon have been only slightly rearranged. The 58 Golden Egg is a good performer for her size and class. With standard 1,080-hp 12V92 diesels she'll cruise at a fast 27–28 knots and reach a top speed of around 30 knots. ❏

SPECIFICATIONS

Length	59'6"
Beam	17'6"
Draft	5'3"
Weight	72,000#
Clearance	NA
Water	220 Gals.
Fuel	1,200 Gals.
Cockpit	165 Sq. Ft.
Hull Type	Modified-V
Designer	D. Martin

Production
1990-Current

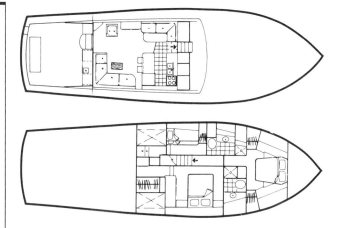

EGG HARBOR 60 CONVERTIBLE

Egg Harbor made a clean break with the past when they introduced their new 60 Sportfisherman in 1986. Designed by David Martin (who also drew the plans for the popular Ocean 55 and 63 sportfishermen among many other tournament-level boats), the Egg Harbor 60's construction is high-tech with balsa-cored hullsides and triaxial/Kevlar composites — an engineering first for Egg Harbor. By moving the engines aft and tightening up the engine room, Martin was able to fit a unique dressing area into the master stateroom and a separate utility room to port. The huge salon/galley layout is impressive in both size and decor. So too is the rest of the interior, including the expansive master stateroom with walkaround queen berth and a forward stateroom with yet another walkaround queen — accommodations on a scale more often found on motor yachts. Outside, the profile of the Egg 60 is classic Jersey-style sportfish with a graceful sheer and generously flared bow. A good performer for a big boat, GM 1,080-hp 12V92 diesels will cruise around 27 knots with a top speed in excess of 30 knots. ❑

SPECIFICATIONS

Length	59'6"
Beam	17'6"
Draft	5'3"
Weight	72,000#
Clearance	18'5"
Water	300 Gals.
Fuel	1200/1500 Gals.
Cockpit	111 Sq. Ft.
Hull Type	Modified-V
Designer	D. Martin

Production
1986–89

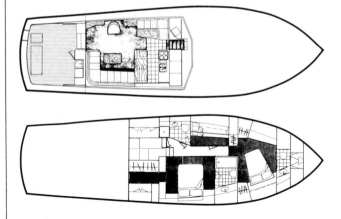

EGG HARBOR

GRAND BANKS

(AMERICAN MARINE PTE., LTD.)

Brief History

The first wooden Grand Banks trawlers were built in Hong Kong in 1964. Their popularity was soon established in the U.S., and the original 32, 36, and 42-foot trawlers were soon followed by a series of successful DeFever-designed Alaskan pilothouse cruisers. Operations were moved to Singapore in 1968. The original American Marine company expanded too swiftly and financial considerations forced the sale of the company to the current owners in 1975. The switch to fiberglass was made in 1973. Worldwide, Grand Banks is recognized as the premium builder of production trawlers.

Selected Inboard Models

Grand Banks 32
Grand Banks 36 Classic (Early)
Grand Banks 36 Classic
Grand Banks 36 Sedan
Grand Banks 36 Europa
Grand Banks 42 Classic (Early)
Grand Banks 42 Classic
Grand Banks 42 Europa

Grand Banks 42 Sports Cruiser
Grand Banks 42 Motor Yacht
Grand Banks 46 Classic
Grand Banks 46 Motor Yacht
Grand Banks 49 Classic
Grand Banks 49 Motor Yacht
Grand Banks 58 Motor Yacht

U.S. Offices

Grand Banks Yachts, Ltd., 563 Steamboat Road, Greenwich, CT 06830
203-869-9274
Grand Banks Yachts, Ltd., 3355 Via Lido, #225, Newport Beach, CA
92663 714-675-5846

225

GRAND BANKS 32

The Grand Banks 32 is one of the most enduring small trawler designs ever produced with nearly 900 built to date. Her exterior profile has remained essentially unchanged since the original wood models were built back in 1965 at the Hong Kong yard. At a distance, it's difficult to distinguish between a mid-1973 mahogany Grand Banks 32 and one of the fiberglass models built thereafter. Powered with a single 6-cylinder Lehman diesel, owners report long hours of 7-knot cruising at less than 3 gph and a cruising range in excess of 500 miles. A full-length skeg protects the underwater gear and hard chines help to stabilize the ride. Below, the 32's layout is simple and practical for a small cruiser with basic accommodations for two people. Storage is quite adequate and visability from the lower helm is very good. Throughout, high-quality hardware, furnishings and systems are very impressive. Grand Banks 32s are dependable and seaworthy boats with immense eye appeal, great popularity and strong resale values. Aside from her various nautical attributes, a new or used GB 32 can often be a good yachting investment. ❑

SPECIFICATIONS

Length	31'11"
Length WL	30'9"
Beam	11'6"
Draft	3'9"
Weight	17,000#
Clearance	NA
Water	110 Gals.
Fuel	225/250 Gals.
Hull Type	Semi-Disp.
Designer	Ken Smith

Production
1965–Current

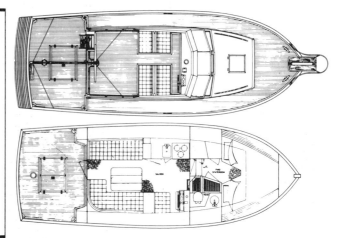

GRAND BANKS 36 CLASSIC (EARLY)

Like all Grand Banks models, the 36 Classic has a reputation for high-quality construction, economical operation, and dependable cruising performance. Built of Philippine mahogany until mid-1973, most have been powered with the durable Lehman 6-cylinder diesel, although some 36s have been equipped with twin engines for greater speed and improved maneuverability. With the single engine, she cruises effortlessly at a steady 8 knots (3 gph) and has a range of up to 1,000 nautical miles depending on conditions. A full-length keel below protects the running gear while providing a great deal of directional stability. Not surprisingly, the interior is traditional and straightforward with teak cabinetry and paneling, teak parquet cabin soles, durable fabrics, and big wraparound salon windows — a completely practical layout for serious long-distance cruising. Note that a Grand Banks 36 Sedan model was introduced in 1986 with a two-stateroom floorplan and less exterior teak trim. Replaced by an all-new, slightly larger 36 Classic in 1988, used GB 36 models hold their values well. ❑

SPECIFICATIONS

Length	36'4"
Length WL	35'0"
Beam	12'2"
Draft	3'11"
Weight	23,300#
Clearance	NA
Water	170 Gals.
Fuel	400 Gals.
Hull Type	Semi-Disp.
Designer	Ken Smith

Production
1965–87

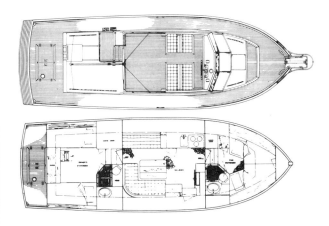

GRAND BANKS 36 CLASSIC

The new Grand Banks 36 Classic has the same profile as the original GB 36 but with an extra 6" added to both the beam and length. These new dimensions allow for a slightly enlarged salon and master stateroom and a stall shower is finally available in the aft head compartment — a big plus for weekenders and serious cruisers alike. Note also that an alternate interior floorplan with a walkaround queen berth aft is now available in the 36 for the first time. In other respects the two boats are nearly identical, although the new GB 36 has a fiberglass bow pulpit instead of

the teak platform of old. It's interesting to observe that, while other builders are constantly introducing newly redesigned models to keep up with the latest trends, Grand Banks simply improves on an already-proven design by making her larger and even more comfortable. Experienced cruisers will immediately recognize the GB 36 as a fine and seaworthy craft built to high standards. With the optional twin 210-hp Cummins diesels, the Grand Banks 36 has a cruising speed of up to 12 knots (8 gph) and a top speed of 14–15 knots. ❑

SPECIFICATIONS

Length	36'10"
Length WL	35'2"
Beam	12'8"
Draft	4'0"
Weight	26,000#
Clearance	NA
Water	140 Gals.
Fuel	400 Gals.
Hull Type	Semi-Disp.
Designer	Amer. Marine

Production
1988–Current

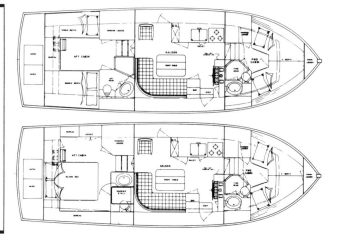

GRAND BANKS 36 SEDAN

While she's never been a notably good-selling model, the Grand Banks 36 Sedan is offered for those who enjoy the practicality of a sedan layout. To many, the profile of the GB 36 Sedan is slightly boxy — a characteristic not shared by other Grand Banks designs. She is, however, a fairly roomy boat inside thanks to her long deckhouse and extended trunk cabin forward. The standard floorplan includes two staterooms and there's an optional single-stateroom layout with a split head compartment. Either way, the galley is up to port in the salon where it's convenient to the lower helm and cockpit. The salon dimensions are on the narrow side due to the wide sidedecks but that's a trade-off that most experienced yachtsmen will gladly accept. The interior woodwork is solid teak in keeping with years of Grand Banks tradition. Outside, raised bulwarks provide exceptional security all around the house. Note that the GB 36 Sedan is basically the same boat as the 36 Europa without the the bridge overhangs and pilaster supports. Single or twin 135-hp Lehman or Cummins 210-hp diesels are offered. ❏

SPECIFICATIONS

Length	36'10"
Length WL	35'2"
Beam	12'8"
Draft	4'0"
Weight	26,000#
Clearance	NA
Water	205 Gals.
Fuel	410 Gals.
Cockpit	NA
Hull Type	Semi-Disp.
Designer	Amer. Marine

Production
1984–Current

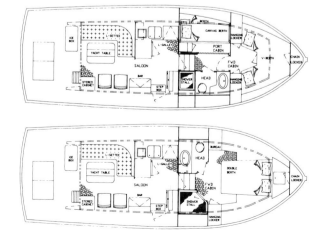

GRAND BANKS

GRAND BANKS 36 EUROPA

Built on the newly enlarged Grand Banks 36 hull, the Europa will appeal to those who enjoy entertaining family and friends aboard a practical and obviously well-crafted small yacht. A good-looking cruiser, the mast remains for those times when a steadying sail is required and serves as a reminder of her traditional Grand Banks trawler heritage. Bridge overhangs protect the aft deck and walkaround decks from the sun and weather. The 36 Europa is basically a downsized version of the Grand Banks 42 Europa, with her deck-level walk-through salon and aft deck area running about two-thirds of the boat's length. Cabin headroom is a full 6'6" and the salon is completely paneled and trimmed with traditional grain-matched teak joinerwork. A single 135-hp Lehman diesel is standard in the 36 Europa and burns an efficient 3 gph at an easy 8-knot cruising speed. Optional twin 210-hp Cummins diesels will power the GB 36 Europa to a top speed of about 15–16 knots. Note that the less-popular Grand Banks 36 Sedan is essentially the same boat without the flybridge overhangs. ❑

SPECIFICATIONS

Length	36'10"
Length WL	35'2"
Beam	12'8"
Draft	4'0"
Weight	26,000#
Clearance	NA
Water	170 Gals.
Fuel	400 Gals.
Cockpit	NA
Hull Type	Semi-Disp.
Designer	Amer. Marine

Production
1988–Current

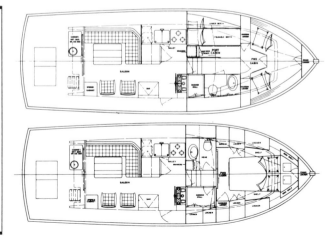

GRAND BANKS

GRAND BANKS 42 CLASSIC (EARLY)

Introduced in 1966, a total of 1,203 Grand Banks 42s were built before she was replaced with a new model in 1991. Indeed, she's the standard by which other bluewater trawlers her size are generally measured. Her enduring popularity and strong resale values can be attributed to superb engineering and construction, apparently timeless styling, and a proven semi-displacement offshore hull design. Her fine entry combined with a moderate beam and full-length skeg keel give the GB 42 excellent seakeeping characteristics in a wide range of conditions. Aside from the obvious change to fiberglass construction in 1973, there have been few major modifications to the basic design. Instead, continuous product refinement can best characterize her evolution from the original mid-1960s wooden version. The two-stateroom interior is finished with rich teak woodwork and her engine room is spacious and well designed. Most Grand Banks 42s have been powered with the reliable 120/135-hp Lehman diesels and cruise economically at 8–9 knots. The optional 375-hp Cats will cruise at around 17 knots and reach top speeds of 20+ knots. ❏

SPECIFICATIONS

Length	41'10"
Length WL	40'6"
Beam	13'7"
Draft	4'2"
Weight	34,000#
Clearance	NA
Water	270 Gals.
Fuel	600 Gals.
Hull Type	Semi-Disp.
Designer	Kenneth Smith

Production
1966–91

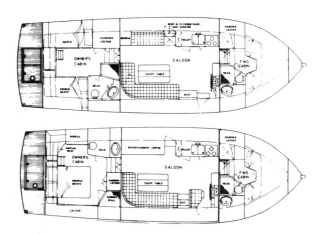

GRAND BANKS

GRAND BANKS 42 CLASSIC

After 25 years, Grand Banks finally retired the molds for the original GB 42 Classic hull in 1991. Beginning with hull #1204, the new 42 Classic is wider and longer than the original model but few will ever notice the difference since both appear the same. The new floorplan options are basically the same as in earlier years as well (the queen berth in the master stateroom is the more popular), although the aft cabin's cockpit access door has now been eliminated. The increased hull dimensions of the new GB 42 are seen in the enlarged galley area, a larger forward cabin, and a slightly enlarged engine room. The extra beam is also noticeable in the salon which is definitely more open and spacious, and in the aft stateroom where there's some extra floor space. Everything else remains the same — the teak decks are still standard, the sidedecks are as wide as before, and the entire boat exudes the quality and workmanship found in all Grand Banks yachts. Designed for serious offshore cruising, 135-hp Lehmans are standard and 210-hp to 375-hp Cats are optional. A cruising speed of around 16 knots is typical of the 375-hp Cats. ❏

SPECIFICATIONS

Length	43'3"
Length WL	41'1"
Beam	14'1"
Draft	4'2"
Weight	34,914#
Clearance	NA
Water	265 Gals.
Fuel	600 Gals.
Hull Type	Semi-Disp.
Designer	Ken Smith

Production
1991—Current

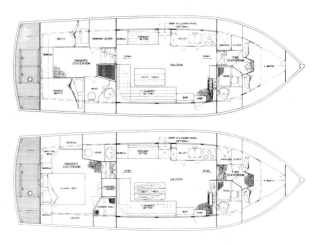

GRAND BANKS 42 EUROPA

The first Grand Banks 42 Europas were built of mahogany in 1970 and 1971 primarily for the European market. Several were built, however she was never a notably popular boat until 1981 when Grand Banks decided to reintroduce the design as a fiberglass production model. Not surprisingly, few changes have been made from the original. The 42 Europa's sedan layout offers the benefits of a spacious salon and a large cockpit. Her two-stateroom floorplan provides comfortable cruising accommodations for two couples, with a double berth fitted in the owner's portside stateroom. Although teak is used extensively throughout the interior of the Europa, the wraparound cabin windows make for an unusually bright and cheerful salon area. An extended hardtop shades the cockpit and flybridge overhangs offer good weather protection for the wide sidedecks. The Europa is built on the standard Grand Banks 42 hull and shares similar power options and performance figures. Note that Grand Banks also offers a 42 Sedan model which is essentially the Europa without the sidedecks and cockpit overhangs. ❏

SPECIFICATIONS

Length	42'7"
Length WL	40'10"
Beam	13'7"
Draft	4'2"
Weight	34,000#
Clearance	NA
Water	270 Gals.
Fuel	600 Gals.
Cockpit	NA
Hull Type	Semi-Disp.
Designer	Kenneth Smith

Production
1978–Current

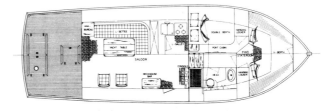

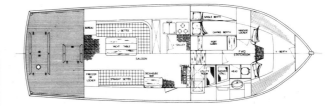

GRAND BANKS 42 SPORTS CRUISER

Sharing the same semi-displacement hull as the famous Grand Banks 42, the 42 Sports Cruiser is a beautifully styled flybridge sedan capable of serious offshore sportfishing or economical family cruising. Her long forward trunk cabin and large house give the Sports Cruiser a distinctive, slightly Downeast profile. Like all Grand Banks boats, the keel provides grounding protection for the running gear and the simulated planked hull is flawlessly finished and topped with a teak caprail. Her practical two-stateroom, galley-up floorplan includes one full head and a deck access door at the lower helm. Grain-matched teak paneling and a beautiful teak parquet sole join with the large wraparound cabin widows to create an open and very traditional salon. Twin teak-framed sliding doors open from the salon into a very large cockpit with a teak sole, transom door, and plenty of room for a tackle center and mounted chair. The sidedecks are wide and well secured with rails and raised bulwarks all around the house. A classy boat with tremendous eye appeal, engine options range from standard 135-hp Lehmans (8-knot cruise) to 375-hp Cats (16-knots cruise).❏

SPECIFICATIONS

Length	42'7"
Length WL	40'9"
Beam	13'7"
Draft	4'2"
Weight	34,000#
Clearance	NA
Water	270 Gals.
Fuel	600 Gals.
Hull Type	Semi-Disp.
Designer	Ken Smith

Production
1989–Current

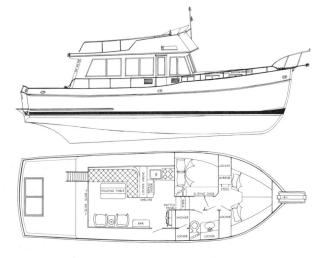

GRAND BANKS

GRAND BANKS 42 MOTOR YACHT

Built on the same hull as the original Grand Banks 42, the principal features of the 42 Motor Yacht are her three-stateroom interior floorplan, an enlarged aft cabin, and a full-width aft deck platform. The master stateroom utilizes the full beam of the boat and allows queen-size sleeping accommodations not found in the trunk cabin GB 42 Classic. The portside guest stateroom is fitted with a double berth and conventional V-berths are in the forward stateroom. While the linear galley in the salon is compact and short on counter space, it's at least adequate for most purposes. There are port and starboard salon deck doors and both heads come with separate stall showers. The 42 MY is certainly a good-looking boat and built to the rigid standards found in all Grand Banks models but this galley-up floorplan results in a crowded salon. The aft deck, however, is a comfortable entertainment platform surrounded by stainless steel safety railings. Several engine options are offered from 135-hp Lehmans to the popular 210 to 375-hp Cats. The big Cats will cruise the Grand Banks 42 at around 16 knots and reach a top speed of 19–20 knots. ❑

SPECIFICATIONS

Length	42'7"
Length WL	40'9"
Beam	13'7"
Draft	4'2"
Weight	34,000#
Clearance	NA
Water	260 Gals.
Fuel	600 Gals.
Hull Type	Semi-Disp.
Designer	Ken Smith

Production
1987—Current

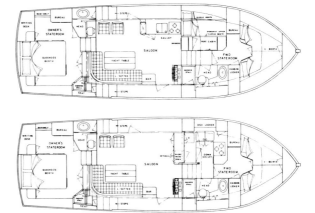

GRAND BANKS

GRAND BANKS 46 CLASSIC

Introduced in 1987 as the 46 Motor Yacht and also marketed as a Cockpit MY, the Grand Banks 46 is now simply referred to as the "Classic," a designation few knowledgeable boaters would dispute. With her elegant trawler profile and proven semi-displacement hull the GB 46 is built with the heavy construction and reliable systems required of a true offshore passagemaker. Notably, her lines are exactly those of the smaller Grand Banks 42 and it's difficult to tell the two apart from a distance. Most 46s have been delivered with a spacious two-stateroom floorplan with the galley-down and an island queen berth in the aft cabin. A three-stateroom layout with the galley-up is also available. The interior is all grain-matched teak, both heads have stall showers, there's 5' headroom in the engine room, the flybridge is quite large, and the walkaround decks are wide and well secured. Note that the deckhouse tooling was changed at hull #43 to provide wider sidedecks aft. Among several engine options, 210 to 375-hp Cats have been the most popular with buyers. The 320-hp Cats, as an example, will cruise at 11 knots (16 gph) and reach a top speed of 14 knots.   ❏

SPECIFICATIONS

Length	47'1"
Length WL	44'9"
Beam	14'9"
Draft	4'2"
Weight	39,000#
Clearance	23'7"
Water	278 Gals.
Fuel	600 Gals.
Hull Type	Semi-Disp.
Designer	Amer. Marine

Production
1987–Current

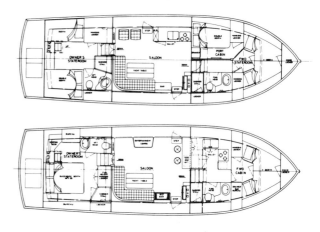

GRAND BANKS 46 MOTOR YACHT

A handsome boat, the Grand Banks 46 Motor Yacht differs from the original (and still current) GB 46 Classic in her raised afterdeck and more spacious aft cabin. Other than that, the two boats are essentially the same. Those who enjoy outdoor entertaining will find the full-width aft deck of the 46 MY a great convenience, although more traditional hands might prefer the flexibility provided by the walkaround decks and cockpit of the 46 Classic. There are two floorplan choices — a standard three-stateroom, galley-up layout or an alternate (and more popular) two-stateroom arrangement with the galley-down. Not surprisingly, the craftsmanship and attention to detail found throughout compare with the best in production yacht building. Standard power for the Grand Banks 46 is a pair of 135-hp Lehman diesels which will cruise economically at 8–9 knots. The optional 375-hp Cats will increase the cruising speed to 13–14 knots and the top speed to around 17 knots. At 9 knots, the fuel consumption is only 6 gph (regardless of engines) and the cruising range exceeds 800 nautical miles. ❑

SPECIFICATIONS

Length	47'1"
Length WL	44'9"
Beam	14'9"
Draft	4'4"
Weight	39,000#
Clearance	23'7" Mast Up
Water	278 Gals.
Fuel	600 Gals.
Hull Type	Semi-Disp.
Designer	Amer. Marine

Production
1990–Current

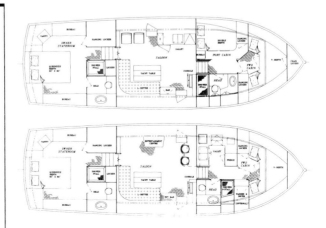

GRAND BANKS 49 CLASSIC

A very popular boat since her introduction in 1980, the GB 49 Classic is a serious long-range cruiser with the characteristic trawler profile and quality workmanship typical of all Grand Banks models. Needless to say, this is not a glitzy yacht with a Eurostyle interior or high-tech construction. Indeed, she comes off as a little old-fashioned when compared to most other modern yachts but the 49 stands apart as a proven passagemaker with probably the most functional and practical three-stateroom, galley-up layout to be found in an offshore cruiser. Highlights: the *full* walkaround decks are secure and easily negotiated; the stand-up engine room is spacious and carefully detailed; the grain-matched teak woodwork is flawless inside and out; hardware, fixtures, and appliances are top quality; the gelcoat is excellent; props and rudders are keel-protected; and her seakindly hull has a long record of handling every kind of weather worldwide. Originally powered with twin 120-hp Lehman diesels, newer models have been delivered with Cat diesels from 210-hp. The popular 375-hp versions will cruise the GB 49 at 13-14 knots. ❑

SPECIFICATIONS

Length	50'6"
Length WL	48'9"
Beam	15'5"
Draft	5'2"
Weight	60,000#
Clearance	NA
Water	500 Gals.
Fuel	1,000 Gals.
Hull Type	Semi-Disp.
Designer	Amer. Marine

Production
1980–Current

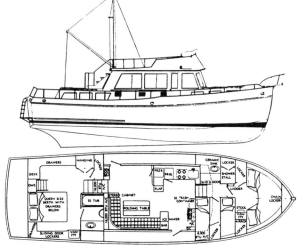

GRAND BANKS

GRAND BANKS 49 MOTOR YACHT

The Grand Banks 49 Motor Yacht is distinguished from the original Grand Banks 49 Classic (introduced in 1980 and still in production) by the addition of a raised afterdeck, which adds about 150 sq. ft. to the usable aft-deck entertainment area. This is a particularly handsome yacht with a plumb bow and graceful sheer, and her engineering and construction are up to the normal high Grand Banks standards. The standard layout includes three staterooms with three heads, a stand-up engine room, luxurious master suite and a spacious main salon with deck-house galley and lower helm. Standard power is a pair of dependable 135-hp Lehman diesels, but the bigger 375-hp Caterpillar diesels have proven to be a popular option since they raise the cruising speed to 12–13 knots and the top speed to around 15 knots. At her 8–9-knot displacement speed, the 6-gph fuel economy is not lost with larger engines. The cruising range at this speed is excellent — over 1,200 nautical miles. Not inexpensive, the Grand Banks 49 Motor Yacht is a traditional long-range cruiser aimed at an affluent clientele. ❏

SPECIFICATIONS

Length	50'6"
Length WL	48'9"
Beam	15'5"
Draft	5'2"
Weight	60,000#
Clearance	NA
Water	500 Gals.
Fuel	1,000 Gals.
Hull Type	Semi-Disp.
Designer	Amer. Marine

Production
1986–Current

GRAND BANKS

GRAND BANKS 58 MOTOR YACHT

The Grand Banks 58 is a flush deck motor yacht with the traditional trawler styling that Grand Banks enthusiasts are sure to love. The solid fiberglass hull is an enlarged version of the standard Grand Banks semi-displacement hull with simulated lapstrake hullsides and a deep, full-length keel. This luxurious yacht is clearly designed with long-range passagemaking in mind and her three-stateroom accommodations provide extravagant liveaboard comforts. The teak-paneled main salon/dining area is a full 210 sq. ft. with the galley conveniently located on the main

deck level. Additional features include a chart table and settee in the pilothouse, a huge flybridge with protective bridge overhangs, secure walkaround sidedecks, a spacious engine room with standing headroom, washer/dryer in the utility room, and a whirlpool in the owner's head compartment. Notably, the Grand Banks 58 MY is designed to be owner-operated and all equipment is installed for easy access. Caterpillar 375-hp diesels are standard for a 9-knot cruising speed and a top speed of 11–12 knots. The cruising range is approximately 1,400 miles. ❑

SPECIFICATIONS

Length	58'11"
Length WL	54'4"
Beam	17'6"
Draft	5'6"
Weight	100,000#
Clearance	17'6"
Water	450 Gals.
Fuel	1,400 Gals.
Hull Type	Semi-Disp.
Designer	Ed Fry

Production
1990–Current

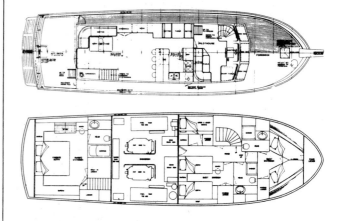

GULFSTAR

Brief History

Gulfstar began production in 1971 in St. Petersburg, FL with a series of displacement motorsailers that were soon turned into a popular line of cruising trawlers. One of the few to build in both power and sail, the company entered the modern motor yacht market in 1981 with the introduction of the 48 Motor Yacht. Sailboat production ended in the mid-1980s. The highly acclaimed 55 Motor Yacht came out in 1987 and confirmed Gulfstar's position as an industry leader in contemporary yacht design and high-tech construction. Gulfstar was acquired by Viking Yachts in 1987.

Selected Gulfstar Models

Gulfstar 36 Trawler	Gulfstar 44 Widebody MY
Gulfstar 38 Motor Cruiser	Gulfstar 48 Motor Yacht
Gulfstar 43 Trawler	Gulfstar 49 Motor Yacht
Gulfstar 44 Motor Cruiser	Gulfstar 53 Trawler
Gulfstar 44 Motor Yacht	

Main Office

No longer in production. Gulfstar was acquired by
Viking Yachts in 1987.

241

GULFSTAR 36 TRAWLER

It's interesting to note that the Gulfstar 36 Trawler was built on the same hull used in the production of the Gulfstar 36 Motorsailer. The twin diesels of the 36 Trawler provide good maneuverability and the increased performance required of a mid-range powerboat. Not that she's fast — her twin 80-hp Perkins diesels will cruise economically at 7.5 knots and reach a top speed of around 9–10 knots. The hull is solid glass and a ballasted keel protects the underwater gear. In 1975, the Gulfstar 36 MK II version was introduced featuring a raised aft deck, a full-beam master stateroom, a slightly larger flybridge, bigger rudders, and a new teak interior to replace the previous wood-grain Formica (or mahogany) paneling. The engines were also relocated further outboard in the MK II model which is said to improve handling. Several two-stateroom floorplans were used in the Gulfstar 36 over the years with the latest having the dinette to port (opposite the galley) and a starboard deck access door. A comfortable and easy-riding boat, the Gulfstar 36 Trawler is economical to operate and requires little maintenance. ❏

SPECIFICATIONS

Length	36'3"
Length WL	31'0"
Beam	12'0"
Draft	3'0"
Weight	16,000#
Clearance	12'0"
Water	100 Gals.
Fuel	250 Gals.
Hull Type	Semi-Disp.
Designer	V. Lazzara

Production
1972–76

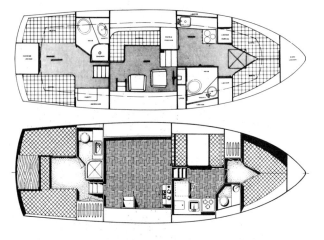

GULFSTAR 38 MOTOR CRUISER

The 38 Motor Cruiser is one of Gulfstar's early applications of cored hull construction in a powerboat — considered reasonably high-tech among production builders in 1980. A good-looking yacht with still-modern lines, the 38 Motor Cruiser weighs only 18,000 lbs. which is light compared to other yachts in this size range. With her relatively narrow 12'5" beam and high deck profile, the 38 can be a bit tender in spite of her long keel and hard aft chines. Below, the galley-down layout features a double berth in both staterooms, a tub in the aft head, full dinette, large galley, and a complete lower helm. Although the salon dimensions are on the small side, the overall accommodations are still impressive for a 38-foot boat. The grain-matched teak woodwork found throughout the interior is notable for its quality and beauty. With twin 4-cylinder 115-hp Perkins diesels, the Gulfstar 38 Motor Cruiser will operate efficiently at 8.5 knots (4 gph) with a top speed of around 10 knots. Perkins 200-hp engines were optional and deliver a cruising speed around 14 knots and 16–17 knots wide open. ❑

SPECIFICATIONS

Length	38'4"
Length WL	33'6"
Beam	12'5"
Draft	3'3"
Weight	18,000#
Clearance	12'6"
Water	150/294 Gals.
Fuel	250 Gals.
Hull Type	Semi-Disp.
Designer	R. Lazzara

Production
1980–84

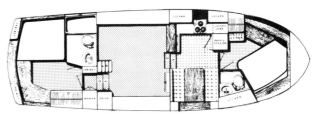

GULFSTAR 43 TRAWLER

Built on the Gulfstar 43 Motorsailer hull, the 43 Trawler is a conservative trawler design made popular in the 1970s during the fuel crisis. Hull construction is solid fiberglass and the use of exterior teak trim was kept to a minimum. Originally a trunk cabin design, in 1975 a raised aft deck version (the 43 MK II pictured above) was introduced with a redesigned flybridge and a full teak interior replacing the previous mica (or mahogany) decor. The full-width aft deck allows for an enlarged master stateroom with a centerline queen berth. A comfortable cruiser, the galley and dinette in the Gulfstar 43 are located down from the salon level. The lower helm is standard and sliding doors port and starboard provide access to the deck. Additional features include near-standing headroom in the engine room, excellent cabin ventilation, and protected underwater running gear. The engines were moved further apart (on 6' centerlines rather than 5') early in production for improved handling and maneuverability. A light boat for her size, she'll cruise economically at 9 knots and reach a top speed of 11–12 knots with 130-hp Perkins diesels. ❏

SPECIFICATIONS

Length	43'4"
Length WL	39'2"
Beam	13'11"
Draft	3'6"
Weight	21,000#
Clearance	12'0"
Water	130 Gals.
Fuel	300 Gals.
Hull Type	Semi-Disp.
Designer	V. Lazzara

Production
1972–77

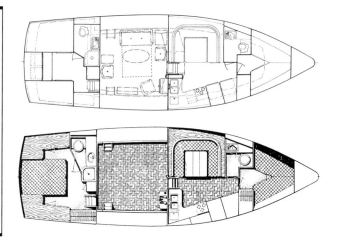

GULFSTAR 44 MOTOR CRUISER

When she was introduced in 1978, the 44 Motor Cruiser marked Gulfstar's initial entry into the modern motor yacht market in spite of her trawler speeds. The 44 remains a good-looking yacht today with her stylish radar arch, raised afterdeck, and modern hardtop. Built on a full displacement hull with a protective keel and flat aft sections, the Gulfstar 44 provides an efficient and comfortable ride. Inside, the floorplan is arranged in the conventional manner with the galley-down and a notably spacious master stateroom. The salon, which is somewhat narrow due to the wide sidedecks, has a lower helm and deck access door to starboard. A ladder leads down into the 44's stand-up engine room and a pump room forward separates the generator and air conditioning units from the motors. Twin 130-hp Perkins diesels were standard in the 44 Motor Cruiser and 160-hp Perkins turbos were optional (although they add little to performance). At her hull speed of 8.5 knots she'll burn only 5-6 gph. With 500 gallons of fuel (in one tank), the 44 has an average cruising range of approximately 700 miles. A total of 105 of these boats were built. ❏

SPECIFICATIONS

Length	44'5"
Length WL	39'0"
Beam	14'6"
Draft	3'6"
Weight	30,000#
Clearance	NA
Water	250 Gals.
Fuel	500 Gals.
Hull Type	Disp.
Designer	V. Lazzara

Production
1978–80

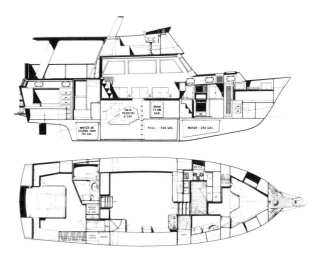

GULFSTAR

GULFSTAR 44 MOTOR YACHT

The Gulfstar 44 Motor Yacht is a downsized version of Gulfstar's popular 49 Motor Yacht. She differs from the 44 MK III model (1986–88) in that she has sidedecks surrounding the fully enclosed afterdeck. As in the Gulfstar 49, this fully enclosed and paneled afterdeck serves as the main salon and entertainment area. In this unique layout the (huge) galley and dinette are located on the lower level. Both staterooms are fitted with centerline double berths and a shower stall is provided in each head. In an innovative departure from the conventional, the aft stateroom has the bed fitted against the *forward* bulkhead. Thus arranged, the Gulfstar 44 has one of the roomiest interior layouts available in any 44-foot yacht ever offered. Space for a washer/dryer is located next to the forward companionway steps where a bulkhead door leads into the stand-up engine room. Note that a seawater intake chest and discharge system is installed to eliminate individual thru-hull fittings. Twin 300-hp Caterpillar diesels will cruise the Gulfstar 44 Motor Yacht around 16 knots with a top speed of 19–20 knots. ❏

SPECIFICATIONS

Length	43'9"
Length WL	39'1"
Beam	15'0"
Draft	3'6"
Weight	36,400#
Clearance	17'0"
Water	200 Gals.
Fuel	400 Gals.
Hull Type	Modified-V
Designer	R. Lazzara

Production
1985–86

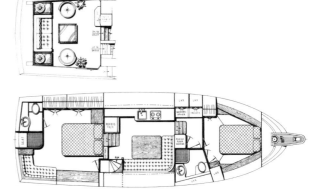

GULFSTAR 44 WIDEBODY MY

Featuring a *full-width*, fully enclosed afterdeck with wing doors, the Gulfstar 44 Widebody (MK II and MK III models) replaced the original 44 Motor Yacht during the 1986 model year. A total of 25 Widebodys were built during her production run and they remain popular today thanks to an innovative and truly practical accommodation plan. Rather than placing the salon amidships in the normal fashion, the Gulfstar 44's salon is located on the raised afterdeck — a fully enclosed, paneled, and air conditioned cabin with a sliding glass door to the small aft deck. This is the same unique floorplan first used in the original Gulfstar 44 MY, only now, by eliminating the sidedecks, the salon dimensions are substantially increased. The mid-level galley/dinette area is huge. The handsome teak interior is notable and there are many who consider this woodwork to be extraordinary in a U.S. production boat. Other changes made in the Widebody include the addition of a radar arch, larger standard engines and a slightly restyled flybridge. Twin 375-hp Cat diesels will cruise at 17–18 knots with a top speed around 21 knots. ❏

SPECIFICATIONS

Length	43'9"
Length WL	39'1"
Beam	15'0"
Draft	3'6"
Weight	36,400#
Clearance	17'0"
Water	200 Gals.
Fuel	400 Gals.
Hull Type	Modified-V
Designer	R. Lazzara

Production
1986–88

GULFSTAR

GULFSTAR 48 MOTOR YACHT

Closely resembling the 44 Motor Cruiser in appearance, the Gulfstar 48 Motor Yacht was the first Gulfstar to be built on a planing hull and powered to attain true motor yacht speeds. Then-state-of-the-art construction techniques — including balsa coring in the hull-sides and unidirectional composite materials — were used in the production of the boat. Inside, her expansive three-stateroom interior is arranged with the galley and dinette down from the salon, queen berths in both aft cabins, and stacked single berths in the forward stateroom. The salon is large enough to accommodate several furniture arrangements and there is near-standing headroom in the engine compartment. Throughout, the teak cabinetry and woodwork found in the Gulfstar 48 are exceptionally beautiful and lavishly applied. A hardtop shades the open aft deck and bench seating is provided forward of the helm on the flybridge. Standard power for the Gulfstar 48 Motor Yacht was GM 6-71Ns (290-hp) with the 390-hp TI versions offered as an option. The latter engines cruise around 17 knots. A total of eighteen 48 MYs were built. ❑

SPECIFICATIONS

Length	48'11"
Length WL	NA
Beam	15'0"
Draft	3'7"
Weight	40,500#
Clearance	14'7"
Water	200 Gals.
Fuel	500 Gals.
Hull Type	Modified-V
Designer	R. Lazzara

Production
1981–83

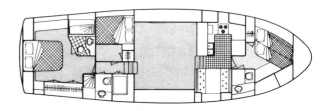

GULFSTAR 49 MOTOR YACHT

The Gulfstar 49 MY was a further refinement of the company's popular 48 Motor Yacht. First introduced in 1984 with 350-hp Perkins diesels, the MK II version (introduced in 1985) featured optional 435-hp 6-71 GM diesels and a unique aft stateroom design with the bed fitted against the forward bulkhead. Updates in 1986 (MK III) include a standard radar arch and bigger standard engines (375-hp Cats), and the MK IV (1987) offered GM 6V92TA diesels as an option. In all models, the *main* salon and entertaining area is the afterdeck — a fully enclosed and teak-paneled indoor living area with wing doors and generous dimensions. This spacious full-width salon allows for elegant entertaining in a truly expansive environment. At the deckhouse level, where the salon is normally found, the area has been converted into a huge galley and dinette. Additional features include a spacious stand-up engine room and a small aft deck for line handling. Cruising speed with the 350-hp Perkins is 14 knots (17 knots top), and with the 435-hp GM 6-71s the Gulfstar 49 will cruise at 16–17 knots with a top speed of about 20 knots. ❑

SPECIFICATIONS

Length	49'0"
Length WL	44'4"
Beam	15'1"
Draft	3'10"
Weight	42,000#
Clearance	17'0"
Water	370 Gals.
Fuel	675 Gals.
Hull Type	Modified-V
Designer	R. Lazzara

Production
1984–87

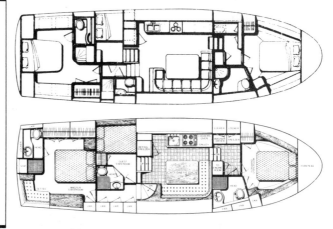

GULFSTAR 53 TRAWLER

L argest of the Gulfstar trawlers, the 53 is built on the same round-bilge displacement hull used in the construction of the Gulfstar 53 Motorsailer. Aside from her tendency to roll in a beam sea (like all displacement trawlers), the Gulfstar 53 is a seakindly boat with good handling characteristics. Her deep bilges allow the fuel tanks to be set low in the hull, thus reducing the center of gravity and making for a more comfortable motion. The 53's standard three-stateroom layout came with a choice of twin berths or a walkaround double in the aft cabin. The lower helm station is located on the centerline in the salon with deck doors port and starboard — a very practical set-up. Both heads have separate stall showers and it's worth noting that while the salon in the Gulfstar 53 Trawler is somewhat compact, the lower level galley and dinette area is very spacious. Additional features include a full teak interior, stand-up engine room, wide sidedecks, foredeck mast, and fully protected underwater running gear. Twin 160-hp Perkins diesels will cruise economically at 8–9 knots burning about 6 gph. Fewer than ten were built. ❏

SPECIFICATIONS

Length	53'2"
Length WL	47'3"
Beam	15'0"
Draft	4'6"
Weight	42,000#
Clearance	14'0"
Water	300 Gals.
Fuel	1,000 Gals.
Hull Type	Disp.
Designer	V. Lazzara

Production
1975–76

HATTERAS

Brief History

The clear leader in the production of quality sportfishermen and motor yachts, Hatteras began operations in 1959 with the all-fiberglass 41 Convertible. Today's Hatteras yachts are built to world-class standards and the company is a major exporter. Once owned by AMF, Hatteras is now owned by Genmar, a marine conglomerate that also operates (among many others) Wellcraft and Carver.

Selected Hatteras Models

Hatteras 32 FB SF
Hatteras 36 C (Early)
Hatteras 36 C
Hatteras 36 SF
Hatteras 37 C
Hatteras 38 C (Early)
Hatteras 38 C
Hatteras 38 DC
Hatteras 40 DC
Hatteras 41 C (Early)
Hatteras 41 C
Hatteras 41 Twin Cabin
Hatteras 42 C
Hatteras 42 LRC
Hatteras 43 C (Early)
Hatteras 43 C
Hatteras 43 DC
Hatteras 43 MY
Hatteras 44 Tri Cabin
Hatteras 45 C (Early)
Hatteras 45 C
Hatteras 46 C (Early)
Hatteras 46 C
Hatteras 48 YF

Hatteras 48 LRC
Hatteras 48 MY (Early)
Hatteras 48 MY
Hatteras 48 CMY
Hatteras 48 C
Hatteras 50 MY
Hatteras 50 C (Early)
Hatteras 50 C
Hatteras 50 C (New)
Hatteras 52 C
Hatteras 52 CMY
Hatteras 53 C
Hatteras 53 MY
Hatteras 53 YF
Hatteras 53 EDMY
Hatteras 54 MY
Hatteras 54 EDMY
Hatteras 54 C
Hatteras 55 C
Hatteras 56 MY
Hatteras 58 TCMY
Hatteras 58 YF
Hatteras 58 LRC
Hatteras 58 MY (Early)

Hatteras 58 CMY
Hatteras 58 MY
Hatteras 58 C
Hatteras 60 C
Hatteras 60 MY
Hatteras 60 EDMY
Hatteras 61 MY
Hatteras 61 CMY
Hatteras 63 MY
Hatteras 63 CMY
Hatteras 64 MY
Hatteras 65 LRC
Hatteras 65 MY
Hatteras 65 C
Hatteras 67 CMY
Hatteras 67 EDCMY
Hatteras 68 CMY
Hatteras 70 MY (Early)
Hatteras 70 EDMY
Hatteras 70 MY
Hatteras 70 CMY
Hatteras 72 MY
Hatteras 77 CMY
Hatteras 82 C

Main Office

Hatteras Yachts, 2100 Kivett Dr., High Point, NC 27261
919-889-6621

251

HATTERAS 32 FLYBRIDGE SF

The Hatteras 32 Flybridge Sport Fisherman was built with the modern good looks and quality touches one expects to find in a Hatteras product. The hull is a Jim Wynne design with recessed propeller pockets and 18° of transom deadrise. The hullsides are balsa-cored from the waterline up and considerable flare is used at the bow. Compared to other boats in her class, the Hatteras 32 is no lightweight. Inside, the cabin is arranged in the conventional manner with a small galley, a roomy head compartment and overnight berths for four. This is perhaps the most finely crafted and stylish interior one is likely to find in a 32-foot fishing boat. The decor is bright and airy with only a modest amount of teak trim. Although not designed with any serious cruising in mind, the Hatteras 32 can provide comfortable accommodations for an extended weekend. Twin 300-hp Caterpillar diesels will cruise at 21–22 knots with a top speed of around 26 knots. Note that the Hatteras 32 Sport Fisherman (with no flybridge) was also available with the same interior layout but smaller cabin windows. ❏

SPECIFICATIONS

Length	32'8"
Beam	12'0"
Draft	3'0"
Weight	18,000#
Clearance	10'6"
Water	50 Gals.
Fuel	265 Gals.
Cockpit	95 Sq. Ft.
Hull Type	Modified-V
Designer	Jim Wynne

Production
1982–86

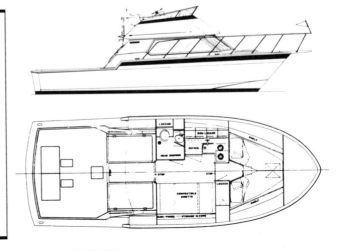

HATTERAS 36 CONVERTIBLE (EARLY)

The original Hatteras 36 Convertible is still a popular boat on the used market in spite of her obviously dated (but still classic) profile and overbuilt hull construction. Equally adept as an offshore fishing boat or comfortable family cruiser, the Hatteras 36 features an all-teak interior with the galley and stateroom three steps down from the salon. A two-stateroom floorplan with deckhouse galley was made available in 1975. While the accommodations are not considered spacious by today's standards, the handcrafted woodwork and quality hardware and systems in-stalled aboard the Hatteras 36 make renovations practical and reasonably inexpensive. The cockpit is large enough for a mounted chair and tack-le center, but the flybridge and (espe-cially) the engine room are both com-pact. Never known for her blinding speed, standard 330-hp gas engines will cruise the Hatteras 36 Convertible at 18 knots (26–27 top), while the optional Caterpillar 3160 diesels cruise around 15 knots with a top speed of 18 knots. Significantly, the fuel capaci-ty was increased in 1971 to 300 gal-lons. ❏

SPECIFICATIONS

Length	36'1"
Beam	12'9"
Draft	3'0"
Weight	19,000#
Clearance	12'11"
Water	70 Gals.
Fuel	240/300 Gals.
Cockpit	NA
Hull Type	Modified-V
Designer	J. Hargrave

Production
1969–77

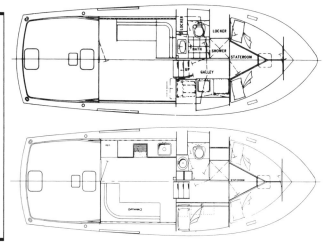

HATTERAS 36 CONVERTIBLE

The Hatteras 36 Convertible (the original 36 Convertible ran from 1969–77) was introduced in 1983. Designed as a replacement for the Hatteras 37, she's built on a heavy Jim Wynne-designed hull with a shallow keel section and propeller pockets below. This is the same hull used in the Hatteras 36 SF — a good open-water design but not especially fuel efficient. Well engineered and impressively finished, the Hatteras 36 makes an excellent family cruiser with her deluxe interior accommodations and stylish decor. Buyers can chose between a single-stateroom floorplan with an open salon and the galley-down or a two-stateroom layout with the galley-up. She has a big tournament-style flybridge with seating forward of the helm but her relatively small cockpit and unimpressive performance have resulted in mixed reviews among hard-core anglers. Standard 454-cid gas engines cruise at just 15 knots and the optional 390-hp 6-71 diesels cruise around 22 knots and reach 26 knots wide open. Note that the 36 Sedan Cruiser (1986–87) is the same boat with a slightly enlarged interior and smaller cockpit. ❑

SPECIFICATIONS

Length......................36'6"
Beam.......................13'7"
Draft ....3'9"
Weight ....26,500#
Clearance ....12'6"
Water................115 Gals.
Fuel ....355 Gals.
Cockpit.........................NA
Hull Type.........Modified-V
Designer ....Jim Wynne

Production
1983–1987

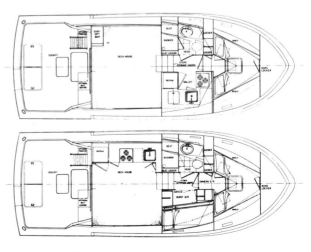

HATTERAS 36 SPORT FISHERMAN

The Hatteras 36 Sport Fisherman is a heavy boat for her size — a fact that doubtless accounts for much of her somewhat sedate performance. Hull construction is solid fiberglass with balsa coring applied in the deck and superstructure. The 36 SF is a Jim Wynne design with recessed propeller pockets below for reduced shaft angles — the same hull used in the production of the Hatteras 36 Convertible (1983–87). Her open bi-level cockpit layout is well suited for serious deepwater fishing and comes standard with a transom door and a built-in fish box. Other features include wide walkaround sidedecks, an elevated helm position, a wraparound windshield, and easy cockpit access to the engines. Three steps down into the cabin reveals a practical layout with stylish fabrics, attractive high-pressure plastic laminates and teak trim. Not only is this interior completely modern and appealing, it's easy to clean as well. The optional 390-hp GM 6-71s will cruise the Hatteras 36 Sport Fisherman around 24 knots and reach a top speed of 27–28 knots. ❑

SPECIFICATIONS

Length	36'6"
Beam	13'7"
Draft	3'9"
Weight	25,000#
Clearance	9'3"
Water	115 Gals.
Fuel	355 Gals.
Cockpit	110 Sq. Ft.
Hull Type	Modified-V
Designer	Jim Wynne

Production
1983–86

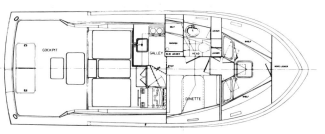

HATTERAS

HATTERAS 37 CONVERTIBLE

The Hatteras 37 Convertible replaced the early Hatteras 36 Convertible in 1977. While she never achieved the widespread popularity of her predecessor, the Hatteras 37 is an excellent family cruiser with the ability to handle weekend service as a competent sportfisherman. She's built on a solid fiberglass hull with twin chines, a long keel, and moderate deadrise at the transom. With only 330 gallons of fuel, she's not a long-range boat. The interior is paneled in teak and an offset double berth was offered in the forward stateroom beginning with the 1982 models. A stall shower is located in the spacious double-entry head compartment. Large wrap-around cabin windows give the salon a surprisingly spacious feeling for a 37-foot boat and her tournament-style flybridge has seating for five. At 29,000 lbs., the Hatteras 37 Convertible is no lightweight. Those powered with the GM 6-71N diesels will cruise 18–19 knots with a top speed of about 21 knots. The optional 390-hp 6-71TIs will cruise the 37 Convertible around 21 knots and reach 23–24 knots wide open. ❏

SPECIFICATIONS

Length	37'0"
Beam	14'0"
Draft	3'3"
Weight	29,000#
Clearance	13'5"
Water	135 Gals.
Fuel	330 Gals.
Cockpit	NA
Hull Type	Modified-V
Designer	J. Hargrave

Production
1977–83

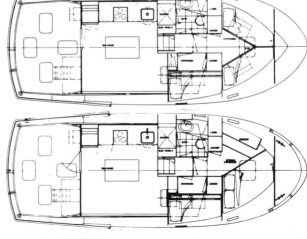

HATTERAS

HATTERAS 38 CONVERTIBLE (EARLY)

The last of the original Hatteras 38 Convertibles were built some fifteen years ago, but used models are still seen regularly in most coastal markets. While only two feet longer than the 36 Convertible (1969–77), the Hatteras 38's interior, flybridge, and engine room dimensions are notably larger. The galley location is unique: arranged athwartship against the aft bulkhead, it's convenient and opens up the salon considerably but severely restricts any view of the cockpit. The salon is fully paneled in teak or mahogany and features a standard lower helm and space for a sofa-bed and a couple of chairs. V-berths are located in the forward stateroom and stacked single berths are fitted in the guest cabin. Outside, the cockpit is on the smallish side although suitable for sportfishing activities. Cockpit freeboard is only 3'4" — boating a fish should be easy. The tournament flybridge has bench seating forward of the console and good cockpit visibility. With the GM8V53N diesels, the 38 Convertible models will cruise around 17 knots and reach 20 knots wide open. ❑

SPECIFICATIONS

Length	38'4"
Beam	13'7"
Draft	3'2"
Weight	29,000#
Clearance	13'4"
Water	148 Gals.
Fuel	300 Gals.
Cockpit	NA
Hull Type	Modified-V
Designer	Jack Hargrave

Production
1968–74

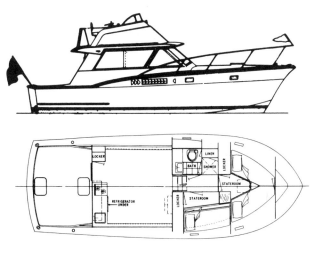

HATTERAS

HATTERAS 38 CONVERTIBLE

The current Hatteras 38 Convertible is one of the few boats in the Hatteras fleet not designed by Jack Hargrave. A handsome boat with an aggressive profile, she's built on a modified-V hull with balsa coring in the hullsides and a keel for stability. Aside from her stylish lines, the Hatteras 38 features a modern glassed-in front windshield and a luxurious two-stateroom teak interior layout with the galley-up in the salon. A centerline double berth is located in the large master stateroom and over/under single bunks are fitted in the guest cabin.

While the cockpit dimensions of the Hatteras 38 are not notably deep, her beam is carried well aft providing ample space for the installation of a full-size tuna chair. A molded tackle center and a transom door and gate are standard in the cockpit and the engine room air intakes are located under the coaming. The aft-raking flybridge windshield is particularly stylish. A good performer with now-standard 485-hp 6-71 diesels, the Hatteras 38 Convertible will cruise at a fast 26–27 knots and reach a top speed of 30+ knots. ❏

SPECIFICATIONS

Length	38'10"
Beam	13'5"
Draft	4'8"
Weight	28,800#
Clearance	12'6"
Water	117 Gals.
Fuel	490 Gals.
Cockpit	103 Sq. Ft.
Hull Type	Modified-V
Designer	Hatteras

Production
1988–Current

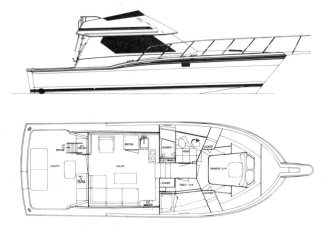

HATTERAS 38 DOUBLE CABIN

The Hatteras 38 Double Cabin is a restyled version of an earlier 38 double cabin cruiser that Hatteras introduced back in 1968. This newer model has a raised aft deck (which results in a full-beam master stateroom) and places the bridge over the deckhouse. An attractive design in spite of her stubby profile, the Hatteras 38 Double Cabin is a comfortable and well-built family cruiser. Her interior accommodations are arranged around a conventional two-stateroom, galley-down layout with large wraparound salon windows and excellent storage.

The owner's stateroom is fitted with twin berths (a double berth was never offered) and V-berths are in the forward stateroom. The interior is fully paneled and finished with teak woodwork, and a lower helm was optional in the salon. Her flybridge is small by today's standards (although the styling is modern) with bench seating to starboard of the helm console. A comfortable and easy-riding boat, with standard GM 6-71N diesels the Hatteras 38 Double Cabin will cruise at 16–17 knots and reach a top speed of around 20 knots. ❏

SPECIFICATIONS

Length	38'4"
Length WL	NA
Beam	13'7"
Draft	3'5"
Weight	33,000#
Clearance	12'10"
Water	145 Gals.
Fuel	300 Gals.
Hull Type	Modified-V
Designer	J. Hargrave

Production
1973–78

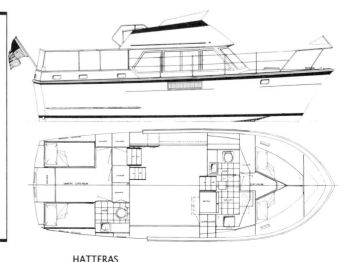

HATTERAS

HATTERAS 40 DOUBLE CABIN

A popular boat since her introduction in 1986, the 40 Double Cabin is built on an in-house hull design with moderate beam, propeller pockets, and 14° of deadrise at the transom. A shallow keel helps tracking and balsa coring is used in the hullsides above the waterline. Her now-standard (since 1990) galley-down floorplan is arranged with a dinette in the salon and stacked single berths in the forward stateroom. Both heads are fitted with stall showers — a major selling point. The original layout (now discontinued) had a slightly smaller salon, no dinette and V-berths forward. These are practical and luxurious accommodations well suited for extended cruising. The extensive use of teak (or ash) paneling and cabinetry is contrasted with rich pastel fabrics and white formica counters in the galley. The flybridge was redesigned in 1990 with a forward helm and swept-back windscreen, and a new full-height entry door to the salon was added at the same time. A poor performer with gas engines (13-14 knots cruise/20 knots top), 375-hp Cats are now standard. They'll deliver a cruising speed of 17 knots and a top speed of around 21 knots.   ❑

SPECIFICATIONS

Length	40'10"
Length WL	NA
Beam	13'7"
Draft	4'8"
Weight	38,000#
Clearance	15'9"
Water	110 Gals.
Fuel	359 Gals.
Hull Type	Modified-V
Designer	Hatteras

Production
1986–Current

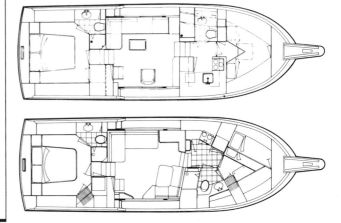

HATTERAS

HATTERAS 41 CONVERTIBLE (EARLY)

Sharing the same hull as the Hatteras 41 Twin Cabin motor yacht, the old Hatteras 41 Convertible continues to be a highly visible and still-popular boat more than two decades after going out of production. Her chief attributes today remain her rugged all-fiberglass construction, a practical two-stateroom interior layout, a sizable fishing cockpit, and quality hardware and fixtures. A lower helm station was standard and the interior is finished in mahogany. While the salon and staterooms aren't notably large, they're still comfortable and can easily be updated at a moderate cost. The Hatteras 41 is, of course, almost totally dated by today's standards — the flybridge is ancient and the ride, while stable, can be wet. Nonetheless, a used Hatteras 41 in good condition can still bring a surprisingly strong resale value in spite of her age. Although 300-hp gas engines were standard, most of the early Hatteras 41s were powered with the 283-hp GM 8V53N diesels (a tight fit in the 41's small engine room). She'll cruise around 17 knots and reach a top speed of about 20 knots. ❑

SPECIFICATIONS

Length	40'9"
Beam	14'0"
Draft	2'11"
Weight	23,000#
Clearance	13'6"
Water	150 Gals.
Fuel	400 Gals.
Cockpit	105 Sq. Ft.
Hull Type	Modified-V
Designer	J. Hargrave

Production
1968–71

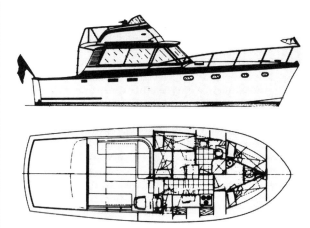

HATTERAS

HATTERAS 41 CONVERTIBLE

When the current Hatteras 41 Convertible was introduced in 1986 she was widely hailed as the beginning of a new series of high-tech Hatteras designs. Notably, the 41 was the first Hatteras to have a completely cored hull (including the bottom) with vacuum-bagging used extensively in the construction process. This new styling was dramatic for a Hatteras. The "new look" deckhouse window treatment, solid front windshield, stepped sheer, and rakish flybridge were the forerunners of today's Hatteras convertible styling. In the original two-stateroom layout, an in-line galley consumes a considerable amount of the salon's living space. (A single-stateroom, galley-down floorplan was also offered.) In 1990 a revised two-stateroom floorplan improved on the original layout by moving the galley to starboard. A light ash interior became available in 1987. The transom door and tackle center were standard and the engine air intakes are located under the gunnels. Fuel tankage was increased to 500 gallons in 1987. A good running boat, standard 465-hp 6-71s diesels cruise at 23–24 knots and the optional 535-hp 6V92s cruise at 26 knots with 29 knots top. ❑

SPECIFICATIONS

Length	41'9"
Beam	14'3"
Draft	4'4"
Weight	35,400#
Clearance	13'9"
Water	150 Gals.
Fuel	400/500 Gals.
Cockpit	120 Sq. Ft.
Hull Type	Modified-V
Designer	J. Hargrave

Production
1986–91

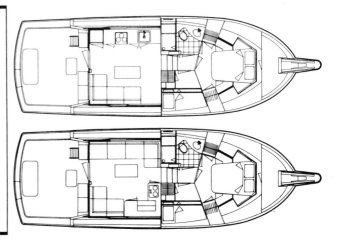

HATTERAS 41 TWIN CABIN

Built on the same hull as the original 41 Convertible, the Hatteras 41 Twin Cabin is a flush deck design with a conventional double-cabin interior layout. Although it's been nearly 20 years since production ceased, used models continue to be popular and many have been extensively updated by their owners. Indeed, Hatteras 41 Twin Cabins have been a particular favorite of those who enjoy renovating older boats. Her primary appeal today is solid construction and above-average engineering. The deck plan features a spacious entertainment area abaft the helm station and wide sidedecks around the house. All of the 41s were built with a short hardtop covering about half of the aft deck area, and all have twin berths in the master stateroom. Additional features include a full-size refrigerator in the galley, a salon wet bar, mahogany interior woodwork, and good storage space. Gasolene engines were standard but most Hatteras 41 Twin Cabins were fitted with the optional GM 8V53N diesels. The cruising speed is around 15–16 knots and the top speed is about 19 knots. ❏

SPECIFICATIONS

Length	40'11"
Length WL	NA
Beam	14'0"
Draft	3'0"
Weight	24,500#
Clearance	12'7"
Water	150 Gals.
Fuel	400 Gals.
Hull Type	Modified-V
Designer	J. Hargrave

Production
1966–71

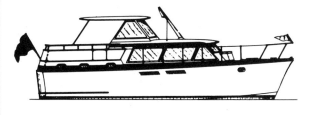

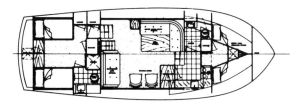

HATTERAS 42 CONVERTIBLE

The Hatteras 42 Convertible replaced the aging 41 Convertible in the Hatteras lineup in 1971. She represented a big step forward in convertible design with her larger, full-width flybridge (the first in any Hatteras model) and her bold and more aggressive exterior profile. Construction was on the heavy side and considerable flare was added at the bow. Her large 110 sq. ft. cockpit easily accommodates a mounted chair and complete tackle center. The Hatteras 42 was offered with only one floorplan: a two-stateroom arrangement with the galley-down to star-board. A stall shower is fitted in the double-entry head, and teak paneling and cabinetry are used throughout. The engine room is tight but routine access is satisfactory. In 1977 the flybridge was restyled, and the galley was rearranged with the refrigerator moved forward (thus opening the galley up to the salon) — big improvements when compared against the earlier models. A comfortable offshore boat, the 42 Convertible will cruise around 20 knots with either the GM 6-71TIs or the Cummins VT-903 diesels. Top speed is 22–23 knots. ❑

SPECIFICATIONS

Length......................42'8"
Beam......................13'10"
Draft ....3'5"
Weight ....31,000#
Clearance.................13'3"
Water.................150 Gals.
Fuel ....400 Gals.
Cockpit............110 Sq. Ft.
Hull Type.........Modified-V
Designer ....J. Hargrave

Production
1971–78

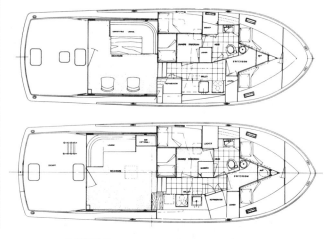

HATTERAS 42 LONG RANGE CRUISER

The Hatteras 42 LRC was introduced as one of the few alternatives to the influx of Asian trawlers imported during the era of fuel shortages. Her hull form features rounded bilges forward that gradually harden to form a shallow "V" aft at the transom. Not surprisingly, the 42 LRC will roll somewhat in a beam sea — a common characteristic of displacement-type hulls but a worthwhile price to pay for her otherwise excellent seakeeping qualities. Her conventional double cabin floorplan includes fore and aft staterooms, each with a head and stall

shower. The deckhouse galley was redesigned in 1979 from an in-line arrangement to port to a convenient U-shaped layout set against the aft salon bulkhead. A full-width afterdeck replaced the walkaround trunk cabin in 1980, and a tapered double berth in the master stateroom became available in 1981. A superb cruising yacht, twin Lehman or GM diesels will cruise the Hatteras 42 Long Range Cruiser at a steady 8 knots (6 gph) with a cruising range of over 1,000 miles. At a reduced 7-knot speed the range is close to 2,000 miles. ❑

SPECIFICATIONS

Length	42'6"
Length WL	38'0"
Beam	14'6"
Draft	3'10"
Weight	36,000#
Clearance	13'6"
Water	220 Gals.
Fuel	700 Gals.
Hull Type	Displacement
Designer	J. Hargrave

Production
1977–85

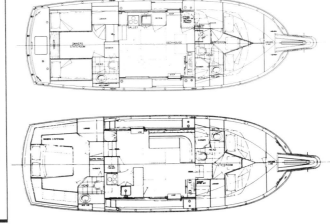

HATTERAS 43 CONVERTIBLE (EARLY)

The Hatteras 43 Convertible was the replacement boat for the earlier Hatteras 42 Convertible. A good-looking boat, her all-new double-chined hull (11° deadrise aft) resulted in an enlarged engine room capable of handling the (then) recently introduced GM 6V92 diesels. In addition, her extra beam allowed for the installation of side-by-side berths in the master stateroom. (A double berth became available in 1982.) Other notable features of the Hatteras 43 Convertible include a spacious teak-paneled salon, an oversize flybridge with seating for eight, under-coaming air intakes in the cockpit, and a transom door with gate. The cockpit, while adequate for serious fishing activities, seems nonetheless small in an otherwise spacious boat. A short-lived European arrangement (crew quarters forward with foredeck access) was offered in 1981–82 models. Never considered a particularly fast boat for her size, the early models with 450-hp 6V92s cruise around 20 knots. In 1981, the high-performance 6V92s (500-hp) were offered for a cruising speed of 23 knots and 26 knots at full throttle. ❏

SPECIFICATIONS

Length	43'8"
Beam	14'6"
Draft	4'2"
Weight	41,000#
Clearance	14'3"
Water	165 Gals.
Fuel	470 Gals.
Cockpit	110 Sq. Ft.
Hull Type	Modified-V
Designer	J. Hargrave

Production
1979–84

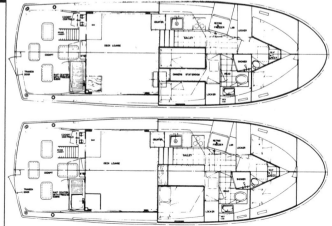

HATTERAS 43 CONVERTIBLE

Sharing the same rakish profile and step-down sheer of her larger sister-ships, the new Hatteras 43 Convertible is a good-looking sportfisherman with the solid construction and improved performance typical of most recent Hatteras designs. She's built on an all-new hull with balsa coring in the hullsides, 10° of transom deadrise, and a shallow keel below. A galley-down, two-stateroom layout is standard and the optional single-stateroom floorplan trades out the guest cabin for a large U-shaped dinette. While the salon dimensions in both layouts are somewhat compact for a 43-footer, the white ash woodwork opens up the interior significantly. A washer/dryer is located in the companionway and there's a stylish curved shower door in the head. Outside, the 43's large cockpit is tournament-grade all the way and includes direct access to the engine room. (Hatteras mistakenly claims the 43 to be the first in her class to offer this feature but the Phoenix 38 and Californian 42 Convertibles had it years before.) A good running boat, the cruising speed with standard 535-hp 6-92s is around 25–26 knots and the top speed is 28 knots. ❏

SPECIFICATIONS

Length	43'2"
Beam	14'3"
Draft	4'4"
Weight	40,000#
Clearance	12'4"
Water	154 Gals.
Fuel	500 Gals.
Cockpit	120 Sq. Ft.
Hull Type	Modified-V
Designer	Hargrave

Production
1991–Current

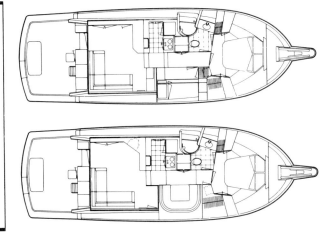

HATTERAS

HATTERAS 43 DOUBLE CABIN

The 43 Double Cabin had a long and very successful production run for Hatteras. She was originally designed to replace the then-aging Hatteras 41 Twin Cabin model back in 1971, and her popularity kept her in production for the next thirteen years. She's built on a solid fiberglass, modified-V hull with 8° of deadrise aft and a long keel for stability. Inside, the 43's accommodations have always been considered among the more comfortable to be found in a yacht of this size. The salon is extremely open and rich teak paneling and cabinetry are found in every cabin. Early models have a stall shower in the forward head; however, the floorplan was changed in 1979 to include a portside dinette (at the expense of that stall shower). A walkaround double berth was first offered in the master stateroom in 1978, and a three-stateroom floorplan became optional in 1980. The flybridge (also optional, but most are so equipped) is small and visibility from the lower helm is very good. With GM 6-71N diesels, the Hatteras 43 will cruise around 14 knots. The larger 390-hp TI versions cruise at 16–17 knots. ❏

SPECIFICATIONS

Length	43'1"
Length WL	37'6"
Beam	14'0"
Draft	3'5"
Weight	34,000#
Clearance	17'10"
Water	130 Gals.
Fuel	375 Gals.
Hull Type	Modified-V
Designer	J. Hargrave

Production
1971–84

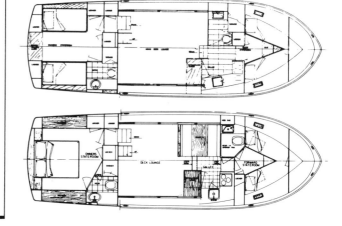

HATTERAS 43 MOTOR YACHT

While she's built on the same hull as the earlier Hatteras 43 Double Cabin, the 43 Motor Yacht is much more than a warmed-over 43 DC. The profile and interior layout are completely revised and the exterior styling of the 43 MY is dramatically improved from that of her predecessor. The plush two-stateroom interior layout features a spacious and open main salon with a mid-level galley to port and separate stall showers in both heads. Modern decorator fabrics and stylish white Formica cabinetry in the galley and heads provide a pleasant contrast to the interior's teak paneling and woodwork. Outside, the aft deck is very roomy for a boat of this size. An optional hardtop and wing doors provide weather protection and wide sidedecks make fore and aft movement secure. The flybridge is arranged with the helm console forward and bench seating is provided for six. The standard 375-hp Cat diesels will cruise the Hatteras 43 MY around 16 knots with a top speed of 20–21 knots. Optional 6-71TIs cruise around 17 knots. With a small fuel capacity the cruising range of is somewhat limited. ❏

SPECIFICATIONS

Length	43'1"
Length WL	37'9"
Beam	14'0"
Draft	3'5"
Weight	34,500#
Clearance	16'7"
Water	130 Gals.
Fuel	375 Gals.
Hull Type	Modified-V
Designer	J. Hargrave

Production
1984–87

HATTERAS

HATTERAS 44 TRI CABIN MY

When the Hatteras 44 MY was introduced in 1967 the market for large fiberglass motor yachts was a Hatteras domain as nearly all manufacturers of the day were still building in wood. Built on the early single-chine Hatteras hull form, construction was solid fiberglass (bulletproof by today's standards) with moderate beam and a shallow, full-length keel below. She's a wet boat when the seas pick up but the ride is comfortable and her three-stateroom, galley-down layout is well arranged. The galley is on the small side but the salon dimensions are quite generous. All of the 44s had twin single berths in the master stateroom. The flush deck design of the Hatteras 44 puts the helm and open afterdeck on the same level with an extended hardtop providing some protection from the elements. Note that a flybridge became available beginning in 1971 but they are comparatively rare on the market. Most Hatteras 44 MYs were powered with either 8V53N diesels or 8V71Ns (14 knots cruise/16 top). A few later models were delivered with optional turbo 8V71Ts which will cruise at a brisk 17–18 knots. ❏

SPECIFICATIONS

Length	44'8"
Length WL	NA
Beam	14'7"
Draft	3'6"
Weight	32,000#
Clearance	16'10"
Water	250 Gals.
Fuel	500 Gals.
Hull Type	Modified-V
Designer	J. Hargrave

Production
1967–72

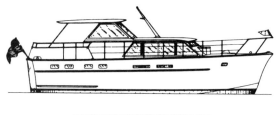

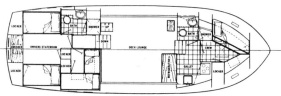

HATTERAS 45 CONVERTIBLE (EARLY)

There always seems to be a market for the old Hatteras 45 Convertible. Her profile is that of a classic sportfisherman with a high foredeck and sweeping sheerline ending with a low-freeboard cockpit. Solid hull construction and good seakeeping qualities have made the 45 Convertible a favorite among tournament-minded anglers. Her conventional two-stateroom, galley-down interior includes a spacious main salon with a complete lower helm station and built-in lounge seating to port. A galley-up model was also available with an open day berth replacing the galley in the companionway. A versatile boat, the spacious cockpit in the Hatteras 45 gets high marks for good all-around fishability. The old-style flybridge, however, is small. (Note that the original centerline pedestal bridge layout was revised in 1970 to a more versatile tournament-style design.) The popular engine choices were 8V71Ns (15–16 knots cruise) and 8V71TIs (around 20 knots at cruise and 23 knots at full throttle). Still a durable boat, the resale values of early Hatteras 45 Convertibles are surprisingly good. ❑

SPECIFICATIONS

Length	45'2"
Beam	14'7"
Draft	3'6"
Weight	37,000#
Clearance	13'10"
Water	180 Gals.
Fuel	650 Gals.
Cockpit	NA
Hull Type	Modified-V
Designer	J. Hargrave

Production
1968–74

HATTERAS 45 CONVERTIBLE

The Hatteras 45 Convertible was originally conceived as an enlarged version of the Hatteras 43 Convertible — basically the same interior layout with the additional length of the 45 going into a larger (and greatly improved) cockpit. The original two-stateroom, galley-down floorplan was available with either a double berth or twin singles in the midships master stateroom. A short-lived "Palm Beach" version of the 45 Convertible (1987 only) featured an optional two-stateroom, two-head layout with a glassed-in front windshield and a choice of soft yellow or light blue hull colors. In 1986 a contemporary light ash interior option became available, and in keeping with the "new look" of Hatteras convertibles the 45 was restyled in 1987 with a new flybridge and window treatment. For 1988 the interior layout was revised to include an S-shaped forward companionway, two heads, and an enlarged master stateroom with a walkaround queen berth. Not known as a particularly fast boat, standard 535-hp 6V92s will cruise the Hatteras 45 Convertible at 23–24 knots and reach 27 knots wide open. ❑

SPECIFICATIONS

Length	45'8"
Beam	14'6"
Draft	4'6"
Weight	45,000#
Clearance	14'3"
Water	165 Gals.
Fuel	590 Gals.
Cockpit	135 Sq. Ft.
Hull Type	Modified-V
Designer	J. Hargrave

Production
1984–91

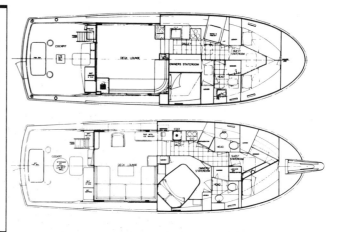

HATTERAS 46 CONVERTIBLE (EARLY)

One of the most popular Hatteras convertibles ever, the 46 was built on the original single chine Hargrave hull design with a deep, full-length keel and moderate transom deadrise. By any standard, the Hatteras 46 Convertible is a handsome boat. Aside from being an excellent fisherman, she's also a popular cruising boat due to her spacious and comfortable interior accommodations. Revised two and three-stateroom floorplans were introduced in 1982 (each with two heads), and a new sliding door replaced the original hinged salon door in the same year. The original 46 Convertibles were powered with 8V71TI diesels and cruise around 20 knots with a top speed of 23-24 knots. In 1982, a high-performance version of the Hatteras 46 (with 650-hp 8V92TIs) featured a beefed-up hull with balsa coring in the hullsides and extra transverse frames in the bottom. The keel was also shortened to improve handling and reduce wetted surface. Speeds with the hi-performance 8V92s are around 26 knots cruise and 29 knots top. Still a popular boat on the used market, resale values are quite strong for this model. ❏

SPECIFICATIONS

Length	46'2"
Length WL	41'3"
Beam	14'9"
Draft	4'2"
Weight	41,000#
Clearance	13'8"
Water	180 Gals.
Fuel	650/710 Gals.
Cockpit	125 Sq. Ft.
Hull Type	Modified-V
Designer	J. Hargrave

Production
1974–85

HATTERAS 46 CONVERTIBLE

Sharing the rakish profile, sculptured bridge, and step-down sheer of all modern Hatteras sportfishermen, the 46 Convertible replaced the long-running 45 Convertible in the Hatteras fleet in 1992. She's heavily built on a conventional modified-V hull with balsa coring in the hullsides, a shallow keel and 10° of transom deadrise. Inside, the upscale white ash interior features a standard two-stateroom, mid-level galley layout with a dinette and single head. The alternate floorplan has a second full head below with the dinette up in the salon. In both arrangements a wash-er/dryer is located in the companion-way forward of the galley and a built-in entertainment center is found in the salon. The large tournament level cockpit comes with molded tackle centers, in-deck fishbox, and transom door with gate. The incredibly well-designed engine room (accessed from the cockpit) is the best we've seen in any Hatteras convertible. Hatteras offers a choice of 720-hp 8V92s or 780-hp MANs for the 46 Convertible. An expensive boat, the cruising speed with the GMs is 25–26 knots and the top speed is around 30 knots. ❑

SPECIFICATIONS

Length	46'10"
Beam	15'7"
Draft	4'8"
Weight	51,000#
Clearance	13'9"
Water	188 Gals.
Fuel	775 Gals.
Cockpit	121 Sq. Ft.
Hull Type	Modified-V
Designer	J. Hargrave

Production
1992–Current

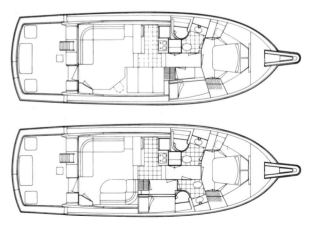

HATTERAS 48 YACHT FISHERMAN

Built on a stretched Hatteras 44 Motor Yacht hull, the 48 Yacht Fisherman enjoyed moderate success during her relatively brief production run in the early 1970s. She was originally developed to offer the spaciousness and comfort of a motor yacht with the sportfishing capability of a convertible — a design that has only grown in popularity over the years. The Hatteras 48 YF came with a choice of two floorplans: a two-stateroom layout with a huge master suite aft, and a more popular three-stateroom arrangement with the extra guest cabin at the expense of the aft stateroom dimensions. Both heads were fitted with separate stall showers, and the interior was completely finished with teak paneling and cabinetry. The main salon of the 48 YF is very roomy with space for several different furniture settings. Outside, the semi-enclosed lower helm and aft deck area overlook the cockpit. The flybridge is small, even by 1970's standards. With the optional 425-hp 8V71TIs, the Hatteras 48 Yacht Fisherman will cruise 17–18 knots and reach 21 knots top. ❏

SPECIFICATIONS

Length	48'9"
Beam	14'7"
Draft	3'7"
Weight	43,500#
Clearance	16'0"
Water	250 Gals.
Fuel	650 Gals.
Cockpit	NA
Hull Type	Modified-V
Designer	J. Hargrave

Production
1972–75

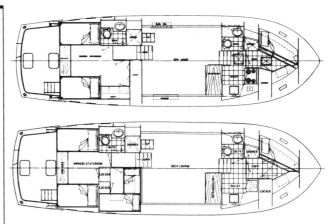

HATTERAS 48 LONG RANGE CRUISER

With her raised pilothouse and sturdy profile, the Hatteras 48 Long Range Cruiser has the strictly business appearance of a serious offshore passagemaker. It is, of course, the raised pilothouse that sets her apart from most of the competition. From here, the 48 LRC can be operated in complete privacy from the rest of the boat. Twin sliding doors provide quick access to the decks, and a settee/watchman's berth is fitted abaft the helm. The 48 LRC is built on a heavy fiberglass hull with a full keel providing protection to the props and rudders. Freeboard — 8'7" forward — is quite high. Featuring a practical two-stateroom layout, the spacious master suite (with a tub in the head compartment) is located directly below the pilothouse. (An optional three-stateroom layout was also available.) The compact galley is to port in the salon, and the small cockpit is fitted with a boarding door. With 112-hp GM or 120-hp Lehman diesels, the Hatteras 48 LRC will cruise at her 8.8 knot hull speed burning only 9 gph. At a 7-knot cruising speed the range exceeds 2,000 miles. ❏

SPECIFICATIONS

Length	48'10"
Length WL	43'4"
Beam	16'6"
Draft	4'6"
Weight	54,000#
Clearance	16'11"
Water	430 Gals.
Fuel	1,390 Gals.
Hull Type	Displacement
Designer	J. Hargrave

Production
1976–81

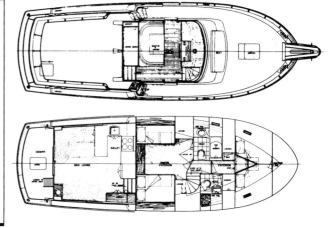

HATTERAS 48 MOTOR YACHT (EARLY)

This good-looking flush deck motor yacht is built on a "dual mode" semi-displacement hull; that is, she's designed for efficient operation at displacement speeds while still having planing-speed ability with the larger 6V92TA engines. The hull is constructed of solid fiberglass and features moderate deadrise aft and a long keel for stability. A standard three-stateroom interior arrangement includes three heads but the only stall shower is reserved for the master stateroom. An optional four-stateroom floorplan replaces the dinette found in the standard layout. The huge afterdeck can be fully enclosed with wing doors to create a full-width entertainment area larger in dimensions than the salon. Standard power for the 48 was GM 6-71N diesels which will deliver an efficient 1 mpg at a 9-knot displacement speed but lack the power to get the 48 on plane with a full load. The larger 425-hp 6V92s will cruise the Hatteras 48 around 16 knots and reach 18–19 knots wide open. Note that the Hatteras 48 Cockpit MY (1981–84) is the same boat without the aft guest stateroom and head. ❏

SPECIFICATIONS

Length	48'8"
Length WL	NA
Beam	15'0"
Draft	3'11"
Weight	45,000#
Clearance	17'2"
Water	190 Gals.
Fuel	590 Gals.
Hull Type	Semi-Disp.
Designer	J. Hargrave

Production
1981–84

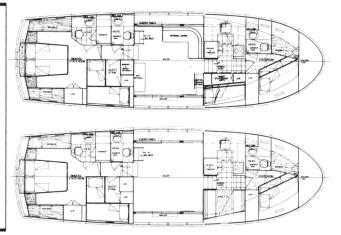

HATTERAS 48 MOTOR YACHT

The Hatteras 48 MY (and her sister-ship, the 52 Cockpit MY) is a modern in-house design with contemporary styling accented with an integral radar arch and hardtop — all one piece. She's heavily built on a modified-V hull with Divinycell coring in the hullsides, and at 63,000 lbs. the Hatteras 48 is certainly no lightweight. The standard galley-down layout allows for three staterooms (two with walkaround double berths) and three full heads. The less popular two-stateroom floorplan replaces the small guest cabin aft with an enlarged master head and adds a walk-in wardrobe to port in the owner's stateroom. A built-in washer/dryer is included in both layouts. The huge aft deck of the Hatteras 48 comes with wing doors and may be fully enclosed and air conditioned. The sidedecks are wide and there's generous guest seating on the bridge behind the wraparound helm. Twin 535-hp 6V92 diesels were standard in very early models (16-knots cruise/19-knots top) but they were quickly replaced with the larger 720-hp 8V92s which cruise the Hatteras 48 MY at a more acceptable 20 knots and reach 23 knots wide open.   ❏

SPECIFICATIONS

Length	48'9"
Length WL	NA
Beam	16'0"
Draft	5'2"
Weight	63,000#
Clearance	16'8"
Water	170 Gals.
Fuel	750 Gals.
Hull Type	Modified-V
Designer	Hatteras

Production
1990–Current

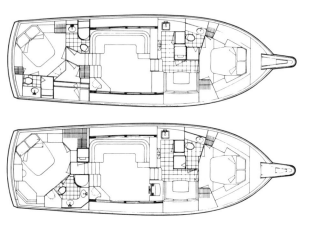

HATTERAS 48 COCKPIT MY

A good-looking yacht with her flush deck profile and raked bridge, the 48 Cockpit MY was not a big seller for Hatteras. She's constructed on the same "dual mode" hull used in the Hatteras 48 MY (1981–84) — basically a semi-displacement configuration with rounded bilges forward, flat aftersections (7° deadrise aft), and a long keel terminating a few feet forward of the transom. Her standard layout included a centerline double berth in the master cabin (twin single berths were optional) and a second stateroom forward with twin over/under berths. An optional three-stateroom floorplan traded out the dinette for a third stateroom while leaving the galley-down. Either way, the aft stateroom dimensions are impressive. Teak woodwork was used throughout the interior and the only stall shower is aft. A lower helm station was optional. Outside, the afterdeck is very roomy with space for several pieces of deck furniture. The cockpit, however, is small. Short on performance, standard 285-hp 6-71Ns will cruise the Hatteras 48 CMY at 12–13 knots and the optional 425-hp 6V92TAs cruise around 15–16 knots. ❑

SPECIFICATIONS

Length	48'8"
Length WL	NA
Beam	15'0"
Draft	3'11"
Weight	47,000#
Clearance	17'2"
Water	190 Gals.
Fuel	590 Gals.
Hull Type	Modified-V
Designer	J. Hargrave

Production
1981–85

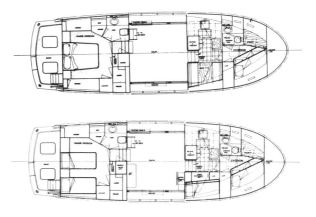

HATTERAS

HATTERAS 48 CONVERTIBLE

Modern construction and contemporary styling are the hallmarks of the Hatteras 48 Convertible — a striking design aimed at the upscale end of the luxury sportfish market. Surprisingly, weight wasn't kept down very much in the Hatteras 48 although Divinycell coring is used in the hullsides and bulkheads. Her tournament-size cockpit came with a wide transom door and tackle center as standard, along with an engine room access door and under-coaming air intakes. Below, the spacious salon is laid out in traditional Hatteras style with a complete entertainment center, stylish fabrics, and teak paneling and cabinetry (light ash woodwork was also available). Both staterooms have roomy head compartments with stall showers, and a convenient raised serving counter divides the salon from the mid-level galley area. Additional features of the 48 include a solid front windshield, side exhausts, wide sidedecks, and a huge tournament flybridge. Standard 720-hp 8V92TA diesels will cruise the Hatteras 48 Convertible about 25–26 knots and turn a top speed of 30 knots. ❏

SPECIFICATIONS

Length	48'8"
Beam	16'0"
Draft	5'5"
Weight	51,500#
Clearance	14'0"
Water	184 Gals.
Fuel	812 Gals.
Cockpit	135 Sq. Ft.
Hull Type	Modified-V
Designer	Jack Hargrave

Production
1987–91

HATTERAS 50 MOTOR YACHT

When the Hatteras 50 MY was introduced in 1965 she was the largest production fiberglass motor yacht built in the world. Obviously dated by today's standards, she was constructed on a solid fiberglass hull with a single chine and an unusually wide keel which houses the fuel and water tankage. Those familiar with latter-day Hatteras designs will find it interesting to note that this was the first Hatteras motor yacht with split engine rooms — almost a trademark design for most subsequent Hatteras motor yachts until the 1990s. Her traditional galley-down, three-stateroom interior features twin single berths in the master stateroom, a decidedly small salon (compared to a modern 50-footer), and a spacious outdoor afterdeck. The wheelhouse is open to the salon in this layout which adds some depth to the deckhouse dimensions. The sidedecks are very wide and a bridge overhang provides weather protection all around the house. There's space on the hardtop model for dinghy storage, but with the flybridge model a dinghy won't fit. Nearly all were powered with 350-hp 8V71N diesels. Cruising speed is 12–13 knots and the top speed is 15 knots. ❏

SPECIFICATIONS

Length	50'3"
Length WL	NA
Beam	15'7"
Draft	4'0"
Weight	42,000#
Clearance	20'6"
Water	250 Gals.
Fuel	550 Gals.
Hull Type	Modified-V
Designer	Hargrave

Production
1965–69

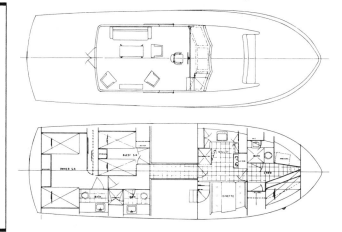

HATTERAS

HATTERAS 50 CONVERTIBLE (EARLY)

Obviously dated by current design standards, the old Hatteras 50 Convertible remains a fairly common occurrence on today's used boat market. She was a popular yacht in her day — the next step up from the Hatteras 41 Convertible when she was introduced in 1967 — and she retained her popularity among sportfishermen until the now-classic 53 Convertible came out in 1969. Like many early Hatteras single-chine hulls, the 50 can be a wet ride when the seas pick up. Below, the three-stateroom, three-head interior is arranged with the owner's cabin to port featuring a stall shower in the private head. Both the guest stateroom to starboard and the bow stateroom are fitted with over/under berths. The galley is to port in the salon, and the interior is finished with mahogany woodwork and cabinetry throughout. The cockpit, with 136 sq. ft. of space, is well suited for fishing activities. No racehorse, GM 8V71N diesels were standard in the early Hatteras 50 Convertibles (14 knots cruise/17 knots top) with GM 12V71Ns (17 knots cruise/20 top) offered as options. ❏

SPECIFICATIONS

Length......................50'0"
Beam.....................15'10"
Draft ....4'0"
Weight ....42,000#
Clearance ....15'2"
Water.................250 Gals.
Fuel ....950 Gals.
Cockpit............136 Sq. Ft.
Hull Type.........Modified-V
Designer ....J. Hargrave

Production
1967–69

HATTERAS

HATTERAS 50 CONVERTIBLE

The Hatteras 50 Convertible (the second of three Hatteras 50 Convertible models) was initially designed to handle the new GM 8V92 diesels. She was, in fact, the first Hatteras to have these engines as standard equipment. Constructed on the traditional Hatteras hull form with full-length double chines, balsa coring from the waterline up, and a long keel running well aft, the Hatteras 50 is widely regarded as a good-looking convertible. Her wide 16'4" beam provides interior accommodations that are truly expansive for a boat of this size. A choice of two floorplans was available: a two-stateroom version with galley-down, and a popular three-stateroom layout with a more convenient deckhouse galley. The cockpit (notably small for a 50' sportfishing boat) features a standard transom door and gate, undercoaming air intakes, and direct engine room access. The full-width flybridge is huge with bench seating for six forward of the helm. The original 550-hp 8V92 diesels will cruise the Hatteras 50 around 20 knots, and the hi-performance 650-hp versions (introduced in the 1982 models) cruise at 23 knots with a top speed of around 26 knots. ❑

SPECIFICATIONS

Length	50'0"
Length WL	45'5"
Beam	16'4"
Draft	4'6"
Weight	56,500#
Clearance	15'10"
Fresh Water	185 Gals.
Fuel	1,065 Gals.
Cockpit	NA
Hull Type	Modified-V
Designer	J. Hargrave

Production
1980–83

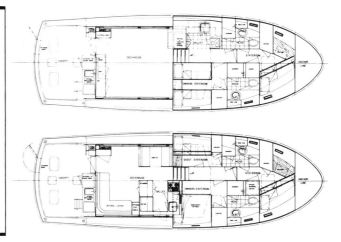

HATTERAS 50 CONVERTIBLE (NEW)

The newest Hatteras 50 — third in the company's three decades of building tournament-level sportfishermen — replaced the very popular 52 Convertible in the Hatteras lineup in 1991. The hull is a stretched version of the 48 Convertible with 8° of deadrise at the transom. A handsome boat with a stepped sheer and raked bridge, the Hatteras 50's standard three-stateroom, galley-up floorplan includes two full heads and a very comfortable midships master suite. This is a much-improved layout from the earlier Hatteras 48 C. By employing lighter woods and a cut-down galley, the deckhouse has a surprisingly open feeling. Note that a galley-down, two-stateroom floorplan is optional. Additional features include cockpit access to the engine room (with near-standing headroom), a huge flybridge, underwater exhausts, and five-bladed props. Performance is good, but at a price. To achieve a 26–27 knot cruising speed the Hatteras 50 requires optional 870-hp 12V71 diesels, since the standard 720-hp 8V92s provide only 23–24 knots at cruise and 26 knots wide open. At 60,000 lbs., the Hatteras 50 is no lightweight but she is a comfortable ride. ❑

SPECIFICATIONS

Length	50'10"
Length WL	NA
Beam	16'1"
Draft	5'9"
Weight	60,000#
Clearance	13'8"
Water	184 Gals.
Fuel	890 Gals.
Cockpit	135 Sq. Ft.
Hull Type	Modified-V
Designer	Hargrave

Production
1991–Current

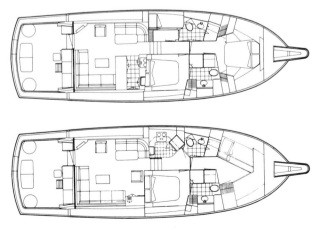

HATTERAS 52 CONVERTIBLE

Introduced in 1984, the Hatteras 52 Convertible is virtually identical to the earlier Hatteras 50 Convertible that she replaced but with a larger cockpit. A popular design with tremendous eye appeal (just over 200 were built), she's constructed on a modified-V bottom with a long keel below and balsa coring in the hullsides and superstructure. In 1987, the 52 was restyled on the outside to reflect the new look of Hatteras convertibles with a fresh deckhouse window treatment, solid front windshield, and a redesigned flybridge. Two floorplans were available— a galley-down layout with two staterooms or a more popular main deck galley arrangement with three staterooms. Both floorplans include two heads with stall showers. A teak interior was standard and light ash woodwork became optional in 1987. The large cockpit features a molded-in tackle center, transom door with gate, and an access door to the spacious engine room. A very successful model, the Hatteras 52 will cruise around 23 knots with GM 720-hp 8V92s and reach a top speed of 26 knots. Notably, she was the first Hatteras convertible to use side exhausts. ❏

SPECIFICATIONS

Length	52'0"
Beam	16'4"
Draft	5'0"
Weight	55,400#
Clearance	15'10"
Water	188 Gals.
Fuel	1,068 Gals.
Cockpit	153 Sq. Ft.
Hull Type	Modified-V
Designer	J. Hargrave

Production
1984–91

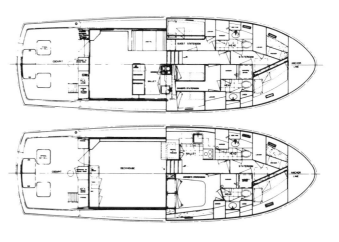

HATTERAS 52 COCKPIT MY

Essentially a Hatteras 48 MY with a cockpit, the 52 CMY is a good-looking design with a modern profile and better-than-average performance. Her modified-V hull is balsa-cored from the chines up and features a fairly steep 14° of deadrise at the transom — a deeper "V" than most previous Hatteras designs. She also has an innovative (and quiet) split exhaust system with side ports for idling and larger underwater ports for speeds above 1,300 rpm. Her galley-down, three-stateroom floorplan is the same as the Hatteras 48's with contemporary teak or light ash wood-work and three *full* heads. An optional two-stateroom layout trades out the aft guest stateroom and one head for a drastically enlarged master suite. Additional features include a spacious engine room, a huge afterdeck with plenty of space for outdoor furnishings, wide sidedecks, standard arch and hardtop, and lounge seating for eight on the flybridge. The cockpit is very small but at least suitable for line handling duties. With standard 720-hp 8V92s the Hatteras 52 Cockpit MY will cruise at a respectable 20–21 knots and reach 24 knots wide open. ❑

SPECIFICATIONS

Length	52'9"
Length WL	NA
Beam	16'0"
Draft	5'0"
Weight	66,000#
Clearance	16'9"
Water	170 Gals.
Fuel	994 Gals.
Hull Type	Modified-V
Designer	Hatteras

Production
1990–Current

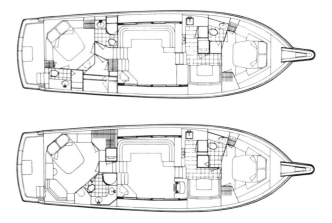

HATTERAS 53 CONVERTIBLE

Until she was retired from the Hatteras fleet in 1980, the 53 Convertible was the standard for over-50' production sportfishing yachts. Her long foredeck and sweeping sheer give the 53 Convertible the low-profile appearance of a thoroughbred sportfisherman, and her massive cockpit has never been improved upon for design and fishability. Indeed, this boat is so well proportioned that she must be seen up close to fully appreciate her size. There have been several three-stateroom, galley-up layouts used in the 53 including a popular U-shaped galley to port with separate under-counter refrigeration. An alternate two-stateroom floorplan has the galley located forward of the dinette in the companionway. Significant updates include increased fuel and prop pockets in 1976 and a restyled flybridge in 1977. A heavy and comfortable boat offshore (but with a sometimes-wet ride), the GM 12V71Ns cruise the Hatteras 53 around 17 knots with a top speed of 20 knots. The 12V71TIs and 8V92TIs provide cruising speeds around 20 knots and a top speed of 23. The Hatteras 53 Convertible remains a popular boat with experienced anglers. ❏

SPECIFICATIONS

Length......................53'7"
Length WL................48'3"
Beam.......................16'0"
Draft ....4'0"
Weight ....61,000#
Clearance ....15'2"
Water.................250 Gals.
Fuel..........950/1100 Gals.
Cockpit............147 Sq. Ft.
Hull Type.........Modified-V
Designer ....J. Hargrave

Production
1969–80

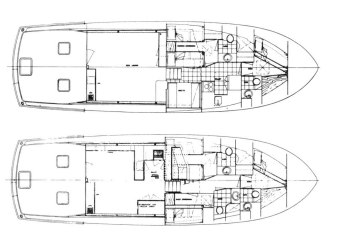

HATTERAS 53 MOTOR YACHT

Over the years some designs have succeeded so well in the marketplace that they have earned the distinction of industry classics. Such a boat is the Hatteras 53 Motor Yacht. Only recently taken out of production after nearly two decades, the Hatteras 53 MY became the standard by which other motor yachts in her size range were measured. Her bi-level, three-stateroom/three-head floorplan is considered ideal in a motor yacht of this size, and the separate engine rooms have become a Hatteras trademark. Notable updates to the 53 MY over the years include the addition of stall showers to the aft guest head and forward head in 1975, a redesigned lower-profile flybridge in 1977, an optional walkaround queen bed in the master stateroom in 1978, and an increase in the fuel capacity (to 700 gals.) in 1980. Early models with the GM 8V71N diesels will cruise at 13 knots and reach 16 knots top. The larger 8V71TIs (and the later [1985] 6V92TAs) improve the cruising speed to around 16 knots with a top speed of 19 knots. Resale values for Hatteras 53 Motor Yachts are very strong in all markets. ❏

SPECIFICATIONS

Length	53'1"
Length WL	NA
Beam	15'10"
Draft	4'0"
Weight	55,000#
Clearance	18'6"
Water	245 Gals.
Fuel	550/600/700 Gals.
Hull Type	Modified-V
Designer	J. Hargrave

Production
1969–88

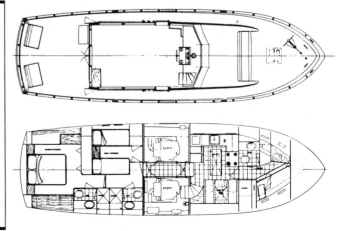

HATTERAS 53 YACHT FISHERMAN

While never achieving the widespread popularity of the larger 58 Yacht Fisherman, the Hatteras 53 Yacht Fisherman nevertheless combines all the comforts of a motor yacht with the added versatility of a cockpit. Interestingly, the 53 YF was withdrawn from production in 1981 only to be reintroduced in 1986 with an enlarged flybridge, updated interior decor, and the new GM 6V92TA diesels. Constructed on the same hull as the Hatteras 53 Motor Yacht and Convertible models, the 53 Yacht Fisherman shares their reputation for being a wet ride offshore. She's available with a choice of two- or three-stateroom interior floorplans with the three-stateroom layout being the most popular. It's worth noting, however, that the owner's cabin in the two-stateroom version is extremely spacious. As with most Hatteras motor yachts, the engine rooms are split by the central passageway leading aft from the galley. With the early GM 8V71TI diesels or the later 6V92TAs, the cruising speed of the Hatteras 53 YF is around 16–17 knots. The fuel capacity was significantly increased in 1980. ❏

SPECIFICATIONS

Length	52'11"
Length WL	47'3"
Beam	15'10"
Draft	4'0"
Weight	55,000#
Clearance	18'6"
Water	235 Gals.
Fuel	825/1,015 Gals.
Hull Type	Modified-V
Designer	J. Hargrave

Production
1978–81, 1986–87

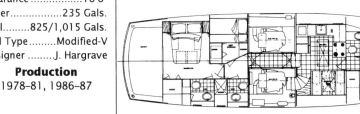

HATTERAS

HATTERAS 53 EXTENDED DECKHOUSE MY

Featuring a completely restyled superstructure from that of the venerable Hatteras 53 Motor Yacht, the Hatteras 53 Extended Deckhouse challenged the older model in buyer popularity soon after she was introduced in 1983. Aside from the dramatic improvement in exterior styling (including a bold new curved windshield), the 53 ED features an extended, full-width main salon with an inside bridge access ladder. Rather than having the lower helm open to the salon area, the 53 ED has an enclosed wheelhouse for salon privacy. The expanded salon dimensions (174 sq. ft. vs. the 53 MY's 112 sq. ft.) create a huge entertainment area for a boat of this size. The walkaround sidedecks of the 53 MY are eliminated in the ED, but a small open-air afterdeck is provided for line handling requirements. The ED's belowdeck floorplan is the same as the 53 Motor Yacht with three staterooms, three heads, and separate engine rooms. GM 6V92TA diesels replaced the 8V71TIs as standard in 1985. Both engines will cruise the Hatteras 53 Extended Deckhouse MY around 16 knots. ❑

SPECIFICATIONS

Length	53'1"
Length WL	NA
Beam	15'10"
Draft	4'0"
Weight	57,000#
Clearance	17'2"
Water	287 Gals.
Fuel	700 Gals.
Hull Type	Modified-V
Designer	J. Hargrave

Production
1983–89

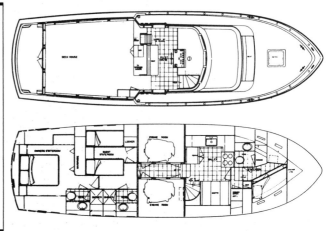

HATTERAS 54 MOTOR YACHT

The Hatteras 54 MY was the first of the "new look" Hatteras motor yachts when she was introduced in 1985. Designed to replace the aging 53 Motor Yacht in the Hatteras fleet, the 54 was built on a newly designed, balsa-cored hull with increased beam and propeller pockets below. Most agree that the 54 MY is a decidedly good-looking boat with her curved wind-shield and rakish, Eurostyle profile. The accommodations are equally well arranged around a practical and roomy floorplan. The lower helm is open to the main salon for an uninterrupted wheelhouse view from bow to stern. The galley is down, and the belowdeck layout includes three staterooms (each with private head and stall shower) and separate walk-in engine rooms. Outside, the semi-enclosed afterdeck is fitted with wing doors and extended windshields for weather protection while a bridge overhang shelters the walkaround sidedecks. Powered by 720-hp GM 8V92 diesels, the Hatteras 54 MY will cruise around 16–17 knots and reach 22 knots wide open. The earlier 650-hp versions cruise around 15 knots. ❏

SPECIFICATIONS

Length	54'9"
Length WL	NA
Beam	17'6"
Draft	4'2"
Weight	62,500#
Clearance	21'3"
Water	250 Gals.
Fuel	800 Gals.
Hull Type	Modified-V
Designer	J. Hargrave

Production
1985–88

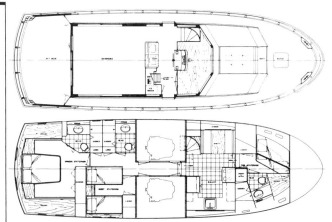

HATTERAS

HATTERAS 54 EXTENDED DECKHOUSE MY

The Hatteras 54 EDMY is a maxi-volume luxury yacht with sleek Mediterranean styling and plenty of eye appeal. By eliminating the sidedecks and moving the salon bulkhead aft, the living quarters and entertainment capabilities of the 54 ED are dramatically increased from the original 54 MY model. Hatteras has gone beyond just improving the salon size; this is an all-new interior layout as well. Gone is the galley-down approach so common in Hatteras motor yacht interiors. Instead, the 54 EDMY has a canted U-shaped galley in the salon with under-counter refrigeration hidden beneath a serving bar. Design changes on the lower level are equally impressive. Unlike most Hatteras motor yachts, the 54 ED has a full-width engine room rather than split compartments. Where the original 54 MY has three staterooms, the EDMY has four — three with walkaround double berths — in what is surely one of the most efficient floorplans to be seen in an under-60' yacht. The new and improved Eurostyle ash interior is completely impressive throughout. With 720-hp 8V92 diesels, the Hatteras 54 EDMY will cruise around 16–17 knots.❏

SPECIFICATIONS

Length	54'9"
Length WL	NA
Beam	17'6"
Draft	4'9"
Weight	76,000#
Clearance	20'11"
Water	250 Gals.
Fuel	1,014 Gals.
Hull Type	Modified-V
Designer	J. Hargrave

Production
1989–Current

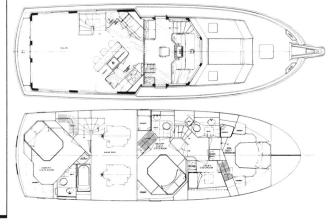

HATTERAS

HATTERAS 54 CONVERTIBLE

The Hatteras 54 — the replacement boat for the popular Hatteras 55 Convertible — is a completely impressive sportfisherman with the luxurious interior accommodations of a fair-size motor yacht. A handsome boat with a super-aggressive profile, stylish (oversize) bridge, and the rakish step-down sheer found in all of the newer Hatteras convertibles, she's built on an all-new hull with balsa coring in the hullsides and 9° deadrise aft. Perhaps the most impressive feature of the Hatteras 54 is her innovative three-stateroom interior with an incredibly open deckhouse and the largest master stateroom seen in a convertible this size. The diagonal galley configuration *really* opens up the salon and adds considerable living and entertaining space. Additional features include an immense flybridge, a helm console designed to flush-mount all necessary electronics, and a spacious walk-in engine room with near-standing headroom. No racehorse, standard 870-hp 12V71s cruise the Hatteras 54 at 22 knots with a top speed of about 24–25 knots. Optional 1,040hp 12V92s will cruise around 25 knots and reach 28+ knots top. ❏

SPECIFICATIONS

Length	54'11"
Beam	17'4"
Draft	5'10"
Weight	70,000#
Clearance	14'8"
Water	200 Gals.
Fuel	1,320 Gals.
Cockpit	157 Sq. Ft.
Hull Type	Modified-V
Designer	Hatteras

Production
1991–Current

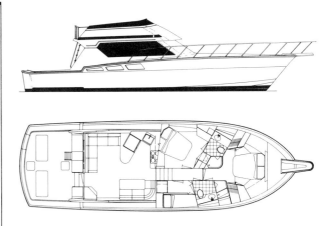

HATTERAS 55 CONVERTIBLE

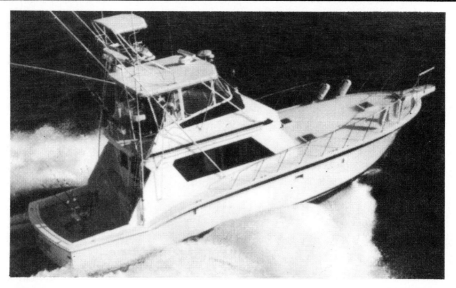

The Hatteras 55 Convertible was introduced in 1980 to bridge the gap between the then-new 50 Convertible and the existing Hatteras 60 Convertible. Her broad, double-chined hull is cored from the waterline up and features extensive internal supports. In 1987, the front windshield was glassed over and the cabin windows and flybridge were restyled in keeping with the current new look of the Hatteras convertibles. Two accommodation plans were offered, with the three-stateroom, galley/dinette-up layout being the more popular. The cockpit is fitted with a standard tackle center and transom door with gate and features direct access to the 55's spacious stand-up engine room. (Note that the air intakes for the engine room are located below the cockpit coaming.) The flybridge on the Hatteras 55 Convertible is huge. GM 12V71TIs were standard from the beginning with high-performance versions available since 1982. Performance with the 650-hp 12V71s is 19–20 knots at cruise and 23 knots wide open. Later models with the 870-hp versions cruise at 23+ knots and reach a top speed of 26 knots. ❑

SPECIFICATIONS

Length	55'8"
Length WL	50'2"
Beam	17'6"
Draft	4'10"
Weight	70,000#
Clearance	16'8"
Water	380 Gals.
Fuel	1,285 Gals.
Cockpit	158 Sq. Ft.
Hull Type	Modified-V
Designer	J. Hargrave

Production
1980–89

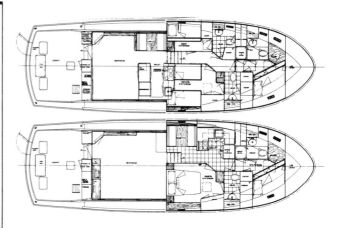

HATTERAS 56 MOTOR YACHT

The Hatteras 56 Motor Yacht is notable in that she was the first Hatteras to use the then-new 18'2"-wide double chine hull design — the same hull mold later used in the production of a dozen Hatteras designs, including the new Hatteras 70 MY. As it developed, the Hatteras 56 was the smallest of all that followed. Wide in the beam, the interior accommodations are quite expansive. Indeed, the spacious mid-level galley/dinette area has the dimensions of the average home kitchen. The lower helm is completely open to the main salon area, and stall showers are provided for each of the two guest staterooms. A corridor dividing the engine rooms leads to the private master stateroom aft. (Interestingly, most Hatteras motor yachts up to this time had two staterooms, not one, aft of the engine rooms.) The flybridge on the Hatteras 56 is huge with bench seating for as many as ten. With standard 8V92TIs, she'll cruise at 15–16 knots and reach 18 knots top. In 1981, a 6' cockpit extension was added to create the 61 Cockpit MY which turned out to be a very popular model. ❑

SPECIFICATIONS

Length	56'3"
Length WL	NA
Beam	18'2"
Draft	4'11"
Weight	74,000#
Clearance	18'10"
Water	350 Gals.
Fuel	1,020 Gals.
Hull Type	Modified-V
Designer	J. Hargrave

Production
1980–85

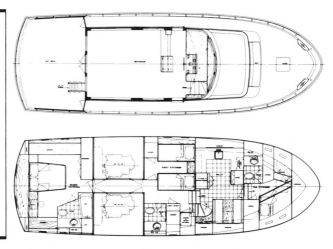

HATTERAS

HATTERAS 58 TRIPLE CABIN MY

The Flagship of the Fleet at the 1971 Miami Boat Show, the Hatteras 58 Triple Cabin was the next step up in size from the Hatteras 53 MY until she was replaced with the 58 Motor Yacht model in 1977. Built on a stretched 53' hull of solid fiberglass construction, the 58 TCMY originally featured an expansive afterdeck area partially protected by wing doors and extended side windshields. The lower helm was enclosed and separated from the aft deck by a fixed bulkhead. This pilot-house/semi-enclosed aft deck arrangement was revised in 1975 when the afterdeck was fully enclosed with only a small line-handling platform left at the stern. In this later floorplan, the lower helm is open to the upper salon area. Notable features of the Hatteras 58 TCMY are the large staterooms, big foredeck, and wide walkaround sidedecks. The bridge is arranged with the helm forward and guest seating port and starboard. The standard GM 8V71Ns will provide a 13-knot cruising speed and the larger 12V71Ns cruise the Hatteras 58 TCMY around 16 knots with a top speed of about 19 knots. ❑

SPECIFICATIONS

Length	58'5"
Length WL	NA
Beam	15'10"
Draft	4'0"
Weight	63,000#
Clearance	18'8"
Water	250 Gals.
Fuel	850 Gals.
Hull Type	Modified-V
Designer	J. Hargrave

Production
1971–76

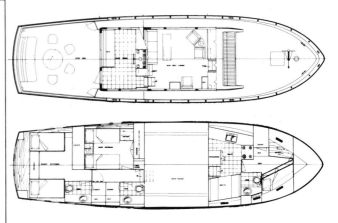

HATTERAS 58 YACHT FISHERMAN

The Hatteras 58 Yacht Fisherman is essentially a 53 Motor Yacht with the addition of a 5' cockpit. She was introduced in 1970 — a year after the Hatteras 53 Motor Yacht — and enjoyed a long and very successful production run during the next twelve years. Inside, her accommodation plan is the same as that found in the 53 MY. Significant improvements came in 1975 with the addition of stall showers in the aft guest and the forward head compartments. The previously optional GM 8V71TI diesels also became standard in 1975. In 1977, the fly-bridge was redesigned, and the fuel and water capacities were each increased in the 1980 models. The aft deck is sheltered by a bridge overhang and fitted with wing doors for spray protection. Note that the Hatteras 58 Cockpit MY (1977–81) differs from the 58 Yacht Fisherman in its extended deckhouse and four-stateroom, galley-up interior layout. Early 58 Yacht Fishermen with 8V71Ns cruise around 13 knots, and the later models with the 8V71TIs cruise at 17 knots. Still a very popular yacht, resale values are excellent. ❏

SPECIFICATIONS

Length	58'4"
Beam	15'10"
Draft	4'9"
Weight	62,500#
Clearance	18'6"
Water	250/300 Gals.
Fuel	825/1,015 Gals.
Cockpit	60 Sq. Ft.
Hull Type	Modified-V
Designer	J. Hargrave

Production
1970–82

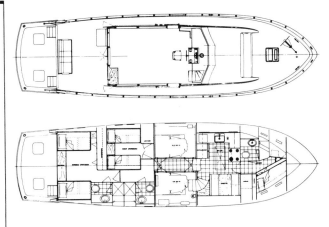

HATTERAS 58 LONG RANGE CRUISER

The Hatteras 58 LRC was the first of four Hatteras trawler-style yachts (the 42, 48 and 65 LRCs followed) built from the mid-1970s through the early 1980s. A serious cruising yacht, the 58's pilothouse is fully enclosed and separated from the main salon by the galley. Across from the galley is a convenient on-deck powder room with sink and toilet. On the lower level, the master stateroom is divided from the forward sections of the boat by an expansive engine room. Both forward staterooms are served by separate heads, each with a stall shower. Outside, wing doors protect the covered aft deck from spray and the small cockpit is fitted with a transom door. The spacious flybridge is accessed from a stairway in the pilothouse. Designed for efficient operation and possessing transatlantic range, the 58 LRC burns only 6 gph at 8.5 knots and 8–9 gph at her 9.5-knot hull speed with standard GM 4-71 diesels. Larger 6-71Ns were optional and are considered desirable for the extra power. Heavily built, the Hatteras 58 LRC is a true go-anywhere cruising yacht. ❑

SPECIFICATIONS

Length	58'2"
Length WL	52'0"
Beam	17'11"
Draft	5'10"
Weight	90,000#
Clearance	18'9"
Water	440/540 Gals.
Fuel	2,390 Gals.
Hull Type	Displacement
Designer	J. Hargrave

Production
1975–81

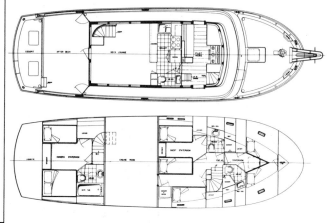

HATTERAS 58 MOTOR YACHT (EARLY)

The Hatteras 58 Motor Yacht replaced the 58 Triple Cabin in the Hatteras fleet in 1977. (Note that an all-new Hatteras 58 Motor Yacht came out in 1985.) Featuring a full-width salon and offered with or without an enclosed aft deck, the Hatteras 58 Motor Yacht was introduced as the next step up from the Hatteras 53 MY. Built on an extended 53-foot hull, the 58 has an enclosed wheelhouse forward of the main salon. A three-stateroom, three-head floorplan with the galley and dinette down from the wheelhouse was standard. An optional (and more popular) four-stateroom layout relocated the galley up to the deckhouse level directly abaft the wheelhouse. Other features of the 58 Motor Yacht include separate stand-up engine rooms, a full-size tub in the owner's stateroom, and a huge flybridge with a reverse venturi windshield and L-shaped lounge seating. GM 8V92TI diesels replaced the original 8V71TIs in 1978 and will cruise at 17–18 knots with a top speed of about 21 knots. An excellent boat for entertaining and cruising, the Hatteras 58 MY still remains popular today. ❏

SPECIFICATIONS

Length	58'3"
Length WL	NA
Beam	15'10"
Draft	4'9"
Weight	74,000#
Clearance	16'10"
Water	300 Gals.
Fuel	775 Gals.
Hull Type	Modified-V
Designer	J. Hargrave

Production
1977–81

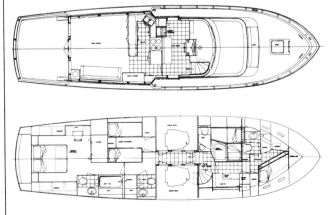

HATTERAS 58 COCKPIT MY

Easily confused with the more popular 58 Yacht Fisherman, the Hatteras 58 Cockpit MY can be identified by her full-width salon and lack of walka-round sidedecks. She's built on a stretched version of the Hatteras 53 MY hull with solid fiberglass construction and a deep keel below. With her enlarged salon area the 58 Cockpit MY also offered an optional galley-up, four-stateroom floorplan (which the 58 YF never had) in addition to the standard galley-down, three-stateroom arrangement. (The galley-down layout outsold the galley-up flooplan by 3 to 1.) Teak paneling and cabinetry are used throughout and both floorplans carry one guest stateroom aft of the separate engine rooms. Port and starboard deck access doors are provided in the enclosed wheelhouse. Additional features include a spacious master stateroom with walk-in closets, transom door and washdown, enclosed wheelhouse with bridge access, small afterdeck, and a modern helm console on the flybridge with dinghy storage aft. With standard 550-hp 8V92s the Hatteras 58 Cockpit MY will cruise around 16 knots and deliver a top speed of 19 knots. ❑

SPECIFICATIONS

Length	58'2"
Length WL	NA
Beam	15'10"
Draft	4'9"
Weight	73,000#
Clearance	21'2"
Water	300 Gals.
Fuel	1,085 Gals.
Hull Type	Modified-V
Designer	Hargrave

Production
1978–81

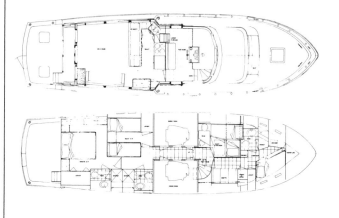

HATTERAS 58 MOTOR YACHT

The most recent Hatteras 58 Motor Yacht (the earlier 58 MY was built on a single-chine hull in the late 1970s) is basically a stretched version of the previous 56 Motor Yacht — the boat she replaced in the Hatteras lineup in 1985. A handsome design, the new 58 has a wider beam than the original 58 model (18'2" vs. 15'10") while retaining the traditional Hatteras motor yacht profile. Her galley-down, three-stateroom layout offered a choice of twin berths or a queen-size berth in the master stateroom, and both guest and forward staterooms are fitted with a stall shower in the head. Throughout, the decor is notably lighter than in previous Hatteras models with greater use made of white, high-pressure laminates in the galley and designer fabrics in the salon and staterooms. The flybridge, stretching for more than half of the boat's LOA, is ideal for large parties. With the standard 8V92TIs, the cruising speed of the Hatteras 58 MY is around 18 knots and the top speed is 21. Also introduced in 1985, the popular Hatteras 63 Cockpit MY is the same boat with a cockpit extension. ❏

SPECIFICATIONS

Length	58'8"
Length WL	NA
Beam	18'2"
Draft	4'11"
Weight	79,000#
Clearance	18'10"
Water	350 Gals.
Fuel	1030 Gals.
Hull Type	Modified-V
Designer	J. Hargrave

Production
1985–87

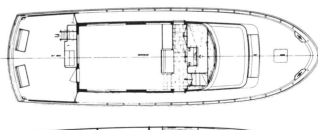

HATTERAS

HATTERAS 58 CONVERTIBLE

The Hatteras 58 Convertible is an in-house design built on a heavy modified-V hull (10° deadrise aft) with cored hullsides and a distinctive step-down sheer. A good-looking boat, her three-stateroom, three head floorplan is arranged with a roomy midships owner's cabin located to starboard, a walkaround queen-size berth forward, and stall showers in each head. The extravagant, high-style salon of the 58 (with a choice of teak or light ash woodwork) is by far the most wide-open and spacious to be found in any Hatteras convertible under 60 feet. Outside, the immense cockpit is set up for tournament-level fishing and includes an oversize transom door and gate, live baitwell, complete tackle center, direct engine room access, and a waist-level fish box built into the transom coaming. The spacious two station flybridge can be fully enclosed and features a beautiful wrap-around electronics console at the helm. A good performer, standard 1,040-hp 12V92 diesels cruise the Hatteras 58 at 22 knots (about 80 gph) with a top speed of 26 knots. More popular 1,350-hp 16V-92s will cruise at a fast 28–29 knots (140 gph) with a top speed of 32 knots. ❑

SPECIFICATIONS

Length	58'10"
Beam	17'9"
Draft	5'9"
Weight	92,000#
Clearance	22'4"
Water	250 Gals.
Fuel	1,660 Gals.
Cockpit	175 Sq. Ft.
Hull Type	Modified-V
Designer	Hatteras

Production
1990–Current

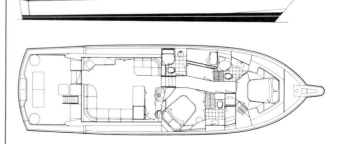

HATTERAS 60 CONVERTIBLE

The Hatteras 60 Convertible was for several years the largest sportfisherman in the Hatteras fleet. Over 100 were built before she was replaced with the new Hatteras 65 Convertible in 1987. Offered with a fully enclosed and air-conditioned flybridge, the 60 Convertible features a luxurious three-stateroom, three-head layout with the galley and dinette located on the deckhouse level. A separate utility room forward of the engine compartment houses the air-conditioning compressors, optional washer/dryer, and a deep-freeze with room to spare.

Notable features include a deep keel for prop protection, fore and aft flybridge helm stations, and a queen berth in the master stateroom. Her massive cockpit (175 sq. ft.) provides direct access to the spacious, stand-up engine room. The high-performance Hatteras 60 model was first offered in 1982 with balsa coring in the hullsides and beefed-up internal strengthening. A comfortable boat offshore, the standard 650-hp 12V71s will cruise the Hatteras 60 Convertible at 17–18 knots, and the high-performance 825-hp versions cruise around 21 knots. ❑

SPECIFICATIONS

Length	60'11"
Beam	18'0"
Draft	4'11"
Weight	82,000#
Clearance	17'1"
Water	490 Gals.
Fuel	1555 Gals.
Cockpit	175 Sq. Ft.
Hull Type	Modified-V
Designer	J. Hargrave

Production
1977–86

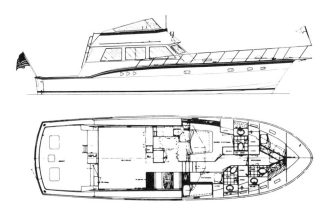

HATTERAS 60 MOTOR YACHT

The Hatteras 60 Motor Yacht (and the 67 Cockpit MY) borrows heavily from the contemporary styling characteristics of the Hatteras 54 MY introduced in 1985. Actually, the Hatteras 60 is a Eurostyled version of the earlier Hatteras 58 Motor Yacht which she replaced and the floorplans are basically the same. Obviously designed for luxurious cruising, the 60 MY shares the same three-stateroom, three full head layout with the galley-down and the helm open to the main salon. The salon measures 15'x12' — an open but not full-width layout which still leaves room outside for wide sidedecks. A door in the salon bulkhead leads to the covered aft deck, where wing doors and extended side windshields provide protection from the weather and spray. Unlike the earlier 58 Motor Yacht, access to the flybridge in the Hatteras 60 is from inside the wheelhouse (much more practical and convenient). The bridge has a stylish aft-raking windshield with plenty of guest seating aft of the helm. A respectable performer, 720-hp 8V92s are standard in the Hatteras 60 Motor Yacht. The cruising speed is around 18 knots and the top speed is 21 knots. ❏

SPECIFICATIONS

Length......................60'9"
Length WL...................NA
Beam.......................18'2"
Draft ....5'0"
Weight ....86,000#
Clearance ....20'9"
Water.................335 Gals.
Fuel ....1,033 Gals.
Hull Type.........Modified-V
Designer ....J. Hargrave

Production
1988–Current

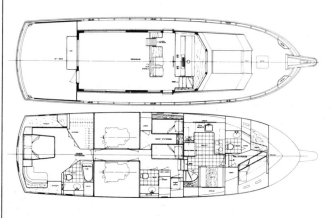

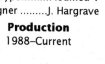

HATTERAS

HATTERAS 60 EXTENDED DECKHOUSE MY

It isn't just the extended deckhouse that sets the Hatteras 60 EDMY apart from the 60 Motor Yacht. She's an entirely different yacht with an on-deck galley, four staterooms, and a full-beam engine room rather than separate walk-in rooms typical of earlier Hatteras motor yachts. Although the extended deckhouse layout widens the salon dimensions, it's notable that the 60 EDMY still has sidedecks — something most extended deckhouse models sadly lack. By eliminating the large open-air afterdeck found in the 60 MY, the EDMY has a spacious 200 sq. ft. deck-house with the galley and dinette wide open to the salon. The wheelhouse, with direct access to the flybridge, is completely enclosed in this layout. A staircase in the salon leads down to a spacious master stateroom and engine room access door. Both the VIP and forward staterooms have double berths and all three heads are fitted with stall showers. Standard 720-hp 8V92s will deliver a cruising speed of 16 knots (19 knots top) and the optional 870-hp 12V71s will cruise the Hatteras 60 EDMY around 18–19 knots and reach 21 knots wide open. ❏

SPECIFICATIONS

Length	60'9"
Length WL	NA
Beam	18'2"
Draft	5'1"
Weight	87,000#
Clearance	21'2"
Water	335 Gals.
Fuel	1,033 Gals.
Hull Type	Modified-V
Designer	Hargrave

Production
1991–Current

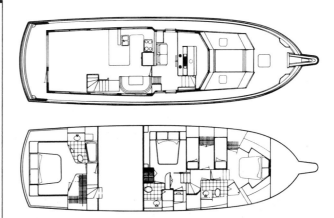

HATTERAS 61 MOTOR YACHT

Noted as having been one of the more popular Hatteras motor yacht models, the 61 MY is constructed on the same hull as the Hatteras 61 Cockpit MY. She was designed as the next step up from the Hatteras 56 MY (1980–85) and features an enlarged four-stateroom layout with two dinettes and four heads. A fixed partition and privacy door separate the salon from the on-deck galley and dinette with another door leading forward into the fully enclosed pilothouse. Utilizing nearly all of her wide 18'2" beam, the teak-paneled living and entertaining areas are expansive indeed. Double doors in the salon bulkhead open onto the small covered aft deck platform, which is primarily used for dockside line handling. The master stateroom is particularly spacious and includes a walk-in wardrobe as well as a full tub in the adjoining private head. Note that the owner's stateroom is the only cabin aft of the separate engine rooms. The flybridge on this boat is huge. Powered with 650-hp GM 12V71 diesels, the Hatteras 61 MY will cruise at 17–18 knots and reach a top speed of around 21 knots. ❑

SPECIFICATIONS

Length	61'3"
Length WL	55'9"
Beam	18'2"
Draft	4'11"
Weight	82,000#
Clearance	18'10"
Water	350 Gals.
Fuel	1,150 Gals.
Hull Type	Modified-V
Designer	J. Hargrave

Production
1981–84

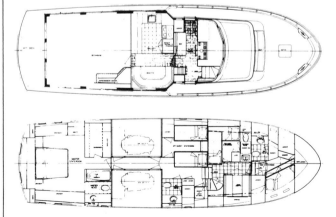

HATTERAS

HATTERAS 61 COCKPIT MY

The 61 Cockpit Motor Yacht has proven to be one of the more popular Hatteras designs since her introduction in 1981. She's basically a stretched-out version of the Hatteras 56 MY (1980–85) with the addition of a 5' cockpit; the hull is the same and so is the three-stateroom, galley-down interior layout. Aside from the fact that a cockpit adds great utility to any motor yacht, the additional length gives the 61 CMY a more attractive profile (and better performance) than the 56 MY. Designed for comfortable cruising and entertaining, the expansive salon has large wraparound tinted windows for superb outside visibility. The helm station is open to the salon and separated by a waist-high divider, while double doors in the after bulkhead lead to the covered afterdeck with extended windshields on both sides, wing doors, and bridge access ladder. A transom door is fitted in the cockpit for fishing and easy stern boarding. Standard power for the Hatteras 61 Cockpit MY is a pair of GM 12V71s for a cruising speed of around 18 knots and a top speed of 21 knots. ❑

SPECIFICATIONS

Length	61'3"
Length WL	55'9"
Beam	18'2"
Draft	4'11"
Weight	85,000#
Clearance	18'10"
Water	350 Gals.
Fuel	1,150 Gals.
Hull Type	Modified-V
Designer	J. Hargrave

Production
1981–84

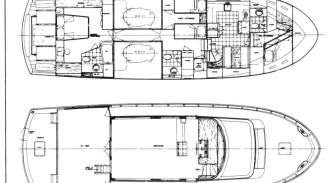

HATTERAS 63 MOTOR YACHT

A good-selling boat for Hatteras (although production lasted only two years), the 63 MY is notable because of her galley-up layout and spacious full-width salon dimensions — desirable features in many of today's modern motor yacht floorplans. The 63 MY (and her sistership, the 68 Cockpit MY) came with a spacious four-stateroom, four head interior with a full-width, extended salon and an enclosed galley/dinette located aft of the wheelhouse. The owner's stateroom in this floorplan is exceptionally large with a separate dressing area, walk-in wardrobes, several dressers, and a full-size tub in the head. There are port and starboard deck doors in the private wheelhouse and the interior s fully paneled and finished with teak woodwork. The maindeck salon of the 63 MY is absolutely enormous with more than 275 sq. ft. of living space — enough to create a formal dining area forward without intruding on the salon's expansive entertainment facilities. A small aft deck provides space for line handling. With standard 650-hp 12V71s the 63 MY will cruise comfortably around 17 knots and reach a top speed of 20 knots. ❏

SPECIFICATIONS

Length	63'10"
Length WL	NA
Beam	18'2"
Draft	5'0"
Weight	92,000#
Clearance	21'3"
Fresh Water	350 Gals.
Fuel	1170 Gals.
Hull Type	Modified-V
Designer	J. Hargrave

Production
1986–87

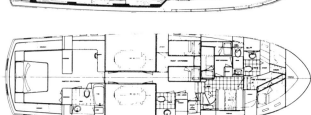

HATTERAS 63 COCKPIT MY

The Hatteras 63 CMY was developed by adding a cockpit to the popular 58 Motor Yacht. The fuel capacity was increased by 140 gallons, larger (and thirstier) 12V71 diesels increase her cruising speed from 18 to 19 knots, and the added versatility of the cockpit speaks for itself. Hull construction is solid glass and a long keel provides prop protection. The accommodations are virtually the same in both boats with the exception of the master stateroom, where the 63 has a little more square footage. (Most 63s have a king-size bed in the master but twin singles were available.) The two guest staterooms are forward of the separate engine rooms and all three heads are fitted with stall showers. The galley and dinette are down leaving the entire upper deck level for the wheelhouse and salon. Those who actually *use* their boats will appreciate the advantages of the 63 Cockpit MYs full walkaround decks and spacious aft deck. The flybridge is huge with adequate space for storing water toys and a Whaler. Note that the lower helm is open to the salon and not separated with a bulkhead. ❏

SPECIFICATIONS

Length	63'8"
Length WL	NA
Beam	18'2"
Draft	4'11"
Weight	79,000#
Clearance	18'10"
Water	375 Gals.
Fuel	1,170 Gals.
Hull Type	Modified-V
Designer	Hargrave

Production
1985–87

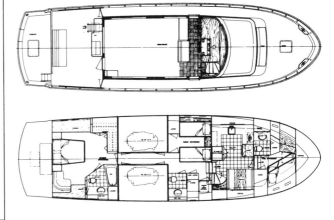

HATTERAS 64 MOTOR YACHT

The Hatteras 64 Motor Yacht is remembered as the only Hatteras ever to use V-drives. Consequently, the 64 hasn't been an especially popular model although she is recognized for her good offshore handling characteristics. A roomy boat, her unusual four-stateroom interior layout has the owner's stateroom amidships (with a tub/shower in the head), two guest cabins aft, and the crew quarters forward. With the enclosed wheelhouse separated from the main salon by the galley, the owner's party can thus enjoy complete privacy from crew, day or night

(or vice versa). Twin doors in the salon's aft bulkhead open onto a covered, semi-enclosed afterdeck with wing doors and extended side windshields. Additional features include a concealed engine room access ladder in the salon, an inside stairway leading to the huge flybridge (which was restyled in 1977), and protected sidedecks. Standard GM 12V71TI diesels will cruise the Hatteras 64 Motor Yacht at 16–17 knots with a top speed of around 19 knots. Interestingly, the 64 is the only Hatteras ever built on this 18'4"-beam hull. ❏

SPECIFICATIONS

Length	64'1"
Length WL	NA
Beam	18'4"
Draft	5'0"
Weight	95,000#
Clearance	22'6"
Water	550 Gals.
Fuel	1440 Gals.
Hull Type	Modified-V
Designer	J. Hargrave

Production
1975–81

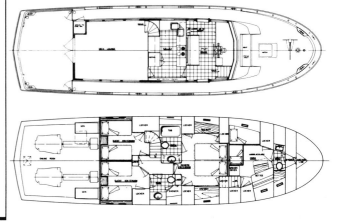

HATTERAS 65 LONG RANGE CRUISER

The largest of the Hatteras Long Range Cruisers, the 65 LRC was built on a stretched 58 LRC hull — a displacement design with a full keel and rounded bilges that harden at the transom for stability. Hull construction is solid fiberglass, and at 114,000 lbs. the Hatteras 65 easily qualifies as a serious heavyweight. She features a spacious four-stateroom layout with a fully enclosed pilothouse and a deckhouse galley open to the main salon. A spiral teak stairway leads down to the extravagant owner's stateroom and nearby engine room access door. The 65 LRC was also offered with an optional extended deckhouse floorplan with the salon lengthened to include the aft deck, an enlarged pilothouse, and a convenient day head opposite the galley. Designed for all-weather long-range cruising, the curved protective bulwark on the foredeck provides protection against oncoming breaking seas. With a range of over 2,500 nautical miles, the Hatteras 65 Long Range Cruiser will cruise comfortably at her 10–knot hull speed burning only 9 gph with GM 6-71N diesels. ❏

SPECIFICATIONS

Length	65'0"
Length WL	58'8"
Beam	17'11"
Draft	4'10"
Weight	114,000#
Clearance	18'9"
Water	455 Gals.
Fuel	2,625 Gals.
Hull Type	Displacement
Designer	J. Hargrave

Production
1981–85

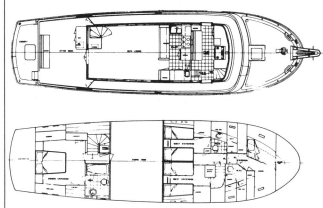

HATTERAS 65 MOTOR YACHT

The Hatteras 65 Motor Yacht was orig-inally designed as an enlarged ver-sion of the earlier Hatteras 63 MY with a new Eurostyle profile and the elimina-tion of the traditional Hatteras sheer stripe. Her full-width salon provides an extravagant 240 sq. ft. of living space at the expense of walkaround sidedecks. Originally offered with a traditional split engine room layout with four-state-rooms and heads (see Hatteras 70 CMY), an optional VIP floorplan was intro-duced in 1990 with a luxurious guest stateroom and a full-width engine room. For 1992 the now-standard VIP layout features an additional centerline queen forward and a rearranged master suite with his-and-hers heads aft. The gal-ley/dinette is separated from the salon and a small aft deck is provided for line handling. The upscale interior of the Hatteras 65 is available with either teak or light ash woodwork. Above, the enor-mous flybridge features an aft-raking windshield and U-shaped lounge seat-ing. Note that the Hatteras 70 Cockpit MY is the same boat with a cockpit extension. Standard 870-hp 12V71s will cruise the Hatteras 65 MY around 17 knots and reach 20 knots top. ❑

SPECIFICATIONS

Length	65'10"
Length WL	NA
Beam	18'2"
Draft	5'4"
Weight	99,000#
Clearance	21'5"
Water	350 Gals.
Fuel	1,170 Gals.
Hull Type	Modified-V
Designer	Jack Hargrave

Production
1988–Current

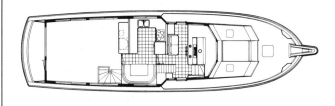

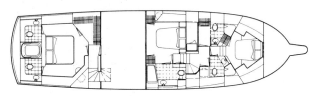

HATTERAS 65 CONVERTIBLE

A great-selling boat (over 75 have been built), the Hatteras 65 Convertible is the most popular 60-foot-plus sportfisherman ever built. She's a step up from the earlier Hatteras 60 Convertible — not only are her lines more aggressive, but the performance is improved as well. The 65's hull is derived from an extension of the mold used in the production of the Hatteras 60 with a finer entry and the addition of lightweight Divinycell coring in the hullsides. Her huge cockpit (among the largest in this size range) comes equipped with a transom door, in-deck livewell, tackle center with freezer, and an engine room access door. A second helm station is located abaft the optional flybridge enclosure for cockpit visibility. Below, the spacious three-stateroom layout is completely luxurious with a salon that many consider to be the ultimate in a production sportfisherman. Standard 1,035-hp 12V92s will cruise the Hatteras 65 Convertible around 23 knots. The optional 1,235-hp MTUs or 1,350-hp 16V92s will cruise at 27–28 knots and reach a top speed of 30+ knots. Note the huge engine room air intakes on the hullsides. ❏

SPECIFICATIONS

Length	65'5"
Beam	18'0"
Draft	5'10"
Weight	102,000#
Clearance	16'4"
Water	460 Gals.
Fuel	1,674 Gals.
Cockpit	183 Sq. Ft.
Hull Type	Modified-V
Designer	J. Hargrave

Production
1987–Current

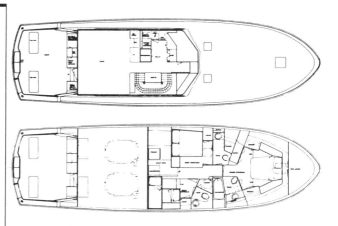

HATTERAS 67 COCKPIT MY

A beautifully proportioned yacht (she is, after all, our Cover Boat), the 67 CMY is basically a Hatteras 60 MY with a cockpit extension. This is the largest factory-installed cockpit found in any of the Hatteras CMY models built on the standard 18'2"-beam hull. Indeed, the extra hull length adds much to the profile of the 67 to say nothing of convenience and versatility. Beautiful as she is, the galley-down layout of the 67 CMY is considered by nany to be out-of-fashion in today's U.S. motor yacht market. (Galley-up floorplans have become the norm.) The standard layout has the wheelhouse separated from the salon by a low divider. The lower level floorplan is traditional for a Hatteras with two guest cabins forward and split engine rooms flanking the corridor leading aft to the (extravagant) master stateroom. Outside, there are full walkaround decks and a spacious semi-enclosed afterdeck with wing doors. Standard 770-hp 12V71s will cruise the 67 CMY 18 knots and reach around 21 knots top. Note that the newer Hatteras 67 Extended Deckhouse CMY has a four-stateroom, galley-up floorplan with an enlarged salon. ❏

SPECIFICATIONS

LOA	67'2"/67'8"
Length WL	NA
Beam	18'2"
Draft	4'11"/5'1"
Weight	90,000#
Clearance	20'3"
Water	375 Gals.
Fuel	1,170 Gals.
Hull Type	Modified-V
Designer	J. Hargrave

Production
1988-Current

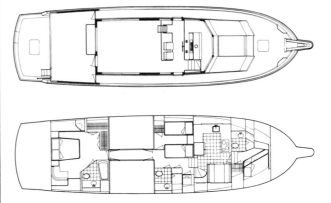

HATTERAS 67 EXTENDED DECKHOUSE CMY

The Hatteras 67 ED CMY has the distinction of being the smallest Hatteras *cockpit* model with the popular deckhouse galley floorplan. Basically, this is simply a Hatteras 60 Extended Deckhouse MY with a 7' cockpit extension. Heavily built with cored hullsides, a long keel, and modest deadrise aft, she retains the convenience of walkaround sidedecks although they're much narrower than in previous Hatteras models. Her extravagant galley-up, four-stateroom floorplan features light ash woodwork throughout and very generous guest accommodations. The dinette and galley are on the deckhouse level and open to the salon, while the wheelhouse — with its flybridge access — is separate. A curved salon staircase leads down to the master stateroom and engine room access door. A small afterdeck overlooks the cockpit and the flybridge dimensions are huge. Aside from the convenience and versatility provided by a cockpit, many feel that the extra hull length makes the 67 a better-looking yacht than the 60 EDMY. Standard 870-hp 12V71s will cruise at 17–18 knots and the optional 1,040-hp 12V92s cruise around 20 knots. ❏

SPECIFICATIONS

Length	67'2"
Length WL	NA
Beam	18'2"
Draft	5'3"
Weight	95,000#
Clearance	21'5"
Water	372 Gals.
Fuel	1,171 Gals.
Hull Type	Modified-V
Designer	Hargrave

Production
1991–Current

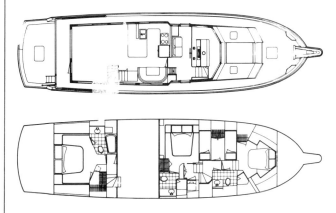

HATTERAS 68 COCKPIT MY

The Hatteras 68 CMY is basically a 63 MY with a cockpit extension. Seven of these yachts were built in her two years of production. The hull is solid fiberglass with a long keel below and the shafts were extended to the transom when the cockpit was added. It's interesting to note that Hatteras did not increase the fuel capacity in the 68 CMY as they have in other cockpit applications. Her four-stateroom floorplan follows the usual Hatteras configuration with a corridor leading aft to the master stateroom flanked on both sides by separate walk-in engine rooms. The spacious 275 sq. ft. full-width salon with its formal dining area and luxurious furnishings dominates the interior. The master suite is enormous with a king-size bed and an athwartships wardrobe (closet) dividing the living area to create a separate dressing room forward. Outside, a small covered afterdeck overlooks the cockpit. Needless to say, the flybridge is huge. Twin 770-hp 12V71 diesels will cruise the Hatteras 68 Cockpit MY at a respectable 17 knots with a top speed of around 19–20 knots. ❏

SPECIFICATIONS

Length	68'10"
Length WL	NA
Beam	18'2"
Draft	5'0"
Weight	96,500#
Clearance	21'3"
Water	350 Gals.
Fuel	1,170 Gals.
Hull Type	Modified-V
Designer	Hargrave

Production
1986–87

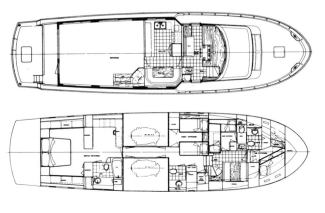

HATTERAS 70 MOTOR YACHT (EARLY)

The Hatteras 70 Motor Yacht was the largest fiberglass production yacht of her time when she was introduced back in 1971. With her classic motor yacht profile and impressive size, the Hatteras 70 is considered a handsome yacht even by today's standards. Because of her length, Hatteras had to open a new plant in New Bern, N.C., from which to launch her (the main Hatteras plant being some 250 miles inland). Designed to be captain-operated and maintained, the Hatteras 70 will accommodate the owner and a small party in three large staterooms aft of the engine room on the lower level. Crew quarters and galley areas are forward, thus affording owner and guests complete privacy. The floorplan arrangement features a spacious formal dining room detached from the galley and an enclosed wheelhouse forward of the main salon. The semi-enclosed afterdeck is fitted with wing doors and extended side windshields for weather protection. No lightweight, standard 12V71TI diesels will cruise the Hatteras 70 MY around 14 knots and provide a top speed of 17 knots. Fuel capacity was increased in 1980. ❏

SPECIFICATIONS

Length	70'2"
Length WL	NA
Beam	18'7"
Draft	5'0"
Weight	109,000#
Clearance	18'10"
Water	400 Gals.
Fuel	1,440/1,650 Gals.
Hull Type	Modified-V
Designer	J. Hargrave

Production
1971–81

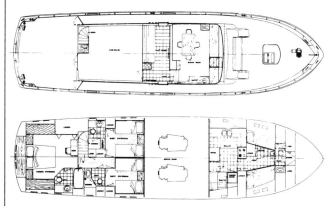

HATTERAS

HATTERAS 70 EXTENDED DECKHOUSE MY

The Hatteras 70 Extended Deckhouse Motor Yacht followed the original 70 Motor Yacht by six years in the Hatteras fleet. Built on the same modified-V hull, the EDMY continued in production until 1983. The Extended Deckhouse model has a completely different superstructure and flybridge profile than the Motor Yacht, with the ED's pilothouse set further forward. The result is a larger main salon with the galley located on the main deck level behind the wheelhouse. While the salon in the 70 ED is longer than in the 70 MY, the semi-enclosed afterdeck areas are similar in size. The crew quarters of the ED are enlarged as well with separate staterooms for a captain and two mates, a small galley and dinette, and direct engine room access. Owner and guest cabin accommodations are the same in both boats, with a spiral staircase leading down from the salon to the staterooms. A heavy boat, 12V71TI diesels will cruise the Hatteras 70 Extended Deckhouse MY around 14 knots and provide a top speed of 17 knots. Note that tuel capacity was increased in 1981. ❏

SPECIFICATIONS

Length	70'2"
Length WL	NA
Beam	18'7"
Draft	5'0"
Weight	109,000#
Clearance	18'10"
Water	400 Gals.
Fuel	1,440/1,650 Gals.
Hull Type	Modified-V
Designer	J. Hargrave

Production
1976–83

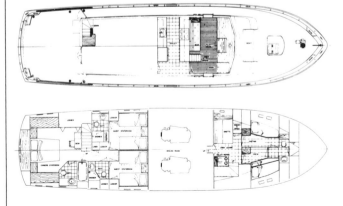

HATTERAS 70 MOTOR YACHT

A popular yacht, the Hatteras 70 MY has the largest superstructure ever to rest on the durable 18'2"-beam hull used in most large Hatteras motor yacht models since 1980. Her graceful profile and contemporary styling are strikingly similar to the smaller 65 MY with the additional 5 feet of length used to create a more spacious 24' salon and an enlarged master stateroom. While all Hatteras 70 MYs have been delivered with semi-custom interiors with four-staterooms as standard, the deckhouse galley layout provides a huge salon of extravagant proportions. The galley/ dinette is separate from the salon and a choice of teak or light ash woodwork is available. On the lower level there's a generous midships VIP cabin and an absolutely opulant owner's suite with a king-size bed, whirlpool tub, and private office/den. The standard salon arrangement offers a small aft deck, however a larger aft deck/smaller salon floorplan is optional. Sidedecks became available in 1990. Standard 870-hp 12V71s will cruise the Hatteras 70 MY at 18 knots and reach 21 knots top. Optional 1,040-hp 12V92 diesels cruise at 20 knots. ❑

SPECIFICATIONS

Length	70'11"
Length WL	NA
Beam	18'2"
Draft	5'6"
Weight	108,000#
Clearance	21'2"
Water	251 Gals.
Fuel	1,596 Gals.
Hull Type	Modified-V
Designer	Hargrave

Production
1988–Current

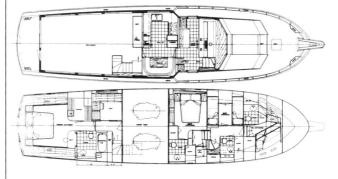

HATTERAS 70 COCKPIT MY

An extremely popular yacht (over 50 have been built) with a beautiful European profile and extravagant accommodations, the 70 CMY is one of the most luxurious production yachts ever offered by Hatteras. She's basically a 65 MY with a 5' cockpit addition (the extra hull length allows for an additional 426 gallons of fuel beneath the cockpit sole). Like most of the newer Hatteras motor yachts, the floorplan is arranged with the galley and dinette on the deckhouse level. The spacious full-width salon (no sidedecks) is extended well aft leaving only a small afterdeck overlooking the cockpit. The wheelhouse and galley are both enclosed in this layout and completely separate from the salon. Originally designed with a standard four-stateroom floorplan with twin engine rooms, recent VIP layouts (see Hatteras 65 MY) have a full-width engine room and more spacious guest accommodations. Note that most 70 CMYs have been semi-customized at the factory to meet an individual owner's requirements. Standard 870-hp 12V71s will cruise the 70 CMY at 17 knots and optional (since 1990) 1,040 12V92s cruise at 21 knots. ❏

SPECIFICATIONS

Length	70'10"
Length WL	NA
Beam	18'2"
Draft	5'4"
Weight	103,000#
Clearance	21'4"
Water	345 Gals.
Fuel	1,596 Gals.
Hull Type	Modified-V
Designer	Hargrave

Production
1988–Current

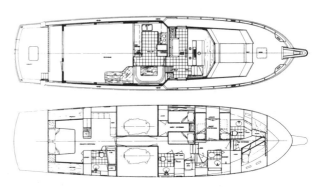

HATTERAS 72 MOTOR YACHT

Using the slightly lengthened hull form of the original Hatteras 70 MY, the 72 Motor Yacht was introduced in 1983 along with two 77-foot models as part of the Hatteras Custom Yacht Program. Each of the models in this series can be customized (to a reasonable extent) within the confines of hull and superstructure. With her modern flybridge and curved wheelhouse windows, the styling of the 72 is contemporary and very appealing. Although she's not marketed as an extended deckhouse model, the spacious salon of the Hatteras 72 is indeed full-width —

the actual dimensions are 14' x 25'. With both the galley and wheelhouse enclosed and separated from the salon area, the owner and guests are allowed complete privacy from any crew interruption. Belowdecks, the roomy walk-in engine room divides the lower deck floorplan with the owner and guest staterooms aft and the crew quarters (two staterooms) forward. A small aft deck for line handling remains at the stern. No lightweight, standard 870-hp 12V71 diesels will cruise the Hatteras 72 MY at 16–17 knots with a top speed of around 20 knots. ❏

SPECIFICATIONS

Length	72'8"
Length WL	NA
Beam	18'7"
Draft	5'3"
Weight	117,000#
Clearance	26'3"
Water	365 Gals.
Fuel	1,650/1,858 Gals.
Hull Type	Modified-V
Designer	J. Hargrave

Production
1983–Current

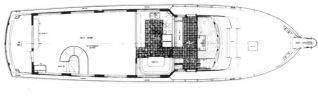

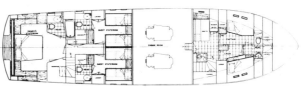

HATTERAS 77 COCKPIT MY

The 77 CMY remains the largest production cockpit motor yacht ever offered by Hatteras. Seven of these opulent yachts were built, two with walkaround decks (pictured above) and five with a full-width salon and no sidedecks. Designed as a fully crewed yacht, the galley is on the deckhouse level and private from the salon. Both guest staterooms and the extravagant master suite are accessed from a salon staircase while the full crew quarters occupy the forward sections of the boat. With the engine room aft, the midships location of the master stateroom is ideal (very quiet). Needless to say, the salon dimensions of the walkaround model are extravagant; in the widebody layout —with its extended deckhouse — they're cavernous. Note that there are wing doors for the aft deck in the walkaround while the widebody's has just a small aft deck. Additional features of the Hatteras 77 CMY include a massive flybridge and cockpit access to the standup engine room with its separate workbench area. Standard 12V71s cruise at 16–17 knots and the optional 12V92s will cruise around 18–19 knots. (Note that one 77 CMY was built with MTUs.) ❏

SPECIFICATIONS

Length	77'8"
Length WL	NA
Beam	18'7"
Draft	5'0"
Weight	140,000#
Clearance	26'3"
Water	496 Gals.
Fuel	2,080 Gals.
Hull Type	Modified-V
Designer	Hargrave

Production
1983–85

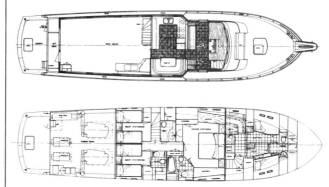

HATTERAS 82 CONVERTIBLE

To begin with, the Hatteras 82 is the largest production convertible available although it's safe to say that most will be customized to meet the needs of her owner. Still, a production fiberglass sportfisherman over 80' was just a dream a few years ago and Hatteras is finding that there's a market for such a boat with some (very) well-heeled sport fishermen. Designed as a crewed yacht (with separate crew quarters beneath the afterdeck), her extravagant triple-deck profile includes a two-stationenclosed bridge, four staterooms with full heads, a vast salon/deckhouse galley living and entertainment area, and a huge tournament-style cockpit. Notable features of the Hatteras 82 include a circular stairwell in the salon for access to the bridge, a full-beam master suite with his-and-her toilet room, a utility/work room, a large observation deck overlooking the cockpit and a convenient day head on the deckhouse level. Powerful 16-cylinder Deutz diesels (2,540-hp each) are available in the Hatteras 82 Convertible as well as smaller DD 16V92s and DD 16V149s. ❏

PRELIMINARY SPECS

Length	82'8"
Beam	21'5"
Draft	6'6"
Weight	172,000#
Clearance	26'0"
Cockpit	NA
Water	840 Gals.
Fuel	4,075 Gals.
Hull Type	Modified-V
Designer	Hatteras

Production
1992–Current

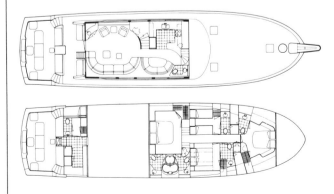

HENRIQUES

Brief History

Henriques is a small family-owner New Jersey builder of production and semi-custom sportfishing boats. Founded in 1978 by Jack Henriques (a Portuguese immigrant whose ancestors were also boatbuilders) the company's first boat was the 35 Main Coaster which remains in production today. As the Henriques line has expanded over the years, so too has their reputation for sturdy, no-nonsense construction. Many of their boats see regular service in charter operations. All Henriques models have been designed by the founder.

Selected Henriques Inboard Models

Henriques 35 Maine Coaster

Henriques 38 Sportfisherman

Henriques 38 El Bravo

Henriques 44 Sportfisherman

Henriques 50 Sportfisherman

Main Office

Henriques Boat Works, Inc., 198 Hilton Ave., Bayville, NJ 08721
908-269-1606 or 269-1180

HENRIQUES 35 MAINE COASTER

The Maine Coaster 35 is a capable long-range diesel sportfisherman with good heavy weather performance, a huge cockpit, and a pleasant interior with weekend accommodations for four. The first production boat from the Henriques yard and their best-selling model ever (about 110 have been sold), she's a durable design that has remained essentially unchanged since her introduction in 1977. The hull is constructed the old-fashioned way — solid fiberglass laminate with a fine entry, deep forefoot, and a flat run aft. The original floor plan had the galley on the deckhouse level, but by 1985 buyers were offered the option of having the galley down. The layout is basic but well finished with off-white laminate countertops and teak cabinetry throughout. The interior dimensions of the Maine Coaster are necessarily modest thanks to her massive 120 sq. ft. cockpit which is unmatched in size by any other production boat in her class. Standard 250-hp Cummins diesels will cruise at 20 knots and reach 23 knots wide open. Note that a 35 Open SF model is also available. ❏

SPECIFICATIONS

Length	35'4"
Beam	12'0"
Draft	3'1"
Weight	22,000#
Clearance	NA
Water	60 Gals.
Fuel	320 Gals.
Cockpit	120 Sq. Ft.
Hull Type	Modified-V
Designer	J. Henriques

Production
1977–Current

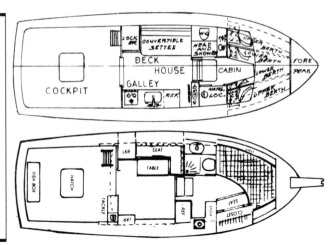

HENRIQUES 38 SPORTFISHERMAN

The Henriques 38 SF is another in the line of strictly-business canyon runners from the Henriques yard. Designed for long-range fishing, the 38 is built on a modified-V hull with 14° of deadrise at the transom. Divinycell foam coring is used from the waterline up. The house, deck and cockpit are constructed in a single seamless mold, and the cockpit is among the largest to be found in any 38' flybridge sportfisherman. Cockpit controls, transom door, tackle center, rod storage, and two 70-gallon recessed fish boxes are all standard. Note the side-facing bridge ladder. Nearly all of the Henriques 38's have been built with the popular single-stateroom layout, although a second stateroom is available (at the expense of the dinette). The interior accommodations are comfortable and tastefully finished with traditional teak cabinetry and woodwork throughout. A fine-looking boat, the Henriques 38 will cruise at 25–26 knots with the 375-hp Cat diesels and reach a top speed of about 30 knots. Note that the 38 El Bravo (an open sportfisherman built on the same hull) was introduced in 1990. ❏

SPECIFICATIONS

Length	38'0"
Beam	13'10"
Draft	3'10"
Weight	28,000#
Clearance	21'0"
Water	75 Gals.
Fuel	415 Gals.
Cockpit	140 Sq. Ft.
Hull Type	Modified-V
Designer	J. Henriques

Production
1988–Current

HENRIQUES 38 EL BRAVO

Based on the hull of the Henriques 38 SF, the El Bravo is a rugged offshore fisherman with an array of features that hard-core anglers will appreciate. Her modified-V hull (14° deadrise aft) has a deep forefoot and Divinycell coring is used in the hullsides. The El Bravo is a good-looking boat and her huge 130 sq. ft. cockpit (with two removable fishboxes, tackle center with circulating baitwell, washdowns, and under-gunnel rod storage port and starboard) is a superb fishing platform. The raised bridgedeck features a fore-and-aft settee to port and a well-designed helm console with electronic controls and in-dash space for flush mounting most electronics (no overhead box required). Combined, the El Bravo's bridgedeck and cockpit consume most of the boat's LOA so the belowdecks accommodations (dinette, galley and berths for four) are necessarily compact. Designed as a pure fishing boat, the El Bravo will have limited appeal as a family cruiser. Fully loaded with tower and gear, she'll cruise economically at 25 knots with optional 425-hp Cats (375-hp Cats are standard) and reach a top speed of 29–30 knots. ❏

SPECIFICATIONS

Length......................38'0"
Beam.....................13'10"
Draft ....3'4"
Weight ....28,000#
Clearance ....9'3"
Water...................60 Gals.
Fuel ....415 Gals.
Cockpit............130 Sq. Ft.
Hull Type.........Modified-V
Designer........J. Henriques

Production
1991–Current

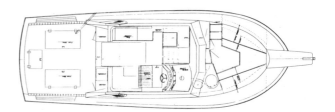

HENRIQUES 44 SPORTFISHERMAN

A proven offshore design, the Henriques 44 SF is built on a modified-V hull (12° deadrise aft) of solid fiberglass construction. A prominent bow pulpit and a solid front windshield accent her lines, and most consider the 44 to be a sturdy and good-looking boat. As sportfishing designs go, the Henriques is remarkably straightforward in her commitment to all-out fishability. Where most builders sacrifice cockpit space for comfortable interior dimensions, Henriques puts the emphasis where serious anglers feel it belongs. In the case of the Henriques 44, that priority translates into a huge uncluttered 12'x14' cockpit — more than enough space to satisfy the requirements of the most demanding tournament activities. Insulated fish boxes, a transom door, tackle center, and teak covering boards are all standard. Several floor-plan options are available with the interior in each fully paneled and finished in traditional teak woodwork. Standard 550-hp 6V92TAs will cruise the Henriques 44 Sportfisherman around 25 knots and turn 28 knots wide open. ❑

SPECIFICATIONS

Length......................44'0"
Beam......................14'10"
Draft ....3'8"
Weight ....37,000#
Clearance ....NA
Water................120 Gals.
Fuel ....600 Gals.
Cockpit............170 Sq. Ft.
Hull Type.........Modified-V
Designer.......J. Henriques

Production
1983–Current

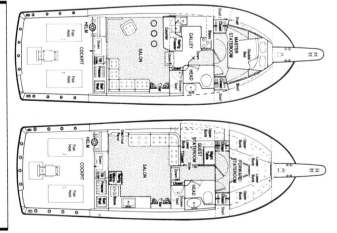

HENRIQUES 50 SPORTFISHERMAN

The Henriques 50 SF is one of the more graceful and well-proportioned production sportfishermen available — a remarkable achievement since most convertibles with closed bridges look pretty bad (except for the new Hatteras 58). She's built on a beamy modified-V hull with cored hullsides, a sweeping sheer and 12° of transom deadrise. Perhaps the most striking feature of the Henriques 50 is her huge 160 sq. ft. fishing cockpit with its on-deck head/shower compartment, giant fishbox and extended bridge overhang. Belowdecks, the accommodations are arranged with the galley down and two staterooms, both with full heads. While the salon dimensions are more confined than other 50-footers (thanks to the large cockpit), the interior is well appointed and finished with traditional teak woodwork throughout. Additional features include underwater exhausts, electronic controls, washer/dryer, and cockpit controls. Because each Henriques 50 will be a semi-custom boat, engine options vary. With 820-hp MANs she'll cruise at a fast 27 knots and reach 30–31 knots wide open. ❏

SPECIFICATIONS

Length	50'0"
Beam	16'6"
Draft	4'8"
Weight	53,000#
Clearance	18'0"
Water	160 Gals.
Fuel	1,000 Gals.
Cockpit	161 Sq. Ft.
Hull Type	Modified-V
Designer	J. Henriques

Production
1983–Current

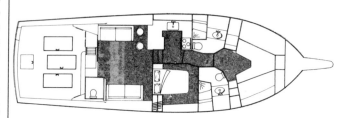

HI-STAR

Brief History

A relatively new company, Hi-Star began production in 1986 and has become one of the major Taiwan exporters of convertibles and motor yachts. Hi-Star production facilities are among the most modern on the island and their boats have earned a reputation for quality engineering and above-average construction standards. Hi-Star yachts are distributed by several East and West Coast dealers.

Selected Hi-Star Models

Hi-Star 42 Convertible   Hi-Star 48 Sundeck

Hi-Star 44 Convertible   Hi-Star 55 Yacht Fisherman

Hi-Star 48 Convertible

Main Office

Hi-Star Marine Co., Ltd., 50 Ta Yeh Rd.
Shaou Kang, Kaohsiung, Taiwan
886-7-871-5286

331

HI-STAR 42 CONVERTIBLE

The Hi-Star 42 Convertible is a good-looking design with crisp European styling and excellent performance. Built on a deep-V hull (18° deadrise aft), construction is solid fiberglass from keel to chine and lightweight Airex coring is used in the hullsides and superstructure. The 42 Convertible is aimed primarily at the upscale family cruiser market although her seakindly hull design, spacious cockpit, and superb engineering should appeal to part-time anglers as well. Two interior floorplans are offered: a two-stateroom, galley-up arrangement and a single-stateroom, galley-down version with a dinette. Like all Hi-Star yachts, the 42 Convertible features meticulous grain-matched interior teak joinerwork and a spacious fully-gelcoated engine room. The 110 sq. ft. cockpit is large enough for serious fishing activities, the side-decks are wide and secure, and the tournament-style flybridge provides a good view of the cockpit from the helm with bench seating forward. A popular boat in Europe, the performance of the Hi-Star 42 Convertible with 375-hp Cat diesels is around 22 knots at cruise and 26 knots wide open. ❏

SPECIFICATIONS

Length	42'3"
Beam	14'9"
Draft	3'2"
Weight	30,000#
Clearance	12'2"
Water	180 Gals.
Fuel	360 Gals.
Cockpit	110 Sq. Ft.
Hull Type	Deep-V
Designer	Chas. Chang

Production
1988–Current

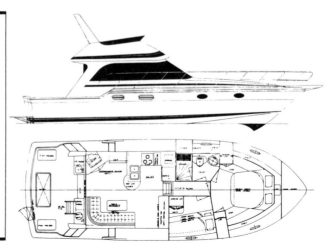

HI-STAR

HI-STAR 44 CONVERTIBLE

The Hi-Star 44 Convertible is designed primarily as a family cruiser and makes no attempt to present herself as a fishing boat. Her profile is fairly conservative and the cockpit is notably small, however it's her superb engineering and modern construction that set her apart. Hi-Star is a good builder and the 44 Convertible is particularly roomy inside where a galley-up, two-stateroom layout provides the living space you generally expect to find in a larger boat. If the guest cabin is tight, the master stateroom is roomy and comfortable. The joinerwork is first class throughout and not as dark as most Asian teak interiors. The engine room is accessed from the folding steps forward of the galley and the detailing and service access are *very* good. The cockpit in this boat really is tight but then the interior is so spacious. The factory tackle centers are way too small (and too low) and the bridge console is a pretty plain-Jane affair compared to other boats in her class. A good running boat with a solid and seakindly hull, optional 375-hp Cats provide an economical 21-knot cruise while burning around 30 gph. Top speed is 23–25 knots. ❑

SPECIFICATIONS

Length	43'9"
Length WL	37'7"
Beam	15'2"
Draft	3'2"
Weight	33,000#
Clearance	NA
Water	250 Gals.
Fuel	500 Gals.
Cockpit	NA
Hull Type	Modified-V
Designer	C. Chang

Production
1986–Current

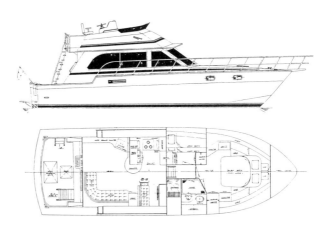

HI-STAR

HI-STAR 48 CONVERTIBLE

A good-looking boat with a long foredeck and a distinctive stepped sheer, the Hi-Star 48 Convertible is built on a modified-V hull (16° deadrise) with cored hullsides and a shallow keel for stability. With over 100 sq. ft. of cockpit space, the Hi-Star 48 is well suited for serious fishing activities (a transom door is standard) and features extra-wide sidedecks and a large flybridge. Her spacious two-stateroom teak interior is arranged with the galley and salon on a single level and separated by a stylish drum-shaped serving counter. A lower helm is standard and wraparound cabin windows provide plenty of natural lighting. Forward, a centerline double berth is located in the large master stateroom and stacked bunks are fitted in the guest cabin. Note that the double-entry stall shower serves both heads — an innovative and space-saving feature. The superb teak interior joinerwork and well-designed engine room are impressive. With standard Caterpillar 375-hp diesels the Hi-Star 48 Convertible will cruise at 19–20 knots and reach a top speed of around 22 knots. ❏

SPECIFICATIONS

Length	47'9"
Length WL	41'3"
Beam	15'2"
Draft	3'3"
Weight	37,000#
Clearance	13'6"
Water	250 Gals.
Fuel	500 Gals.
Cockpit	108 Sq. Ft.
Hull Type	Modified-V
Designer	Chas. Chang

Production
1986–Current

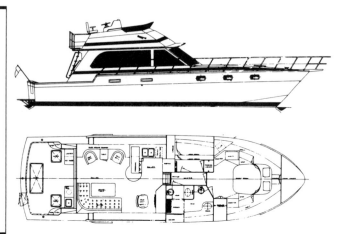

HI-STAR 48 SUNDECK MY

Since her introduction in 1987, the Hi-Star 48 Sundeck has become one of the more popular Asian imports currently available in the U.S. market. Built on a modified-V hull with a fairly deep 16° of deadrise aft, the 48 Sundeck is constructed on a solid fiberglass bottom with Airex coring used from the waterline up. Her styling is contemporary and a close-up inspection reveals above-average glasswork in the hull and superstructure. Designed as a luxury cruising yacht, the Hi-Star 48 has a conventional two-stateroom interior layout with the galley and dinette down a few steps from the salon level. Both staterooms are fitted with centerline double berths, and the interior is finished with grain-matched teak paneling and cabinetry. Indeed, Hi-Star's joinerwork rivals the best to be found in any production boat. Equally notable is the 48's meticulously arranged engine room with easy access to the motors and mechanical systems. A good performer with standard 375-hp Cats, the 48 Sundeck will cruise 18-19 knots and reach 22 knots wide open. Note that the popular 55 Yacht Fisherman is the same boat with a 7' cockpit. ❏

SPECIFICATIONS

Length	47'9"
Length WL	41'3"
Beam	15'2"
Draft	3'3"
Weight	37,000#
Clearance	13'6"
Water	250 Gals.
Fuel	500 Gals.
Hull Type	Modified-V
Designer	Chas. Chang

Production
1986–Current

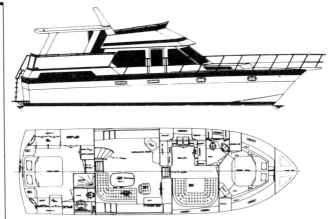

HI-STAR 55 YACHTFISHERMAN

The 55 Yachtfisherman is basically a Hi-Star 48 MM with a 7' cockpit extension, additional fuel, and a more attractive profile. A cockpit is a useful addition to just about any motor yacht as it provides easy access to the water and much more civilized boarding procedures. The aft deck of the Hi-Star 55 is huge and comes with a wet bar and plenty of room for outdoor tables and chairs. The two-stateroom/dinette interior is teak, of course, and the only real complaint about the layout is the lack of a stall shower in the forward head (a boat of this length *should* have two stall showers). A gorgeous lower helm station is standard in the 55 Yachtfisherman along with a convenient deck access door and wide sidedecks. The curved staircase from the aft deck is definitely a nice touch. Additional features include two centerline queen berths, a spacious galley, and an attractive hardtop. Airex coring is used above the waterline and the boat weighs in at just 39,000 lbs. which helps explain her good performance with only 375-hp Cats. Loaded, the Hi-Star 55 YF will cruise economically at a respectable 17–18 knots and reach a top speed of 22 knots. ❑

SPECIFICATIONS

Length	54'9"
Beam	48'3"
Draft	3'3"
Weight	39,000#
Clearance	NA
Water	250 Gals.
Fuel	800 Gals.
Hull Type	Modified-V
Designer	C. Chang

Production
1986–Current

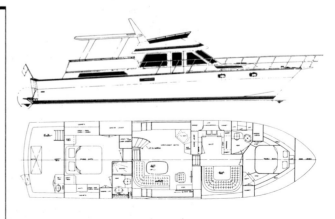

JEFFERSON

Brief History

While many U.S. importers represent boats from several Asian yards in their lineup, all Jefferson yachts come from a single builder — Her Shine Marine in Taiwan. Her Shine began as a builder of commercial fishing boats in the 1960s and made the transition to yacht production in the early 1980s. The first Jefferson model, the 45 Motor Yacht, was introduced in 1982 and today Jefferson distributes a full selection of moderately priced cruising boats for the American market. Her Shine sells their boats in the European market under their own name.

Selected Jefferson Models

Jefferson 37 Viscount MY

Jefferson 42 Sundeck MY

Jefferson 42 Viscount MY

Jefferson 43 Marlago Sundeck

Jefferson 45 Motor Yacht

Jefferson 46 Sundeck MY

Jefferson 46 Marlago Sundeck

Jefferson 48 Rivanna MY

Jefferson 52 Monticello MY

Jefferson 52 Marquessa MY

Jefferson 60 Motor Yacht

Main Office

Jefferson Yachts, Inc., PO Box 790,
106 W. Court Ave., Jeffersonville, IN 47131
812-282-8111

337

JEFFERSON 37 VISCOUNT MY

The Jefferson 37 Viscount is an affordable aft cabin family cruiser with contemporary lines and an impressive list of standard equipment. As with most Jeffersons, the 37 is free of exterior teak. Below, however, an abundance of teak trim and cabinetry blends with off-white mica counters and surfaces for an attractive and very nautical decor. The floorplan is arranged in the conventional manner with double berths in both staterooms, a comfortable salon with a built-in sofa and lower helm. A dinette is opposite the galley a few steps down from the salon level and a stall shower is fitted in the aft head. This is a workable layout — it's no mean feat to design a roomy double cabin boat on only a 37' hull — and most families will find the Jefferson 37 to be a comfortable weekend retreat. Standard features include an aft-deck hardtop, transom shower, swim platform and bow pulpit. Standard 250-hp Cummins diesels will cruise the 37 Viscount around 18 knots (21–22 knots top) with a fuel consumption of approximately 1 mpg. Note that the Jefferson 40 Viscount is the same boat with a (very) small cockpit extension. ❏

SPECIFICATIONS

Length	36'10"
Length WL	32'6"
Beam	14'5"
Draft	3'0"
Weight	27,000#
Clearance	NA
Water	100 Gals.
Fuel	350 Gals.
Hull Type	Modified-V
Designer	Robt. Harris

Production
1988–Current

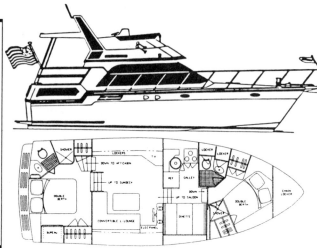

JEFFERSON 42 SUNDECK

The Jefferson 42 Sundeck was built using the same hull as the Jefferson 42 Convertible. She's a fairly straightforward double cabin design with attractive lines and a choice of interior floorplans. In the popular "A" Plan, the layout features a large master stateroom aft with a walkaround queen berth and an offset double berth in the forward stateroom. A tub/shower is included in the head adjoining the owner's aft stateroom while a separate stall shower is found in the forward head. With the galley down and to port, the main salon in this floor-plan is quite large and includes a built-in breakfast bar opposite the lower helm station. Large wraparound windows add plenty of natural lighting, and good-quality teak joinerwork is used throughout the interior. Outside, the 42 Sundeck has wide sidedeck passageways and the full-width aft deck is big enough for comfortable dockside entertaining. A reasonably priced and popular boat, the optional 260-hp Caterpillar diesels will cruise the Jefferson 42 Sundeck at 17–18 knots and provide a top speed of around 20 knots. ❏

SPECIFICATIONS

Length	41'8"
Length WL	37'8"
Beam	14'3"
Draft	3'7"
Weight	30,000#
Clearance	NA
Water	200 Gals.
Fuel	350 Gals.
Hull Type	Modified-V
Designer	Robt. Harris

Production
1985–89

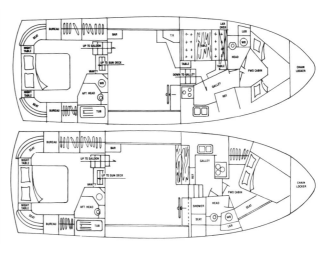

JEFFERSON 42 VISCOUNT MY

Built on a conventional modified-V hull with fiberglass construction, the Jefferson 42 Viscount is a straightforward double cabin design with a modern profile and a practical accommodation plan. Designed for family cruising, the interior features a two-stateroom layout with the galley and dinette down from the salon. A lower helm is standard and the interior is finished with teak paneling, moldings, doors, and cabinets. (Note that it's necessary to enter the forward stateroom to use the head.) There's a tub/shower in the aft head and the fuel tanks are aluminum rather than the black iron found in so many Asian yachts. The full-width aft deck of the 42 Viscount is very spacious and bench seating is provided on the flybridge aft of the helm. At only 28,000 lbs., the Jefferson 42 is a light boat for her size. Twin 300-hp Cummins diesels are standard in the newer models (around 19 knots cruise/22 knots top) and 375-hp Cats (21 knots cruise/24–25 knots wide open) are optional. A more affordable "SE" (Special Edition) model has been available since 1991 with less standard equipment. ❏

SPECIFICATIONS

Length	41'8"
Length WL	37'8"
Beam	14'5"
Draft	3'0"
Weight	28,000#
Clearance	NA
Water	100 Gals.
Fuel	350 Gals.
Hull Type	Modified-V
Designer	Robt. Harris

Production
1990–Current

JEFFERSON 43 MARLAGO SUNDECK

A good-looking boat with her low-profile deckhouse and modern lines, the 42 Marlago is a comfortable family cruiser with a lot of standard features included in her affordable price. She's built on a solid fiberglass hull with modest transom deadrise and a good deal of flare at the bow. The Marlago's floorplan is arranged in the conventional manner with staterooms fore and aft and the galley and dinette down. Both staterooms have double berths (note the tub/shower in the aft head compartment) and a lower helm is standard in the salon. Making the most of her 15' beam, the 43 Marlago is a roomy boat for her size although the forward stateroom is somewhat compact. There's plenty of space on the aft deck for a variety of deck furniture and the flybridge is arranged with built-in guest seating behind the helm. Additional features include a teak interior, radar arch, swim platform, and a particularly attractive hardtop design. Cummins 250-hp diesels are standard (around 14 knots cruise) and Cat diesels to 425-hp are optional. Note that the 46 Marlago Cockpit MY is the same boat with a (very) small cockpit extension. ❏

SPECIFICATIONS

Length	42'10"
Length WL	NA
Beam	15'0"
Draft	3'10"
Weight	31,000#
Clearance	12'9"
Water	200 Gals.
Fuel	420 Gals.
Hull Type	Modified-V
Designer	Robt. Harris

Production
1991–Current

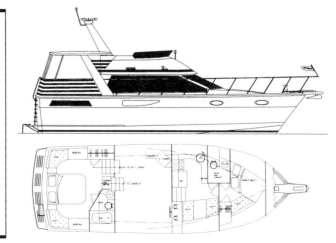

JEFFERSON

JEFFERSON 45 MOTOR YACHT

The Jefferson 45 Motor Yacht was the first boat imported and sold under the Jefferson name. A popular model (55 were sold during her 7-year production run), the 45 is constructed on a solid fiberglass, modified-V hull with a flared bow, hard aft chines, and a long keel for directional stability. Although the Jefferson 45 MY is a fairly conventional boat and her dockside appearance is unlikely to stir the emotions, the secret of her success can be traced to a low price and her practical two-stateroom, galley-down interior. The owner's cabin is spacious and features a centerline queen berth plus good storage space. A lower helm is standard and the interior decor is total teak throughout. Note that the original floorplan was updated in 1985 to include the tub/shower aft and a stall shower in the forward head. The large, full-width afterdeck has plenty of space for furniture and the sidedecks are wide enough for secure passage. Twin 200-hp Perkins diesels were standard in the Jefferson 45 MY (12 knots at cruise/15 top) and 320-hp Cats (16 knots cruise/19 knots top) were a popular option. ❑

SPECIFICATIONS

Length	45'3"
Length WL	41'0"
Beam	15'2"
Draft	4'5"
Weight	41,000#
Clearance	17'10"
Water	300 Gals.
Fuel	600 Gals.
Hull Type	Modified-V
Designer	Robt. Harris

Production
1982–89

JEFFERSON 46 SUNDECK MY

While the Jefferson 46 Sundeck Motor Yacht doesn't have a notably attractive profile, she's been a popular model due in part to her moderate price and spacious interior accommodations. Like the rest of the Jefferson fleet, the 46 Sundeck is built at the Her Shine yard in Taiwan on a conventional modified-V hull form. A choice of four interior floorplans is available with either two or three staterooms. (Note the absence of a stall shower in the forward head.) Teak paneling and cabinetry are used extensively throughout the interior. The afterdeck of the Jefferson 46 is huge — easily one of the largest to be found in any boat of this size and a superb outdoor entertainment platform. The flybridge is arranged with the helm forward and guest seating for six. The 46 comes standard with a swim platform, transom shower, deck washdown, bow pulpit, and lower helm station. Small diesels are standard, but most Jefferson 46 Sundecks were sold with the 375-hp Cats which provide a cruising speed of 19–20 knots. The Jefferson 52 Cockpit Motor Yacht is the same boat with a 6' cockpit extension. ❑

SPECIFICATIONS

Length	45'8"
Length WL	41'8"
Beam	14'3"
Draft	3'7"
Weight	43,000#
Clearance	NA
Water	200 Gals.
Fuel	350 Gals.
Hull Type	Modified-V
Designer	Robt. Harris

Production
1985–89

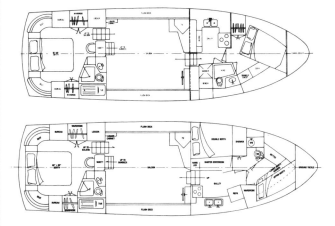

JEFFERSON 46 MARLAGO SUNDECK

The Jefferson 46 Marlago Sundeck is the latest in a new series of sundeck motor yachts from Jefferson aimed at the family cruising market. Built on a solid fiberglass hull, the main selling features of the 46 are a roomy interior and an attractive selling price. Her standard layout consists of two staterooms with the galley and dinette down, and an alternate plan has a mid-level galley with no dinette, a larger salon, and space forward for a washer/dryer. Both staterooms are quite spacious with walkaround double berths and full heads. (To use the forward head it's necessary to enter the stateroom — an inconvenient arrangement.) A lower helm is standard and there's a tub/shower in the aft head compartment. There is less interior teak cabinetry and trim in the 46 Marlago than in previous Jefferson models. Additional features include wing doors, a spacious afterdeck, adequate sidedecks and a swim platform. Standard power for the 46 Marlago is 250-hp Cummins but most buyers will likely choose the larger 375-hp or 425-hp Cats. Cruising speeds with the Cats is around 15–16 knots. The fuel capacity is a little light for a boat this size. ❏

SPECIFICATIONS

Length	45'10"
Length WL	NA
Beam	15'0"
Draft	3'10"
Weight	34,700#
Clearance	14'8"
Water	200 Gals.
Fuel	420 Gals.
Hull Type	Modified-V
Designer	Robt. Harris

Production
1991–Current

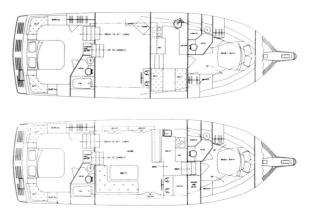

JEFFERSON 48 RIVANNA MY

With her modern lines and low-profile appearance, the Jefferson 48 Rivanna MY is the first of a new series of Rivanna models from 48' to 56' aimed at the family cruising market. She's built on a conventional one-piece, modified-V hull with 6° deadrise aft and a shallow keel below for directional stability. A good-looking boat, the Rivanna is available with a conventional two-stateroom layout or a three-stateroom version with the second (small) guest cabin located aft. The roomy master stateroom features a centerline queen berth and a tub/shower in the head. The interior is finished with plenty of good-quality Asian teak joinerwork, and a lower helm station is standard in the salon. Additional features include a hardtop and radar arch, wing doors, and a swim platform. Twin 250-hp Cummins diesels are standard in the 48 Rivanna but most owners will probably select the more powerful 425-hp Caterpillar 3208TAs. Performance with these engines is 16 knots at cruise and 19 knots wide open. A cockpit version of this boat — the 52 Rivanna — is also offered. ❑

SPECIFICATIONS

Length	48'4"
Length WL	NA
Beam	16'0"
Draft	4'0"
Weight	42,500#
Clearance	13'4"
Water	200 Gals.
Fuel	600 Gals.
Hull Type	Modified-V
Designer	In-House

Production
1990–Current

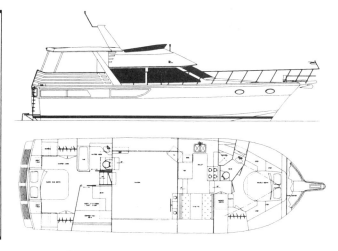

JEFFERSON

JEFFERSON 52 MONTICELLO MY

Displaying a traditional flush deck profile, the 52 Monticello is a moderately priced luxury cruising yacht with generous interior accommodations considering her relatively narrow beam. Her single-piece fiberglass hull shows considerable flare at the bow and includes a long keel below for good directional stability. The Monticello has a fully enclosed afterdeck and pilothouse area (actually, the main salon) which is easily the most popular entertaining spot in the boat. An inside ladder next to the helm leads up to the flybridge where two large L-shaped lounges provide excellent guest seating for as many as eight. The lowerdeck salon is arranged with a built-in dinette, and the large mid-level galley is forward. Most 52's were delivered with a three-stateroom interior which includes a spacious master stateroom and three heads, each with a stall shower enclosure. Teak paneling and cabinetry are used throughout the interior. Twin Caterpillar 375-hp diesels will cruise the Monticello at a sedate 15–16 knots, and the top speed is around 20 knots. She was replaced in mid-1989 with the new 52 Marquessa MY. ❏

SPECIFICATIONS

Length	51'6"
Length WL	47'0"
Beam	15'2"
Draft	3'7"
Weight	NA
Clearance	NA
Water	300 Gals.
Fuel	600 Gals.
Hull Type	Modified-V
Designer	Robt. Harris

Production
1986–89

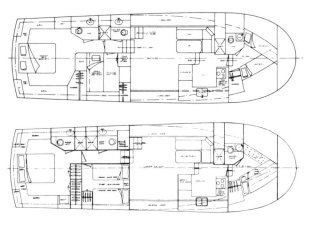

JEFFERSON 52 MARQUESSA MY

The Jefferson 52 Marquessa is an extended deckhouse motor yacht with modern styling, an attractive price tag, and a notably spacious three-stateroom interior layout. Like all Jefferson yachts, the Marquessa is constructed in Taiwan on a modified-V hull design with a shallow keel and moderate deadrise at the transom. Inside, the dominant feature is the huge deckhouse salon — a full-width living and entertainment area of expansive proportions. The staterooms are reached from the companionway leading down from the pilothouse. V-berths are forward, and a

large guest cabin and king-size master stateroom are aft on the lower level. All feature a private head with stall shower. The engines are located in separate engine rooms accessed from the corridor leading to the aft stateroom. Not only is this a spacious layout for a 52' yacht; it's practical as well. An attractive feature of the Marquessa is the willingness of the importer to customize the interior to the buyer's specs. Standard 550-hp 6V92 diesels will cruise the 52 Marquessa at an impressive 19–20 knots and deliver a top speed of around 22 knots.   ❏

SPECIFICATIONS

Length	52'5"
Length WL	NA
Beam	16'0"
Draft	4'0"
Weight	55,800#
Clearance	19'6"
Water	200 Gals.
Fuel	700 Gals.
Hull Type	Modified-V
Designer	Robt. Harris

Production
1989–Current

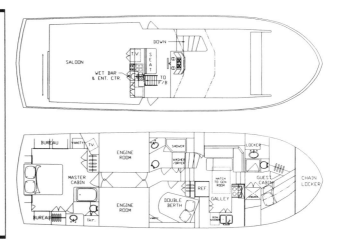

JEFFERSON

JEFFERSON 60 MOTOR YACHT

The Jefferson 60 Motor Yacht has become a popular boat since her 1987 introduction. She's built on a modified-V hull with balsa coring used in the hullsides from the waterline up. A long keel is added for maneuverability and a wide beam ensures a stable and comfortable ride. The standard interior layout includes a spacious master stateroom aft of the engine rooms and three additional staterooms forward, each with a private head. A fifth head is conveniently placed in the main salon abaft the flybridge stairway. While still very large, the Jefferson 60's salon is not of the full-width variety, nor is the salon's aft bulkhead extended to the transom. Instead, wide sidedecks are preserved for safe movements fore and aft, and a semi-enclosed afterdeck is provided for open-air enjoyment. Teak woodwork is used extensively throughout the Jefferson 60, and the joinerwork is up to the usual high Asian standards. With standard 6V92s, the cruising speed is around 13–14 knots. The more popular 735-hp 8V92s provide 17–18 knots of cruising speed. Note that the 65 Cockpit MY is the same boat with a cockpit extension. ❑

SPECIFICATIONS

Length....................59'10"
Beam.........................17'6"
Draft ....4'7"
Weight ....88,000#
Clearance ....18'3"
Water.................400 Gals.
Fuel ....1000 Gals.
Hull Type.........Modified-V
Designer ....Robt. Harris

Production
1987–Current

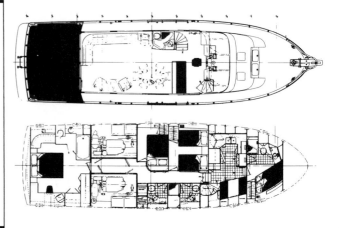

JERSEY

Brief History

Jersey Yachts was founded in 1954 by Fred McCarthy and the company remained a family-owned operation until it was sold to new owners in 1989. The transition to fiberglass began in 1969 with the introduction of the Jersey 31 SF — a landmark boat for the company which was soon offered in seven different configurations. Jersey has always been a limited-production builder of traditional sportfishermen. To date, all of their designs have been drawn by the founder, Fred McCarthy.

Selected Jersey Inboard Models

Jersey 36 Convertible SF   Jersey 44 Devil SF
Jersey 40 Dawn Convertible   Jersey 47 Convertible
Jersey 42 Convertible SF

Main Office

Jersey Yachts, Inc., P.O. Box 588, Lumberton, NJ 08048
609-267-9200

349

JERSEY 36 CONVERTIBLE SF

A handsome sportfisherman with flowing, almost custom lines, the Jersey 36 is built on a solid fiberglass hull with substantial flare at the bow and 10° of transom deadrise. Her original single-stateroom interior (still available) is arranged with the galley-down, a large head with stall shower, and an offset double berth forward. A new floorplan introduced in the 1991 models offers a centerline double berth forward with the addition of a dinette (or second stateroom) at the expense of the stall shower and some engine room and salon space. The bridge layout was also rearranged in 1991 with the helm console now on the centerline rather than to starboard — a big improvement. The 36 comes with a long list of standard equipment including a factory hardtop. Her large fishing cockpit features very low freeboard (only 3') with plenty of room for an optional bait prep center and mounted chair. With standard 350-hp gas engines, the Jersey 36 will cruise at 19–20 knots and turn 30 knots wide open. The optional 375-hp Cat diesels cruise at 24–25 knots and top out around 28 knots. ❏

SPECIFICATIONS

Length.....................36'4"
Beam........................13'4"
Draft ....3'2"
Weight ....23,500#
Clearance ....11'0"
Water...................75 Gals.
Fuel ....365 Gals.
Cockpit..............90 Sq. Ft.
Hull Type.........Modified-V
Designer ....F. McCarthy

Production
1986–Current

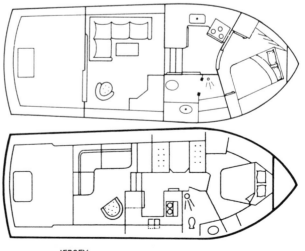

JERSEY 40 DAWN CONVERTIBLE

No longer in production, the 40 Dawn is a straightforward sportfisherman designed for offshore anglers. Her solid fiberglass hull construction and relatively deep keel and generous bow flare insure stable offshore handling characteristics in poor weather, and a large cockpit provides plenty of space for tournament-level fishing activities. Two interior floorplans were offered with the single-stateroom, dinette layout proving more popular than the two-stateroom, galley-up version. While the cabin dimensions of the Jersey 40 are not large by today's standards, the interior is finished with teak woodwork and cabinetry. (Note that the switch from woodgrain mica to an all-teak interior was made in 1979.) Standard features include bow pulpit, air conditioning, generator, stereo, and color TV. Still popular among Northeast fishermen, many of the Jersey 40s were powered with economical 235-hp Volvo diesels which cruise the 40 around 18 knots at 18 gph, or 1 mile per gallon. Later models offering the 325-hp Cats are capable of cruising around 20 knots and reaching 23–24 knots wide open. ❑

SPECIFICATIONS

Length	40'0"
Beam	14'6"
Draft	3'5"
Weight	28,000#
Clearance	NA
Water	100 Gals.
Fuel	400 Gals.
Cockpit	NA
Hull Type	Modified-V
Designer	F. McCarthy

Production
1973–88

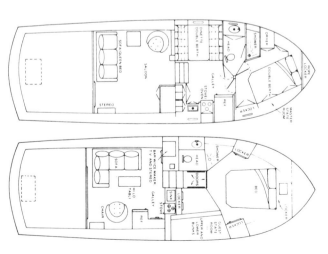

JERSEY 42 CONVERTIBLE SF

The Jersey 42 is a handsome sportfisherman designed for tournament sportfishing activities. She's constructed on a relatively flat-bottom hull (10° deadrise aft) and like all Jersey yachts, her styling is notably graceful with exceptional flare at the bow and a modern convertible profile (note the open front windshield). With her sweeping sheerline and long foredeck, the Jersey 42 presents the businesslike appearance of a custom Carolina-style yacht. Aside from building a tough, solid fiberglass hull, the new Jersey boats have very tastefully finished interiors. Several accommodation plans are offered: the single-stateroom layout includes two heads and a mid-level dinette while the two-stateroom versions offer a choice of a dinette or a second head compartment. Throughout, the interior is luxuriously paneled with dark teak woodwork and cabinetry. The large fishing cockpit is free of obstructions and a factory hardtop and flybridge enclosure are standard. Caterpillar 375-hp diesels will cruise the Jersey 42 around 22 knots with a top speed of 26. The optional 485-hp 6-71s cruise at a fast 27 knots and reach 30 knots wide open. ❏

SPECIFICATIONS

Length	42'4"
Beam	15'8"
Draft	3'6"
Weight	30,500#
Clearance	14'0"
Water	100 Gals.
Fuel	400 Gals.
Cockpit	114 Sq. Ft.
Hull Type	Modified-V
Designer	F. McCarthy

Production
1989–Current

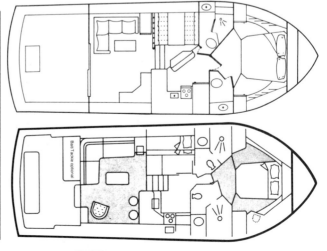

JERSEY DEVIL 44 CONVERTIBLE

When it comes down to cockpit size, the Jersey Devil 44 Convertible is simply in a class by herself. Eight of these durable canyon runners were built during a 6-year production run, and several can be found today operating as charter boats along the East Coast. She was built using a stretched version of the Jersey 40 Dawn's modified-V hull with a deep entry and a slightly rounded bottom that flattens out aft. Transom deadrise is a modest 10°. The basic two-stateroom interior of the Jersey Devil 44 is arranged with the galley-up on the salon level and the front windshield panels are glassed over. Early interiors were finished with simulated teak laminates, but Jersey went to an all-teak interior in 1979. A very useful feature is the huge storage bin below the galley sole — large enough for an inflatable and extra ground tackle. The cockpit has lockable rod racks under the gunwales and a tackle center to port. A good-running boat, all Jersey Devil 44s were powered with 450-hp GM 6-71 diesels. She'll cruise around 24–25 knots and run 27 knots wide open. ❑

SPECIFICATIONS

Length	44'0"
Beam	14'6"
Draft	14'6"
Weight	34,800#
Clearance	14'2"
Water	100 Gals.
Fuel	400 Gals.
Cockpit	154 Sq. Ft.
Hull Type	Modified-V
Designer	F. McCarthy

Production
1980–85

JERSEY 47 CONVERTIBLE

Introduced in 1989, the Jersey 47 Convertible is the largest boat in the fleet of this small New Jersey manufacturer. Notably, Jersey is one of the few builders that hasn't abandoned single-skin fiberglass hull construction, thus avoiding the complexities of cored hulls. The graceful profile of the Jersey 47 is immediately distinctive and her extra-long foredeck and cockpit bridge overhang make her an easy boat to recognize. The front windows are glass — another departure from the norm as most modern sportfisherman have fiberglassed-over windshields (al-though that option is available). Three interior plans are offered with the three-stateroom, galley-up layout being the more popular. Both guest state-rooms are small, but the heads are very large and fitted with shower stalls. Traditional teak woodwork is used extensively throughout the interior. Outside, the cockpit is arranged for serious fishing pursuits and the fly-bridge is huge, with seating for eight. GM 6-71 (485-hp) are standard and the 47 Convertible will cruise at a fast 26–27 knots with a top speed of 30 knots. ❑

SPECIFICATIONS

Length	47'4"
Beam	15'8"
Draft	3'10"
Weight	36,000#
Clearance	17'0"
Water	150 Gals.
Fuel	600 Gals.
Cockpit	124 Sq. Ft.
Hull Type	Modified-V
Designer	F. McCarthy

Production
1987–Current

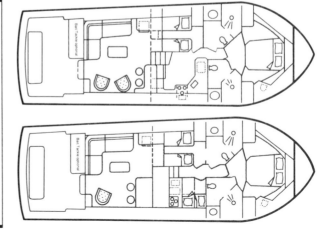

KONG & HALVORSEN

Brief History

Kong & Halvorsen Marine (now called Halvorsen Marine) was formed in 1975 between Joseph Kong and Lars Halvorsen. Kong had been production manager at Grand Banks and Halvorsen was a well-known Australian builder of commercial and pleasure craft. Until recently, most Halvorsen models were built in Hong Kong. In 1980 the company made the decision to shift some production to new facilities in the nearby Shekou Industrial Zone (Mainland China) where, since 1990, all of their boats have been constructed.

Selected Kong & Halvorsen Models

Island Gyspy 30 Sedan

Island Gypsy 32 Sedan

Island Gypsy 32 Sport Fisher

Island Gypsy 36 Aft Cabin

Island Gypsy 40 Flush Aft Deck

Island Gypsy 44 Flush Aft Deck

Island Gypsy 44 Motor Cruiser

Island Gypsy 49 Pilothouse

Island Gypsy 51 Motor Yacht

Main Office

Halvorsen Marine, Ltd.,
Box 79259, Mongkok Post Office, Kowloon, Hong Kong

355

ISLAND GYPSY 30 SEDAN

The Island Gypsy 30 Sedan is a salty little trawler-style design with a handsome, upright appearance. She enjoyed a good deal of popularity some years ago when high fuel prices and the strength of the U.S. dollar combined to spur the importation of efficient Asian trawlers. Built in three different configurations, the Sedan (pictured above) began with a mahogany hull and superstructure and switched to all-fiberglass construction sometime in 1978. The hull is a hard-chined, semi-displacement form with a sharp entry and a long, deep keel for directional stability and prop protection. Inside, the straightforward cabin layout includes a lower helm position opposite the galley, V-berths forward, and excellent storage space. Teak paneling and cabinetry are used liberally throughout the interior and the joinerwork is to high standards. A flybridge overhang affords some aft deck weather protection, and wide, protected teak side-decks provide secure foredeck access. The standard 120-hp Lehman diesel will cruise the Island Gypsy 30 at her 7-knots cruising speed while burning only 2 gph. ❏

SPECIFICATIONS

Length	30'0"
Length WL	27'9"
Beam	11'6"
Draft	3'8"
Weight	14,400#
Clearance	NA
Water	120 Gals.
Fuel	250 Gals.
Hull Type	Semi-Disp.
Designer	H. Halvorsen

Production
1975–85

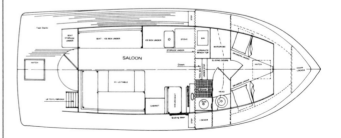

KONG & HALVORSEN

ISLAND GYPSY 32 SEDAN

Like all current Island Gypsy models, the 32 Sedan is built in Mainland China at a yard owned largely by Kong & Halvorsen. She has a distinctive trawler yacht hull shape — hard-chined with a deep skeg, broad in the beam with a flared bow, and an upright, handsome profile. Construction is solid fiberglass (the grooved hullsides require a 2-piece mold), and shallow aft sections provide for semi-displacement performance. The interior plan of the Island Gypsy 32 is arranged in the conventional manner with a single-stateroom forward (choice of V-berths or an offset double berth), galley-up in the salon, and large wraparound cabin windows. All of the woodwork is teak, and a sliding deck access door is located next to the helm station. The aft deck is small but uncluttered and has a single seat in the shelter of the bridge overhang. The decks are teak and the deck hardware is bronze. A single Lehman 135-hp diesel will cruise the Island Gyspy 32 Sedan at 8 knots or so, and the twin 90-hp Lehmans cruise at 8.5 knots. A single 225-hp Lehmans will cruise at 11–12 knots and reach a top speed of 15. ❑

SPECIFICATIONS

Length	32'1"
Length WL	29'8"
Beam	11'6"
Draft	3'8"
Weight	15,000#
Clearance	NA
Water	120 Gals.
Fuel	250 Gals.
Hull Type	Semi-Disp.
Designer	H. Halvorsen

Production
1981–Current

ISLAND GYPSY 32 SPORT FISHER

A great-looking little boat with a distinctive profile, the Island Gypsy 32 Sport Fisher uses the same semi-displacement hull used in the 32 Sedan model as well as the same flybridge mold. Said to be based on a traditional Australian fishing boat design, the 32 SF is built at the Kong & Halvorsen yard in mainland China. This is a fairly new model for K&H and most would agree that she's a handsome little fisherman with a spacious cockpit and a business-like appearance. The accommodations, suitable for two anglers, include V-berths forward, an enclosed head with stand-up shower, galley, and dinette. The lower helm (optional) is uniquely located just inside the cockpit door where forward and portside visibility are limited. The flybridge is small with passenger seating aft of the helm. Engine access is from inside the cabin as well as a raised cockpit hatch, and the transom door and swim platform are standard. A single 275-hp Lehman diesel will cruise the Island Gypsy 32 Sport Fisher at an economical 15 knots and deliver a top speed of 17–18 knots.❏

SPECIFICATIONS

Length	32'1"
Length WL	29'8"
Beam	11'6"
Draft	3'8"
Weight	13,000#
Clearance	NA
Water	120 Gals.
Fuel	250 Gals.
Cockpit	110 Sq. Ft.
Hull Type	Semi-Disp.
Designer	H. Halvorsen

Production
1987–Current

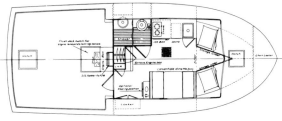

KONG & HALVORSEN

ISLAND GYPSY 36 AFT CABIN

Introduced in 1977, the Island Gypsy 36 Aft Cabin was originally built of wood (fiberglass construction first became available in 1978) and boasted a unique three-stateroom interior floorplan in addition to her handsome trawler-style profile. She's currently built in Mainland China on a semi-displacement hull with a deep keel below for stability and prop protection. A popular model, the original three-stateroom layout is still offered (with two heads but no stall shower) and a two-stateroom floorplan with an enlarged salon, stall showers fore and aft, and a double berth in the forward cabin is also available. The galley is located in the salon in both layouts along with a lower helm and deck access door. Standard features include an all-teak interior, teak overlay on the aft deck and walkways, mast and boom, swim platform, and a 3-kw generator. Powered with twin 135-hp Lehman diesels, the Island Gypsy 36 Aft Cabin will cruise at 8–9 knots and reach a top speed of 11 knots. Note that her sistership, the Island Gypsy 36 Sedan, is built on the same hull mold. ❏

SPECIFICATIONS

Length	36'0"
Length WL	32'10"
Beam	12'6"
Draft	3'11"
Weight	23,320#
Clearance	NA
Water	200 Gals.
Fuel	450 Gals.
Hull Type	Semi-Disp.
Designer	H. Halvorsen

Production
1977–Current

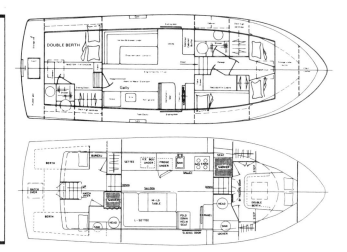

KONG & HALVORSEN

ISLAND GYPSY 40 FLUSH AFT DECK

The Island Gypsy 40 Flush Aft Deck is a fairly conventional double-cabin design with a trawler-style profile and a semi-displacement hull form. The boat is built of fiberglass at the company's China yard, and the workmanship and detailing appear to be in line with traditional high-quality Kong & Halvorsen standards. The interior is arranged with two staterooms, each of about the same size, with centerline double berths and private heads with separate stall showers. The L-shaped galley is aft to port in the salon and a lower helm (with deck access door) is standard. All of the woodwork is well-crafted Burmese teak — very traditional and typical of Asian-built boats. The small aft deck platform will handle a few folding chairs, and the bridge provides seating for six forward of the helm. The deck areas are non-skid fiberglass but the teak overlay has proven a popular option. Standard engines are 135-hp Lehman diesels (8 knots at cruise/11 knots top). Twin 275-hp Lehmans (14 knots cruise/17 top) and 375-hp Cats (18 knots cruise/22 knots top) are available as options. ❏

SPECIFICATIONS

Length	40'0"
Length WL	35'3"
Beam	14'3"
Draft	3'6"
Weight	30,000#
Clearance	NA
Water	200 Gals.
Fuel	400 Gals.
Hull Type	Semi-Disp.
Designer	H. Halvorsen

Production
1986–Current

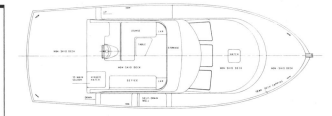

KONG & HALVORSEN

ISLAND GYPSY 44 FLUSH AFT DECK

Aside from her handsome, trawler-style looks and rugged construction, the Island Gypsy 44 Flush Aft Deck can claim a successful Atlantic crossing — a feat few similar boats of her size would ever attempt. She's built on a fiberglass semi-displacement hull form with fairly high freeboard, a graceful sheer, sharp entry and a well-flared bow. A long, deep keel protects the running gear and aids in tracking. Her accommodation plan provides for six in three double staterooms and two more on a berth made by converting the settee in the salon. Note that the L-shaped galley is conveniently located aft and to port in the salon, right next to the steps leading up to the aft deck. Both head compartments have stall showers, and the interior is lavishly finished with well-crafted teak woodwork and cabinetry throughout. Outside, the full-width afterdeck is quite large, and a hi-low table is provided for entertaining on the bridge. A good-selling model, twin 135-hp Lehman diesels are standard and the 44 will cruise economically at 10 knots. Optional 275-hp Lehmans cruise at 13 knots and reach a top speed of 16–17 knots. ❏

SPECIFICATIONS

Length	44'3"
Length WL	38'9"
Beam	15'0"
Draft	4'3"
Weight	32,000#
Clearance	NA
Water	400 Gals.
Fuel	800 Gals.
Hull Type	Semi-Disp.
Designer	H. Halvorsen

Production
1979–Current

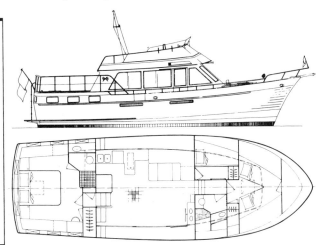

KONG & HALVORSEN

ISLAND GYPSY 44 MOTOR CRUISER

With her rakish profile and generous three-stateroom accommodation plan, the Island Gypsy 44 Motor Cruiser is a practical family sedan with several attractive features. She's built in mainland China on a semi-displacement hull with a fine bow entry and a deep keel with sufficient depth to protect the props and running gear. An extended bridge overhang covers the aft deck and results in a flybridge of unusual dimensions with space for dinghy storage or a sun lounge. Note that the helm is set well aft with wraparound bench seating forward of the console. A unique fold-out ladder provides quick access from the flybridge to the foredeck. Inside, the interior of the 44 Motor Cruiser is completely finished in teak and features a U-shaped galley to port in the salon, with a lower station and deck access door opposite. A good-selling model, several diesel engine options have been available with the 375-hp Caterpillar diesels currently being among the more popular. With these engines, the Island Gypsy 44 Motor Cruiser will cruise at 16–17 knots and reach 21 knots wide open. ❏

SPECIFICATIONS

Length	44'3"
Length WL	38'9"
Beam	15'4"
Draft	4'3"
Weight	35,000#
Clearance	NA
Water	320 Gals.
Fuel	720 Gals.
Hull Type	Semi-Disp.
Designer	H. Halvorsen

Production
1983-Current

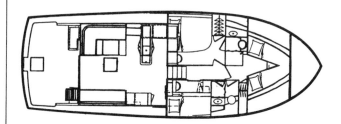

KONG & HALVORSEN

ISLAND GYPSY 49 RAISED PH

The Island Gypsy 49 is the first true pilothouse design for Kong & Halvorsen, a company well-known in the U.S. for their traditional series of cruising trawlers. She's constructed on an all-fiberglass, semi-displacement hull with a prominent bow, hard chines, and a fairly deep keel below. Note the bulwarks protecting the walkaround in front of the house. Her floorplan is arranged with the galley in the salon and three staterooms forward — a layout often seen in raised pilothouse boats allowing for a low-profile house. The master stateroom is quite roomy and both heads have stall showers. There are port and starboard deck doors in the wheelhouse along with bridge access steps and a settee/dayberth. Additional features include standing headroom in the engine room; teak interior woodwork; teak and holly cabin soles; and a large 200 sq. ft. flybridge with settee, table and radar mast. The sidedecks and aft deck are weather protected by bridge overhangs. A handsome boat, twin 375-hp Cat diesels cruise the Island Gypsy 49 Pilothouse at 13–14 knots and reach about 17 knots top. ❏

SPECIFICATIONS

Length	49'0"
Length WL	43'6"
Beam	15'4"
Draft	4'5"
Weight	46,000#
Clearance	NA
Water	400 Gals.
Fuel	800 Gals.
Hull Type	Semi-Disp.
Designer	Halvorsen

Production
1991–Current

ISLAND GYPSY 51 MOTOR YACHT

Constructed on a wide 16'6" beam, the Island Gypsy 51 MY is a roomy cruising yacht with attractive lines and a handsome profile. She's built on a solid fiberglass hull (early models used a cored hull) and features a practical three-stateroom, three-head floorplan with a spacious walk-in engine room. The galley is on the deckhouse level, and the lower helm is open to the salon so as not to separate the owner/helmsman from his guests. Interior paneling and trimwork are traditional Burmese teak and large cabin windows provide all-around visibility from the helm and salon. Double doors in the salon bulkhead open to the large protected afterdeck with wing doors and a wraparound dodger panel. The flybridge of the Island Gypsy 51 MY is huge and includes some 320 sq. ft. of sundeck area. All deck areas are overlaid with teak (including the flybridge) as standard equipment. Several diesel options are available for the Island Gypsy 51 MY including the popular 375-hp Cats (11-knots at cruise and 14-knots top). With 1,200 gallons of fuel the cruising range at hull speed is about 1,000 miles. ❏

SPECIFICATIONS

Length......................51'0"
Length WL...............44'10"
Beam.........................16'6"
Draft ....4'2"
Weight ....49,000#
Clearance ....NA
Water.................600 Gals.
Fuel ....1,200 Gals.
Hull Type.........Modified-V
Designer.......H. Halvorsen

Production
1983–Current

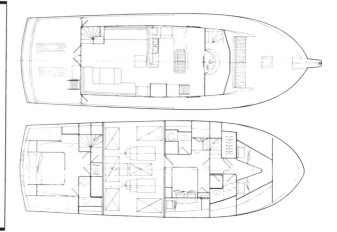

LUHRS

Brief History

Originally known as Henry Luhrs Sea Skiffs, Luhrs began building mahogany runabouts and cruisers in the early 1950s from their facilities in Morgan, New Jersey. A fiberglass 29-footer in 1965 made Luhrs one of the early builders to use this material in a production boat. Bangor Punta acquired Luhrs in 1965 and the family repurchased the company in 1981.

SELECTED LUHRS INBOARD MODELS

Luhrs Tournament 290 (Early)

Luhrs Tournament 290

Luhrs Tournament 290 Open SF

Luhrs Alura 30

Luhrs Tournament 300 SF

Luhrs Tournament 320

Luhrs 340 Sportfisherman

Luhrs Tournament 342

Luhrs 3400 Motor Yacht

Luhrs 3420 Motor Yacht

Luhrs Alura 35

Luhrs Tournament 350

Luhrs Tournament 380

Luhrs Tournament 380 Open

Luhrs Tournament 400

Main Office

Luhrs Corp., 255 Diesel Road, St. Augustine, FL 32086
904-829-0500

365

LUHRS TOURNAMENT 290 (EARLY)

The first Luhrs Tournament 290 (there have been three) is a businesslike sportfisherman with good performance and an attractive price. Options were few; the 290 came with a marlin tower complete with rocket launchers and controls. She's built on a modified-V hull with a double chine and a steep 17° of deadrise at the transom. An out-and-out fishing boat, the Tournament 290 has a large bi-level cockpit with roughly 60 sq. ft. of fishing area on the lower level. Three lift-out fish boxes provide good access to the rudder posts and bilges, and a cockpit washdown and coaming padding were standard. The raised helm seat is on the centerline with a companion seat to port and an overhead electronics box. The accommodations below are simple but nicely finished with oak paneling and a teak and holly sole. Cabin headroom is 6'2". The full-width of the cabin results in narrow sidedecks and walking forward to the bow is difficult. Twin 270-hp Crusaders were standard with GM 6.2 diesels offered as an option. The 270s will cruise the Luhrs Tournament 290 around 24 knots with a top speed of 30+. ❏

SPECIFICATIONS

Length	29'0"
Beam	10'9"
Draft	2'5"
Weight	9,000#
Clearance	14'6"
Water	40 Gals.
Fuel	200/260 Gals.
Cockpit	60 Sq. Ft.
Hull Type	Modified-V
Designer	Mike Peters

Production
1986–88

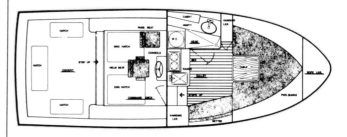

LUHRS TOURNAMENT 290

With her large cockpit and full walkaround deck layout, the Luhrs Tournament 290 was designed primarily for the active sportfisherman. The second of three 29' open express models from Luhrs, she was built on the same hull as the original Tournament 290 (1986–88) with a relatively deep 17° of deadrise at the transom and solid fiberglass hull construction. Dedicated anglers will appreciate the wide sidedecks and efficient cockpit layout. Fishing features include rod storage under the gunwales, a drop curtain to enclose the lower helm, standard bait center, a large livewell in the transom, and a standard factory tower with controls. Note the lack of a windshield at the helm. Below, the cabin of the Tournament 290 is surprisingly spacious for a walkaround design. The dinette converts to a double berth, and the galley and head are adequate for weekend service. The seat at the lower helm also folds out when two extra berths are required. A fast boat with standard 270-hp Crusaders, the Luhrs Tournament 290 will cruise around 23 knots and reach 31–32 knots wide open. ❑

SPECIFICATIONS

Length	29'6"
Length WL	24'7"
Beam	10'9"
Draft	2'5"
Weight	7,480#
Clearance	NA
Water	40 Gals.
Fuel	250 Gals.
Cockpit	NA
Hull Type	Modified-V
Designer	Mike Peters

Production
1989–91

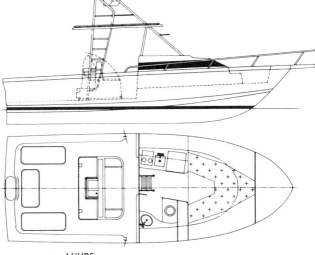

LUHRS

LUHRS TOURNAMENT 290 OPEN SF

The Tournament 290 Open Sport-fisherman is a scaled-down version of the Tournament 380 introduced in 1991. Luhrs is building some good-looking fishing boats these days and the 290 Open will appeal to anglers seeking a capable offshore fishing platform at an affordable price. She's built on a lightweight deep-V hull design (18° of transom deadrise) with a wide 11'6" beam and cored hullsides. Her cockpit is large enough for a full-size chair and includes two in-deck fishboxes, a unique lift-out transom door, and a smaller fishbox built into the transom. The helm is located on the centerline (very practical) and the bridgedeck sole lifts up for easy access to the step-down engine room. There are overnight accommodations for four in the small cabin, which is arranged with the head in the forepeak. Notable features include a full tower with buggy top and controls, electronics box, entertainment center, bait prep station, and side exhausts. A neat boat, standard 350-cid gas engines will cruise the Tournament 290 at 21-22 knots and reach a top speed of around 30 knots. ❏

SPECIFICATIONS

Length	29'10"
Beam	11'6"
Draft	2'9"
Weight	8,000#
Clearance	16'6"
Water	30 Gals.
Fuel	300 Gals.
Cockpit	NA
Hull Type	Deep-V
Designer	Luhrs

Production
1992–Current

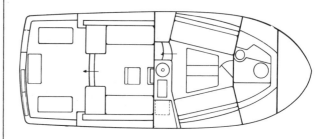

LUHRS ALURA 30

Featuring a distinctive Downeast profile, the Alura 30 is a versatile weekend-type boat with a large cockpit and very comfortable cabin accommodations. The Alura is built on a semi-displacement hull of solid fiberglass construction and moderate deadrise aft. Her long keel provides a measure of prop protection while providing good handling characteristics at low speeds. Although the Alura 30 is not considered a beamy boat, the cockpit is exceptionally large and includes built-in baitwells and fish boxes. Helm visibility is good, and the windshield may be opened for ventilation. Her wide sidedecks are also notable. Inside, the cabin layout is clean and simple, and the teak and holly sole is especially attractive. Two people can cruise aboard this boat for a few days without problem. A good all-purpose design, the Alura 30 will do well as a dive boat or as an inexpensive fisherman and weekend cruiser. Note that the keel was redesigned in 1988 to reduce vibration problems. Her single 270-hp gas engine provides an efficient cruising speed of 14–15 knots and a top speed of around 22 knots. ❏

SPECIFICATIONS

Length	30'0"
Length WL	28'0"
Beam	10'3"
Draft	2'11"
Weight	7,800#
Clearance	NA
Water	38 Gals.
Fuel	196 Gals.
Cockpit	110 Sq. Ft.
Hull Type	Semi-Disp.
Designer	Luhrs

Production
1987–90

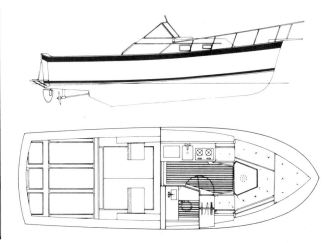

LUHRS TOURNAMENT 300 SF

The Tournament 300 SF is an updated version of the earlier Tournament 290, with several improvements including a windshield and molded swim platform. With her reverse transom and standard hardtop and tower, the 300 is a good-looking boat. Built on a deep-V hull (18° deadrise aft) with cored hullsides, her cockpit is large enough to handle a fighting chair and comes standard with an in-deck fishbox, tackle drawers, bait prep center, rod locker (lockable), and two built-in seats with rod gimbals. The helm is set behind a center-vent windshield and there's space in the console for flush-mounting electronics. A baitwell is located on the transom platform and the full-length helm seat features a hydraulic lift mechanism for easy access to the (tight) engine compartment. Cabin accommodations include a dinette that converts to a double berth, small galley, and a stand-up head with shower — a generous layout considering that this is a full walkaround boat. Twin 350 cid gas engines are standard. With optional 170-hp Yanmar diesels the Tournament 300 will cruise economically at 22 knots (14 gph) and reach a top speed of 25–26 knots. ❑

SPECIFICATIONS

Length	31'6"
Beam	10'9"
Draft	2'6"
Weight	12,000#
Clearance	11'6"
Water	40 Gals.
Fuel	250 Gals.
Cockpit	NA
Hull Type	Deep-V
Designer	Luhrs

Production
1991–Current

LUHRS TOURNAMENT 320

The Luhrs Tournament 320 has the profile and distant appearance of a high-dollar custom sportfisherman. Indeed, her lines are very attractive, and the affordable price of the Tournament 320 has already made her a popular boat in a short period of time. She's built on a double-chined hull with lightweight balsa coring and 15° of deadrise at the transom. Primarily a fishing boat, her surprisingly roomy cabin can accommodate six overnighters by converting the dinette and settee. An island berth is fitted in the forward stateroom, and a complete gal-ley and head compartment (no shower stall) round out the floorplan. The flybridge is fitted with bench seating forward of the helm console. The 320's large, uncluttered fishing cockpit has enough room for a small mounted chair. Standard equipment includes built-in fish boxes, livewell, tackle center with controls, fresh and saltwater washdowns, and a transom door. Standard 320-hp Crusader gas engines will cruise the Luhrs Tournament 320 around 21 knots and reach a top speed of 30–31 knots. Note that the interior was upgraded (no dinette) in 1992. ❏

SPECIFICATIONS

Length	31'6"
Beam	12'8"
Draft	3'1"
Weight	11,800#
Clearance	NA
Water	60 Gals.
Fuel	300 Gals.
Cockpit	NA
Hull Type	Modified-V
Designer	Luhrs

Production
1988–Current

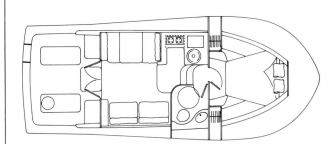

LUHRS 340 SPORTFISHERMAN

The Luhrs 340 Sportfisherman was built on the same hull as the Silverton 34 Convertible — a proven and well-tested design with generous flare at the bow and about 15° of deadrise at the transom. She was marketed as an inexpensive and fully equipped fisherman with a marlin tower, fish boxes, salt and freshwater washdown, cockpit coaming, and recessed rod storage in the cabin — all standard. The Luhrs 340 has a large bi-level cockpit (the bridgedeck is raised two feet) resulting in good helm visibility and adequate working space in the engine compartment. Note that the helm console is set on the centerline with the companionway offset to starboard. Below, the 340's cabin is arranged in the normal fashion with a convertible dinette and V-berths in the stateroom. Teak-trimmed white mica cabinetry and a teak and holly sole highlight the interior. Side exhaust ports keep potentially dangerous fumes from collecting in the cockpit or cabin area. Optional 210-hp GM 8.2 diesels will cruise the Luhrs 340 SF around 23 knots and reach 25–26 knots wide open. ❏

SPECIFICATIONS

Length	34'0"
Beam	12'6"
Draft	3'0"
Weight	12,300#
Clearance	11'5"
Water	60 Gals.
Fuel	260 Gals.
Cockpit	67 Sq. Ft.
Hull Type	Modified-V
Designer	J. Fielding

Production
1983–87

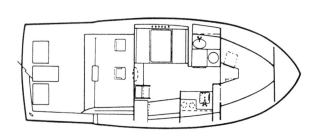

LUHRS TOURNAMENT 342

The Luhrs Tournament 342 shares the same hull as the Luhrs 340 but with a different superstructure and a much larger interior. Like all of the current Luhrs products, the 342 was offered as a fairly complete package in keeping with the Luhrs' practice of marketing a well-equipped boat at an affordable price. Her cockpit will handle a mounted chair and comes equipped with fresh and saltwater washdowns, fishboxes (small), and padded coaming. The fly-bridge is particularly spacious with bench seating forward of the console. The original layout featured two state-rooms, a deckhouse dinette, and oak woodwork. A new and much-revised layout was introduced in 1988 with only one stateroom, a more open salon/galley arrangement, and an updated decor with an absence of any wood. The 342 also has a unique cabin ventilation system with hidden air intakes located beneath the forward bridge overhang. A good-running boat with brisk acceleration, the Luhrs Tournament 342 will cruise at 21–22 knots with standard 454-cid Crusaders gas engines and reach a top speed of 30 knots. ❑

SPECIFICATIONS

Length	34'0"
Beam	12'6"
Draft	3'2"
Weight	13,500#
Clearance	11'5"
Water	60 Gals.
Fuel	300 Gals.
Cockpit	67 Sq. Ft.
Hull Type	Modified-V
Designer	J. Fielding

Production
1986–89

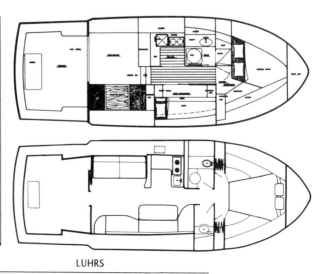

LUHRS 3400 MOTOR YACHT

The Luhrs 3400 Motor Yacht is built on the same modified-V hull as the earlier Tournament 340 and 342 models. What Luhrs engineers have done is to give the 3400 a much larger interior volume by moving the salon bulkhead well aft into the cockpit and designing the new layout with a modern Eurostyle decor. The result is a spacious family cruiser with the galley and dinette down, wraparound windows in the salon, a complete entertainment center, and a queen-sized island berth in the stateroom — all in a fairly attractive and moderately priced package. Calling this boat a "Motor Yacht" is wishful thinking at its best; the 3400 is actually a flybridge sedan with larger-than-average interior dimensions. The cockpit is too small for any serious fishing activities but the flybridge is huge and includes a convenient walkthrough to the foredeck (which compensates for the boat's somewhat narrow sidedecks). Standard 320-hp Crusader gas engines will cruise the Luhrs 3400 MY at 19–20 knots and reach about 28 knots wide open. Twin 300-hp Cummins diesels are optional. ❑

SPECIFICATIONS

Length......................34'0"
Beam........................12'6"
Draft ....3'2"
Weight ....13,500#
Clearance ....22'0"
Water...................60 Gals.
Fuel ....300 Gals.
Cockpit........................NA
Hull Type.........Modified-V
Designer ....J. Fielding

Production
1990–Current

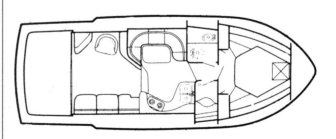

LUHRS 3420 MOTOR YACHT

Closely resembling the 3400 MY, the newer Luhrs 3420 has a larger cockpit, a smaller salon, and a revised flybridge layout without the foredeck walk-thru. For just a 34' hull, there's a lot of interior volume in the 3420. The floorplan is arranged with the mid-level galley open to the salon and there's a centerline double berth in the stateroom. With the dinette and salon settee converted, there are overnight accommodations for six. Note that the head is divided with the shower stall to starboard. The interior is attractively finished with colorful pastel fabrics and carpeting accented with a modest amount of teak trim. Outside, the cockpit is small — useful enough for open-air entertaining but not suitable for any serious fishing pursuits. Guest seating is provided forward of the helm console on the flybridge and the aluminum arch is standard. Additional features include a built-in TV, VCR, and stereo; oak parquet galley sole; fishbox; washdown; cockpit bridge overhang; and a swim platform with molded bait well. Twin 454-cid gas engines will cruise the Luhrs 3420 at 19–20 knots and reach a top speed of around 28 knots. ❑

SPECIFICATIONS

Length	34'0"
Beam	12'6"
Draft	3'2"
Weight	13,500#
Clearance	22'0"
Water	60 Gals.
Fuel	300 Gals.
Cockpit	50 Sq. Ft.
Hull Type	Modified-V
Designer	Luhrs

Production
1991–Current

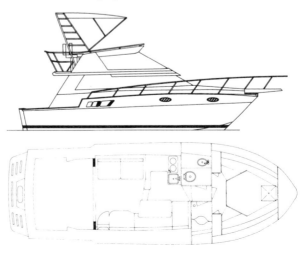

LUHRS ALURA 35

The appealing Downeast character of the original Alura 30 is missing from the more recent Alura 35. Here, the styling is more contemporary and the accent is on the popular "sportboat" image. As such, the Alura 35 was designed to appeal to the price-conscious buyer. This is a very straightforward design without the curved windshield, fancy radar arch, or elaborate swim platform found in many of today's modern sportboats. What the Alura 35 does provide is a lot of boat for the money. The Eurostyle interior accommodations are roomy and very comfortable with a private mid-cabin fitted aft below the raised bridgedeck. The decor is light and airy, and the urethaned teak and holly cabin sole is especially attractive. Outside, the 35's large, bi-level cockpit is well suited for fishing, and anglers will appreciate the bait prep center with cutting board behind the helm seat. A bow pulpit and anchor well were standard. A practical and low maintenance family cruiser, twin 270-hp Crusader gas engines will cruise the Alura 35 at around 18 knots with a top speed of 26–27 knots.   ❑

SPECIFICATIONS

Length	35'5"
Length WL	32'5"
Beam	12'2"
Draft	2'11"
Weight	12,800#
Clearance	NA
Water	55 Gals.
Fuel	260 Gals.
Cockpit	NA
Hull Type	Modified-V
Designer	Luhrs

Production
1988–89

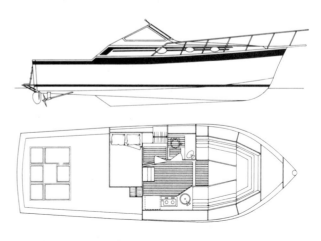

LUHRS TOURNAMENT 350

Luhrs has had a good deal of success with their Tournament series of sportfishing boats since 1988 when the first of these models — the Tournament 320 — was introduced. Designed to fill the gap between the 320 and 380 models, the Tournament 350 is built on an all-new hull design with balsa coring in the hullsides and a steep 17° of transom deadrise. The aggressive profile and custom-style appearance of the 350 are accented by her darkly tinted, wrap-around windows and a rakish flybridge with its stylish cockpit overhang. She features a spacious single-stateroom floorplan with a mid-level galley which is open to the salon. A pedestal berth is forward, and the large head includes a separate stall shower. While the interior of the Tournament 350 seems large for only a 35' boat, the cockpit is still big enough for the installation of a fighting chair and a full tackle center. A transom door and in-deck fish boxes are standard. Twin 320-hp Crusader gas engines will cruise the Tournament 350 at 17 knots with a top speed of around 25-26 knots. The optional 300-hp GM diesels cruise around 23 knots and reach 26 knots top. ❏

SPECIFICATIONS

Length	35'0"
Beam	12'10"
Draft	3'4"
Weight	13,700#
Clearance	16'0"
Water	93 Gals.
Fuel	390 Gals.
Cockpit	94 Sq. Ft.
Hull Type	Deep-V
Designer	Luhrs

Production
1990–Current

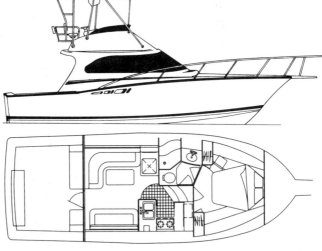

LUHRS

LUHRS TOURNAMENT 380

The Tournament 380 is another in the Luhrs series of popularly priced off-shore sportfishermen. She's built on a wide beam, deep-V hull with generous flare at the bow, a steep 18° of transom deadrise, and balsa coring in the hull-sides. A handsome boat with plenty of eye appeal, the Luhrs 380 has the classic profile of an expensive custom-built sportfisherman. The half-tower is standard, and her tournament-style fly-bridge and large cockpit with molded tackle center should satisfy the demands of most serious anglers. The original two-stateroom interior was arranged with a serving counter separating the galley from the salon area. The standard floorplan was restyled in 1990 when the galley was redesigned and the salon opened up to provide more usable floor space — a notable and practical improvement. Interestingly, the front windows are real and not fiberglassed-over although the wraparound deckhouse mask does a good job of concealing them. Crusader 454-cid gas engines were standard (15 knots cruise) until 1991 when 425-hp J&T 6-71s became standard (22 knots cruise/27 knots top). ❑

SPECIFICATIONS

Length	38'1"
Beam	14'11"
Draft	3'7"
Weight	NA
Clearance	12'0"
Water	100 Gals.
Fuel	450 Gals.
Cockpit	100 Sq. Ft.
Hull Type	Deep-V
Designer	Luhrs

Production
1989–Current

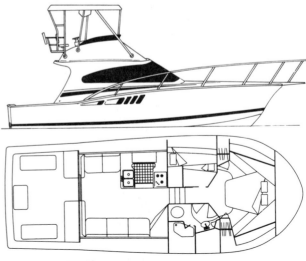

LUHRS TOURNAMENT 380 OPEN

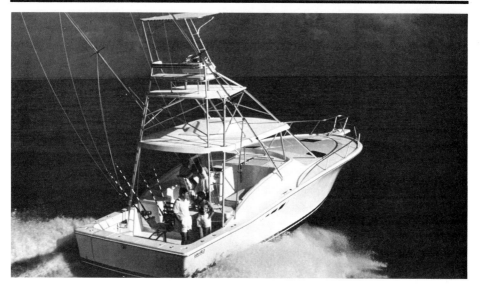

Luhrs has come up with a real beauty in the Tournament 380 Open, a versatile and feature-packed fishing machine with a very inviting price tag. Open sportfishermen are growing in length and popularity in recent years and this is becoming a very competitive market. Built on a wide, low-profile hull with cored hullsides and a steep 18° of deadrise aft, the 380 Open is a roomy and capable offshore boat. Her large bi-level cockpit layout includes a unique centerline helm console, flanking full-length lounge seating with rod storage under, molded transom fishbox, and

P&S molded tackle centers which double as bait-watching seats. The interior of the Tournament 380 is notable for its spacious layout, varnished teak cabinetry, and stylish decor — impressive indeed for a serious fishboat. Additional features include a full tuna tower with hardtop, hydraulic bridgedeck lift mechanism for superb engine room access, pop-up electronics display at the helm, and side exhausts. A good-running boat with excellent range, standard 485-hp 6-71 diesels cruise the 380 Open around 26 knots and deliver 29–30 knots wide open. ❑

SPECIFICATIONS

Length	37'10"
Beam	14'11"
Draft	3'7"
Weight	24,000#
Clearance	22'0"
Water	85 Gals.
Fuel	600 Gals.
Cockpit	100 Sq. Ft.
Hull Type	Deep-V
Designer	Luhrs

Production
1991–Current

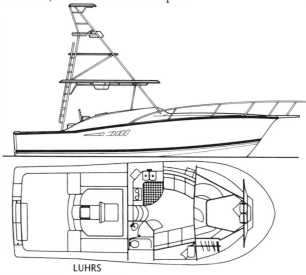

LUHRS

LUHRS TOURNAMENT 400

Built on the same hull as the Silverton 40 Convertible, the Luhrs Tournament 400 was a moderately priced convertible sportfisherman with aggressive lines and comfortable accommodations below. With her rakish flybridge and black wraparound deckhouse mask, the Luhrs 400 has a very distinctive profile. A roomy boat, her two-stateroom interior is arranged with the galley-down and an L-shaped dinette located in the salon. The forward stateroom has an offset double berth, and over/under bunks are fitted in the guest cabin. The 400's interior originally featured oak paneling but was revised in 1988 with updated fabrics and off-white mica surfaces trimmed in teak. Fishing accessories in the cockpit include fresh- and saltwater washdowns, an in-deck fish box, rocket launchers, and flush rod holders. The half-tower is a standard feature of the Tournament 400 and the flybridge is notably large compared to other convertibles her size. With 454-cid Crusader gas engines, she'll cruise at 15–16 knots (around 25 knots top). Optional 375-hp Cats cruise the Tournament 400 around 22 knots and reach 26 wide open. ❏

SPECIFICATIONS

Length	40'0"
Beam	14'0"
Draft	3'2"
Weight	25,500#
Clearance	14'0"
Water	100 Gals.
Fuel	400 Gals.
Cockpit	NA
Hull Type	Modified-V
Designer	Bob Rioux

Production
1987–90

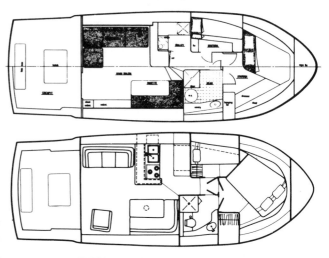

LUHRS

MAINSHIP

Brief History

Today's Mainship Company is a spin-off of the original Mainship series of trawlers introduced by Silverton in 1978. During most of the 1980s, Mainship was known for its efficient trawler-style family cruisers. In 1988 the company surprised the industry with their super-Eurostyle Mediterranean series. Mainship is recognized today as a volume builder of moderately priced family cruisers.

Selected Mainship Models

Mainship 34 Sedan
Mainship 34 II
Mainship 34 III
Mainship 35 Convertible
Nantucket 36 Double Cabin
Nantucket 36 Sedan
Mainship 36 Express

Mainship 36 Sedan Bridge
Mainship 39 Express
Nantucket 40 Double Cabin
Mainship 41 Grand Salon
Mainship 41 Convertible
Mainship 47 Motor Yacht

Main Office

Luhrs Corp., 255 Diesel Road, St. Augustine, FL 32086
904-829-0500

381

MAINSHIP 34 SEDAN

The Mainship 34 Sedan is one of the most popular small cruisers ever built in the U.S. She was constructed on a solid fiberglass semi-displacement hull design with a fine bow entry and a full-length keel below. First of the Mainship series, the appeal of the 34 Sedan had much to do with her trawler-style profile and affordable price tag, but her greatest attraction remains her superb economy. With a single 160-hp Perkins 6-cylinder diesel, the Mainship's easily driven hull will cruise at 10–11 knots while burning only 6 gph. At a more relaxed 7-knot speed, the fuel consumption drops to a remarkable 2 gph. Besides her impressive economy, the Mainship 34 also features a practical single-stateroom floorplan well suited to the needs of a cruising couple. A lower helm was standard in the salon, the galley is large enough for serious food preparation, and a stall shower is included in the head. Outside, the flybridge extends aft to provide weather protection for the cockpit. Considered a low-maintenance boat, the Mainship 34 Sedan continues to enjoy great popularity in most markets. ❏

SPECIFICATIONS

Length	34'0"
Length WL	NA
Beam	11'11"
Draft	2'10"
Weight	14,000#
Clearance	13'6"
Water	50 Gals.
Fuel	220 Gals.
Cockpit	80 Sq. Ft.
Hull Type	Semi-Disp.
Designer	Cherubini

Production
1978–82

MAINSHIP 34 II

With her clean-cut profile, seakindly hull, and attractive interior, the Mainship II is a practical family cruiser with a cockpit large enough for some light-tackle fishing pursuits. She's built on the same fuel-efficient hull used in the production of the original Mainship 34 — a lightweight semi-displacement design with a distinctive trawler-style profile. Her single-stateroom layout is arranged with the U-shaped galley-down and a stall shower is found in the head compartment. A lower helm is standard in the salon and there's a convenient pass-through serving counter from the galley below. This is basically the same layout used in the Mainship 34 but the salon is smaller in order to provide for the larger cockpit. Additional features include a roomy engine compartment, wide sidedecks, full wraparound cabin windows, foredeck mast, and teak interior trim. The flybridge is quite small with bench seating for two. A single turbocharged 160-hp Perkins diesel was standard in the Mainship 34 II. She'll cruise easily around 11 knots (burning just 6 gph) and reach a top speed of 14 knots. ❏

SPECIFICATIONS

Length	34'0"
Length WL	NA
Beam	11'11"
Draft	2'10"
Weight	14,000#
Clearance	13'6"
Water	50 Gals.
Fuel	220 Gals.
Cockpit	78 Sq. Ft.
Hull Type	Semi-Disp.
Designer	Cherubini

Production
1980–82

MAINSHIP 34 III

The Mainship 34 III is a refined and more stylish version of the original Mainship 34 Sedan. (There was also a fishing version called the Mainship 34 II, which met with only limited success.) In the 34 III, the salon has been lengthened by some 9" to add interior space, and the extended hardtop of the original 34 Sedan was eliminated in favor of a more open cockpit. The same basic interior (updated from teak to light oak trimwork in 1985) was retained with a slightly larger galley and bigger salon windows. While the cockpit of the 34 III is somewhat smaller than the earlier Mainship 34, a transom door and swim platform were made standard. Every Mainship 34 is powered with a single diesel engine (usually a 165-hp or 200-hp Perkins) capable of cruising at 7 knots at 2 gph, or 13–14 knots at only 6–7 gph. The fuel efficiency of this coastal cruiser is truly impressive and used Mainship 34 IIIs are always in demand. In all, over 900 Mainship 34s were built including the original Sedan and 34 II models, and these boats remain a benchmark in owner popularity. ❑

SPECIFICATIONS

Length	34'0"
Length WL	NA
Beam	11'11"
Draft	3'6"
Weight	14,000#
Clearance	13'6"
Water	40 Gals.
Fuel	190 Gals.
Cockpit	NA
Hull Type	Semi-Disp.
Designer	Cherubini

Production
1983–88

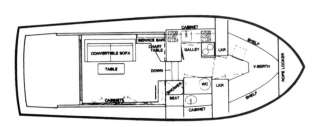

MAINSHIP 35 CONVERTIBLE

The Mainship 35 Convertible (called the Mediterranean 35 "Cockpit" until 1992) is a modern family cruising sedan with one of the largest interior layouts in her class. The clean profile of the Mainship 35 speaks for itself — European, streamlined, and very distinctive. Built on a solid glass hull with a modest 12° deadrise aft, the sleek styling gives her the appearance of a bigger boat. The original single-stateroom floorplan was replaced with a two-stateroom dinette layout in 1992 when the boat was restyled. Further updates for 1992 included white windshield frames (replacing the earlier black frames), a bigger flybridge with additional seating, and new interior colors. While there are few 35' boats with two staterooms *and* a dinette, the Mainship even manages a roomy salon — very impressive. The cockpit is small with a transom door, engine compartment hatches, and molded-in bridge steps. Note the single-piece Eurostyle rails and step-down window styling. Standard 454-cid Crusader gas engines will cruise the Mainship 35 at 17–18 knots with a top speed of around 28 knots. ❑

SPECIFICATIONS

Length	34'11"
Beam	12'8"
Draft	2'10"
Weight	16,000#
Clearance	15'0"
Water	80 Gals.
Fuel	250 Gals.
Cockpit	80 Sq. Ft.
Hull Type	Modified-V
Designer	Mike Peters

Production
1988–Current

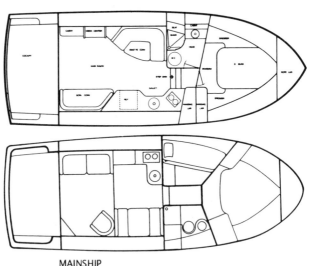

MAINSHIP

NANTUCKET 36 DOUBLE CABIN

A popular boat, the Nantucket 36 Double Cabin is a conservative design with an attractive profile and an efficient cabin layout. Built on a solid fiberglass hull with moderate deadrise aft, her profile displays a hint of trawler styling. The interior accommodations aboard the Nantucket 36 are arranged with the galley and dinette down a few steps from the salon level. V-berths are forward, and a walkaround double berth is fitted in the aft stateroom. Large, wraparound deckhouse windows provide an abundance of natural light-ing. In 1985, the original teak interior was replaced with light oak woodwork. Outside, the 36 has a full-width after-deck with nearly 90 sq. ft. of entertain-ment area. The bridge is only three steps up and will seat four. Included in a long list of standard equipment was a gener-ator, lower helm station, bow pulpit, and swim platform. With only twin 270-hp Crusader gas engines, the Nantucket 36 Double Cabin has a relatively good turn of speed. She'll cruise comfortably at a respectable 17 knots and reach a top speed of around 25–26 knots. ❑

SPECIFICATIONS

Length	36'2"
Length WL	NA
Beam	13'0"
Draft	2'2"
Weight	20,000#
Clearance	11'3"
Water	100 Gals.
Fuel	240 Gals.
Hull Type	Modified-V
Designer	Mainship

Production
1984–89

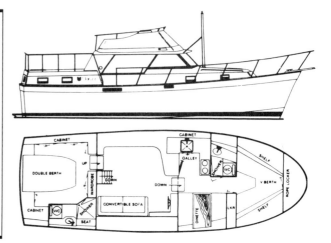

MAINSHIP

NANTUCKET 36 SEDAN

Sharing the same hull as the 36 Double Cabin, the Nantucket 36 Sedan has the interior space and comfort of a much larger boat. Indeed, the salon dimensions are unusually generous due to the fact that the salon bulkhead is designed well aft to increase the interior dimensions at the expense of cockpit space. Although a comfortable cruising boat, the profile of the 36 Sedan is on the boxy side. There are two staterooms on the lower level as well as a stall shower in the head, and both the galley and dinette are located in the salon. The decor features attractive light oak woodwork, and with the dinette converted, there are overnight accommodations for as many as six. Outside, a second benefit of her extended main salon is seen in the spacious flybridge where L-shaped lounge seating is provided aft of the helm. A good performer with standard Crusader 270-hp gas engines, she'll cruise at 17 knots and reach 25–26 knots wide open. Approximately 50 Nantucket 36 Sedans were built before she was replaced in 1988 with the new Mainship Mediterranean 35. ❏

SPECIFICATIONS

Length	36'2"
Beam	13'0"
Draft	3'0"
Weight	20,000#
Clearance	11'3"
Water	100 Gals.
Fuel	240 Gals.
Cockpit	NA
Hull Type	Modified-V
Designer	Mainship

Production
1986–88

MAINSHIP

MAINSHIP 36 EXPRESS

The Mainship 36 Express (originally called the 35 Open when she was introduced in 1990) is a Eurostyle express cruiser with a large cockpit and a practical mid-cabin interior layout. Her high freeboard and lack of a curved wraparound windshield keep the 36 Express from being a truly attractive and modern design in our eyes, and her portside helm is unusual (most builders place the helm to starboard). Because about half of the boat's length is devoted to the spacious cockpit, the interior dimensions are fairly modest compared with other express cruisers in this size range. The two-stateroom floorplan (upgraded in 1992) is arranged with a step-down mid-cabin aft, compact galley, and stall shower in the head compartment. The absence of interior bulkheads adds to the impression of space although there are no privacy doors for the staterooms. The real appeal of this boat is the cockpit with its sexy helm console, contoured sun lounge, walk-through transom, and seating for a crowd. A hatch in the sole provides good access to the engines and V-drives. Crusader 454-cid gas engines will cruise at 19 knots and reach a top speed of 27–28 knots. ❑

SPECIFICATIONS

Length	36'5"
Length WL	NA
Beam	12'5"
Draft	2'8"
Weight	13,500#
Clearance	10'6"
Water	75 Gals.
Fuel	250 Gals.
Hull Type	Modified-V
Designer	Mike Peters

Production
1990–Current

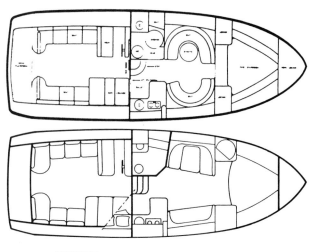

MAINSHIP 36 SEDAN BRIDGE

While maximum interior volume is obviously the theme of this model, the egg-shaped exterior styling of the Mainship 36 Sedan Bridge is very unorthodox. Appearances aside, the full-width interior of this boat is cavernous and ideally suited to entertaining on a grand scale. The Mainship 36 is built on the same modified-V hull (12° of transom deadrise) used in the production of the 35 Convertible. (Note that she was originally called the 35 "Open Bridge" when introduced in 1990.) The single-level interior is set well below the cockpit level and the headroom throughout is extraordinary. Indeed, these are comfortable accommodations for a 36' boat and the facing salon settees are notable. The only outside natural lighting comes through the glass salon bulkhead and overhead hatches as the cabin windows are tiny. Additional features include a walk-through from the bridge to the foredeck, attractive cherry interior trim, and wraparound bridge seating. Standard 454-cid gas engines will cruise the 36 Sedan Bridge at a respectable 17–18 knots and deliver a top speed of around 28 knots. ❏

SPECIFICATIONS

Length	36'0"
Length WL	NA
Beam	12'5"
Draft	2'8"
Weight	13,500#
Clearance	10'0"
Water	85 Gals.
Fuel	250 Gals.
Hull Type	Modified-V
Designer	K. Boehler

Production
1990–Current

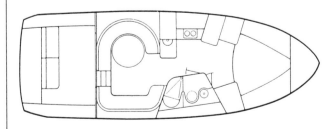

MAINSHIP 39 EXPRESS

The Mainship 39 Express (originally called the 39 Open) has the bold and seductive profile of a modern Italian sportboat although the absence of a stylish curved windshield is a little disappointing. She's built on a solid glass hull with a wide beam and a modest 12° transom deadrise. Not surprisingly, the Mainship 39's two-stateroom interior layout is lavish and extremely spacious. The convertible dinette and settee provide seating for a crowd and outside natural lighting is excellent thanks to a series of translucent overhead deck hatches. The single-level cockpit of the Mainship 39 is huge with a contoured sun lounge next to the Eurostyle helm, full wet bar, and wrap-around lounge seating for a dozen people. Additional features include a unique bi-level transom design, twin foredeck sun pads, side exhausts, and radar arch. Note that the sidedecks are extremely narrow on this boat and going forward is a dicey proposition while underway. With V-drives and 502-cid Crusader gas engines, the Mainship 39 Express will cruise at a respectable 21 knots and reach a top speed of 28–29 knots. ❑

SPECIFICATIONS

Length......................39'2"
Beam........................14'1"
Draft ....3'4"
Weight ....15,000#
Clearance ....8'0"
Water...................80 Gals.
Fuel ....320 Gals.
Cockpit........................NA
Hull Type........Modified-V
Designer.........Mike Peters

Production
1989–Current

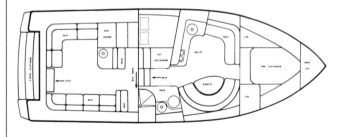

NANTUCKET 40 DOUBLE CABIN

In 1981, Silverton introduced the Mainship 40 Sedan — a handsome design with a huge interior but just one stateroom. Only twenty were sold in three years. The Nantucket 40 Double Cabin was built on the same hull as the earlier 40 Sedan, and this time the results were more to Mainship's liking. While the 40 DC has a distinctive Downeast profile, her performance and interior accommodations are similar to those of a modern motor yacht. The salon is particularly spacious and the absence of a dinette in this layout is interesting and per-haps even a welcome change from the norm. Instead of a dinette, the Nantucket 40 has a handy breakfast bar which takes up considerably less space. An attractive light oak interior replaced the original teak woodwork in 1985. Both staterooms are arranged in the conventional manner, and a tub/shower is fitted in the aft head. Constructed on a modified-V hull with very little deadrise aft, the Nantucket 40 Double Cabin will cruise around 18 knots with her standard 350-hp Crusader gas engines and reach a top speed of 27 knots. ❏

SPECIFICATIONS

Length	40'0"
Length WL	NA
Beam	14'0"
Draft	3'4"
Weight	24,000#
Clearance	17'6"
Water	140 Gals.
Fuel	300 Gals.
Hull Type	Modified-V
Designer	Mainship

Production
1984–88

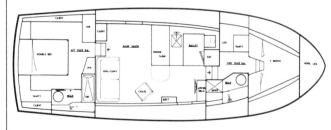

MAINSHIP 41 GRAND SALON

The Mainship 41 Grand Salon is an unorthodox Eurostyle cruiser that might better be described as a floating condo. The design emphasis was obviously on the mega-volume interior. Built on a solid glass hull with 12° of transom deadrise, there were two versions of the Mainship 41: the Double Cabin with a master stateroom aft, and the Grand Salon with an enormous full-length salon stretching for almost two-thirds of the boat's length. Either layout is very impressive with probably the most stylish European decor package ever attempted in a popular-priced pro-duction boat. Indeed, the interior of the Mainship 41 was more than just innovative — it was a giant step toward Mainship's vision of the future in mid-size U.S. yacht designs. Her boxy profile and townhouse-sized accommodations, however, failed to impress the market and production lasted only two years. Standard 454-cid Crusader gas engines will cruise the Mainship 41 Grand Salon/Double Cabin at 16–17 knots (around 25 knots top), and the optional Cat 375-hp diesels cruise around 23 knots and reach 27 knots wide open. ❏

SPECIFICATIONS

Length	40'11"
Length WL	NA
Beam	14'5"
Draft	3'6"
Weight	23,000#
Clearance	15'0"
Water	130 Gals.
Fuel	375 Gals.
Hull Type	Modified-V
Designer	Mike Peters

Production
1989–90

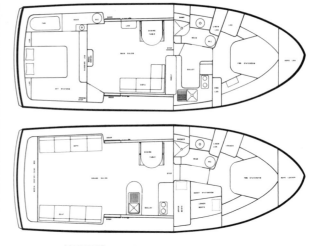

MAINSHIP 41 CONVERTIBLE

Featuring one of the largest interior layouts found in a boat of this size, the Mainship 41 Convertible is a modern Eurostyle family cruiser with an affordable price tag. She was built on a solid fiberglass, modified-V hull with 12° of transom deadrise. At only 22,000 lbs., the Mainship 41 is definitely a light boat for her size. Her chief attraction is undoubtedly the cavernous interior — an appealing array of stylish appliances, designer fabrics, pastel colors, and rounded corners. Originally designed with the dinette open to the salon, an alternate layout (introduced in 1991) has the galley and dinette two steps down from the salon area. While the guest stateroom is a tight fit, the master stateroom is quite spacious and fitted with a big pedestal berth. The unique fold-down transom door (with molded boarding steps) offers easy access to the swim platform. The flybridge on this boat is huge (note the cockpit overhang). Standard 454-cid gas engines will cruise the Mainship 41 at 15–16 knots and deliver a top speed of around 24 knots. Optional 375-hp Cat diesels will cruise at 22–23 and reach 26 knots top. ❏

SPECIFICATIONS

Length	40'11"
Beam	14'5"
Draft	3'6"
Weight	22,000#
Clearance	11'4"
Water	130 Gals.
Fuel	375 Gals.
Cockpit	75 Sq. Ft.
Hull Type	Modified-V
Designer	Mike Peters

Production
1989–92

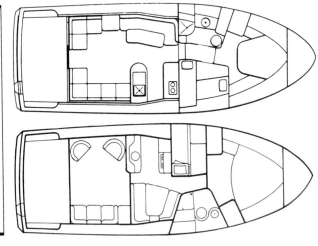

MAINSHIP 47 MOTOR YACHT

The largest yacht ever built by Mainship, the 47 Motor Yacht is a modern flush deck design with a distinctive European profile and an innovative layout. Her modified-V hull has 12° of deadrise aft and is cored from the waterline up. Inside, the contemporary European look continues with modern decorator fabrics, off-white wallcoverings and counters, and upscale furnishings and hardware — an altogether impressive decor with no trace of teak anywhere. The large salon includes a dining area forward, and the stylish step-down galley features a hardwood floor and overhead track lighting. The forward guest stateroom adjoins an office/stateroom with a built-in desk and two pull-out berths. This entire forward area is unique in its ability to combine stateroom and office into an expansive suite. Topside, the semi-enclosed aft deck has a wet bar and the bridge will seat up to seven. The sidedecks are wide, and a sun pad is fitted on the foredeck. Overall, the Mainship 47 is a pretty plain-Jane boat. Standard 485-hp 6-71 diesels cruise around 22 knots and deliver a top speed of 25 knots.   ❑

SPECIFICATIONS

Length	46'10"
Length WL	NA
Beam	15'5"
Draft	3'10"
Weight	44,000#
Clearance	19'6"
Water	200 Gals.
Fuel	600 Gals.
Hull Type	Modified-V
Designer	Mike Peters

Production
1990-Current

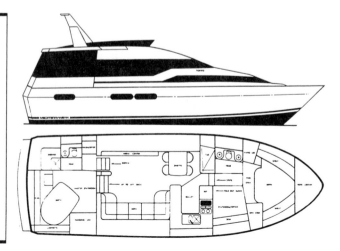

MARINE TRADER

Brief History

Marine Trading International (MTI) is best known for its line of inexpensive Taiwan trawlers. The company began in 1969, and by the early 1970s MTI was well positioned to take advantage of the huge demand for efficient trawlers during the years of the oil shortages. The company still imports Taiwan-built yachts and recently began building boats in Argentina. Always privately-owned, MTI has imported over 3,000 boats (more than any other importer in the country) since they began operations.

Selected Marine Trader Models

Marine Trader 34 Double Cabin
Marine Trader 34 Sedan
Marine Trader 36 Double Cabin
Marine Trader 36 Sedan
Marine Trader 36 Sundeck
Marine Trader 38 Double Cabin
Marine Trader 38/42 Sedan
Marine Trader 39 Tradewinds
Marine Trader 40 Double Cabin
Marine Trader 40 Sedan

Marine Trader 40/44 Sundeck MY
Marine Trader 43 LaBelle
Marine Trader 43/47 Tradewinds
Marine Trader 44 Tri Cabin
Marine Trader 46 Double Cabin
Marine Trader 47 Tradewinds
Marine Trader 48 Med 14 Meter
Marine Trader 49 Pilothouse
Marine Trader 50 Motor Yacht
Marine Trader 56 Montecristo

Main Office

Marine Trading International, Route 166, Toms River, NJ 08754-5300
201-286-4000

MARINE TRADER 34 DOUBLE CABIN

The Marine Trader 34 Double Cabin was the best-selling small trawler ever imported and sold in the U.S. market. Built by Chung Hwa (CHB) in Taiwan, there were other importers besides Marine Trader and she may be recognized on the West Coast as the La Paz, CHB, Eagle or Puget Trawler 34. She enjoyed her best years during the fuel crisis of the 1970s when power-boats with big fuel-guzzling engines were out of favor. With only a single diesel engine and a favorable exchange rate, Marine Trader 34s were inexpensive to buy in spite of her lavish full teak interior and abundant exterior teak trim. Equally important, they were solidly built and very fuel efficient (2–3 gph at 7 knots) with a standard 120-hp Lehman diesel. Inside, the tri-cabin floorplan includes a double berth in the aft cabin, two heads, and an efficient salon and galley area with a lower helm to starboard. Note the passageway from the aft cabin to the cockpit — very convenient. Used 34s are found easily in most markets and the prices are very reasonable. Those built before 1975 were constructed with glass-over-plywood decks and house. ❏

SPECIFICATIONS

Length.....................33'6"
Length WL ....30'3"
Beam........................11'9"
Draft ....3'6"
Weight ....17,000#
Clearance ....NA
Water.................150 Gals.
Fuel ....300 Gals.
Hull Type ....Semi-Disp.
Designer ....Floyd Ayers

Production
1972–91

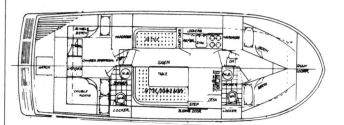

MARINE TRADER 34 SEDAN

Upgraded in 1991 with a restyled fly-bridge and deckhouse profile and updated interior, the 34 Sedan has had a long and successful production run for Marine Trader. Except for the first couple of years (when the deckhouse was glass-over-plywood) the construction is all fiberglass. The original floorplan has V-berths forward and the galley forward in the salon. The current layout has a greatly enlarged master stateroom with a walkaround island berth, less hanging locker space, and the galley has been moved aft in the salon where it's more convenient to the cockpit. The entire interior is paneled and finished with dark teak woodwork and large cabin windows let in plenty of outside natural lighting. The sidedecks are wide and secured by raised bulwarks all around the house. Most Marine Trader 34 Sedans have been powered with a single 135-hp Lehman diesel (120-hp in older models) and she'll cruise very efficiently at 6 knots burning only 2.5 gph. Like the Marine Trader 34 DC (her sistership), the cruising range of this boat can exceed 700 miles. ❏

SPECIFICATIONS

Length	33'6"
Length WL	NA
Beam	11'9"
Draft	3'6"
Weight	19,600#
Clearance	NA
Water	150 Gals.
Fuel	300 Gals.
Hull Type	Semi-Disp.
Designer	Floyd Ayers

Production
1973–Current

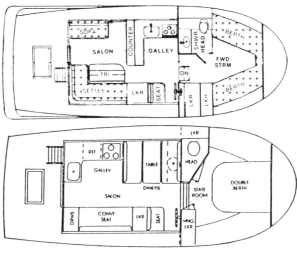

MARINE TRADER

MARINE TRADER 36 DOUBLE CABIN

The Marine Trader 36 is your generic low-priced, double cabin Taiwan trawler with a complete teak interior and full walkaround teak decks. Like most of the popular imported trawler designs, the MT 36 is built on a semi-displacement hull with hard aft chines, a flared bow, and a long keel below. (*Real* trawlers are displacement hulls with rounded bilges and full keels.) The success of this model can be traced to her attractive price, economical operation, and a practical two-stateroom interior. The original layout was modified in 1977 with changes in the aft cabin (including a tub in the private head) and in the placement of the galley. A lower helm was standard and there's also a companionway in the aft stateroom for direct deck access. The boat has good storage for her size and the engine room is large and easy to get around in. Other features of the Marine Trader 36 Double Cabin include a mast and boom, teak swim platform, wide sidedecks and a distinctive teak foredeck hatch. Most all were fitted with a single Lehman diesel (120 or 135-hp) although twins were available. At an 8-knot cruising speed the range is around 750 miles. ❏

SPECIFICATIONS

Length	36'0"
Length WL	NA
Beam	12'2"
Draft	3'6"
Weight	21,000#
Clearance	NA
Water	150 Gals.
Fuel	400 Gals.
Hull Type	Semi-Disp.
Designer	Unknown

Production
1975–Current

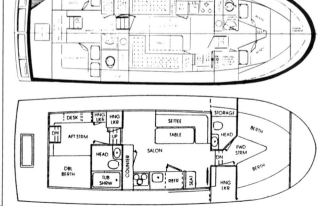

MARINE TRADER

MARINE TRADER 36 SEDAN

People buy boats like the Marine Trader 36 Sedan because they like the looks of a sedan-style boat and because they're on a budget. For years Marine Trading International staked their success on importing inexpensive Taiwan trawlers for the masses (ex-sailboaters and retired people being among the most prominent) and the strategy has obviously worked since these guys have been selling Taiwan-built boats for better than 20 years now. The MT 36 Sedan is a straightforward sedan cruiser with a classic trawler profile and practical accommodations. The layout in-cludes two staterooms with the master stateroom to port rather than forward. There's a tub/shower in the head and the galley can be aft or forward in the salon. A sliding door at the lower helm provides quick access to the decks and everything inside is finished with teak. Note the traditional bridge overhangs that shelter the sidedecks and the aft deck. With the extended flybridge there's space aft of the helm for a small dinghy. Most 36 Sedans have been powered with a single 135 or 120-hp Lehman diesel although twin screw applications are common. ❑

SPECIFICATIONS

Length	36'0"
Length WL	NA
Beam	12'2"
Draft	3'6"
Weight	21,000#
Clearance	NA
Water	150 Gals.
Fuel	350 Gals.
Hull Type	Semi-Disp.
Designer	F. Ayers

Production
1975–Current

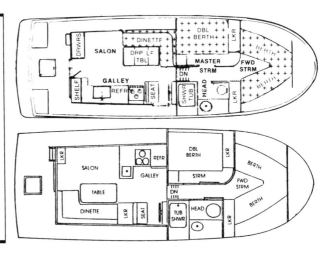

MARINE TRADER

MARINE TRADER 36 SUNDECK

A popular cruising boat, the Marine Trader 36 Sundeck is an inexpensive trawler-style design with a balanced profile and a modern appearance. Built in Taiwan, she features a conventional two-stateroom layout with the galley and dinette down a few steps from the salon level. The forward stateroom is fitted with a space-saving offset double berth while the master stateroom features a walkaround double as well as a built-in vanity/desk and a tub/shower in the head. The interior of the Marine Trader 36 Sundeck is completely finished in teak with well-crafted paneling and cabinetry on display throughout. With the galley and dinette down, the main salon aboard the 36 features a sliding deck access door at the lower helm. Outside, there's space on the full-width sundeck for a few chairs, and there's additional seating for five on the flybridge. Engine choices (there have been several over the years) for the 36 Sundeck include twin 90-hp or 135-hp Lehman diesels or a single 210-hp Cummins diesel. All will provide an economical 7–8 knot cruising speed and good cruising range. ❏

SPECIFICATIONS

Length	36'0"
Length WL	NA
Beam	12'2"
Draft	3'6"
Weight	19,000#
Clearance	NA
Water	150 Gals.
Fuel	350 Gals.
Hull Type	Semi-Disp.
Designer	Floyd Ayers

Production
1985–Current

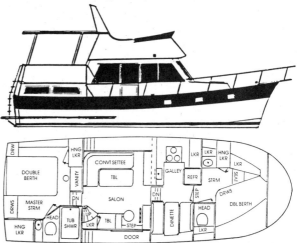

MARINE TRADER

MARINE TRADER 38 DOUBLE CABIN

For those still attracted to the classic profile of a traditional trunk cabin trawler, the Marine Trader 38 Double Cabin is one of only a handful of such designs still being actively imported from Taiwan. Although the market for trawlers has clearly declined in recent years, the Marine Trader 38 continues to sell thanks to her moderate price and economical operating costs. Inside, the spacious main salon features an in-line galley to starboard, a sliding deck access door at the helm, convertible settee, and a teak high-low table to port. (A galley-down floorplan is also offered.) V-berths are forward, and a centerline double berth is in the owner's aft stateroom. As is the case with most Asian trawlers, the interior of the 38 is completely finished in rich teak woodwork. Nearly all have been powered by a single 120/135-hp Lehman diesel, and fuel consumption at a leisurely 7–8 knots is only 3 gph. With the optional twin 210-hp Cummins diesels, the Marine Trader 38 DC will cruise at 12 knots and reach a top speed of 16 knots. Note that a 38 Sedan model is also offered on this same hull. ❏

SPECIFICATIONS

Length	38'0"
Length WL	NA
Beam	12'10"
Draft	4'0"
Weight	22,000#
Clearance	NA
Water	250 Gals.
Fuel	300 Gals.
Hull Type	Semi-Disp.
Designer	Floyd Ayers

Production
1980–Current

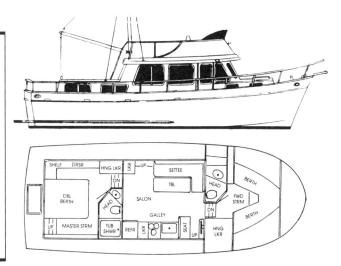

MARINE TRADER

MARINE TRADER 38/42 SEDAN

Sedan trawlers — with their roomy salons and walkaround sidedecks — are practical and comfortable cruisers for those who don't require the luxury of a private aft stateroom. The Marine Trader 38 Sedan and the 42 Sedan (pictured above) are basically the same boat with the 42 having the convenience of a much larger cockpit. A handsome boat with a classic trawler profile, the 38 Sedan features an all-teak interior with two staterooms and the galley forward in the salon. The master stateroom is quite spacious and includes a walkaround double berth while the small guest cabin has over/under single berths. There's a deck access door at the lower helm and the head is fitted with a tub/shower. While the cockpit area in the 38 is adequate for a couple of deck chairs, the step-down cockpit in the 42 is big enough for casual fishing activities. Additional features include a large flybridge with room for an inflatable, protective bridge overhangs for the decks, and a swim platform. A single (or twin) 135-hp Lehman diesel will cruise the Marine Trader 38/42 Sedan at an economical 8 knots at 4–5 gph. ❑

SPECIFICATIONS

Length	38'0"/42'0"
Length WL	NA
Beam	12'10"
Draft	4'0"
Weight	22,000#
Clearance	NA
Water	250 Gals.
Fuel	300 Gals.
Hull Type	Semi-Disp.
Designer	MTI

Production
1987–Current

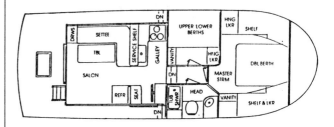

TRADEWINDS 39 SUNDECK

Because nearly all under-40' double cabin motor yachts cause a certain amount of eye strain, one can hardly fault the Tradewinds 39 Sundeck for lacking the modern profile found in larger Tradewinds models. (The problem is always the hardtop; owners love them and rightly so, but they distort the profile of any small motor yacht.) Like all Tradewinds models, the 39 is built for Marine Trader in Taiwan by Lien Hwa — a heavyweight among Taiwanese manufacturers. Her modified-V hull is constructed of solid fiberglass with balsa coring used in the deck and superstructure. Inside, the conventional galley-down floorplan of the Tradewinds 39 is designed for comfortable family cruising and features double berths in both staterooms. The interior gets the full Asian teak treatment, and large cabin windows admit plenty of outside lighting. With over 14' of beam, the accommodations are roomy in spite of the wide sidedecks. Twin 135-hp Lehman diesels are standard. Among several engine options, the popular 225-hp Lehmans will cruise the Tradewinds 39 around 14–15 knots. ❑

SPECIFICATIONS

Length	38'10"
Length WL	NA
Beam	14'4"
Draft	3'1"
Weight	NA
Clearance	NA
Water	300 Gals.
Fuel	500 Gals.
Hull Type	Modified-V
Designer	Lien Hwa

Production
1989–Current

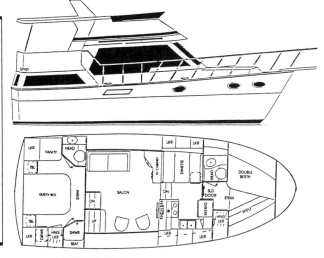

MARINE TRADER

MARINE TRADER 40 DOUBLE CABIN

Although she remained in production until 1986, the Marine Trader 40 Double Cabin enjoyed her greatest popularity during the fuel crisis years of the late 1970s. Trawler sales were on a roll back then as the public turned toward the efficiency and traditional styling inherent in such a design. The Marine Trader 40 has the proper trawler "look" with enough teak trim and interior woodwork to sink a lesser boat. Plus, she was very affordable when compared to similar imported trawlers available at the time. Indeed, used models can often be found on today's market at equally attractive prices. Inside, her accommodation plan is arranged in the normal double cabin configuration with overnight berths for as many as six. Engine room access is very good, storage is excellent, the deck hardware is sturdy and the glasswork is average. The interior decor is teak on teak. A single 120-hp Lehman diesel was standard power for the Marine Trader 40 DC, and at 7–8 knots she burns about 3 gph. Twin-screw models will cruise about a knot faster and reach a top speed of 11–12 knots. ❑

SPECIFICATIONS

Length	40'0"
Length WL	36'7"
Beam	13'8"
Draft	4'0"
Weight	30,000#
Clearance	NA
Water	250 Gals.
Fuel	400 Gals.
Hull Type	Semi-Disp.
Designer	Floyd Ayers

Production
1974–86

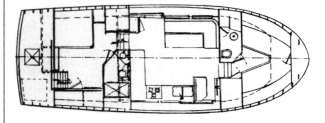

MARINE TRADER 40 SEDAN

For those seeking the more open layout of a sedan floorplan, the Marine Trader 40 can make a lot of sense. A good-looking boat with a salty profile, construction is solid glass although some of the earliest models were built with a glass-over-plywood deckhouse. The MT 40 Sedan has a traditional two-stateroom, full-teak interior layout with a double berth in the master stateroom and a tub/shower stall in the head. All of these boats have a lower helm station with a sliding deck access door. The galley in the Marine Trader 40 is very large and takes up about half of the salon

space. With the dinette converted and the salon settee used as a single berth, the boat can sleep up to seven people. Outside, the wide sidedecks and part of the aft deck are protected with a bridge overhang. All of the decks are overlaid with teak and there's plenty of exterior teak trim as well. With her long deckhouse, the flybridge can easily accommodate a dinghy aft of the helm. An economical boat to operate, standard power for the Marine Trader 40 Sedan was a single 120-hp Lehman diesel (7–8 knots cruise) and twin engines (9–10 knot cruise) were optional. ❏

SPECIFICATIONS

Length	39'8"
Length WL	36'5"
Beam	13'8"
Draft	4'0"
Weight	24,200#
Clearance	NA
Water	200 Gals.
Fuel	400 Gals.
Hull Type	Semi-Disp.
Designer	Floyd Ayers

Production
1978–86

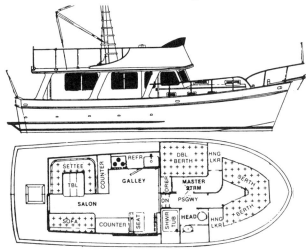

MARINE TRADER

MARINE TRADER 40/44 SUNDECK MY

A popular boat, the Marine Trader 40 Sundeck and the 44 Cockpit model (pictured above) are good-looking Taiwanese imports with simulated lapstrake hullsides, a rakish bridge overhang, and a solid fiberglass semi-displacement hull design. Her standard two-stateroom, galley-down floorplan is arranged with double berths in both cabins, an open salon with a serving counter overlooking the galley, and a lower helm to starboard with a sliding deck access door. The entire interior of the 40/44 is finished with the same good-quality teak woodwork and cabi-netry found in nearly all Taiwan imports regardless of price. The master stateroom is surprisingly large and includes a tub/shower in the head and plenty of storage and locker space. Additional features include a large aft deck with teak sole, wide sidedecks, hardtop, teak handrails, and a teak swim platform. The cockpit in the 44 is small but adds much to the boat's versatility. Twin 135-hp Lehman diesels (a single Lehman is standard) will cruise either boat at an economical 7–8 knots burning only 5–6 gph with a top speed of about 10 knots. ❏

SPECIFICATIONS

Length	39'4"
Length WL	NA
Beam	12'11"
Draft	4'0"
Weight	NA
Clearance	NA
Water	250 Gals.
Fuel	350 Gals.
Hull Type	Semi-Disp.
Designer	MTI

Production
1986–Current

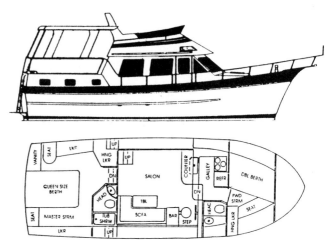

MARINE TRADER

LABELLE 43 MOTOR YACHT

Marine Trader sold enough LaBelle 43 Motor Yachts (as well as the smaller LaBelle 40 model) to insure their presence on the used markets for some time to come. The LaBelle series was built by the Bestway yard in Taiwan — an oddly named company still actively marketing boats in the U.S. under their own name. She's an easy boat to recognize due to her very low freeboard and somewhat topheavy profile. Hull construction is solid fiberglass using a semi-displacement design with a long keel for stability and generous flare at the bow. Most of the LaBelle 43s were sold with the two-stateroom layout featuring a lower helm in the salon and the galley and dinette down. The interior is completely finished in good-quality teak paneling and cabinetry. Outside, the LaBelle's raised sundeck has a teak sole and abundant entertaining space. An affordable price, generous interior space, and her traditional teak interior made her a popular boat. With a pair of 165-hp Volvo diesels, the Marine Trader 43 LaBelle Motor Yacht will cruise at a comfortable 10 knots with a top speed of 13–14 knots. ❏

SPECIFICATIONS

Length	43'0"
Length WL	NA
Beam	14'2"
Draft	4'2"
Weight	NA
Clearance	NA
Water	250 Gals.
Fuel	450 Gals.
Hull Type	Semi-Disp.
Designer	NA

Production
1983–1988

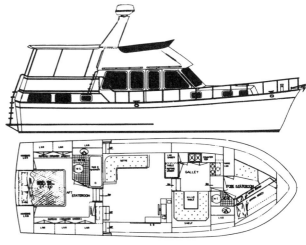

TRADEWINDS 43 MY/47 YACHTFISHERMAN

The Tradewinds 43 MY (pictured above) and the 47' cockpit version are two of the newer Marine Trader imports with modern motoryacht styling and planing speed performance. Unlike most previous Marine Trader yachts, the Tradewinds models are free of exterior teak trim. She's built in Taiwan at the Lien Hwa yard on a modified-V bottom with a solid fiberglass hull and balsa coring in the deck and superstructure. To date, the Tradewinds 43/47s have proven popular with the public thanks to their contemporary styling and a very affordable price.

Below, the interior accommodations are completely finished in teak. The galley-down, two-stateroom layout is fairly conventional and well arranged for cruising. On the downside, the only stall shower is aft in the master stateroom. Standard features include the aft deck hardtop, radar arch, swim platform, and bow pulpit. With the twin 210-hp Cummins diesels the cruising speed of both the Tradewinds 43 MY and 47 YF is about 14 knots and the top speed is around 17 knots. The larger 275-hp Lehmans will cruise at 16–17 knots and reach 20 knots wide open. ❏

SPECIFICATIONS

Length	42'6"
Length WL	NC
Beam	14'11"
Draft	3'10"
Weight	27,500#
Clearance	NA
Water	320 Gals.
Fuel	500 Gals.
Hull Type	Modified-V
Designer	Lien Hwa

Production
1986–Current

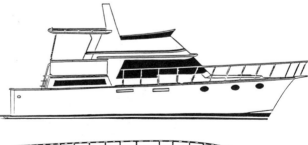

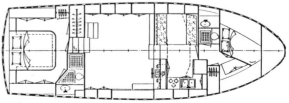

MARINE TRADER 44 TRI CABIN

Easily one of the better-looking trawler-style boats available, the Marine Trader 44 Tri Cabin became a popular design some years ago due to her comfortable accommodations and low price. The 44 was built at the well-known C&L yard in Taiwan. While not actually a real full-displacement trawler, she does have the right trawler "look" and a keel of sufficient depth to protect the running gear in the single-screw version. Construction is solid fiberglass with a teak overlay on the decks and an abundance of teak trim. Indeed, a Marine Trader 44, with prop-

erly oiled decks and varnished trim, will be a stand out on any dock and a source of great owner pride if he survives the maintenance. Inside, the decor is entirely teak. Two layouts were offered with the two-stateroom, galley-down version being the most popular, but many were sold with the optional three-stateroom floorplan. Features include sliding deck doors in the salon, a tub/shower in the aft head, and deck access from the aft cabin. Single or twin 120-hp Lehman diesels will cruise the 44 Tri Cabin very economically at 8–9 knots. ❏

SPECIFICATIONS

Length	43'6"
Length WL	38'8"
Beam	14'4"
Draft	4'2"
Weight	33,000#
Clearance	NA
Water	250 Gals.
Fuel	500 Gals.
Hull Type	Semi-Disp.
Designer	Floyd Ayers

Production
1977–88

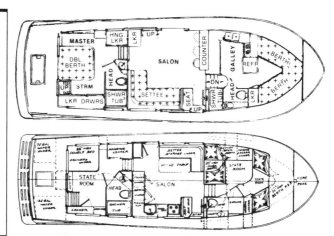

MARINE TRADER 46 DOUBLE CABIN

These days, Marine Trading International just about owns the low-price end of the Taiwan trawler market in the U.S. Few importers continue to sell trawler-style yachts these days but the new Marine Trader 46 DC is a reminder that some demand still exists. Actually, the 46 only looks like a trawler — given the proper horsepower she'll achieve true planing speed with no problem thanks to her semi-displacement, hard-chined hull bottom. Below, the full teak interior is arranged in the traditional double cabin configuration with centerline queen berths fore and aft, two heads, and galley and dinette down. A lower helm is standard and storage space is excellent. Engine access is fairly tight on the outboard sides due to the location of the fuel tanks. The full walkaround sidedecks, afterdeck, and flybridge are all teak planked but the window frames are aluminum. Twin Lehman 135-hp diesels are standard but won't achieve planing speeds. The optional twin 210-hp Cummins diesels can cruise the Marine Trader 46 DC comfortably at 11–12 knots and reach a top speed of around 15 knots. ❏

SPECIFICATIONS

Length	46'2"
Length WL	NA
Beam	14'7"
Draft	3'8"
Weight	35,000#
Clearance	14'2"
Water	220 Gals.
Fuel	600 Gals.
Hull Type	Semi-Disp.
Designer	MTI

Production
1990–Current

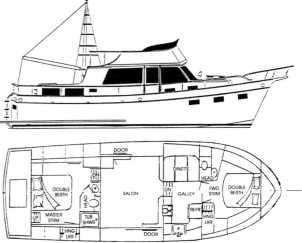

MARINE TRADER

TRADEWINDS 47 MOTOR YACHT

The Tradewinds 47 Motor Yacht from Marine Trader is basically an enlarged version of the popular Tradewinds 43 MY. Built by the Lien Hwa yard in Taiwan, the 47 incorporates an attractive Eurostyle profile, affordable price, and a modern modified-V hull design. Until 1989 the standard floorplan had three staterooms with the galley-down and the second guest cabin aft of the salon. The current two-stateroom interior is arranged with the galley and dinette down although a third stateroom can be ordered at the expense of the dinette. The lack of a stall shower in the forward head should be noted. A lower helm is standard as is a deck access door — an item seldom found on modern motor yachts. Standard features include a roomy afterdeck with wing doors, radar arch, and a full teak interior. Twin 135-hp Lehman diesels are standard and several diesel options are available. The popular twin 300-hp Cummins will attain a cruising speed of around 14 knots and a top speed of 18–19 knots. Note that the Tradewinds 47 was restyled in 1989 with a new superstructure and flybridge and without the original simulated lapstrake hullsides. ❏

SPECIFICATIONS

Length	46'6"
Length WL	NA
Beam	14'11"
Draft	3'6"
Weight	30,500#
Clearance	NA
Water	320 Gals.
Fuel	500 Gals.
Hull Type	Modified-V
Designer	Lien Hwa

Production
1986–Current

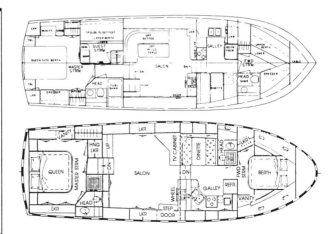

MED YACHT 14 METER

Built in Argentina, the Eurostyle Med Yacht 14 Meter is a big departure from the Taiwanese trawlers and motor yachts that have always characterized Marine Trader imports in the past. She definitely has the right Mediterranean "look" with her streamlined, low-profile appearance, oval ports, stainless-steel-and-glass cabin bulkhead, and reverse swim platform — complete with Med-style transom hardware, no less. The 14 Meter is built on a conventional modified-V hull (15° transom deadrise) with solid fiberglass construction. The sweeping reverse sheer and bold graphics are quite appealing. Her sedan layout is available with two staterooms and the galley-down (most popular to date), or with three staterooms and the galley-up in the salon. Two heads are included with either floorplan but only one has a separate stall shower. Additional features include a large flybridge (note the extended cockpit overhang) with wraparound venturi, huge sunpad on the foredeck, low-profile arch and roomy cockpit. With optional 412-hp 6-71 diesels the Med 14 Meter will cruise at 21 knots and reach a top speed of 23–24 knots. ❑

SPECIFICATIONS

Length	48'6"
Length WL	NA
Beam	14'5"
Draft	3'11"
Weight	26,450#
Clearance	12'4"
Water	160 Gals.
Fuel	475 Gals.
Hull Type	Modified-V
Designer	MTI

Production
1991–Current

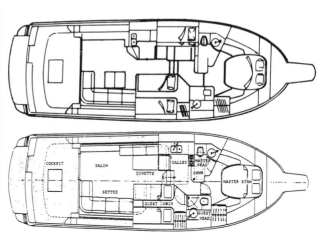

MARINE TRADER

MARINE TRADER 49 PILOTHOUSE

A salty design with a prominent bow and high bulwarks around the house, the Marine Trader 49 is a classic pilothouse trawler with an attractive profile and long-range capability. Construction is all fiberglass with hard chines aft, relatively flat aftersections, and simulated planking in the hull-sides. The 49's interior is similar to most pilothouse floorplans, with two staterooms below, galley to port in the salon, and a raised wheelhouse. There's a comfortable watch berth behind the U-shaped dinette in the pilothouse and the midships master stateroom includes a tub in the adjoining head. The side-decks are wide and weather-protected with a bridge overhang. Typically, the entire interior is teak and so are the decks and cabintop. Price-wise, these were fairly inexpensive boats and the detailing is not overly impressive. Note that Marine Trader also offered a 49 Sundeck model (1983–90) on the same hull but with a full-width salon and no sidedecks. A few 49s were powered with a single diesel but twin 135-hp Lehmans (8-knot cruise) were standard. Optional 160-hp Perkins diesels cruise around 10 knots. ❑

SPECIFICATIONS

Length	48'6"
Length WL	NA
Beam	15'0"
Draft	4'6"
Weight	46,000#
Clearance	NA
Water	375 Gals.
Fuel	700 Gals.
Hull Type	Semi-Disp.
Designer	Unknown

Production
1979–90

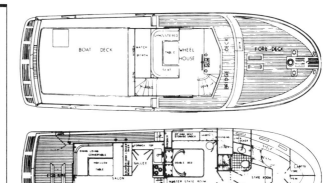

MARINE TRADER

MARINE TRADER 50 MOTOR YACHT

The largest trawler-style yacht ever offered by Marine Trader, the Marine Trader 50 is a moderately priced, long-range cruiser with comfortable accommodations and traditional styling. She's built at the Lien Hwa shipyard in Taiwan which has turned out some very large production motor yacht designs over the years. The standard Marine Trader 50 has full walkaround sidedecks and a covered aft deck. In 1985, she was joined by the 50 Wide Body model with an enlarged, full-width and extended main salon. Both versions share the same three-stateroom floorplan on the lower level while a convenient day head is added in the salon of the Wide Body. The engines are located in separate compartments on either side of the central corridor leading to the aft cabin. Traditional teak paneling and cabinetry are used extensively throughout the yacht's interior. A comfortable (if slow) offshore cruiser, standard 135-hp Lehman diesels will cruise around 9–10 knots. With 750 gallons of fuel capacity, the cruising range of the Marine Trader 50 Motor Yacht can exceed 1,000 miles. ❏

SPECIFICATIONS

Length	50'0"
Length WL	44'0"
Beam	15'5"
Draft	4'8"
Weight	46,000#
Clearance	16'6"
Water	380 Gals.
Fuel	750 Gals.
Hull	Displacement
Designer	Floyd Ayers

Production
1979–Current

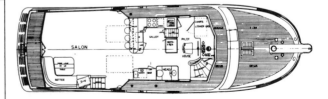

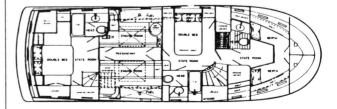

MED 56 MONTECRISTO

The Med 56 Montecristo is a modern and comfortable cruising yacht with expansive interior accommodations and an attractive motor yacht profile. Imported by Marine Trading, Int'l. from Taiwan, the 56 Montecristo is constructed on a somewhat narrow, modified-V hull with 15° of deadrise at the transom. The hull is solid fiberglass and balsa coring is applied in the decks and superstructure. Her most prominent feature is a fully enclosed and teak-paneled aft deck which serves as the main salon and entertainment center of the boat. Below, the lower salon can be arranged as a formal dining room and includes a helm station to starboard. The master stateroom and aft guest stateroom have private heads, but share a common shower stall in a manner reminiscent of the old Hatteras motor yachts. Both the galley and dinette are down from the salon level, and the interior of the Montecristo is finished in teak. A good performer but a little light on fuel, 210-hp Cummins diesels are standard. The optional 485-hp GM 6-71TIBs will cruise the Med 56 Montecristo around 20 knots with a top speed of 23 knots. ❏

SPECIFICATIONS

Length......................55'6"
Length WL....................NA
Beam........................16'0"
Draft ....4'7"
Weight ....48,400#
Clearance ....NA
Water.................200 Gals.
Fuel ....500 Gals.
Hull Type.........Modified-V
Designer ....H. Appolinio

Production
1987–Current

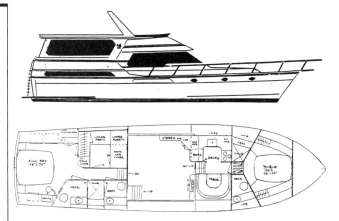

MATTHEWS

Brief History

Matthews is one of the oldest names in the marine business. The company began building wooden boats in Port Clinton, Ohio in 1906, and by 1969 Matthews had introduced their first 46-foot fiberglass models. A 56-foot Hargrave-designed hull followed in 1971. All of their fiberglass hulls were built by Halmatic, Ltd. in England and sent to the U.S. for finishing and delivery. Financial difficulties forced the closing of Matthews in 1976.

Selected Matthews Models

Matthews 46 Flush Deck MY   Matthews 56 Sportfisherman
Matthews 46 Sportfisherman   Matthews 56 Motor Yacht
Matthews 56 Offshore

Main Office

Based in Port Clinton, Ohio, Matthews ceased production in 1976.

417

MATTHEWS 46 FLUSH DECK MY

The Matthews nameplate used to mean something in yachting circles, especially around the Great Lakes where the boats were assembled in Port Clinton, Ohio. The 46 Motor Yacht (originally called the Matthews 45 MY) was one of the first all-fiberglass Matthews boats (although a few of the early hulls had wood deckhouses) and her competitors — products from Hatteras, Chris-Craft, and Concorde — were some of the earliest fiberglass motor yachts built in this country. The hulls were built by Halmatic in England and shipped to Port Clinton for assem-

bly. The Matthews 46 MY was a popular model and remained in production until the company went out of business. With her traditional flush deck floorplan (including a huge master stateroom) the interior arrangements are clearly dated. A flybridge was available in later models. Several power options were offered. Popular 8V53N diesels will provide a cruising speed of 13–14 knots and a top speed of around 16 knots. Those fitted with the 370-hp Cummins will cruise around 17-18 knots. Note the limited fuel capacity and large galley. ❏

SPECIFICATIONS

Length	46'0"
Length WL	41'2"
Beam	14'10"
Draft	3'6"
Weight	34,000#
Clearance	15'11"
Water	100 Gals.
Fuel	320 Gals.
Hull Type	Modified-V
Designer	Hargrave

Production
1969–75

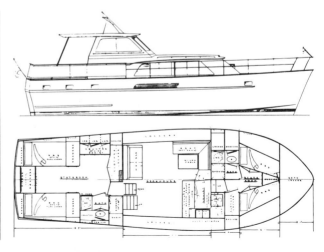

MATTHEWS 46 SPORTFISHERMAN

Although many of the old wood-built Matthews boats have disappeared, the company's switch to fiberglass in 1970 insured that used Matthews products will be with us for a few more years. Designed by Jack Hargrave (then becoming famous for his work with Hatteras), the Matthews 46 Sportfisherman is still admired for her classic convertible profile — a long foredeck, aggressive bow, and well-proportioned house. She shares the same Halmatic fiberglass hull used in the production of the 46 Motor Yacht with slack chines and a deep keel. She rolls a lot and she's wet, but the ride is soft. Indeed, the hull is notably efficient and easily driven. Early models of the Matthews 46 SF (called a 45-footer in 1970–71) were built with a two-stateroom, galley-down layout. In 1973, a revised three-stateroom, galley-up floorplan became available. The cockpit is roomy and the bridge (with the helm forward) is small. Optional 320-hp V-903 Cummins diesels cruise the 46 SF around 17–18 knots and provide a top speed of 21 knots. Standard fuel was only 320 gallons and 520 gallons was optional. ❑

SPECIFICATIONS

Length	46'0"
Length WL	41'2"
Beam	14'10"
Draft	3'6"
Weight	34,000#
Clearance	14'2"
Water	100 Gals.
Fuel	320/520 Gals.
Cockpit	NA
Hull Type	Modified-V
Designer	Hargrave

Production
1970–75

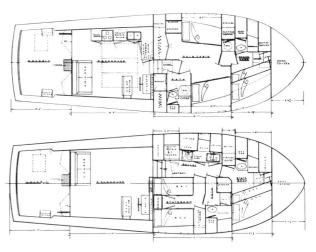

MATTHEWS 56 OFFSHORE

With her low-profile deckhouse and old-fashioned mast assembly, it's unlikely that anyone will confuse the Matthews 56 Offshore with a modern-day yachtfisherman. Nonetheless, she was designed for long-range fishing expeditions with the interior accommodations of a motor yacht. Constructed on a solid fiberglass hull with a wood superstructure, early production hulls had glass–over–wood decks. Later models (after 1973) were built with a fiberglass cabintop and decks. Carrying the beam well forward, the narrow afterbody and rounded chines of the 56

Offshore result in an efficient and easily driven hull form. Below, her three-stateroom floorplan includes a spacious salon with the galley-down and crew quarters forward. Large cabin windows provide good visibility from the lower helm and make the salon seem larger than it actually is. There's direct access to the owner's stateroom from the cockpit, and the stand-up engine room provides excellent access to the motors. Five 56 Offshores were built, and all were powered with the 435-hp GM 8V71TIs. She'll cruise around 18 knots and reach a top speed of 20–21 knots. ❑

SPECIFICATIONS

Length	56'0"
Length WL	48'7"
Beam	16'0"
Draft	4'3"
Weight	63,000#
Clearance	NA
Water	300 Gals.
Fuel	700 Gals.
Cockpit	NA
Hull Type	Modified-V
Designer	Hargrave

Production
1971–75

MATTHEWS

MATTHEWS 56 SPORTFISHERMAN

Basically an enlarged version of the Matthews 46 Sportfisherman, the 56 Sportfisherman is one of four different Matthews models built on the same 56' fiberglass hull (the other three were motor yacht designs) from 1971–75. These were heavily constructed, modified-V hulls with tapered aftersections, slightly rounded bilges, and a deep keel for directional stability. The superstructure of the 56 SF is wood, and the decks are fiberglass over wood. Besides being a good fisherman, the 56 is a comfortable cruising yacht in spite of her slight rolling characteristics. The floorplan includes three staterooms with the large master stateroom located to starboard. The galley is on the salon level, and the two head compartments are fitted with stall showers. Outside, the cockpit is large enough for a full-size fighting chair. The flybridge is very spacious although the helm console is located forward, thus limiting cockpit sightlines. Only three 56 Sportfisherman were built, and all were equipped with GM 8V71TI diesels. She'll cruise in the 18-knot range and reach a top speed of around 21 knots. ❑

SPECIFICATIONS

Length	56'0"
Length WL	48'7"
Beam	16'0"
Draft	4'1"
Weight	63,000#
Clearance	14'5"
Water	300 Gals.
Fuel	700 Gals.
Cockpit	NA
Hull Type	Modified-V
Designer	Hargrave

Production
1972–75

MATTHEWS 56 MOTOR YACHT

Of the four models built on the Matthews 56-foot hull, the Motor Yacht carries the greatest expanse of accommodations and liveaboard luxury. Constructed on a fiberglass hull with a wood superstructure, this is a traditional motor yacht design with a full-width deckhouse salon followed by an even larger covered afterdeck which is easily enclosed. The athwartships dinette and galley are forward of the salon, and sliding deck doors open from the wheelhouse to the teak sidedecks and foredeck. A staircase leads from the salon down to the extravagant master suite (larger than the salon) complete with a king-size bed, dressing area, and tub. Two additional staterooms are forward of the engine room with the bow stateroom serving as crew quarters in the original design. Additional features include a spacious bridge area with an extended hardtop, molded foredeck seating, and teak interior paneling. A total of thirteen were built, and all were powered with GM 8V71TI diesels for a 16-knot cruising speed. Not known as a particularly dry boat, the built-in sprayrails knock down the worst of the spray. ❑

SPECIFICATIONS

Length	56'0"
Length WL	48'7"
Beam	16'0"
Draft	4'3"
Weight	68,000#
Clearance	14'7"
Water	300 Gals.
Fuel	700 Gals.
Cockpit	NA
Hull Type	Modified-V
Designer	Hargrave

Production
1971–75

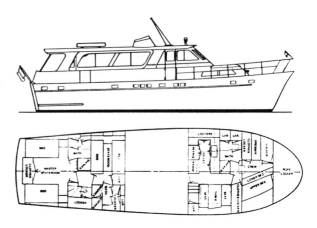

OCEAN

Brief History

Ocean Yachts was founded in 1977 by a group of ex-Pacemaker employees headed by Jack Leek. Their first boat was the Ocean 40 SS which established the company's reputation for building low-cost, high-performance convertibles. All Ocean models have been designed by David Martin. Recent years have seen the rapid expansion of Ocean Yachts and today the firm is recognized as one of the largest builders of sportfishermen in the country.

Selected Ocean Models

Ocean 29 Super Sport
Ocean 32 Super Sport
Ocean 35 Super Sport
Ocean 35 Sport Cruiser & SF
Ocean 38 Super Sport (Early)
Ocean 38 Super Sport
Ocean 40 Super Sport
Ocean 40+2 Trawler
Ocean 42 Super Sport (Early)
Ocean 42 Super Sport
Ocean 42 Sunliner
Ocean 44 Super Sport
Ocean 44 Motor Yacht

Ocean 46 Super Sport
Ocean 46 Sunliner
Ocean 48 Super Sport (Early)
Ocean 48 Super Sport
Ocean 48 Motor Yacht
Ocean 50 Super Sport
Ocean 53 Motor Yacht
Ocean 53 Super Sport
Ocean 55 Super Sport
Ocean 55 Sunliner
Ocean 56 Cockpit MY
Ocean 58 Super Sport
Ocean 63 Super Sport

Main Office

Ocean Yachts, Inc., P.O. Box 312, Egg Harbor, NJ 08215
609-965-4616

OCEAN 29 SUPER SPORT

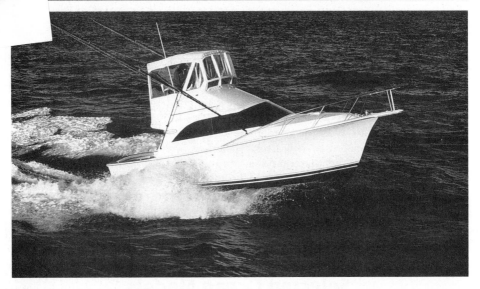

The Ocean 29 SS shares the distinction (with the Blackfin 29 FB and Phoenix 29 Convertible) of being the smallest convertible sportfisherman currently offered by a major builder. Her lines incorporate the classic styling characteristics found in Ocean's larger boats, and like the earlier 32 and 35 SS models, the 29 Super Sport carries a little more transom deadrise (14°) than most previous Ocean hulls. Inside, the floorplan includes a real salon/dinette area with a step-down galley to starboard and an offset double berth in the stateroom. The interior is very attrac-

tively furnished with varnished teak woodwork, wall-to-wall carpeting, mini-blinds, and decorator fabrics. Air conditioning is standard along with a central vacuum system, microwave, and stereo. A good sized fishing cockpit is fitted out with an in-deck fish box, tackle center, and rod lockers. Standard 230-hp gas engines deliver a cruising speed of around 23 knots and a top speed of 30 knots and the larger 350-hp gas engines cruise around 26–27 knots (35-knots top). Optional 250-hp Cummins diesels provide 26 knots at cruise (at only 16 gph) and 30 knots wide open. ❏

SPECIFICATIONS

Length	29'0"
Beam	11'6"
Draft	2'5"
Weight	13,500#
Clearance	10'6"
Water	35 Gals.
Fuel	215 Gals.
Cockpit	68 Sq. Ft.
Hull Type	Modified-V
Designer	D. Martin

Production
1990–Current

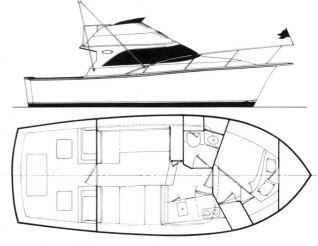

OCEAN

OCEAN 32 SUPER SPORT

The Ocean 32 has the classic raked-back appearance and solid performance of the larger boats in Ocean's fleet. She is, in fact, a good-looking small convertible with a roomy cockpit and a surprisingly open interior layout. The fact that she has a real salon/lounge areas is notable in a boat of this size. The Ocean 32 is built on a modified-V hull with a moderate 13° of deadrise at the transom. Like all previous Ocean yachts, she comes with an impressive list of standard equipment considered optional in most other boats including a central vacuum system, microwave oven, bimini with enclosure panels, basic electronics, and teak covering boards in the cockpit. Twin 320-hp Crusader gas engines are standard (23 knots cruise/30 top) with Cummins diesels available as options. Performance with the economical 250-hp Cummins is excellent: 22 knots at cruise (at 1 mpg) and 25–26 knots wide open. The larger 300-hp Cummins will cruise at a fast 26 knots. The engine room is tight. A classy little convertible, the Ocean 32 SS should prove popular with those looking for a small, well-styled sportfisherman at a competitive price. ❑

SPECIFICATIONS

Length	32'0"
Beam	12'4"
Draft	2'6"
Weight	17,043#
Clearance	11'1"
Water	60 Gals.
Fuel	280 Gals.
Cockpit	NA
Hull Type	Modified-V
Designer	D. Martin

Production
1989–Current

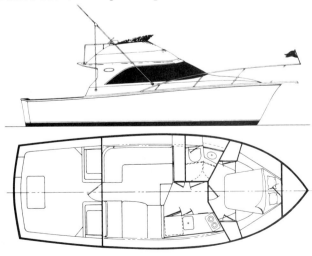

OCEAN

OCEAN 35 SUPER SPORT

The Ocean 35 Super Sport is a fast convertible sportfisherman with the sleek, Jersey-style profile of the larger Ocean yachts. Built on a modified-V hull with considerable beam and more transom deadrise (13°) than previous Oceans, the hullsides are cored with Divinycell foam for reduced weight. The interior is roomy for a 35' sedan with the salon open to the galley and the dinette. An extensive list of standard equipment includes generator, air conditioning, and central vacuum system. The use of interior teak woodwork is notably scaled-back in the 35 SS when compared to other Ocean models. Engine room access below the salon sole is tight. Outside, the cockpit is fitted with a standard transom door, molded-in tackle center, side lockers, and teak covering boards. The 35 does not have the teak cockpit sole or toe rail found in previous Ocean yachts. Standard 320-hp Crusaders will cruise at 21 knots and reach 30 knots wide open. The optional 300-hp Cummins diesels will cruise the Ocean 35 SS around 25 knots at an economical 23 gph and still reach 30 knots top. ❏

SPECIFICATIONS

Length	35'0"
Beam	13'0"
Draft	2'5"
Weight	19,800
Clearance	11'9"
Water	70 Gals.
Fuel	320 Gals.
Cockpit	NA
Hull Type	Modified-V
Designer	D. Martin

Production
1988–Current

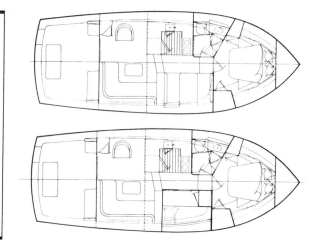

OCEAN 35 SPORT CRUISER & SF

In general, the open dayboat-type sportfishermen offered by major builders tend to be at the high end of the price spectrum. The Ocean 35 Sport Fish (and her sistership, the 35 Sport Cruiser) should fill this void rather nicely as both are priced in the moderate category. Based on the Ocean 35 Super Sport hull, the basic difference between these two express models is the additional cockpit seating and radar arch found in the Sport Cruiser and the teak covering boards, tackle lockers, and hinged transom gate of the SF. The interiors are identical in both boats with a centerline double berth in the forward stateroom, a nifty mid-cabin fitted beneath the bridgedeck, head with shower stall, and a small portside galley with dinette opposite. The 35 Sport Fish comes with an impressive list of standard equipment including air conditioning, generator, salt- and freshwater washdowns, rod storage, and bimini with enclosure. Twin 320-hp gas engines will cruise at 22–23 knots and exceed 30 knots wide open. The optional 300-hp Cummins diesels cruise around 26 knots with a top speed of 29–30 knots. ❏

SPECIFICATIONS

Length	35'0"
Beam	13'0"
Draft	2'11"
Weight	18,000#
Clearance	8'9"
Water	55 Gals.
Fuel	280 Gals.
Cockpit	74 Sq. Ft.
Hull Type	Modified-V
Designer	D. Martin

Production
1990–Current

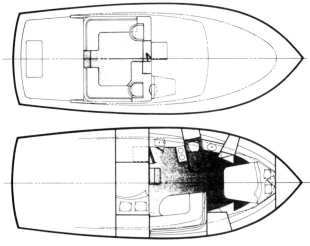

OCEAN

OCEAN 38 SUPER SPORT (EARLY)

The 38 Super Sport was one of Ocean's best-selling models with 158 built during her 7-year production run. A handsome design, she's a big boat for her length with the speed and performance of a sportfisherman and the luxurious accommodations of a family cruiser. Indeed, the 38 SS has the aggressive good looks that many other convertibles in her size range can only admire. Note the glassed-in front windshield and black wraparound deckhouse mask. Most 38s have been delivered with the two-stateroom layout (a single-stateroom, galley-down layout was offered) and the varnished teak interior is impressive. One of the more appealing aspects of the Ocean 38 is her large and well-arranged engine room. The cockpit is set up for serious fishing and includes a standard tackle center, freezer, teak sole, and teak covering boards. A sistership — the Ocean 38 Super Sportfisherman (1984–87) — was also available with a larger cockpit and no fixed salon bulkhead. The optional 375-hp Caterpillar diesels will cruise at a fast 26–27 knots and turn 30+ knots wide open. ❑

SPECIFICATIONS

Length	38'4"
Beam	13'8"
Draft	3'2"
Weight	23,000#
Clearance	13'1"
Water	80 Gals.
Fuel	354 Gals.
Cockpit	NA
Hull Type	Modified-V
Designer	D. Martin

Production
1984–91

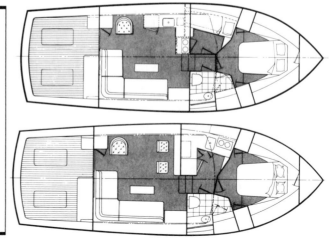

OCEAN 38 SUPER SPORT

The new Ocean 38 Super Sport looks a lot like the original Ocean 38 SS on the outside but she's an entirely different boat below. Built on a slightly wider (and heavier) hull with a sharper entry, cored hullsides, and modest transom deadrise, the new 38 has a smaller cockpit than her predecessor but a much larger interior. Indeed, the two-stateroom floorplan is innovative and completely unique for a boat of this size. Stepping into the salon, one is confronted with a surprisingly spacious and efficient layout with the dinette positioned forward (beneath the windshield panels) and an open galley to starboard. The companionway is all the way to port (there's a 7' rod locker in the outside wall) and leads down to a *midships* master stateroom of truly remarkable proportions. The dinette above the bed intrudes into the overhead but who cares — this is a superb master stateroom arrangement. The engine room, however, is a tight fit. Note that the hardtop is standard. The Ocean 38 SS comes standard with a choice of 425-hp Cats (22–23 knots cruise/28 knots top) or the hot new 430-hp Volvo diesels (26-knots cruise/31 top). ❏

SPECIFICATIONS

Length	38'9"
Beam	14'2"
Draft	3'8"
Weight	27,000#
Clearance	15'6"
Water	80 Gals.
Fuel	400 Gals.
Cockpit	85 Sq. Ft.
Hull Type	Modified-V
Designer	D. Martin

Production
1992–Current

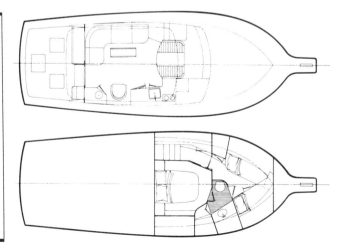

OCEAN 40 SUPER SPORT

The Ocean 40 Super Sport was the first production design built by Ocean Yachts. Introduced to enthusiastic reviews in 1977, the 40 SS was a breakthrough boat capable of reaching a top speed of 30 knots — unheard-of performance in a production boat this size back in 1977. The cockpit is adequate for serious fishing activities and is fitted with a teak sole and teak covering boards. Delivered with a long list of standard equipment (generator, air conditioning, cockpit freezer, etc.), the Ocean 40 Super Sport was available with a two-stateroom, galley-down floorplan or a two-stateroom, galley-up layout providing a day berth in the companionway. The interior is a blend of varnished teak woodwork and vinyl wall coverings, and the large cabin windows in the salon allow for plenty of natural lighting. A good-running boat, with the standard 410-hp 6-71 diesels, the Ocean 40 will cruise around 26 knots and reach a top speed of 29–30 knots. Stretched to 42 feet in 1980, the Ocean 40 Super Sport was the beginning of a popular breed of East Coast sportfishermen. ❏

SPECIFICATIONS

Length.....................40'2"
Beam.......................14'4"
Draft ....3'0"
Weight ....30,000#
Clearance ....12'0"
Water.................100 Gals.
Fuel ....450 Gals.
Cockpit..............80 Sq. Ft.
Hull Type.........Modified-V
Designer ....D. Martin

Production
1977–80

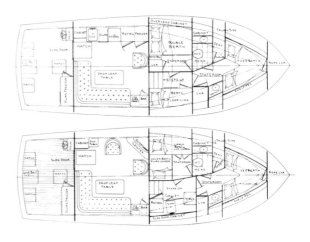

OCEAN 40+2 TRAWLER

The Ocean 40+2 Trawler uses a modified version of the original Ocean 40 Super Sport hull. The swim platform is an integral part of the hull (the + 2 in the model designation), and a unique reverse curve below the waterline at the stern aids in getting the boat on plane. Nominally called a "dual mode" hull, the 40+2 Trawler is a semi-displacement cruiser with a distinct trawler profile and untrawlerlike performance. The teak interior layout is fairly conventional with private staterooms fore and aft, a deckhouse galley, and a lower helm station. Air conditioning was standard along with a central vacuum system and a convertible dinette in the salon. Outside, the walkaround sidedecks are protected by a teak rail, and the spacious flybridge can easily accommodate eight people. Most of the Ocean 40+2 Trawlers were powered with twin 160-hp Perkins diesels. Cruising speed is 12–13 knots (14 gph), and the top speed is around 15 knots. Not an especially popular design on today's used markets, there were fewer than thirty Ocean 40+2 Trawlers built during her short 3-year production run. ❏

SPECIFICATIONS

Length	42'0"
Length WL	38'0"
Beam	14'4"
Draft	3'6"
Weight	30,000#
Clearance	12'6"
Water	100 Gals.
Fuel	450 Gals.
Hull Type	Semi-Disp.
Designer	D. Martin

Production
1978–1980

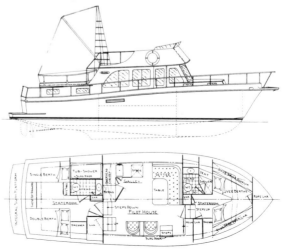

OCEAN 42 SUPER SPORT (EARLY)

The 42 Super Sport is a stretched version of the original Ocean 40 Super Sport with the additional length used to create a full 100 sq. ft. fishing cockpit (vs. 80 sq. ft. in the 40 Super Sport). A good-looking sportfisherman with a clean-cut profile and excellent performance, her nearly flat bottom (1.5° of transom deadrise) helps provide a nice turn of speed with relatively small engines but makes for a hard ride in a chop. Oceans are noted for their attractive teak interiors and the 42 is no exception. The standard two-stateroom layout is well arranged

and suited to the needs of serious anglers as well as family cruisers. Standard features included a cockpit control station, tackle center, freezer, transom door, teak cockpit sole, central vacuum system, and a generator. On the downside, the engine room is a tight fit and there's plenty of exterior teak trim to maintain. The 42 Super Sport will cruise at 27 knots and reach a top speed of 30+ knots with standard 6-71TIs. A popular design at the time, the Ocean 42 Super Sport became one of the best-selling Oceans ever built. ❏

SPECIFICATIONS

Length......................42'0"
Length WL ....38'0"
Beam.......................14'4"
Draft ....3'4"
Weight ....30,000#
Clearance ....12'0"
Water...............100 Gals.
Fuel ....480 Gals.
Cockpit...........100 Sq. Ft.
Hull Type.........Modified-V
Designer ....D. Martin

Production
1980–83

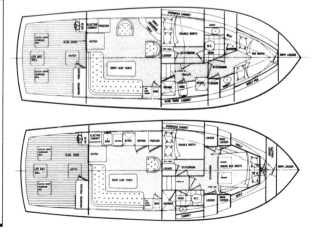

OCEAN 42 SUPER SPORT

In the past, Ocean's Super Sport models have been distinctive boats with rakish profiles, lush teak interiors, nearly-flat aftersections, and plenty of exterior teak trim. The "new generation" Super Sports, while still affordably priced, are quite different. The 42 SS has a more streamlined deckhouse than earlier models plus an all-new hull design with a little more transom deadrise and shallower (longer) keel, and most of the outside teak trim is gone. But the real story is inside where the Ocean 42 lays claim to one of the more impressive galley-up salon layouts to be found in a boat of this size. It's an overused refrain, but this is a spacious floorplan. The master stateroom is quite large and the unique midships guest stateroom extends beneath the salon sole and includes a double *and* single berth. Additional features include a restyled hardtop, separate pump room below the galley sole, a huge fishbox in the cockpit, and good service access to the engines. Cat 425-hp diesels are standard in the Ocean 42 (24 knots cruise/27 knots top) and 485-hp 6-71s (26 knots cruise/30 top) are optional. Chances are the 42 SS is headed for a successful production run.   ❑

SPECIFICATIONS

Length	42'0"
Beam	15'0"
Draft	3'7"
Weight	35,466#
Clearance	12'0"
Water	100 Gals.
Fuel	466 Gals.
Cockpit	100 Sq. Ft.
Hull Type	Modified-V
Designer	D. Martin

Production
1991–Current

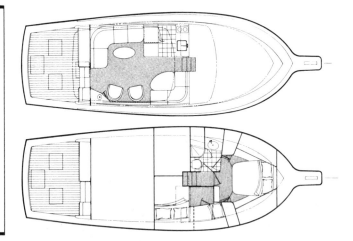

OCEAN

OCEAN 42 SUNLINER

The Ocean 42 Sunliner was built on the same hull as the popular Ocean 42 Super Sport with the aft cabin replacing the Super Sport's cockpit. A good-performing family cruiser, she features a raised aft deck entertainment area and a full-beam master stateroom below with a walkaround queen-sized berth. V-berths are fitted in the forward cabin and both head compartments are equipped with separate stall showers. The 42 Sunliner came with few options. Standard equipment included a generator, garbage disposal, washer/dryer, vacuum system, instant hot water, microwave oven, and much more. Like the 42 Super Sport from which she was designed, the engine room in the Sunliner is compact with limited outboard engine access. Interior accommodations are comfortable and attractively finished with teak cabinetry and woodwork throughout. Several diesel options were offered. Those powered with the GM 6-71TIs will cruise around 26 knots and reach a top speed of 29–30 knots. Though no award-winner, the 42 is easily the best-looking of the Ocean Sunliner series. ❑

SPECIFICATIONS

Length	42'0"
Length WL	38'0"
Beam	14'4"
Draft	3'6"
Weight	28,000
Clearance	12'0"
Water	100 Gals.
Fuel	480 Gals.
Hull Type	Modified-V
Designer	D. Martin

Production
1981–85

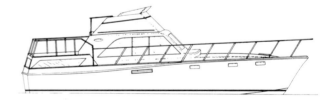

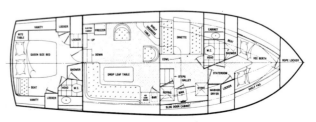

OCEAN 44 SUPER SPORT

The Ocean 44 Super Sport was built on a shortened 46 Super Sport hull with a restyled deck and superstructure. A popular boat (111 were built during her production run) and with a particularly handsome profile, she was designed to replace the original 42 SS in 1985. With her nearly flat bottom (1.5° transom deadrise) the 44 is quick to accelerate but a hard ride in a chop. Her upscale teak interior includes a spacious main salon area with the galley-down, two staterooms, and two full heads. A walkaround queen berth is fitted in the forward stateroom and the galley arrangement in the Ocean 44 is particularly open and spacious. Also notable is the serviceable engine room in the 44 — a big improvement from that found in the previous Ocean 42s. The oversized fishing cockpit (a full 130 sq. ft.) comes standard with a tackle center, control station, freshwater washdown, teak sole, and teak covering boards. Later models powered with the 485-hp versions of the GM 6-71s will cruise around 27 knots and reach 30+ knots top. Earlier 450-hp versions of the same engines are about a knot slower. ❏

SPECIFICATIONS

Length	44'0"
Beam	15'2"
Draft	3'6"
Weight	36,000#
Clearance	13'3"
Water	100 Gals.
Fuel	480 Gals.
Cockpit	130 Sq. Ft.
Hull Type	Modified-V
Designer	D. Martin

Production
1985–91

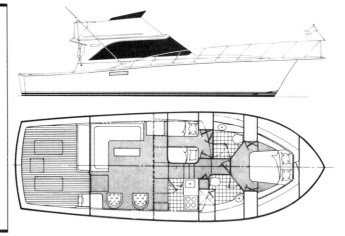

OCEAN 44 MOTOR YACHT

The Ocean 44 MY is a high-performance aft cabin design with a stylish profile and a very innovative floorplan. She's built on a typical Dave Martin hull — tapered at the stern with the maximum beam well forward, very modest transom deadrise (5°) and generous flare at the bow. Most motor yachts in this size range incorporate two staterooms with the galley-down, however the Ocean 44 has three staterooms with the galley and dinette on the deckhouse level. The starboard guest stateroom extends below the salon dinette (at the expense of engine room dimensions) and features a double berth as well as a single upper berth that slides out for use. (Note that this is the same forward stateroom arrangement as used in the current 42 SS model.) Both heads are fitted with stall showers and clever use of the doors provides either of the two forward staterooms with private head access. Additional features include a built-in radar arch, comfortable bridge seating and a very upscale interior decor. A superb performer with optional 485-hp 6-71s (425-hp Cats are standard), she'll cruise around 25 knots and reach a top speed of 27–28 knots. ❑

Specifications	
Length	44'0"
Length WL	38'9"
Beam	15'0"
Draft	3'7"
Weight	40,000#
Clearance	12'0"
Water	100 Gals.
Fuel	466 Gals.
Hull Type	Modified-V
Designer	D. Martin

Production
1992–Current

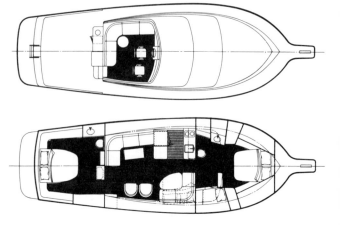

OCEAN

OCEAN 46 SUPER SPORT

The Ocean 46 Super Sport was introduced in 1983 as a bridge between the 42' and 50' Super Sport models. Like most Ocean Yacht hull designs, the 46 has a relatively light displacement for her size and a flat bottom for quick planing and high performance. Inside, the decor is lush with beautiful teak woodwork and cabinetry highlighting the salon and staterooms. While a conventional two-stateroom layout was available, the popular three-stateroom arrangement with mid-level galley is an unusual find in a 46' convertible. The list of standard equipment was equally impressive — teak cockpit sole and covering boards, molded-in tackle center, freezer, vacuum system, etc. The factory hardtop with an overhead electronics cabinet was a popular option. Access to the engines and generator is good. A fast boat, the Ocean 46 Super Sport will cruise at a solid 26 knots and reach a top speed of 30 knots with the standard 450-hp 6-71s. Optional 475-hp 6V92s have a top speed of 32 knots. With over 160 built, the 46 Super Sport became one of Ocean's best-selling models. ❏

SPECIFICATIONS

Length.....................46'0"
Beam........................15'2"
Draft ....3'6"
Weight ....40,000#
Clearance ....13'3"
Water..................150 Gals.
Fuel ....580 Gals.
Cockpit........................NA
Hull Type.........Modified-V
Designer ....D. Martin

Production
1983–85

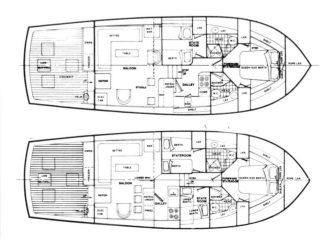

OCEAN 46 SUNLINER

The Ocean 46 Sunliner is a high-performance aft cabin motor yacht built on the hull of the 46 SS convertible. Whether one likes or dislikes her exterior lines, few will argue with the Sunliner's beautiful interior decor and luxurious appointments. The teak cabinetry and woodwork found in the salon and staterooms are well crafted and very impressive. A roomy boat, the 46 Sunliner's two-stateroom, galley-down floorplan includes double berths in both staterooms and a comfortable salon with built-in settee seating. (An optional three-stateroom interior trades the dinette for a third stateroom.) Both heads are fitted with separate shower stalls, and the galley is quite large with a full-sized U-shaped dinette opposite. Standard features included a central vacuum system, wet bar, entertainment center, washer/dryer, and garbage disposal. The flybridge is three steps up from the aft deck with lounge seating for eight. A fast and economical boat for her size, the Ocean 46 Sunliner will cruise at around 24–25 knots with standard GM 6-71TI diesels and reach a top speed of 28 knots. ❑

SPECIFICATIONS

Length	46'0"
Length WL	NA
Beam	15'2"
Draft	3'6"
Weight	40,000#
Clearance	13'3"
Water	150 Gals.
Fuel	480 Gals.
Hull Type	Modified-V
Designer	D. Martin

Production
1983–86

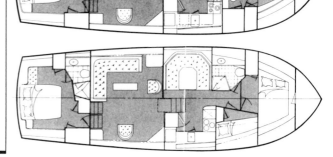

OCEAN

OCEAN 48 SUPER SPORT (EARLY)

The second-best-selling Ocean model ever, the 48 SS was built on a stretched 46 Super Sport hull with upgraded deck and superstructure styling. Her Jersey-style lines are unquestionably handsome and the rakish black mask sweeping around the solid front windshield and both sides of the house is distinctive. Most notable of all, however, is the fact that the she can turn an honest 30 knots with only 485-hp GM 6-71 diesels. That spells economy. At a hard 27-knot cruising speed she's burning only 44–46 gph. Built on a lightweight hull with a narrow beam and 2° of transom deadrise, she's quick to accelerate but has a stiff ride in a chop thanks to her flat-bottom design. Ocean 48s were offered with a very popular three-stateroom, mid-galley interior layout (unusual in a 48' convertible) in addition to a conventional two-stateroom, galley-down floorplan. The interior cabinetry and woodwork are varnished teak and the array of standard equipment included cockpit controls, tackle center with freezer, teak cockpit sole, and teak covering boards. A total of 167 Ocean 48 Super Sports were built during her 5-year production run. ❏

SPECIFICATIONS

Length......................48'0"
Beam........................15'2"
Draft ....3'6"
Weight ....40,000#
Clearance ....13'3"
Water.................150 Gals.
Fuel ....580 Gals.
Cockpit............152 Sq. Ft.
Hull Type.........Modified-V
Designer ....D. Martin

Production
1986–90

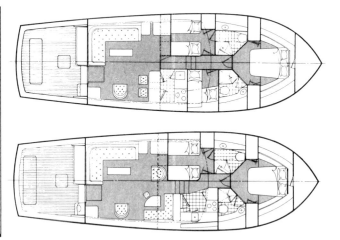

OCEAN 48 SUPER SPORT

The new Ocean 48 SS is basically a restyled version of the original 48 SS model (1986–90) with a more streamlined deck and superstructure, a built-in hardtop with radar arch, less exterior teak, and a completely revised three-stateroom interior layout. The hull (with just 2° transom deadrise), tankage, power, and performance remain unchanged. The urethaned teak interior of the new 48 is lush and impressively decorated with designer-style fabrics and appliances. The galley is open to the salon in this floorplan and the result is a very spacious and well-appointed living area with a built-in entertainment center and full dinette. The midships location of the master stateroom is ideal although the deep overhead intrusion from the dinette above is discomforting. There's a double berth in the forward stateroom and both heads are fitted with stall showers. Additional features include good engine room access, a new cockpit layout with optional teak decking, and a long list of standard equipment. Priced well below the competition, she'll cruise at 26–27 knots with 485-hp 6-71 diesels and reach a top speed of 30+ knots. ❏

SPECIFICATIONS

Length	48'0"
Beam	15'2"
Draft	3'6"
Weight	40,000#
Clearance	13'3"
Water	150 Gals.
Fuel	580 Gals.
Cockpit	NA
Hull Type	Modified-V
Designer	D. Martin

Production
1991–Current

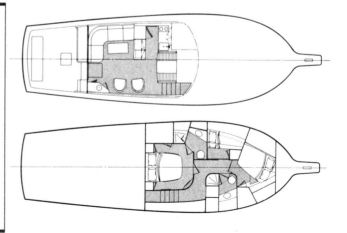

OCEAN 48 MOTOR YACHT

Introduced at the 1989 Miami Boat Show, the Ocean 48 MY is a scaled-down version of the Ocean 53 MY with one less stateroom, a smaller salon, and a boxier profile. She's a true double deck motor yacht (a rare layout in such a small boat) with a full-width salon, deckhouse galley, and three staterooms — each with a full head. Indeed, these accommodations are so expansive and well designed that it's hard to believe the yacht is only 48' long. The master stateroom is accessed via a spiral staircase aft in the salon, and another staircase forward leads up to the bridge. The galley and helm are open to the salon and the rich teak woodwork and decorator furnishings are lush. Notably, both guest staterooms have double berths and are quite large. A door in the midships guest stateroom provides access to the stand-up engine room, and a small deck abaft the salon leaves room for line handling. Standard 485-hp 6-71 diesels will cruise the Ocean 48 MY at 23–24 knots and reach 27 knots wide open. The newer 56 Cockpit MY is basically same boat with a reworked hull bottom and an 8' cockpit extension. ❏

SPECIFICATIONS

Length	48'6"
Length WL	NA
Beam	16'4"
Draft	4'0"
Weight	51,000#
Clearance	14'10"
Water	150 Gals.
Fuel	500 Gals.
Hull Type	Modified-V
Designer	D. Martin

Production
1989–Current

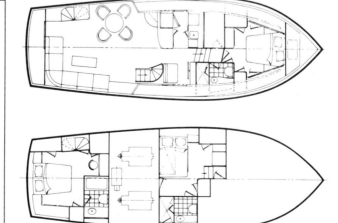

OCEAN

OCEAN 50 SUPER SPORT

The Ocean 50 Super Sport was built on a shortened 55 Super Sport hull with balsa coring in the hullsides and a flat 5° of deadrise at the transom. The result is a fast and easily powered yacht capable of a good turn of speed with the standard 675-hp 8V92 diesels. Unlike the early 55 Super Sports, the front windshield of the Ocean 50 is glassed-in. The cockpit is rigged for serious fishing and features a molded-in tackle center, freezer, baitwell, transom door, and a teak sole. The engine room is entered directly from the cockpit but service access to the engines and generator is poor — a real problem in this boat. Two floorplans were offered with the two-stateroom version notable for its huge master stateroom. Both interiors feature a large salon with the galley-down to starboard. A good-running boat, at a normal cruising speed of 25–26 knots the Ocean 50 SS burns about 55 gph and she'll reach a top speed of around 29 knots. Unfortunately, the Ocean 50 Super Sport is not considered to be a particularly popular boat on the used market and resale values are generally below average. ❑

SPECIFICATIONS

Length	50'0"
Beam	16'0"
Draft	4'2"
Weight	50,000#
Clearance	14'2"
Water	200 Gals.
Fuel	750 Gals.
Cockpit	NA
Hull Type	Modified-V
Designer	D. Martin

Production
1982–85

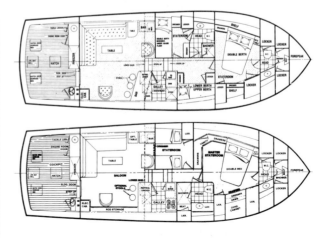

OCEAN 53 MOTOR YACHT

Introduced in 1988, the Ocean 53 Motor Yacht represented an obvious departure from Ocean's tradition of building Jersey-style sportfishing boats. The first of a new series of Ocean motor yachts, the 53 was built on a relatively flat-bottom hull design with 5° of transom deadrise and lightweight Divingcell coring in the hullsides, deck, and superstructure. Aside from her luxurious and innovative interior accommodations, the Ocean 53 MY has the distinction of being one of the fastest production motor yachts available. With a pair of 750-hp 8V92s, she'll cruise around 27 knots and reach a top speed of 30+ knots. Two floorplans were offered, each with four state-rooms. Plan "A" has a fully extended, full-width main salon of impressive size, and Plan "B" shortens the salon area while leaving a semi-enclosed afterdeck. Lacking sidedecks or a workable aft deck area in Plan A, line-handling space is severely restricted. The moderate price and surprising performance of the Ocean 53 Motor Yacht do much to offset her somewhat boxy appearance. A total of 29 were built during her four-year production run. ❑

SPECIFICATIONS

Length	53'0
Length WL	NA
Beam	17'2"
Draft	4'6"
Weight	64,000#
Clearance	16'0"
Water	300 Gals.
Fuel	750 Gals.
Hull Type	Modified-V
Designer	D. Martin

Production
1988–91

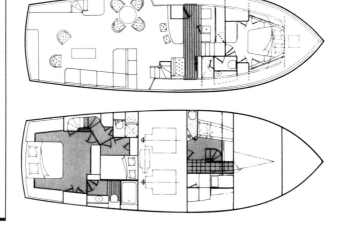

OCEAN 53 SUPER SPORT

Replacing the *very* popular 55 Super Sport will be no easy task but the new 53 SS is already off to a good start. Built on an all-new hull design with a sharper entry and slightly deeper (8°) transom deadrise, the 53 SS is a better headsea boat than her predecessor — a feature sure to be noted by most 55 owners. The standard three-stateroom, galley-up layout is arranged with a midships master suite and another double berth forward. The alternate (and less popular) two-stateroom floorplan has the galley-down and a large salon dinette. While the salon dimensions are slightly smaller than the 55 SS, the furnishings and decor are plush in the extreme. The 53's cockpit has been redesigned with a new-style transom door and the fishbox has been repositioned behind the chair for improved access to the rudder posts. Competitively priced, additional features include a new-style factory hardtop, molded pulpit, enlarged tackle centers, and the elimination of exterior teak trim. An fast boat with just 760-hp 8V92s, the Ocean 53 Super Sport will cruise at 27–28 knots and reach a top speed of 31+ knots. ❑

SPECIFICATIONS

Length	53'0"
Beam	16'4"
Draft	4'4"
Weight	50,000#
Clearance	16'3"
Water	200 Gals.
Fuel	860 Gals.
Cockpit	118 Sq. Ft.
Hull Type	Modified-V
Designer	D. Martin

Production
1991–Current

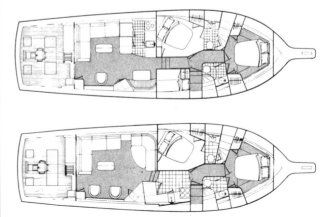

OCEAN 55 SUPER SPORT

The Ocean 55 Super Sport combines two of the most essential elements of any successful modern sportfisherman: speed and beauty. Key to the 55's success is her excellent performance and moderate cost compared to the competition. Whereas most big sportfishermen in this size range require the heavier 12-cylinder diesels to reach the magic 30-knot number, the Ocean gets the job done with lighter, more efficient (and far less expensive) 8V92TAs. Her sleek profile is pure Jersey-style sportfish. The three-stateroom layout with three heads and deckhouse galley proved more popular than the galley-down version with two heads and a roomier salon. The 55 was restyled in 1986 with a new flybridge, a solid front windshield, and a black mask running around both sides of the deckhouse. The foredeck seat was also eliminated in 1986 for a more streamlined appearance. Inside — luxury on a grand scale. Top speed with the 735-hp versions of the 8V92 diesels is 31 knots and she'll cruise at a fast 27 knots. A total of 170 of the Ocean 55 Super Sports were sold making her the most popular Ocean yacht ever built. ❏

SPECIFICATIONS

Length	55'8"
Length WL	50'0"
Beam	16'4"
Draft	4'4"
Weight	58,000#
Clearance	14'6"
Water	200 Gals.
Fuel	1,000 Gals.
Cockpit	130 Sq. Ft.
Hull Type	Modified-V
Designer	D. Martin

Production
1981–9

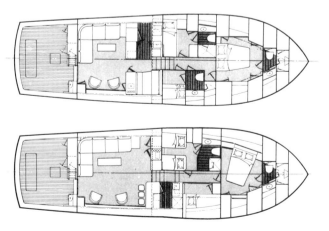

OCEAN 55 SUNLINER

The 55 Sunliner was built using the same hull and deckhouse as the Ocean 55 Super Sport. While she's a good performer for a motor yacht, her profile is certainly less than inspiring. Like many of her counterparts in the industry, the 55 Sunliner *looks* like she was originally designed as a convertible. It is unusual, however, to see this conversion attempted in such a large boat. Below, the accent is clearly on upscale entertaining and cruising accommodations. Dollar for dollar, Ocean yachts have some of the most extravagant interiors in the business, and the amenities aboard the 55 Sunliner are nothing if not impressive. The long list of standard features includes a dishwasher and disposal in the galley, a tub/shower in the master stateroom head, and a washer/dryer in the passageway aft. The large aft deck area is fitted with wing doors and soft enclosure panels for weather protection. GM 8V92s were standard and the 600-hp versions will cruise the Ocean 55 Sunliner at 22–23 knots. The more powerful 675-hp versions cruise around 25 knots and turn 28+ wide open. ❏

SPECIFICATIONS

Length	55'8"
Length WL	50'0"
Beam	16'4"
Draft	4'4"
Weight	60,000#
Clearance	14'6"
Water	200 Gals.
Fuel	750 Gals.
Hull Type	Modified-V
Designer	D. Martin

Production
1983–86

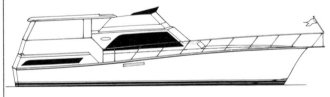

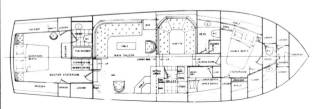

OCEAN 56 COCKPIT MY

The Ocean 56 Cockpit MY is basically a 48 MY with an 8' cockpit extension. To create this boat, the original 48's hull mold was lengthened and a small skeg has been added to the bottom to improve steering. Note that the running gear is located eight feet forward of the transom. Constructed on a fairly flat-bottom hull with Divinycell coring above the waterline, the tapered hull design of the Ocean 56 CMY carries her maximum beam well forward of the salon. Her efficient galley-up, three-stateroom floorplan includes three full heads and a large salon open to the helm. There's a sliding deck door at the lower helm and a staircase in the salon leads up to the spacious flybridge. The small afterdeck of the 48 MY has been preserved in the 56 CMY (shaded by a bridge overhang) and overlooks the cockpit below. At a full 8' x 10', this is a large cockpit (for a motor yacht at least) with room for a couple of light tackle anglers. A molded tackle center and transom door are standard. A good performer, standard 485-hp 6-71 diesels will cruise the Ocean 56 Cockpit MY around 23 knots and reach a top speed of 25–26 knots. ❑

SPECIFICATIONS

Length .... 56'0"
Beam .... 16'4"
Draft .... 4'0"
Weight .... 54,500#
Clearance .... 14'10"
Water .... 150 Gals.
Fuel .... 525 Gals.
Cockpit .... 80 Sq. Ft.
Hull Type .... Modified-V
Designer .... D. Martin

Production
1991–Current

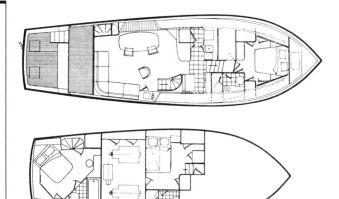

OCEAN 58 SUPER SPORT

First of the "new generation" Ocean yachts, the 58 Super Sport is built on a newly modified bottom with greater transom deadrise, cored hullsides, and more bow flare than seen in most previous Ocean models. Belowdecks, her innovative three-stateroom, three head layout is arranged with the huge, full-width master stateroom located *beneath* the raised salon sole — a giant departure from conventional convertible floorplans. Like all Ocean models, the 58 Super Sport features a beautiful varnished teak interior with upscale furnishings and color-coordinated fabrics throughout. The tournament-sized cockpit features a tackle center with freezer and sink, cockpit controls, teak covering boards, transom door, and direct engine room access. The 58's flybridge is extremely large with three helm chairs and U-shaped lounge seating forward of the modern helm console. A factory option allows the flybridge to be fully enclosed and air conditioned. A good-running boat, standard 1,080-hp DDA 12V-92 diesels (or 12-cylinder MANs) will cruise the fully loaded Ocean 58 Super Sport at a fast 30+ knots. ❏

SPECIFICATIONS

Length	58'0"
Beam	17'6"
Draft	4'10"
Weight	72,215#
Clearance	14'11"
Water	250 Gals.
Fuel	1,100 Gals.
Cockpit	131 Sq. Ft.
Hull Type	Modified-V
Designer	D. Martin

Production
1990–Current

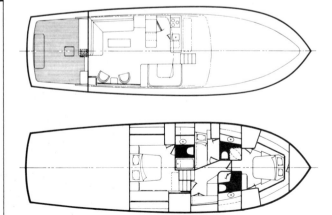

OCEAN 63 SUPER SPORT

Once the top of the line boat for Ocean (a new 66 SS will debut in late 1992) the handsome 63 SS was for a time one of the largest production sportfisherman built in the U.S. Constructed on a relatively lightweight, flat-bottom hull with balsa coring in the hullsides, the 63 SS is a classic Jersey-style sportfishing design but a hard ride in a chop. Below, her four-stateroom interior is extravagant. The opulent master stateroom and spacious guest cabin are both fitted with a walkaround queen berth. An eye-catching back-lit and glass-enclosed rod locker is recessed into the wall in the forward passageway. Outside, the massive fly-bridge (with seating for a dozen) and tournament cockpit are fitted with an impressive array of standard features. While the 63 SS has all of the beauty and fishability expected in a convertible of this size, she also has the speed. With standard 900-hp 12V71s she'll cruise at 25–26 knots. Optional 1,050-hp 12V92s cruise around 28 knots with a top speed of 32 knots. During 1990–91 optional MAN 1,050-hp diesels were available (32–33 knots top). A total of 32 Ocean 63s were built. ❏

SPECIFICATIONS

Length......................63'0"
Beam........................17'8"
Draft ....4'8"
Weight ....74,000#
Clearance ....14'9"
Water.................300 Gals.
Fuel ....1,200 Gals.
Cockpit............150 Sq. Ft.
Hull Type.........Modified-V
Designer ....D. Martin

Production
1986–91

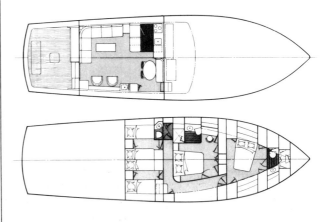

OCEAN ALEXANDER

Brief History

Beginning with the 50 Pilothouse in 1977, Ocean Alexander has become recognized as a premier Taiwanese yacht builder. All Ocean Alexanders are designed by Ed Monk, Jr. and reflect distinct Pacific Northwestern styling influences in addition to their European lines. The company builds production and semi-custom yachts in excess of 70 feet. Notably, Ocean Alexander is one of the few Asian builders to market their products worldwide under their own name.

Selected Ocean Alexander Models

Alexander 38 Double Cabin

Alexander 390 Sundeck

Alexander 40 Double Cabin

Alexander 40 Sedan

Alexander 420/440 Cockpit

Alexander 42/46 Sedan

Alexander 43 Trawler

Alexander 456 Classico

Alexander 48 Yachtsman

Alexander 48/50 Sedan

Alexander 50 Pilothouse

Alexander 50 MK II Pilothouse

Alexander 50/54 Motor Yacht

Alexander 51/53 Sedan

Alexander 520/540 Pilothouse

Alexander 60 Motor Yacht (Early)

Alexander 60 Motor Yacht

Alexander 600 Motor Yacht

Alexander 60 Pilothouse

Alexander 63 Motor Yacht

Alexander 66 Motor Yacht

Main Office

Alexander Marine Co., Ltd., P.O. Box 29-84
Shaou Kang, Kaohsiung, Taiwan

451

OCEAN ALEXANDER 38 DC

The Ocean Alexander 38 is good-quality double cabin trawler with a clean profile and traditional trunk cabin layout. She was built on a solid fiberglass semi-displacement hull with hard aft chines and a moderate keel deep enough to provide protection to the props and rudders. Note that her exterior is relatively free of teak for reduced maintenance. Her belowdecks accommodations are typical of those found in most double cabin trawlers with the exception of the unusual mid-level galley configuration to port in the salon. A lower helm is standard and there are two sliding deck doors in the salon. The master stateroom comes with a centerline queen berth, separate shower and head compartments, and a convenient cockpit deck access door. Teak woodwork is used throughout the interior and the joinerwork is excellent. Outside, raised bulwarks provide protection for the walkaround decks and the flybridge has adequate guest seating. There's space on the cabintop for a dinghy and a radar mast was standard. Powered with the popular 135-hp Lehman diesels, the 38 DC will cruise economically at 7–8 knots. ❑

SPECIFICATIONS

Length	38'4"
Length WL	NA
Beam	13'4"
Draft	3'2"
Weight	21,500#
Clearance	NA
Water	200 Gals.
Fuel	300 Gals.
Hull Type	Semi-Disp.
Designer	Monk

Production
1984–87

OCEAN ALEXANDER

OCEAN ALEXANDER 390 SUNDECK

The introduction of the 390 Sundeck in late 1987 marked the beginning of what has become a successful series of mid-size Alexander sundeck models. Indeed, the only real difference between the original 390 and her larger 42- and 44-foot sisterships is the 390's lack of a cockpit. The two-stateroom, galley-down floorplans are basically the same for all three models and the modern, low-profile design of the 390 makes her a more attractive boat than many of her competitors. For those not wanting the extra length of a cockpit, the Alexander 390 has a superb cruising layout with queen berths in both staterooms, a fairly large aft deck, roomy flybridge, wide sidedecks and a standard lower helm with deck access door. The salon dimensions are more than adequate for a boat of this size and the interior can be finished with teak or light oak woodwork. Several engine options have been offered for over the years including 250-hp GMs, 306-hp Volvos, and now 250-hp Cummins. Depending upon the engines, cruising speeds range from 15–17 knots and top speeds are around 19–21 knots. ❏

SPECIFICATIONS

Length	39'3"
Length WL	NA
Beam	13'11"
Draft	3'2"
Weight	24,800#
Clearance	14'0"
Water	150 Gals.
Fuel	300 Gals.
Hull Type	Modified-V
Designer	Ed Monk, Jr.

Production
1987–Current

OCEAN ALEXANDER

OCEAN ALEXANDER 40 DOUBLE CABIN

A good-looking flush deck cruiser with a clean-cut profile, the Ocean Alexander 40 Double Cabin was introduced some years ago (during the fuel crisis) to meet the public demand for fuel-efficient trawlers. She's built on a solid fiberglass semi-displacement hull with hard chines aft and a keel of sufficient depth to offer good protection to the props and running gear. The Ocean 40 has an abundance of exterior teak (decks, doors, and rails), and the interior is finished in precisely matched teak cabinetry and woodwork. Indeed, those who enjoy the nautical appeal of a well-crafted teak interior will find much to admire in the Alexander 40 DC. Her tri-cabin layout is fairly traditional with a walkaround queen berth in the master stateroom and V-berths in the forward cabin. The galley is aft in the salon, and sliding deck doors are located port and starboard. Access and serviceability are good in the large engine room. A well-built boat, twin 120-hp Lehman diesels will cruise Ocean Alexander 40 DC at 7–8 knots at only 6 gph for a cruising range of approximately 500 miles. ❏

SPECIFICATIONS

Length.....................40'10"
Length WL.................36'0"
Beam.........................13'4"
Draft ....3'6"
Weight ....22,500#
Clearance ....NA
Water.................240 Gals.
Fuel....................400 Gals.
Hull Type.........Semi-Disp.
Designer........Ed Monk, Jr.

Production
1980–85

OCEAN ALEXANDER

OCEAN ALEXANDER 40 SEDAN

Built on the same hull as the Ocean 40 Double Cabin, the Ocean 40 Sedan is a great-looking sedan-style family cruiser with distinctive lines and a handsome, slightly European profile. Her open sedan layout will appeal to those looking for the convenience and improved entertaining capabilities of a larger salon with direct aft deck access. In the 40 Sedan, the galley is located forward, a step up from the salon level, to accommodate the engines below. A raised double berth is located in the large master stateroom forward, and over/under bunks are fitted into the small guest cabin. Both staterooms are served by a double-entry head with a separate stall shower. The interior is finished with solid teak woodwork in every cabin and the joinerwork is impressive throughout. Outside, the modest aft deck has room for a couple of folding chairs but that's about it. The sidedecks are wide and well protected with bridge overhangs and raised bulwarks. Notably, the flybridge is very spacious for a 40-footer. With the standard twin 120-hp Lehman diesels, the Ocean 40 Sedan will cruise economically at 7–8 knots. ❑

SPECIFICATIONS

Length	40'10"
Length WL	36'0"
Beam	13'4"
Draft	3'6"
Weight	22,500#
Clearance	NA
Water	240 Gals.
Fuel	400 Gals.
Hull Type	Semi-Disp.
Designer	Ed Monk, Jr.

Production
1980–85

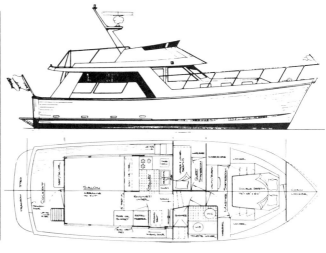

OCEAN ALEXANDER

OCEAN ALEXANDER 420/440 COCKPIT

The Alexander 420 and 440 are basically the same boat as the original 390 Sundeck with the addition of cockpits accounting for the different lengths. (The 420 is pictured above and the 440 has just a slightly longer cockpit.) All three models share the same balsa-cored hull with a shallow keel and moderate transom deadrise. Inside, the modern two-stateroom layout with two heads and the galley-down is well arranged and very appealing. The interior is finished in teak or optional light oak woodwork and the joinerwork is excellent throughout. Both heads are fitted with stall showers and a lower helm is standard. The afterdeck has enough space for a table and a few chairs and the flybridge will seat six. Both the 420 and 440 have been popular boats and Alexander now offers a new variation — the 460 Euro with a sexy reverse transom that transforms the small cockpit into a useful swim or dive platform. Several diesel options have been offered over the years including 250-hp GMs and Cummins (14–15 knots cruise/19 knots top) and 375-hp Cats which will cruise around 20 knots reach a top speed of 24 knots. ❑

SPECIFICATIONS

Length ....42'3"/43'9"
Beam......................13'11"
Draft ....3'2"
Weight ....27,000#
Clearance ....NA
Water.................150 Gals.
Fuel ....300 Gals.
Hull Type.........Modified-V
Designer ....Ed Monk, Jr.

Production
1987–Current

OCEAN ALEXANDER

OCEAN ALEXANDER 42/46 SEDAN

Beginning as the 390 Sedan in 1985, Alexander stretched the hull a couple of years later to create the popular 42 Sedan and today this model is marketed as both the 42 and 46 Sedan (pictured above). The layout are very similar with the 46 having a slightly larger salon and cockpit. Built on a lightweight hull design with a shallow keel and balsa coring in the hullsides, the 42/46 Sedan is a practical and stylish family cruiser with good overall performance. While she isn't a notably beamy boat, the salon and living areas are well proportioned and beautifully finished.

Two staterooms and one head are forward along with a unique storage room where the engine room access door is found. The galley is forward and up one step, and full wraparound cabin windows create a surprisingly open salon with a choice of light oak or teak woodwork. Note that the lower helm is standard. Updates in 1990 included a new Eurostyle superstructure, exaggerated radar arch, wider sidedecks, and a more modern interior with less wood. Standard 250-hp Cummins will cruise at 13–14 knots and the optional 425-hp Cats will cruise at 22–23 knots. ❏

SPECIFICATIONS

Length	42'10"/46'0"
Beam	14'4"
Draft	3'2"
Weight	23/26,000#
Clearance	11'6"
Water	150 Gals.
Fuel	500 Gals.
Cockpit	NA
Hull Type	Modified-V
Designer	Ed Monk, Jr.

Production
1987–Current

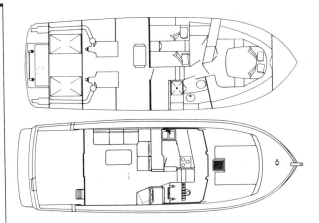

OCEAN ALEXANDER 43 DC TRAWLER

The Ocean Alexander 43 Double Cabin earned a reputation early on for top-quality exterior gelcoat finish and outstanding interior cabinetry and woodwork. Along with the earlier 50 Pilothouse, the 43 DC did much to establish the Ocean Alexander name in the minds of many brokers and dealers. Not just another inexpensive Taiwan import, the Ocean 43s stand up to the demands of the more discriminating owner. Aside from her decks, the 43 is free of excessive outside teak trim. Her large aft deck allows space below for a luxurious, full-width master stateroom with a walkaround double berth. The galley is down, leaving a large and comfortable salon area. As previously noted, the teak joinerwork found throughout the interior of the Ocean Alexander 43 is superb. Fore and aft head compartments — each with a shower stall — round out this practical cruising interior. Twin 120-hp Lehmans were standard, and the 43 will cruise efficiently at 7–8 knots (6 gph) with a cruising range of about 600 miles. The 43 Double Cabin continues to be a popular trawler-style design with good resale value. ❑

SPECIFICATIONS

Length	42'6"
Length WL	38'2"
Beam	14'6"
Draft	3'6"
Weight	29,000#
Clearance	NA
Water	200 Gals.
Fuel	500 Gals.
Hull Type	Semi-Disp.
Designer	Ed Monk, Jr.

Production
1980–85

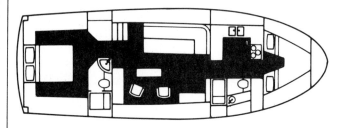

OCEAN ALEXANDER 456 CLASSICO

The Alexander 456 Classico (some name) is a modern, low-profile performance trawler with plenty of eye appeal. By setting the house well forward the Classico is able to offer a spacious layout in a traditional trunk cabin design. She's built on a fairly wide-beam hull with a cutaway keel for prop protection, double chines (very unusual in a trawler-style design), and balsa coring in the hullsides. The mid-level galley is open to the salon in this floorplan which creates a spacious living and entertainment area. The master stateroom is equally spacious and both heads have shower stalls. Burmese teak cabinetry, teak parquet flooring, brass hardware, and varnished woodwork provide soft, warm styling to the Classico's interior. Additional features include a sturdy radar mast, a large flybridge with L-shaped seating, teak handrails (the only exterior teak trim), a deep step-down cockpit, and space on the aft cabintop for dinghy storage. With standard 210-hp Cummins diesels the Alexander 456 will cruise very economically around 11 knots and reach 15 knots top. No lightweight, her cruising range exceeds 600 miles at hull speed. ❏

SPECIFICATIONS

Length	45'6"
Length WL	NA
Beam	15'8"
Draft	4'0"
Weight	40,000#
Clearance	12'9"
Water	250 Gals.
Fuel	550 Gals.
Hull Type	Semi-Disp.
Designer	Ed Monk, Jr.

Production
1992–Current

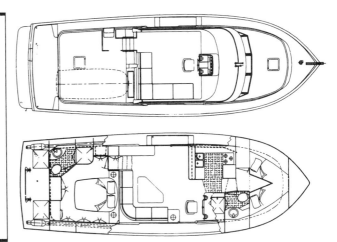

OCEAN ALEXANDER

OCEAN ALEXANDER 48 YACHTSMAN

Like all of the new Ed Monk, Jr. designs that make up the current Ocean Alexander fleet, the 48 has the sleek, low-profile styling seen in more and more modern mid-size cruising yachts. Stretched from her original 46-foot length in 1988, the 48 was built on a modified-V hull with a solid fiberglass bottom and balsa coring in the hullsides and superstructure. The addition of a cockpit makes the 48 Yachtsman a good selection for those who enjoy swimming and diving activities (to say nothing of her fishing potential). Below-decks, the conventional floorplan is arranged with a queen berth in each stateroom, stall showers in both heads and a mid-level galley separated from the salon by a convenient serving bar. The interior woodwork is teak or light ash and a sliding door at the standard lower helm provides easy access to the deck. The transom door, radar arch, swim platform, foredeck washdown, and hardtop were all standard. No longer in production, the 320-hp Cummins VT555 diesels were a popular option in the 48 Yachtsman. Cruising speeds are in the 17-knot range and the top speed is around 20 knots. ❑

SPECIFICATIONS

Length	48'7"
Length WL	NA
Beam	15'6"
Draft	3'10"
Weight	41,500#
Clearance	NA
Water	210 Gals.
Fuel, Std	500 Gals.
Cockpit	NA
Hull Type	Modified-V
Designer	Ed Monk, Jr.

Production
1988–90

OCEAN ALEXANDER 48/50 SEDAN

The Ocean Alexander 50 Sedan (pictured above) began in 1985 as the Ocean 48 Sedan. Already a handsome yacht with arguably the best styling of any recent Alexander production yacht, the additional two feet of length of the 50 only improves her modern profile while providing her crew with the luxury of a larger cockpit and a slightly enlarged galley/salon area. Like all of the newer Ocean Alexander yachts, the 50 Sedan is built on an easily-driven modified-V hull with lightweight balsa coring used in the hullsides. Her two-stateroom interior includes a very spacious salon with the U-shaped galley forward and opposite the helm. Large wraparound cabin windows allow an abundance of natural lighting and twin sliding glass doors open into the cockpit. The sidedecks aboard the 48/50 Sedan are wide enough for easy foredeck access and a bridge overhang provides a measure of weather protection in the cockpit. For her length, the Ocean Alexander 48/50 Sedan is a good performer with either the 375-hp Cats or the 400-hp 6V53 diesels. She'll cruise around 18 knots and reach a top speed of 21–22 knots. ❑

SPECIFICATIONS

Length ....48'0"/50'0"
Beam........................15'6"
Draft ....4'6"
Weight ....38,000#
Clearance ....NA
Water.................210 Gals.
Fuel............410/500 Gals.
Cockpit........................NA
Hull Type.........Modified-V
Designer........Ed Monk, Jr.

Production
1988–91

OCEAN ALEXANDER 50 PILOTHOUSE

The Ocean Alexander 50 Pilothouse was a hugely successful design. She was first imported from Taiwan in 1977, and by the time she was replaced in 1984 with the all-new 50 MK II version, over 90 of the original models had been sold. It's interesting to note that this was the first of what went on to become a very popular series of Ocean Alexander yachts. Her appeal had much to do with her size — at 50'3" LOA, the Ocean 50 PH can easily be handled by an experienced owner. Perhaps most importantly, the price was affordable. As a practical Pacific Northwest cruising yacht, the 50 PH was equipped with a large, elevated pilothouse and a substantial bow to deal with rough sea conditions. Inside, the teak woodwork and cabinetry provide the proper nautical setting expected in a traditionally styled cruising yacht. The spacious owner's cabin in her two-stateroom layout is impressive. Twin salon doors open to the protected cockpit where a swim platform and transom door were standard. A good performer, the 50 Pilothouse will cruise around 14 knots with the optional 270-hp Cummins diesels. ❏

SPECIFICATIONS

Length	50'3"
Length WL	45'8"
Beam	15'6"
Draft	4'6"
Weight	46,500#
Clearance	19'0"
Water	420 Gals.
Fuel	1,000 Gals.
Hull Type	Modified-V
Designer	Ed Monk

Production
1977–83

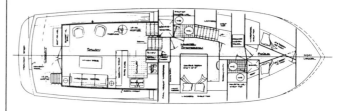

OCEAN ALEXANDER 50 MK II PH

A good-looking yacht, the Ocean 50 MK II Pilothouse replaced the original Ocean 50 Pilothouse in the Alexander lineup in 1984. Already a popular yacht in her own right, the 50 MK II displays a modern Eurostyle appearance in contrast to the traditional profile of the original Ocean 50 PH model. She was built in Taiwan with lightweight balsa coring in the hullsides and superstructure and a solid fiberglass bottom. The MK II featured a spacious three-stateroom layout with double berths in two of the cabins, two full heads (including a tub/shower in the owner's head), and a fully enclosed raised pilothouse. The luxurious teak-paneled salon and galley are separated by a full-size breakfast bar and are within easy reach of the cockpit. Ocean Alexanders have always had a reputation for quality interior woodwork, and the MK II is no exception. The grain-matched teak paneling, countertops, and cabinets are of custom furniture quality. A good performer with 375-hp Caterpillar diesels, the Ocean Alexander 50 MK II will cruise at around 17–18 knots and reach a top speed of 20 knots. ❏

SPECIFICATIONS

Length	50'0"
Beam	15'6"
Draft	4'6"
Weight	42,000#
Clearance	NA
Water	220 Gals.
Fuel	600 Gals.
Cockpit	NA
Hull Type	Modified-V
Designer	Ed Monk, Jr.

Production
1984–90

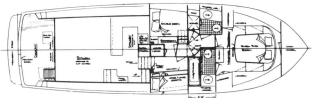

OCEAN ALEXANDER

OCEAN ALEXANDER 50 MY/54 CMY

With her sturdy, slightly boxy appearance the Alexander 50 MY (pictured above) lacks the low-profile styling common to most Alexander designs. She was built on a modified-V hull with moderate beam and balsa coring in the hullsides — the same seakindly hull used in the popular Alexander 50 Pilothouse. The 50 MY's tri-level floorplan is unusual in a motor yacht of this size. The salon is aft and up from the intermediate level where the galley and lower helm are located. The result is a spacious galley and dining area and a completely separate full-width salon. A small afterdeck is provided for line handling and a staircase is located forward in the salon for easy bridge access. There are three staterooms on the lower level and both aft staterooms share a common head — an unusual compromise in a 50' MY. The interior is fully teak paneled and the engine room is quite spacious. The flybridge is comfortably arranged and there's room on the hardtop for a dinghy. Among several engine options, 450-hp 6-71s will deliver a 15-knot cruising speed and 17–18 knots top. The 54 Cockpit MY is the same boat with a cockpit addition. ❏

SPECIFICATIONS

Length	50'0"/54'0"
Length WL	NA
Beam	15'6"
Draft	4'6"
Weight	48,000#
Clearance	NA
Water	230/260 Gals.
Fuel	540/700 Gals.
Hull Type	Modified-V
Designer	Monk

Production
1985–88

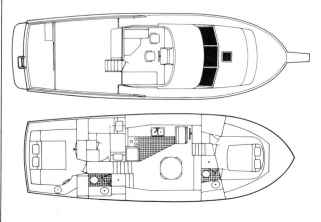

OCEAN ALEXANDER 51/53 SEDAN

This good-looking sport cruiser from Ocean Alexander features an aggressive Eurostyle profile and a raised pilothouse floorplan — a potent combination in today's upscale yachting market where pilothouse designs are becoming increasingly popular. The 51 Sedan (pictured above) has a conventional squared-off transom while the newer 53 model (introduced in 1991) has a modern reverse transom that adds an extra two feet to the boat's LOA. Instead of locating the galley-down on the salon level — the traditional layout in pilothouse floor-plans — the 51/53 has the galley to port on the pilothouse level in European fashion. The result is a huge salon with extravagant entertaining capabilities. The decor is luxurious throughout with a choice of teak or light oak interior wood-work. The master stateroom is forward in this layout and both guest cabins are located a few steps down beneath the pilothouse. Additional features include a large cockpit, roomy flybridge (with a greatly exaggerated radar arch, and a foredeck sunpad. Standard 400-hp 6V53s will cruise the 51/53 at 16 knots and optional 735-hp 8V92s will cruise at a fast 24–25 knots. ❑

SPECIFICATIONS

Length	51'1"/53'0"
Length WL	NA
Beam	16'4"
Draft	3'2"
Weight	45,500#
Clearance	12'6"
Water	250 Gals.
Fuel	500 Gals.
Hull Type	Modified-V
Designer	Ed Monk, Jr.

Production
1989–Current

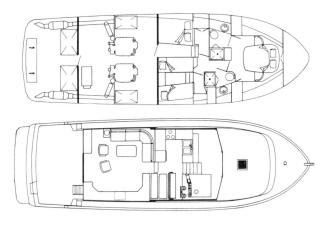

OCEAN ALEXANDER 520/540 PH

The Ocean Alexander 520/540 is a high-quality and completely impressive pilothouse design with absolutely no trace of her Asian heritage. Indeed, even those who persist in believing that Taiwan yachts just don't measure up to their U.S. counterparts are impressed with the 540's classy Eurostyle transom and custom hardware and fixtures. Introduced in 1991 as the 520, the 540 model (pictured above) incorporates the Euro transom which adds an extra two feet to the LOA. (Her 15'6" beam is somewhat narrow for a 54-footer.) There are two floorplans offered — both with the same three-stateroom layout on the lower level. The original interior has a dinette opposite the helm in the raised pilothouse, and the other (less popular) layout has no dinette and P&S pilothouse deck access doors. The spacious master stateroom is forward and both guest cabins are beneath the pilothouse. A good-running boat with standard 400-hp 8V53s (or 425-hp Cats) she'll cruise at 17–18 knots and reach a top speed of about 20 knots. The optional 485-hp 6-71s are reported to cruise at 21–22 knots. ❑

SPECIFICATIONS

Length	52'5"/54'0"
Length WL	NA
Beam	15'6"
Draft	4'0"
Weight	42,500#
Clearance	14'0"
Water	300 Gals.
Fuel	600 Gals.
Hull Type	Modified-V
Designer	Ed Monk, Jr.

Production
1991–Current

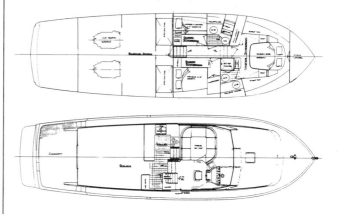

OCEAN ALEXANDER 60 MY (EARLY)

The first of two 60' motor yacht models from this builder, the Ocean Alexander 60 MY was at one time the largest boat in the Alexander fleet. Designed by Ed Monk, Jr. on an efficient modified-V hull form with simulated lapstrake hullsides, the Alexander 60 is a handsome yacht with a rugged and sturdy character. The rakish bridge overhangs and wraparound bulwarks forward of the house only add to her appearance. Her roomy galley-up pilothouse floorplan is arranged with four staterooms on the lower level including a VIP queen stateroom forward. Note the convenient deckhouse day head. A staircase in the salon leads down to the master stateroom with its queen-size berth, tub/shower and access to the large engine room. Additional features include full teak decks, P&S pilothouse doors, foredeck seating, wide sidedecks and a unique transom that opens to provide access to the swim platform via molded steps. While 550-hp 6V92 diesels were standard, most Alexander 60 MYs were delivered with the larger 650-hp 8V92s. The cruising speed is around 16 knots and the top speed is 18–19 knots. ❏

SPECIFICATIONS

Length	60'0"
Length WL	NA
Beam	18'0"
Draft	4'10"
Weight	65,000#
Clearance	17'0"
Water	365 Gals.
Fuel (Std.)	1,200 Gals.
Hull Type	Modified-V
Designer	Ed Monk, Jr.

Production
1984–87

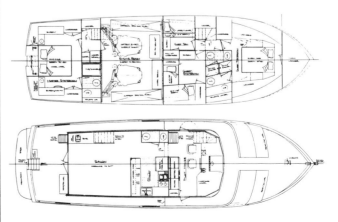

OCEAN ALEXANDER 60 MY

Unlike the earlier Alexander 60 MY model (with its four-stateroom floorplan), the Alexander 60 pictured above is a modern flush deck motor yacht with a full-width salon and three staterooms below. A good-looking design, she was built on an efficient modified-V hull form with a wide beam, full-length keel, and cored hull-sides. The Alexander 60's spacious galley-up layout and her generous salon and master stateroom dimensions are impressive. The wheelhouse is separated from the salon and there's a deck-house day head opposite the galley. A unique office alcove located beneath the wheelhouse comes at the expense of a third head on the lower level — a huge sacrifice in our eyes. The engine room is reached from the huge master stateroom aft with its king-size bed and apartment-size head. The dinette is ideally located next to the lower helm and traditional teak woodwork and paneling are used extensively throughout the interior. Although 550-hp 6V92 diesels were standard, most Alexander 60 MYs were powered with the optional 735-hp 8V92s for a 17–18 knot cruising speed. ❏

SPECIFICATIONS

Length	60'0"
Length WL	NA
Beam	18'0"
Draft	4'10"
Weight	65,000#
Clearance	17'0"
Water	365 Gals.
Fuel (Std.)	1,000 Gals.
Hull Type	Modified-V
Designer	Ed Monk, Jr.

Production
1989–91

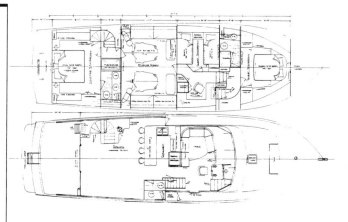

OCEAN ALEXANDER 600 MY

The 600 MY is Alexander's newest model with the first hull delivered in mid-1992. As the artist's rendering above shows, she's clearly a beautifully-styled pilothouse yacht with sweeping European lines, modern reverse transom, straight sheer and a dramatic motor yacht appearance. The flybridge sits well aft on the house where it tends to reduce the profile of the 600, although at the expense of the bridge dimensions. The interior layout is arranged with the galley and dinette abaft the helm on the pilothouse level a few steps above the salon. The midships master stateroom is huge and comes with a Jacuzzi tub. There are two guest staterooms forward and crew quarters are aft beneath the cockpit sole with twin berths, an enclosed head, and access to the engine room. Additional features include full walkaround sidedecks (weather-protected with a bridge overhang); a large afterdeck; twin curved stairways molded into the transom; sliding pilothouse deck doors; and an opulant interior decor. Standard engines are 735-hp 8V92s which should cruise the Alexander 600 at around 18–19 knots. ❑

SPECIFICATIONS

Length	60'3"
Length WL	NA
Beam	17'6"
Draft	4'4"
Weight	68,000#
Clearance	NA
Water	300 Gals.
Fuel	1,000 Gals.
Hull Type	Modified-V
Designer	Ed Monk, Jr.

Production
1992–Current

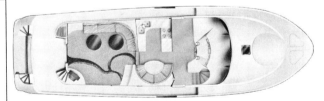

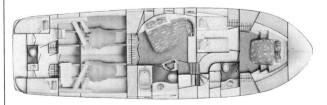

OCEAN ALEXANDER 60 PILOTHOUSE

The Ocean Alexander 60 Pilothouse is a stretched version of the earlier Ocean 56 Pilothouse model introduced in 1986. Designed by Ed Monk, Jr. on an efficient wide-beam hull form, the 60 has balsa coring in the hullsides and superstructure and a molded sprayrail at the bow to keep the decks dry. A good-looking yacht with a distinct European character, nearly all Alexander 60 PHs (a total of ten were built) were ordered with custom interior layouts to suit the owner's requirements. Three staterooms were suggested in the standard floorplan with the enclosed

pilothouse featuring a dinette/settee abaft the helm position and deck access doors. A serving counter separates the galley from the main salon, and a choice of teak or ash woodwork was offered. Most of the extra length of the 60 PH is used to create an enlarged cockpit area with space below for a combination washer/dryer and the ship's generator. Engine room access is via a watertight hatch in the lazarete. With standard 735-hp 8V92TA diesels, the Ocean Alexander 60 Pilothouse will cruise around 18 knots with a top speed of about 20 knots. ❑

SPECIFICATIONS

Length	56'0"
Length WL	NA
Beam	18'0"
Draft	4'10"
Weight	66,000#
Clearance	16'0"
Water	365 Gals.
Fuel	1,000 Gals.
Hull Type	Modified-V
Designer	Ed Monk, Jr.

Production
1988–91

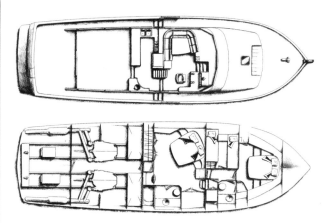

OCEAN ALEXANDER 63 MY

A popular boat for Ocean Alexander, the 63 MY was introduced in 1986 and is one of their longest-running production yachts. She's built on the same modified-V hull used in other large Alexander models with balsa-cored hullsides and 12° of transom deadrise. Key to the 63's success is her enormous full-width salon and enclosed afterdeck. When the salon's aft sliding doors are opened, the entire deckhouse level is wide open all the way forward past the galley and dinette to the helm. The standard four-stateroom layout is arranged with the master stateroom aft and

accessed via a circular staircase in the salon. A VIP cabin is amidships and there are four full heads. (Note that most 63s have been delivered with customized interiors.) Additional features include a circular bridge access stairway in the salon, engine room workbench, and a huge flybridge. Standard power is 550-hp 6V92s but most 63's have been powered with the 735-hp 8V92s which will cruise around 15 knots. Note: The Alexander 63 YF is the same boat with a cockpit and smaller salon and engine room, and the Alexander 70 CMY model is a 63 MY with a cockpit. ❑

SPECIFICATIONS

Length	63'0"
Length WL	NA
Beam	18'0"
Draft	4'10"
Weight	65,200#
Clearance	23'3"
Water	400 Gals.
Fuel	1,200 Gals.
Hull Type	Modified-V
Designer	Ed Monk, Jr.

Production
1986–Current

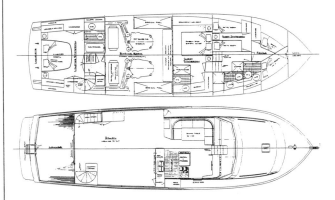

OCEAN ALEXANDER 66 MY

With her striking European profile and aggressive mega-yacht appearance, the Ocean Alexander 66 is certainly one of the best-looking production motor yachts in her size range. And if the published weight of 71,000 lbs. is even close, she's also one of the lightest — a fact which helps to account for her good performance with only 8V92 diesels for power. Built on a modified-V hull, the 66 MY is cored from the waterline up, and the transom deadrise is a moderate 12°. Inside, the four-stateroom layout is spacious and very luxurious. A full-width salon and glass-enclosed afterdeck provide ideal motor yacht accommodations with the added convenience of an on-deck day head. For maximum privacy, the galley is separate from the salon and formal dining area. Additional features include four full heads (two with tubs), a well-arranged engine room, deckhouse galley, and enough space on the flybridge for a cocktail party. At a cruising speed of 17 knots the Alexander 66 MY has a range of around 350 miles. Beautifully proportioned and built to high production standards, eight of these yachts have been built to date. ❏

SPECIFICATIONS

Length	66'0"
Length WL	NA
Beam	18'0"
Draft	4'10"
Weight	71,000#
Clearance	NA
Water	400 Gals.
Fuel	1,300 Gals.
Hull Type	Modified-V
Designer	Ed Monk, Jr.

Production
1986–Current

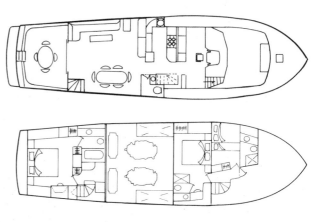

OCEAN ALEXANDER

HIGH-TECH

1993 MODELS
86 EURO
70 EURO
63 EURO
56 EURO
42 EURO

Left and above:
The beautiful 63 Euro, shown with optional Jet Ski docking platform, dinghy davits, and hard top

HIGH-TECH INVITES COMPARISON!

- All HIGH-TECH yachts are built to A.B.S. specifications, from components and raw materials manufactured in the U.S.A.
- Standard equipment includes GPS, VHF, Autopilot, and Radar.
- Custom layouts available Interiors finished to your specifications

HIGH-TECH YACHT & SHIP BROKERS

We are a a full service yacht brokerage specializing in quality preowned AZIMUT, BROWARD, HATTERAS, HIGH-TECH and VIKING yachts.

1535 SE 17th Street (Quay), Fort Lauderdale, FL 33316
305-524-6911• FAX 305-524-7107

HIGH-TECH

CAVEAT EMPTOR

(let the buyer beware)

Many good boats have *hidden* deficiencies.
The seller may not know the defects exist.
Do not acquire someone else's *problems*!

Let a true professional assist you in the determination
of the *actual* condition of your next boat.

NATIONAL ASSOCIATION
OF
MARINE SURVEYORS

1 800 822 NAMS (6267)

NAMS was the *first* group in the marine industry to
organize professional marine surveyors.
NAMS was the *first* to establish stringent requirements
and testing for membership.
NAMS was the *first* to enforce mandatory continuing
education for a surveyor's field of expertise.

NAMS has the most knowledgable surveyors in the
marine industry.

Call, *before you buy*!

For information on our National
and International membership. **Toll Free**....

 800 822 6267

BEFORE BUYING YOUR NEW BOAT, MAKE SURE IT'S EQUIPPED WITH THIS ESSENTIAL PART.

We build the big 3

MARINE TRADER TRAWLERS
20 Models – 34' to 50'

From traditional cruising trawlers and versatile motor yachts to sleek Euro-styled high performance yachts MARINE TRADING INTERNATIONAL provides you with the most in VALUE AND SELECTION.

No other yacht builder has so much to offer.

TRADEWINDS MOTORYACHTS
4 Models – 38' to 47'

NEW MED YACHT SERIES
12 to 19 Meters

We maintain a large inventory of new and used MTI Yachts for our customers, dealers, and brokers

DEALER
INQUIRIES
WELCOMED

MARINE TRADING INTERNATIONAL
World Renowned Yacht Builder. First In Value.

Route 166, South Toms River, NJ
Telephone (908) 286-4000

Mail: Post Office Box 5300
Toms River, NJ 08754-5300

BOAT
FINANCING

WOFFORD ASSOCIATES
INCORPORATED

1 - 800 - 256 - 0860
HOUSTON

WE'LL KEEP YOU IN THE LOOP

Product. When it comes to new Hatteras Inventory, the Allied Marine Hatteras Dealer Association proudly offers a full array of Hatteras Sportfishing Convertible and Motoryacht models. From 43' to 125', Hatteras in Miami, Hatteras of Lauderdale, Hatteras in Palm Beach and Stuart Hatteras is prepared to deliver the Hatteras of your choice.

Financing. The purchase of your new or pre-owned Hatteras just became easier with the introduction of Genmar Financing, an exclusive in-house dealer financing program. Now the Allied Marine Group can offer you competitive rates to assist in your yacht purchasing decisions.

Service. Perhaps your most cherished investment, we can assure you of the finest service programs available. With two complete yards, our service professionals are prepared to safeguard your investment

and protect it's resale value. Layout customizations and cockpit extensions are our specialties.

Brokerage. With four sales facilities and twenty five sales executives, our brokerage program is currently host to over three hundred listings. Perhaps the most successful pre-owned sales facility in the industry, Allied Marine sells more quality, used Hatteras yachts than anyone in the business.

Advertising. To keep you up to date on available product, our four color advertisements run monthly in national yachting magazines. Inventory, current market trends, news items and yachting events are covered bi-monthly in MAKIN WAKE, Allied's in-house magazine.

Allied Marine is Hatteras in Miami, Hatteras of Lauderdale, Hatteras in Palm Beach and Stuart Hatteras.

2550 S. Bayshore Drive
Coconut Grove, FL 33133
(305) 854-1100

401 S.W. 1st Avenue
Ft. Lauderdale, FL 33301
(305)462-5557

401 PGA Blvd., Suite 155
Palm Beach Gardens, FL 33410
(407) 775-3531

110 N. Federal Highway
Stuart, FL 34994
(407) 692-1122

THE MARINE GROUP

• HATTERAS
• VIKING
   MOTORYACHTS

From the large corporate yacht to the family cruiser, we are the experts who can best assist you in your purchase.

• HATTERAS
• BERTRAM
• VIKING
   SPORTFISH

We are Central agents for the latest and best in the world of production sportfishing yachts. Call for our latest offerings.

EXPRESS SPORTFISH & CRUISERS
• TOPAZ • TIARA
• SEA RAY • BLACKFIN

We have access to the finest express boats in today's market. Either cruise or fish rigged according to your specifications.

The Marine Group is committed to offering the finest yacht brokerage services available today. Our Buyers can attest to our reputation and so can the Sellers who have experienced our timely, professional results. We offer our clients a tried and true marketing program that produces! National, regional and local advertising, informative seasonal newsletters, a targeted direct mail program, discount brokerage dockage, and the best personal service available are some of the advantages we offer our Sellers. If you are a serious seller and want results, call us!

THE MARINE GROUP

MEGA MOTORYACHTS

We specialize in large, fiberglass Pacific Northwest built vessels. We are agents for new construction or brokerage.

CUSTOM SPORTFISH

This unique market is one of our specialties. We are Central agents for the fastest and finest in the world today.

FAMILY CRUISERS
- CALIFORNIAN
- CHRIS CRAFT
- TOLLYCRAFT

Call us for our latest inventory and take advantage of our ability to offer the best possible opportunities.

GULF COAST OFFICE

Orange Beach Marina
P.O. Box 650
ORANGE BEACH, AL 36561

(205) 981-9200 Fax (205) 981-9137

PALM BEACH OFFICE

Soverel Harbour
2401 PGA Blvd. Suite 104
PALM BEACH GARDENS, FL 33410

(407) 627-9500 Fax (407) 627-9503

Yacht Sales - Finance - Insurance - Full Service Yard

World's Largest Yacht Broker

Miami
(305) 633-9761
Fax: 634-9071
3660 N.W. 21st Street
Miami, FL 33142

Fort Lauderdale
(305) 467-8405
Fax: 763-2675
651 Seabreeze Boulevard
Ft. Lauderdale, FL 33316

Palm Beach
(407) 625-1045
Fax: 625-0939
2385 PGA Boulevard
Palm Beach Gardens, FL 33410

Ocean Reef
(305) 367-3267
Fax: 252-0698
Ocean Reef Club
Key Largo, FL 33037

Dealers For

Bertram Yacht   *Viking Yachts*

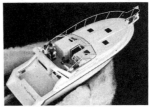

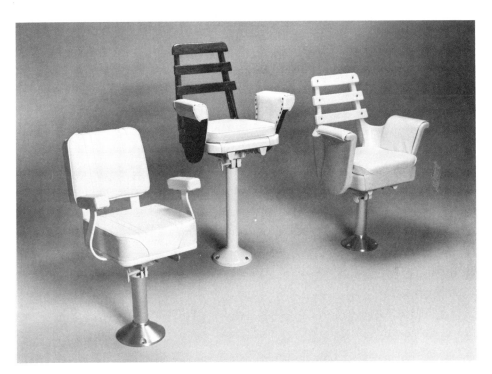

You deserve the best no matter how little it costs.

A close look at Murray Brothers helm chairs...the materials, heavy duty slide assemblies, seams that defy splitting, powder-coated arms and backrests...tells you that you're getting good-as-gold quality you'd expect to pay more for.

We make chairs that outlive most helmsmen at prices most helmsmen can live with. On the left is our all-poly-based custom-upholstered model. No plywood inside to rot. Removable cushions you can wash down without hidden moisture.

On the right is its contour-cushioned slatback sister. As comfortable to own as it is to sit in. In the middle, the Taj Mahal of helm chairs. Collector quality teak finished to rival the finest salon furniture.

New or used boat, fitting out or upgrading, Murray Brothers chairs will add value to your boat. So call today. (407) 845-1366. The service will warm your seat as much as the quality.

DO YOU FIT THIS CRUISING PROFILE?

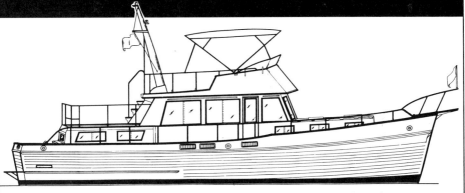

If you fit the cruising lifestyle, you want to cruise in a Grand Banks. Because with over 25 years of satisfied owner feedback, each layout, system and new feature has been developed to make cruising more enjoyable, more comfortable and safer than ever.

With a resale value among the highest in the industry, a new or previously owned Grand Banks is one of the best buys in boating today. To find out how well you fit the Grand Banks cruising profile, contact a GB dealer listed below or write: Grand Banks Yachts, Dept AMP, 563 Steamboat Road, Greenwich, CT 06830.

GRAND BANKS®

The bad news

The good news

PACEMAKER

Brief History

Pacemaker was founded in the late 1940s by John Leek, father of the current-day owner of Ocean Yachts. The company experienced a period of rapid growth from 1957–68, during which time the line was expanded to 27 models. In 1968 Pacemaker was sold to Fuqua Industries, and in 1973 the company was sold again to Mission Marine, a Californian conglomerate that allowed the company to stagnate. Pacemaker ceased production in 1980 when Mission Marine was unable to find a buyer. In 1983, a new Pacemaker Company began production of several updated Pacemaker convertible models.

Selected Pacemaker Models

Pacemaker 30 Express Cruiser
Pacemaker 30 Sportfisherman
Pacemaker 32 Convertible Sedan
Pacemaker 34 Convertible
Pacemaker 36 Sportfisherman
Pacemaker 37 Sportfisherman
Pacemaker 40 Motor Yacht

Pacemaker 40 Sportfisherman
Pacemaker 46 Motor Yacht
Pacemaker 48 Sportfisherman
Pacemaker 57 Motor Yacht
Pacemaker 62 MY & CMY
Pacemaker 66 Motor Yacht

Main Office

Pacemaker Yachts, 110 E. Cushman Ave., Berlin, NJ 08009
609-768-1860

473

PACEMAKER 30 EXPRESS CRUISER

Sharing the same hull as the Pacemaker 30 Sportfisherman (1973–80), the Pacemaker 30 Express Cruiser was introduced as an inexpensive model aimed at the growing market for family convertibles. Her ability to sleep six — plus a roomy cockpit and open lower helm — made the Pacemaker 30 Express a popular boat with those who enjoyed the utility offered in such a design. Her profile is, of course, completely dated by today's standards, but the appeal of a used Pacemaker 30 is the affordable price and all-purpose layout. Her main cabin sleeps six when the dinette and sofa are converted. A folding door separates the forward cabin and offers a degree of privacy. Outside, a small flybridge with bench seating overlooks a fair-size cockpit. With a pair of 270-hp Crusaders the Pacemaker 30 will cruise economically around 23 knots and reach 30 knots wide open. With only 140 gallons of fuel the cruising range is very limited. In 1978, the superstructure and interior were revised, and Pacemaker changed the model designation to Concept 30 Express Cruiser. ❑

SPECIFICATIONS

Length	30'8"
Length WL	28'5"
Beam	11'6"
Draft	2'6"
Weight	10,000#
Clearance	11'8"
Water	30 Gals.
Fuel	140 Gals.
Cockpit	NA
Hull Type	Modified-V
Designer	Pacemaker

Production
1973–80

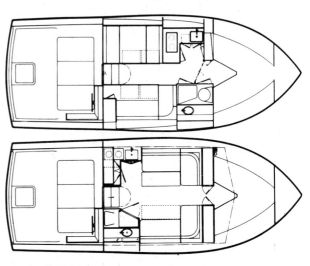

PACEMAKER 30 SPORTFISHERMAN

The Pacemaker 30 Sportfisherman is a good-looking boat with a still-modern profile and comfortable accommodations below. She was offered with or without the lower helm station, which came at the expense of one of the salon settees. Both floorplans have the galley and head aft in the salon where access from the cockpit is the most convenient. The Pacemaker 30 Sportfisherman proved to be a popular design due to her clean lines and affordable price. A competent sportfishing boat, her large cockpit should easily satisfy the requirements of most weekend anglers. Notably, in 1978 Pacemaker engineers combined the flybridge into the deck/cabin mold thus making the bridge an integral part of the superstructure. Standard 225-hp Chryslers cruise at 18–19 knots and the top speed is around 27 knots. The current Pacemaker 31 Convertible (introduced by the new Pacemaker Yachts in 1988 and no relation to the old Pacemaker company) uses the same Pacemaker 30 tooling but includes several modern updates and design improvements. ❏

SPECIFICATIONS

Length	30'8"
Length WL	28'5"
Beam	11'6"
Draft	2'6"
Weight	10,000#
Clearance	9'11"
Water	20 Gals.
Fuel	140 Gals.
Cockpit	80 Sq. Ft.
Hull Type	Modified-V
Designer	Pacemaker

Production
1973–80

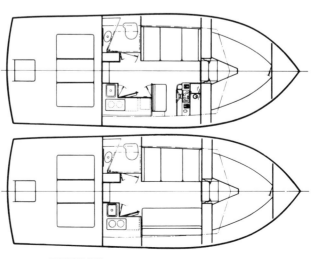

PACEMAKER 32 CONVERTIBLE SEDAN

Pacemaker built three 32' models on this durable modified-V hull design. The original hardtop cruiser introduced in 1971 was quickly followed by the family oriented Pacemaker 32 Convertible Sedan and Sport Cruiser models. The 32 Convertible Sedan soon became a popular all-around family cruiser and weekend fisherman because of her practical interior and affordable price. Her old-style cabin profile is obviously dated by today's standards, but her cabin accommodations are comfortable and reasonably complete.

Anglers who prefer the express cruiser version (with an open lower helm and more usable cockpit space) will give up the enclosed salon of the Convertible Sedan. Either way, the factory interiors of the Pacemaker 32 are nothing to get excited about — plain fabrics, early-1970s mica decor, etc. Several engine options were made available over the years. The standard 220-hp Crusaders will cruise efficiently at 17 knots (17 gph) and reach 27 knots wide open. Range, with only 150 gallons of fuel, is limited. ❏

SPECIFICATIONS

Length	32'3"
Length WL	26'9"
Beam	12'4"
Draft	2'4"
Weight	12,200#
Clearance	11'11"
Water	50 Gals.
Fuel	150 Gals.
Cockpit	NA
Hull Type	Modified-V
Designer	Pacemaker

Production
1972–80

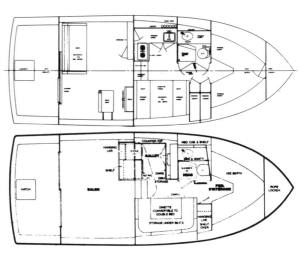

PACEMAKER 34 CONVERTIBLE

The Pacemaker 34 has more beam than any other convertible-style boat of her size. Originally called the Pacemaker 33, she's built on the same solid glass (8° aft deadrise) hull used for the larger Pacemaker 37 SF. Not surprisingly, the Pacemaker's interior dimensions are spacious indeed, and the fact that she has a *real* salon is notable in just a 34' boat. There's also a separate dinette (not jammed into the salon) as well as a stall shower in the head compartment. The raised foredeck makes for good headroom in the stateroom. Completely finished with teak cabinetry, doors, and woodwork, the full wraparound cabin windows provide plenty of natural lighting. The cockpit is too small for a fighting chair, although there's room for a couple of light-tackle anglers. Teak covering boards, washdowns, and a transom door are standard. Price-wise, the Pacemaker 34 is an inexpensive boat compared with other convertibles her size. Standard 454-cid gas engines cruise at 20–21 knots with a top speed of around 30 knots. Note that the 34 SF model is the same boat with a larger cockpit and reduced salon dimensions. ❏

SPECIFICATIONS

Length	33'10"
Beam	13'10"
Draft	3'6"
Weight	15,000#
Clearance	12'0"
Cockpit	75 Sq. Ft.
Water	85 Gals.
Fuel	340 Gals.
Hull Type	Modified-V
Designer	Pacemaker

Production
1988–Current

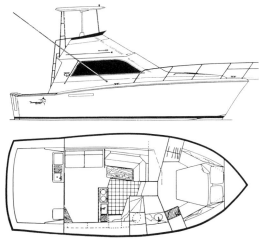

PACEMAKER 36 SPORTFISHERMAN

In the eyes of many experienced sportfishermen, the Pacemaker 36 has always been a good-looking and practical boat. Introduced back in 1973, she has the traditional sportfish profile of today's modern designs. Her large tournament flybridge and a roomy fishing cockpit have made the Pacemaker 36 popular with a great many anglers over the years. Early models came with a standard two-stateroom floorplan with a deckhouse galley and a stall shower in the head. The interior was redesigned in 1976 with the galley relocated down from the salon and offering the option of replacing the guest stateroom with a full dinette. This later floorplan results in a more open salon with room for additional seating to port. Either layout offers comfortable family cruising and adequate storage for brief trips. Several power options were offered. The standard 270-hp gas engines will run at 16–17 knots cruise and 25 knots top. Twin 350-hp Crusaders gas engines will cruise the Pacemaker 36 Sportfisherman around 17–18 knots and reach 26 knots wide open. ❑

SPECIFICATIONS

Length	36'0"
Beam	13'3"
Draft	2'3"
Weight	17,100#
Clearance	12'2"
Water	75 Gals.
Fuel	260 Gals.
Cockpit	80 Sq. Ft.
Hull Type	Modified-V
Designer	Pacemaker

Production
1973–80

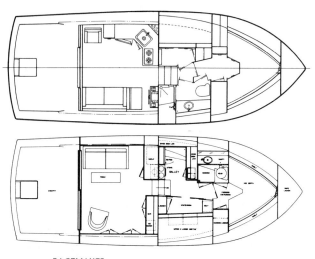

PACEMAKER 37 SPORTFISHERMAN

First introduced in 1988 as the Pacemaker 36 Convertible, the 37 SF is a classic Jersey-style sportfisherman with conservative lines and the traditional Pacemaker profile. She's available in two versions: The Sportfisherman (pictured above) came out in 1990 with a huge cockpit, optional front windshield and standard hardtop; and the original Convertible with a smaller cockpit, increased interior dimensions, and standard front cabin windshield. Hull construction is solid fiberglass with a deep forefoot and a modest 8° of transom deadrise. The oversize cockpit of the 37 SF (one of the biggest in her class) mandates a rather small interior for a boat of this size. Several floorplans are available and the factory will accommodate those seeking semi-custom layouts. The interior is finished out with plenty of teak woodwork and there's a big fishbox in the cockpit along with molded tackle centers and a transom door. Standard 454-cid gas engines will cruise the Pacemaker 37 SF around 19–20 knots and reach 29 knots top. Optional 450-hp Merlin diesels (very popular) deliver a cruising speed of 25 knots and 29 knots wide open. ❏

SPECIFICATIONS

Length	36'10"
Beam	14'0"
Draft	3'8"
Weight	22,000#
Clearance	16'6"
Cockpit	110 Sq. Ft.
Water	85 Gals.
Fuel	450 Gals.
Hull Type	Modified-V
Designer	Pacemaker

Production
1990–Current

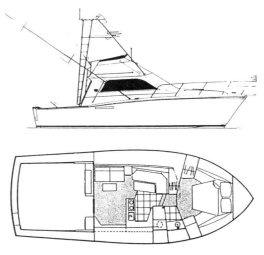

PACEMAKER

PACEMAKER 40 MOTOR YACHT

Sharing the same hull as the Pacemaker 40 Sportfisherman, the Pacemaker 40 Motor Yacht proved to be a popular boat among many motor yacht enthusiasts. Her traditional flush deck profile is obviously dated, but she's a comfortable boat inside with enough room for cruisers and liveaboards alike. Early models had a deckhouse galley interior with twin single berths in the aft stateroom. In 1976, teak replaced the mahogany interior, and the layout was revised with the galley moved forward from the salon for a notably larger and more open entertainment area. A walkaround queen berth in the master stateroom also became available in 1976. Seating for five is provided on the flybridge, and visibility from both helm positions is very good. Wide sidedecks make fore and aft passage especially easy and safe. Standard 454-cid gas engines will cruise the Pacemaker 40 Motor Yacht at 15–16 knots and reach a top speed of around 23 knots. The GM 6-71N diesels (17–18 knots cruise) were a popular option. The fuel capacity was increased to 300 gallons in 1977. ❑

SPECIFICATIONS

Length	39'11"
Length WL	NA
Beam	13'11"
Draft	2'11"
Weight	24,000#
Clearance	12'10"
Water	82 Gals.
Fuel	260/300 Gals.
Hull	Modified-V
Designer	Pacemaker

Production
1972–80

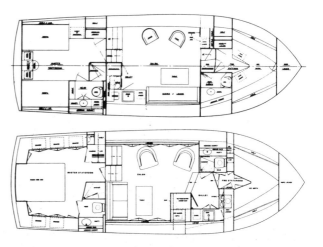

PACEMAKER 40 SPORTFISHERMAN

Featuring classic sportfish styling and a handsome profile, the Pacemaker 40 Sportfisherman has the appearance of a much larger boat. She's built on a solid glass hull with balsa coring in the deck and cabintop. Typical of Jersey-style boats, the Pacemaker 40 has a flared bow and a notably attractive sheer. The modern tournament-style flybridge offers an excellent view of the large cockpit where a full-size fighting chair can easily be installed. Two basic floorplans were offered in later models: a two-stateroom layout (popular); and a single-stateroom version with a dinette replacing the guest cabin. The galley is down in both arrangements and the head has a shower stall. The engine room is small enough when equipped with the standard gas engines but becomes too small with diesels. Even with the optional 330-gallon fuel capacity, the cruising range is limited for a sportfisherman. At around 21,000 lbs., the Pacemaker 40 SF is a light boat for her size. GM 6-71TIs will cruise her around 23 knots (32 gph) with a top speed of 25–26 knots. ❑

SPECIFICATIONS

Length	39'11"
Beam	13'10"
Draft	2'8"
Weight	20,098#
Clearance	12'3"
Water	69 Gals.
Fuel, Std	260 Gals.
Fuel, Opt	330 Gals.
Cockpit	NA
Hull Type	Modified-V
Designer	Pacemaker

Production
1973–80

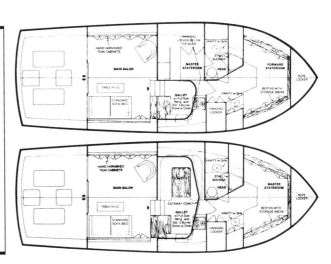

PACEMAKER

PACEMAKER 46 MOTOR YACHT

There are many who believe the Pacemaker 46 to be one of the best-looking flush deck motor yachts ever designed. (Indeed, when Pacemaker went out of business in 1980, the molds to the 46 were picked up by Uniflite and later by Chris Craft.) She's built on a solid fiberglass hull with flat aftersections (just 4° of transom deadrise), moderate beam ,and an almost-flat sheerline. Her standard three-stateroom floorplan is uniquely arranged: Most were built with *two* salons, with the aft deck fully enclosed and paneled. The step-down galley is open to the salon,

and the forward head is located in the forepeak. A guest cabin adjacent to the master stateroom easily doubles as a den/office since it's fitted with a writing desk, bookshelves, and cabinets. The interior is finished with traditional teak woodwork, and large cabin windows provide good natural lighting. Additional features include wide sidedecks, wing doors, foredeck seating, and a roomy bridge. A good performer, 435-hp 8V71 diesels will cruise the Pacemaker 46 MY at a respectable 19–20 knots and deliver a top speed of about 22 knots.   ❏

SPECIFICATIONS

Length	46'3"
Length WL	NA
Beam	15'3"
Draft	4'0"
Weight	42,000#
Clearance	17'1"
Water	160 Gals.
Fuel, Std.	300 Gals.
Fuel, Opt.	500 Gals.
Hull Type	Modified-V
Designer	D. Martin

Production
1977–80

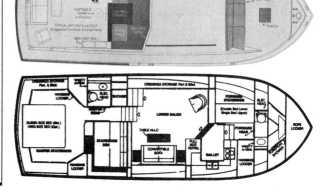

PACEMAKER 48 SPORTFISHERMAN

The largest sportfishing model ever built by Pacemaker (and by far the best-looking), the Pacemaker 48 SF was also one of the first boats to offer the new GM 8V92TI diesels as an option back in 1978. A pure tournament machine in all that the name implies, the 48 is a big boat designed for serious deepwater pursuits. She has the profile of a typical Jersey-style fisherman with a long foredeck and graceful sheer. The large and uncluttered cockpit has a teak sole and teak covering boards, transom door, and molded tackle centers. Two basic interior arrangements were available — either galley-down with two staterooms or galley-up with three — and large wraparound salon windows add to the impact of the spacious interior dimensions. The flybridge was restyled in 1976 and the fuel was increased to 880 gallons in 1978. Many Pacemaker 48 Sportfishermen were powered with the 425-hp GM 8V71s and cruise at 19–20 knots. Later models equipped with the GM 8V92TIs are capable of 24-knot cruising speeds and around 26–27 knots wide open. ❑

SPECIFICATIONS

Length	48'4"
Beam	14'11"
Draft	3'10"
Weight	40,000#
Clearance	NA
Water	155 Gals.
Fuel	610/700/880
Cockpit	105 Sq. Ft.
Hull Type	Modified-V
Designer	Pacemaker

Production
1971–1980

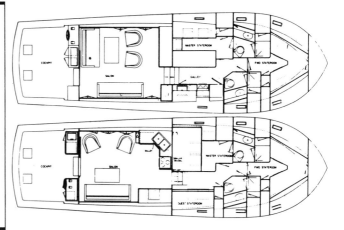

PACEMAKER 57 MOTOR YACHT

The Pacemaker 57 Motor Yacht is best described as an updated Pacemaker 62 Cockpit MY minus the cockpit. Like the earlier Pacemaker 62 with her combination glass-over-wood and fiberglass superstructure, the Pacemaker 57 MY is built with a fiberglass hull and flybridge, with full teak decks and teak toe rails. Introduced early in the 1977 model year, she features the same interior layout as the 62 CMY with the owner and guest staterooms aft and the crew quarters forward. The mid-level salon and separate galley area are three steps down from the wheelhouse. This lower salon may be used as a private formal dining room. On the deckhouse level the spacious full-width main salon is completely open to the helm and extends aft nearly to the transom. A small afterdeck on the 57 leaves room for line-handling duties. The crew quarters forward are fitted with stacked single berths with an adjoining head and stall shower. A washer/dryer unit and engine room access door are also forward. The standard GM 8V71TI diesels provide a comfortable cruising speed of 16–17 knots at around 45 gph. ❑

SPECIFICATIONS

Length	57'2"
Length WL	52'0"
Beam	17'2"
Draft	4'0"
Weight	66,300£
Clearance	NA
Fuel	980 Gals.
Hull Type	Modified-V
Designer	D. Martin

Production
1977–80

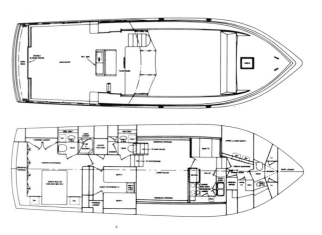

PACEMAKER 62 MY & CMY

The Pacemaker 62 MY and Cockpit MY are traditional flush deck designs constructed with a fiberglass hull and flybridge and a combination of fiberglass and glass–over–mahogany superstructure. With beautiful teak decks and a handsome profile, many consider the Pacemaker 62s to be among the most beautiful of the classic flush deck motor yachts. The interior layouts are similar in both boats, with the 62 Cockpit model giving up one of the guest staterooms (and some space in the main salon) for the convenience and versatility of the cockpit. Both have a mid-level salon/dining area three steps down from the wheelhouse. Owner and guest staterooms are aft, and crew quarters are forward. The galley and dinette are further forward and engine room access is via the crew stateroom. The enclosed deckhouse salon in each model extends full-width and is completely open to the helm. A full-height door in the master stateroom of the CMY leads directly into the cockpit. With standard 8V71TIs, the Pacemaker 62s cruise at 15–16 knots and reach a top speed of around 19 knots. ❏

SPECIFICATIONS

Length	62'0"
Length WL	NA
Beam	17'2"
Draft	4'0"
Weight	73,000#
Clearance	NA
Water	300 Gals.
Fuel	980 Gals.
Hull Type	Modified-V
Designer	D. Martin

Production
1973–80

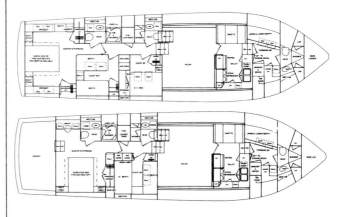

PACEMAKER 66 MOTOR YACHT

The Pacemaker 66 Motor Yacht has the classic upper-class elegance that few other limited production motor yachts can match. Sharing the same construction characteristics as the Pacemaker 62, the hull is rounded at the chines and employs only 5–6° of deadrise at the transom. The 66 MY remained popular right up until Pacemaker went out of business in March, 1980. Uniflite then acquired the molds, but before they delivered the first boat (three years later), Uniflite had itself gone under. Chris Craft then took over, eventually building two boats. With her extended full-beam main salon, separate formal dining area, two guest staterooms, a palatial master stateroom, crew quarters, and three heads, the Pacemaker 66 Motor Yacht offers extravagant entertaining and cruising possibilities. While the aft deck is somewhat small, the flybridge dimensions are expansive. Standard power was a pair of GM 12V71N diesels for a cruising speed of 15–16 knots and a top speed of about 18 knots. The larger 650-hp TI versions of the same motors cruise at 19–20 knots. The fuel capacity was increased in 1978. ❏

SPECIFICATIONS

Length	66'0"
Length WL	60'10"
Beam	17'2"
Draft	4'0"
Weight	73,000#
Clearance	NA
Water	300 Gals.
Fuel	1,100/1,400 Gals.
Hull Type	Modified-V
Designer	D. Martin

Production
1977–1980

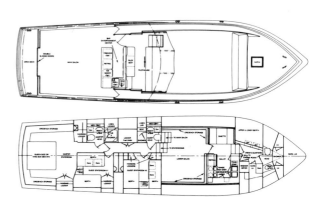

PHOENIX

Brief History

Phoenix Marine began production in 1977 with the introduction of the popular Phoenix 29 Convertible. Since then the line has expanded to include a series of sportfishing models (and one cruiser — the Blackhawk 909) from 27 to 37 feet. Notably, all Phoenix boats are built with a full-length inner liner and prop pockets, and all have been designed by the late Jim Wynne. Phoenix Marine is a privately held company.

Selected Phoenix Models

Phoenix 27 Weekender

Phoenix 27 Tournament

Phoenix 29 Convertible

Phoenix 29 SF Convertible

Phoenix Blackhawk 909

Phoenix 33 Convertible & SFX

Phoenix 33 Tournament

Phoenix 37 Convertible

Phoenix 38 Convertible

Main Office

Phoenix Marine, Inc., 1775 W. Okeechobee Rd., Hialeah, FL 33010
305-887-5625

487

PHOENIX 27 WEEKENDER

Long a popular boat, the Phoenix 27 Weekender is a straightforward offshore open express without a lot of frills. Construction is solid fiberglass with a full-length inner liner bonded to the hull for added strength. As with other Jim Wynne designs, the Phoenix 27 has propeller pockets recessed into her deep-V (21° deadrise aft), solid fiberglass hull. Since over half of the boat's length is devoted to the single-level cockpit, the interior is necessarily compact with V-berths, a small galley, and stand-up head with shower. The engines are located under raised engine boxes that double as bait-watching seats. In addition to the Weekender model, the 27 was offered in a "Fishbuster" version (1979–89) with the galley/tackle center located forward and to port in the cockpit — a practical and accessible layout in a small fisherman (see layout below). A good running-boat with a seakindly hull, standard 350-cid gas engines provide a cruising speed of about 24 knots and a top speed of 31+ knots. Optional 200-hp Volvo diesels will cruise around 25 knots and deliver a top speed of 29-30 knots. The Weekender is also available with outboards. ❑

SPECIFICATIONS

Length	27'3"
Length WL	23'6"
Beam	9'10"
Draft	1'10"
Weight	7,200#
Clearance	6'9"
Water	24 Gals.
Fuel, Std	200 Gals.
Fuel, Opt	250 Gals.
Cockpit	NA
Hull Type	Deep-V
Designer	Jim Wynne

Production
1979–Current

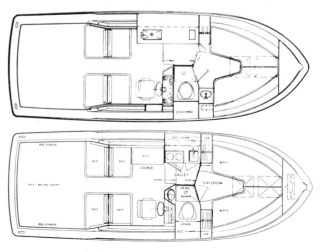

PHOENIX 27 TOURNAMENT

Built on the same hull as the Phoenix 27 Weekender, the 27 Tournament is a good-looking, raised deck open express with a clean and uncluttered fishing layout. She's built on a rugged deep-V hull with prop pockets and a steep 21° of transom deadrise. Her bi-level cockpit eliminates the engine boxes found in the Weekender while providing much-improved helm visibility. Below, the cabin accommodations include a U-shaped lounge/dinette forward converting into a double berth. There's standing headroom in the galley and head compartment and the inte-rior is carpeted and tastefully finished with teak trim and off-white mica lami-nates. Additional features include a molded bow pulpit, transom door and gate, in-deck fishbox, seawater wash-down, full wraparound rubrail, lock-able rod storage under the cockpit coaming, and good access to the engines. Twin 350-cid Crusader gas engines are standard (23 knots cruise/30 knots top), and Volvo 200-hp diesels are optional (25 knots cruise/29 knots wide open). Note that the Phoenix 27 Tournament is also offered with outboard engines. ❏

SPECIFICATIONS

Length	27'3"
Length WL	23'6"
Beam	9'10"
Draft	2'0"
Weight	8,200#
Clearance	7'6"
Water	24 Gals.
Fuel, Std	220 Gals.
Fuel, Opt	290 Gals.
Cockpit	90 Sq. Ft.
Hull Type	Deep-V
Designer	Jim Wynne

Production
1990–Current

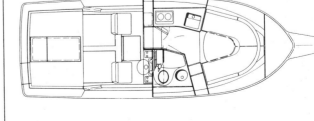

PHOENIX 29 CONVERTIBLE

The Phoenix 29 Convertible had a long and successful production run before being replaced with an all-new model in 1988. Over 700 of the original 29s were built, and during that time she earned the respect of many anglers for her clean styling and durable construction. Below, she has a surprisingly large interior for a boat of her size and type. There's plenty of elbow room throughout the cabin, and both the head and galley are conveniently located just inside the salon door. Overnight berths are provided for four adults and two kids. Topside, a bench seat on the flybridge will seat three. The cockpit is free of obstructions and clearly designed for fishing. Because of her recessed prop pockets, shaft angles are significantly reduced allowing her to run in reasonably shallow waters. On the downside, some consider the Phoenix 29 to be a bit tender. Several engine choices were offered over the years. The optional 124-hp Volvo diesels (very popular) will cruise 18–19 knots (14 gph) and turn 23 knots wide open. Later models with the 165-hp Volvos cruise at around 20–21 knots. ❑

SPECIFICATIONS

Length	28'10"
Length WL	24'10"
Beam	10'0"
Draft	2'4"
Weight	8,500#
Clearance	9'6"
Water	50 Gals.
Fuel, Std	160 Gals.
Fuel, Opt	260 Gals.
Cockpit	75 Sq. Ft.
Hull Type	Modified-V
Designer	Jim Wynne

Production
1977–87

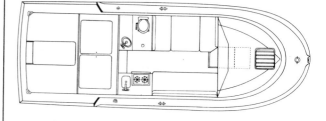

PHOENIX 29 SF CONVERTIBLE

The Phoenix 29 SF Convertible is an updated and restyled version of the original Phoenix 29 (1977–87). She replaces the straightforward and businesslike profile of her predecessor with the more aggressive lines of the larger 33 Convertible. Indeed, the 29's oversized flybridge seems almost *too* large for a 29-footer. Phoenix has introduced a number of desirable features in the new 29 including a transom door, molded-in bow pulpit, aluminum rails, and a revamped and updated interior layout with overnight berths for six. Stoutly built, the all-new hull features a slightly wider beam at the waterline, a redesigned entry, and extra strakes for improved lift and stability. Inside, the elimination of the forward stateroom bulkhead results in a more open interior. Borrowing from the 33 Convertible, a unique air duct system is used to rid the cockpit of exhaust fumes while underway. Standard 350-cid gas engines will cruise the Phoenix 29 at about 22 knots (30 knots top). Optional 200-hp Volvo diesels cruise about 25 knots (30 knots top), and the newer Volvo 225-hp diesels cruise at 27–28 knots (32 top). ❏

SPECIFICATIONS

Length	31'11"
Beam	10'0"
Draft	2'4"
Weight	9,450#
Clearance	9'6"
Water	50 Gals.
Fuel, Std	180 Gals.
Fuel, Opt	300 Gals.
Cockpit	75 Sq. Ft.
Hull Type	Deep-V
Designer	Jim Wynne

Production
1988–Current

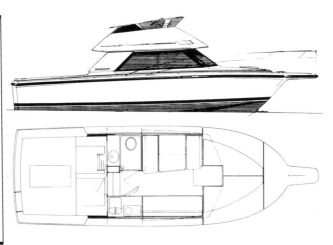

PHOENIX

PHOENIX BLACKHAWK 909

Phoenix has a reputation for building good fishing boats, so it was a surprise when they introduced the Eurostyle Blackhawk 909 express cruiser in 1985. Sharing the same prop-pocket hull as the Phoenix 27, the 909 was a stern-drive boat (a first for any Phoenix model) until 1986 when inboards were offered. This is a three-piece boat with a molded inner liner forming the interior shape while adding to the strength of the hull. Below deck, a U-shaped lounge/dinette at the bow will seat five and converts into a large double berth at night.

Another couple can sleep in the small mid-cabin tucked beneath the bridge-deck. While the absence of interior bulkheads makes the interior seem very open, the lack of natural cabin lighting and ventilation is apparent. Features include a unique sliding transom door, curved windshield, good headroom below, and an integral swim platform and bow pulpit. Twin 350 cid gas inboards cruise the Blackhawk at 22 knots with a 31-knot top speed. Twin 200-hp Volvo diesels are also available. About 60 have been built. Note the limited fuel capacity. ❏

SPECIFICATIONS

Length w/Pulpit	32'5"
Length on Deck	30'1"
Beam	10'0"
Draft	1'10"
Weight	9,150#
Clearance	8'0"
Water	40 Gals.
Fuel	140 Gals.
Hull Type	Modified-V
Designer	Jim Wynne

Production
1985–Current

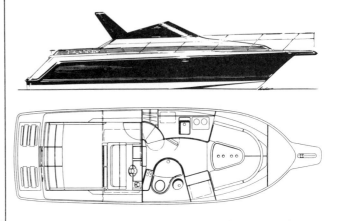

PHOENIX

PHOENIX 33 CONVERTIBLE

When the time comes to pick a rugged 33' convertible for serious fishing and family cruising, the Phoenix 33 is going to be a very tough boat to beat. Well built and realistically priced, the 33 is loaded with the kind of features sure to please hard-core anglers and cruisers alike. Beginning with her aggressive good looks, the Phoenix 33 has a huge flybridge overlooking her 114 sq. ft. cockpit, where a transom door and lockable rod storage are standard. Underway, a unique vent ducting system directs fresh air into the cockpit to disperse fumes that might collect in that area. The stylish decor is impressive with berths for six and several thoughtful design features. The hull is solid fiberglass (17° deadrise aft) with recessed prop pockets below, and a full-length inner liner is bonded to the hull for increased rigidity. Standard 454-cid gas engines cruise the Phoenix 33 at 19 knots and reach a top speed of 30. The optional 425-hp Cats cruise around 26 knots. Note that the Phoenix 33 SFX (1991–current) has a larger salon (but no stall shower), full teak interior, and a revised helm with more room for flush-mounting electronics. ❏

SPECIFICATIONS

Length......................33'9"
Beam.......................13'0"
Draft ....2'9"
Weight ....20,520#
Clearance ....10'9"
Water...................70 Gals.
Fuel ....300 Gals.
Cockpit............114 Sq. Ft.
Hull Type ....Deep-V
Designer ....Jim Wynne

Production
1987–Current

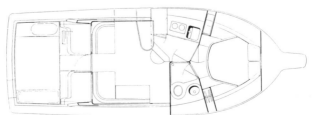

PHOENIX 33 TOURNAMENT

Designed for serious anglers, the Phoenix 33 is a good-looking express with a very low profile and a large, unobstructed fishing cockpit. She's built on the same hull as the 33 Convertible — a rugged deep-V with 17° of deadrise aft, a full inner liner, and recessed prop pockets. The single-level cockpit of the 33 is arranged with a convenient dinette/lounge for guests opposite the helm, complete bait and tackle center, and a lockable rod storage compartment. The engine boxes double as excellent bait-watching seats. Additional cockpit features include an in-deck fishbox, seawater washdown, excellent non-skid, and a transom door with gate. (A reinforcing plate is provided in the cockpit sole for the installation of a mounted chair.) Below, the small (but very upscale) cabin can be fitted with an island berth or conventional V-berths. While 454-cid gas engines are standard, most anglers will likely go for one of the several diesel options offered for the 33 Tournament. The popular 375-hp Cats cruise at 26–27 knots (30 knots top) and the newer 412-hp Cats will cruise at a fast 28 knots and reach 32 knots wide open. ❑

SPECIFICATIONS

Length.....................33'9"
Beam........................13'0"
Draft ....2'9"
Weight ....20,520#
Clearance ....8'4"
Water...................70 Gals.
Fuel, Std ....300 Gals.
Fuel, Opt ....400 Gals.
Cockpit...........114 Sq. Ft.
Hull Type ....Deep-V
Designer ....Jim Wynne

Production
1990–Current

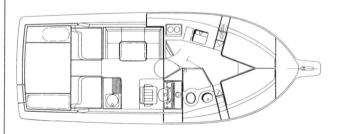

PHOENIX 37 CONVERTIBLE

Bold styling and rugged construction characterize the Phoenix 37 Convertible, a recent entry in the Phoenix fleet of sportfishermen. The 37 is built on basically the same hull as the Phoenix 38 (the boat she replaced) with the full inner liner, extended keel, recessed prop pockets, and a steep 18° of deadrise at the transom. New features include a molded-in bow pulpit, enlarged salon dimensions, a revised flybridge profile, and recessed trim tabs. Her two-stateroom, galley-up interior is arranged with a centerline double berth forward and stacked single berths in the guest stateroom. Teak or white ash interior woodwork is offered. A glassed-in front windshield is optional. With her large and uncluttered cockpit the 37 is designed to meet the needs of serious fishermen. A transom door and gate are standard along with a molded tackle center, livewell, rod storage, and two insulated in-deck fish boxes. With the optional 375-hp Cat diesels, the Phoenix 37 will cruise at 22–23 knots and reach a top speed of 26 knots. The 485-hp 6-71s will cruise around 26–27 knots and turn 30 knots wide open. ❑

SPECIFICATIONS

Length	37'10"
Beam	14'0"
Draft	3'7"
Weight	30,800#
Clearance	12'7"
Water	110 Gals.
Fuel	440 Gals.
Cockpit	93 Sq. Ft.
Hull Type	Modified-V
Designer	Jim Wynne

Production
1989–Current

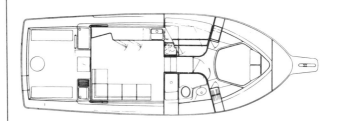

PHOENIX 38 CONVERTIBLE

Like all Phoenix designs, the 38 Convertible was constructed with a full-length inner liner that shapes the boat's interior and greatly strengthens the hull from stem to stern. Hull construction is solid fiberglass with prop pockets below and a relatively steep 18° of deadrise aft. Most observers agree that the Phoenix 38 is a well-engineered and finely finished sportfisherman with an especially handsome profile. Note that the salon's aft bulkhead is angled to improve the flow of fresh air in the cockpit while underway. Her wide sidedecks, roomy cockpit, and excellent bridge layout make the Phoenix 38 a comfortable boat to fish. Her two-stateroom interior layout is, however, on the small side. Engine room access is via a hatch in the cockpit — an innovative approach in a 38' boat but still a tight fit. (Interestingly, this is the smallest production boat with a cockpit engine room door.) A solid front windshield became optional in 1988. The 375-hp Cats cruise at 20 knots and reach 24 at the top. The optional 485-hp 6-71s cruise the Phoenix 38 about 23 knots and push her 26 knots wide open. ❑

SPECIFICATIONS

Length	38'0"
Beam	14'0"
Draft	3'7"
Weight	25,000#
Clearance	12'1"
Water	100 Gals.
Fuel	400 Gals.
Cockpit	NA
Hull Type	Deep-V
Designer	Jim Wynne

Production
1982–88

POST

Brief History

Founded in 1957 by Russel Post, Post Marine is a limited-production builder of traditional Jersey-style sportfishing boats. Early models were built of wood, but the boat that established the company's name was the Post 42 Sportfisherman, introduced in 1974. Their largest model — the Post 50 — came out in 1989. Russel Post sold the company in 1974 and Post Marine remains a privately held company today.

Selected Post Models

Post 42 Sportfisherman
Post 43 II Sportfisherman
Post 44 Sportfisherman

Post 46 II Sportfisherman
Post 50 Sportfisherman

Main Office

Post Marine Company, 36 Post Road, Mays Landing, NJ 08330
609-625-2434

497

POST 42 SPORTFISHERMAN

With over 230 built, the Post 42 Sportfisherman is the best-selling Post design ever. She was introduced in 1975 as a replacement for the all-wood Post 40 and she shares her predecessor's beautiful Jersey-style profile. As a fishing platform, most tournament veterans will rank the Post 42 high among the best of the mid-range sportfishermen. Her flat (4° deadrise) aftersections and flared bow produce a relatively dry boat, quick to plane and fast across the water. The glassed-in windshield seen in later models first became available in 1979. Inside, mahogany wood-work was standard (a teak interior became optional in 1979), and the salon appears much larger than the dimensions might suggest. Her two-stateroom layout has the master stateroom located amidships and stacked single berths in the forward stateroom. Always built on a solid fiberglass hull, the Post 42 was constructed with a glass-over-wood deck and superstructure until mid-1976. Nearly all Post 42s were delivered with 310-hp 6-71N diesels (18–19 knots cruise/22 knots wide open) or 410-hp 6-71s (22–23 knots cruise/ 26 knots top).   ❑

SPECIFICATIONS

Length	42'0"
Length WL	38'0"
Beam	15'9"
Draft	3'0"
Weight	30,000#
Clearance	12'6"
Water	120 Gals.
Fuel	460/500 Gals.
Cockpit	115 Sq. Ft.
Hull Type	Modified-V
Designer	Russel Post

Production
1975–83

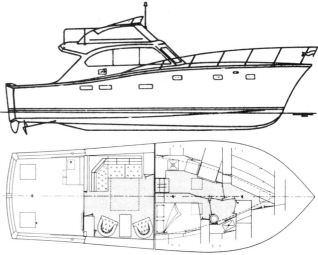

POST

POST 43 II SPORTFISHERMAN

The Post 43 II is a revised and updated version of the classic Post 42 Sportfisherman. Introduced in 1984, the Post 43 underwent significant design changes for 1989 when she became the 43 II. Featuring a redesigned bottom with a deeper forefoot and slightly increased transom deadrise (7° aft), the Post 43 II also received a revised flybridge layout, more fuel, and a molded-in tackle center. The previously optional solid front windshield became standard, and a second sprayrail was added for improved lift and a dryer ride. Her two-stateroom interior is a tasteful blend of traditional teak woodwork and decorator fabrics. The cockpit (at a 125 sq.ft.) is very large and includes a bait freezer, teak covering boards, a transom door, and two in-deck fish boxes. Like all Posts, the bridge ladder is stepped on the tackle center and leads through a (small) opening in the flybridge overhang — a Post trademark. GM 6-71 diesels rated at 485-hp will cruise the Post 43 II around 25 knots with a top speed of 28 knots. The optional 550-hp 6V92s cruise at a fast 28 knots and reach 32 knots wide open. ❑

SPECIFICATIONS

Length	43'8"
Beam	15'9"
Draft	3'6"
Weight	33,000#
Clearance	13'7"
Water	120 Gals.
Fuel	500/550 Gals.
Cockpit	125 Sq. Ft.
Hull Type	Modified-V
Designer	W. Nickerson

Production
1984–89

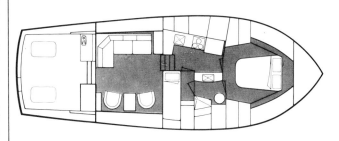

POST 44 SPORTFISHERMAN

The profile of the Post 44 is virtually identical from that of the 43 II model, the boat she replaced in the Post lineup in 1990. Indeed, both are built on the same hull, and the cockpit dimensions and bridge layout are identical. But where the Post 43 II has a two-stateroom, galley-down layout, the newer 44 has a two-stateroom, two-head floorplan with a more open salon/mid-level galley and private head access from the guest cabin. While the actual salon dimensions of the Post 44 are modest, the meticulous woodwork (including a handsome built-in entertainment center) and upscale decor are characteristic of Post's elegant teak interiors. Built for the serious angler, the cockpit has a molded tackle center with top-loading refrigerator/freezer, two in-deck fish boxes, transom door, and teak covering boards. The helm console and flybridge layout are state-of-the-art. Cockpit engine room access was added beginning with the 1992 models. A limited-production boat, only 10–12 Post 44s are built annually and most have had the optional 550-hp 6V92s. She'll cruise at an honest 28 knots and deliver a top speed of 32 knots. ❑

SPECIFICATIONS

Length	43'9"
Beam	15'9"
Draft	3'6"
Weight	33,000#
Clearance	13'7"
Water	120 Gals.
Fuel	570 Gals.
Cockpit	125 Sq. Ft.
Hull Type	Modified-V
Designer	W. Nickerson

Production
1990–Current

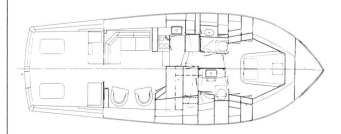

POST 46 II SPORTFISHERMAN

The original Post 46 was introduced back in 1978 as an enlarged version of the popular Post 42. Using the 42's reworked hull, the extra length of the Post 46 resulted in a second head and the additional luxury of a dinette. The standard interior layout was changed in 1985 (the dinette was moved into the salon, and the master stateroom was relocated forward). since 1989, the 46 II has featured a new bottom with slightly increased deadrise and a deeper forefoot. The flybridge was also rearranged in 1989 when a solid front windshield became standard and a molded-in tackle center was added in the cockpit. In 1992, cockpit access to the engine room became standard. Below, her lush two-stateroom teak interior remains unchanged. Since the beginning, the Post 46 has been recognized as a premium tournament design with a classic Jersey-style profile long admired in the sportfishing community. With the now-standard 550-hp 6V92 diesels, the Post 46 II will cruise around 27 knots and reach 30 knots wide open. Earlier models with the 450-hp 6-71TIs will cruise around 24 knots with a top speed of 27 knots. ❑

SPECIFICATIONS

Length	46'9"
Beam	15'9"
Draft	3'6"
Weight	36,000#
Clearance	13'7"
Water	120 Gals.
Fuel	640 Gals.
Cockpit	NA
Hull Type	Modified-V
Designer	W. Nickerson

Production
1978–Current

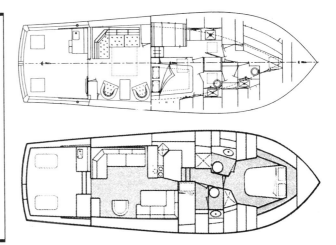

POST 50 SPORTFISHERMAN

There are many who find the distinctive, classic profile of a Post design to be unmatched for beauty and sex appeal. The Post 50 SF is the latest (and biggest) model from this time-honored New Jersey builder of tournament-class sportfishermen. Introduced in mid 1989 and offered on a limited production basis (17 have been built to date), the Post 50 is built on an all-new cored hull with nearly 17 feet of of beam and 8° of transom deadrise. Her three-stateroom, mid-level galley floorplan is unique in a convertible of this size (most three-stateroom 50' convertibles have the galley-up). Completely finished with hand-rubbed teak woodwork, the elegant salon includes a dinette, and the single berths in the aft stateroom can be converted into a large double. The cockpit is set up for serious fishing with a full tackle center, refrigerator/freezer, cockpit controls, teak covering boards, and direct access to the engine room (where the overhead is very low but outboard access is good). The performance of the Post 50 with standard 735-hp 8V92s is excellent — an honest 29 knots at cruise and 33 knots wide open. ❑

SPECIFICATIONS

Length	50'7"
Length WL	45'0"
Beam	16'11"
Draft	4'0"
Weight	43,000#
Clearance	13'10"
Water	240 Gals.
Fuel	800 Gals.
Cockpit	147 Sq. Ft.
Hull Type	Modified-V
Designer	W. Nickerson

Production
1989–Current

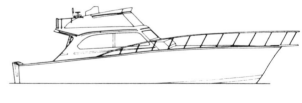

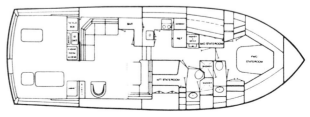

RAMPAGE

Brief History

The Rampage series of sportfishing boats began in 1985 with the introduction of the Rampage 31. Further models were well received, and by 1990 Rampage offered a total of five different designs — the high point for the company's operations. Rampage boats were originally built by the well-regarded Tillotson-Pearson yard in Rhode Island (manufactures of Freedom, Alden and J-Boat sailboats). The company was purchased by Cruisers, Inc., in early 1990, and production has now been moved to Cruisers' Oconto, Wisconsin facility.

Selected Rampage Models

Rampage 28 Sportsman   Rampage 36 Sportfisherman

Rampage 31 Sportfisherman   Rampage 42 Sportfisherman

Rampage 33 Sportfisherman

Main Office

Rampage Yachts, 800 Pecor Street, Oconto, WI 54153
414-834-2211

503

RAMPAGE 28 SPORTSMAN

The Rampage 28 Sportsman is a beamy and well-styled fishing boat with attractive lines and an aggressive profile. It's unlikely that anyone will confuse the Rampage 28 with a family cruiser; she's a pure sportfisherman with a big fishing cockpit and plenty of offshore performance. The Rampage is built on a high-tech cored hull with a modified-V bottom and a relatively sharp entry. A wide 11' beam gives her the look and feel of a bigger boat. About half of her length is given over to a superb cockpit layout with plenty of room for a mounted fighting chair.

A large baitwell and transom door are standard. Inside, the accommodations are basic as befits a no-nonsense sportfishing boat. The portside backrest of the dinette/settee swings up for a total of three single berths. Both galley and head are small with teak-trimmed mica surfaces. Separate engine boxes below the helm and companion seats provide good access to the motors. Twin Volvo 260-hp gas engines cruise the Rampage 28 around 24–25 knots and top out at around 34 knots. The range at full cruise is approximately 260 miles. ❑

SPECIFICATIONS

Length	28'0"
Beam	11'0"
Draft	2'6"
Weight	8,200#
Clearance	NA
Water	25 Gals.
Fuel	240 Gals.
Cockpit	80 Sq. Ft.
Hull Type	Modified-V
Designer	Dick Lema

Production
1986–Current

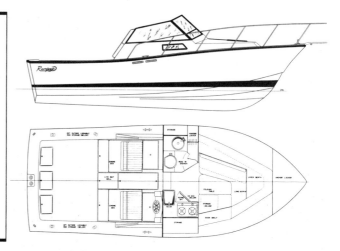

RAMPAGE

RAMPAGE 31 SPORTFISHERMAN

The Rampage 31 is a good example of how a modern yard combines the stringent requirements of an offshore fishing boat with the modern construction techniques rapidly taking hold throughout the industry. Like all Rampage designs, the 31 is beamy. Her cored hull is built on a modified-V bottom with a modest 10° of deadrise at the transom. Trolling stability is said to be exceptional, and a generously flared bow helps ensure a remarkably dry ride. Below, the cabin is snug but adequate for the needs of four anglers. The dinette/settee converts into a V-berth, and the backrests fold up to become bunks — a total of four berths. The cockpit of the Rampage 31 is particularly well designed with an extra-wide transom door, lockable rod storage, and a huge in-deck 85-gallon circulating live well. Notable, too, is the unique system of sliding hatches to access both engines and the service area between. Twin 454-cid gas engines will cruise around 24 knots, but most will choose the 300-hp GM 8.2 diesels which will cruise the Rampage 31 at a fast 28 knots with a top speed of 31–23 knots. ❏

SPECIFICATIONS

Length	30'10"
Beam	11'11"
Draft	2'9"
Weight	12,000#
Clearance	NA
Water	50 Gals.
Fuel	256 Gals.
Cockpit	114 Sq. Ft.
Hull Type	Modified-V
Designer	Dick Lema

Production
1985–Current

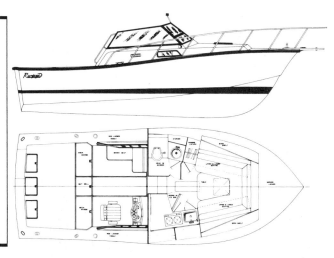

RAMPAGE

RAMPAGE 33 SPORTFISHERMAN

The Rampage 33 Sportfisherman is new for 1990. Like other models in the Rampage fleet, the 33 is designed for experienced anglers who don't mind paying for the quality that goes into a Rampage boat. The 33 has a deep-V hull with 18° of deadrise at the transom and her wide beam insures a stable platform at trolling speeds. The Rampage 33 is a serious canyon runner, and her high-tech construction features the use of bi-directional fabrics as well as a balsa-cored hull. Belowdecks, the roomy cabin is arranged to sleep four and includes a stand-up head, U-shaped dinette, and compact galley. The 33 is loaded with thoughtful features sure to appeal to hard-core fishermen: good engine access, an oversized transom door, big in-deck fish boxes, lockable rod storage, hinged helm console, underwater exhausts, windshield vents, and a completely removable aft cockpit sole. Cummins 291-hp diesels are standard for the Rampage 33, and she'll cruise at 24–25 knots and reach about 29 knots wide open. Optional 320-hp Caterpillar diesels will cruise at about the same speeds. ❏

SPECIFICATIONS

Length	32'4"
Beam	12'4"
Draft	2'7"
Weight	14,500#
Clearance	11'2"
Water	58 Gals.
Fuel	300 Gals.
Cockpit	77 Sq. Ft.
Hull Type	Deep-V
Designer	Rampage

Production
1990–Current

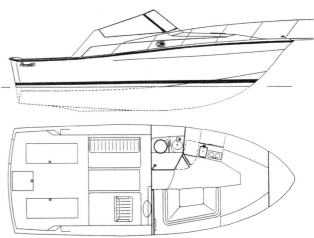

RAMPAGE 36 SPORTFISHERMAN

The 36 Sportfisherman is another in the growing Rampage fleet of high-performance offshore fishing boats. Built on a deep-V hull with 17° of deadrise aft, she offers a large, bi-level cockpit with two insulated 70-gal. fish boxes, concealed rod storage, a livewell, an extra-large transom door, and four tackle centers. The helm position is elevated and features a lockable electronics panel and excellent visibility. A convenient settee is abaft the companion seat, and easy engine access is provided via a centerline hatch in the cockpit sole. While the Rampage 36 is primarily designed for fishing, her cabin layout is comfortable (the cherry wood paneling is elegant) and well arranged with a small galley, a full-sized convertible dinette, and an enclosed head with the toilet concealed in the shower stall. Constructed on a cored hull, the Rampage 36 is a high-quality sportfisherman with obvious eye appeal. Note the side exhausts and molded bow pulpit. With 291-hp Cummins diesels the Rampage 36 will cruise efficiently around 22–23 knots (26 knots top), and with 425-hp Cats she'll cruise around 25 knots and reach 29 knots wide open. ❏

SPECIFICATIONS

Length	35'6"
Beam	13'9"
Draft	2'9"
Weight	19,000#
Clearance	8'10"
Water	70 Gals.
Fuel	435 Gals.
Cockpit	100 Sq. Ft.
Hull Type	Deep-V
Designer	Rampage

Production
1989–Current

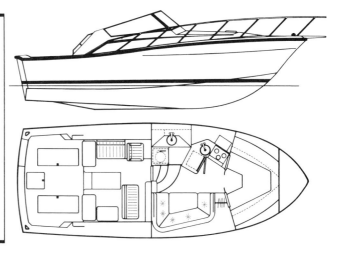

RAMPAGE 42 SPORTFISHERMAN

The Rampage 42 is a lightweight, high-performance fisherman with a wide beam and an upscale price tag. Her styling is unusual in that she features a raised trunk cabin rather than the conventional flush foredeck seen in most modern convertibles of this size. Originally built as the Rampage 40 (1988–89), the hull is fully cored and provides an 18" keel for stability and tracking. Rampage's largest boat to date, the 42 differs from the 40 only in her larger cockpit (102 sq. ft. vs. 142 sq. ft.). Unique underwater exhausts are located midships, just below the salon.

The wraparound helm console has two large electronics lockers properly angled for easy viewing. In the cockpit a transom door, circulating livewell, bait prep station, and two fish boxes were all standard. The appealing cherry wood interior has the galley conveniently located just inside the companionway and a cavernous rod locker is built into the salon overhead. A high-quality boat, 485-hp 6-71s will cruise the Rampage 42 around 23–24 knots. The bigger 550-hp 6V92 diesels will cruise at 27 knots and reach about 30 knots top. ❏

SPECIFICATIONS

Length......................41'8"
Beam.......................15'2"
Draft ....3'6"
Weight ....25,000#
Clearance.................13'3"
Water................100 Gals.
Fuel ....575 Gals.
Cockpit............142 Sq. Ft.
Hull Type.........Modified-V
Designer ....Rampage

Production
1990 Only

SEA RAY

Brief History

Sea Ray was founded in 1959 by C.N. Ray when he bought a small fabrication shop in Detroit that made a 16' fiberglass runabout. By 1986 he had built the business into the second largest powerboat builder in the country (behind Bayliner) with an output of 16,000 boats. Sea Ray was sold to Brunswick in 1986 and Ray stepped down as president in 1988. At peak production, Sea Ray's seven manufacturing facilities can turn out some 25,000 boats annually from 16 to 65 feet.

Selected Sea Ray Inboard Models

Sea Ray 300 Weekender
Sea Ray 300 Sedan Bridge (Early)
Sea Ray 300 Sedan Bridge
Sea Ray 310 Express Cruiser
Sea Ray 310 Sundancer
Sea Ray 310 Amberjack
Sea Ray 310 Sport Bridge
Sea Ray 340 Sedan Bridge (Early)
Sea Ray 340 Sedan Bridge
Sea Ray 340 Express Cruiser
Sea Ray 340 Sundancer
Sea Ray 350 Express Bridge
Sea Ray 355T Sedan
Sea Ray 360 Express
Sea Ray 360 Aft Cabin
Sea Ray 350/370 Express Cruiser

Sea Ray 350/70 Sundancer
Sea Ray 370 Sedan Bridge
Sea Ray 380 Aft Cabin
Sea Ray 390 Sedan SF
Sea Ray 390 Express Cruiser
Sea Ray 400 Express Cruiser
Sea Ray 420/440 Sundancer
Sea Ray 440 Aft Cabin
Sea Ray 440 Convertible
Sea Ray 460 Convertible
Sea Ray 460 Express Cruiser
Sea Ray 480/500 Sundancer
Sea Ray 500/550 Sedan Bridge
Sea Ray 600/630 Super Sun Sport
Sea Ray 650 Motor Yacht

Main Office

Sea Ray Boats, Inc., 2600 Sea Ray Blvd., Knoxville, TN 37914
615-522-4181

509

SEA RAY 300 WEEKENDER

A popular and versatile family cruiser, the Sea Ray 300 Weekender remained pretty much the same boat throughout her 5-year production run. She's built on the standard Sea Ray deep-V hull with a fine entry, recessed propeller pockets, and a deep 21° of deadrise at the transom. While the 300's contemporary sportboat styling is appealing, her lack of a modern integral swim platform during her last few years of production is notable. Because she carries the greater part of her beam well aft, the cockpit is very spacious and capable of seating six or eight passengers with the optional bench seating. Below, the cabin is on the smallish side since the beam narrows considerably forward of the helm. Off-white mica cabinets and countertops and light-grain teak trim make the Weekender interior decor quite appealing. Twin 260-hp gas engines cruise the 300 Weekender at 25 knots with a top speed of around 32 knots. The fuel capacity was increased in 1987 to 200 gallons. Sea Ray also offered a 300 Sundancer model during this time — basically the same boat with a mid-cabin layout and stern drives. ❏

SPECIFICATIONS

Length	29'8"
Beam	11'0"
Draft	2'4"
Weight	9,600#
Clearance	NA
Water	40 Gals.
Fuel	140/200 Gals.
Cockpit	NA
Hull Type	Deep-V
Designer	Sea Ray

Production
1985–89

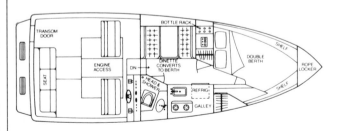

SEA RAY 300 SEDAN BRIDGE (EARLY)

The Sea Ray 300 Sedan Bridge is a good-looking flybridge cruiser with a well-balanced combination of comfort and performance. Designed primarily for the family market, the 300 features an efficient and practical floorplan with overnight accommodations for as many as six. An offset double bed is fitted in the forward stateroom in place of the normal V-berths, and both the dinette and salon sofa convert to double berths. Most of these boats were sold with the optional lower helm. Note that the interior is laid out a step down from the cockpit level as the engines are located aft, under the cockpit sole, and driven through V-drives. Three lift-out hatches provide good access to the engines, and a transom door and swim platform were standard. Topside, the flybridge of the 300 Sedan Bridge is arranged with the helm forward and bench seating aft for four guests. Twin 260-hp MerCruiser gas engines will cruise the Sea Ray 300 Sedan Bridge around 21 knots and the top speed is 28–29 knots. A new Sea Ray 300 Sedan Bridge replaced this model in 1988. ❏

SPECIFICATIONS

Length ....29'1"
Beam ....11'0"
Draft ....2'5"
Weight ....10,500#
Clearance ....NA
Water ....40 Gals.
Fuel ....140 Gals.
Cockpit ....NA
Hull Type ....Deep-V
Designer ....Sea Ray

Production
1985–87

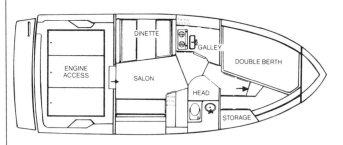

SEA RAY 300 SEDAN BRIDGE

Sea Ray's advertising claimed that their 300 Sedan Bridge (first called the 305 Sedan Bridge when introduced in 1988) embodies "spectacular styling" among her attributes. Spectacular, indeed — the unusual styling of the Sea Ray 300 Sedan Bridge is surely a matter of opinion. She was built on a wide beam hull with propeller pockets, and aimed at the expanding market for maxi-cube family cruisers. Her interior accommodations are, in fact, quite spacious for a 31-footer. With a unique mid-cabin tucked away beneath the raised dinette, the 300 Sedan Bridge can boast of two private staterooms. The athwartships double-berth arrangement in the forward stateroom is innovative in its use of space, and the concealed galley is particularly appealing. The head is located aft in the salon, just inside the companionway door, where access from the outside is easiest. The cockpit itself is very small, but the flybridge (with its overhang) is exceptionally large. Standard 260-hp MerCruiser gas engines will cruise around 22 knots and have a top speed of 29 knots. Note that this model remained in production for only two years. ❏

SPECIFICATIONS

Length	29'10"
Beam	12'0"
Draft	2'6"
Weight	11,500#
Clearance	NA
Water	60 Gals.
Fuel	200 Gals.
Cockpit	NA
Hull Type	Deep-V
Designer	Sea Ray

Production
1988–89

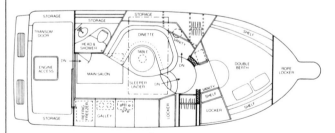

SEA RAY 310 EXPRESS CRUISER

A good-looking boat, the 310 Express Cruiser (EC) replaced the 300 EC in the Sea Ray fleet for 1990. Built on a deep-V (17°) prop-pocket-type hull with greater beam and significantly increased interior volume, the 310 EC incorporates the stylish integral swim platform and rounded windshield typical of modern sportboat designs. Although the 310 EC and her sistership, the 310 Sundancer, look the same on the outside, the interiors are entirely different. Lacking a mid-cabin, the more open salon of the EC makes her a more practical day boat. The long salon sofa offers increased entertainment space, and the wider entryway is a convenient plus compared to the narrow passageway of the Sundancer. The cockpit seating is also different with double helm and companion seats and a little more free space for moving around. A hatch in the sole provides access to the engines and a transom door was standard. Note that stern drives were standard in the Sea Ray 310 EC and the desirable inboard 260-hp gas engines were optional. With the inboards, the cruising speed is 24–25 knots and the top speed is around 32 knots. ❑

SPECIFICATIONS

Length.......................31'6"
Length WL.....................NA
Beam.........................11'5"
Draft (V-drives)..........2'3"
Weight ....10,000#
Clearance ....NA
Water...................40 Gals.
Fuel ....200 Gals.
Hull Type ....Deep-V
Designer...............Sea Ray

Production
1990–91

SEA RAY 310 SUNDANCER

Built on an easy-running deep-V hull with prop pockets, side exhausts, and 17° of transom deadrise, the Sea Ray 310 Sundancer incorporates the integral swim platform and rounded windshield typical of modern sportboat designs. Clearly, this is a stylish family cruiser and a great improvement over the earlier Sundancer 300 model with its stern drives. Below, the mid-cabin layout provides privacy for two couples with room for an additional couple when the large U-shaped dinette is converted. The use of privacy curtains opens up the cabin considerably and the rounded corners, pastel fabrics, and off-white laminates make for a very attractive decor. A portside entryway door leaves plenty of room for cockpit seating, including the elevated helm position with bench seating for three. Stern drives were standard and the inboard 260-hp gas engines (with V-drives) were an option. With the inboards, the 310 Sundancer will have a cruising speed of 23–24 knots and a top speed of around 31 knots. Note that the 310 Sundancer and Express Cruiser models both share the same exterior profile. ❑

SPECIFICATIONS

Length	31'6"
Length WL	NA
Beam	11'5"
Draft (V-drives)	2'3"
Weight	10,000#
Clearance	NA
Water	40 Gals.
Fuel	180 Gals.
Hull Type	Deep-V
Designer	Sea Ray

Production
1990–91

SEA RAY 310 AMBERJACK

Anglers are going to find a lot to like in the 310 Amberjack besides just her affordable price tag. This is a very good-looking boat with the aggressive low-profile silhouette of a small Bertram or Blackfin. She's built on a solid glass deep-V hull with cored hull-sides, a wide beam, prop pockets, and 18° of transom deadrise. Like any well planned day boat, the Amberjack's emphasis is clearly in the spacious bi-level cockpit — a wide-open affair consuming well over half of the boat's LOA. There's plenty of guest seating forward with its sunpad and dinette (note the aft-facing companion seat), and the cockpit can be fitted with in-deck fishboxes, rod holders, and transom livewell. While cabin space belowdecks is at a premium, the 310 AJ manages to include overnight berths for two, plus a stand-up head with shower, a small galley, and convertible dinette. Hinged motor boxes provide good access to the engines and the sidedecks are a foot wide. A good performer with optional 454-cid gas engines (350-cid inboards are standard), she'll cruise at 24 knots and reach 31–32 knots top. ❑

SPECIFICATIONS

Length	31'2"
Beam	11'5"
Draft	3'1"
Weight	10,500#
Cockpit	57 Sq. Ft.
Clearance	NA
Water	40 Gals.
Fuel	296 Gals.
Hull Type	Deep-V
Designer	Sea Ray

Production
1991–Current

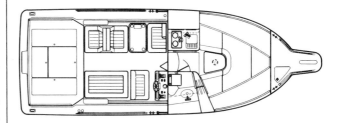

SEA RAY 310 SPORT BRIDGE

A great-looking boat with aggressive styling and a low-profile appearance, the 310 Sport Bridge is basically a 310 Amberjack with a flybridge and semi-enclosed lower helm. She's built on a deep-V hull with a wide beam, side exhausts, prop pockets, and 18° of deadrise at the transom. Like any well-planned sedan fisherman, she comes with a spacious cockpit — a wide-open affair consuming well over half of the boat's LOA. There's plenty of guest seating forward including a sunpad and dinette (note the aft-facing companion seat), and the cockpit can be fitted with in-deck fishboxes, rod holders, and a transom livewell. While cabin space is at a premium, the 310 manages to include overnight berths for two, plus a stand-up head with shower, a small galley and convertible dinette. The bridge is small (as it should be) with seating for two. Hinged motor boxes provide good access to the engines and the sidedecks are a foot wide. Optional 454-cid gas engines (350-cid inboards are standard) will cruise at 23 knots (30–31 knots top) and 291-hp Cummins diesels will cruise around 27 knots (31 knots top). ❏

SPECIFICATIONS

Length	31'2"
Beam	11'5"
Draft	3'1"
Weight	11,500#
Clearance	9'6"
Cockpit	57 Sq. Ft.
Water	40 Gals.
Fuel	296 Gals.
Hull Type	Deep-V
Designer	Sea Ray

Production
1992–Current

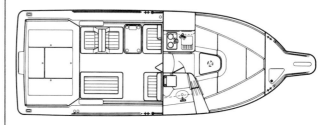

SEA RAY 340 SEDAN BRIDGE (EARLY)

340 Sedan Bridge

The Sea Ray 340 Sedan Bridge is a capable family cruising boat with a modern convertible profile and comfortable interior accommodations. She was built on a solid fiberglass deep-V hull with recessed propeller pockets and 21° of deadrise at the transom — the same hull used in the popular 340 Express Cruiser. The salon is dominated by an attractive drum-shaped bottle-and-glass cabinet with circular tambour doors and a grabrail. Although optional, most Sea Ray 340 Sedans were sold with the lower helm station. The MSD (toilet) is located in the shower stall in the head compartment (a space-saving idea later seen in other models), and a bi-fold privacy door closes off the forward stateroom. Large wraparound cabin windows give the 340's interior a notably spacious appearance and most will find the layout to be functional and ideally suited for family cruising. Outside, the cockpit is average in size and comes with a transom door and swim platform as standard equipment. The optional 350-hp Crusader gas engines will cruise the Sea Ray 340 Sedan Bridge at 20–21 knots with a top speed of around 30 knots. ❑

SPECIFICATIONS

Length	33'7"
Beam	11'11"
Draft	2'6"
Weight	11,400#
Clearance	NA
Water	80 Gals.
Fuel	204 Gals.
Cockpit	NA
Hull Type	Deep-V
Designer	Sea Ray

Production
1983–87

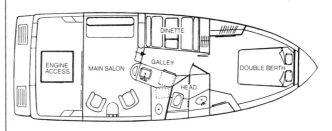

SEA RAY 340 SEDAN BRIDGE

Lasting only two years in production, the Sea Ray 340 Sedan Bridge incorporated the same unusual exterior styling found in the smaller 300 Sedan Bridge. The oversized flybridge — with its unusual cockpit overhang — is different, to say the least. The newer 340 Sedan Bridge (the original model ran from 1983–87) was built on a wide-beam hull design with prop pockets and is not an update of the original 340 Sedan Bridge. Inside, the two-stateroom floorplan includes a private mid-cabin located below the raised dinette with partial standing headroom. Additional features include a modern interior decor with an efficient galley in the salon, a transom door, and a swim platform with boarding ladder. The cockpit is somewhat small but should be adequate for most cruising families, and the integral bow pulpit adds considerably to the 340's profile. Standard power was a pair of 340-hp MerCruiser gas engines which will cruise the Sea Ray 340 Sedan Bridge around 22–23 knots and turn 30+ knots wide open. Note that this model was originally introduced as the 345 Sedan Bridge in 1988. ❏

SPECIFICATIONS

Length	33'9"
Beam	12'6"
Draft	3'9"
Weight	16,500#
Clearance	NA
Water	100 Gals.
Fuel	250 Gals.
Cockpit	NA
Hull Type	Deep-V
Designer	Sea Ray

Production
1988–89

SEA RAY 340 EXPRESS CRUISER

The 340 Express Cruiser (and her sistership, the 340 Sundancer) proved to be an extremely popular model for Sea Ray during her six-year production run. She's built on a solid fiberglass, deep-V hull with a relatively wide beam, prop pockets below, and a steep 21° of deadrise at the transom. Aimed at the family sportboat market, there were several changes and modifications during her lifetime. The galley and dinette were rearranged in 1986, and the original centerline double berth in the stateroom was dropped in the 1988 models in favor of a full-width bed and (optional) built-in entertainment center. Notable, too, was the increase in fuel capacity to 250 gallons in 1987. Standard features included a swim platform, transom door, radar arch, and side exhausts. The styling of the 340 Express is attractive, although somewhat dated compared to many of the newer sportboat designs now on the market. With standard 340-hp gas engines, she'll cruise at 24 knots and reach 33 knots wide open. Note that the Sea Ray 340 Sport Fisherman (1984–86) is the same boat as the 340 EC but with the addition of a flybridge. ❏

SPECIFICATIONS

Length	33'7"
Beam	11'11"
Draft	2'5"
Weight	10,100#
Clearance	NA
Water	52 Gals.
Fuel	204/250 Gals.
Cockpit	NA
Hull Type	Deep-V
Designer	Sea Ray

Production
1984–89

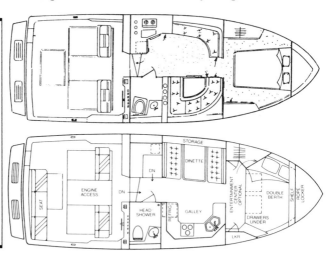

SEA RAY

SEA RAY 340 SUNDANCER

The Sea Ray 340 Sundancer has the same deep-V hull (21° deadrise aft with prop pockets) and exterior profile as the 340 Express Cruiser (EC), the difference being that the Sundancer has a mid-cabin located beneath the bridgedeck. The Sundancer's additional interior space is made possible by using V-drives to move the engines aft under the cockpit sole. The popular mid-cabin layout made the Sundancer a better-selling model than the EC and these boats remain in demand in the brokerage market. Inside, the forward stateroom and mid cabin are both fitted with double berths, but any privacy is limited to a couple of draw curtains — not the most desirable setup for weekend cruising. The Sundancer's cockpit is quite roomy and includes a companion seat next to the helm, a transom door, and a swim platform. Two lift-out hatches in the cockpit sole provide access to the engines, however the transom bench seat must first be removed to get at them. Standard 454-cid gas engines provide a cruising speed of 23 knots and a top speed of about 32 knots. The fuel capacity of only 172 gallons results in a limited cruising range. ❑

SPECIFICATIONS

Length	33'7"
Beam	11'11"
Draft	2'5"
Weight	10,500#
Clearance	NA
Water	52 Gals.
Fuel	172 Gals.
Cockpit	NA
Hull Type	Deep-V
Designer	Sea Ray

Production
1984–89

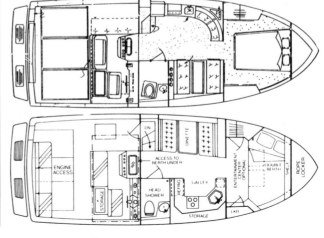

SEA RAY 350 EXPRESS BRIDGE

So-called "Express Bridge" models have become popular weekend cruisers with families because of their sunken, full-width interiors (no sid-edecks) and easy bridge access (molded steps rather than a ladder). Carver began the trend with the Mariner 36 some years ago and the competition has been joined recently by Wellcraft, Cruisers, and now Sea Ray with the 350 Express Bridge. Like others of her type, she has a spacious interior arranged on a single-level with facing semi-circular settees dominating the salon and a single stateroom forward. While the layout is indeed cavernous for a 35-footer, the lack of a separate stall shower in the head is notable. The bridge is very large and features a fold-down door for easy access to the foredeck. Interestingly, the cabin windows are larger than those found in other express-bridge models and the interior seems less confining. Note that 260-hp stern drives are standard in the 350 Express Bridge — a poor choice in our opinion for a boat this size. Optional 454-cid gas inboards (with V-drives) will cruise around 22–23 knots and reach 32 knots wide open. ❏

SPECIFICATIONS

Length ....35'4"
Beam.........................11'5"
Draft ....3'1"
Weight ....11,500#
Clearance ....NA
Water...................60 Gals.
Fuel ....200 Gals.
Cockpit........................NA
Hull Type ....Deep-V
Designer...............Sea Ray

Production
1992–Current

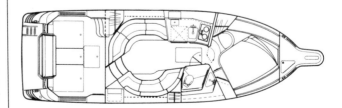

SEA RAY 355T SEDAN

The Sea Ray 355T (the "T" stands for Trawler) is a roomy cruising sedan with a spacious interior and the largest master stateroom seen in any sedan under 40'. She was built on the same hull used later in the production of the popular 360 Aft Cabin — a modified-V with prop pockets, side exhausts, and a shallow keel below. With her stepped sheer, rakish bridge and Eurostyle cabin windows, the 355T is an unusual and somewhat distinctive boat. Rather than providing the usual two-stateroom layout in a boat this size, Sea Ray opted for a more open single-stateroom floorplan.

This master stateroom is enormous with a walkaround island berth, lots of dressing space, and a large hanging locker. A convenient serving counter separates the step-down galley from the salon, and the optional lower helm is to port rather than starboard (where it belongs). The carpeted overhead and teak-and-mica interior woodwork are unimpressive. Outside, the bridge is very roomy and the cockpit is tiny. Single and twin engines, gas and diesel, were offered. With twin 135-hp Perkins diesels she'll cruise economically at 10–11 knots. ❑

SPECIFICATIONS

Length	36'3"
Beam	12'6"
Draft	2'11"
Weight	13,000#
Clearance	10'3"
Water	120 Gals.
Fuel	270 Gals.
Cockpit	36 Sq. Ft.
Hull Type	Modified-V
Designer	Sea Ray

Production
1982–83

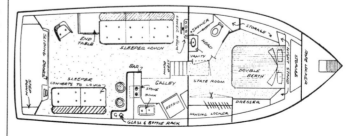

SEA RAY 360 EXPRESS CRUISER

An innovative and somewhat unusual design, the Sea Ray 360 Express Cruiser is distinguished by her unique T-shaped hardtop and spoiler section. Supported by the windshield, the forward end of the top provides wind protection while underway. To get all-weather protection, the slots in the T-top can be closed with clear snap-in vinyl inserts or plexiglass panels. She's equally innovative below, where angled bulkheads give the staterooms and head compartment unusual shapes — a notable departure from the rigid, squared-off interiors found in most boats of the early 1980s. The salon of the Sea Ray 360 EC is quite open and spacious thanks to her extra-wide beam. The interior woodwork is a simulated-teak plastic laminate trimmed with natural teak. She'll sleep up to six and the head compartment is fitted with a stall shower. Outside, the cockpit is very large with seating for eight to ten people. Standard power was a pair of big block 454 gas engines. No racehorse, the 360's cruising speed is around 17 knots and the top speed is 26–27 knots. Note that the Sea Ray 360 Sedan (1980–83) was built on the same hull. ❏

SPECIFICATIONS

Length	36'6"
Beam	13'11"
Draft	2'7"
Weight	17,900#
Clearance	9'7"
Water	100 Gals.
Fuel	300 Gals.
Cockpit	NA
Hull Type	Deep-V
Designer	Sea Ray

Production
1979–83

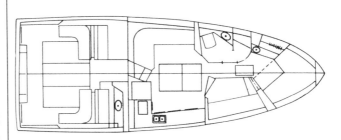

SEA RAY 360 AFT CABIN

The Sea Ray 360 Aft Cabin was built on a "dual mode" hull capable of providing trawler-style economy at 7–8 knot displacement speeds while still able to achieve planing-speed performance. The hull has about 9° of deadrise at the transom, propeller pockets, moderate beam, and a shallow keel for maneuverability. The 360 Aft Cabin was a fairly popular model due to her efficient twin-cabin accommodation plan and reasonable price. Her layout is somewhat unusual in that a walka-round double bed is located in the forward cabin while twin berths are fitted into the smallish aft stateroom (a dou-ble berth in the aft cabin was optional). The stall shower is found in the forward head, and the galley is a couple of steps down from the salon level, making for a roomy living and entertainment area. The small afterdeck has enough room for a few deck chairs and most 360s were sold with the optional hardtop. Standard 260/270-hp gas engines cruise the Sea Ray 360 Aft Cabin around 15 knots and reach a top speed of 23–24 knots. Optional 200-hp Perkins diesels provide an efficient cruising speed of 15–16 knots. ❏

SPECIFICATIONS

Length	36'3"
Length WL	NA
Beam	12'6"
Draft	2'11"
Weight	15,100#
Clearance	NA
Water	120 Gals.
Fuel	270 Gals.
Hull Type	Modified-V
Designer	Sea Ray

Production
1983–87

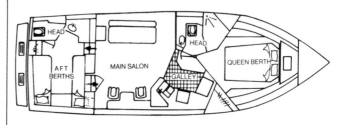

SEA RAY 350/370 EXPRESS CRUISER

Called the 350 Express Cruiser (EC) until 1992, Sea Ray's 370 EC is a modern family cruiser with contemporary sportboat lines and a very spacious interior layout. She's built on a good-running, deep-V hull with prop pockets, side exhausts, and a steep 21° of transom deadrise. While she has the same exterior profile of the 370 Sundancer (her sistership), the EC has a larger salon with an extended settee, bigger galley, and indoor entertaining space for a crowd. There's a separate stall shower in the head and a built-in TV can be pulled out and viewed from the salon to the forward cabin. On the downside, only a curtain provides privacy in the stateroom. Note that the 350/370 Express Cruiser has straight drives while the Sundancer has V-drives. Additional features include good interior headroom throughout, integral bow pulpit, and a stylish, curved wrap-around windshield. Like all current Sea Ray express cruisers, the swim platform is an integral and functional part of the boat. Standard 454-cid gas engines will cruise the Sea Ray 370 EC around 20 knots and reach a top speed of 29 knots. ❏

SPECIFICATIONS

Length	36'10"
Length WL	NA
Beam	12'4"
Draft	2'5"
Weight	13,000#
Clearance	NA
Water	70 Gals.
Fuel	250 Gals.
Hull Type	Deep-V
Designer	Sea Ray

Production
1990–Current

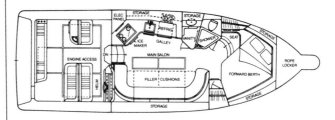

SEA RAY 350/370 SUNDANCER

Called the 350 Sundancer until 1992, the Sea Ray 370 is an upscale family cruiser with modern sportboat lines and a mid-cabin interior layout. She's built on a good-running deep-V hull design with prop pockets below, side exhausts and a steep 21° of deadrise at the transom. While she has the same exterior profile as the 370 Express Cruiser (her sistership), the Sundancer has a more compact (albeit still wide open) salon to make room for the sunken mid-cabin floorplan. There's a separate stall shower in the head compartment and a built-in TV can be pulled out and viewed from the salon to the forward cabin. On the downside, only draw curtains provide privacy for the staterooms. Unlike the EC model, the Sundancer is driven with V-drives and access to the engines is further aft in the cockpit. (Stern drives are available — a poor choice in a boat this size.) Additional features include good interior headroom, integral bow pulpit and swim platform, transom door, and a stylish, curved wraparound windshield. Standard 454-cid gas engines will cruise the 370 Sundancer around 20 knots and reach a top speed of about 29 knots. ❏

SPECIFICATIONS

Length	36'10"
Length WL	NA
Beam	12'4"
Draft	2'5"
Weight	13,500#
Clearance	NA
Water	70 Gals.
Fuel	250 Gals.
Hull Type	Deep-V
Designer	Sea Ray

Production
1990–Current

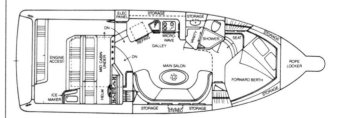

SEA RAY 370 SEDAN BRIDGE

With her long foredeck and relatively small cockpit, the Sea Ray 370 Sedan Bridge is a modern flybridge cruiser with a conservative profile and spacious interior layout. She's built on the same hull used in the 370 EC and Sundancer models — a deep-V affair with a steep 21° of transom deadrise, prop pockets, moderate beam ,and side exhausts. Her two-stateroom, galley-down floorplan features fairly expansive salon dimensions (for a 37-footer) with a full-length settee, removable dinette table, breakfast bar, and large wraparound cabin windows. There's an offset double berth in the master stateroom forward, and the portside guest cabin has another double berth extending below the salon sole. The cockpit is too small for any serious fishing and comes with a transom door, coaming padding and optional bench seating. Note that the helm console is all the way forward on the flybridge, with L-shaped lounge seating aft. Additional features include an arch, swim platform, and integral bow pulpit. Standard 454-cid gas engines will cruise the 370 Sedan Bridge at 19 knots and deliver a top speed of around 28 knots. ❏

SPECIFICATIONS

Length ....36'10"
Beam.......................12'4"
Draft ....2'7"
Weight ....14,500#
Clearance ....NA
Water...................70 Gals.
Fuel ....250 Gals.
Cockpit........................NA
Hull Type ....Deep-V
Designer...............Sea Ray

Production
1991–Current

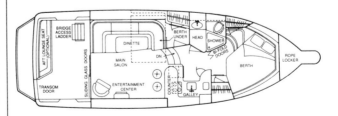

SEA RAY 380 AFT CABIN

The Sea Ray 380 Aft Cabin is a modern, maxi-cube family cruiser with a slightly top-heavy profile and a very spacious interior layout. Built on a new Sea Ray hull design with nearly 14 feet of beam, prop pockets, and an integral bow pulpit, the 380 Aft Cabin has as much living and entertaining space below as most 40-footers. Indeed, the accommodations are very impressive for a 38' boat, with large staterooms (each with a double berth), full dinette, and a wide-open salon capable of seating six or eight in comfort. A contemporary blend of pastel fabrics, Formica countertops and cabinetry, and traditional teak trim presents an appealing and upscale interior decor. Features include a vanity in the forward stateroom, a stall shower enclosure in the aft head, and a convenient serving counter overlooking the large, U-shaped galley. Outside, the flybridge will seat six and the aft deck is large enough for several deck chairs. A popular boat, twin 340-hp MerCruiser gas engines were standard. With these engines, the Sea Ray 380 Aft Cabin will cruise around 16 knots and reach a top speed of 25+ knots. ❏

SPECIFICATIONS

Length	37'9"
Length WL	NA
Beam	13'11"
Draft	2'7"
Weight	20,000#
Clearance	NA
Water	100 Gals.
Fuel	300 Gals.
Hull Type	Deep-V
Designer	Sea Ray

Production
1989–91

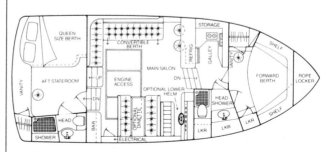

SEA RAY 390 SEDAN SF

The Sea Ray 390 Sedan Sportfisherman is actually a stretched version of the 360 Sedan model that Sea Ray built from 1980 to 1983. The extra length went into the cockpit, which is easily the boat's most impressive feature. She was built on the same one-piece fiberglass hull as the 360 and 390 Express Cruisers — a deep-V design with a wide beam, 19° of deadrise at the transom, and propeller pockets below. The original floorplan was updated in 1985 to include a centerline queen berth in the forward stateroom and a more open salon area. Stacked single berths are located in the guest cabin and a serving counter separates the galley from the salon. The comfortable interior arrangements of the 390 Sedan make her an excellent all-purpose family cruiser, and with 400 gallons of fuel and an oversized tournament cockpit, she's equally well suited for offshore fishing activities. Standard 350-hp gas engines will cruise around 16 knots and reach a top speed of 25 knots. The optional 320-hp Cat diesels cruise the Sea Ray 390 Sedan SF at an economical 21 knots and reach 24 knots top. ❑

SPECIFICATIONS

Length	39'0"
Beam	13'11"
Draft	2'5"
Weight	18,400#
Clearance	NA
Water	100 Gals.
Fuel	400 Gals.
Cockpit	116 Sq. Ft.
Hull Type	Deep-V
Designer	Sea Ray

Production
1983–86

SEA RAY 390 EXPRESS CRUISER

The Sea Ray 390 EC is one of the most popular family express boats ever built. First of the big production sportboats when she came out in 1984 (she was a stretched version of the prop pocket 360 EC hull), her sleek lines and European styling attracted a lot of attention among upscale buyers and within the industry itself. Her expansive two-stateroom interior is arranged with a queen berth in the forward stateroom and a combined galley-and-breakfast bar facing the curved settee in the salon. The guest cabin is unique. It is separated from the galley by a retractable mirrored bulkhead and has bunk berths that can be converted into a sofa during the day and the area used for additional seating within the main cabin. The interior was updated twice over the years, changing from the original wood-grain mica to teak in 1986 and to a white-mica/teak-trim decor in 1988. Outside, the huge cockpit provides seating for as many as ten passengers. With standard 454-cid gas engines the 390 EC will cruise at 18–19 knots and reach about 28 knots wide open. Optional 375-hp Cat diesels will cruise at 25 knots with a top speed of about 29 knots. ❏

SPECIFICATIONS

Length	39'0"
Beam	13'11"
Draft	2'4"
Weight	16,400#
Clearance	NA
Water	100 Gals.
Fuel	300 Gals.
Cockpit	NA
Hull Type	Deep-V
Designer	Sea Ray

Production
1984-91

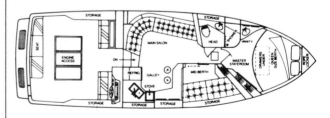

SEA RAY 400 EXPRESS CRUISER

The 400 Express Cruiser (EC) is the long-awaited replacement for Sea Ray's hugely popular 390 EC, which ran from 1984 to 1991. With her stylish curved windshield, integral swim deck, and sleek hull profile, the 400 EC is truly a handsome boat and a big step up from her predecessor in appearance. It's interesting to note that the new hull (solid fiberglass with prop pockets, side exhausts, and 19° deadrise aft) is narrower by a foot than the 390's and interior and cockpit dimensions are reduced accordingly. The good news is that the 400 EC basically retains the 390's innovative two-stateroom floorplan, albeit completely updated and restyled. A sliding wall partition opens the guest cabin's convertible settee to the salon for additional seating during the day — a very practical design feature. Outside, the cockpit is fitted with an elevated helm, wet bar, and plenty of guest seating, and there's an optional bolt-on extended platform attachment with fender storage available. Standard 454-cid gas engines will cruise the Sea Ray 400 Express Cruiser about 18 knots and reach a top speed of 27–28 knots. ❑

SPECIFICATIONS

Length ....40'4"
Beam........................13'0"
Draft ....3'3"
Weight ....16,000#
Clearance ....NA
Water.................100 Gals.
Fuel ....300 Gals.
Cockpit........................NA
Hull Type ....Deep-V
Designer...............Sea Ray

Production
1992–Current

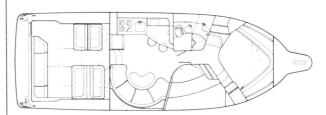

SEA RAY 420/440 SUNDANCER

Introduced in late 1989 as the 420 Sundancer, Sea Ray made some hull changes and reintroduced this boat in 1992 as the 440 Sundancer. Construction is solid glass with 17° of deadrise aft — basically the same hull used in the long-running 390 EC. Note that the current 440 hull has prop pockets while the original 420 model did not. Her sleek sportboat profile is beautifully accented with a modern curved windshield, and her stylish boarding-platform/transom adds much to her graceful lines. The Sundancer's wide-open cabin is a blend of curved bulkheads, white Formica cabinetry in the galley, and light oak trimwork throughout. Offering complete cruising privacy for two couples, a unique wraparound door closes off the mid-cabin at night and the forward stateroom is fitted with a huge double bed and vanity. Facing lounge seating in the cockpit provides plenty of guest seating. V-drives are used in all engine installations. Originally powered with standard 454-cid gas engines (17 knots cruise/26 top), 300-hp Cummins diesels are now standard (21 knots cruise/25 top). Optional 425-hp Cats will cruise around 25 knots. ❑

SPECIFICATIONS

Length	41'7"/44'0"
Beam	13'11"
Draft	3'3"
Weight	20,000#
Clearance	NA
Water	100 Gals.
Fuel	400 Gals.
Cockpit	NA
Hull Type	Deep-V
Designer	Sea Ray

Production
1989–Current

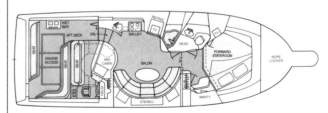

SEA RAY 440 AFT CABIN

The Sea Ray 440 Aft Cabin began life in 1986 as the 410 Aft Cabin. (Note that for 1988 she was called the "415.") The hull was stretched in 1989 and the final "440" designation reflected her increased length. With her dramatic styling and sporty profile, the 440 Aft Cabin has that distinctive Sea Ray look and many consider her a good-looking boat. She's constructed on a deep-V hull with 17° of transom deadrise and recessed prop pockets below — the same hull used in the 440 Convertible. Inside, her floorplan is arranged in the conventional manner with an offset double berth in the forward stateroom instead of the over/under bunks found in the earlier 410/415 models. In 1990, off-white laminates replaced the teak paneling and cabinetry used in previous years. The dinette was also eliminated in favor of a stylish wraparound deckhouse lounge. Outside, both the flybridge seating and aft deck dimensions are limited. A very popular model, standard 454-cid gas engines cruise the Sea Ray 440 around 15 knots with a top speed of 24 knots. Optional 375-hp Cats will cruise at 20 knots and reach 24 knots wide open. ❏

SPECIFICATIONS

Length	43'6"
Length WL	NA
Beam	13'11"
Draft	3'2"
Weight	25,000#
Clearance	15'3"
Water	150 Gals.
Fuel	420 Gals.
Hull Type	Deep-V
Designer	Sea Ray

Production
1986–91

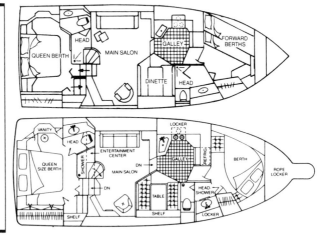

SEA RAY

SEA RAY 440 CONVERTIBLE

Designed to appeal to the sportfisherman, the Sea Ray 440 Convertible was styled after the larger 460 Convertible (1987–88) with a low foredeck, stepped sheer, and modern deckhouse profile. Introduced in 1988 as the 430 Convertible, the 440 designation was added in the 1989 models. Below, the high-style European interior theme of the 440 (no teak anywhere) was updated in 1990 with a modest amount of teak trim and compares well with many of today's contemporary family convertibles. The floorplan — with its athwartships guest stateroom — is unusual and innovative.

Also unusual in any 43' boat is the cockpit engine room access where a hatch just aft of the salon door reveals a three-step ladder leading into the somewhat tight engine compartment. Her bridge layout and tournament-sized cockpit are obviously designed with fishing in mind. Additional features include a transom door, removable fish box, salon and flybridge wet bars, cockpit shower, and a swim platform. With the optional 375-hp Cat diesels, the Sea Ray 440 will cruise around 21 knots and turn 25 knots at full throttle. A nice-looking boat but no tournament monster. ❑

SPECIFICATIONS

Length	43'6"
Beam	13'11"
Draft	2'8"
Weight	23,000#
Clearance	10'9"
Water	132 Gals.
Fuel	500 Gals.
Cockpit	NA
Hull Type	Deep-V
Designer	Sea Ray

Production
1988–91

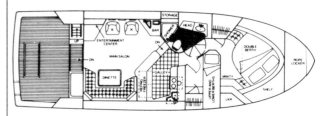

SEA RAY 460 CONVERTIBLE

The 460 Convertible was Sea Ray's first venture into the serious sportfishing market and represented a bold departure from the company's past devotion to family oriented cruisers and sportboats. Her lightweight construction was suitably high-tech and modern, and her aggressive, Eurostyle appearance remains attractive today. Still, the 460 Convertible wasn't a big seller and production lasted only two years until she was replaced in 1988 with the less-expensive 440 model. A comfortable boat, her two-stateroom interior is plush in the extreme (too plush for some anglers) with an appealing combination of ultrasuedes and vinyls matched with pastel grey Formica galley counters and cabinetry — a Eurostyle decor with luxury touches seldom found in an offshore fisherman. Outside, the 105 sq. ft. cockpit is large enough for a mounted chair and the flybridge ladder is mounted sideways to save space. Caterpillar diesels were standard but the best performance is achieved with the 550-hp 6V92s. With those engines, the Sea Ray 460 Convertible will cruise around 24 knots and reach 27 knots at full throttle. ❏

SPECIFICATIONS

Length	45'6"
Beam	14'11"
Draft	3'2"
Weight	34,000#
Clearance	13'1"
Water	150 Gals.
Fuel	700 Gals.
Cockpit	105 Sq. Ft.
Hull Type	Modified-V
Designer	Sea Ray

Production
1987–88

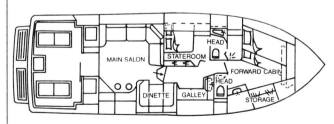

SEA RAY 460 EXPRESS CRUISER

Back in the mid '80s the Sea Ray 460 Express Cruiser (EC) was the largest production express-type sportboat available anywhere. With her aggressive low profile hull, long foredeck, and reversed radar arch, the 460 EC was one of the best looking express models in the Sea Ray fleet. Below, the cabin accommodations are laid out on a grand and luxurious scale. Originally offered with a one- or two-stateroom floorplan, Sea Ray settled on a spacious single-stateroom arrangement in 1988 with an absolutely huge main salon. This is an elaborate interior with wraparound suede sofas, overhead track lighting, high-pressure laminate counters and cabinetry, and no teak anywhere — a completely modern European decor with very attractive detailing. Outside, the bi-level cockpit is massive with room for a dozen guests. Twin 375-hp Caterpillar diesels were standard and provide about 21 knots at cruise and 24–25 knots top. When powered with the optional 550-hp 6V92s, the Sea Ray 460 Express Cruiser will cruise at a fast 28 knots with a top speed of 30–31 knots. ❏

SPECIFICATIONS

Length	45'6"
Beam	14'11"
Draft	3'2"
Weight	25,000#
Clearance	9'9"
Water	150 Gals.
Fuel	420 Gals.
Cockpit	NA
Hull Type	Modified-V
Designer	Sea Ray

Production
1985–89

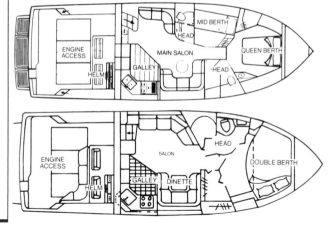

SEA RAY

SEA RAY 480/500 SUNDANCER

A great-looking boat, the 500 Sundancer (called the 480 until 1992) is one of the larger production express cruisers on the market. With her long foredeck, curved wraparound windshield, and sleek profile, the 500 is a crowd-stopper at any dock. Her sheer size is impressive enough, but it's the 480's huge Eurostyle interior layout that causes first-time viewers to catch their breath in surprise. Here, laid out on a single level and presenting a panorama of curved bulkheads and designer-style furnishings, the accommodations rival those found in a small motor yacht.

There are two private staterooms, two heads (each with a stall shower), a plush U-shaped sofa below the bridgedeck, and a wide-open salon with good headroom throughout. The cockpit — with its raised helm, wet bar, and built-in lounge seating — can seat up to a dozen guests. Running on a solid glass deep-V hull with 17° of deadrise aft, standard 485-hp 6-71 diesels will cruise the 500 Sundancer at 24 knots, and optional 735-hp 8V92s will deliver a fast 29 knots at cruise and 32 knots wide open. Note that V-drives are used in this model. ❑

SPECIFICATIONS

Length	50'1"
Length WL	NA
Beam	15'0"
Draft	4'0"
Weight	32,000#
Clearance	NA
Water	150 Gals.
Fuel	500 Gals.
Hull Type	Deep-V
Designer	Sea Ray

Production
1990–Current

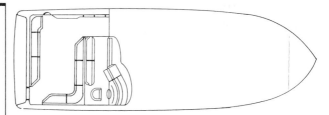

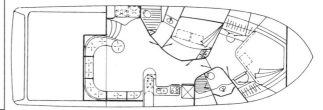

SEA RAY

SEA RAY 500/550 SEDAN BRIDGE

Built on a fully cored, deep-V (17° deadrise aft) hull, the 500 Sedan Bridge and the newer 550 model (introduced in 1992 and pictured above) are basically the same boat with the 550 having a reverse transom with integral swim platform. Her wide-open floorplan includes three private staterooms forward while still managing to provide a very expansive main salon/galley area with plenty of floor space. The spacious salon is furnished with a wraparound sofa, free-standing dinette table and a built-in wet bar. Eye-catching European fixtures and white formica cabinets highlight the galley, which is separated from the salon by a breakfast bar. Additional features include stall showers in both heads, lower helm and a spacious engine room. The interior decor is a stylish blend of curved bulkheads, textured wall coverings, light oak trimwork, and designer fabrics. The cockpit is small but the flybridge is big and features lounge seating behind the helm. A good performer with the standard 550-hp 6V92 diesels, the 500/550 will cruise around 25 knots with a top speed of 28+ knots. Larger 735-hp 8V92 diesels are optional. ❑

SPECIFICATIONS

Length	49'11"/54'10"
Length WL	NA
Beam	15'0"
Draft	4'2"
Weight	40/45,000#
Clearance	17'6"
Water	200 Gals.
Fuel	600 Gals.
Hull Type	Deep-V
Designer	J. Michalak

Production
1989–Current

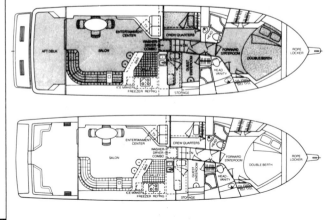

SEA RAY 600/630 SUPER SUN SPORT

Largest full-production express cruiser (Magnums and Tempests, etc. are semi-custom boats), the 630 Super Sun Sport is a completely impressive boat with a stunning profile (note the long foredeck and low-profile inboard rails) and the interior accommodations of a small motor yacht. Introduced as the 600 Super Sun Sport in 1991, she's built on a fully cored, deep-V hull with 19° of transom deadrise. The massive salon of the 630 is dominated by a sculptured ceiling and a huge 23' leather sofa, while the lush decor is a blend of pickled-oak veneers, beige fabrics, and white Formica counters. The standard layout includes one stateroom and two heads, and an alternate floorplan replaces the dinette with a second private stateroom. Note the crew quarters hidden beneath the transom and accessed through the half-moon cockpit sunpad. Additional features include a reverse arch, two transom doors, extravagant cockpit lounge seating, and a well-arranged engine room with push-button access. A great performer with standard 1,080-hp 12V92s, the 630 SSS will cruise at a fast 31-32 knots (about 100 gph) and reach a top speed of 35 knots.   ❏

SPECIFICATIONS

Length	62'6"
Beam	15'9"
Draft	5'0"
Weight	52,000#
Clearance	12'9"
Water	200 Gals.
Fuel	800 Gals.
Cockpit	NA
Hull Type	Deep-V
Designer	Sea Ray

Production
1991–Current

SEA RAY 650 MOTOR YACHT

Largest Sea Ray ever, the 650 MY is an impressive creation from a company that only a decade ago ranked a 36' express as their largest model. She's an elegant yacht with a Mediterranean profile and a superb (and unusual) interior layout. The 650 MY is constructed on a fully cored hull with a wide beam and a steep 18° of deadrise at the transom. Her double-deck floorplan is arranged with four staterooms below and a deckhouse galley open to the salon. What makes this layout unusual is the aft engine room — only a few builders have ever built a motor yacht with V-drives (and fewer still have been successful in the market). The Eurostyle interior of the 650 MY can completely opulent and includes a Jacuzzi-style tub in the owner's head, a huge master stateroom, and a full-width salon with a formal dining area to port and a bridge stairway forward. The cockpit is quite roomy and provides access to the engine room below. The flybridge is small compared to some 65' motor yachts. The performance of the 650 MY is very good. With standard 870/900-hp 12V71s, she'll cruise at 21–22 knots and deliver 25 knots wide open. ❑

SPECIFICATIONS

Length	64'6"
Beam	18'1"
Draft	4'10"
Weight	67,500#
Clearance	25'3"
Water	275 Gals.
Fuel	1,000 Gals.
Cockpit	95 Sq. Ft.
Hull Type	Deep-V
Designer	Sea Ray

Production
1992–Current

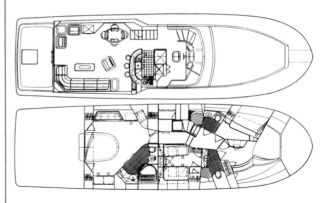

SILVERTON

Brief History

Originally called Silverton Sea Skiffs, Silverton was formed in 1969 by John Luhrs. Their first all-fiberglass boat — the Silverton 28 — was introduced in 1973, and the hugely successful Mainship 34 came out in 1978 spawning the Mainship Company. Silverton expanded into the affordably-priced motor yacht and express cruiser market during the 1980s.

Selected Silverton Inboard Models

Silverton 28 Sedan

Silverton 29 Sportcruiser

Silverton 30X Express

Silverton 31 Convertible (Early)

Silverton 31 Gulfstream

Silverton 31 Conv/Mid Cabin

Silverton 33 Sport Sedan

Silverton 34 Sedan

Silverton 34 Convertible (Early)

Silverton 34 Conv/Mid Cabin

Silverton 34X Express (Early)

Silverton 34 Express

Silverton 37 Convertible (Early)

Silverton 37 Convertible

Silverton 37 Motor Yacht

Silverton 38X Express

Silverton 40 Aft Cabin

Silverton 40 Convertible

Silverton 41 Convertible

Silverton 41 Aft Cabin

Silverton 46 Motor Yacht

Main Office

Silverton Marine Corporation, Riverside Drive, Millville, NJ 08332-6798
609-825-4117

541

SILVERTON 28 SEDAN

Although she's been out of production for over a decade, the Silverton 28 Sedan remains a popular boat on the used market due to her low price and generous interior accommodations. Compared with most modern 28' flybridge boats, the Silverton has a fairly low profile and her lines are quite aggressive. Inside, the step-down floorplan is laid out on a single level with both the galley and head placed aft in the cabin, just inside the salon bulkhead door. A lower helm was standard and the dinette converts into a double berth in the normal fashion.

This is not the most expansive interior to be found in a 28-footer, but practical nonetheless and certainly adequate for weekend family cruising. The cockpit is very large for a boat of this length with room for some light-tackle fishing or a few deck chairs. Access to the engines and V-drives is via hatches in the salon sole. Among several power options offered (including single-screw installations), the twin 225-hp Chryslers will cruise the Silverton 28 Sedan at 21 knots and reach about 30 knots wide open. Note the limited fuel capacity. ❏

SPECIFICATIONS

Length	28'0"
Beam	10'6"
Draft	2'8"
Weight	9,500#
Clearance	9'6"
Water	37 Gals.
Fuel	130 Gals.
Cockpit	90 Sq. Ft.
Hull Type	Modified-V
Designer	Silverton

Production
1975–78

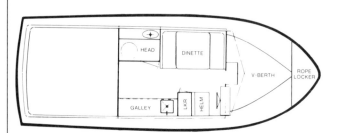

SILVERTON 29 SPORTCRUISER

Silverton's 29 Sportcruiser was a popular family weekender with comfortable interior accommodations and excellent fuel economy. She lasted for only three years until being replaced in 1988 by the more glamorous Silverton 30X, but the 29 Sportcruiser is worthy of note for several interesting design features. Styling-wise, her conservative lines are not much to get excited about. The Sportcruiser's unique interior floorplan, however, includes a private aft cabin with standing headroom (which is unusual) in addition to an expansive full-length galley running along the starboard side of the cabin from the companionway forward. The rest of the cabin is tight and moving around-space is at a premium. Prop pockets in the hull reduce the boat's draft and allow the engines to be located beneath the cockpit sole without the need for V-drives. Standard V6 gas engines will cruise the Silverton 29 Sportcruiser at a very satisfactory 17–18 knots while burning only 12 gph — better than a mile-and-a-half per gallon! That puts her near the top of the class in economy. ❑

SPECIFICATIONS

Length	29'2"
Beam	10'10"
Draft	1'7"
Weight	7,800#
Clearance	8'2"
Water	40 Gals.
Fuel	150 Gals.
Cockpit	50 Sq. Ft.
Hull Type	Modified-V
Designer	M. Peters

Production
1985–87

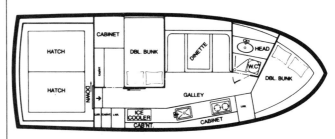

SILVERTON 30X EXPRESS

The 30X was second in the series of Euro-express "X" designs introduced by Silverton, beginning with the original 34X in 1987. In spite of the 30's shorter length, the addition of a reverse swim platform makes her a better-looking boat than her predecessor. Indeed, the sleek profile of the 30X is very much in step with today's trends in modern sportboat design. Designed primarily as a day boat but capable of comfortable weekend family cruising, the interior layout is fairly conventional for a boat of this type with facing settees in the salon, a com-pact head and galley, and an offset dou-ble berth forward. With the dinette and settee converted there are overnight accommodations for six. The decor is a plain-Jane blend of pastel fabrics and textured wall coverings and there's no teak in sight. Outside, a companion seat to port and bench seating along the tran-som will seat five guests. The perfor-mance of the 30X is very good. With standard 270-hp gas engines she'll cruise about 24 knots and reach a top speed of 31–32 knots. Note that she remained in production for only two years. ❏

SPECIFICATIONS

Length......................30'8"
Length WL....................NA
Beam......................10'10"
Draft ....3'0"
Weight..................9,100#
Clearance ....8'5"
Water..................37 Gals.
Fuel ....185 Gals.
Hull Type.........Modified-V
Designer ....M. Peters

Production
1988–89

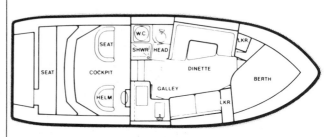

SILVERTON 31 CONVERTIBLE (EARLY)

The appeal of the Silverton 31 Convertible (production ran for a full decade) had much to do with her roomy accommodations, attractive design, and an affordable price tag. Compared with other convertibles and family sedans of her size, the Silverton 31 gets high marks for a spacious salon area — a rare luxury in a boat this small — with enough room to seat four cramped. Her large cockpit provides a good platform for swimming and casual fishing activities. On the downside, the flybridge is notably small with seating for just three persons. The Silverton 31 Convertible received a major styling update in 1982 when the deckhouse was redesigned with a much-improved profile. Light oak interior woodwork was added in the 1985 model. Throughout her long production run the Silverton 31 Convertible retained the same basic interior floorplan with the galley and head forward and down from the salon. Twin 220-hp gas engines with V-drives will provide a cruising speed of around 17–18 knots and a cruising speed of about 27 knots. ❑

SPECIFICATIONS

Length	31'0"
Length WL	25'0"
Beam	11'11"
Draft	2'11"
Weight	11,400#
Clearance	10'8"
Water	40 gals.
Fuel	220 Gals.
Cockpit	82 Sq. Ft.
Hull Type	Modified-V
Designer	Silverton

Production
1977–87

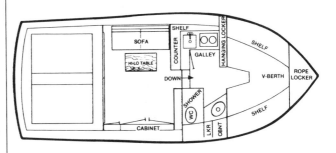

SILVERTON 31 GULFSTREAM

When the Silverton 31 Gulfstream was introduced in 1979, she represented a dramatic break from Silverton's past market reliance on affordable convertible sedan cruisers. Designed as a family sportboat with no serious fishing ambitions, the 31 Gulfstream will appeal to those seeking an inexpensive family express boat with attractive lines and basic cabin accommodations. This is a pretty straightforward design by today's maxi-cube, Eurostyle sportboat standards. Interestingly, V-drives were used through the 1982 model year, and in 1983 she was reintroduced with straight inboards. The 31 Gulfstream was never offered with a modern radar arch or a stylish curved windshield, but she does have a large cockpit capable of handling six or eight passengers without being crowded (which is more than might be said for a few of her more modern counterparts in this size range). Standard power in the Gulfstream was twin 270-hp Crusaders (18–19 knots cruise/28 top) with the larger 350-hp gas engines (around 24 knots cruise/32–33 knots top) offered as an option. ❑

SPECIFICATIONS

Length......................31'0"
Length WL................25'0"
Beam......................11'11"
Draft ....2'11"
Weight..................9,500#
Clearance ....NA
Water..................40 Gals.
Fuel ....250 Gals.
Cockpit............115 Sq. Ft.
Hull Type.........Modified-V
Designer..........Bob Rioux

Production
1979–86

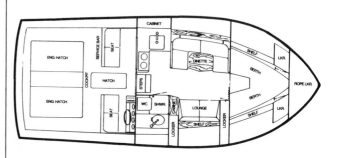

SILVERTON 31 CONV. & MID CABIN

A modern family convertible at a very attractive price, the Silverton 31 is one of the roomiest sedan cruisers in her size range. Introduced as the 31 Mid Cabin in 1991, the Convertible made its debut in 1992. Both share the same slightly top heavy exterior profile (note the very high foredeck), small cockpit dimensions, and compact flybridge. Inside, however, the spacious interior is a genuine surprise in just a 31' boat. Of the two layouts, the Convertible has the larger and more appealing salon. The Mid Cabin's elevated dinette provides some needed headroom for the small stateroom below (accessed from a door in the galley) but robs the salon of some of its wide-open appeal. Both models have a pedestal island berth in the master stateroom and a stall shower is included in the head compartment. Headroom is very good in this boat and large cabin windows let in plenty of natural lighting. Attractive light oak woodwork and decorator fabrics are used throughout. Standard 350-cid gas engines will cruise the Silverton 31 at a respectable 18-19 knots and deliver a top speed of about 28 knots. ❏

SPECIFICATIONS

Length	31'2"
Beam	11'8"
Draft	3'0"
Weight	11,000#
Clearance	11'9"
Cockpit	48 Sq. Ft.
Water	84 Gals.
Fuel	250 Gals.
Hull Type	Modified-V
Designer	Silverton

Production
1992–Current

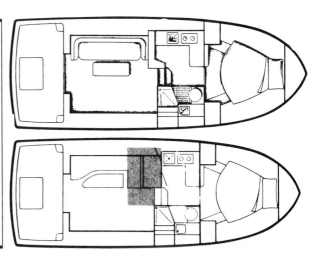

SILVERTON 33 SPORT SEDAN

The 33 Sport Sedan was the top-of-the-line cruiser for Silverton back in the early 1970s. Because of her low price and generally adequate construction, she turned out to be a fairly popular boat and used models are often encountered on the brokerage market. The modified-V hull (14° deadrise), flybridge, and cockpit liner are constructed of molded fiberglass, and the deck and superstructure are marine plywood with a glass overlay. The 33 Sport Sedan will sleep up to six in two cabins — two forward in the V-berth and the others on the convertible dinette and fold-out settee. A lower helm was standard and the cabin floor is a step down from the cockpit level. Both the head and galley are aft in the salon where they're easily reached from the outside — a very practical floorplan for any small family cruiser. Large hatches in the cockpit sole provide good access to the engines and V-drives. The elevated cockpit itself is surprisingly spacious. Twin 225-hp Chrysler gas engines offer a cruising speed of around 19 knots and a top speed in the neighborhood of 28–29 knots. ❑

SPECIFICATIONS

Length......................33'8"
Length WL ....28'7"
Beam........................12'6"
Draft ....2'10"
Weight ....12,000#
Clearance ....11'1"
Water..................40 Gals.
Fuel ....220 Gals.
Cockpit..............86 Sq. Ft.
Hull Type.........Modified-V
Designer ....J. Fielding

Production
1973–76

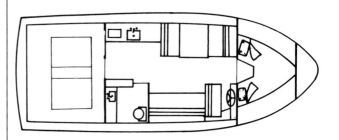

SILVERTON 34 SEDAN

The Silverton 34 Sedan was intro-duced in 1977 as an inexpensive family cruiser with overnight accom-modations for as many as six. She's built on a solid fiberglass hull design with moderate transom deadrise, a faily flat sheer, and considerable flare at the bow. A comfortable boat, the 34 Sedan's interior accommodations are arranged on a single level (no steps leading down to the forward stateroom) which creates the impression of a very large and open cabin. The inside helm was a standard feature on the Silverton 34 Sedan and the visibility from this lower station is quite good considering the lowered salon level. Both the galley and head are located aft, just inside the salon door where they're within easy reach of those outside. The cockpit is a step up from the salon level and measures a good 10'x10' — large for a 34-foot boat. Hatches in the cockpit sole provide good access to the motors and V-drive units. Chrysler 250-hp gas engines were standard, with 270-hp Crusaders offered as options. Cruising speeds for both are in the neighborhood of 17 knots and top speeds are around 26–27 knots. ❑

SPECIFICATIONS

Length......................34'0"
Beam.......................12'6"
Draft ....3'1"
Weight ....12,500#
Clearance ....11'6"
Water....................40 Gals.
Fuel ....220 Gals.
Cockpit............100 Sq. Ft.
Hull Type.........Modified-V
Designer.............Silverton

Production
1977–81

SILVERTON 34 CONVERTIBLE (EARLY)

After a decade in production, the Silverton 34 Convertible has proven to be Silverton's most popular model ever. She's constructed on a modified-V hull with considerable flare at the bow and 15° of deadrise at the transom. In her original form, the 34 Convertible presents a somewhat conservative appearance — a white fiberglass cruiser with a sturdy, plain-Jane profile. That changed in 1983 when Silverton redesigned this boat by adding a modern new deck and super-structure and eliminating the V-drives of previous years in favor of a conventional straight-drive engine installation. In 1985 a stall shower and double berth were added below along with a new light oak interior. With the dinette and sofa converted, there are overnight berths for up to six. Several engine options were offered over the years with the 270-hp Crusaders being among the most frequently seen in used models. A good performer, the Silverton 34 will cruise around 18 knots with a top speed of 27–28 knots. Note that the fuel capacity was increased from 220 to 250 gallons in 1983. ❏

SPECIFICATIONS

Length......................34'0"
Beam.......................12'6"
Draft ....3'1"
Weight ....12,500#
Clearance.................13'3"
Water...................40 Gals.
Fuel ....250 Gals.
Cockpit..............70 Sq. Ft.
Hull Type.........Modified-V
Designer ....J. Fielding

Production
1978–88

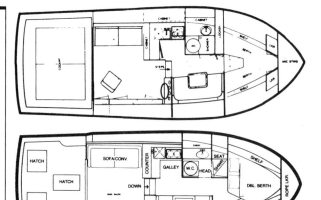

SILVERTON 34 CONV. & MID CABIN

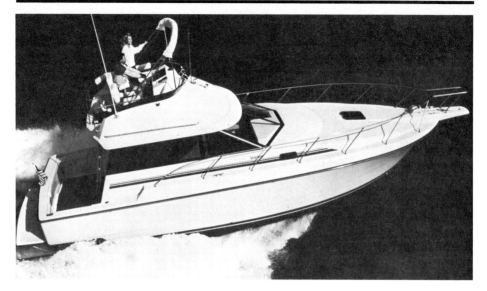

The current Silverton 34 Convertible isn't just an updated version of the original 34 Convertible she replaced in 1989. She's an entirely new boat with a sleeker profile, greater transom deadrise (17°), and a revised interior layout. In 1991, Silverton updated the deckhouse to give her a more contemporary look and restyled the original Convertible layout . In the newer Mid Cabin model (introduced in 1991), the extra stateroom replaces the Convertible's dinette, which is relocated in the salon. Inside, the light oak (or ash) woodwork, wraparound cabin windows, and pastel fabrics make for a bright and attractive interior. Additional upgrades in 1991 included a restyled helm console, wider sidedecks, and a bigger head compartment. The cockpit is small but adequate for modest fishing pursuits and visibility from the flybridge helm position is good. Aimed at the family cruiser market, the Silverton 34 is very attractively priced compared to other boats in her size range. No racehorse, with standard 454-cid gas engines she'll cruise around 16 knots and reach a top speed of 26–27 knots. ❏

SPECIFICATIONS

Length	34'6"
Beam	12'7"
Draft	3'2"
Weight	13,500#
Clearance	13'5"
Water	40 Gals.
Fuel	300 Gals.
Cockpit	56 Sq. Ft.
Hull Type	Modified-V
Designer	M. Peters

Production
1989–Current

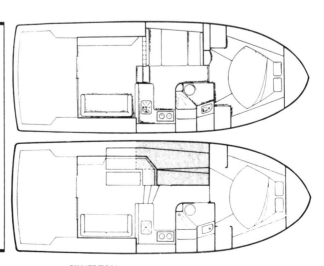

SILVERTON

SILVERTON 34X EXPRESS (EARLY)

The original Silverton 34X Express was a contemporary sportboat design with traditional styling and generous interior accommodations. She was built on a solid fiberglass hull (the same hull used in the production of the new 34 Convertible) with a relatively deep 17° of deadrise at the transom. Aimed at the family cruiser market, her raised bridgedeck provides room for a private mid-cabin below with a stand-up entryway and a door instead of a privacy curtain. The attractive decor of the 34X is Eurostyle with light-colored mica laminates and pastel wall coverings applied throughout. The cockpit provides plenty of outdoor space for guests, and a cut-out in the transom provides easy boarding. Visibility from the raised helm position is excellent and a sunpad is fitted on the foredeck. V-drives allow the engines to be located aft where access is gained via the normal cockpit hatches. Twin 350-hp Crusader gas engines will cruise the Silverton 34X around 22 knots and reach a top speed of 30+ knots. This model was replaced in 1990 with a new and completely restyled Silverton 34X. ❏

SPECIFICATIONS

Length......................34'6"
Beam........................12'7"
Draft ....3'8"
Weight ....11,000#
Clearance ....12'7"
Water..................40 Gals.
Fuel ....250 Gals.
Cockpit.............62 Sq. Ft.
Hull Type........Modified-V
Designer ....M. Peters

Production
1987–89

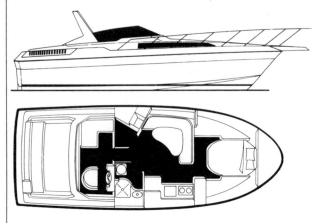

SILVERTON 34 EXPRESS

The current Silverton 34 Express (which replaced the original 34X in 1990) is a mid-cabin family cruiser with a profile similar to most modern sport-boat designs. She's built on a reworked version of the modified-V hull (17° deadrise aft) used by her predecessor and the integral swim platform and reduced hull graphics give the new 34 a softer, more contemporary appearance. Although the layout below is only slightly changed from that found in the original 34, the U-shaped settee and relocated entertainment center result in a more open appearance. The new decor has been updated with modern high-pressure laminates and a complete absence of interior woodwork. Only a privacy curtain divides the forward stateroom from the salon, while a door closes off the mid cabin. The bi-level cockpit of the 34 features a raised helm with an L-shaped lounge to port and an aft deck wet bar. Additional features include a hydraulically operated engine access hatch, foredeck sunpad, stall shower and transom door. Driven through V-drives, 454 cid gas engines deliver a cruising speed of about 21 knots and a top speed of 27–28. ❏

SPECIFICATIONS

Length	34'3"
Beam	12'8"
Draft	3'1"
Weight	16,500#
Clearance	9'3"
Water	47 Gals.
Fuel	254 Gals.
Cockpit	62 Sq. Ft.
Hull Type	Modified-V
Designer	M. Peters

Production
1990–Current

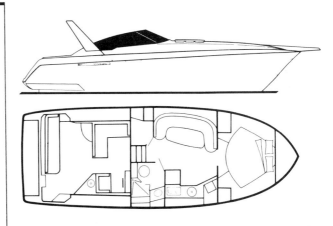

SILVERTON 37 CONVERTIBLE (EARLY)

The Silverton 37 is a modern family cruiser with an attractive profile and plenty of interior space. She's built on a solid glass, modified-V hull with a fairly wide beam, 14° of deadrise at the transom and considerable flare at the bow. Unlike many other convertibles this size, the Silverton 37 has a single-stateroom interior floorplan with a very large salon area and a full-size dinette in place of a second stateroom. Other interior features include a stall shower in the head, a convenient service counter above the dinette, sliding glass cockpit doors, and light oak paneling and cabinetry throughout. (Teak woodwork is found in pre-1985 models.) Her tournament-style flybridge is arranged with bench seating forward of the helm and provides excellent visibility in all directions. Twin 200-hp Perkins diesels were standard in early models, but the majority of Silverton 37 Convertibles have been powered with twin 350-hp Crusader gas engines. The cruising speed is 18–19 knots and the top speed is around 29 knots. Note that the V-drives were dropped for both gas- and diesel-powered models in 1983. ❏

SPECIFICATIONS

Length	37'0"
Length WL	31'4"
Beam	14'0"
Draft	3'7"
Weight	20,000#
Clearance	12'6"
Water	100 Gals.
Fuel	300 Gals.
Cockpit	75 Sq. Ft.
Hull Type	Modified-V
Designer	Bob Rioux

Production
1980–89

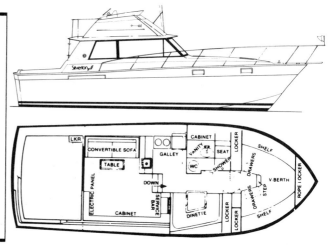

SILVERTON 37 CONVERTIBLE

With her contemporary profile and improved interior layout, the newest Silverton 37 (the original 37 Convertible ran from 1980 to 1989) is one of the most affordable family cruisers available in her size range. Like most Silverton models, she's a lot of boat for the money. Her solid fiberglass, modified-V hull has a shallow keel and a fairly steep 17° of deadrise at the transom. Belowdecks, the spacious single-stateroom interior is arranged with the galley and dinette down and but still open to the salon. The light oak interior woodwork, white galley laminates, pastel fabrics, and wraparound cabin windows create a bright and pleasant interior. The cockpit is too small for a fighting chair but coaming pads, an in-deck fishbox, and a transom door and swim platform are standard. The flybridge seats six with bench seating forward of the helm and the well-planned console has space for flush-mounting most basic electronics. No racehorse, the performance of the Silverton 37 Convertible with standard 454 gas engines is a modest 15–16 knots at cruise and the top speed is about 25 knots. ❏

SPECIFICATIONS

Length	37'4"
Beam	13'11"
Draft	3'9"
Weight	21,000#
Clearance	14'0"
Water	100 Gals.
Fuel	375 Gals.
Cockpit	80 Sq. Ft.
Hull Type	Modified-V
Designer	M. Peters

Production
1990–Current

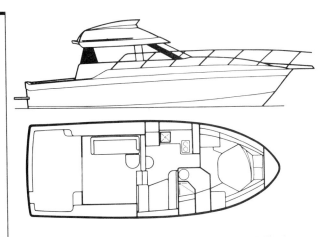

SILVERTON 37 MOTOR YACHT

Motor yachts under 40 feet have been popular in recent years and the Silverton 37 MY was one of the more affordable (if least attractive) models available. Built on a conventional modified-V hull, the interior dimensions of the 37 MY are very impressive. Both staterooms have pedestal queen berths and the forward stateroom is nearly as spacious as the master stateroom. Notably, a separate stall shower is found in each head — an unexpected convenience in a 37' boat. The galley is only a step down from the salon/dinette level, thus opening up the interior considerably. The light oak paneling and woodwork applied in each cabin are especially attractive. Topside, the theme of comfortable family cruising is continued in the huge bridge with lounge seating for up to ten. Boarding is somewhat difficult, however, due to the raised aft deckhouse configuration and the cabin entrance is from the flybridge. The cruising speed of the Silverton 37 MY with the standard 350-hp Crusaders is around 15 knots and the top speed is 23–24 knots. Note that this boat remained in production for only two years.   ❏

SPECIFICATIONS

Length	37'6"
Length WL	NA
Beam	13'9"
Draft	3'8"
Weight	22,000#
Clearance	16'0"
Water	100 Gals.
Fuel	300 Gals.
Hull Type	Modified-V
Designer	M. Peters

Production
1988–89

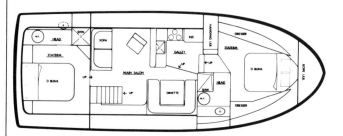

SILVERTON 38 EXPRESS

Introduced in 1990, the Silverton 38 Express is built on the same solid fiberglass, modified-V (17° transom deadrise) hull first used in the production of the Silverton 40X model (1989 only). A good-looking boat with sculptured lines and an attractive sportboat profile, she was designed to compete with similar upscale products from Sea Ray, Mainship, and Trojan. Sold with a long list of standard equipment, the 38 has a well arranged bi-level cockpit with a companion seat and sun lounge opposite the helm. A wet bar and ice maker are standard, and a walk-through transom door opens to the integral swim platform. Below, natural lighting is excellent with a cluster of six overhead skylights plus a large opening hatch. The floorplan includes an island berth in the forward stateroom and a double bed in the private aft cabin. The decor is an eye-catching blend of contemporary pastel colors and off-white Formica countertops. Twin 502 cid Crusader gas engines (with V-drives) are standard in the 38. The cruising speed is 22–23 knots and the top speed is around 30 knots. Note that 425-hp Cats are optional. ❏

SPECIFICATIONS

Length	37'7"
Length WL	NA
Beam	13'11"
Draft	3'7"
Weight	21,000#
Clearance	9'9"
Water	110 Gals.
Fuel	300 Gals.
Hull Type	Modified-V
Designer	M. Peters

Production
1990–Current

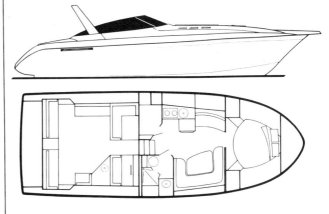

SILVERTON 40 AFT CABIN

Introduced in 1982, the Silverton 40 Aft Cabin was Silverton's first double cabin design. She was built on a solid fiberglass, modified-V hull with relatively high freeboard, considerable bow flare and 14° of deadrise at the transom. Her styling is contemporary and she has a conservative, clean-cut appearance. Below, her twin-stateroom interior is arranged in the conventional manner with the galley and dinette down a few steps from the salon level. The owner's aft cabin includes a walka-round queen berth and V-berths are found in the forward stateroom. Both heads in the Silverton 40 are fitted with shower stalls, and light oak interior woodwork replaced the original teak interior beginning with the 1985 models. The 80 sq. ft. aft deck is on the small side for a boat of this size, and the compact flybridge (with seating for only three) further restricts outside accommodations. Too, the companionway from the aft deck is a tight fit for most people. An affordable and good-selling boat, standard 454-cid Crusader gas engines deliver a cruising speed around 17 knots and a top speed of 25–26 knots. ❑

SPECIFICATIONS

Length	40'0"
Length WL	NA
Beam	14'0"
Draft	3'0"
Weight	24,000#
Clearance	13'6"
Water	100 Gals.
Fuel	300 Gals.
Hull Type	Modified-V
Designer	Bob Rioux

Production
1982–90

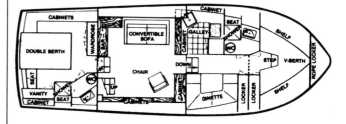

SILVERTON 40 CONVERTIBLE

Sharing the same hull as the Silverton 40 Aft Cabin, the Silverton 40 Convertible is an attractively-styled family sedan with a spacious interior and a sizable cockpit suitable for light tackle fishing or open-air entertaining. She was clearly designed to appeal to the weekend cruiser market and came equipped with nearly everything required for immediate use. The price of the Silverton 40 was quite attractive compared with other boats her size, and maintenance requirements are minimal. During her first few years of production, a well-arranged two-stateroom floorplan had the galley, dinette, and salon on essentially one level, with the staterooms and head forward. In 1989, this floorplan was revised ,with the galley and dinette moved forward and down two steps from the salon and a single stateroom. Wraparound deckhouse windows and a sliding glass door aft provide excellent natural lighting and the salon is very open and spacious. The flybridge is arranged with bench seating forward of the helm console. Twin 454-cid gas engines provide a cruising speed of 16–17 knots and the top speed is around 26 knots. ❏

SPECIFICATIONS

Length	40'0"
Beam	14'0"
Draft	3'0"
Weight	23,000#
Clearance	13'6"
Water	100 Gals.
Fuel	300 Gals.
Cockpit	79 Sq. Ft.
Hull Type	Modified-V
Designer	Bob Rioux

Production
1985–90

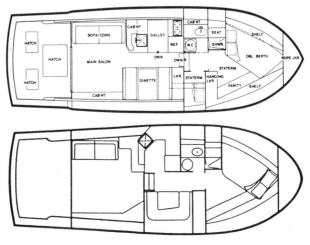

SILVERTON 41 CONVERTIBLE

The Silverton 41 Convertible is a moderately-priced sedan cruiser with a clean-cut profile and a practical two-stateroom interior layout. With her long foredeck, step-down sheer, and raked bridge, the 41 Convertible has the look of a serious sportfisherman although Silvertons have never been noted for building tournament-level designs. The cockpit is large enough for a fighting chair and there's a good-size fishbox below the sole. Inside, the full wraparound cabin windows provide excellent natural lighting. The modern light oak interior is arranged with the galley and (big) dinette down from the salon level, a double-entry head with a stall shower, over/under single berths in the small guest cabin and a large pedestal berth in the master stateroom. Additional features include a reasonably spacious flybridge with plenty of seating, side exhausts, transom door and swim platform. Standard 502-cid gas engines will cruise the Silverton 41 Convertible at 19–20 knots (about 28 knots top), and the optional 425-hp Caterpillar diesels will cruise at 24–25 knots and reach 28 knots wide open. ❑

SPECIFICATIONS

Length	41'3"
Beam	14'10"
Draft	3'9"
Weight	27,000#
Clearance	15'5"
Cockpit	98 Sq. Ft.
Water	200 Gals.
Fuel	516 Gals.
Hull Type	Modified-V
Designer	Silverton

Production
1991–Current

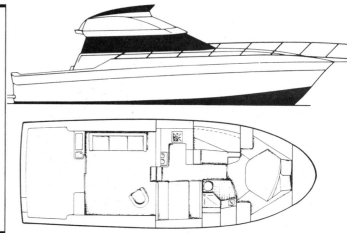

SILVERTON

SILVERTON 41 AFT CABIN

A modern and notably-affordable flush deck cruiser, the Silverton 41 Motor Yacht is in many ways a scaled-down version of the larger Silverton 46 MY. She's built on a solid fiberglass, modified-V hull with plenty of beam, a shallow keel, and 17° of transom deadrise. Silverton has packed a lot of floorplan into the 41 MY including queen berths in both staterooms, a fair-size salon, dinette, and stall showers in both head compartments. (Note that the forward head is larger than the aft head — a practical feature for cruising with guests.) A tempered glass partition divides the galley from the salon and light oak woodwork and cabinetry are applied throughout. While the aft deck isn't very deep, it is wide and roomy enough for most open-air activities. Additional features include side exhausts, a tubular radar arch, and adaquate sidedecks. The standard 502-cid gas engines are barely up to the job in a boat this large and it takes a thirsty 3,500 rpm to get a respectable 15–16 knot cruising speed (at 35 gph!). Because the Silverton 41 MY is a basically price boat, it's unlikely that many will opt for the optional 375-hp Cat diesels. ❑

SPECIFICATIONS

Length ....41'3"
Length WL....................NA
Beam.....................14'10"
Draft ....3'9"
Weight ....28,000#
Clearance ....16'3"
Water.................200 Gals.
Fuel ....408 Gals.
Hull Type.........Modified-V
Designer.............Silverton

Production
1991–Current

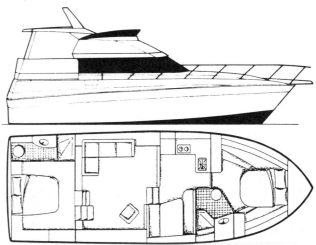

SILVERTON 46 MOTOR YACHT

Introduced in mid-1989, the 46 Motor Yacht is the largest boat Silverton has ever produced. She's built on a new double-chined hull with Divinycell foam coring in the deck and hullsides. With a fairly steep 17° of transom deadrise, she rides on a seakindly hull with better-than-average handling characteristics (for a motor yacht, at least). Overall, the Silverton 46 is a conventional aft-cabin design with a modern profile and a spacious three-stateroom layout. The exterior lines are contemporary if not elegant, and the floorplan is designed for comfortable family cruising. Two of the three staterooms are fitted with walkaround doubles, and the dinette is a convenience always appreciated by those who spend any time aboard. Other features include a covered aft deck, molded foredeck seating, washer/dryer, and a bathtub in the owner's head. Standard 485-hp 6-71s will cruise the Silverton 46 MY around 22 knots with a top speed of 25 knots. True to Silverton's long-standing reputation for building affordable boats, the 46 MY comes standard with items normally considered options on other boats. ❑

SPECIFICATIONS

Length	46'8"
Length WL	NA
Beam	16'2"
Draft	3'9"
Weight	40,500#
Clearance	17'8"
Water	200 Gals.
Fuel	580 Gals.
Hull Type	Modified-V
Designer	M. Peters

Production
1989-Current

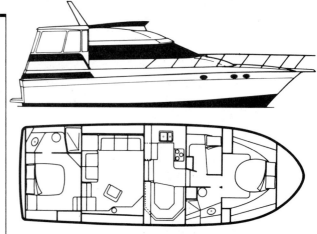

STRIKER

Brief History

Founded in 1951, Strikers were built of steel until 1959, when the company became the first yachtbuilder to use marine aluminum in the construction of pleasureboats. First built in the U.S., production shifted to Holland in 1957 and to Norway in 1961. Note that Strikers have also been built in Australia, New Zealand, Korea, Chile, and Argentina. After a series of business difficulties in recent years, today the company is again in the hands of the founder and several partners.

Selected Striker Models

Striker 34 Canyon Runner   Striker 54 Sportfisherman
Striker 37 Canyon Runner   Striker 58/60 Sportfisherman
Striker 41 Sportfisherman   Striker 62 Sportfisherman
Striker 44 Sportfisherman   Striker 70 Sportfisherman
Striker 50 Sportfisherman

Main Office

Striker Yacht Corp., 1535 SE 17th St., Suite 117B,
Ft. Lauderdale, FL 33316
305-523-8600

563

STRIKER 34 CANYON RUNNER

The Striker 34 was introduced in 1973 as a scaled-down version of the popular Striker 44' and 54' sportfishermen. She was built in Norway of welded aluminum, and utilized the same exclusive Pentapolymeric hull design of the bigger Strikers. With her serious profile and ship-like construction, the 34 set the tone for future models in the Canyon Runner series, including the new Striker 37. She was specifically designed for the type of offshore running typical of the Jersey and Maryland coasts. Her wide beam provides a stable fishing platform, and the 34 has the range to go long distances without refueling. The cabin is arranged to meet the practical overnight needs of a couple of anglers with V-berths, a convertible dinette area, and a small galley and head. The interior is trimmed with teak woodwork and Formica counters — not a particularly stylish decor, but maintenance is easy. A rugged little vessel still occasionally found on the used market, the Striker 34 Canyon Runner with the 240-hp V555M Cummins diesels will cruise at 15 knots and reach a top speed of 18–19 knots.   ❑

SPECIFICATIONS

Length......................34'0"
Beam.......................13'7"
Draft ....2'3"
Weight ....16,500#
Clearance ....NA
Water.................100 Gals.
Fuel...................400 Gals.
Cockpit............100 Sq. Ft.
Hull Type.........Modified-V
Construction ....Aluminum
Designer..........T. DeGroot

Production
1973–75

STRIKER 37 CANYON RUNNER

The Striker 37 Canyon Runner is an enlarged version of the original 34 Canyon Runner (1973–75). She started out as a 36-foot prototype in 1987 but was lengthened the following year to gain additional cockpit space. Like all Strikers, the 37's hull and superstructure are heavy-gauge welded marine aluminum. The beam is unusually wide, and the deepest part of the keel provides protection for the props. She was built in the U.S., making her the only domestically-manufactured Striker ever produced. The 37 can be characterized as a serious gamefishing machine with battleship construction and several innovative features. What appears to be a window in the aft bulkhead is actually a complete fold-up bait prep center. Inside, the 37's compact layout has a single stateroom forward, small head (no shower stall), convertible dinette, and mini galley. The decor is contemporary, and the woodwork and fabrics top quality. A good-looking boat, standard 485-hp 6-71s will cruise at 28–29 knots. Note the large 750-gallon fuel capacity. For the record, the Striker 37 Canyon Runner was at the top of the scale when it came to price. ❑

SPECIFICATIONS

Length	37'4"
Beam	14'7"
Draft	2'8"
Weight	24,000#
Clearance	13'1"
Water	150 Gals.
Fuel	750 Gals.
Cockpit	100 Sq. Ft.
Hull Type	Modified-V
Construction	Aluminum
Designer	T. DeGroot

Production
1988–90

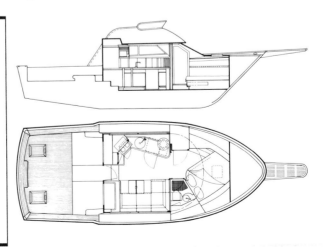

STRIKER 41 SPORTFISHERMAN

A good-looking boat with a stepped sheer, rakish flybridge, and distinctive bow pulpit, the Striker 41 SF is a stable offshore fisherman built for serious tournament-level pursuits. She was constructed of aluminum on a wide-beam hull with shallow draft, and at only 16,250 lbs. she's an incredibly light boat for her size. Her two-stateroom layout is very spacious (in spite of plenty of dark teak woodwork and cabinetry) and includes *two* heads as well as a roomy galley on the lower level. There's a sink in the guest stateroom and a U-shaped settee is to port in the salon. Thanks to her wide beam, the generous interior accommodations of the Striker 41 don't intrude into the cockpit where there's room for a complete set of tackle centers and a mounted chair. The flybridge is large for a 41-footer and the sidedecks are very wide. Additional features include a teak cockpit sole and covering boards, foredeck seating, sturdy tubular deck rails, and a big engine room with good outboard service access. All six Striker 41s were fitted with 410-hp 6-71s and cruise around 23 knots and reach a top speed of 26–27 knots. ❑

SPECIFICATIONS

Length	41'0"
Draft	2'4"
Beam	14'9"
Weight	16,250#
Clearance	13'6"
Water	100 Gals.
Fuel, Std	650 Gals.
Cockpit	NA
Hull Type	Modified-V
Construction	Aluminum
Designer	T. DeGroot

Production
1981–83

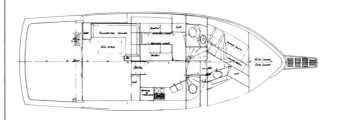

STRIKER 44 SPORTFISHERMAN

Although she's been out of production for years, the Striker 44 Sportfisherman remains the best-selling Striker ever. A total of 99 were built at the Striker yard in Norway, and used models always seem to be in demand around serious sportfishing markets. Her popularity stems from the rugged, welded aluminum construction and the massive brawn common to all Striker yachts. The 44 quickly gained a reputation as a capable offshore sportfisherman with a distinctive profile and superb offshore handling. As a fishing boat she has very good range, a first

class working cockpit, and wide side-decks with beefy deck hardware and rails. The more popular two-stateroom, galley-down layout is well suited to the needs of extended cruising. Among many notable features are a sea chest to eliminate unnecessary through-hull fittings, a serviceable engine room, an expansive flybridge, teak cockpit sole, and teak covering boards. Most Striker 44s were powered with 310-hp 6-71s and cruise at around 17 knots with a top speed of 20 knots. The 370-hp Cummins cruise at 21 knots and top out at 24. ❏

SPECIFICATIONS

Length	44'0"
Beam	15'9"
Draft	2'9"
Weight	20,000
Clearance	14'6"
Water	235 Gals.
Fuel, Std	470 Gals.
Fuel, Opt	705 Gals.
Cockpit	NA
Hull Type	Modified-V
Construction	Aluminum
Designer	Tom DeGroot

Production
1968–75

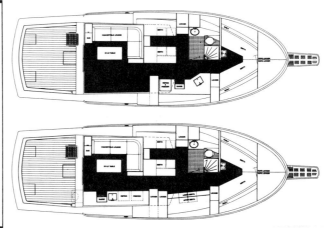

STRIKER

STRIKER 50 SPORTFISHERMAN

The first Striker 50s were built in Korea beginning in 1979. Five were constructed through 1982, and each was a semi-custom yacht built to suit the needs of her owner. Production was resumed in 1987 with the boats then being constructed in Chile. This new, updated Striker 50 incorporated major design changes in the deckhouse, cockpit, engine room, and flybridge. Her two-stateroom interior was available with the galley up or down, the difference being the size of the owner's stateroom and the salon arrangement. Featuring a luxurious decor, the spacious accommodations available in the Striker 50's living areas are most impressive. The cockpit is set up for serious fishing with cockpit controls and a teak sole standard, together with direct access to the engine room. Other notable features include very wide sidedecks with sturdy rails, an upright rod locker in the cockpit, a huge flybridge, and a modern profile. A proven tournament performer with a handsome profile, the Striker 50 Sportfisherman will cruise at 25 knots and reach a top speed of 28 with 735-hp GM 8V92TIB diesels. ❏

SPECIFICATIONS

Length	49'11"
Beam	16'8"
Draft	3'9"
Weight	41,000#
Clearance	12'6"
Water	250 Gals.
Fuel	1,100 Gals.
Cockpit	100 Sq. Ft.
Hull Type	Modified-V
Construction	Aluminum
Designer	T. DeGroot

Production
1979–82, 1987–89

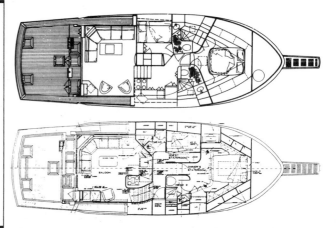

STRIKER 54 SPORTFISHERMAN

The Striker 54 evolved from the successful Striker 36' and 44' sportfishermen. All were designed for long-range, tournament-level events. A total of 18 of these yachts were built in Norway. Her distinctive profile, welded aluminum construction, super-wide beam, and unique (and very seaworthy) modified-V hull design set her quite apart from the competition. The first impression of a Striker 54 is of size — she's a very big 54-footer. Her three-stateroom interior layout is finished in solid teak and features an expansive 20'-long salon area with an open, U-shaped galley forward. Each stateroom is fitted with twin berths and each has a private head (with stall showers in all three after 1973). Like all Strikers, the 54 features a sea chest to eliminate through-hull fittings, self-cooling integral fuel tanks, protection for the underwater running gear, very wide sidedecks, and massive aluminum rails for on-deck security. Still in demand as a used boat, she'll cruise at 17 knots and run 20 knots wide open with 12V71N diesels. With the larger 12V71TI versions, she'll cruise at 21 knots and reach 24 knots top. ❏

SPECIFICATIONS

Length	54'0"
Beam	17'0"
Draft	3'6"
Weight	34,000#
Clearance	14'9"
Water	350 Gals.
Fuel, Std	925 Gals.
Fuel, Opt	1,275 Gals.
Cockpit	170 Sq. Ft.
Hull Type	Modified-V
Construction	Aluminum
Designer	T. DeGroot

Production
1970–75

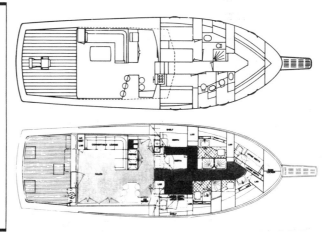

STRIKER 58/60 SPORTFISHERMAN

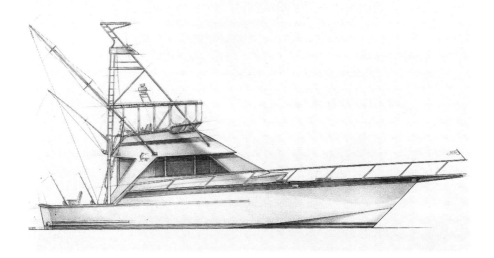

Built in Chile, the Striker 58 SF is actually a revised and updated version of the earlier Striker 60 SF which was built in Korea from 1979–82. She has the same hull and specifications, but changes were made to the deckhouse, cockpit, engine room, and flybridge. Like all Striker yachts, she was constructed of welded marine aluminum on a wide-beamed hull with the shallow keel providing protection to the props and running gear. Her classic Striker profile is immediately recognized everywhere and is generally one of the more respected in the industry.

At heart, the Striker 58/60 is a world-class tournament fisherman with the strength and endurance to match any boat in the fleet. The spacious cockpit is set up for serious fishing and — as with the Striker 62 and 70 models— the 58 also has a unique on-deck day head. While all were delivered with semi-custom layouts, the interior of the 58 was redesigned early in her production run (see lower floorplan) and featured an all-new decor package. A good-running boat, 1,080-hp 12V92s will cruise the Striker 58/60 at 26 knots and reach a top speed of around 28 knots. ❏

SPECIFICATIONS

Length	58'6"
Beam	19'6"
Draft	3'11"
Weight	51,480#
Clearance	15'6"
Water	315 Gals.
Fuel	1,550 Gals.
Cockpit	149 Sq. Ft.
Hull Type	Modified-V
Construction	Aluminum
Designer	T. DeGroot

Production
1988–90

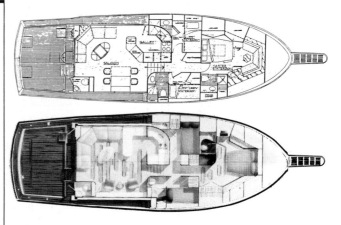

STRIKER 62 SPORTFISHERMAN

Only a few production yachts received the media attention of the Striker 62 SF when she was introduced in 1986. Aside from the fact that she was at the time the largest all-aluminum sportfisherman ever built, what set the 62 apart from earlier Striker yachts was her lush interior decor and incredible 21-foot beam. Built in Holland, the Striker 62 was priced at the top of the chart compared to other similar yachts in her size range. Nevertheless, she become a successful design, and a total of nine were built during her production years. Not surprisingly, the Striker 62 is packed with innovative design features. The salon steps in the cockpit can be raised hydraulically for engine room access. Electronics are hidden within the flybridge helm console until needed. The extravagant three-stateroom accommodations available in the Striker 62 Sportfisherman are the equal of the most luxurious motor yacht. Standard 1,080-hp 12V92s cruise about 23 knots (at around 100 gph) and reach a top speed of 26–27 knots. Optional 1,300-hp MTUs offer a 27-knot cruising speed and around 30 knots wide open. ❏

SPECIFICATIONS

Length.......................62'0"
Beam.........................21'0"
Draft ....3'10"
Weight ....68,000#
Clearance ....NA
Water.................315 Gals.
Fuel ....2,280 Gals
Cockpit............146 Sq. Ft.
Hull Type.........Modified-V
Construction ....Aluminum
Designer.........T. DeGroot

Production
1986–90

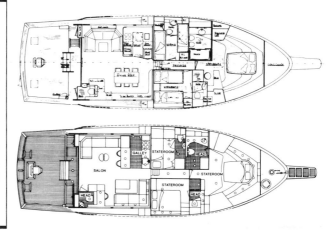

STRIKER 70 SPORTFISHERMAN

The 70 Sportfisherman was the largest model ever offered by Striker Yachts. A total of seven of these custom yachts were built — two in Korea and five in Holland. This is one of the world's largest semi-production sportfishing yachts and she's considered among the finest of her size ever built. Not surprisingly, the 70 is built like a small ship, with the offshore performance to take her owner to some of the most remote fishing grounds in the world. With 4,000 gallons of fuel, the range is impressive. The 221-sq. ft. cockpit is awesome in size and comes equipped with a vast array of features, including the popular day head. The salon steps lift up at the touch of a button to provide direct cockpit access to the engine room, and like all Strikers, the gin pole serves as an air duct to ventilate the engine room. The interior layout and decor of the 70 are generally customized to meet the tastes of the owner. The salon and cabin accommodations are enormous. Those powered with the 1,300-hp MTUs will cruise at 17–18 knots. The 1,900-hp MTU diesels will cruise the Striker 70 at 22 knots and reach a top speed of 25 knots. ❏

SPECIFICATIONS

Length......................70'6"
Beam........................23'6"
Draft ....3'4"
Weight ....75,000#
Clearance.................17'4"
Water.................450 Gals.
Fuel...............4,000 Gals.
Cockpit............221 Sq. Ft.
Hull Type.........Modified-V
Designer..........T. DeGroot

Production
1983–89

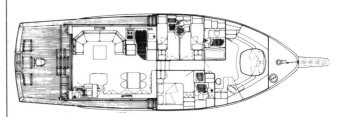

TIARA

Brief History

Tiara traces its roots back to 1954 when Leon Slikkers quit his job at the Chris Craft plant in Holland, MI and began the Slickcraft Boat Company. By the late 1960s the company had caught the eye of the AMF Corporation, which purchased the operation and kept Slikkers on to run it. In 1973 he left AMF and started S2 Yachts, specializing in sailboats. Since then, S2 has prospered and today the company builds the Tiara and Pursuit line of convertibles and sportfishermen (sailboat production ended in the mid-1980s). Tiara is one of the largest family-owned boatbuilding companies in the country.

Selected Tiara Inboard Models

Tiara 2700 Open

Taira 3100 Open (Early)

Tiara 3100 Open

Tiara 3100 Convertible

Pursuit 3250 Open

Tiara 3300 Open

Tiara 3300 Flybridge

Tiara 3600 Open

Tiara 3600 Convertible

Tiara 4300 Convertible

Tiara 4300 Open

Main Office

Tiara Yachts, Inc., 725 East 40th Street, Holland, MI 49423
616-392-7163

573

TIARA 2700 OPEN

Originally called the 2700 Pursuit, the Tiara 2700 Open is a scaled-down version of the company's successful 3100 Open fisherman. She's built on a deep-V hull design with moderate beam, balsa-cored hullsides, and a steep 22° of deadrise at the transom. The 2700 is a good-quality offshore express capable of fast and comfortable running in choppy seas. Her large fishing cockpit is fitted with rod storage under the gunnels and the non-skid on the cockpit sole provides outstanding traction when wet. The 2700 Open's wide side-decks provide an added measure of safety when moving forward to the bow. Engine boxes beneath the helm and companion seats allow for easy access to the power plants. Below, the compact layout includes V-berths, a small galley area, and a stand-up head with shower. The 2700's decor is notably plush for a fishing boat. Additional features include optional cockpit bench seating, anchor locker, molded pulpit, and swim platform. A fine-running boat with excellent sea-keeping characteristics, standard 350 cid gas engines will cruise around 24 knots with a top speed of 31–32 knots. ❏

SPECIFICATIONS

Length	27'0"
Beam	10'0"
Draft	2'0"
Weight	7,300#
Clearance	7'0"
Water	20 Gals.
Fuel	240 Gals.
Cockpit	NA
Hull Type	Deep-V
Designer	L. Slikkers

Production
1982–Current

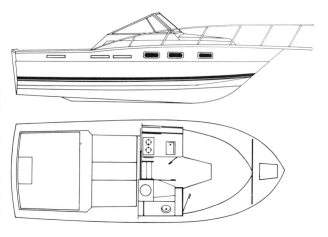

TIARA 3100 OPEN (EARLY)

Originally called the 3100 Pursuit when she was introduced, the Tiara 3100 Open has long been considered a serious tournament-level contender in coastal sportfishing circles. After more than a decade in production, she remained basically unchanged until she was replaced with a new 3100 model in 1992. Her popularity derives from her large cockpit and good offshore handling, but behind her reputation as a fishing boat is the realization that she's well engineered and built to high standards. The addition of the optional radar arch, swim platform, and bench seating in the cockpit transforms the 3100 into a conservative but good-looking family sportboat with genuine eye appeal. Although more than half of her LOA is committed to the cockpit, the interior accommodations are plush if somewhat compact. Built on a modified-V hull (16° deadrise aft), standard 454 gas engines will cruise the 3100 Open at 22–23 knots and reach a top speed of around 32 knots. The 300-hp GM 8.2 diesels have been a popular option (22–23 knots cruise). Note that the 3100 FB Convertible model is the same boat with a flybridge. ❑

SPECIFICATIONS

Length	31'3"
Beam	12'0"
Draft	2'9"
Weight	10,500#
Clearance	7'6"
Water	36 Gals.
Fuel, Std	196 Gals.
Cockpit	144 Sq. Ft.
Hull Type	Modified-V
Designer	L. Slikkers

Production
1979–92

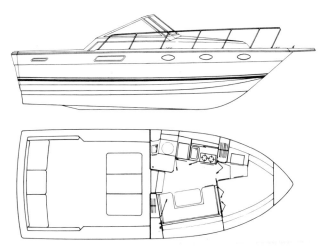

TIARA

TIARA 3100 OPEN

The new Tiara 3100 Open is a complete update of the original (and very popular) 3100 Open. Her reworked solid glass hull features a sharper entry, additional transom deadrise (18° vs. 16°), greater bow flare for a dryer ride, and prop pockets for shallow draft. The 3100 also has a new bi-level cockpit layout which allows for the installation of optional Volvo, Cat, or Cummins diesels in an enlarged engine compartment. Tiara has always been a conservative builder and it's no surprise that the new 3100 looks a lot like the original — basically a no-glitz express with good-quality construction, systems, and hardware. The slightly enlarged interior of the 3100 has more headroom than before and there's also a bigger U-shaped dinette. A stable and durable offshore fisherman, the addition of an arch and optional cockpit seating turns the 3100 into a stylish family cruiser. Other updates include increased fuel, recessed trim tabs, and a large in-deck fishbox and livewell in the cockpit. Standard 454-cid gas engines will cruise at 21-22 knots (30 knots top) and 291-hp 3116 Cats cruise at an efficient 25 knots (20 gph) and deliver 30 knots wide open. ❏

SPECIFICATIONS

Length	31'3"
Beam	12'0"
Draft	2'9"
Weight	10,500#
Clearance	7'9"
Cockpit	NA
Water	36 Gals.
Fuel	206 Gals.
Hull Type	Modified-V
Designer	L. Slikkers

Production
1992–Current

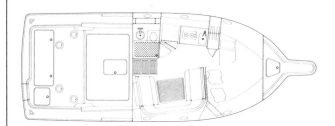

TIARA 3100 CONVERTIBLE

The Tiara 3100 Convertible can be characterized as an upscale family cruiser with attractive lines and good overall performance. She was originally introduced in 1982 as the 3100 Continental, a designation that lasted through 1986. Built on the same hull used for the 3100 Open with 16° of transom deadrise, the Convertible offers the added comforts of a salon and an enclosed helm along with the ability to sleep six persons overnight. The salon is fully carpeted, and a removable hatch in the sole provides access to the motors. Below, the stylish decor is a blend of quality fabrics and teak trim with modern off-white mica cabinets featured in the galley. This is, in fact, one of the more appealing interiors to be found in any 31' convertible and most will find it well suited to the demands of family cruising. A sliding glass door opens to the cockpit, where there's sufficient room for recreational fishing activities. The flybridge has bench seating forward of the helm console for three guests. Standard 454 gas engines will cruise the Tiara 3100 Convertible at 20–21 knots with a top speed of about 30 knots. ❏

SPECIFICATIONS

Length	31'3"
Beam	12'0"
Draft	2'11"
Weight	13,200#
Clearance	12'2"
Water	36 Gals.
Fuel, Std	206 Gals.
Fuel, Opt	286 Gals.
Cockpit	NA
Hull Type	Modified-V
Designer	L. Slikkers

Production
1982–Current

TIARA

PURSUIT 3250 OPEN

Largest of the Pursuit series of off-shore fishing boats, the 3250 Open is an upscale canyon runner designed to appeal to well-heeled anglers with a taste for quality. She's built on a reworked version of the popular Tiara 3300 hull, a modified-V (18° deadrise aft) with a shallow keel and balsa coring in the hullsides and deck. An inner liner is used to create a rugged one-piece hull of extraordinary strength. Below, the cabin layout is conventional with V-berths forward, compact galley, dinette, and stand-up head amidships. A teak and holly sole is standard, and the teak trim and off-white mica cabinetry are finished to high standards. The 3250's bi-level fishing cockpit features an oversize transom door, big in-deck fishbox, livewell, molded steps, and fresh- and saltwater washdowns. Push a button and hydraulic hatches rise to expose both engines. Gas engines are standard (15 knots cruise/24 top) but most 3250s will surely have one of several optional diesel installations. The 300-hp Cummins, 296-hp Volvos and 300-hp Cats all cruise around 26-28 knots and deliver top speeds of 30+ knots. ❏

SPECIFICATIONS

Length	33'0"
Beam	12'6"
Draft	2'8"
Weight	13,500#
Clearance	8'4"
Water	50 Gals.
Fuel	305 Gals.
Cockpit	115 Sq. Ft.
Hull Type	Modified-V
Designer	L. Slikkers

Production
1990–Current

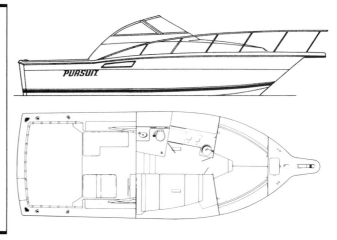

TIARA

TIARA 3300 OPEN

Tiara's 3300 Open is a stylish family sportcruiser with several features that should make her attractive to experienced owners who are willing to trade some of the modern sportboat glitz for a more conservative design. She's built on a proven modified-V hull (18° deadrise aft) with a shallow skeg for stability and balsa coring in the hullsides. Unlike the Tiara 3100 Open, the 3300 is not designed as a sportfisherman. Instead, she's more at home in the family-cruiser role, where her plush interior and sportboat profile are most appreciated. Her well-designed interior features overnight berths for six in a cabin of unusual elegance and luxury. The interior is finished with grain-matched teak joinerwork and the galley features white Formica cabinetry. In spite of her generous interior dimensions, the 3300 still manages to provide an excellent fishing cockpit with a transom door, inwale padding, and cockpit washdown as standard equipment. With standard 454 gas engines the Tiara 3300 Open will cruise at 22–23 knots with a top speed of 32 knots. Optional 300-hp GM 8.2 diesels will cruise at 24–25 knots. ❏

SPECIFICATIONS

Length	32'10"
Beam	12'6"
Draft	2'3"
Weight	11,500#
Clearance	8'11"
Water	46 Gals.
Fuel	295 Gals.
Cockpit	NA
Hull Type	Modified-V
Designer	L. Slikkers

Production
1988–Current

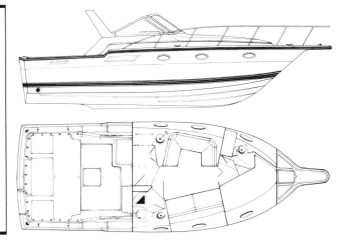

TIARA

TIARA 3300 FLYBRIDGE

A great-looking design with a modern profile and a big fishing cockpit, the Tiara 3300 Flybridge is 33 feet of solid construction and quick, agile performance. Her rakish profile and glassed-in windshield combine with a practical deck layout in making the Tiara 3300 FB an extremely capable sportfisherman. Note the offset companionway hatch which allows space in the cockpit for the raised tackle center. The hull (a modified-V with a steep 18° of deadrise aft) is balsa-cored above the waterline and side exhausts exit just forward of the transom. The ride is dry and comfortable with good lateral stability at trolling speeds. The upscale cabin in the 3300 is modest but well-suited to the needs of up to four anglers. Unlike other Tiaras with their abundant teak woodwork, the interior in the 3300 uses off-white Formica laminates and pastel fabrics for a bright, cheerful look. A hydraulically-operated hatch in the raised deck provides excellent access to the motors. Standard 454-cid Crusaders will cruise the Tiara 3300 FB at 20–21 knots and optional 300-hp GM 8.2 diesels (or 320-hp Cats) cruise around 24–25 knots. ❏

SPECIFICATIONS

Length	32'10"
Beam	12'6"
Draft	2'8"
Weight	13,000#
Clearance	11'6"
Water	46 Gals.
Fuel	295 Gals.
Cockpit	75 Sq. Ft.
Hull Type	Modified-V
Designer	L. Slikkers

Production
1986–91

TIARA

TIARA 3600 OPEN

A hugely popular boat, the 3600 Open is a wide-beamed express with conservative lines, top-shelf construction, and plush interior accommodations. What sets the 3600 apart from some of her more glitzy Eurostyle counterparts is her excellent fishability and outstanding offshore performance. Her modified-V hull (18° of deadrise at the transom) features a shallow skeg for excellent tracking and balsa coring in the hullsides for reduced weight. The spacious bi-level cockpit is fitted with a big fish box on the centerline, a pair of circulating livewells, rod storage, and a transom door. The interior accommodations are finished with traditional teak cabinetry and designer fabrics throughout. An island berth is forward in the original "A" Plan, and the alternate "B" layout (new in 1989) has a settee opposite the dinette and overnight berths for six, but no stall shower. The bridgedeck has an hydraulic lift for easy access to the engines. Standard 454 gas engines provide a 21–knot cruising speed and a top speed of about 30 knots. Optional 375-hp Cats offer cruising speeds at a fast 27–28 knots and reach 32+ knots wide open.   ❏

SPECIFICATIONS

Length	36'8"
Beam	13'9"
Draft	2'11"
Weight	16,500#
Clearance	9'7"
Water	85 Gals.
Fuel	396 Gals.
Cockpit	NA
Hull Type	Modified-V
Designer	L. Slikkers

Production
1985–Current

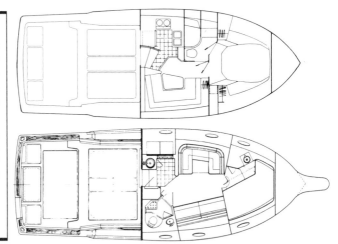

TIARA

TIARA 3600 CONVERTIBLE

Based on the hull of the 3600 Open, the Tiara 3600 Convertible is a good-looking flybridge sedan with an upscale interior and good offshore performance. A stepped sheer and oval portlights give her a modern and slightly aggressive appearance at dockside. The gelcoat is superb — about as good as it gets in a production boat. The glassed-in front windshield is optional, as is a lower station, and the light-grain interior woodwork and decorator fabrics create stylish and very luxurious accommodations below. Two interior layouts are available in the 36 Convertible: a two-stateroom arrangement or a single-stateroom floorplan with a dinette. Both have a mid-level galley and include a stall shower in the head. The cockpit is equipped with a transom door and gate, and wide walkaround decks provide safe access to the bow. The roomy tournament-style flybridge can seat six. A popular boat with both cruisers and anglers, standard 454 gas engines cruise the 3600 Convertible at 19-20 knots and reach 28 knots wide open. Optional Cat 375-hp diesels cruise at 25 knots and deliver a top speed of around 29–30 knots. ❏

SPECIFICATIONS

Length	36'8"
Beam	13'9"
Draft	3'0"
Weight	18,300#
Clearance	12'6"
Water	85 Gals.
Fuel	396 Gals.
Cockpit	NA
Hull Type	Modified-V
Designer	L. Slikkers

Production
1987–Current

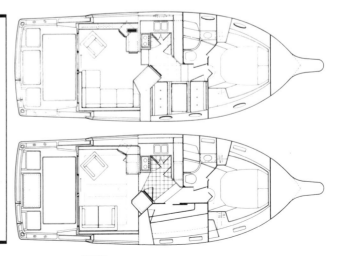

TIARA

TIARA 4300 CONVERTIBLE

Designed to hold her own against the likes of the Viking 43 and Bertram 43, the Tiara 4300 is a superb combination of elegant styling and top-quality construction and engineering. She's built on a beefy, modified-V hull with balsa coring above the WL, wide chine flats aft, and 16° of transom deadrise. Two floorplans are offered. The original two-stateroom, two-head layout has the mid-level galley separated from the salon by a breakfast bar. A dinette floorplan introduced in 1992 trades out the guest cabin for a large U-shaped dinette and an enlarged master stateroom. Rod storage is located in the (sculptured) salon overhead and the interior is finished with an abundance of teak woodwork and cabinetry. While the 4300 can certainly be viewed as a luxurious family cruiser, her real objective is tournament-level sportfishing. The uncluttered cockpit is equipped with a wide transom door and gate, baitwells, and in-deck fishbox. Topside, the stylish wraparound helm console features raised panels for flush-mounting electronics. The Tiara 4300 will clock 24–25 knots at cruise with standard 550-hp 6V92s and top out around 28 knots. ❑

SPECIFICATIONS

Length	43'2"
Beam	15'2"
Draft	4'0"
Weight	31,000#
Clearance	13'5"
Water	160 Gals.
Fuel	640 Gals.
Cockpit	121 Sq. Ft.
Hull Type	Modified-V
Designer	J. Garland

Production
1990–Current

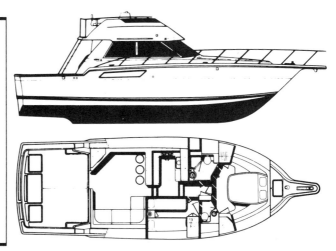

TIARA

TIARA 4300 OPEN

While the Tiara 4300 Open isn't the largest express cruiser on the market, she's in a class of her own when it comes to quality and engineering. Built on the same rugged offshore hull used in the 4300 Convertible (with cored hull-sides and 16° of transom deadrise), the 4300 Open is aimed primarily at the cruising market although she can be converted easily into a serious fishing platform. Her luxurious interior (the finest we've seen in any boat of this type) includes light ash cabinetry and woodwork, leather upholstery, teak and holly cabin sole, hydraulically operated dinette, and a huge master stateroom with a walkaround island berth and built-in TV. Outside, 4300's bi-level cockpit provides seating for ten and space in the helm console for flush-mounting electronics. There's plenty of room for a fighting chair and a tackle center and baitwell are optional. Additional features include rod storage, superb nonskid on the decks, excellent engine room access, and a fold-out bench seat at the transom. A good-running boat with 535-hp 6V92s, she'll cruise around 27 knots and reach 30 knots wide open. ❑

SPECIFICATIONS

Length	43'2"
Beam	15'2"
Draft	4'0"
Weight	28,000#
Clearance	10'4"
Cockpit	167 Sq. Ft.
Water	150 Gals.
Fuel	525 Gals.
Hull Type	Modified-V
Designer	J. Garland

Production
1992–Current

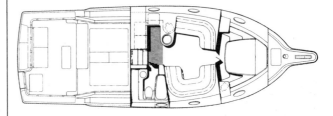

TOLLYCRAFT

Brief History

Founded in the early 1930s by R.F. Tollefson, Tollycraft began as a regional builder of wooden cruisers aimed primarily at the West Coast market. The conversion to fiberglass was made in the early 1960s, and the company expanded its sales activities during the 1980s to include East Coast and Great Lakes markets. Long considered a conservative, good-quality builder, all of the current Tollycraft models are designed by Ed Monk, Jr. Tollefson retired and the company was sold in 1988 (and again in 1990) to independent investors.

Selected Tollycraft Inboard Models

Tollycraft 26 Sedan
Tollycraft 30 Sedan
Tollycraft 30 Sport Cruiser
Tollycraft 34 Sedan
Tollycraft 34 Tri Cabin
Tollycraft 34 Convertible Sedan
Tollycraft 34 Sundeck
Tollycraft 34 Sport Sedan
Tollycraft 37 Convertible
Tollycraft 39 Sport Yacht

Tollycraft 40 Tri Cabin MY
Tollycraft 40 Sundeck MY
Tollycraft 40 Sport Sedan
Tollycraft 43 Cockpit MY
Tollycraft 44 Cockpit MY
Tollycraft 48 Cockpit MY
Tollycraft 48 Convertible
Tollycraft 53/57 Motor Yacht
Tollycraft 61 Motor Yacht

Main Office

Tollycraft Yacht Corp., 2200 Clinton Ave., Kelso, WA 98626
206-423-5160

585

TOLLYCRAFT 26 SEDAN

Tollycraft's all-time best-selling boat, the 26 Sedan attracted a loyal following over the years due to her roomy interior and rugged all-fiberglass construction. She's a tough little family cruiser (and big for only 26'), equally at home on inland waters or heading offshore for a day of casual fishing. At 9,000 lbs., the Tollycraft 26 is no lightweight for her size. A 10-foot beam provides good stability and a well-flared bow helps to keep the deck dry. The cabin arrangement is simple but adequate, and the decor was updated from wood-grain mica to teak in 1982. The convertible dinette and V-berths forward sleep a total of four. There's a stand-up head and visibility from the lower helm is excellent. The cabin windows in the 26 Sedan are very large and the interior is surprisingly open for such a small boat. Five people can sit on the bridge and the cockpit is large enough for a couple of anglers and their gear. Nearly all of the Tollycraft 26s were equipped with a single 270-hp gas engine with a V-drive (stern drives were also offered). The cruising speed is around 18 knots and the top speed is 24–25 knots. ❏

SPECIFICATIONS

Length	26'8"
Beam	10'0"
Draft	2'10"
Weight	9,000#
Clearance	10'0"
Water	33 Gals.
Fuel	140 Gals.
Cockpit	49 Sq. Ft.
Hull Type	Modified-V
Designer	Ed Monk, Jr.

Production
1973–85

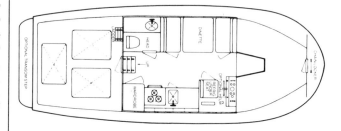

TOLLYCRAFT 30 SEDAN

The stout little Tollycraft 30 Sedan may come up a little short on sex appeal, but she's certainly long on interior volume and living space. The house and flybridge are exceptionally large for a 30-footer, and at 13,500 lbs. she's a heavy boat for her size. By building on a wide-beam hull and extending the salon bulkhead well into the cockpit, Tollycraft designers were able to create a spacious and very open interior with first-class accommodations for one couple. As with all Tollycraft designs, the sidedecks are wide and extra-large cabin windows provide plenty of natural lighting as well as good lower helm visibility. Storage is also impressive and includes a full wardrobe locker opposite the head. The interior decor was updated from imitation teak mica to real teak in 1982 and the woodwork and cabinetry are well crafted throughout. The cockpit is too small for any serious fishing, although the transom door and platform are fine for swimming. Most Tollycraft 30 Sedans were built with twin 270-hp Crusader gas engines. The cruising speed is 23–24 knots and the top speed is about 30 knots. ❏

SPECIFICATIONS

Length ....29'11"
Beam.......................11'9"
Draft ....2'6"
Weight ....13,500#
Clearance.................11'8"
Water....................58 Gals.
Fuel ....200 Gals.
Cockpit ....NA
Hull Type.........Modified-V
Designer........Ed Monk, Jr.

Production
1977–84

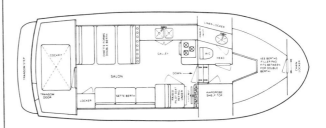

TOLLYCRAFT 30 SPORT CRUISER

The 30 Sport Cruiser was an all-new design when she was introduced in 1985. Built on Tollycraft's efficient Quadra-Lift hull (10° deadrise aft), the Sport Cruiser is a quick ride (25 knots at cruise/about 32 knots top) with standard 260-hp MerCruiser gas engines. Her styling is attractive and her crisp lines and rakish profile are quite appealing. The cabin is arranged with both the galley and head conveniently located just inside the cockpit door. V-drives permit the engines to be moved aft, thus lowering the Sport Cruiser's profile and allowing the interior to be arranged on a single level. A dinette and facing settee dominate the cabin and each will convert into a double berth at night. A lower helm (optional) is to starboard and V-berths are located forward. The teak cabinetry and quality fabrics are up to Tollycraft's normal above-average production standards. The cockpit is large enough for a few anglers and the transom door opens onto a stylish integral swim platform. Seating is available for up to six on the roomy flybridge. Note that the fuel capacity was increased in 1988 to 198 gallons. ❏

SPECIFICATIONS

Length	30'6"
Beam	11'6"
Draft	2'7"
Weight	11,500#
Clearance	11'8"
Water	42 Gals.
Fuel	150/198 Gals.
Cockpit	45 Sq. Ft.
Hull Type	Modified-V
Designer	Ed Monk, Jr.

Production
1985–Current

TOLLYCRAFT 34 SEDAN

Long out of production, the Tollycraft 34 Sedan remains a popular West Coast design with a graceful profile and a comfortable cabin layout. Hull construction is solid fiberglass with 16° of deadrise at the transom. V-drives are used to maximize the interior space. Features include a full 6'4" of headroom in the salon, a stall shower in the head, a huge 5'-wide clothes locker, and overnight accommodations for six. Mahogany woodwork was used throughout the interior until the 1977 models, when wood-grain mica cabinetry became standard. The salon in the 34 Sedan is on the same level as the galley and dinette. This open floorplan — together with the large cabin windows — provides a very spacious interior with good natural lighting. A lower station with full instrumentation was standard and engine access is via hatches in the cockpit sole. Topside, the flybridge has seating for five. With standard 270-hp Crusader gas engines, the cruising speed is around 20 knots and the top speed is 27–28 knots. A durable boat, the Tollycraft 34 has earned a reputation as an economical and practical family cruiser. ❏

SPECIFICATIONS

Length ....33'7"
Beam.......................12'3"
Draft ....2'6"
Weight ....15,000#
Clearance ....NA
Water...................50 Gals.
Fuel ....160 Gals.
Cockpit ....NA
Hull Type.........Modified-V
Designer........Ed Monk, Jr.

Production
1972–80

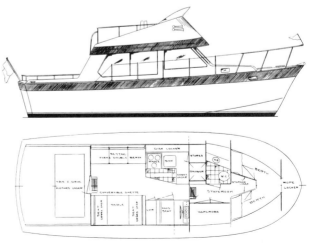

TOLLYCRAFT 34 TRI CABIN

Although she's been out of production for several years, the Tollycraft 34 Tri Cabin is one of the most desirable small aft cabin cruisers to be found on the used market. She's built on a modified-V bottom with a moderate 13° of transom deadrise. Her traditional lines are somewhat trawlerlike and at 17,000 lbs., the 34 Tri Cabin is a heavy boat for her size. Tollycraft designers managed to pack some 280 sq. ft. of living space inside the 34, including two heads (with a stall shower aft), a complete lower helm station with a deck access door, and excellent storage. The large salon windows provide an abundance of natural lighting and visibility from the lower helm is good. Early models have twin single berths in the aft cabin and a more popular double bed became standard in 1982. An all-teak interior was introduced in 1984 — a big improvement over the teak-grain mica veneers of earlier models. The non-skid is a unique imitation-teak fiberglass surface and the wide sidedecks make passage around the house very secure. With twin 270-hp gas engines, the 34 Tri Cabin will cruise at 17–18 knots with a top speed of around 25 knots. ❑

SPECIFICATIONS	
Length	34'0"
Length WL	30'6"
Beam	12'6"
Draft	2'10"
Weight	17,000#
Clearance	12'0"
Water	77 Gals.
Fuel	200 Gals.
Hull Type	Modified-V
Designer	Ed Monk, Jr.

Production
1975–85

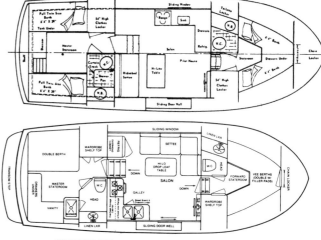

TOLLYCRAFT

TOLLYCRAFT 34 CONVERTIBLE SEDAN

Now out of production, the Tollycraft 34 Convertible Sedan has been a popular West Coast design for a number of years. Attractively styled with a rakish bridge overhang and a stepped sheer, her chief qualities consist of a practical interior layout, rugged construction, and a very seaworthy hull design. The single-stateroom layout is arranged with the galley down, and teak woodwork replaced the original teak-grained mica veneers beginning with the 1982 models. Note that a tournament-style flybridge option became available in 1985 for the East Coast market and the simulated teak non-skid deck surface was dropped the same year. Additional features include a good-size cockpit with transom door and swim platform, a very roomy flybridge, a stall shower in the head, and extra-large cabin windows that provide plenty of natural lighting. Offshore, the sturdy hull of the Tollycraft 34 Convertible enables her to comfortably handle a fairly wide range of weather conditions. Standard 270-hp Crusader gas engines will cruise at 18–19 knots and reach a top speed of around 26 knots. ❏

SPECIFICATIONS

Length	34'0"
Length WL	30'6"
Beam	12'6"
Draft	2'10"
Weight	17,000#
Clearance	12'2"
Water	100 Gals.
Fuel	200 Gals.
Cockpit	72 Sq. Ft.
Hull Type	Modified-V
Designer	Ed Monk, Jr.

Production
1981–1986

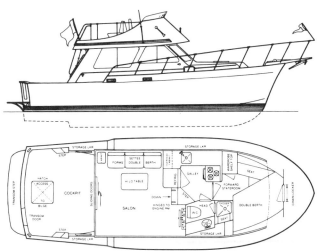

TOLLYCRAFT

TOLLYCRAFT 34 SUNDECK

The 34 Sundeck Cruiser was introduced in 1986 as a replacement for Tollycraft's aging 34 Tri Cabin. This all-new model received a fresh deckhouse and flybridge design resulting in a very stylish profile — maybe the best-looking of her type under 35 feet. Below, the interior remains similar to the older Tri Cabin layout but with an enlarged aft cabin featuring a walka-round double berth and a rearranged head compartment. The teak woodwork and cabinetry are well crafted throughout and the fabrics, hardware, and appliances are all top quality components. The efficient use of interior space in the 34 Sundeck is quite remarkable, and when combined with the rich furnishings it would be easy to confuse this interior with that of a larger boat. Built on the then-new Quadra-Lift hull, the Tollycraft 34 Sundeck weighs in at a hefty 17,000 lbs. and provides a dry, stable ride in most sea conditions. She'll cruise around 20 knots with 350-hp gas engines and reach a top speed of approximately 28 knots. Note the significant fuel increase to 296 gallons in 1988 (the final year of production). ❏

SPECIFICATIONS

Length......................34'0"
Length WL ....30'6"
Beam........................12'6"
Draft ....2'10"
Weight ....17,000#
Clearance ....12'0"
Water...................77 Gals.
Fuel............200/296 Gals.
Hull Type.........Modified-V
Designer........Ed Monk, Jr.

Production
1986–88

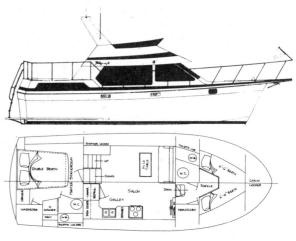

TOLLYCRAFT 34 SPORT SEDAN

Introduced in 1987 as the 34 Convertible SF, the Tollycraft 34 Sport Sedan is a versatile family cruiser with a sturdy and distinctive dockside appearance. Built on the efficient Quadra-Lift hull with 13° of deadrise aft, the 34 Sport Sedan is well suited to recreational fishing or diving activities in addition to having a luxurious and innovative two-stateroom cruising layout. A walka-round double berth is forward, stacked single berths are in the guest cabin to port, and a separate stall shower is fitted in the head compartment. The traditional teak interior woodwork is fashionable and extremely well finished, and over-size cabin windows make the interior seem wide open and bright. Outside, an insulated fish box is built into the cock-pit sole and molded steps provide easy access to the wide sidedecks. Two fly-bridge layouts are offered for the 34 Sport Sedan: An aft helm for the East Coast with seating forward, and a for-ward helm console with seating aft for the Pacific market. With standard 454 gas engines, the cruising speed is around 20 knots and the top speed is 28–29 knots. Fuel and water were increased in the 1988 models. ❑

SPECIFICATIONS

Length	34'0"
Beam	12'6"
Draft	2'10"
Weight	17,000#
Clearance	13'11"
Water	77/116 Gals.
Fuel	200/296 Gals.
Cockpit	72 Sq. Ft.
Hull Type	Modified-V
Designer	Ed Monk, Jr.

Production
1987–Current

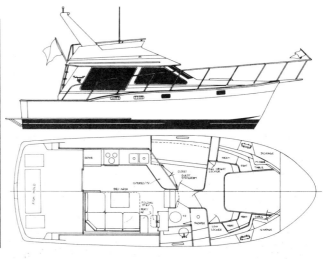

TOLLYCRAFT

TOLLYCRAFT 37 CONVERTIBLE

The Tollycraft 37 Convertible is one of those rare boats whose good reputation has grown over the years. Introduced in 1974 and enjoying a long and successful production run, this models remains popular because of her sturdy construction, practical layout, and low maintenance demands. Showing a distinctive West Coast profile, her relatively heavy displacement and a sharp entry allow the Tollycraft 37 to handle adverse sea conditions with confidence. With nearly 90 sq. ft. of space, the cockpit is large enough for serious fishing activities. Two interior layouts were offered with the galley-up floor-plan having an extra guest stateroom forward in place of the dinette. Early models were fitted with a wood-grain mica decor; a more appealing full teak interior became standard in 1977. Sliding glass doors separate the salon from the cockpit and the deck surfaces were given Tollycraft's imitation-teak non-skid treatment. Twin 454 cid gas engines will cruise the Tollycraft 37 Convertible at 20–21 knots (about 30 knots top) while optional 210-hp Cat diesels cruise efficiently at 16–17 knots with a top speed of around 21 knots. ❏

SPECIFICATIONS

Length	37'4"
Beam	13'2"
Draft	3'0"
Weight	22,000#
Clearance	12'6"
Water	140 Gals.
Fuel	300 Gals.
Cockpit	89 Sq. Ft.
Hull Type	Modified-V
Designer	Ed Monk, Jr.

Production
1974–85

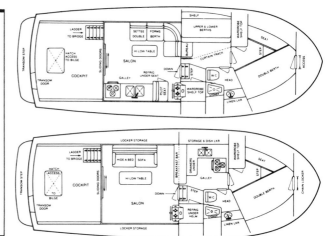

TOLLYCRAFT 39 SPORT YACHT

When she came out in 1990, the 39 Sport Yacht combined a modern Eurostyle appearance and a somewhat unusual deck plan in a manner not seen in previous Tollycraft products. Built on a solid fiberglass hull with a wide beam, 10° of transom deadrise, and a stylish reverse transom, the 39 Sport Yacht can be described as a 34' double cabin with a big cockpit, tiny flybridge, and a worthless aft deck. Her low-profile deckhouse is made possible because V-drives get the engines beneath the cockpit rather than placing them below the salon sole in the conventional manner — a unique arrangement in a boat of this type. The salon is all screwed up — the galley counter juts into the middle of the room — although the bleached ash woodwork and big windows make for a bright interior. The engine compartment is *tight* and working space is at a premium. Standard 454-cid gas engines will cruise around 17–18 knots with a top speed of 24 knots. Optional 250-hp 8.2 Detroits cruise at 17 knots and reach about 20 knots wide open. Just over twenty Tollycraft 39s were built during her short production run. ❑

SPECIFICATIONS

Length	38'11"
Beam	14'8"
Draft	3'0"
Weight	25,500#
Clearance	14'7"
Water	140 Gals.
Fuel	400 Gals.
Cockpit	44 Sq. Ft.
Hull Type	Modified-V
Designer	Ed Monk, Jr.

Production
1990–91

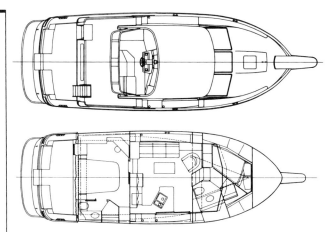

TOLLYCRAFT 40 TRI CABIN MY

The Tollycraft 40 Tri Cabin Motor Yacht was the first big yacht ever built by the Tollycraft company. A conservative design, she features a conventional double-cabin interior layout with the galley up in the salon and full wraparound cabin windows. The aft stateroom is particularly spacious and was offered with a choice of twin single berths or an optional double bed. Sliding deck access doors are fitted in the salon, and the interior woodwork was updated from African mahogany to teak in 1977. Notable in the Tollycraft 40 Tri Cabin is the conve-nient cockpit area with its transom door and swim platform. Her large 100 sq. ft. aft deck is useful for entertaining or dinghy storage while cruising. Typical of West Coast boats, the Tollycraft 40 Tri Cabin has extra-wide sidedecks and a complete lower helm station. Construction is solid fiberglass and the engineering and workmanship are first rate. Standard 454-cid gas engines provide a cruising speed of 16–17 knots and a top speed of about 26. The optional 210-hp Caterpillar diesels will average an efficient 1 mpg at a 15-knot cruising speed. ❏

SPECIFICATIONS

Length	40'2"
Beam	13'4"
Draft	3'2"
Weight	30,000#
Clearance	NA
Water	150 Gals.
Fuel	440 Gals.
Cockpit	40 Sq. Ft.
Hull Type	Modified-V
Designer	Ed Monk, Jr.

Production
1970–79

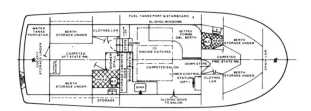

TOLLYCRAFT 40 SUNDECK MY

A good-selling model, the 40 Sundeck is a modern double-cabin yacht with attractive styling and a first-rate interior layout. Aimed at the upscale family cruiser market, the 40's profile has not been subjected to the Eurostyle overkill seen recently in many other boats her size. Like all Tollycraft designs, her modified-V hull (10° transom deadrise) handles well and her construction ranks high in the production industry. Inside, the large deckhouse windows combine with a well-crafted teak interior and designer fabrics to create a very open and upscale decor. The U-shaped galley and dinette are down, and there's a sliding deck door in the salon (a lower helm is optional). Note that a new queen forward layout (with a very small head) became available in 1992. Outside, the aft deck provides a full 130 sq. ft. of entertainment space with additional seating for six on the flybridge. Standard 454-cid gas engines cruise at 17–18 knots (26 knots top). Optional 375-hp Cat diesels will cruise around 23 knots (27 top) and the 400-hp 6V53s cruise around 24 knots (27 top). Note that the fuel capacity was increased in 1991. ❏

SPECIFICATIONS

Length	40'2"
Length WL	NA
Beam	14'8"
Draft	3'0"
Weight	26,000#
Clearance	12'0"
Water	140 Gals.
Fuel	300/398 Gals.
Hull Type	Modified-V
Designer	Ed Monk, Jr.

Production
1985–Current

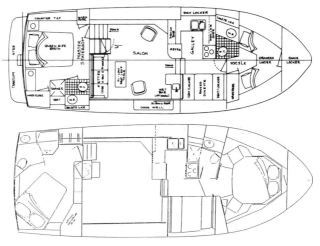

TOLLYCRAFT

TOLLYCRAFT 40 SPORT SEDAN

A good sea boat, the 40 Sport Sedan is the first really serious sportfishing design ever offered by Tollycraft. Introduced in 1987 as the Convertible Sportfisherman, she's built using the modified-V hull originally designed for the Tollycraft 40 Sundeck MY. In 1989 Tollycraft gave the boat a new profile and a revised interior layout while toning down the emphasis on fishing and renaming her as the "Sport Sedan." Her slightly reduced cockpit (101 sq. ft. vs. the previous 112 sq. ft.) is still large enough to accommodate a mounted chair and tackle center, and molded steps provide easy access to the wide sidedecks. The original two-stateroom, galley-up floorplan was revised in 1989 with the galley moved forward to a mid-level position, thus creating an even more spacious salon. (Note that a dinette can be ordered in place of the guest cabin.) The 40 Sport Sedan is available with the helm aft on the flybridge or forward in the West Coast style. Caterpillar 375-hp diesels will cruise at 23 knots (27 top) and the 485-hp GM 6-71s will cruise around 27 knots and deliver 29–30 knots wide open. ❑

SPECIFICATIONS

Length	40'2"
Beam	14'8"
Draft	3'0"
Weight	26,000#
Clearance	12'4"
Water	140 Gals.
Fuel	500 Gals.
Cockpit	101 Sq. Ft.
Hull Type	Modified-V
Designer	Ed Monk, Jr.

Production
1987–Current

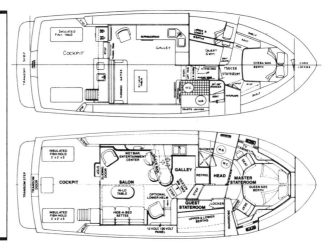

TOLLYCRAFT 43 COCKPIT MY

For those who are really serious about their cruising and who value seaworthiness over the glitz of some of today's Eurostyle bay boats, the Tollycraft 43 Cockpit Motor Yacht should receive strong consideration. Built on a rugged, semi-displacement, solid fiberglass hull and bearing a distinct trawler-style profile, the 43 CMY is widely regarded as a superior heavy-weather boat. A sharp entry and a full-length keel provide excellent handling characteristics, while her flat aftersections allow the 43 to cruise efficiently at 15 knots (15 gph) with the small 210-hp Cat diesels. The accommodations are well organized with double berths in each stateroom and a serving bar separating the salon from the lower-level galley. A lower helm and deck access door were standard and the interior is finished with well-crafted teak cabinetry and paneling throughout. Other features include a transom door, wide walkaround sidedecks, radar mast and top-quality appliances, furnishings, and hardware. A proven design, the Tollycraft 43 Cockpit MY is a classic Pacific Northwest cruiser with considerable eye appeal. ❏

SPECIFICATIONS

Length .... 43'4"
Length WL .... 39'5"
Beam .... 14'2"
Draft .... 3'5"
Weight .... 30,000#
Clearance .... 13'9"
Water .... 140 Gals.
Fuel .... 400 Gals.
Cockpit .... NA
Hull Type .... Semi-Disp.
Designer .... Ed Monk, Jr.

Production
1980–86

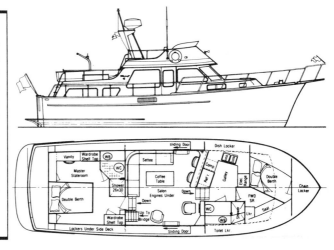

TOLLYCRAFT 44 COCKPIT MY

The addition of a cockpit to the Tollycraft 40 Sundeck has created the 44 Cockpit MY, a handsome design with great appeal for the cruising yachtsman. Cockpits add a lot of versatility to any motor yacht and can often add an extra knot or two of performance besides. In the case of the Tollycraft 44, her lines are somewhat rakish and many consider her to be one of the best-looking cruising yachts available in her size range. The accommodations are the same as in the Tollycraft 40 Sundeck — a two-stateroom layout with galley and dinette down, spacious salon dimensions, and (since 1992) a choice of V-berths or an island berth forward. A transom door makes boarding an easy matter and the cockpit also allows the generator to be moved from the engine room to below the cockpit sole. Standard 454-cid gas engines cruise at 18–19 knots (27 knots top). Optional 375-hp Cat diesels will cruise around 23 knots (about 26 top), and the 400-hp 6V53s cruise around 24 knots (27 knots top). Note that the fuel was increased in 1991. With over 100 built to date, the 44 Cockpit MY is one of Tollycraft's best-selling yachts. ❑

SPECIFICATIONS

Length	44'2"
Beam	14'8"
Draft	3'0"
Weight	28,000#
Clearance	12'0"
Cockpit	42 Sq. Ft.
Water	140 Gals.
Fuel	300/398 Gals.
Hull Type	Modified-V
Designer	Ed Monk, Jr.

Production
1986–Current

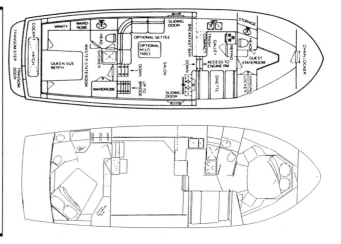

TOLLYCRAFT 48 COCKPIT MY

Long regarded as a top-quality West Coast cruiser, the 48 Cockpit MY was reintroduced into the Tollycraft lineup in 1991. Not much has changed — the interior layout is basically the same (the decor has been updated) and her rugged semi-displacement hull with rounded chines and 10° deadrise aft remains the same. Capable of long-distance passages in a wide range of weather conditions, the 48 CMY is built for those who place a priority on serious cruising. The efficient two-stateroom layout is arranged with the galley and dinette down, a lower helm with two deck access doors in the salon, and a comfortable master stateroom. Exterior features include a cockpit transom door, wide walkaround sidedecks with protective bulwarks, and space for dinghy storage on the cabintop. Styling changes to the flybridge were made in 1985. Early models with 320-hp Cat diesels will cruise at 16 knots (around 20 knots top), and the newer boats with 300-hp Cummins or 3116 Cats cruise at about the same speed. Eighty 48 Cockpit MYs were built before the original production run ended in 1986 and used models are very sellable. ❏

SPECIFICATIONS

Length	48'2"
Beam	15'2"
Draft	3'8"
Weight	42,000#
Clearance	17'0"
Water	188 Gals.
Fuel	600 Gals.
Cockpit	65 Sq. Ft.
Hull Type	Semi-Disp.
Designer	Ed Monk, Jr.

Production
1976–86
1991–Current

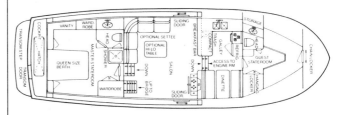

TOLLYCRAFT 48 CONVERTIBLE

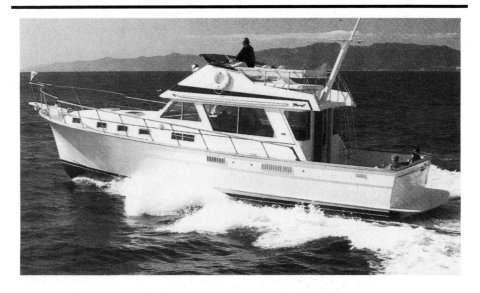

Sharing the same semi-displacement hull as the 48 Cockpit Motor Yacht, the Tollycraft 48 Convertible is a truly handsome yacht with traditional styling and go-anywhere construction. With her fine entry, moderate 10° transom deadrise, and long keel, the Tolly 48 cuts through head seas and tracks steadily in a beam or following sea. Not developed as an out-and-out sportfisherman, she's designed instead for part-time anglers who enjoy a comfortable family cruising yacht with offshore fishing capabilities. Among her features are two staterooms and heads, a complete

lower helm station, cored hull construction, a *giant* cockpit with transom door, and an enormous flybridge. The owner's stateroom in the 48 is huge and rivals those found in many motor yachts for size and comfort. Her easy-running hull will cruise efficiently at 16 knots with any of the diesel options, and the big 8V92TIs will reach a top speed of nearly 30 knots. With 600 gallons of fuel capacity and a cruising economy of close to 1 mpg at 15 knots, the 48 Convertible is indeed a long-range yacht. Note that a tournament-style flybridge was never offered. ❏

SPECIFICATIONS

Length	48'2"
Beam	15'2"
Draft	3'8"
Weight	40,000#
Clearance	14'3"
Water	200 Gals.
Fuel	600 Gals.
Cockpit	120 Sq. Ft.
Hull Type	Semi-Disp.
Designer	Ed Monk, Jr.

Production
1982–85

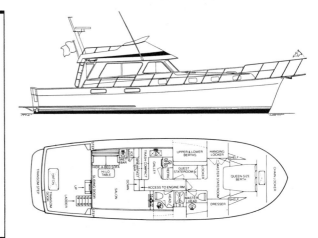

TOLLYCRAFT 53/57 COCKPIT MY

With the 53 and 57 MYs, Tollycraft made a clean break from their image as a conservative West Coast builder. This is a completely innovative design with an aggressive profile and dramatic styling features never before seen in a Tollycraft product. The 53 and 57 are basically the same boat with the 57 having a larger cockpit and additional fuel. They're built on Tollycraft's efficient Quadra-Lift hull — a modified-V design with 11° of deadrise aft and balsa coring above the waterline. The floorplan is unique: the pilothouse shares space with the galley, and a single port-side wing door in the salon complements the starboard sliding door in the pilothouse. The staterooms are forward (the full-width master is opulent), and both guest cabins share a common head. The engine room is entered from the cockpit — not the stand-up variety, but outboard access is excellent. The teak joinerwork in the salon and pilothouse is superb and the flybridge dimensions are extravagant. Early models with 550-hp 6V92s cruise around 18–19 knots. Optional 735-hp 8V92s cruise at 23 knots and the now-standard 665-hp MTUs cruise at 20–21 knots. ❑

SPECIFICATIONS

Length	52'11"/57'0"
Beam	16'11"
Draft	3'6"
Weight	55/58,000#
Clearance	16'3"
Water	280 Gals.
Fuel	800/1,200 Gal.
Cockpit	75/122 Sq. Ft.
Hull Type	Modified-V
Designer	Ed Monk, Jr.

Production
1989–Current

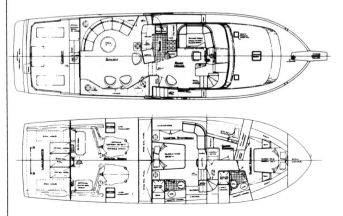

TOLLYCRAFT 61 MOTOR YACHT

Flagship of the Tollycraft fleet, the popular 61 MY is a handsome pilothouse design with tremendous eye appeal and excellent seakeeping qualities. Unlike conventional double-deck motor yachts this size, the 61's low profile keeps guests and crew at the water level for much of the boat's length. Built on an efficient hull with 10° of transom deadrise, her three-stateroom layout is extremely practical and the raised pilothouse floorplan offers obvious advantages for cruising in cold or wet weather. While the 61 was designed with Pacific Northwest passages in mind, her graceful profile and economical operation appeal to experienced yachtsmen in virtually every market. Practical features include covered sidedecks, a shallow keel for prop protection, cored hull construction, and a traditional teak interior. Most have been sold with optional 650-hp 8V92s (20 knots cruise/23 top) or the 735-hp 8V92s (22 knot cruise/25 top), although she's still a good performer with the 485-hp 6-71s (15–16 knots at cruise/19 knots top). The new 665-hp MTUs will cruise at 20 knots and hit 23 knots top. ❑

SPECIFICATIONS

Length ....61'2"
Beam.......................17'8"
Draft ....4'0"
Weight ....65,000#
Clearance ....17'6"
Water.................400 Gals.
Fuel ....1,160 Gals.
Cockpit..............64 Sq. Ft.
Hull Type.........Modified-V
Designer........Ed Monk, Jr.

Production
1983–Current

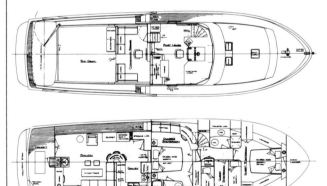

TOPAZ

Brief History

Topaz was founded in the mid-1970s by Pat Patterson, who previously had been building small boats from his fiberglass shop in Davidsonville, Maryland. His first production boat was a 28-foot open offshore fisherman. Always a small, limited-production builder (about 500 boats were built), the company was purchased by industry giant OMC in 1991. The prolonged industry recession caused OMC to temporarily discontinue production of Topaz models in late 1991.

Selected Topaz Models

Topaz 29 Sportfisherman   Topaz 37 Sportfisherman

Topaz 32 Sportfisherman   Topaz 39 FB Sportfisherman

Topaz 32 Royale   Topaz 39 Royale

Topaz 36 Sportfisherman   Topaz 44 FB Sportfisherman

Main Office

Topaz Boats, P.O. Box 68, Swansboro, NC 28584
919-326-1200

TOPAZ 29 SPORTFISHERMAN

The Topaz 29 Sportfisherman proved to be a popular boat over the years due to her rugged construction and single-minded approach to serious sportfishing activities. Like all Topaz models, the cockpit dominates the 29's layout and measures about half of her LOA. There is adequate room for a full-size marlin chair and a large insulated fish box is built into the sole. The raised bridgedeck conceals the engines and provides good visibility from the helm. A companion seat/tackle center (optional) is to port, and engine access is via a removable centerline hatch. Topaz offered an extensive list of optional gear to allow the boat to be set up according to her owner's requirements. Below, the cabin is simple and straightforward with upper and lower berths forward that will sleep three plus a mini galley and head. Recognized as a competent offshore fisherman, most Topaz 29s were sold with the factory tower and Volvo diesels. The 200-hp TAMD41s cruise at a fast 26–27 knots and reach a top speed of around 30 knots. Topaz sold the molds in 1988 and today the boat is in production as the Bimini 29. ❏

SPECIFICATIONS

Length	29'0"
Beam	10'3"
Draft	2'6"
Weight	8,100#
Clearance	NA
Water	30 Gals.
Fuel	225 Gals.
Cockpit	65 Sq. Ft.
Hull Type	Modified-V
Designer	Topaz

Production
1983–88

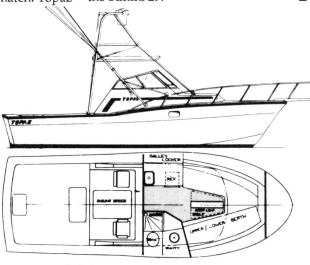

TOPAZ

TOPAZ 32 SPORTFISHERMAN

The Topaz 32 is an attractive open sportfisherman with a large cockpit, stable handling characteristics and good-quality construction. She was built on a conventional modified-V hull with 18° of transom deadrise, a relatively wide beam, and considerable flare at the bow. The hull is solid fiberglass and beefy aluminum frames support the engine mounts. Inside, the cabin accommodations are comfortable and extremely well finished with durable fabrics and superb teak joinerwork throughout. Notably, the V-berth cabin is private. The 32's bi-level cockpit is quite spacious and reinforced to handle a mounted fighting chair. An in-deck removable fish box is just forward of the transom and two roomy storage bins are also built into the cockpit sole. The raised bridgedeck provides excellent visibility from the helm console and a hatch between the seats offers good access to the diesel engines. (The entire bridgedeck can be raised for major engine work.) The Topaz 32 is available with 306-hp Volvo or 320-hp Cat diesels. She'll cruise around 25 knots with the Cats and reach a top speed of 29 knots. ❏

SPECIFICATIONS

Length	32'8"
Beam	12'2"
Draft	2'1"
Weight	16,500#
Clearance	NA
Water	40 Gals.
Fuel	300 Gals.
Cockpit	NA
Hull Type	Modified-V
Designer	Pat Patterson

Production
1986–91

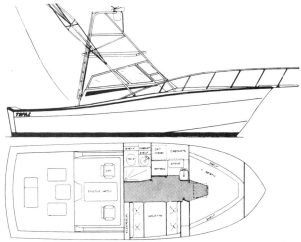

TOPAZ

TOPAZ 32 ROYALE

The Topaz 32 Royale incorporates the same dramatic styling and sleek European profile seen in the larger (and very popular) 39 Royale. Indeed, with her sweeping sheer and curved windshield, the Royale is easily one of the most stylish boats in her class. Designed to meet the needs of sportboat enthusiasts as well as the demands of offshore fishermen, the Royale is built on the proven modified-V hull (18° transom deadrise) used for the Topaz 32 SF. She features a bi-level cockpit layout with the engines located below the bridgedeck. Visibility from the raised portside helm position is excellent, and a lounge/dinette opposite provides seating for guests and anglers. The cockpit is large enough for a fighting chair and includes an in-deck fish box and removable floor. Below, the small cabin is arranged with V-berths (which double as a settee during the day), stand-up head, and a compact galley. No lightweight, many Royales were sold with 320-hp Cat diesels which will cruise at 21–22 knots. Larger 375-hp Cats cruise at 23 knots and reach a top speed of around 27–28 knots. ❑

SPECIFICATIONS

Length	32'8"
Beam	12'2"
Draft	2'1"
Weight	16,500#
Clearance	NA
Water	40 Gals.
Fuel	350 Gals.
Cockpit	NA
Hull Type	Modified-V
Designer	Pat Patterson

Production
1990-91

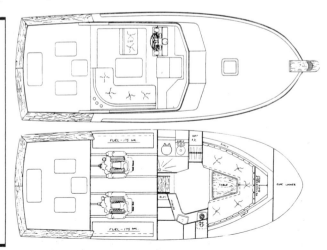

TOPAZ 36 SPORTFISHERMAN

Forerunner of the popular Topaz 37 and a good-selling boat in her own right, the Topaz 36 established the company's name with offshore fishermen in the early 1980s. She was constructed on a solid glass hull with a fairly wide beam and modest transom deadrise. With her low center of gravity, the 36 is a stable boat with a tower but her relatively flat aftersections can mean a hard ride in a chop and some extra steering in a following sea. She was designed as a dedicated sportfisherman and her spacious bi-level cockpit is arranged to meet the requirements of tournament-level anglers. There's room for a full-size tuna chair in the cockpit, and a large in-deck fishbox and teak covering boards were standard. Her belowdecks accommodations are comfortable and adequate for overnight expeditions with V-berths, convertible dinette, small galley, and stand-up head compartment with stall shower. The Topaz 36 was available with a variety of diesel engine options from Volvo, GM, and Caterpillar. The popular 355-hp Cats will cruise economically at 23 knots and reach 26–27 knots wide open. ❏

SPECIFICATIONS

Length......................36'2"
Beam.......................13'0"
Draft ....2'5"
Weight ....17,800#
Clearance ....NA
Water..................50 Gals.
Fuel ....300 Gals.
Cockpit........................NA
Hull Type.........Modified-V
Designer ......Pat Patterson

Production
1980-85

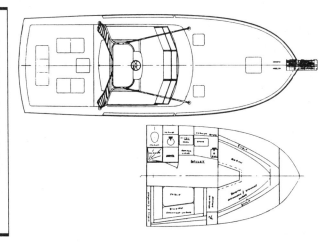

TOPAZ 37 SPORTFISHERMAN

A good-selling boat, the Topaz 37 Sportfisherman is a reworked version of the popular, tournament-proven Topaz 36 (1980–1985) with additional fuel, increased bow flare (for a dryer ride), a new and larger interior, and improved performance. Like all Topaz designs, the 37 was built on a modified-V bottom of solid fiberglass construction. Offshore, she has a reputation for a solid ride and good handling characteristics. The Topaz 37 is a stable boat at trolling speeds thanks to a low center of gravity and a wide 13' beam. The cockpit is a bi-level arrangement with the engines located beneath the raised bridgedeck. (Access to the engines is much improved from the Topaz 36.) The open helm provides good visibility and there's room on the console for flush-mounting electronics not fitted in an overhead cabinet. The cabin is set up to sleep four and includes a U-shaped dinette, complete galley, and a separate stall shower in the head. The only engines installed in the Topaz 37 were 375-hp Cat diesels. A good performer, she'll cruise at 25 knots and reach a top speed of around 28–29 knots. ❏

SPECIFICATIONS

Length......................37'6"
Beam.........................13'0"
Draft ....3'4"
Weight ....19,800#
Clearance ....NA
Water..................60 Gals.
Fuel ....350 Gals.
Cockpit..............81 Sq. Ft.
Hull Type.........Modified-V
Designer ......Pat Patterson

Production
1986–91

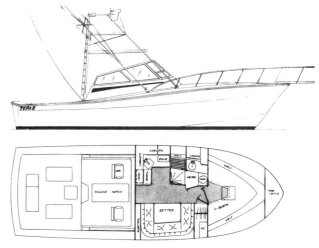

TOPAZ

TOPAZ 39 FB SPORTFISHERMAN

Featuring the distinctive profile of a pure-bred South Florida custom boat, the Topaz 39 Flybridge is an updated and much-improved version of the original Topaz 38 Flybridge (1984–87) with a new interior layout and enlarged engine room. She was built on a modified-V hull with a steep 17° of deadrise at the transom, moderate beam, and solid fiberglass construction. Aside from her outright sex appeal, serious anglers are attracted to the Topaz 39's large and uncluttered fishing cockpit (with standard tackle center, washdown and flush fish box) and her reliable offshore performance. Unlike most convertibles in this size range, the Topaz 39 was available only with a single-stateroom interior layout offering the convenience of a full-size dinette rather than a second guest cabin. A serving counter separates the mid-level galley from the main salon area, and the interior is finished with hand-rubbed teak woodwork and quality fabrics and hardware throughout. A good performer with 485-hp 6-71s, the Topaz 39 Flybridge Sportfisherman will cruise at a fast 27 knots and turn 30 knots wide open. ❏

SPECIFICATIONS

Length......................39'1"
Beam.......................13'0"
Draft ....3'5"
Weight ....24,500#
Clearance ....NA
Water................100 Gals.
Fuel ....400 Gals.
Cockpit.......................NA
Hull Type.........Modified-V
Designer ......Pat Patterson

Production
1987–91

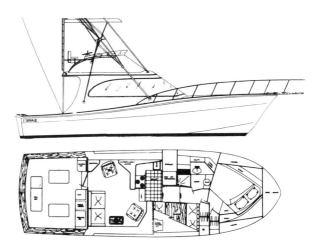

TOPAZ 39 ROYALE

Before Topaz ceased operations in 1991, the 39 Royale was one of the best-selling boats in the Topaz fleet. Designed to appeal to the upscale end of the family express cruiser market as well as the style-conscious sportfisherman, the 39 Royale is an extremely handsome sportboat design with an aggressive low-profile appearance and outstanding performance. She was built on a modified-V hull form with generous flare at the bow and 17° of deadrise at the transom — the same hull used in the production of the Topaz 39 FB. Her graceful lines are enhanced by the beau-tiful Eurostyle wraparound windshield and oval portlights in the hullsides. The cabin accommodations in the Royale are compact but still comfortable with berths for four or five depending on the floorplan. The head is fitted with a stall shower and the interior is finished with mica counters and teak woodwork. A popular sportboat, the 39 Royale is equally at home as a fisherman and comes equipped with a molded tackle center and a large in-deck fish box. A fast ride, the 39 Royale will cruise 30 knots with 485-hp 6-71s and reach 33–34 knots top.   ❏

SPECIFICATIONS

Length	39'1"
Beam	13'0"
Draft	3'1"
Weight	21,900#
Clearance	NA
Water	60 Gals.
Fuel	400 Gals.
Cockpit	NA
Hull Type	Modified-V
Designer	Pat Patterson

Production
1988–91

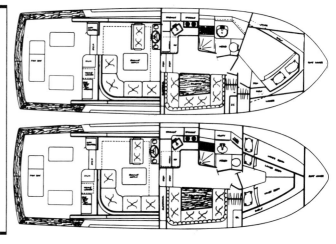

TOPAZ 44 FB SPORTFISHERMAN

A real attention-getter on any dock, the Topaz 44 never became a big seller (ony a few were built) in spite of her classic sportfish profile. Topaz introduced this model in 1987 in a further departure from the company's past reliance on the open skiff-type day boats. Retained, however, was the traditional Topaz emphasis on performance and offshore fishability. The cockpit is somewhat larger than most boats her size (the beam is carried well aft), and features a huge in-deck fishbox, molded tackle center with freezer, cockpit controls, and teak covering boards. A flybridge overhang provides protection from the weather, and the bridge ladder is mounted flush against the salon bulkhead. The flybridge is large for a 44-footer and features bench seating forward and starboard of the helm console. The 44's fashionable two-stateroom interior is composed of a spacious teak-paneled salon with the mid-level galley area divided from the salon by a breakfast bar. Easily serviced in a spacious engine room, the standard 565-hp 6V92 diesels will cruise the Topaz 44 at 26–27 knots and reach a top speed of around 30 knots.   ❏

SPECIFICATIONS

Length	44'3"
Beam	15'4"
Draft	3'11"
Weight	37,500#
Clearance	12'8"
Water	125 Gals.
Fuel	640 Gals.
Cockpit	152 Sq. Ft.
Hull Type	Modified-V
Designer	Topaz

Production
1987–89

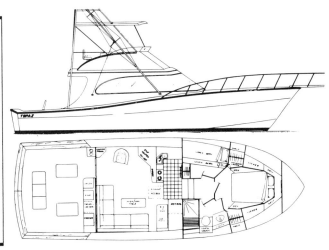

TOPAZ

TROJAN

Brief History

Trojan Yachts was founded in 1949 in Lancaster, PA, an area of strong Amish influence. Early boats were small wooden runabouts, and in 1961 the company introduced the famous 31' Sea Voyager, building some 3,000 over the next decade. Trojan purchased the old Shepherd Boat Company (of Canada) in 1966, thereby moving into the motor yacht market. The conversion to fiberglass was made in 1970. The late 1970s were bad times for Trojan, but in 1981 the company was revitalized with the introduction of the then-revolutionary International series of Eurostyle express boats. Today Trojan is in trouble again and production was suspended in early 1992.

Selected Trojan Inboard Models

Trojan 28 Sedan Cruiser
Trojan 30 Sport Cruiser
Trojan 30 FB Express
Trojan 32 Sedan
Trojan 10 Meter Express
Trojan 10 Meter Sedan
Trojan 10 Meter Mid Cabin
Trojan 10.8 Meter Convertible
Trojan 36 Tri Cabin
Trojan 36 Convertible
Trojan 11 Meter Express (Early)

Trojan 11 Meter Express
Trojan 11 Meter Sedan
Trojan 12 Meter Convertible
Trojan 12 Meter Motor Yacht
Trojan 12 Meter Express
Trojan 40 Motor Yacht
Trojan 13 Meter Express
Trojan 44 Convertible
Trojan 44 Motor Yacht
Trojan 14 Meter Convertible

Main Office

Trojan Yachts, P.O. Box 3571, Lancaster, PA 17603
717-397-2471

615

TROJAN 28 SEDAN CRUISER

The Trojan 28 Sedan is a *big* boat for her length. Indeed, her wide 12'3" beam would be considered normal for most 32-footers. The use of V-drives allows the cabin level to be two steps lower than the cockpit sole, which results in an attractive, somewhat low-profile appearance. Inside, the 28 Sedan boasts overnight berths for seven — five in the main cabin (the settee backrests fold up) and two forward. The lower helm and galley are fitted in the main cabin area together with a dinette. The head compartment is a tight fit. While the cockpit is small, five persons can find seating on the flybridge. Normally that much weight on the flybridge of any 28' boat would be too much, but the 28's wide beam seems to handle it reasonably well. On the downside, the standard fuel tankage is only 100 gallons (an additional 50 gallons was optional), and the cabin windows are made of plastic. Those equipped with twin 225-hp Chrysler engines will cruise at around 20 knots and burn 21 gph. Top speed is 27–28 knots at 35 gph. Overall, the Trojan 28 is a versatile family cruiser for inland lakes and coastal cruising. ❑

SPECIFICATIONS

Length	28'2"
Length WL	23'11"
Beam	12'3"
Draft	2'0"
Weight	7,700#
Clearance	11'6"
Water	60 Gals.
Fuel	100 Gals.
Cockpit	NA
Hull Type	Modified-V
Designer	Trojan

Production
1976–79

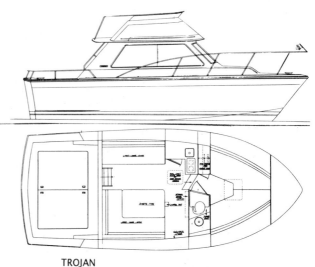

TROJAN

TROJAN 30 SPORT CRUISER

When she was introduced in 1973, the Trojan 30 Sport Cruiser was something of a radical design. Trojan ads began by saying, "Don't laugh. The more serious you are about fishing, the less strange she looks." The Sport Cruiser was built on a solid fiberglass hull with a fairly wide beam and 12° of deadrise at the transom. With her large bi-level cockpit and spacious, full-width tournament-style flybridge, the Sport Cruiser (called the Clean Machine by many) can indeed be fished, but with a 160-gallon fuel supply she's not heading too far offshore. (Early models had only 100 gallons of fuel.) The cabin layout sleeps six and includes a convertible dinette and settee, V-berths forward, and a small galley area. The head compartment is located just inside the salon door for easy outside access. The teak interior cabinetry and woodwork are nicely done but storage space is limited both in the cabin and the cockpit. Up to four persons can be seated comfortably on the flybridge. Twin 225-hp Chrysler gas engines (318-cid) will cruise the Sport Cruiser at 20 knots at only 17–18 gph. Top speed is about 27 knots. ❏

SPECIFICATIONS

Length	30'2"
Beam	11'1"
Draft	2'2"
Weight	8,100#
Clearance	9'5"
Water	33 Gals.
Fuel	160 Gals.
Cockpit	80 Sq. Ft.
Hull Type	Modified-V
Designer	Trojan

Production
1973–79

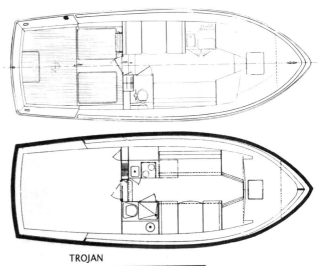

TROJAN

TROJAN 30 FB EXPRESS

The Trojan 30 Flybridge Express was a moderately priced cruiser designed to appeal to the family market. Available in either a hardtop or flybridge version, these were fairly basic boats with an open lower helm and practical cabin accommodations with berths for six. Early models carried only 100 gallons of fuel which severely limited the cruising range of the Trojan 30s. In 1978, a number of design changes were made to the boat, including the removal of the foredeck bench seating in favor of windows to brighten up the interior. The head was also relocated and expanded by 10", and a built-in stove was added in the galley. The cockpit is roomy enough for entertaining or weekend fishing activities and the small flybridge has seating for three. Engine access is via removable hatches in the cockpit sole. A choice of single or twin gas engines was offered. With the popular 225-hp Chrysler gas inboards, the Trojan 30 FB Express can be expected to cruise around 20 knots with a top speed of about 27 knots. The larger 250-hp Chryslers will add one or two knots to those speeds. ❏

SPECIFICATIONS

Length......................30'0"
Beam........................11'0"
Draft ....2'1"
Weight..................8,100#
Clearance ....11'9"
Water...................33 Gals.
Fuel...........100/160 Gals.
Cockpit........................NA
Hull Type.........Modified-V
Designer ....Trojan

Production
1975–79

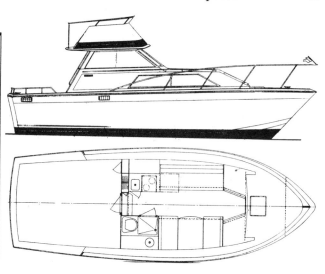

TROJAN

TROJAN 32 SEDAN

There have been more Trojan 32s built than any other fiberglass boat over 30 feet. (For the record, some 2,700 have been sold to date.) Her appeal has always been the combination of an affordable price tag, contemporary design, a roomy interior, good handling, and generally low operating costs. As a versatile family cruiser the Trojan 32 obviously met the demands of a great many owners. There have been several configurations offered over the years including a hardtop express model, a flybridge express, and the Flybridge Sedan pictured above. The Sedan — with its large salon and a relatively small cockpit — became the most popular because of her spacious interior accommodations. The solid fiberglass, modified-V hull (9° deadrise aft) planes easily and incorporates considerable flare at the bow. A stable and good-running boat, cruising speed with 250-hp Chrysler engines is approximately 18–19 knots and the top speed is around 25 knots. Add 1–2 knots for more recent models equipped with the 270-hp Crusaders. The previously optional 220-gallon fuel capacity became standard in 1984. ❑

SPECIFICATIONS

Length	32'0"
Length WL	27'0"
Beam	13'0"
Draft	2'6"
Weight	12,000#
Clearance	12'6"
Water	40 Gals.
Fuel	120/220 Gals.
Cockpit	NA
Hull Type	Modified-V
Designer	Trojan

Production
1973–92

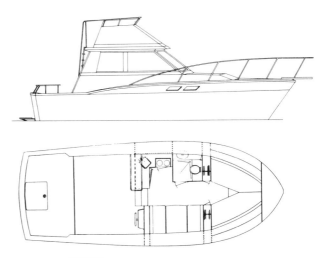

TROJAN 10 METER EXPRESS

The first of Trojan's International series, the 10 Meter Express was a breakthrough design when she was introduced in 1981. Boldly styled and featuring all-new modular construction, the "experts" at first had a field day with the Trojan 10 Meter calling her too wide and too glitzy for the conservative American market. Nevertheless, the 10 Meter quickly captured the public's imagination and soon became a marketing success. The original, somewhat gaudy interior was toned down in later years but her Mediterranean styling, curved bulkheads, and lush Eurostyle decor marked the beginning of today's modern family sportboats. The 10 Meter (and all subsequent Trojan International models) was built on a patented DeltaConic hull design which provides a dry and remarkably stable ride across a wide range of sea conditions. Note the side exhaust ports. In 1982, a 10 Meter Aft Cabin model became available, lasting only through the 1985 model year. Standard Crusader 454-cid gas engines cruise the Trojan 10 Meter Express at a steady 19–20 knots with a top speed of around 28 knots. ❏

SPECIFICATIONS

Length	33'0"
Beam	13'0"
Draft	2'0"
Weight	11,250#
Clearance	9'4"
Water	40 Gals.
Fuel	242 Gals.
Cockpit	NA
Hull Type	Modified-V
Designer	H. Schoell

Production
1981–89

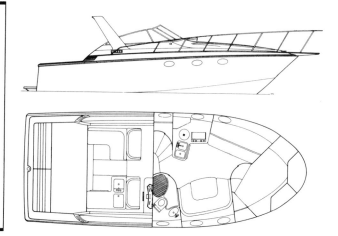

TROJAN

TROJAN 10 METER SEDAN

The Trojan 10 Meter Sedan was built on the same DeltaConic hull form used in the original 10 Meter Express — a comfortable design providing a dry and stable ride. A good-looking family sedan, the cockpit is reasonably large and the extra-wide 13' beam provides exceptional interior volume below. In the original Sedan, the layout from the companionway forward was the same as in the early 10 Meter Express models. The resulting chopped-up floorplan proved unpopular with the public and a revised interior evolved in 1984 with a more open salon/dinette layout with

teak trim replacing the earlier brushed aluminum and bare fiberglass surfaces. The interior was updated again in 1988 and these later 10 Meter Sedans feature a luxurious and more contemporary decor. Good quality hardware, fabrics, appliances and furnishings are found throughout. With standard 454-cid Crusader gas engines, the cruising speed of the 10 Meter Sedan is 18 knots and the top speed is around 27–28 knots. Note that Trojan also offered the 10 Meter in Flybridge Express and Aft Cabin models built on this same hull mold. ❏

SPECIFICATIONS

Length	33'0"
Beam	13'0"
Draft	2'0"
Weight	14,250#
Clearance	12'2"
Water	40/55 Gals.
Fuel	242 Gals.
Cockpit	60 Sq. Ft.
Hull Type	Modified-V
Designer	H. Schoell

Production
1982–89

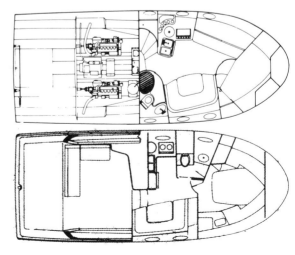

TROJAN

TROJAN 10 METER MID CABIN

Sharing the same hull and exterior profile as the 10 Meter Express, the Trojan 10 Meter Mid Cabin featured a private stateroom located beneath the raised bridgedeck. The interior accommodations provide owner and guests with a modern Eurostyle well-arranged for weekend family cruising. The interior of the 10 Meter Mid Cabin is impressive — white high-pressure laminates and pastel colors dominate the decor and curved cabinets and bulkheads mark her modern styling. The U-shaped settee in the mid cabin converts to a comfortable double berth at night.

The modern, all-white galley of the Trojan is fitted with top-quality hardware and stylish fixtures. Outside, the cockpit will seat four at the helm and companion seats, and another four at the transom with the optional bench seating. A new and very appealing instrument panel was added in 1989, and in 1990 a new bolt-on swim platform and powder-coated white rails became standard. With the standard 454-cid gas engines, the Trojan 10 Meter Mid Cabin will cruise at a respectable 17–18 knots with a top speed of around 26 knots. ❑

SPECIFICATIONS

Length	33'0"
Beam	13'0"
Draft	2'0"
Weight	12,500#
Clearance	9'4" w/Arch
Water	55 Gals.
Fuel	250 Gals.
Cockpit	NA
Hull Type	Modified-V
Designer	H. Schoell

Production
1986–92

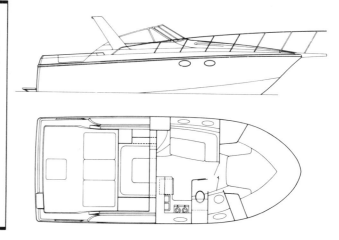

TROJAN

TROJAN 10.8 METER CONVERTIBLE

The Trojan 10.8 Meter Convertible is essentially a stretched version of the earlier 10 Meter Sedan. Both are good-looking designs with dramatic European styling and attractive profiles. The single-piece hull construction and interior layouts are the same in both boats, the difference being the larger cockpit and additional fuel capacity of the 10.8 Meter. Although not designed as a sportfishing boat, a transom door and bait prep-center were standard equipment and the cockpit is large enough for a couple of anglers. Indeed, the added cockpit space is a big improvement over her predecessor and makes the 10.8 Meter a more versatile family cruiser. Inside, the salon flows easily into the galley and dinette area and wraparound cabin windows provide an abundance of natural lighting. A two-stateroom floorplan became available in 1991. Note that the engine room in this boat is a tight fit and access to the motors is difficult. The flybridge will seat four and a Eurostyle helm console was introduced in 1989. Standard 454-cid gas engines will cruise at 17–18 knots and reach around 26 knots wide open. ❑

SPECIFICATIONS

Length	35'4"
Beam	13'0"
Draft	2'4"
Weight	15,000#
Clearance	12'2"
Water	55 Gals.
Fuel	325 Gals.
Cockpit	87 Sq. Ft.
Hull Type	Modified-V
Designer	H. Schoell

Production
1986–92

TROJAN

TROJAN 36 TRI CABIN

Trojan introduced this durable aft cabin design back in 1970 as the 36 Sea Raider. Built on a fiberglass hull with a wooden deckhouse and teak cockpit and decks, the transition to all-fiberglass construction was made in 1972, when she was renamed the 36 Tri Cabin. Her durable modified-V hull (9° deadrise) was also used in the production of the Trojan 36 Convertible. The long-running popularity of the Cabin has much to do with both the price and the privacy afforded by her double-cabin floorplan. Three galley-up layouts were offered over the years with the lat-est (introduced in 1986) featuring centerline double berths fore and aft and a new U-shaped galley in the salon. Although diesels were an option, the majority of the Tri Cabins were sold with twin gas power. Note that the Sea Raider and a few of the early model Tri Cabins were fitted with V-drives with the engines located beneath the berths in the owner's stateroom (!). With the 250-hp Chryslers, the 36 Tri Cabin will cruise at 16 knots and reach about 23 knots wide open. During 1976–78 a flybridge model was offered with the same interior layout.   ❏

SPECIFICATIONS

Length	36'0"
Length WL	NA
Beam	13'0"
Draft	2'11"
Weight	17,500#
Clearance	12'3"
Water	66/85 Gals.
Fuel	150/220/300 Gals.
Hull Type	Modified-V
Designer	Trojan

Production
1970–87

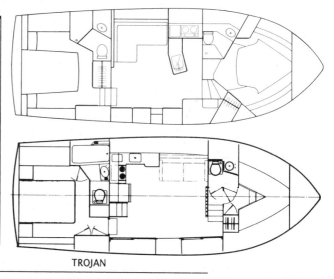

TROJAN

TROJAN 36 CONVERTIBLE

The Trojan 36 Convertible has been one of the most popular boats in her size range for many years. Both her lines and basic interior layout remained essentially the same since she was introduced back in 1972. The standard floorplan in the Trojan 36 includes a comfortable salon with optional lower helm, a convenient mid-level galley, and a full dinette. An optional two-stateroom interior was also offered which traded the dinette for a small guest cabin. The cockpit is adequate for fishing but becomes small in a hurry when a chair is mounted. Above, the tournament-style flybridge provides seating for up to five. All Trojan 36 Convertibles were built with a solid fiberglass hull (9° deadrise) and cored decks and super-structure. A teak cockpit sole was standard through 1976. Up until the last few years of production, the standard fuel capacity was only 250 gallons with an extra 100 gallons optional. Always a popular and affordable boat on the used market, most were powered with 454-cid Chrysler or Crusader gas engines. The average cruising speed is around 19 knots at and the top speed is 27–28 knots. ❏

SPECIFICATIONS

Length	36'0"
Beam	13'0"
Draft	2'11"
Weight	16,000#
Clearance	13'0"
Water	80 Gals.
Fuel	250/350 Gals.
Cockpit	75 Sq. Ft.
Hull Type	Modified-V
Designer	Trojan

Production
1972–89

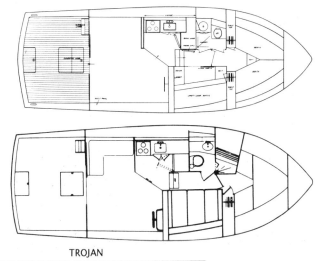

TROJAN

TROJAN 11 METER EXPRESS (EARLY)

The 11 Meter Express was the third in the series of International designs following the original 10 Meter Express in 1981 and the less-successful 9 Meter Express in 1982. Modular construction allowed the 11 Meter hull to be built in four different model configurations: an open express, a flybridge sedan, an express aft cabin, or a sedan aft cabin. She was built on a wide hull with 14° of deadrise at the transom. The 11 Meter series was the first to use balsa coring in the hull bottom in addition to the hullsides and deck. The stylish interior accommodations are a blend of round-ed corners, indirect lighting, modern fabrics, and bright-colored laminates. The curved doors to the stateroom and head are pneumatic — push a button and they automatically open or close. Outside, the bi-level cockpit places the helm in an elevated position for good visibility. Crusader 454-cid gas engines were standard in the 11 Meter Express (19 knots cruise/28 knots top), with 375-hp Cat diesels (24 cruise/28 knots top) and 485-hp 6-71s (29 knots cruise/ 32 top) offered as options. She was replaced in 1990 with a new 11 Meter Express model. ❏

SPECIFICATIONS

Length	37'6"
Beam	14'0"
Draft	3'3"
Weight	16,800#
Clearance	9'4"
Water	100 Gals.
Fuel	350 Gals.
Cockpit	NA
Hull Type	Modified-V
Designer	H. Schoell

Production
1983–89

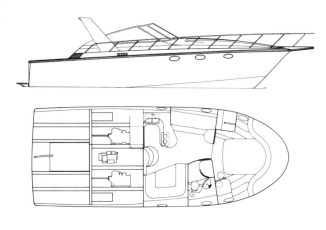

TROJAN 11 METER EXPRESS

In 1989 the highly acclaimed 12 Meter Express put Trojan back on top in American sportboat design. The newer 11 Meter Express (built on the original 11 Meter hull) incorporates the same graceful lines and balanced profile of the 12 Meter, but the cabin layout is a clear departure from those of other express cruisers in her class. Instead of trotting out yet another mid-cabin design, the 11 Meter has a real portside master stateroom with private access to a very roomy head and shower. Guests can sleep in the (non-private) lounge/dinette area forward — no guessing about who sleeps well on this boat. The 11 Meter's layout is unique and manages to provide a great owner's cabin without intruding into the expansive salon. Features include an integral swim platform, award-winning helm, fold-away stern seat, spacious cockpit, and walk-through transom door. A pair of 360-hp (502 cid) gas engines will cruise at 18 knots and reach a top speed of around 27–28 knots. Diesel options include 425-hp Cats (24 knots cruise/28 knots top) and 485-hp 6-71TIs (29 knots cruise/32 knots wide open). ❏

SPECIFICATIONS

Length	39'0"
Length WL	NA
Beam	14'0"
Draft	3'3"
Weight	16,800#
Clearance	9'4"
Water	100 Gals.
Fuel	350 Gals.
Hull Type	Modified-V
Designer	H. Schoell

Production
1990–92

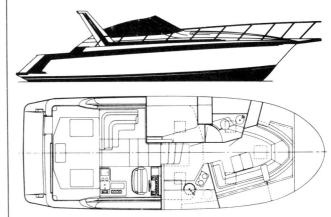

TROJAN 11 METER SEDAN

A sleek profile and dramatic hull graphics make the Trojan 11 Meter Sedan a real eye-catcher at dockside. Her wide DeltaConic hull is fully cored and features 14° of transom deadrise and side-dumping exhausts. Along with the Trojan 10 Meter Sedan introduced in 1982, the 11 Meter Sedan was one of the early Med-style convertibles introduced to the American market. The modern European interior accommodations are plush and very appealing. A wet bar and railing separate the salon from the step-down galley and dinette. A stall shower is included in the head and a tapered island berth dominates the luxurious forward stateroom. In most respects, the 11 Meter Sedan is more family cruiser than sportfisherman. The cockpit is large enough for light tackle fishing but most anglers will find it too small for serious bluewater activities. With standard 454-cid Crusader gas engines, the Trojan 11 Meter Sedan will cruise at around 18 knots and reach a top speed of 27–28 knots. Caterpillar 375-hp diesels were a popular option: they cruise around 23 knots and reach 26–27 knots top. ❏

SPECIFICATIONS

Length	37'6"
Beam	14'0"
Draft	3'5"
Weight	18,000#
Clearance	12'6"
Water	100 Gals.
Fuel	350 Gals.
Cockpit	NA
Hull Type	Modified-V
Designer	H. Schoell

Production
1985–88

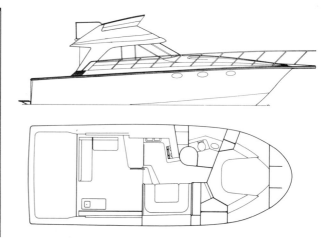

TROJAN

TROJAN 12 METER CONVERTIBLE

Trojan's 12 Meter Convertible was clearly aimed at the upscale end of the sportfishing market. She retains the bold styling and luxurious accommodations of others in the International series but the cockpit is much larger than in the earlier sedan models. The 12 Meter is, in fact, a good-looking 40-footer with a profile that even the most hard-core angler will appreciate. Since the accent is on fishability, the cockpit is set up with built-in fish boxes, seawater washdown, transom door, and tackle center. Her low-profile flybridge provides a good view of the cockpit action below and the stylish interior comes standard with a built-in entertainment center, wet bar, and icemaker. Until 1989, the dinette in the single-stateroom version could be replaced with a guest cabin for a two-stateroom floorplan. A revised two-stateroom layout with a deckhouse settee was introduced for 1990. Crusader 454-cid gas engines were standard. Optional 375-hp Cats deliver a cruising speed of 22 knots. The larger 485-hp 6-71s will cruise the 12 Meter at a fast 27 knots and reach around 30 knots wide open. ❑

SPECIFICATIONS

Length	39'9"
Beam	14'3"
Draft	3'6"
Weight	19,000#
Clearance	12'6"
Water	100 Gals.
Fuel	400 Gals.
Cockpit	110 Sq. Ft.
Hull Type	Modified-V
Designer	H. Schoell

Production
1986–92

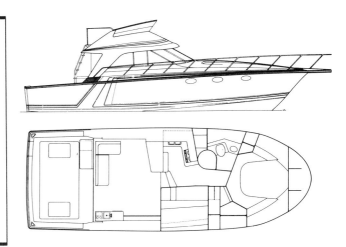

TROJAN

TROJAN 12 METER MOTOR YACHT

Built on the same DeltaConic hull used in the production of the 12 Meter Convertible, the Trojan 12 Meter MY is a modern flush deck family cruiser with attractive lines and a very upscale interior. Indeed, the interior appointments aboard the 12 Meter MY are slightly overwhelming to the first-time visitor. The expansive salon has a decidedly high-fashion decor with a unique wraparound dinette and quality fabrics and appliances throughout. Trojan's engineers obviously went the extra mile in designing this yacht and the detailing is quite good. A hidden entertainment center rises from a counter in the salon at the touch of a button and distinctive European galley fixtures add to the impression of luxury. The spacious salon dimensions come at the expense of somewhat small staterooms, but Trojan has managed to include a stall shower in each head plus an exceptionally large galley area. Optional 375-hp Cat diesels provide a cruising speed of 19–20 knots, and 450-hp 6-71s will cruise the Trojan 12 Meter MY at a fast 24 knots with a top speed of around 27 knots. ❑

SPECIFICATIONS

Length	39'9"
Length WL	NA
Beam	14'3"
Draft	3'8"
Weight	19,000#
Clearance	NA
Water	150 Gals.
Fuel	400 Gals.
Hull Type	Modified-V
Designer	H. Schoell

Production
1987–92

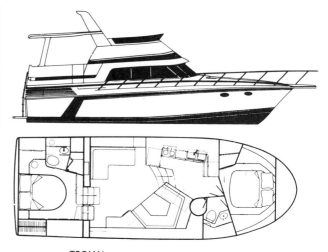

TROJAN

TROJAN 12 METER EXPRESS

Any rumblings heard in recent years to the effect that Trojan's express models were beginning to show their age were dispelled with the introduction of the Trojan 12 Meter Express in 1989. Built on a fully cored hull with prop pockets and plenty of beam, the 12 Meter inherited the modern styling of earlier International models with several innovative features of her own. Prominent among them is a stylish integral swim platform with an open transom and hidden storage lockers. The 12 Meter's beautifully curved windshield adds much to her sleek profile and the huge cockpit is fitted with an hydraulically operated in-deck storage well for an inflatable. The twin lounges in the cockpit can seat a dozen and a wet bar is standard. Notable, too, are the all-white deck hardware and rails, and especially her space-age helm console. The wide open Eurostyle interior features a port side settee that uniquely converts into a private stateroom — a rather innovative design feature. With optional 485-hp 6-71s, the Trojan 12 Meter Express will cruise at a fast 27 knots with a top speed of around 30 knots. ❑

SPECIFICATIONS

Length	41'0"
Beam	14'3"
Draft	3'8"
Weight	18,000#
Clearance	NA
Water	95 Gals.
Fuel	325 Gals.
Cockpit	NA
Hull Type	Modified-V
Designer	H. Schoell

Production
1989–92

TROJAN

TROJAN 40 MOTOR YACHT

Designed with a "dual mode" hull capable of economical operation at slower displacement speeds and higher speed planing performance with larger engines, the 40 MY was Trojan's response to the fuel uncertainties of the late 1970s. The hull form has a slight hump forward on the underbody (which is quite unique) with wide 8" chine flats for lift. The relatively long waterline length results in an expansive interior floorplan. The spacious salon measures a full 10'x13' and is separated from the galley by a convenient serving bar. Teak paneling and trim were used throughout the interior. A notable feature of the Trojan 40 Motor Yacht is the quiet underwater exhaust system — only a few production builders were using them in the early 1980s. Several diesel options were offered with gas engines as standard. The popular GM 6-71Ns (rated at 310-hp from J&T) burn 7–8 gph at an 8-knot displacement speed and cruise at approximately 14–15 knots. Top speed is 17 knots. Note that the Trojan 47 Yacht Fisherman (the same boat with the addition of a 7' cockpit) runs about two knots faster with the same engines. ❏

SPECIFICATIONS

Length	40'3"
Length WL	NA
Beam	14'3"
Draft	3'10"
Weight	29,000#
Clearance	15'6" w/Arch
Water	125 Gals.
Fuel	445 Gals.
Hull Type	Modified-V
Designer	Jim Wynne

Production
1979–84

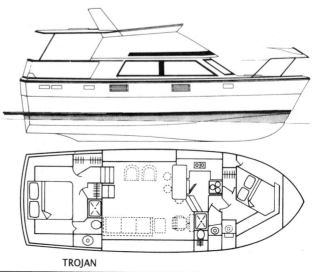

TROJAN

TROJAN 13 METER EXPRESS

The most notable feature of the Trojan 13 Meter Express is her massive beam — the cockpit and cabin proportions in this boat are truly immense. Indeed, the 13 Meter is so wide that she'll be a tight fit in many 45' slips. The expanded DeltaConic hull (12° transom deadrise) is fully cored with end-grain balsa for weight reduction and increased strength, and the exhausts exit from the hullsides at the waterline. Inside, her ultra-modern two-stateroom interior is a tasteful blend of designer fabrics and curved Formica surfaces. The dinette table lowers electrically at the touch of a switch when an extra double berth is required. Additional features include push-button pneumatic sliding doors, a stylish helm console, colorful hull graphics, and a convention-size cockpit. Visibility from the raised helm position is excellent and a center section of the windshield can be opened electrically for ventilation. Optional 735-hp 8V92 diesels will provide an honest 30-knot cruising speed and a top speed of 32+ knots. Note that a short-lived Trojan 13 Meter FB Sedan model ran from 1986–87. ❏

SPECIFICATIONS

Length	43'0"
Beam	16'3"
Draft	3'2"
Weight	24,000#
Clearance	10'1"
Water	175 Gals.
Fuel	510 Gals.
Cockpit	NA
Hull Type	Modified-V
Designer	H. Schoell

Production
1984–90

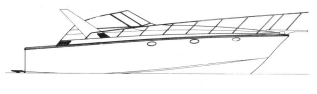

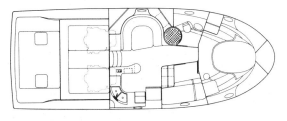

TROJAN 44 CONVERTIBLE

The Trojan 44 Convertible was built on the same hull as the Trojan 44 Motor Yacht — a modified-V affair with a modest 8° of deadrise aft, plenty of bow flare, and a long skeg ending just forward of the shaft struts. With her sweeping sheer, the profile of the 44 Convertible is quite handsome. Notably, this was Trojan's first (and only) attempt at a serious sportfisherman prior to the International series. There were two interior arrangements: Plan "A" was a Mediterranean version with crew quarters forward with one head for the huge master stateroom and guest cabin; Plan "B" (which became standard) is a more conventional layout with a deckhouse galley, two staterooms, and two heads. Outside, the 44's cockpit is huge with room for a mounted chair and optional tackle center and controls. Several diesel options were available during her production run. The Cummins VT-903-Ms (400-hp) provide a top speed of 23 knots and an average cruising speed of about 19 knots. Market-wise, the Trojan 44 Convertible was not considered a notably successful sportfishing design. ❑

SPECIFICATIONS	
Length	43'3"
Beam	14'11"
Draft	3'9"
Weight	33,750#
Clearance	12'6"
Water	200 Gals.
Fuel, Std	400 Gals.
Fuel, Opt	700 Gals.
Cockpit	150 Sq. Ft.
Hull Type	Modified-V
Designer	Trojan

Production
1974–78

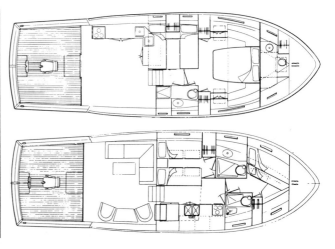

TROJAN 44 MOTOR YACHT

The original Trojan 44 MY was introduced in 1974 as an all-fiberglass replacement for the highly successful Trojan 42 mahogany-planked motor yacht. She was extensively redesigned in 1978 (see above) with an all-new superstructure, wing doors for the afterdeck, and a revised wraparound bridge profile and she's a much-improved boat from the early model. The hull has a sharp entry forward, a well-flared bow, innovative underwater exhausts, and hard chines aft. A long keel and deep rudders aid in tracking. (Both the 44 MY and 44 Convertible share this same hull.) Wide sidedecks allow for secure passage around the house and there's guest seating on the foredeck. The interior accommodations are about average for a 44' motor yacht with a walkaround queen berth in the aft stateroom, traditional teak paneling in the salon, a U-shaped galley, and two head compartments. (A guest cabin replaced the dinette in the three-stateroom model.) Used Trojan 44 MYs are often found with the popular 310-hp GM 6-71N diesels. These engines provide a cruising speed of 15–16 knots and a top speed of around 18 knots. ❏

SPECIFICATIONS

Length	44'3"
Length WL	38'0"
Beam	14'11"
Draft	4'0"
Weight	32,000#
Clearance	17'2"
Water	120 Gals.
Fuel	420/520 Gals.
Hull Type	Modified-V
Designer	Trojan

Production
1974–84

TROJAN

TROJAN 14 METER CONVERTIBLE

The Trojan 14 Meter Convertible was built on a stretched 13 Meter hull with 12° of deadrise at the transom, fairly low freeboard, and a wide 16'3" beam. She has essentially the same interior floorplan as the previous 13 Meter Sedan (1986–87) with the extra three feet of length used to create a much larger cockpit area. A stylish and completely modern convertible design, everything about the 14 Meter Convertible is on a grand scale. The extra beam creates huge volumes of space in both the cockpit and the interior. Although aimed at the sportfishing market, her luxurious two-stateroom floorplan features an extravagant main salon, a spacious galley and two staterooms — each with a double berth and private head compartment with stall shower. Outside, the uncluttered fishing cockpit is arranged for tournament-level activities with a transom door and tackle center to port. The huge flybridge has its own wet bar and seating for as many as ten. Optional 750-hp 8V92s will cruise the Trojan 14 Meter Convertible at 26 knots and reach a top speed of 29 knots. ❑

SPECIFICATIONS

Length	46'3"
Beam	16'3"
Draft	3'6"
Weight	34,000#
Clearance	13'7"
Water	175 Gals.
Fuel	710 Gals.
Cockpit	130 Sq. Ft.
Hull Type	Modified-V
Designer	H. Schoell

Production
1988–92

TROJAN

UNIFLITE

Brief History

Uniflite's first production moldel was a 17-foot runabout introduced in 1957. Uniflite was among the first to build in fiberglass and by the early 1970s the company was one of the largest builders on the West Coast and the Navy's biggest supplier of fiberglass boats. Conservative designs built to rugged standards, Uniflites were plagued with gelcoat blistering problems during their last decade of production. The company closed in 1984 and their molds were acquired by Chris Craft the following year.

Selected Uniflite Models

Uniflite 28 Salty Dog   Uniflite 37 Coastal Cruiser
Uniflite 28 Mega   Uniflite 38 Convertible
Uniflite 32 Sport Sedan   Uniflite 42 Double Cabin
Uniflite 34 Sport Sedan   Uniflite 42 Convertible
Uniflite 36 Sport Sedan   Uniflite 48 Convertible
Uniflite 36 Double Cabin   Uniflite 48 Yacht Fisherman

Main Office

Uniflites were built in Bellingham, WA.
The company is no longer in production.

UNIFLITE 28 SALTY DOG

The Uniflite 28 Salty Dog has long been recognized as a sturdy and well-crafted day fisherman. With nearly 100 sq. ft. of usable space in her bi-level cockpit, the Salty Dog has one of the best fishing platforms in her size range. A molded-in fish well was standard, and the engine access is very good. Although the Salty Dog is rather a plain-Jane boat in her stock form, she is nonetheless a very capable little fishing machine and the addition of a tower and outriggers adds much to her appearance. The cabin accommodations are close to the bare basics but still com-fortable for an occasional offshore weekend. The elevated portside helm is close to the action and visibility is excellent. The Salty Dog came with several power options including single and twin installations of either gas or diesel engines. The standard single Crusader 270-hp gas engine will cruise at 17 knots (25 knots top), and the twin 220s cruise at around 22 knots and reach 30+ wide open. Note that the fuel capacity was increased in 1982. Following Uniflite's demise in 1984, the Salty Dog enjoyed brief resurgence as Chris Craft 282 SF in 1985–86. ❏

SPECIFICATIONS

Length	28'2"
Length WL	24'5"
Beam	10'10"
Draft	2'10"
Weight	9,000#
Clearance	8'0"
Water	30 Gals.
Fuel	150/210 Gals.
Cockpit	NA
Hull Type	Modified-V
Designer	Uniflite

Production
1971–1984

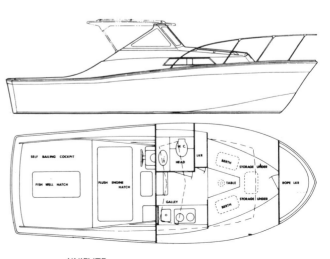

UNIFLITE 28 MEGA

Built on the 28-foot hull of the Salty Dog, the Uniflite 28 Mega is a compact family cruiser with attractive lines and a fairly roomy accommodation plan. With nearly 11 feet of beam, the Mega offers a comfortable salon area complete with an L-shaped dinette and a facing settee. Most were sold with the optional lower helm station to port. The large wraparound cabin windows provide good outdoor visibility and abundant natural lighting, and the teak joinerwork and cabinetry are well crafted. The galley in the Mega 28 is two steps down from the salon level and a compact stand-up head with shower is opposite to port. Outside, the cockpit area is on the small side but large enough for a couple of folding fishing chairs. Access to the engines and V-drives is via removable hatches in the cockpit sole. Seating for five people is provided on the bridge although a prudent helmsman is unlikely to want that much weight topside in anything but calm water. Like many Uniflites of her era, gelcoat blisters are a common problem. Twin 220-hp Crusaders cruise the Uniflite 28 Mega at 20–21 knots with a top speed of around 27 knots. ❏

SPECIFICATIONS

Length	28'2"
Length WL	25'5"
Beam	10'10"
Draft	2'10"
Weight	10,500#
Clearance	10'0"
Water	50 Gals.
Fuel	140 Gals.
Cockpit	NA
Hull Type	Modified-V
Designer	Uniflite

Production
1977–84

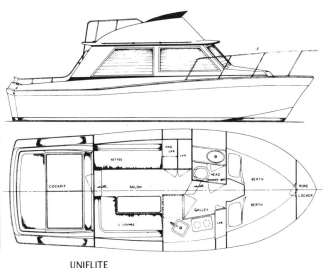

UNIFLITE

UNIFLITE 32 SPORT SEDAN

A versatile and popular boat for many years, the Uniflite 32 Sport Sedan was clearly designed with family cruising in mind. She was built on a solid, one-piece fiberglass hull with a wide beam and 15° of deadrise at the transom. V-drives are used in the 32 to locate the engines aft under the cockpit sole thus lowering her exterior profile. The styling is conservative (like all Uniflites) and most consider the 32 Sport Sedan to have a generally attractive — if functional — appearance. The cabin arrangements are quite expansive for a boat of this size. The layout is very practical with both the head and galley located just inside the companionway door where they're easily reached from the cockpit. Topside, the flybridge is unusually spacious with plenty of room abaft the forward helm position. Construction is on the heavy side and quality is above average. When powered with twin 270-hp Crusaders, the Uniflite 32 will cruise around 19 knots and top out at 27–28 knots. Trim tabs are required to keep her running angles down at planing speeds since her tendency is to run bow-high. Cruising range is only about 150 miles. ❑

SPECIFICATIONS

Length	31'8"
Length WL	27'8"
Beam	11'11"
Draft	2'8"
Weight	15,000#
Clearance	11'0"
Water	75 Gals.
Fuel	200 Gals.
Cockpit	NA
Hull Type	Modified-V
Designer	Uniflite

Production
1975–84

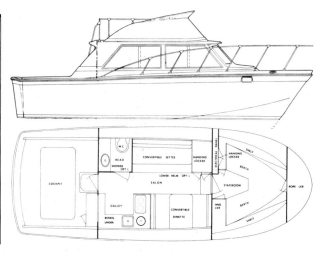

UNIFLITE

UNIFLITE 34 SPORT SEDAN

The Uniflite 34 was introduced in 1974 in two models: the 34 Tournament Fisherman, with helm aft on the bridge and extra fuel capacity (300 gallons); and the 34 Sport Sedan, with the helm console forward in the West Coast fashion. Her lines are more attractive than those of the Uniflite 32 (whose hull was stretched in the design of the 34). She was built on a solid fiberglass, modified-V hull with generous flare at the bow and about 15° of deadrise at the transom. The result was a rugged family cruiser and offshore fisherman with conservative lines and good sea-keeping characteristics. The basic galley-down interior layout features a stall shower in the head, a roomy galley area, well-crafted teak interior woodwork, and wraparound salon windows. When the dinette and sofa are converted, the 34 Sport Sedan provides overnight berths for up to six. In a notable update, the original sliding glass salon doors were replaced in 1977 with a single hinged door. With the 454-cid Crusader gas engines, the Uniflite 34 Sedan will cruise around 20 knots and reach 29–30 knots at full throttle. ❑

SPECIFICATIONS

Length	34'2"
Beam	11'11"
Draft	2'9"
Weight	17,000#
Clearance	11'11"
Water	100 Gals.
Fuel	200 Gals.
Cockpit	75 Sq. Ft.
Hull	Modified-V
Designer	Uniflite

Production
1974–84

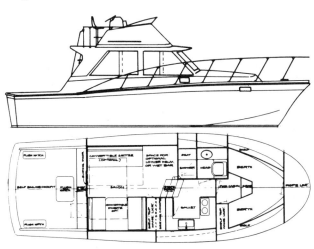

UNIFLITE

UNIFLITE 36 SPORT SEDAN

The Uniflite 36 Sport Sedan is a very traditional sedan-style design with a smart profile and a rugged personality. Built on the same solid fiberglass hull as the 36 Double Cabin (a modified-V with single chines and 11° of deadrise at the transom), she was offered with two basic interior layouts during her production years. The two-stateroom version has an in-line galley to port in the main salon. In the single-stateroom arrangement, the galley replaces the guest stateroom on the lower level and the salon is considerably enlarged. Wraparound cabin windows and a sliding glass cockpit door provide an abundance of natural lighting inside. The cockpit is large enough for fishing and the wide sidedecks are notable. The flybridge is exceptionally large for a 36' boat with the helm console set all the way forward in the West Coast fashion. Standard Crusader 454-cid gas engines will cruise the Uniflite 36 Sport Sedan around 19 knots and reach a top speed of 28–29 knots. The optional 210-hp Caterpillar diesels cruise at 16 knots a(about 18 gph) and reach a top speed of about 18–19 knots. ❑

SPECIFICATIONS

Length	36'0"
Length WL	32'0"
Beam	12'4"
Draft	3'4"
Weight	20,000#
Clearance	NA
Water	100 Gals.
Fuel, Std	216 Gals.
Fuel, Opt	300 Gals.
Cockpit	80 Sq. Ft.
Hull Type	Modified-V
Designer	A. Nordtvedt

Production
1970–84

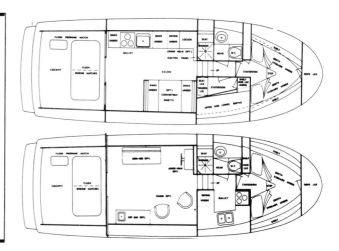

UNIFLITE 36 DOUBLE CABIN

Sharing the same hull as the 36 Sport Sedan, the Uniflite 36 Double Cabin was one of the earliest double cabin yachts to incorporate the now-popular raised aft deck design. She remained a good seller for Uniflite for many years. Her standard galley-down floorplan remained relatively unchanged during her long production run with only minor updates in the galley and master stateroom arrangements. Engineering and construction were held to high standards and fire-retardant resin was used in the laminate. Standard 454-cid gas engines will cruise the Uniflite 36 at 19 knots with a top speed of almost 30 knots. In 1984, the 36 II version was introduced with a fully cored hull, a new flybridge profile, and a revised interior layout. The weight savings (3,000 lbs.) allowed the smaller 350-cid (270-hp) gas engines to nearly match the performance of the larger 454s used in the earlier models. When Uniflite closed in 1984, Chris Craft picked up the molds and reintroduced this boat as the Chris 362 Catalina. Note that the Uniflite 41 Yacht Fisherman (1981–84) is a 36 DC with a cockpit addition. ❑

SPECIFICATIONS

Length	36'0"
Length WL	32'0"
Beam	12'4"
Draft	2'8"
Weight	21,000#
Clearance	12'3"
Water	100 Gals.
Fuel, Std	200 Gals.
Fuel, Opt	300 Gals.
Hull Type	Modified-V
Designer	A. Nordtvedt

Production
1972–84

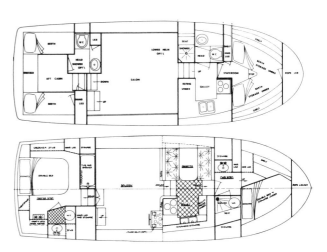

UNIFLITE 37 COASTAL CRUISER

The 37 Coastal Cruiser was Uniflite's response to the need for fuel-efficient family cruisers in the late 1970s and early 1980s. Although her handsome lines are those of a modern trawler, her semi-displacement hull design and shallow keel give the Uniflite 37 a good turn of speed when the throttles are advanced. (Note that the exhaust ports of the Coastal Cruiser are underwater.) Below, the all-teak interior features a spacious salon with large wraparound cabin windows for plenty of natural lighting. A service bar separates the salon area from the mid-level galley. The second "stateroom" is actually a lounge in the passageway with a privacy curtain (the backrest swings up to create over/under berths at night). The large double-entry head is fitted with a shower stall. Outside, a bridge overhang affords some weather protection for the cockpit and the huge flybridge has seating for eight. Standard power was a single 192-hp Volvo diesel (11-knots cruise), but most Coastal Cruisers were sold with twin 124-hp Volvos for a cruising speed of 14–15 knots and a top speed of about 17 knots. ❏

SPECIFICATIONS

Length	37'9"
Length WL	33'9"
Beam	12'9"
Draft	3'10"
Weight	21,000#
Clearance	12'0"
Water	160 Gals.
Fuel	300 Gals.
Cockpit	58 Sq. Ft.
Hull Type	Semi-Disp.
Designer	Uniflite

Production
1979–84

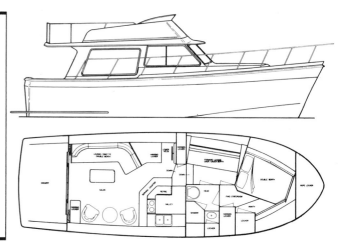

UNIFLITE

UNIFLITE 38 CONVERTIBLE

The Uniflite 38 Convertible is a comfortable family cruising yacht and a competent offshore sportfisherman. Heavily built, she was available with two basic floorplans: a single-stateroom, galley-down arrangement, and the standard two-stateroom, galley-up plan — the latter being somewhat notable due to the small galley which Uniflite tucked into the forward corner of the salon. Both layouts had the convenience of a double-entry head, stall shower, and large staterooms. The 38's salon is spacious for a boat of this size. The portside lower helm station was an option and most were so equipped. As a sportfisherman, the 38 has a large and uncluttered cockpit with a molded-in fish box and wide sidedecks. East Coast anglers will want the tournament-style bridge layout with the helm console aft. While the 400-gallon fuel capacity is adequate in the diesel-powered models, those with gas engines carry only 300 gallons. Optional 310-hp J&T 6-71Ns will cruise the Uniflite 38 at a steady 19 knots and reach 22 knots at full throttle. In 1985, Chris Craft reintroduced this boat as the 382 Commander. ❏

SPECIFICATIONS

Length	38'0"
Length WL	33'0"
Beam	13'11"
Draft	3'8"
Weight	24,000#
Clearance	12'8"
Water	100 Gals.
Fuel	400 Gals.
Cockpit	92 Sq. Ft.
Hull Type	Modified-V
Designer	Uniflite

Production
1977–84

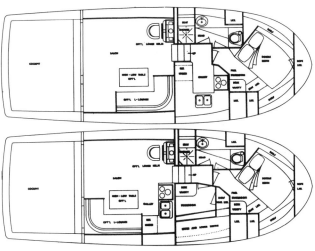

UNIFLITE 42 DOUBLE CABIN

The Uniflite 42 Double Cabin was one of the early production motor yachts to be designed with a raised, full-width aft deck. A proven cruiser, the 42's hull and deck molds are currently used in the production of the Chris Craft 427 Catalina Double Cabin. Uniflite 42s remain popular today on the used market because of their sturdy construction, open accommodation plan, and conservative lines. The standard interior includes twin berths in the aft cabin, a galley down with dinette, a deck access door at the optional lower helm, and teak interior woodwork throughout. Those models built after 1978 have a stall shower in the forward head and a rearranged galley/dinette area. Quality systems and hardware make used Uniflite 42 DCs a good candidate for refits and interior upgrades. In 1984, the 42 MK II SE version appeared with a new cored hull and a revised interior layout which is still used in today's Chris Craft 427. The popular 310-hp J&T 6-71s will cruise the Uniflite 42 Double Cabin at 18 knots with a top speed of 20–21 knots. Note that the fuel capacity was increased in 1977 to 500 gallons. ❑

SPECIFICATIONS

Length	42'0"
Length WL	37'7"
Beam	14'9"
Draft	3'9"
Weight	35,000#
Clearance	12'10"
Water	160 Gals.
Fuel	400/500 Gals.
Hull Type	Modified-V
Designer	A. Nordtvedt

Production
1971–84

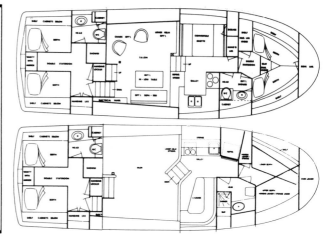

UNIFLITE 42 CONVERTIBLE

The Uniflite 42 is a rugged and good-looking convertible with genuine offshore sportfishing capabilities. Constructed on the same solid fiberglass, modified-V hull as the 42 Double Cabin, the 42 Convertible has a large fishing cockpit with plenty of room for a tackle center and mounted fighting chair. With the optional 600 gallon fuel capacity, the 42 has the ability to range far offshore. There were two basic interior layouts over the years. The original plan has the galley and dinette at the lower level with a single stateroom forward. Later models have a two-state-room layout with the galley down (no dinette) and a choice of one or two heads. A lower station is generally found in the salon. Standard 350-hp (454-cid) gas engines cruise at 17 knots and run about 24 knots wide open. The optional 310-hp 6-71s cruise around 18–19 knots, and the more powerful 410-hp 6-71 diesels will cruise the Uniflite 42 Convertible at a solid 24 knots. Note that the standard fuel capacity increased to 500 gallons in 1977. A tournament-style flybridge (with the helm aft) was offered for East Coast markets. ❑

SPECIFICATIONS

Length	42'0"
Length WL	37'7"
Beam	14'9"
Draft	3'9"
Weight	35,000#
Clearance	12'10"
Water	160 Gals.
Fuel	450/500 Gals.
Cockpit	102 Sq. Ft.
Hull Type	Modified-V
Designer	A. Nordtvedt

Production
1972–84

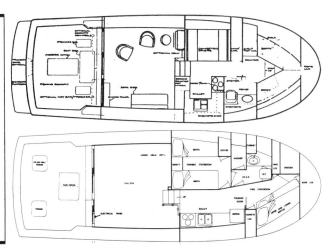

UNIFLITE 48 CONVERTIBLE

The Uniflite 48 Convertible is a handsome and good-running offshore sportfisherman built to compete in tournament-level events. She's constructed on a conventional modified-V hull design (14° deadrise aft) with balsa coring in the hullsides from the waterline up. The 48 Convertible was Uniflite's largest (and last) foray into the big-boat sportfishing market. Once considered a relatively fast boat, she was one of the first production applications of the then-new 8V92 diesels. A good-looking boat, the hull molds were later used by Chris Craft in the construction of their 482 Commander. The popular three-stateroom interior layout has the galley forward and to starboard in the salon. Other accommodation plans were available and the 48's flexible floorplan allowed the master stateroom to be located either amidships or forward. The huge cockpit provides direct access to the engine room, and the flybridge is arranged with the helm console aft on the centerline with bench seating forward. Known for her agile handling, 550-hp 8V92 diesels will cruise the Uniflite 48 at 24–25 knots and reach 28 knots wide open. ❏

SPECIFICATIONS

Length	48'10"
Beam	15'9"
Draft	4'9"
Weight	48,000#
Clearance	13'9"
Water	200 Gals.
Fuel	780 Gals.
Cockpit	133 Sq. Ft.
Hull Type	Modified-V
Designer	A. Nordtvedt

Production
1980–84

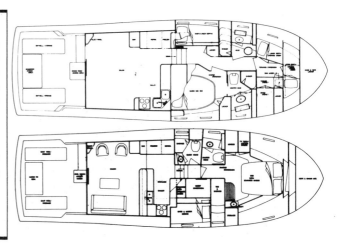

UNIFLITE 48 YACHT FISHERMAN

Built on a stretched Uniflite 42 Double Cabin hull, the 48 Yacht Fisherman adds the flexibility of a 6' fishing cockpit to the comfortable interior accommodations of the 42. With similar power, the extra waterline length of the 48 YF results in a slightly faster hull. A second advantage of the cockpit is the ability to fit the generator under the cockpit sole where the cabin noise is considerably reduced. In a practical design feature, a door in the cockpit leads directly into the aft stateroom for convenient access to the interior. The floorplan layouts are the same as offered in the Uniflite 42 Double Cabin. Her long profile is extremely well proportioned and the 48 Yacht Fisherman presents an attractive appearance at dockside. Built on a notably efficient hull, she'll cruise at 19+ knots (about 22 knots top) with the 310-hp GM 6-71s, and at 23–24 knots (26 knots top) with the larger 410-hp 6-71TI versions. When the Uniflite factory closed the tooling and molds were acquired by Chris Craft, and in 1985 the Uniflite 48 YF began a long and very successful production run as the Chris Craft 480 Catalina. ❏

SPECIFICATIONS

Length	48'0"
Length WL	43'9"
Beam	14'9"
Draft	3'9"
Weight	39,000#
Clearance	12'10"
Water	160 Gals.
Fuel	690 Gals.
Cockpit	80 Sq. Ft.
Hull Type	Modified-V
Designer	A. Nordtvedt

Production
1980–84

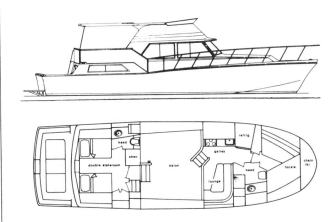

VIKING

Brief History

Viking Yachts dates back to the early 1950s when the company built wooden cruisers under the name of Viking Builders. In 1964 the company was acquired by the Healey family, and the switch to fiberglass was made in 1971. During the past two decades Viking Yachts has seen continued growth, and the purchase of Gulfstar Yachts in 1987 moved Viking into the large motor yacht market. Considered one of the best of the production manufacturers, Viking Yachts is today one of the largest privately owned builders in the U.S.

Selected Viking Models

Viking 33 Convertible
Viking 35 Convertible
Viking 35 Sportfisherman
Viking 38 Convertible
Viking 40 Sedan
Viking 41 Convertible
Viking 43 Convertible
Viking 43 Double Cabin
Viking 44 Motor Yacht
Viking 45 Convertible
Viking 46 Convertible
Viking 48 Convertible
Viking 48 Motor Yacht
Viking 50 Motor Yacht

Viking 50 Convertible
Viking 53 Convertible
Viking 54 Motor Yacht
Viking 55 Motor Yacht
Viking 57 Convertible
Viking 57 Extended Aft Deck MY
Viking 58 Convertible
Viking 63 Motor Yacht
Viking 63 Cockpit MY
Viking 65 Extended Aft Deck MY
Viking 65 Cockpit MY
Viking 72 Motor Yacht
Viking 72 Cockpit MY

Main Office

Viking Yacht Co., Route 9, New Gretna, NJ 08224
609-296-6000

651

VIKING 33 CONVERTIBLE

The introduction of the Viking 33 Convertible in 1971 marked the end of wood construction at Viking Yachts. The 33 Convertible was built on a solid fiberglass hull with 21° deadrise at the transom, a flat keel section, and a shallow skeg — a somewhat thirsty hull as it turned out, but an otherwise fine seaboat with good handling characteristics. Many of the features introduced in the Viking 33, such as the steel engine mounts and grid-type stringer system, have gone on to become key elements in the make up of today's modern Viking Yachts. While the she isn't considered particularly graceful and her cockpit is too small for any serious fishing, her interior accommodations are comfortable with berths for six in the two-stateroom layout or four in the single-stateroom floorplan. With the optional 454-cid gas engines, the 33 is capable of reaching a top speed of about 27 knots with a normal cruising speed of 17–18 knots. The engines are located beneath the cockpit sole and V-drives are used to deliver the power. With just 200 gallons of fuel, the range of the Viking 33 Convertible is limited to around 125 miles. ❏

SPECIFICATIONS

Length	33'0"
Length WL	28'3"
Beam	12'9"
Draft	2'7"
Weight	15,300#
Clearance	11'4"
Water	50 Gals.
Fuel	200 Gals.
Cockpit	68 Sq. Ft.
Hull Type	Modified-V
Designer	Viking

Production
1971–74

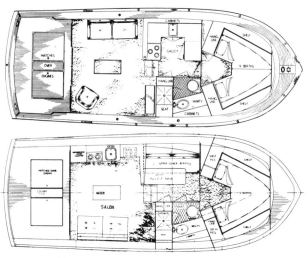

VIKING

VIKING 35 CONVERTIBLE

A popular and durable family convertible, the Viking 35 has been recognized as a successful design since her introduction in 1975. She combines the essential elements of modern convertible styling with an attractive interior layout, superior construction, and proven offshore capability. Built on a beefed-up modified-V hull with 15.5° of deadrise aft, the hullsides are balsacored for weight reduction and strength. She was extensively redesigned and updated in 1985 with a solid front windshield, a completely restyled flybridge, and a luxurious teak interior with a choice of one or two staterooms. (The original wood-grain mica interior was replaced with teak in 1980.) Also in 1985, the generator was relocated from beneath the cockpit to the engine room. With her tournament-style flybridge, uncluttered cockpit, and comfortable interior accommodations, the Viking 35 easily doubles as a weekend fisherman or family cruiser. Standard 454-cid Crusader gas engines will cruise at 18–19 knots with a top speed of nearly 30 knots. Cat 375-hp diesels provide a cruising speed of 24–25 knots and 28 knots top. ❏

SPECIFICATIONS

Length	35'0"
Length WL	33'2"
Beam	13'1"
Draft	2'5"
Weight	20,000#
Clearance	12'4"
Water	75 Gals.
Fuel	275/300 Gals.
Cockpit	80 Sq. Ft.
Hull Type	Modified-V
Designer	Viking

Production
1975–Current

VIKING

VIKING 35 SPORTFISHERMAN

The 35 Sportfisherman was Viking's first (and only) entry into the growing market for express-type offshore fishing boats. Designed with a roomy and completely uncluttered cockpit and featuring modest interior comforts, the 35 Sportfisherman was built using the same durable hull as Viking's existing 35 Convertible. Her large bi-level cockpit is equipped with two in-deck fish boxes, a built-in tackle cabinet, and full-length lounge seating port and starboard. Engine access, however, is not one of her selling points — working space is at a premium and access is tight. Below, the stylish teak interior provides overnight accommodations for four with a single stateroom and a convertible dinette. Note that the MSD (toilet) is fitted in the shower stall compartment to save space, just as in the Viking 35 Convertible. Standard gas engines will cruise around 19 knots with a top speed of 28. The 355-hp Cats cruise at a fast 27 knots and reach over 30 knots wide open. With 32 Viking 35 Sportfishermen built in three years of production, the model was discontinued in 1986 for lack of demand. ❏

SPECIFICATIONS

Length	35'0"
Length WL	33'2"
Beam	13'1"
Draft	2'5"
Weight	19,000#
Clearance	8'6"
Water	70 Gals.
Fuel	300 Gals.
Cockpit	NA
Hull Type	Modified-V
Designer	Viking

Production
1984–86

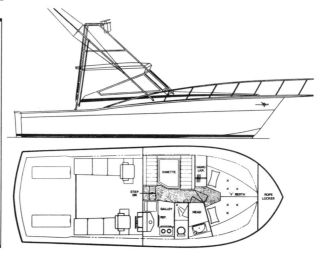

VIKING

VIKING 38 CONVERTIBLE

Although she's the smallest model in the current Viking line up, the 38 Convertible could easily be compared to most 42-footers (note her 39'4" LOA). She's built on a modified-V hull (balsa-cored from the waterline up) with 15.5° of transom deadrise and better than 14 feet of beam — wide for a 38-footer. A decidedly handsome boat with a superb profile and excellent handling characteristics, the expansive interior of the Viking 38 — with its rich teak paneling and luxurious decorator fabrics — is the largest to be found in a boat of this size.

Two floorplans are offered (a choice not always available in this size range), and both retain the convenient mid-level galley and double-entry head. In the dinette layout, the salon takes on seemingly immense proportions. The cockpit has over 100 sq. ft. of uncluttered space and the large flybridge has a state-of-the-art helm console and seating for six. Crusader gas engines were standard until 1992 when they were replaced with 485-hp 6-71 diesels. A great-running boat, the Viking 38 will cruise around 26-27 knots and reach 30 knots wide open.❑

SPECIFICATIONS

Length......................39'4"
Length WL................35'5"
Beam........................14'2"
Draft ....4'1"
Weight ....32,890#
Clearance ....11'10"
Water.................110 Gals.
Fuel ....430 Gals.
Cockpit............108 Sq. Ft.
Hull Type.........Modified-V
Designer ....B. Wilson

Production
1990–Current

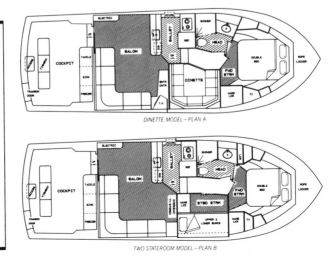

DINETTE MODEL – PLAN A

TWO STATEROOM MODEL – PLAN B

VIKING

VIKING 40 SEDAN

A major sales success for Viking with over 400 sold, the 40 Sedan Fisherman contributed mightily to Viking's reputation as a quality East Coast builder. Boasting an aggressive profile and rugged hull construction, the Viking 40's cockpit and spacious interior are big for a 40' boat. Notable, too, are the balsa-cored hullsides — the Viking 40 was one of the early production boats to pioneer this technology. Steel engine mounts were also employed and have now become a Viking trademark. Three interior layouts were offered with the differences affecting only the lower living area. Early models featured a simulated-wood laminate interior, but in 1982 Viking switched to a more luxurious teak interior. Another update (this one in 1980) moved the generator from under the cockpit to the engine room. Gas power was standard but most Viking 40 Sedans were equipped with diesels. The popular 310-hp J&T 6-71Ns and 300-hp Cats will cruise around 20 knots (23–24 knots top), and the larger 410-hp 6-71TIs cruise at 24 knots (26 knots top). A proven design, used models generally maintain stable resale values. ❑

SPECIFICATIONS

Length	40'4"
Length WL	38'6"
Beam	14'6"
Draft	3'6"
Weight	30,000#
Clearance	11'9"
Water	90 Gals.
Fuel	300/350 Gals.
Cockpit	100 Sq. Ft.
Hull Type	Modified-V
Designer	B. Wilson

Production
1973–83

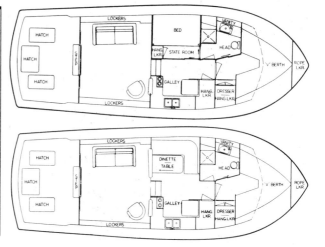

VIKING

VIKING 41 CONVERTIBLE

The Viking 41 Convertible replaced the 40 Sedan Fisherman in the Viking line up in 1983. She was built on a cored, modified-V hull form with 15.5° of deadrise at the transom. A good-looking boat, the Viking 41 is a serious tournament contender and a proven sportfishing design. Her large and unobstructed cockpit is fitted with in-deck fish boxes and a tackle center as standard equipment. Like all modern Viking yachts, the 41 Convertible features an elegant teak interior. She was offered with a two-stateroom layout or a popular single-stateroom arrange-ment with a full dinette — one of the finest arrangements we've seen in a boat of this size. With its wide open dinette and galley, this floorplan gives the interior of the Viking 41 the appear-ance of a *much* larger boat. The matched teak woodwork and top-quality fabrics and hardware are impressive. Fast and agile and possessing good seakeeping characteristics, the Viking 41 Con-vertible will turn an honest 30+ knots wide open and cruise at 26–27 knots with the 485-hp 6-71 diesels. This model was replaced in 1990 with the Viking 43 Convertible. ❏

SPECIFICATIONS

Length	41'2"
Length WL	36'0"
Beam	14'10"
Draft	4'3"
Weight	32,000#
Clearance	12'0"
Water	125 Gals.
Fuel	380/430 Gals.
Cockpit	108 Sq. Ft.
Hull Type	Modified-V
Designer	Viking

Production
1983–89

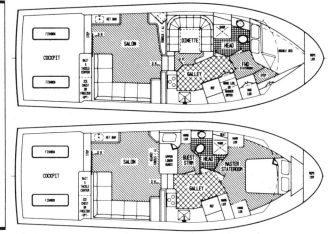

VIKING 43 CONVERTIBLE

Replacing the popular 41 Convertible in 1990, the Viking 43 shares the same aggressive flybridge and deckhouse styling seen in the latest generation of Viking Convertibles. Built on a modified-V hull (15.5° deadrise aft), the deck mold is one piece from pulpit to cockpit liner. She features more beam and fuel capacity than the 41, and like her predecessor she's powered with economical 6-71s and offers a choice of a dinette layout in lieu of a second stateroom. In either arrangement, the mid-level galley is open to the huge salon, and the head and master stateroom are both very large. The interior is finished with rich teak woodwork and the accommodations are upscale indeed. The flybridge is among the largest in her class (with an excellent helm console), and the cockpit includes a transom door, molded tackle center, and a big 8' in-deck fishbox. Designed as a tournament sportfisherman or competent family convertible, the Viking 43 is available with a factory hardtop. Standard 485-hp 6-71s will cruise at around 24 knots (28 top) and optional 550-hp 6V-92s cruise at 27 knots and reach 31 knots top. ❑

SPECIFICATIONS

Length	43'0"
Length WL	37'6"
Beam	15'3"
Draft	4'3"
Weight	38,595#
Clearance	12'3"
Water	115 Gals.
Fuel	525 Gals.
Cockpit	116 Sq. Ft.
Hull Type	Modified-V
Designer	B. Wilson

Production
1990–Current

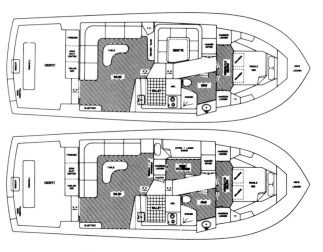

VIKING 43 DOUBLE CABIN

Viking's first fiberglass motor yacht design, the 43 Double Cabin was built on a stretched Viking 40 Convertible hull and incorporated the same interior floorplan from the salon forward. The additional length was used to provide a full-width aft stateroom together with a large railed-in afterdeck. Notably, her wood-grain mica interior was finally upgraded to teak in 1982 — the last year of production. Although some consider the styling a compromise, the Viking 43's quality engineering and muscular construction have made used models popular in most markets. Principal features include excellent storage space, two stall showers, molded steps (not a ladder) leading up to the bridge, and top-quality deck hardware and exterior glasswork. The helm console is set well aft on the flybridge with bench seating forward. Gas engines were standard, but diesels were the choice of most buyers. With 310-hp GM 6-71Ns, the Viking 43 DC will cruise at 19 knots, and the larger 410-hp 6-71s cruise at 22–23 knots. Over 250 Viking 43 Double Cabins were sold and resale values are still better than average. ❏

SPECIFICATIONS

Length	42'8"
Length WL	NA
Beam	14'9"
Draft	3'9"
Weight	34,000#
Clearance	12'0"
Water	100 Gals.
Fuel	350 Gals.
Hull Type	Modified-V
Designer	Viking

Production
1975–82

VIKING

VIKING 44 MOTOR YACHT

The Viking 44 Motor Yacht replaced the popular 43 Double Cabin in the Viking fleet in 1982. Designed for comfortable family cruising and showing the improved styling characteristics of the Viking 46 Convertible, the 44 MY is slightly larger inside than the 43 Double Cabin and carries more fuel and additional water. While the floorplans are similar, the 44 has a larger main salon with the forward companionway offset to starboard. The result is a larger dinette area and a big forward head compartment. The elegant teak interior is a superb blend of natural woodwork and top-quality fabrics and furnishings. Outside, the 44's flybridge is arranged with passenger seating forward and to starboard of the raised helm console. Additional features include a spacious afterdeck, optional hardtop and arch, balsa coring in the hullsides, and steel engine mounts — a Viking trademark. A good-running boat with optional 485-hp 6-71s, the 44 Motor Yacht will cruise at a fast 24 knots and turn 28+ knots wide open. Note that the Viking 50 Cockpit MY is a stretched 44 with a 6' cockpit extension. ❏

SPECIFICATIONS

Length	44'0"
Length WL	37'10"
Beam	15'0"
Draft	4'0"
Weight	40,000#
Clearance	14'6"
Water	180 Gals.
Fuel	460 Gals.
Hull Type	Modified-V
Designer	B. Wilson

Production
1982–91

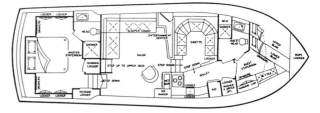

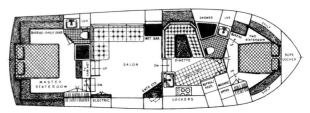

VIKING 45 CONVERTIBLE

The Viking 45 Convertible is one of those rare cases where the product is so well matched to the market that her success is assured. This is a good example of what many believe a modern Jersey-style sportfisherman should look like. More than that, the Viking 45 offers a superb blend of good speed and great interior space utilization. She's constructed on Viking's standard modified-V hull form with 15.5° of deadrise aft and balsa-cored hullsides. Originally offered with two staterooms and two heads, in late 1988 a spacious two-stateroom dinette layout became available at the expense of one of the head compartments. Both floorplans feature a mid-level galley and the beautiful teak interior woodwork and stylish decor package are most impressive. The cockpit is set up for serious fishing (molded tackle center, transom door, etc.), and the big tournament flybridge will seat eight comfortably. A good performer with standard 485-hp 6-71s, she'll cruise at 24 knots and turn 27+ knots on the wall. The 550-hp 6V92s (available since 1990) will cruise at a fast 28 knots and reach a top speed of 31 knots. ❏

SPECIFICATIONS

Length	45'5"
Length WL	39'3"
Beam	15'0"
Draft	4'0"
Weight	44,400#
Clearance	12'5"
Water	160 Gals.
Fuel	600 Gals.
Cockpit	120 Sq. Ft.
Hull Type	Modified-V
Designer	B. Wilson

Production
1987–Current

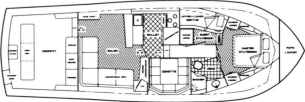

VIKING 46 CONVERTIBLE

The first to display the graceful profile of today's modern Viking yachts, the 46 Convertible is a good-looking canyon runner with plenty of muscle and speed. Built on the standard Viking hull design with a moderate 15.5° of transom aft and reversed chines, the hull bottom is grid-reinforced and the engines rest on rigid steel beds. The Viking 46 has a reputation for being agile as well as strong, although the ride can be a little hard in a chop. Her lush two-stateroom, galley down interior includes an incredibly spacious master stateroom. A triple-stateroom layout — unusual in any convertible below 50' — became available in 1982. The interior is finished with traditional teak woodwork and top-quality furnishings, appliances, and hardware. The tournament-sized cockpit is uncluttered and the large flybridge will seat six comfortably. The engine room air intakes are located under the gunnels (and the engine room itself is a little tight). Originally offered with 500-hp 6V92s (24 knots cruise/28 top), 675-hp 8V92s became available in 1983 raising the cruising speed to a fast 28 knots and the top speed to 31 knots. ❑

SPECIFICATIONS

Length	46'6"
Length WL	41'8"
Beam	16'0"
Draft	4'0"
Weight	44,000#
Clearance	NA
Water	200 Gals.
Fuel	620/750 Gals.
Cockpit	120 Sq. Ft.
Hull Type	Modified-V
Designer	B. Wilson

Production
1981–85

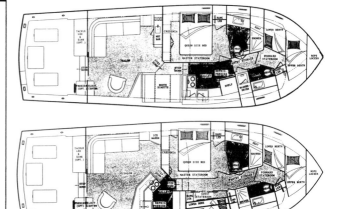

VIKING 48 CONVERTIBLE

Built on a lengthened and reworked Viking 46 hull, the popular 48 Convertible used the additional 2' to create a huge 144 sq. ft. fishing cockpit. Unlike the 46 Convertible, the Viking 48 has a solid front windshield and a much-improved engine room. In the original floorplan, the galley and booth-style dinette are at mid-level. A three-stateroom version replaced the dinette with a small private cabin with over/under berths. In 1989, the Plan "C" arrangement offered an L-shaped dinette on the deckhouse level and two very spacious staterooms. The 48's big cockpit is fitted with recessed fish boxes, a tackle center (with freezer), and a transom door — all standard. The tournament flybridge has seating for eight. Other features include a central vacuum system, washer/dryer unit, molded bow pulpit, and an optional hardtop. A fast-running boat with a fairly stiff ride in a chop, the Viking 48 Convertible will cruise at around 23–24 knots with the 550-hp 6V92s with a top speed of around 26 knots. With the 735-hp 8V92s (standard in later models), she'll cruise at a fast 27–28 knots and reach 31 knots wide open. ❑

SPECIFICATIONS

Length	48'7"
Length WL	44'4"
Beam	16'0"
Draft	4'7"
Weight	45,500#
Clearance	12'5"
Water	200 Gals.
Fuel	680 Gals.
Cockpit	144 Sq. Ft.
Hull Type	Modified-V
Designer	B. Wilson

Production
1985–90

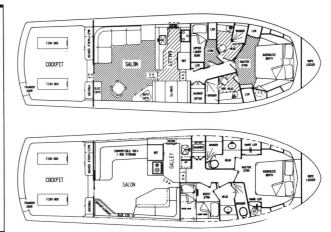

VIKING 48 MOTOR YACHT

Utilizing the 48 Viking Convertible's hull and deckhouse, the 48 Motor Yacht combines surprisingly brisk performance and traditional motor yacht comfort in what most will agree is a good-looking cruising yacht. Her elegant three-stateroom interior accommodations are finished with the same teak cabinetry and woodwork that are now synonymous with Viking quality. A centerline queen berth is fitted in the forward stateroom and offset single berths are in the portside guest cabin. Another walkaround queen berth is located in the owner's stateroom aft.

The Viking 48's raised aft deck is a fully enclosed *second salon* complete with wing doors, wet bar, and an L-shaped lounge. Her big flybridge (also borrowed from the 48 Convertible) will seat up to eight passengers with bench seating forward of the helm. The 48 Motor Yacht came standard with GM 6V92TIs for a cruising speed of 21–22 knots. The optional 8V92TIBs provide a fast 25-knot cruising speed and around 28 knots wide open. Note that the Viking 55 Cockpit MY is the same boat with a 7' cockpit extension but only a few were built. ❑

SPECIFICATIONS

Length	48'7"
Length WL	44'4"
Beam	16'0"
Draft	4'7"
Weight	48,500#
Clearance	12'5"
Water	200 Gals.
Fuel	645 Gals.
Hull Type	Modified-V
Designer	B. Wilson

Production
1986–88

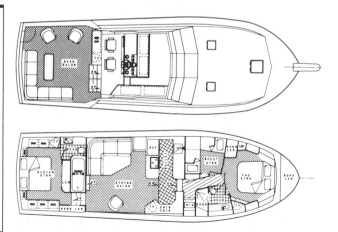

VIKING 50 MOTOR YACHT

The Viking 50 Motor Yacht is a stylish double-deck yacht in spite of her high deckhouse profile. Designed to be owner-operated, the hull is a high-tech blend of modern knitted fabrics, pre-preg composites, and vacuum-bagging in the layup. The big news with the Viking 50 MY, however, is her expansive and well-designed floorplan. There are three full levels (including the bridge) and three double staterooms, each with a head and stall shower. The spacious midships VIP guest suite warrants no apologies and is separated from the master stateroom by the full-width engine room. The galley/dinette area is very large and features deck access doors and an optional lower helm. The salon is open to the galley and includes a staircase (instead of a ladder) leading up to the flybridge. Outside, the spacious aft deck — a full 86 sq. ft. — is an ideal outdoor entertaining platform with room for a crowd. There's room on the extended flybridge for a Whaler and a dozen guests. No lightweight, standard 735-hp 8V92 diesels will cruise the Viking 50 MY around 18–20 knots and reach a top speed of 23 knots. ❑

SPECIFICATIONS

Length	50'6"
Length WL	43'1"
Beam	16'4"
Draft	4'3"
Weight	65,000#
Clearance	20'0"
Water	250 Gals.
Fuel	770 Gals.
Hull Type	Modified-V
Designer	B. Wilson

Production
1990–Current

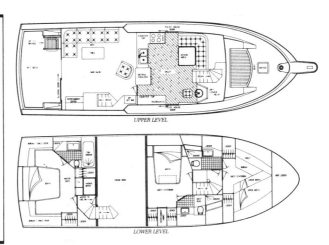

UPPER LEVEL

LOWER LEVEL

VIKING 50 CONVERTIBLE

Replacing the very popular 48 Convertible, the Viking 50 is a scaled-down version of the hot-selling Viking 53 Convertible introduced the previous year. Indeed, her three-stateroom layout is virtually identical with only slightly reduced dimensions. Construction is state-of-the-art and it's worth noting that the 50's deck, superstructure, and cockpit are a single molding. The hullsides are cored with balsa and transom deadrise is 15°. A very handsome boat with a sweeping sheer and sculptured profile, the Viking 50's stunning teak interior is certainly one of her most attractive features. The spacious midships master stateroom comes at the expense of two rather compact guest cabins. (A two-stateroom floorplan is also available.) Other features include an excellent stand-up engine room, an unobstructed cockpit with a *huge* in-deck fishbox, and a superb bridge layout. At 60,000 lbs. the Viking 50 is no lightweight. Standard power in 1991 was 730-hp 8V92s (27–28 knots cruise/31 top), however they were replaced in 1992 with 820-hp MANs. A great-running boat, she'll cruise at a fast 30 knots and deliver a top speed of 33 knots. ❑

SPECIFICATIONS

Length	50'7"
Length WL	NA
Beam	16'4"
Draft	4'9"
Weight	58,814#
Clearance	13'10"
Water	208 Gals.
Fuel	850 Gals.
Hull Type	Modified-V
Designer	B. Wilson

Production
1991–Current

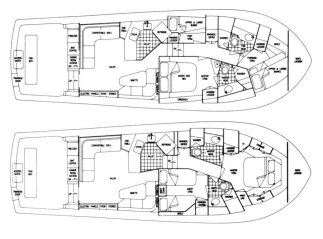

VIKING 53 CONVERTIBLE

A good-selling boat, the Viking 53 is a sleek and well-proportioned sportfisherman with the angular good looks and aggressive profile common to all modern Viking designs. She's built on a rugged modified-V hull form (15.5° deadrise aft) with cored hullsides, wide chines, and a shallow keel. The galley-up floorplan for the Viking 53 includes three staterooms and two heads with the master stateroom located to starboard. (Note that in 1991 the galley was rearranged, and in 1992 a queen bed forward became standard.) The salon is completely open to the gal-ley and includes an L-shaped dinette and seating for a crowd. With its elegant decor, lush teak woodwork, and clever use of mirrors, the high-style interior is slightly overwhelming for a tournament-level fisherman. The cockpit features a full tackle center, transom door, in-deck fish box, and access to an award-winning engine room. The flybridge is equally large and features a superb helm console. Standard 845-hp MANs will cruise at a fast 27–28 knots (33 knots top), and 1,000-hp MANs (optional in 1992) cruise at 31 knots and deliver 35 knots top. ❑

SPECIFICATIONS

Length	53'7"
Length WL	48'3"
Beam	16'7"
Draft	4'10"
Weight	68,000#
Clearance	13'4"
Water	200 Gals.
Fuel	900/1,100 Gals.
Cockpit	148 Sq. Ft.
Hull Type	Modified-V
Designer	B. Wilson

Production
1990–Current

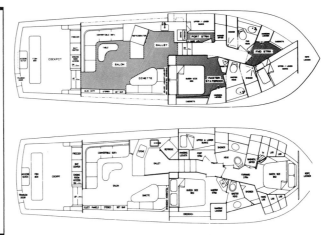

VIKING 54 MOTOR YACHT

Designed to offer Viking motor yacht owners the next step up from the now-discontinued 44 and 48 MY models, the new Viking 54 is a great-looking high-performance cruiser with clean lines and a very handsome profile. Her good performance is due in part to the fact that she rides on a reworked version of the high-tech 53 Convertible hull (with cored hullsides, reverse outer chines, and 15.5° of transom deadrise), and because her center of gravity and windage are much lower than her double-deck counterparts. Accommodations include a spacious and beautifully appointed salon, mid-level galley with dinette opposite, and three heads, each with a stall shower. The upscale decor of the 54 MY is finished with traditional teak woodwork and cabinetry with top-quality appliances, hardware, and fabrics throughout. Additional features include a roomy stand-up engine room, spacious flybridge with wraparound helm console, washer/dryer, and a very large aft deck with wing doors. A good-running boat, 845-hp MANs will cruise around 23–24 knots and deliver a top speed of about 28 knots. ❏

SPECIFICATIONS

Length	54'1"
Length WL	47'9"
Beam	17'5"
Draft	4'10"
Weight	75,000#
Clearance	NA"
Water	200 Gals.
Fuel	900 Gals.
Hull Type	Modified-V
Designer	Viking

Production
1992–Current

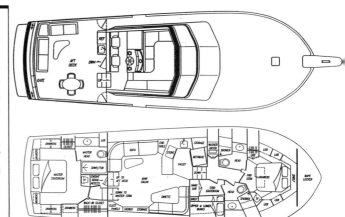

VIKING 55 MOTOR YACHT

Introduced in 1987 as the Gulfstar 55, the Viking 55 MY was a break-through design in terms of modern engineering and lightweight construction. Gulfstar was known as a technology-driven company when they were acquired by Viking in late 1987, and the 55 went on to become a very successful motor yacht. Built on a fully cored hull with moderate transom deadrise, the 55 is noted for her good performance, excellent interior space utilization, and a somewhat noisy master stateroom while underway. Her standard four-stateroom layout (three with double berths) has the main salon/dining area separated from the galley and wheelhouse. Other attractive features include a salon staircase leading up to the flybridge (a big improvement over the normal wheelhouse ladder), and the separate utility room with washer/dryer and workbench. Originally designed with walkaround sidedecks, the full-width salon layout became standard in 1989, and the Extended Aft Deck model (with a much smaller salon) came out in 1990. Standard 735-hp 8V92s cruise at 19–20 knots and reach 23 knots top. A total of 40 were built. ❏

SPECIFICATIONS

Length	55'7"
Length WL	47'2"
Beam	17'4"
Draft	4'5"
Weight	56,000#
Clearance	21'5"
Water	350 Gals.
Fuel	770 Gals.
Hull Type	Modified-V
Designer	R. Lazzara

Production
1987–90

VIKING 57 CONVERTIBLE

The Viking 57 Convertible is easily one of the best-looking tournament boats in her class. She was built on the standard Viking hull form with a wide, flat keel section, reversed outer chines, and 15.5° of deadrise at the transom. The foredeck, house, and cockpit are all one mold which adds strength to the hull and beauty to her profile. Inside, the three-stateroom accommodation plan is luxurious on a grand scale with the huge salon and deckhouse galley dominating the layout. Features include three heads (each with a stall shower), built-in washer/dryer, superb teak woodwork, and a very stylish and modern interior decor. The huge tournament fishing cockpit is completely unobstructed and fitted with a molded-in tackle center with freezer, transom door, teak covering boards, and direct access to the spacious (and well arranged) stand-up engine room. All were built with 1,080-hp 12V92s which cruise the Viking 57 around 28 knots and deliver a top speed of 32 knots. Fast and agile but wet in a headsea, the Viking 57 was replaced in 1992 with the new 58 Convertible. A total of 29 were built. ❏

SPECIFICATIONS

Length	57'2"
Length WL	52'0"
Beam	18'0"
Draft	5'3"
Weight	69,000#
Clearance	14'6"
Water	250 Gals.
Fuel	1,500 Gals.
Cockpit	176 Sq. Ft.
Hull Type	Modified-V
Designer	B. Wilson

Production
1989–91

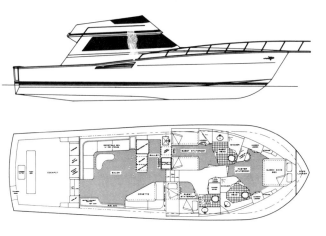

VIKING 57 EXTENDED AFT DECK MY

Replacing the 55 MY, the Viking 57 MY is a high-tech cruising yacht with a spacious four-stateroom layout and good performance. She's built on a fully cored hull with a sharp entry and moderate deadrise aft. The salon is arranged with a circular staircase aft leading to the master stateroom, and is separate from the galley area. Another staircase leads up to the bridge and there are deck doors in the wheelhouse. The salon is large enough for a formal dining area, and the big 100 sq. ft. aft deck is protected by a bridge overhang. Two of the three guest staterooms forward are fitted with queen berths, while a king-size bed is located in the master stateroom. The huge engine room is entered from the utility room aft. The decor of the Viking 57 is a blend of elegant teak woodwork, Corian countertops, and high-quality fabrics — completely impressive. There are narrow 10" service decks around the house, and quiet, lift-type mufflers (not the baffled exhausts of the 55 MY) in the engine room. Standard 820-hp MANs will cruise at 19–20 knots (23 knots top), and optional 730-hp 8V92s cruise at 18 knots (21 knots top). ❏

SPECIFICATIONS

Length	57'7"
Length WL	49'6"
Beam	17'4"
Draft	4'5"
Weight	78,000#
Clearance	21'2"
Water	350 Gals.
Fuel	750 Gals.
Hull Type	Modified-V
Designer	R. Lazarras

Production
1991–Current

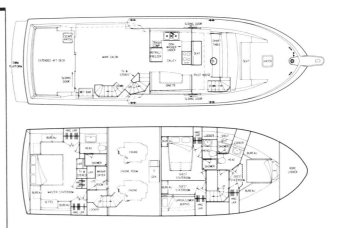

VIKING 58 CONVERTIBLE

The Viking 58 is basically an updated and improved version of the previous 57 Convertible with increased flare in the bow, a sharper entry, and a redesigned transom. She's a dryer boat than her predecessor with slightly better headsea and backing-down characteristics. Her modified-V hull retains the same 15.5° of transom deadrise, and the hullsides are cored with balsa. The superstructure — from pulpit to cockpit — is a single-piece mold. Inside, the deckhouse layout of the Viking 58 is similar to the 57, however the companionway has been moved slightly to star-board resulting in a larger galley (at the expense of the dinette) with more counter space and storage. The master stateroom is now midships rather than forward. All three heads have stall showers, and a built-in washer/dryer is fitted in the hallway. The engine room is a showcase example of Viking's commitment to engineering excellence. Both the cockpit and bridge are designed for tournament sportfishing and are among the best in their class. Standard 12-cylinder 1,100-hp MANs will cruise at a fast 29–30 knots and deliver a top speed of about 33 knots.   ❏

SPECIFICATIONS

Length ....58'11"
Beam.........................18'0"
Draft ....5'3"
Weight ....81,500#
Clearance ....14'6"
Water.................260 Gals.
Fuel ....1,500 Gals.
Cockpit............165 Sq. Ft.
Hull Type.........Modified-V
Designer ....B. Wilson

Production
1991–Current

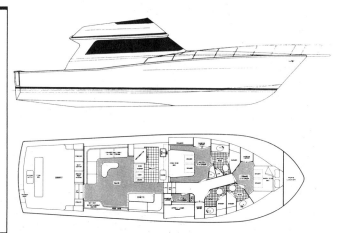

VIKING 63 MOTOR YACHT

An enlarged version of the successful Viking 55 MY, the 63 MY was offered in three versions: the original Walkaround model with full sidedecks and a small aft deck; a Widebody version with a full-width main salon, small aft deck, and no sidedecks; and lastly, an Extended Aft Deck model with walkaround decks, a smaller salon, and enlarged afterdeck. A good-looking yacht, she features a spacious four-stateroom layout below very similar to that found in the 55 MY. The additional length of the 63 is used to extend the main salon on the deckhouse level and to create a huge and opulent master stateroom. The high-style decor is a blend of traditional teak woodwork, luxurious furnishings, and rich designer fabrics. A utility room aft contains a washer/dryer and workbench, as well as access to the spacious engine room. Topside, the huge flybridge is fitted with enough wraparound lounge seating for a crowd. Standard 735-hp 8V92s will deliver a cruising speed of 17–18 knots and a top speed of about 20 knots. With the popular 900-hp 12V71s, she'll cruise at 20–21 knots and reach 23 knots top. ❏

SPECIFICATIONS

Length	62'6"
Length WL	54'2"
Beam	17'4"
Draft	4'9"
Weight	61,500#
Clearance	21'5"
Water	350 Gals.
Fuel	1,080 Gals.
Hull Type	Modified-V
Designer	R. Lazzara

Production
1988–91

VIKING 63 COCKPIT MY

The Viking 63 Cockpit MY began life in 1987 as the Gulfstar 63 CMY — basically a Gulfstar 55 MY with a cockpit extension. Gulfstar built only a couple of these models before the company was acquired by Viking late in 1987. Reintroduced as the Viking 63, the deckhouse was slightly redesigned but the luxurious four-stateroom interior remained unchanged. This is an expansive floorplan with a deckhouse galley, separate wheelhouse with deck access doors, and two salon staircases — one leading up to the bridge, and the other for access to the master stateroom. Two of the three forward staterooms have queen berths, and a utility room aft contains a washer/dryer and workbench. Viking offered the 63 Cockpit MY in a Walkaround (with full sidedecks) and Widebody (with a spacious full-width salon and no sidedecks) configurations. The aft deck is small, but the cockpit is large enough for deck chairs or fishing. Additional features include a big engine room, foredeck seating, and a formal dining area in the salon. Standard 735-hp 8V92s cruise at 18 knots and optional 900-hp 12V71s cruise around 21 knots. ❏

SPECIFICATIONS

Length	62'6"
Length WL	54'4"
Beam	17'4"
Draft	4'9"
Weight	61,500#
Clearance	21'5"
Water	350 Gals.
Fuel	1,080 Gals.
Hull Type	Modified-V
Designer	R. Lazzara

Production
1987–91

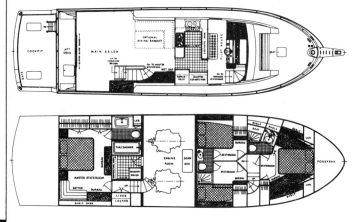

VIKING 65 EXTENDED AFT DECK MY

Built from the Viking 72 MY mold, the 65 EAD combines a lavish four-stateroom floorplan with a spacious aft deck and huge flybridge to create a versatile and extremely good-looking luxury cruiser. The styling is clearly improved over the 63 MY with a sweeping flybridge profile and raised wraparound bulwarks. There are many highlights in this boat — the full walkaround sidedecks and convenient on-deck day head will be appreciated by experienced owners — but the opulent master suite with its walk-in wardrobe, home-size head, and floor-to-ceiling entertainment center (with refrigerator and wineglass storage, no less) simply dominates the layout. A sliding glass salon door opens to the roomy aft deck (125 sq. ft.), and the sliding (not hinged) wing doors are unique. Topside, the extended flybridge has a wraparound helm, and lounge seating for a dozen guests. The large engine room allows space for lift mufflers — much quieter than the baffled exhausts used in earlier Viking 55 and 63 MYs. A good seaboat, standard 1,000-hp MANs cruise at 20 knots and deliver a top speed of about 23 knots. ❑

SPECIFICATIONS

Length ....64'7"
Length WL ....55'0"
Beam........................17'4"
Draft ....4'9"
Weight ....94,000#
Clearance ....20'8"
Water................300 Gals.
Fuel ....1,030 Gals.
Hull Type.........Modified-V
Designer ....R. Lazarra

Production
1991–Current

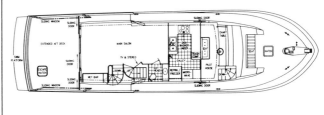

VIKING 65 COCKPIT MY

Nearly all cockpit motor yachts today are derived from already-existing motor yacht models. The Viking 65 CMY is a notable exception to this rule in that she is her own model and not simply a cockpit version of one of Viking's smaller motor yachts. Constructed on the same modified-V hull form used in the production of the 65 and 72 MY models, she's a good-looking design with a rakish flybridge and a bold Eurostyle profile. Her plush four-stateroom floorplan is arranged with three full heads and a utility room on the lower level — similar to the Viking 65 MY layout. The salon is full width and boasts a practical day head forward and a wet bar aft. The galley is separate from the salon in this layout and a sliding glass salon door opens to a small observation deck overlooking the cockpit below. Additional features include a utility room with direct access to the stand-up engine room, good-looking raised bulwarks, cockpit storage lockers, foredeck seating, and a spacious flybridge with wraparound helm. Standard 1,000-hp MAN diesels will cruise the Viking 65 Cockpit MY around 20–21 knots and reach 24 knots wide open. ❑

SPECIFICATIONS

Length	64'7"
Length WL	55'0"
Beam	17'4"
Draft	4'9"
Weight	91,000#
Clearance	20'8""
Water	300 Gals.
Fuel	1,030 Gals.
Hull Type	Modified-V
Designer	R. Lazzara

Production
1991–Current

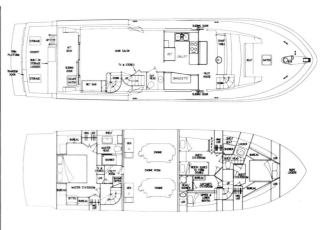

VIKING 72 MOTOR YACHT

The state-of-the-art construction displayed in the Viking 72 MY is evidence that by eliminating weight, designers can increase interior space while decreasing the size of the engines and tankage requirements. Built on a modified-V (16° deadrise aft) fully-cored hull, the Viking 72 weighs in at a relatively lightweight 84,000 lbs. There are three luxurious staterooms below and the extravagant master suite includes his-and-hers heads divided by a common Jacuzzi tub. The crew quarters include a private kitchenette and access to the engine room. Sliding glass doors separate the large semi-enclosed aft deck from the full-width salon with convenient on-deck head. The accommodations aboard the Viking 72 are those of a much larger boat and the contemporary furnishings and meticulous finish work are very much in keeping with her upscale base price. The real surprise, however, is the Viking 72's exceptional 21-knot cruising speed with standard 870-hp 12V71 diesels (24 knots top). Optional 1,040-hp 12V92s cruise at 23 knots (26 top). Simply stated, no other comparably powered production motor yacht this size will run with her.❑

SPECIFICATIONS

Length	72'0"
Length WL	NA
Beam	17'5"
Draft	4'10"
Weight	107,000#
Clearance	21'2"
Water	280 Gals.
Fuel	1,470 Gals.
Hull Type	Modified-V
Designer	R. Lazarra

Production
1989–Current

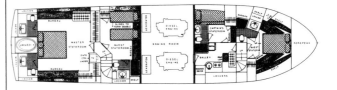

VIKING 72 COCKPIT MY

Not a stretched Viking 63 Motor Yacht, the new Viking 72 Cockpit MY is built from the 72 MY mold and features the same distinctive raised bulwarks forward. Gone, however, are the 72 MY's crew-quarters area, although the floorplan is arranged to provide a separate crew cabin with private head. The huge master stateroom is comparable with that found on much larger yachts. The deckhouse level features a day head, separate dining area, and an opulent and completely extravagant full-width salon. A utility room is aft (adjoining the master suite) with engine room access. The 72 CMY's large cockpit includes tackle lockers, a transom door, swim platform with ladder, and a fresh-water shower — everything required for fun on the water. In a successful effort to maintain a low center of gravity, Viking has gone to great measure to reduce flybridge and deckhouse weight. The Viking 72 Cockpit MY is quick to plane, and with only 870-hp 12V71s, she has a fast cruising speed of 21 knots. The stronger 1,040-hp 12V92TAs are available for a cruising speed of around 23 knots and a top speed of 26 knots. ❑

SPECIFICATIONS

Length	72'0"
Length WL	NA
Beam	17'5"
Draft	4'10"
Weight	105,000#
Clearance	21'2"
Water	350 Gals.
Fuel	1,470 Gals.
Cockpit	92 Sq. Ft.
Hull Type	Modified-V
Designer	R. Lazarra

Production
1990–Current

WELLCRAFT

Brief History

Beginning as a regional boatbuilding company in 1955, Wellcraft was acquired by the Aegis Corporation in 1969. The first of the popular Scarab series was introduced in 1976, and three years later the company built their first inboard cruiser, the Wellcraft 310. Investor Irwin Jacobs purchased the assets of Aegis in 1984, and today Wellcraft is a part of Jacob's Genmar Industries which also owns Hatteras and Carver among other major builders.

Selected Inboard Wellcraft Models

Wellcraft 2800 Coastal

Wellcraft 2900 Express

Wellcraft 2900 Sport Bridge

Wellcraft 3100 Express

Wellcraft 310 Flybridge Sedan

Wellcraft 3200 Coastal

Wellcraft 3200 St. Tropez (LXC)

Wellcraft 33 St. Tropez

Wellcraft 3300 Coastal

Wellcraft 3300 Sport Bridge

Wellcraft 3400 Gran Sport

Triumph 34 Bridgedeck

Triumph 34 Americus

Wellcraft 3500 Corsair

Wellcraft 3700 Cozumel

Wellcraft 37 Corsica

Wellcraft 43 Portifino

Wellcraft 43 San Remo

Wellcraft 46 Cockpit MY

Main Office

Wellcraft Marine, 1651 Whitfield Ave., Sarasota, FL 34243
813-753-7811

679

WELLCRAFT 2800 COASTAL

The Wellcraft 2800 Coastal is a versatile multi-purpose boat with an attractive profile and several notable design features. Built on a conventional modified-V hull with 16° of deadrise aft, she's a capable sportfisherman able to meet the needs of most weekend anglers. While the Coastal has wide sidedecks and a large unobstructed fishing cockpit, she still manages to provide a surprisingly spacious interior layout with good headroom, a small galley area, compact head with shower, and overnight berths for four. For most, however, the chief attraction of the 2800 Coastal is her practical and well-arranged deck plan. The large bi-level cockpit has a fiberglass liner for easy clean up and comes standard with removable in-deck fish boxes and a transom door. The helm seat is mounted on an above-deck livewell, and the companion seat pod contains a tackle center with sink. The 2800 Coastal was updated in 1990 with a fresh deckhouse window treatment, new interior decor, and restyled tackle centers. With the standard 350-cid gas engines she'll cruise around 21 knots and reach 28–29 knots top. Volvo diesels are optional. ❑

SPECIFICATIONS

Length	27'7"
Beam	9'11"
Draft	2'4"
Weight	8,200#
Clearance	7'6"
Water	20 Gals.
Fuel	182 Gals.
Cockpit	55 Sq. Ft.
Hull Type	Modified-V
Designer	B. Collier

Production
1986–Current

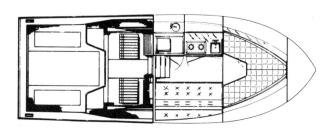

WELLCRAFT 2900 EXPRESS

The Wellcraft 2900 Express was originally called the 288 Suncruiser when she was introduced back in 1980. She was designed as an inexpensive family cruiser with conservative lines, a spacious cockpit layout, and comfortable accommodations below for four. The original 288 Suncruiser model was dropped from production in 1983, and the newly styled Wellcraft 2900 Express took her place. Aside from the hull graphics and several decor updates, she's basically the same boat as her predecessor. Further changes were made in 1985 with the addition of new interior fabrics and modern high-gloss mica laminates. The 2900 was built on a solid fiberglass hull with 16° of deadrise at the transom — the same hull later used for the Wellcraft 2900 Sport Bridge model. The relatively wide beam provides a comfortable and open floorplan with a full galley and convertible dinette and a stand-up head with shower. Twin 230-hp MerCruiser gas engines will cruise the Wellcraft 2900 at an economical 19–20 knots and reach 29 knots at full throttle. Note the very limited fuel capacity. ❏

SPECIFICATIONS

Length	28'8"
Beam	10'8"
Draft	2'6"
Weight	9,000#
Clearance	7'4"
Water	28 Gals.
Fuel	120 Gals.
Cockpit	NA
Hull Type	Modified-V
Designer	B. Collier

Production
1980–87

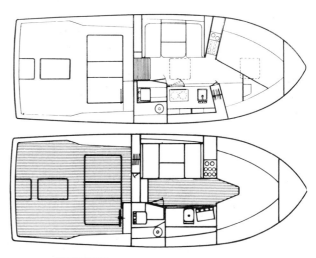

WELLCRAFT

WELLCRAFT 2900 SPORT BRIDGE

The Wellcraft 2900 Sport Bridge is a good-looking flybridge sportfisherman with a large fishing cockpit and an attractive low-profile appearance at dockside. She was built on a conventional modified-V hull form with 16° of deadrise at the transom and generous flare at the bow. The compact cabin layout of the Sport Bridge is straightforward and efficient with the head conveniently located just inside the cabin door. The small galley is to port across from the convertible dinette and V-berths are fitted in the forward stateroom. This is a practical layout for a small convertible and one that will suit the needs of family cruisers as well as a couple of overnight anglers. Engines are accessed via hatches in the raised engine deck, and the flybridge will accommodate three with a bench seat. Additional features include rod holders, swim platform, and a well-arranged and unobstructed fishing cockpit. A popular and very affordable boat, the Wellcraft 2900 Sport Bridge will cruise economically around 20 knots and reach 28 knots top with the optional Crusader 270-hp (or Volvo 260-hp) gas engines. ❏

SPECIFICATIONS

Length	28'8"
Beam	10'8"
Draft	2'6"
Weight	9,200#
Clearance	NA
Fresh Water	45 Gals.
Fuel	200 Gals.
Cockpit Area	NA
Hull Type	Modified-V
Designer	B. Collier

Production
1983–86

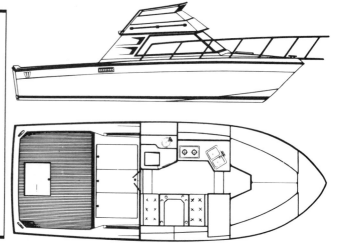

WELLCRAFT 3100 EXPRESS

The Wellcraft 3100 Express evolved from the original Wellcraft 310 Suncruiser introduced back in 1979. Conservatively styled by today's standards, she was built on a deep-V hull form with a steep 19° of deadrise at the transom. The profile of the 3100 Express shows considerable freeboard resulting in a full 6'5" of headroom in the main cabin. Teak trim and attractive fabrics are used throughout and overnight berths are provided for as many as six. Always a comfortable layout, a new Eurostyle interior was installed in the 1985 models with curved bulkheads and shiny off-white mica surfaces. Removable hatches in the cockpit sole access the reversed engines (V-drives are used) which are somewhat close together due to the outboard fuel tanks. Performance with the optional 454-cid big-block gas engines (350-hp) is around 22 knots at cruise and 31+ knots wide open. Note that trim tabs are generally required for the 3100 Express to obtain proper running angles. The Wellcraft 310 Sedan Cruiser (1981–83) was essentially the same boat with the addition of a flybridge and salon.

SPECIFICATIONS

Length	31'3"
Beam	11'6"
Draft	2'11"
Weight	10,200#
Clearance	8'1"
Water	28 Gals.
Fuel	160 Gals.
Cockpit	NA
Hull Type	Deep-V
Designer	R. Cole

Production
1979–85

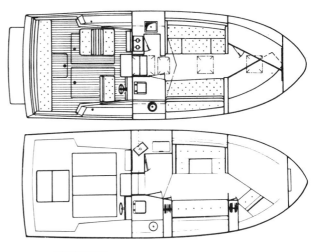

WELLCRAFT 310 FLYBRIDGE SEDAN

Based on the hull of the 3100 Express, the 310 FB Sedan is a conservative design aimed at the weekend cruiser market. Notably, her deep-V hull (with a steep 19° of deadrise at the transom) gives her above-average seakeeping characteristics offshore and the ability to run well in a chop — unusual in a small family cruiser. The interior of the 310 is functional and well arranged with the compact galley and full dinette down and an offset double berth in the stateroom. There's enough floor space in the salon for a sofa and chairs, and a sliding glass door opens into the cockpit. Owners could choose between a wet bar or optional lower helm station. While the cockpit isn't designed for any serious fishing activities, it's still adequate for a couple of light tackle anglers. The helm console is forward on the bridge with bench seating aft. Additional features include wide side-decks, black anodized cabin window frames, teak covering boards, and a teak pulpit. The 310 FB Sedan was offered with a variety of gas and diesel engines. Among them, 350-cid gas engines (with V-drives) will cruise at 18 knots and reach 24–25 knots top.   ❏

SPECIFICATIONS

Length	31'3"
Beam	11'6"
Draft	2'11"
Weight	11,200#
Clearance	11'0"
Water	50 Gals.
Fuel	200 Gals.
Cockpit	NA
Hull Type	Deep-V
Designer	R. Cole

Production
1981–83

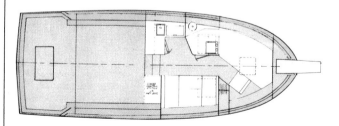

WELLCRAFT 3200 COASTAL

A popular boat with anglers and one of the early fishboat designs from Wellcraft, the 3200 Coastal is a good-looking express fisherman with a well-arranged deck plan and a comfortable interior layout. She was built on a solid fiberglass, modified-V hull form (14° deadrise at the transom) and features wide walkaround sidedecks and a molded bow pulpit. No longer in production, 3200 Coastals are popular today because of a solid and dry ride, good all-around handling qualities and a large, unobstructed fishing cockpit. Below, the roomy teak-paneled cabin will sleep four and includes a full galley and a stand-up head with shower. The Coastal's bi-level cockpit includes a 19" transom door (that unfortunately opens into the cockpit rather than out), and rod storage beneath the gunwales. An optional 60 gallons of fuel (or a generator instead) provide a cruising range of close to 300 miles. Twin 350-hp Crusaders will cruise the 3200 Coastal around 22 knots with a top speed of 30 knots. The Wellcraft 3200 Sport Bridge (1985–86) is essentially the same boat with a flybridge and salon.   ❏

SPECIFICATIONS

Length	32'0"
Beam	11'6"
Draft	3'0"
Weight	13,200#
Clearance	8'3"
Water	80 Gals.
Fuel	290 Gals.
Cockpit	71 Sq. Ft.
Hull Type	Modified-V
Designer	B. Collier

Production
1984–86

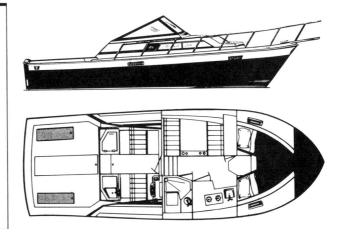

WELLCRAFT 3200 ST. TROPEZ (LXC)

One of the most popular Wellcraft designs ever, the St. Tropez was scheduled to go out of production in 1990 with the introduction of the new 3300 St. Tropez model. She's still available today, however, only with a new name: Now she's called the 3200 LXC. A handsome boat with a rakish profile, she offers a surprisingly spacious and open interior for a boat her size — a layout made possible by Wellcraft's use of an integral cabin liner which eliminates any structural bulkheads. The floorplan has remained essentially unchanged over the years and the decor is a blend of modern Formica surfaces, pastel colors, and designer-style fabrics. A bolt-on swim platform and transom door were added in 1988, and the side exhausts tubes (also introduced in 1988) were eliminated in 1989. Upgrades in 1990 included reduced hull graphics and a stylish white-on-white helm, and the current LXC model has an updated interior and a redesigned transom configuration. Standard 350-cid gas engines (using V-drives) will cruise around 21 knots with a top speed of 29 knots, and optional 454-cid engines will cruise at a fast 26–27 knots. ❑

SPECIFICATIONS

Length	31'8"
Length WL	NA
Beam	11'8"
Draft	2'10"
Weight	10,300#
Clearance	8'5"
Water	40 Gals.
Fuel	180 Gals.
Cockpit	NA
Hull Type	Modified-V
Designer	B.Collier

Production
1985–Current

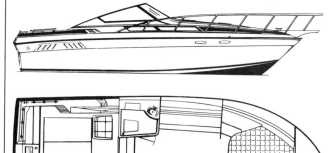

WELLCRAFT 33 ST. TROPEZ

The newest Wellcraft St. Tropez (the original 3200 St. Tropez came out in 1985 and is today called the LXC) is built on the same modified-V hull (16° deadrise aft) as her predecessor, with a bolt-on swim platform accounting for the increased length. Her European lines and sleek wraparound windshield are very modern, although her high profile gives the 33 St. Tropez a somewhat bulky appearance. To maximize forward headroom and improve lighting below, Wellcraft raised the foredeck and added a tinted wraparound cabin window to the deckhouse. Inside, the already-stylish accommodations of the original 3200 have been updated in the new St. Tropez, and the wide-open interior layout (no internal bulkheads) is retained. Originally offered with a walkaround berth forward, an offset double bed is now standard. The cockpit is large with adequate guest seating, and a unique walk-through windshield provides easy access to the foredeck. A pair of 350-cid gas engines (with V-drives) will cruise the Wellcraft 33 St. Tropez at 20 knots with a top speed of around 29 knots. ❏

SPECIFICATIONS

Length	33'7"
Length WL	NA
Beam	11'8"
Draft	2'10"
Weight	11,200#
Clearance	8'6"
Water	40 Gals.
Fuel	180 Gals.
Hull Type	Modified-V
Designer	B. Collier

Production
1990–Current

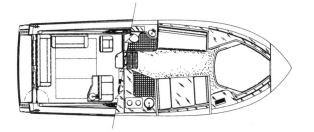

WELLCRAFT

WELLCRAFT 3300 COASTAL

Together with the 3300 Sport Bridge, the 3300 Coastal is the largest model in Wellcraft's current fleet of fishing boats. Introduced in 1989, she's constructed on a modified-V hull form with 16° of deadrise aft and prop pockets below (side exhausts were added in 1992). Designed as a dedicated sportfisherman, the 3300 Coastal comes standard with synchronized throttle controls, insulated in-deck fish boxes, bow pulpit, and the same inward-opening transom door found on the earlier 3200 Coastal. A factory marlin or tuna tower is optional. The bi-level cockpit is fitted with under-gunwale storage and padded coaming. Both helm and companion seats are mounted on raised boxes (with built-in livewell and bait prep station) that swing back for engine access. Overnight berths are provided for four with V-berths forward and a convertible dinette. Although she's primarily a fishing boat, the accommodations aboard the 3300 Coastal are suitable for weekend cruising. Standard 454-cid gas engines will cruise at 20–21 knots with a top speed of about 30 knots. Optional 375-hp Cat diesels will cruise around 25 knots. ❏

SPECIFICATIONS

Length	33'4"
Beam	12'8"
Draft	2'8"
Weight	13,800#
Clearance	8'4"
Water	52 Gals.
Fuel	300 Gals.
Cockpit	NA
Hull Type	Modified-V
Designer	Wellcraft

Production
1989–Current

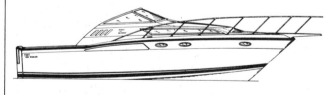

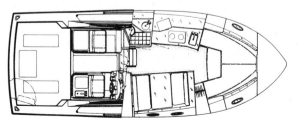

WELLCRAFT 3300 SPORT BRIDGE

A good-looking boat with a big fishing cockpit and an affordable price tag, the 3300 Sport Bridge is built on the same wide-beam hull (16° deadrise aft) used in the production of the 3300 Coastal. Although the Sport Bridge seems most at home as a fisherman, her upscale decor makes her an equally competent family cruiser. The floorplan is arranged with an island berth in the master stateroom and the galley opposite the L-shaped settee in the main cabin. The salon is quite roomy and open, and there's rod storage below the sole. Outside, there's seating for five on the small bridge, and the cockpit includes in-deck fish boxes, tackle center, rod storage, and an inward-opening transom door (a dubious feature that Wellcraft designers seem to favor in their fishing boats). Prop pockets in the hull allow the engines to be located aft of the salon bulkhead where they're accessible via flush hatches in the forward part of the cockpit. This design allows for a lower overall deckhouse profile without the use of engine boxes. Standard 454-cid gas engines will cruise the 3300 Sport Bridge at 19 knots and deliver a top speed of around 27 knots.❑

SPECIFICATIONS

Length	33'4"
Beam	12'8"
Draft	2'10"
Weight	15,300#
Clearance	9'9"
Water	50 Gals.
Fuel	274 Gals.
Cockpit	104 Sq. Ft.
Hull Type	Modified-V
Designer	Wellcraft

Production
1991–Current

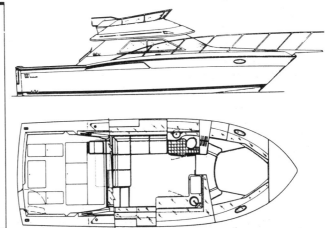

WELLCRAFT

WELLCRAFT 3400 GRAN SPORT

The Wellcraft 3400 Gran Sport is one of the more popular family express cruisers in a field rapidly becoming crowded with competition. She's built on a conventional modified-V hull form with moderate beam and 16° of deadrise at the transom. An integral hull liner is bonded to the solid fiberglass hull and eliminates the need for structural interior bulkheads. She was first introduced in 1984 as the 3400 Express Cruiser. In 1988 a new bolt-on swim platform was added along with side exhaust channels (later dropped in the 1989 models). A wet bar is standard in the cockpit, and the wide-open interior is in keeping with current sportboat trends although the lack of any real privacy in the stateroom is notable and the lack of a stall shower lamentable. The Gran Sport was again updated in 1990 with new hull graphics, a fresh interior decor and a stylish white-on-white helm console. A good-looking sportboat with clean lines and a stylish curved windshield, standard 454-cid gas engines will cruise the 3400 Gran Sport around 22 knots and reach a top speed of 30+ knots. ❏

SPECIFICATIONS

Length......................33'7"
Beam........................12'6"
Draft ....3'0"
Weight ....13,400#
Clearance ....9'4"
Water...................75 Gals.
Fuel ....270 Gals.
Cockpit.........................NA
Hull Type........Modified-V
Designer............B. Collier

Production
1984–Current

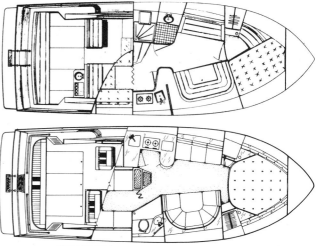

WELLCRAFT

WELLCRAFT TRIUMPH 34 BRIDGEDECK

Introduced as the first model of an all-new boat company in 1990, the Triumph 34 Bridgedeck was quickly blended into the Wellcraft fleet by parant company Genmar. In a lot of ways she resembles Carver's 34 Santego, although she's a little better-looking thanks to her larger cabin windows, cleaner deckhouse, and truly integral swim platform. It's belowdecks that the Triumph will satisfy the skeptics with a spacious, full-width, single-level salon and pit-style wraparound seating. Having the galley open to the salon makes the Triumph a superb entertaining boat, and large families will enjoy this layout for weekend cruising. A recessed bi-fold door provides privacy in the forward stateroom and a hidden curtain does almost the same for the portside settee/berth. There's a unique overhead pass-thru from the galley to the bridge — very practical. The flybridge has space for a crowd, and additional seating can be added in the cockpit. Built on a solid glass hull with 14° of transom deadrise and V-drives to deliver the power, optional 454-cid gas engines will cruise at a sedate 15–16 knots and reach a top speed of 26 knots. ❏

SPECIFICATIONS

Length w/Pulpit	36'9"
Length on Deck	34'0"
Beam	12'6"
Draft	3'0"
Weight	15,700#
Clearance	9'9"
Water	60 Gals.
Fuel	256 Gals.
Cockpit	60 Sq. Ft.
Hull Type	Modified-V
Designer	B. Collier

Production
1990–Current

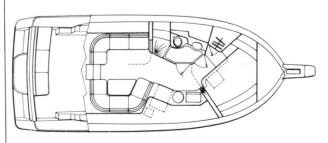

WELLCRAFT TRIUMPH 34 AMERICUS

The 34 Americus follows by a year the introduction of the Triumph 34 Bridgedeck and uses the same solid glass hull with a wide beam and shallow skeg. The Americus is a mid-cabin family cruiser with a modern profile and a big interior. Unlike most mid-cabin models, the windows in the Americus are large enough to provide an open and well-lit salon. The below-decks layout is fairly conventional with a double berth in the forward stateroom and an athwartships berth in the mid-cabin. The decor is a blend of pickled oak woodwork and white Formica cabinetry creating a light and upscale look. Headroom throughout the single level interior is better than average. The cockpit features a wet bar and plenty of lounge seating, along with an oversize wraparound windshield that helps keep the helmsman dry in wet weather. There's also a sunpad on the foredeck and fender storage in a transom box. The sidedecks are hard to find. The Americus is an average performer with standard 454-cid gas engines and V-drives. She'll cruise around 17 knots and run at 27–28 knots wide open.   ❏

SPECIFICATIONS

Length w/Pulpit	36'9"
Length on Deck	34'0"
Beam	12'6"
Draft	3'0"
Weight	15,000#
Clearance	9'3"
Water	46 Gals.
Fuel	226 Gals.
Cockpit	60 Sq. Ft.
Hull Type	Modified-V
Designer	B. Collier

Production
1991–Current

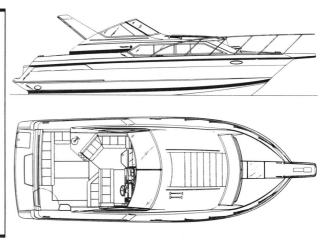

WELLCRAFT 3500 CORSAIR

The Corsair is the newest Wellcraft entry into the hot-selling family sportboat market. She's built on the same modified-V hull used in the production of the Gran Sport with moderate beam, 16° of transom deadrise, and side exhausts. The Corsica's raised foredeck gives her a lot of headroom below (at some expense to her profile) and the lack of sidedecks is notable (foredeck access is via a door in the windshield). The full-width interior layout of the Corsica is quite spacious and includes an offset double berth in the stateroom, stall shower in the head, and accommo- dations for six. Where many sportboats have separate helm and companion seats in the cockpit, the Corsica has a single three-place seat with the companionway to port. There's also lounge seating at the transom, and an aft-facing, fold-away bench seat behind the helm. Additional features include an integral reverse swim platform, stylish grillwork over the forward cabin windows, and cockpit access to the V-drives and engines. Optional 502-cid gas engines will cruise the Corsica at about 20 knots and reach 30-31 knots wide open. ❏

SPECIFICATIONS

Length	33'10"
Length WL	NA
Beam	12'6"
Draft	2'9"
Weight	14,400#
Clearance	9'9"
Water	76 Gals.
Fuel	270 Gals.
Hull Type	Modified-V
Designer	Wellcraft

Production
1992–Current

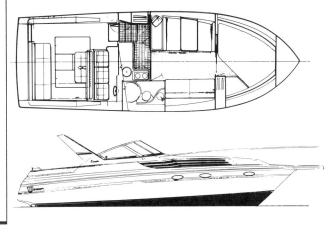

WELLCRAFT 3700 COZUMEL

The Wellcraft 3700 Cozumel was aimed at the growing market for modern, high-style sportfishing boats. Her striking profile features a solid front windshield, elliptical portlights, a sweeping sheer, and generally rakish lines. Inside, the two-stateroom layout with mid-level galley is a contemporary blend of white mica surfaces and attractive fabrics — a stylish decor for a fishing boat with some of the glitz and personality of the luxurious Portifino and San Remo interiors. The Cozumel's hull was designed with 16.5° of deadrise at the transom and propeller pock-

ets were recessed into the hull. Her large and uncluttered cockpit came equipped with lockable rod storage compartments, a transom door, inwale padding, and a fish box. A recessed lounge cushion is provided on the foredeck for sunbathing. Topside, the tournament-style flybridge provides good cockpit visibility and includes bench seating forward of the helm console. Gas engines were standard. The optional 375-hp Cat diesels will cruise the 3700 Cozumel around 24 knots with a top speed of 28 knots. Note the short production run.   ❏

SPECIFICATIONS

Length	36'11"
Beam	13'6"
Draft	3'3"
Weight	21,000#
Clearance	12'3"
Water	90 Gals.
Fuel	400 Gals.
Cockpit	90 Sq. Ft.
Hull Type	Modified-V
Designer	B. Collier

Production
1988–89

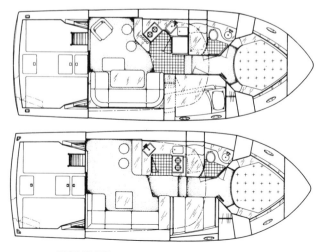

WELLCRAFT 37 CORSICA

With her long foredeck, curved windshield, and stylish (bolt-on) swim platform, the Wellcraft 37 Corsica has the graceful and sweeping profile characteristic of modern family sportboat designs. She was built on a solid fiberglass, modified-V hull (also used for the 3700 Cozumel model) with relatively high freeboard and 16° of deadrise at the transom. The floorplan of the Corsica is divided evenly between the cabin and cockpit. Inside, her wide beam and good headroom make the salon seem more open and spacious than the dimensions actually suggest.

Note the breakfast bar in lieu of the normal dinette. A step-down mid-cabin is abaft the salon, and there are overnight accommodations for a total of six. The salon seating was revised in 1991. The Corsica's cockpit is very large and features an L-shaped lounge with removable table to port in addition to a good-looking Eurostyle helm. A wet bar and walk-through transom door were standard. An average performer with the optional 502-cid gas engines, the Wellcraft 37 Corsica will cruise at 20 knots and reach a top speed of around 29 knots. ❏

SPECIFICATIONS

Length	36'11"
Length WL	NA
Beam	13'6"
Draft	3'1"
Weight	16,800#
Clearance	9'9"
Water	100 Gals.
Fuel	300 Gals.
Hull Type	Modified-V
Designer	B. Collier

Production
1989-91

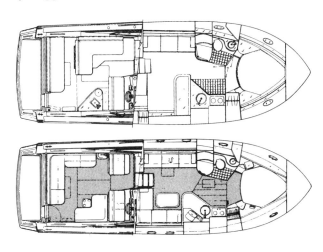

WELLCRAFT 43 PORTIFINO

A good-selling boat, the 43 Portifino is one of the more impressive mega-express sportcruisers on the market. With her sleek low-profile appearance, ultramodern interior, and huge cockpit, the Portifino projects the upscale elegance and Mediterranean styling typically found in boats of this type. She's constructed on a beamy modified-V hull with 14° of transom deadrise, side exhausts, and prop pockets below. The Portifino's original wide-open, single-stateroom layout was redesigned in 1992 to include a second private stateroom and dinette, but at the expense of the superb galley and break-fast bar found in earlier models. Outside, the Portifino's huge bi-level cockpit provides seating for a dozen. Note that hull graphics were reduced and the helm console upgraded in 1990. An opening hatch on the bridgedeck centerline reveals a ladder leading down into the large engine room. With standard 454-cid gas engines, the 43 Portifino has a (barely respectable) cruising speed of 16 knots and a top speed of about 25 knots. Optional 375-hp Cat diesels will cruise about 23 knots and reach 27 knots wide open. ❏

SPECIFICATIONS

Length	42'10"
Length WL	NA
Beam	14'6"
Draft	3'0"
Weight	18,200#
Clearance	10'3"
Water	100 Gals.
Fuel	300 Gals.
Hull Type	Modified-V
Designer	B. Collier

Production
1987–Current

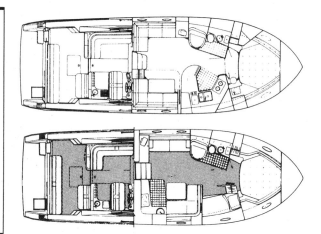

WELLCRAFT 43 SAN REMO

The Wellcraft 43 San Remo was the first motor yacht to bear the Wellcraft name since the Californian series was spun off several years ago. She uses the Portifino's modified-V hull (14° deadrise aft) with prop pockets and side exhaust *tunnels* on the hullsides. The San Remo's lines are low and sleek in spite of her raised deckhouse configuration, and her reverse transom is especially attractive. Below, the interior dimensions are expansive with emphasis placed in the stylish main salon. There were two floorplans available, the difference being that one has rounded sofas and countertops in the salon, and the other offers a more conventional layout with an L-shaped sofa and fewer curves. Either way, the San Remo's salon is an impressive display of high-style contemporary yacht design. The aft stateroom is not particularly spacious by motor yacht standards. Updates in 1990 included reduced hull graphics, a fresh interior decor package, and a stylish all-white Euro-style helm console. Optional Cat 375-hp diesels will cruise the San Remo around 20 knots with a top speed of 23–24 knots. ❑

SPECIFICATIONS

Length	42'10"
Length WL	NA
Beam	14'6"
Draft	3'2"
Weight	25,000#
Clearance	12'6"
Water	120 Gals.
Fuel	300/400 Gals.
Hull Type	Modified-V
Designer	B. Collier

Production
1988–90

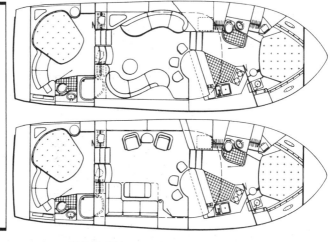

WELLCRAFT 46 COCKPIT MY

With the addition of a small cockpit, Wellcraft's 43 San Remo MY was transformed into the 46 Cockpit MY, currently the largest model in the Wellcraft fleet. Cockpit motor yachts have become increasingly popular in recent years due to the increased versatility they offer. Boarding is made much easier, and it's also possible to do a little fishing or diving from this convenient platform. Equally important, the extra length of the cockpit makes the Wellcraft 46 a slightly better-looking yacht than the original San Remo. The interior layouts of both boats are the same. Two floorplans are offered: a "Eurostyle" salon layout with facing S-shaped salon settees, and a more contemporary arrangement with a more open salon. There's also a cockpit access door added to the aft cabin — a very practical feature. Too, the 46 eliminated the distracting side exhaust tunnels found on the San Remo. Gas engines have been standard in the Wellcraft 46 CMY although most buyers will surely want diesel power in a boat of this size. Caterpillar 425-hp diesels will cruise at 21 knots with a top speed of about 25 knots. ❏

SPECIFICATIONS

Length	46'3"
Beam	14'6"
Draft	3'2"
Weight	27,000#
Clearance	14'0"
Water	120 Gals.
Fuel	400 Gals.
Cockpit	46 Sq. Ft.
Hull Type	Modified-V
Designer	B. Collier

Production
1990–Current

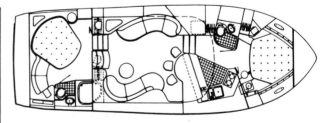

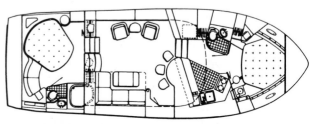

NOTABLE DESIGNS

Many of the most popular inboard powerboat designs have traditionally come from small, limited-production builders or high-volume manufacturers who produce only a few inboard models at the top of their line. Recent years have also seen the entry of several well-known sailboat builders like Sabre, Cape Dory, and Shannon into the powerboat market. The 'Notable Designs' chapter is devoted to boats from some of the above-mentioned builders — companies offering a limited selection of inboard models who may not be counted among the major production powerboat manufacturers.

Boats listed in this chapter are presented first in order of size, and then alphabetically. Address and telephone numbers for the manufacturers are listed at the chapter's conclusion. Those experienced in the business will note that many of the selections are not actually full-production models. Wilbur 38s, for example, are nearly always semi-custom yachts, as are the Little Harbor 36 and the Donzi 65. These models are included because of their interest to the reader as well as to the industry. Many are classics — the Dyer 29 and the Krogan 42 to name only a couple — and others like the Davis 47 and 61 compete directly with the best of the large manufacturers. In a few cases, the design is so unusual that the authors simply couldn't ignore it. All, however, have achieved a level of popularity or importance sufficient to warrant their inclusion in this edition of the PowerBoat Guide.

699

BIMINI 245 TOURNAMENT

Not only is the Bimini 245 the *only* twin-inboard express currently available in this size range (the North Coast 24 is now out of production) — she's also a great-looking fisherman and trailerable as well. Built on the proven modified-V hull (17° of deadrise aft) of the single-inboard Topaz 24, the Bimini 245 is otherwise a completely different boat with a raised deckhouse, prominent wraparound windshield, and superb cockpit layout with room for a small chair and a couple of anglers. The single-level fishing cockpit is among the largest in its class and comes with two in-deck fishboxes, knee-level gunwales, and removable engine boxes that double as baitwatching seats. A well-arranged helm console provides space for flush-mounting basic electronics. Since the Bimini is a dedicated fisherman, the cabin accommodations for two are modest but attractively finished and adequate for weekend expeditions. An agile and good-running boat, twin 140-hp (4-cyl) Volvo gas engines will cruise around 24 knots (at better than 2 mpg!) and deliver a top speed of about 30 knots. ❑

SPECIFICATIONS

Length	24'4"
Beam	8'0"
Draft	2'2"
Weight	5,000#
Clearance	NA
Water	None
Fuel	140 Gals.
Cockpit	45 Sq. Ft.
Hull Type	Modified-V
Designer	B. Walker

Production
1991–Current

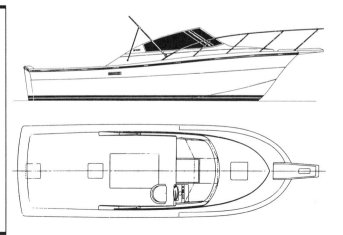

NORDIC 26 TUG

The Nordic 26 Tug (no relation to the Nordic motor yachts) is a salty little character vessel built in the state of Washington. When asked to describe her tugboat lines, most people reply that she's a good-looking little cruiser. And so she is with her plumb bow and upright superstructure — a handsome craft with surprising performance. More than just an eye-catching design, she's well constructed and quite able to head offshore for extended coastal cruising. Her seaworthy semi-displacement hull features a full-length keel for directional stability and grounding protection. Inside, the aft cabin is actually the main living area with the galley to port and a convertible lounge opposite. The pilothouse is raised two steps from the salon (engine access is below), and V-berths are installed in the stateroom. With a 50-hp diesel, the Nordic 26 Tug will cruise effortlessly at 7–8 knots burning about 1 gph. Speeds of up to 16 knots are available with an optional 100-hp diesel engine. About 150 have been built to date. The popularity of the Nordic 26 led to the introduction in 1985 of the Nordic 32 Tug. ❏

SPECIFICATIONS

Length......................26'4"
Length WL....................NA
Beam..........................9'6"
Draft ....2'0"
Weight..................6,200#
Clearance ....9'6"
Water..................50 Gals.
Fuel ....75 Gals.
Hull Type ....Semi-Disp.
Designer............L. Senour

Production
1981–Current

CAPE DORY 28 POWERYACHT

Long known for building a quality line of Alberg-designed sailboats, Cape Dory entered the powerboat market in 1985 with the introduction of the Cape Dory 28, a classy Downeast-style cruiser with a lobster boat heritage. She's built on a seaworthy solid fiberglass hull with rounded bilges and a full-length keel for handling and prop protection. The Cape Dory has a roomy cockpit for a 28-footer and she's very much at home as a weekend fisherman. A full-height door leads from the cockpit into the compact pilothouse, where the accommodations are simple but finished with the quality teak joinerwork and paneling typical of a Cape Dory product. The majority have been equipped with a single 200-hp Volvo diesel rather than the standard gas engine. The cruising speed with the diesel is 16–17 knots and the top speed is around 20 knots. Note that Cape Dory has offered three other models based on this same 28' hull, including the very handsome Open Fisherman. A workboat version is also built for commercial fishermen. Over 220 Cape Dory 28s (mostly flybridge models with a single diesel) have been built. ❑

SPECIFICATIONS

Length	27'11"
Length WL	25'11"
Beam	9'11"
Draft	2'11"
Weight	8,000#
Clearance	11'2"
Water	45 Gals.
Fuel	76 Gals.
Cockpit	56 Sq. Ft.
Hull Type	Semi-Disp.
Designer	Cape Dory

Production
1985–Current

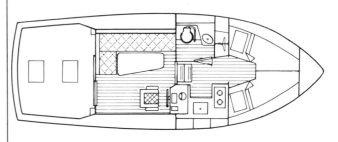

AQUASPORT 290 TOURNAMENT SF

The Aquasport 290 Tournament Master is a durable sportfisherman with a factory tuna tower and an impressive array of standard equipment. There were actually two Aquasport 290 models offered — the Express Fisherman lacks the tower and fishing package found on the Tournament Master (pictured above). Both have notably large (nearly 100 sq. ft.) cockpits thanks to the wide beam. The Tournament Master's cockpit was outfitted with a tackle center, a removable in-deck fish box, and salt and freshwater washdowns. An overhead electron-ics box is located at the helm, and the tower has a full set of controls. Inside, the dinette can be converted into a dou-ble berth in the normal manner, and the hinged bench backs swing up to create two additional bunk berths. Rod racks were placed in the overhead, and the head is quite large. Engine access is via hatches in the cockpit. Twin 350-cid gas engines will cruise the Aquasport 290 around 25 knots with a top speed of 34 knots. Note that Aquasport also offered the similarly styled 270 Tournament model (1984–87) with inboard or out-board engines. ❑

SPECIFICATIONS

Length....................31'0"
Beam......................11'0"
Draft ....2'6"
Weight..................9,500#
Clearance ....8'0"
Water..................32 Gals.
Fuel ....300 Gals.
Cockpit.........................NA
Hull Type ....Deep-V
Designer ....Aquasport

Production
1984–91

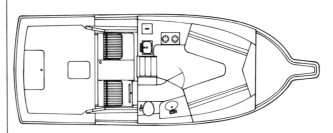

BIMINI 29 CUDDY

Bimini Marine acquired the rights to the former Topaz 29 hull in 1989, and she's been marketed as the Bimini 29 ever since. These are popular and affordable boats with proven fishability and very economical performance. Hull construction is solid fiberglass. The layout of the Bimini is basically the same as the earlier Topaz model with a well-arranged bi-level fishing cockpit and a small cabin below. A large hatch on the bridgedeck provides access to the engines, and visibility from the helm is excellent. The lower level of the cockpit is large enough for a mounted chair, and a large in-deck fishbox and below-deck storage area keep the cockpit free of clutter. Inside, there are berths for three in the cabin along with a compact galley and a roomy stand-up head with shower. Most Bimini 29s have been equipped with the optional factory tower. Several gas and diesel engines have been offered in the Bimini 29 over the years. The popular 200-hp Volvo diesels will cruise at a fast 26-27 knots with a top speed of around 30 knots. Note that a 29 Sport with an enlarged bridgedeck and smaller cabin is also available. ❏

SPECIFICATIONS

Length	29'0"
Beam	10'3"
Draft	2'6"
Weight	8,100#
Clearance	NA
Water	30 Gals.
Fuel	225 Gals.
Cockpit	65 Sq. Ft.
Hull Type	Modified-V
Designer	P. Patterson

Production
1989–Current

NOTABLE DESIGNS

DYER 29

Designed for weekend cruising and fishing or as a general utility boat, the durable Dyer 29 is a industry design classic. Production began over 35 years ago (in 1955), making her *the* longest-running fiberglass design in the history of the business. Each of the over 300 Dyer 29s sold has been customized to some extent, and the boat has seen many updates over the years. At only 6,700 lbs., the Dyer would be considered a light boat were it not for her narrow beam. She's built on a soft-chined hull with moderate bow flare, fine entry, protected prop, and an uncommonly graceful sheer. The ability of the Dyer's hull to tackle heavy sea conditions is legendary. Those who own Dyers tolerate her tight cabin quarters and inconvenient engine box and delight in the fingertip control and positive response of this easily driven hull. Among numerous engine options, a single 200-hp Volvo diesel (now standard) will cruise the Dyer 29 around 16 knots and reach a top speed of approximately 20–21 knots. In addition to the popular Trunk Cabin model (pictured above), the 29 is available in a hardtop or open fishing version.   ❑

SPECIFICATIONS

Length	28'6"
Length WL	26'0"
Beam	9'5"
Draft	2'6"
Weight	6,700#
Clearance	6'0"
Water	24 Gals
Fuel	110 Gals.
Cockpit	NA
Hull Type	Semi-Disp.
Designer	Nick Potter

Production
1955–Current

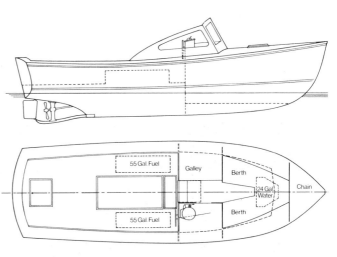

STRIKE 29 SPORTFISHERMAN

The Strike 29 SF displays good-quality workmanship and simplicity of layout that serious anglers always admire. Built on a low-profile, deep-V hull (20° deadrise) with propeller pockets, the Strike 29 has the look and feel of a custom sportfishing machine. The center-console/cuddy deckplan is ideal for fishermen who want overnight capability while still retaining the walkaround fish-fighting attributes of a center console. The cuddy's accommodations are basic — V-berths with a head under — but well finished and sufficient for an occasional offshore weekend. The forward section of the huge center console lifts up for easy access to the diesels. The cockpit itself (with padded coaming) is large enough for the installation of a full-size fighting chair. The Strike 29 can easily handle the addition of a full tower thanks to her wide beam and low center of gravity. A total of 35 were built, and the original teak cockpit sole was replaced with a fiberglass liner beginning with hull #5. Twin 240-hp Perkins diesels (optional) deliver a 25-knot cruising speed (29 knots top) and a range of 350–400 miles. ❑

SPECIFICATIONS

Length	29'0"
Beam	10'11"
Draft	2'6"
Weight	7,500#
Clearance	NA
Water	20 Gals.
Fuel	215 Gals.
Cockpit	NA
Hull Type	Deep-V
Designer	J. Fourtney

Production
1985–89

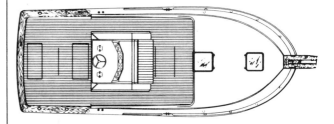

BLACK WATCH 30 SPORTFISHERMAN

Introduced in 1986, the Black Watch 30 has been extremely well received among anglers for her extraordinary handling abilities, handsome profile, and high-tech construction. Built on a deep-V bottom design with 18° of deadrise at the transom, the hull and stringers of the Black Watch 30 are foam cored, and high-strength unidirectional fabrics are used throughout. The result is a solid, seaworthy hull capable of slugging it out in some pretty mean seas. Her layout is dedicated to serious fishing with the large, unobstructed cockpit set low to the water.

Access to the engines is excellent, and the entire cockpit liner is removable for major service. Cabin accommodations are fairly basic with two berths, an enclosed head, and a small galley area. The Black Watch 30 is a very good performer. With the optional 454-cid gas engines, she'll cruise around 26 knots (34 knots top), and the lightweight 250-hp Cummins 6BTA diesels (also optional) will cruise at a fast and very economical 28 knots and reach 33 knots wide open. A flybridge model built on the same hull was introduced in 1989. ❏

SPECIFICATIONS

Length	30'1"
Beam	10'11"
Draft	2'10"
Weight	9,000#
Clearance	7'0"
Water	50 Gals.
Fuel	240 Gals.
Cockpit	120 Sq. Ft.
Hull Type	Deep-V
Designer	Hunt Assoc.

Production
1986–Current

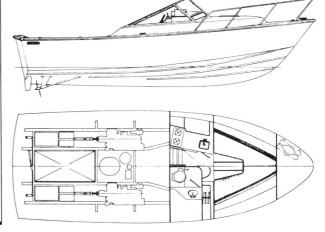

BLACK WATCH 30 FLYBRIDGE

Serious anglers, whose lust for a high-performance sportfisherman conflicts with the family's demand for a comfortable interior, will quickly appreciate the Black Watch 30 Flybridge. A little top-heavy in appearance but an otherwise rugged-looking boat, she's built on the same Baltec-cored deep-V (18°) hull as the Open Fisherman model. Features include an oversize flybridge with bench seating forward of the helm, a well-appointed cabin with the galley to starboard, dinette settee to port, V-berths forward, and an enclosed head with shower just inside the cabin door. The interior is notably roomy for only a 30-footer and the headroom is a full 6'4" in the salon. Outside, the cockpit is adequate for big-game fishing activities. A big fishbox runs athwartships across the after part of the cockpit, and clever roll-back engine boxes provide above-average service access to the engines. Standard power for the Black Watch 30 is 454-cid gas engines, but the optional 300-hp Cummins diesels provide outstanding performance and economy at a hard 28-knot cruise. Top speed with these engines is about 32–33 knots. ❏

SPECIFICATIONS

Length	30'1"
Length WL	25'7"
Beam	10'11"
Draft	3'0"
Weight	12,000#
Clearance	9'6"
Water	40 Gals.
Fuel	270 Gals.
Cockpit	80 Sq. Ft.
Hull Type	Deep-V
Designer	Hunt Assoc.

Production
1989–Current

CAPE DORY 30 POWERYACHT

Designed to fill the gap between the Cape Dory 28 and 33 models, the Cape Dory 30 shares the same Downeast profile and New England styling characteristics. She was built on a hardchined modified-V hull of solid fiberglass. Her hull form differs from the 28's more traditional semi-displacement design, and although she's only slightly longer than the 28, the wider beam results in a much larger interior — some 40& more interior space than in the 28, according to the company. The traditional cabin woodwork is impressive and includes a full teak-and-holly sole with an ash ceiling and plenty of teak trim. Three large hatches in the salon sole provide good access to the engines. A solid teak sliding door opens to the small cockpit, where teak covering boards and two large in-deck storage lockers are found. Chrysler gas engines were standard, however nearly all were equipped with the optional 200-hp Volvo diesels. She'll cruise economically at 19–20 knots with a top speed of around 22 knots. This was a costly boat to build (almost as much as the larger 33-footer) and she was discontinued after a short production run. ❏

SPECIFICATIONS

Length	30'3"
Length WL	27'8"
Beam	12'0"
Draft	3'0"
Weight	12,500#
Clearance	12'3"
Water	62 Gals.
Fuel	230 Gals.
Cockpit	NA
Hull Type	Modified-V
Designer	Clive Dent

Production
1990–91

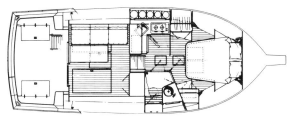

INNOVATOR 30

The Innovator 30 is a well-built West Coast design with a single-minded objective: catching fish. Introduced in 1988 as the Innovator 31, she was extensively updated in late 1991, and today she's now called the Innovator 30. (About 35 Innovator 31s were built.) While her rugged modified-V hull (12° deadrise aft) remains the same, there have been significant changes in the construction process and to the interior layout (which is said to provide a 20% increase in cabin space). A structural grid system replaced the original stringers, and a one-piece deck/cockpit mold

is now used rather than the earlier five separate molds. The cockpit is arranged for serious fishing pursuits with two in-deck fishboxes and *two* bridge ladders. Engine boxes provide excellent access to the motors and molded cockpit steps at the corners lead to extra-wide sidedecks. Inside, the cabin has berths for four along with a small galley and stand-up head. Gas engines are standard, but most are sold with one of several diesel options. Among them, Cummins 210-hp diesels will deliver an impressive cruising speed of 23–24 knots and a top speed of around 28 knots.   ❏

SPECIFICATIONS

Length	30'10"
Beam	10'4"
Weight	11,000#
Clearance	9'0"
Water	60 Gals.
Fuel	265 Gals.
Cockpit	75 Sq. Ft.
Hull Type	Modified-V
Designer	Ed Monk, Jr.

Production
1988–Current

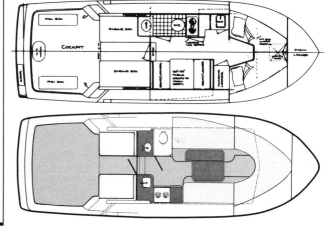

PORTSMOUTH 30 CRUISER

The origins of the Portsmouth 30 go back to 1978 when the late Royal Lowell (perhaps the best-known designer of Downeast boats) drew the lines for the Sisu 30, an inboard lobster fisherman with a reputation for seaworthy and dependable operation. Sisu went out of business in 1987 and the molds were acquired by Portsmouth. Built on a semi-displacement hull with a deep, full-length prop-protecting keel, the Portsmouth hulls are balsa cored and the boats are turned out on a semi-production basis in New Hampshire. There are several versions of the Portsmouth 30 offered including sportfisherman, hardtop, and commercial workboat models, however the Cruiser (pictured above) has been the most popular to date. The floorplan has the galley in the salon behind the helm and a convertible dinette opposite. There's a shower in the stand-up head and the teak woodwork and teak-and-holly flooring give the cabin a very traditional feel. Outside, the cockpit is large enough for some serious fishing and the sidedecks are protected by high railings. A single 250-hp Cummins diesel will cruise at 16 knots at 8–9 gph. ❏

SPECIFICATIONS

Length	29'9"
Length WL	28'2"
Beam	10'6"
Draft	2'11"
Weight	10,000#
Clearance	NA
Water	64 Gals.
Fuel	180 Gals.
Cockpit	NA
Hull Type	Semi-Disp.
Designer	R. Lowell

Production
1989–Current

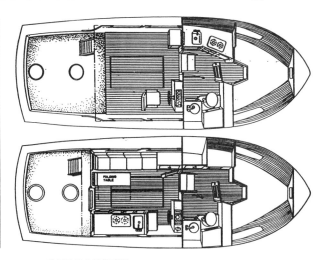

WILLARD 30/4 TRAWLER

The Willard 30/4 is a salty-looking little trawler with a true displacement hull and a ballasted keel. In spite of her topheavy appearance, she's won a lot of hearts over the years for her cozy accommodations and super-economical operation. Her double-ended hull design and heavy displacement provide a secure and comfortable ride in a variety of sea conditions. With only 30'6" of LOA, the Willard provides a surprising amount of living space for her size. There's a compact salon with the galley aft and an L-shaped settee/dinette to port. The lower helm is stan-

dard of course, and V-berths with a small head compartment are forward. Never a full production boat (none were built from 1982–87), the new Willard 30 (1988–current) features a direct-drive engine (replacing the V-drive of previous models) and internal lead ballast rather than external cast iron. With a 50-hp Perkins diesel, the efficiency of the Willard 30/4 is truly phenomenal — at 6 knots she's actually burning less than 1 gph! With only 150 gallons of fuel capacity, her average cruising range is still over 1,000 nautical miles. ❑

SPECIFICATIONS

Length	30'6"
Length WL	27'6"
Beam	10'6"
Draft	3'6"
Weight	17,000#
Clearance	NA
Water	80 Gals.
Fuel	150 Gals.
Cockpit	NA
Hull Type	Displacement
Designer	Willard

Production
1977–Current

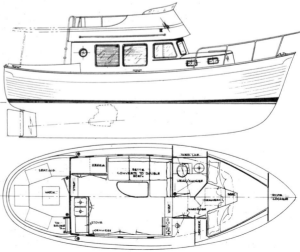

BLUE SEAS 31

The Blue Seas 31 was one of the last introductions for the now-defunct Hinterhoeller Yachts, the Canadian builder best known for their high-quality series of Nonsuch sailboats. The Blue Seas was first introduced at the 1988 Toronto boat show by the original builder, the Blue Seas Boat Co. of Clinton, Ontario. Production under the Hinterhoeller nameplate commenced in late 1989. A lobster-boat design with a Downeast heritage, the Blue Seas was built on a single-piecs fiberglass hull with three watertight compartments, a nearly plumb bow, rounded bilges, full-length skeg, and a graceful low-profile sheerline. Inside, the deckhouse is separated from the lower level with a privacy door. Originally offered with a shortened deckhouse and larger cockpit, the "long house" version became standard in later models. The cockpit is still large, and the Blue Seas makes a good long-range fisherman. The single 210-hp Cummins diesel engine will cruise economically at 14 knots (8 gph) and reach a top speed of around 17–18 knots. Offered with or without a flybridge, the Blue Seas 31 is well constructed and very easy on the eye. ❏

SPECIFICATIONS

Length	30'8"
Length WL	29'2"
Beam	11'6"
Draft	3'0"
Weight	11,000#
Clearance	9'2"
Water	80 Gals.
Fuel	200 Gals.
Cockpit	NA
Hull Type	Semi-Disp.
Designer	R. Lowell

Production
1988–91

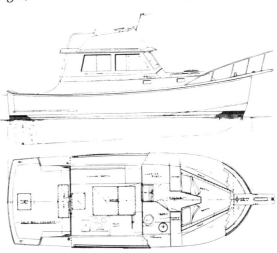

NOTABLE DESIGNS

BOSTON WHALER 31L

The fact that you can't sink the Boston Whaler 31 will appeal to safety-conscious anglers who can afford to own this well-built inboard sportfisherman. Constructed on a rugged deep-V hull (20° of transom deadrise), a layer of urethane foam bonds the inner liner to the outer hull acting as a stiffener as well as providing enough flotation to keep the 31 afloat even when fully swamped! This is a proven offshore design that provides good trolling stability and better-than-average performance in rough water. Introduced in 1988, she was completely redesigned in 1991 with a new deckhouse profile, relocated engines, and fresh interior and cockpit layouts. (The private stateroom in early models was a rarity in a fishing boat of this size.) Designed for tournament-level activities, the revised bi-level cockpit features an in-deck fishbox, bait-prep center, lockable rod storage, and a fold-down jumpseat. The hinged bridgedeck tilts up for excellent engine access. Most early 31s were powered with 250-hp Cummins diesels (23 knots cruise/27 top). The now-standard 300-hp Cummins cruise at 25 knots and deliver around 29 knots wide open. ❏

SPECIFICATIONS

Length	31'9"
Beam	11'10"
Draft	2'8"
Weight	12,500#
Clearance	7'6"
Water	40 Gals.
Fuel	313 Gals.
Cockpit	74 Sq. Ft.
Hull Type	Deep-V
Designer	Whaler

Production
1988–Current

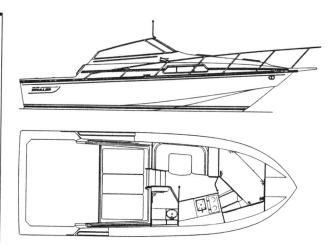

NORTH COAST 31 SPORTFISHERMAN

Several builders inaccurately apply the "Deep-V" label to their hulls in an attempt to curry favor with sportfishermen convinced of the superiority of a deep-V design. In the case of the North Coast 31, the claim is more than just advertising hype. The hull is designed by Charles Jannace (who also designs Blackfins), and with 23° of deadrise aft, the 31 really is a deep-V. In a field crowded with small inboard sportfisherman, the North Coast 31 has several notable features that anglers will admire. The helm visibility is particularly good, and the unique console provides space for flush-mounting most electronics. (Note that the throttles and shift levers are uniquely arranged to starboard, slightly forward of one another.) The cockpit has molded steps for easy access to the recessed sidedecks, and there are two 60" removable fishboxes in the sole. Below, the well-finished cabin has a teak-and-holly sole, attractive light ash trimwork, and a head with stall shower. A good performer, the popular 250-hp Cummins diesels will cruise the North Coast 31 at an economical 25 knots with a top speed of about 29 knots. ❏

SPECIFICATIONS

Length	30'8"
Beam	12'0"
Draft	3'2"
Weight	11,300#
Clearance	8'0"
Water	50 Gals.
Fuel, Std	275 Gals.
Fuel, Opt	410 Gals.
Cockpit	77 Sq. Ft.
Hull Type	Deep-V
Designer	C. Jannace

Production
1988–90

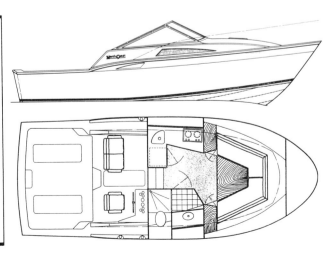

NOTABLE DESIGNS

SHAMROCK 31 GRAND SLAM

Shamrock Marine is a well-regarded South Florida builder of small fishing and utility boats featuring unique "keel drive" hull designs. But unlike the rest of the Shamrock series, the 31 Grand Slam is built on a deep-V hull with 19° of deadrise at the transom. At first glance, she appears to be a fairly standard open sportfisherman with attractive lines and a large fishing cockpit. A closer look reveals several interesting features. The helm seat, for example, can be converted into a leaning post. Engine access is good — a unique central service bay houses all the mechanical and electrical systems. The cockpit features modular tackle centers, rod holders, and storage bins. For accommodations, there are four single berths below (the dinette seatbacks convert to single bunks) and a stand-up head with shower. Standard gas engines have not popular with buyers. Early models with optional 250-hp Cummins diesels cruise at 28 knots (2 mpg!) and reach 33 wide open. Cummins 300-hp diesels (available since 1990) cruise at 31 knots and deliver 34–35 knots top. Over 160 have been built to date. ❏

SPECIFICATIONS

Length	31'0"
Beam	11'4"
Draft	3'4"
Weight	9,250#
Clearance	18'0"
Water	40 Gals.
Fuel, Std	290 Gals.
Fuel, Opt	340 Gals.
Cockpit	142 Sq. Ft.
Hull Type	Deep-V
Designer	Shamrock

Production
1987–Current

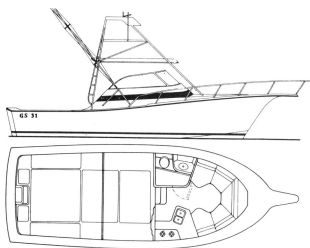

NOTABLE DESIGNS

ALBEMARLE 32 FLYBRIDGE

From a distance the Albemarle 32 has the bold and aggressive profile of a larger boat. Her solid front windshield is painted to carry the "black mask" effect around the deckhouse and she has the appearance of a custom boat. Those who have been aboard the smaller Albemarle 27 will not be surprised with the quality engineering built into the 32 Flybridge. Her deep-V hull (18° transom deadrise) is solid fiberglass and reinforced on the bottom with an grid stringer system. The unobstructed cockpit is set up for serious fishing and includes two fish boxes under the sole.

Inside, there's a real salon with room for a sofa and chairs — very unusual in just a 32- fishing boat. A double berth is fitted in the stateroom of early models (V-berths are now standard) and a stall shower is located in the head. Attractively decorated and featuring plenty of teak cabinetry and trim, this is a surprisingly spacious interior. Standard (but less popular with buyers) 454-cid gas engines will cruise at 22 knots and reach 32 knots top. Optional 300-hp Cummins diesels cruise at a fast 29 knots and deliver 33 knots wide open. ❏

SPECIFICATIONS

Length	32'2"
Beam	10'11"
Draft	3'0"
Weight	18,000#
Clearance	NA
Water	49 Gals.
Fuel	309 Gals.
Cockpit	85 Sq. Ft.
Hull Type	Deep-V
Designer	Albemarle

Production
1988–Current

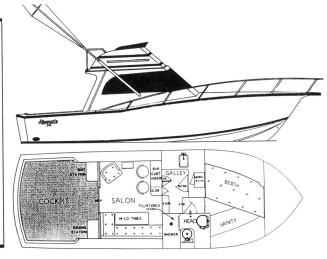

NOTABLE DESIGNS

LBEMARLE 32 EXPRESS FISHERMAN

A modification of the earlier 32 Flybridge model, the Albemarle 32 Express is a rugged day boat that will provide several advantages over her convertible sistership for serious anglers. Without the flybridge the center of gravity is lower, and the weight savings translates into better performance and economy. Albemarle has a history of building no-nonsense fishing boats and the 32 Express is a very substantial platform indeed. Aside from her good looks and solid construction, she's loaded with practical features. The cockpit is large and completely unob-structed — no protruding cleats or hatches anywhere. The raised helm provides excellent visibility, and the helm console is efficient and well arranged. There are two large in-deck fish boxes with macerator pumps and washdowns under the gunnels. For engine access, the entire bridgedeck can be hydraulically raised at the flick of a switch. If the belowdecks accommodations are limited, they're tastefully finished and include berths for four and a stand-up head. Powered with 300-hp Cummins diesels, she'll cruise at a fast 30 knots and reach 35 knots top. ❏

SPECIFICATIONS

Length ....32'2"
Beam......................10'11"
Draft ....3'0"
Weight ....13,500#
Clearance ....NA
Water..................50 Gals.
Fuel..................320 Gals.
Cockpit.........................NA
Hull Type ....Deep-V
Designer.........Albelmarle

Production
1990–Current

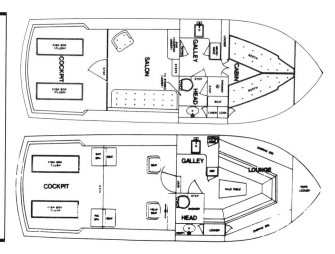

BRENDAN 32 SPORT SEDAN

The Shannon 32 was the first power-boat design from the Shannon Boat Company after years of building luxurious sailing yachts. Offered in Sport Sedan and open Express Sport Fisherman models, the 32s have been reasonably popular boats in recent years and over 40 have been sold. Constructed on a modified-V hull and cored from the chines up, the Brendan 32 is designed primarily as a small family cruiser, although her cockpit is large enough for some light tackle fishing. A transom door is standard and there are two in-deck fish boxes in the cockpit sole. The belowdecks layout has an efficient galley and dinette down and a lower helm in the small salon. The well-crafted teak woodwork (including a teak parquet sole) and a full 360° view creates an open and very traditional interior. The flybridge is notably small and, while well arranged at the helm, it's definitely not designed for a crowd. Several diesel options are available in the Brendan 32, however the 205-hp GM 6.2s have proven most popular. These engines will cruise the boat around 18 knots and reach 23 knots wide open. ❑

SPECIFICATIONS

Length	32'10"
Beam	12'0"
Draft	2'9"
Weight	13,500#
Clearance	11'3"
Water	80 Gals.
Fuel	250 Gals.
Cockpit	NA
Hull Type	Modified-V
Designer	W. Schultz

Production
1986–Current

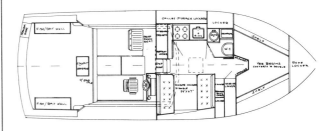

EAGLE 32 TUG

The salty lines and commercial work-boat profile of the Eagle 32 portray a sense of confidence unique to tugboat designs. Indeed, the Eagle looks like she was born for the sea. Built in Taiwan by Transpacific Marine, construction is on a solid fiberglass, semi-displacement hull with a full-length skeg for prop and rudder protection. Her slightly rounded transom moderates the effects of a following sea, while a hard chine and long keel provide stability. The traditional teak interior of the Eagle is well finished and impressively detailed. Visibility from the raised pilothouse is excellent and a door closes off the salon for glare-free nightime running. The stateroom is a little tight, but there's a stall shower in the head compartment and the open salon and aft deck areas are comfortable indeed. Note the upper helm hidden within the false stack on the bridge and the functional mast and boom assembly. A single Lehman 90-hp diesel will cruise the Eagle 32 Tug at about 7 knots (burning just over 1 gph), resulting in an incredible 750–800 miles of range with just 150 gallons of fuel! An optional 135-hp Lehman will cruise at 9–10 knots. ❑

SPECIFICATIONS

Length	32'0"
Length WL	28'0"
Beam	11'6"
Draft	3'4"
Weight	16,000#
Clearance	NA
Water	100 Gals.
Fuel	150 Gals.
Hull Type	Semi-Disp.
Designer	K. Hankinson

Production
1985–Current

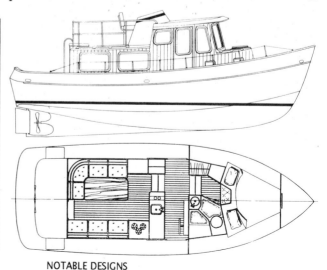

NOTABLE DESIGNS

ELLIS 32 EXTENDED TOP CRUISER

The Ellis Boat Company is an old-time builder of hand-crafted Down-east cruisers and lobster boats operating from a small family-owned yard in Manset, Maine. The Ellis 32 is the newest and largest of their designs, and the first boat was completed in 1991. (She's also offered in a Flybridge and Bass boat model.) The hull is a semi-displacement design with a deep, prop-protecting keel, generous beam, and solid fiberglass construction. The Ellis 32 is a straightforward, basic boat with a pretty trunk cabin profile, superb detailing, and plenty of traditional teak trim.

With nearly 12' of beam, she's a roomy boat inside with overnight accommodations for up to six depending on the floorplan. Note that the galley is located just inside the salon door where it's easily accessed from the cockpit. The fore-cabin has two large V-berths, and the seat back of the settee opposite the large head folds up to create an upper berth. The ceilings are light ash and the cabin sole throughout the interior is solid teak. Built on a semi-custom basis, a single 300-hp Volvo diesel will cruise the Ellis 32 at 18 knots and deliver a top speed of 23–24 knots. ❏

SPECIFICATIONS

Length	32'1"
Beam	11'9"
Draft	3'9"
Weight	13,000#
Clearance	NA
Water	25 Gals.
Fuel	160 Gals.
Cockpit	NA
Hull Type	Semi-Disp.
Designer	R. Ellis

Production
1991–Current

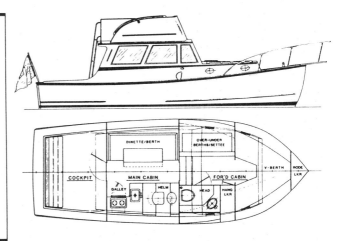

MARINETTE 32 SEDAN

With over 1,800 built, the Marinette 32 Sedan has proven to be a very popular and enduring design since she was introduced back in 1976. While she's beginning to show her age, she makes up for any lack of contemporary styling with her sturdy welded aluminum construction and lively performance. Indeed, the Marinette 32 is (as she was intended to be) a versatile and all-purpose family cruiser. Her interior layout is practical, the flybridge is large, and there's enough room in her modest cockpit for occasional light tackle fishing activities. With the dinette and salon settee converted the 32 Sedan will sleep six in comfort. The salon is large for a 32-footer, and the wraparound cabin windows add to the spacious effect. A portside lower helm is standard. At only 10,500 lbs., it's no surprise that her performance is brisk. With just 240-hp Chrysler gas engines, the Marinette 32 will cruise at 22 knots and turn 30+ at full throttle. For those who worry that aluminum boats are prone to corrosion in both fresh and salt water, Marinette equips their boats with a standard galvanic monitoring system. ❏

SPECIFICATIONS

Length	32'6"
Beam	12'0"
Draft	2'0"
Weight	10,500#
Clearance	9'2"
Water	35 Gals.
Fuel	150 Gals.
Cockpit	NA
Hull Type	Modified-V
Construction	Aluminum
Designer	Marinette

Production
1976–90

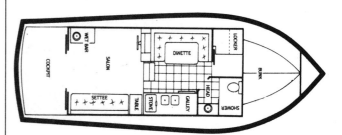

NORDIC 32 TUG

The Nordic 32 has the same graceful tugboat profile and semi-displacement, full-keeled hull as the smaller Nordic 26. Built in America, these are true raised pilothouse designs with an elevated helm position and excellent visibility. Both the 26 and 32 share similar interior layouts, but where the 26 is a little tight in some areas the accommodations aboard the Nordic 32 are quite roomy. This is especially true in the salon where the large windows and traditional teak woodwork combine to produce a charming Old World ambience. Forward (through the pilothouse),

a stall shower is found in the head compartment and the stateroom has an offset double berth. Nowhere below is the headroom less than 6'4". Because the salon uses nearly the full width of the hull's beam, the sidedecks are not walkarounds. The construction of the Nordic 32 Tug is substantial, and she's a genuine offshore cruiser. Several diesel engines (100 to 120-hp) have been standard over the years. With the currently optional 210-hp Cummins, she'll cruise efficiently at 13 knots and reach a 16-knot top speed. Over 60 have been built to date. ❏

SPECIFICATIONS

Length	32'2"
Length WL	32'0"
Beam	11'0"
Draft	3'0"
Weight	13,500#
Clearance	10'2"
Water	100 Gals.
Fuel	115 Gals.
Hull Type	Semi-Disp.
Designer	L. Senour

Production
1985–Current

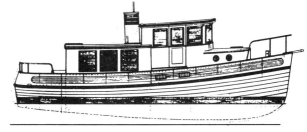

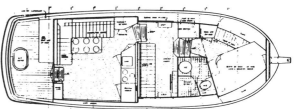

NOTABLE DESIGNS

PERFORMER 32

The Performer 32 is easily recognized in any crowd with her aggressive low-profile appearance, black feature stripe, and strictly business fishing cockpit. She's built on a true deep-V hull (23° deadrise aft) using some of the most advanced construction techniques in the business. The beam is narrow and prop pockets are used to reduce the shaft angle for better speed and efficiency. The result is a rugged and seaworthy fishing platform that can haul ass. With optional J&T 300-hp GM 8.2s, the Performer will cruise at an honest 30 knots and reach 36–37 knots top *with* a tower. The compact bi-level cockpit can still handle a marlin chair, and also provides an in-deck fishbox. The helm is superbly arranged with a full array of instruments set into a shaded dash and a comfortable booster-type helm seat. The interior dimensions are limited (but the layout is efficient) and the molded fiberglass surfaces, brushed aluminum trim, and a snap-out carpeting make clean-up easy. A good-looking boat that lives up to her ambitious name, the Performer 32 will appeal primarily to experienced anglers who have been around the block a few times. ❏

SPECIFICATIONS

Length ....31'6"
Beam........................10'3"
Draft ....2'4"
Weight ....12,500#
Clearance ....NA
Water...................30 Gals.
Fuel............210/320 Gals.
Cockpit..............86 Sq. Ft.
Hull Type ....Deep-V
Designer ....Performer

Production
1987–Current

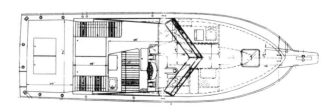

STAMAS 32 FLYBRIDGE SF

The Stamas 32 has a reputation for being a durable sportfisherman as well as a dependable no-frills family cruiser. Originally introduced in 1977, she's built on a solid fiberglass hull with substantial beam and a moderate 12° of deadrise at the transom. Stamas offered the 32 in a Sport Sedan version (with a salon bulkhead), or as a Flybridge Sportfisherman (with no aft bulkhead and a semi-enclosed deckhouse). She features a big fishing cockpit, comfortable interior accommodations and a proven track record as a durable offshore fishing platform. Her good all-around handling qualities are well known by now and the ride is dry and stable in most conditions. Attention to practical details is evident in the extra-wide sidedecks and cockpit coaming. Visibility from the lower helm is excellent and the cockpit is open and completely unobstructed. Inside, the layout is arranged with Vee berths forward, an efficient galley area, and a roomy head compartment with a shower. No lightweight, the Stamas 32 will cruise at 20–21 knots and top out around 30 knots with optional 454-cid gas engines. ❏

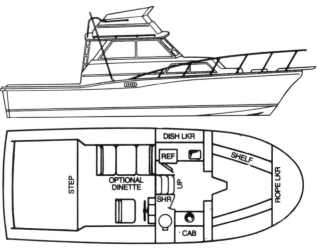

SPECIFICATIONS

Length	32'3"
Length WL	28'0"
Beam	12'0"
Draft:	2'9"
Weight	12,800#
Clearance	11'6"
Water	55 Gals.
Fuel	250 Gals.
Cockpit	90 Sq. Ft.
Hull Type	Modified-V
Designer	Stamas

Production
1977–87

CAPE DORY 33 POWERYACHT

The Cape Dory 33 is a handsome trunk cabin sedan with an eye-catching Downeast character, and a proud, upright profile. She's built on a solid fiberglass, modified-V hull with a full-length keel of sufficient depth to provide protection to the running gear. Inside, the 33's salon is completely surrounded by large cabin windows. The visibility from the lower helm is excellent, and a full 6'5" of headroom makes the salon seem larger than it really is. The interior is finished with traditional grain-matched teak woodwork and cabinetry and a separate stall shower is found in the head compartment. While the Cape Dory 33's floorplan is fairly standard for a boat of this size, the finish work and detailing are noteworthy. An island berth in the stateroom became optional in 1992. The cockpit is large enough to satisfy the needs of most weekend anglers (the angled bridge ladder is a nice touch, as are the port and starboard cockpit steps leading to the sidedecks). The Cape Dory 33 is offered with single or twin engines, gas or diesel. Twin 200-hp Volvos have proven popular and will cruise 17 knots and reach 21 knots top. ❏

SPECIFICATIONS

Length	32'10"
Length WL	30'0"
Beam	12'2"
Draft	2'11"
Weight	13,500#
Clearance	12'8"
Water	100 Gals.
Fuel	260 Gals.
Cockpit	65 Sq. Ft.
Hull Type	Modified-V
Designer	Clive Dent

Production
1988–Current

NOTABLE DESIGNS

ALLMAND 34 CLASSIC

The Allmand 34 is an all-fiberglass family cruiser with a roomy interior, decent performance (for her era), and a better-than-average ride in a chop. She was built on a deep-V hull with a fairly narrow beam and a shallow skeg. In order to maximize interior volume the Allmand 34s deckhouse is set well forward giving her a slightly awkward look. These were affordable family cruisers during the 70s and quite a number were sold. There were several interior layouts offered, but most were arranged with a single stateroom forward giving with the galley and dinette down and a standard lower helm. The teak and mica laminates used in the 34 make for a rather dated interior by today's standards. While she's not designed as a fisherman, her cockpit is suitable for a couple of anglers (but not tackle centers). The bridge is small and the sidedecks are narrow. The Allmand 34 was offered as a flybridge sedan (the "Classic" pictured above), or as a Sportfish model with a much larger cockpit. Diesels were available but most were sold with 225-hp gas inboards which cruise around 17 knots and reach a top speed of 25 knots. ❏

SPECIFICATIONS

Length	34'0"
Beam	11'0"
Draft	2'8"
Weight	12,000#
Clearance	12'2"
Water	120 Gals.
Fuel	170 Gals.
Hull Type	Deep-V
Designer	Allmand

Production
1971–81

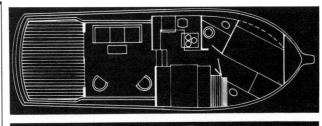

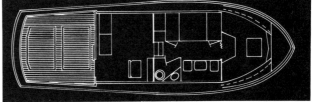

CATALINA 34 CONVERTIBLE

The Catalina 34 Convertible began life as the Pearson 34 (1990–91), a good-looking cruiser with notably high production standards. Catalina picked up the molds when Pearson went bankrupt in 1991, and the first of the new 34s was introduced in 1992. The interior layout has been rearranged (see lower floorplan), and gas engines are now standard, and she retains her good-looking profile and modern appearance. She's constructed on a true deep-V hull with 19° of transom deadrise — a key factor in her ability to run well in poor weather. The original Pearson floorplan had the galley down and a single stateroom, while the new Catalina 34 has opted for the galley up and two staterooms. Either way, she's a beamy boat and there's a lot of room below. The cockpit is on the small side but still adequate for some light-tackle fishing. The bridge will seat five and the wide sidedecks are a definite plus. Note that 320-hp Cats (24 knots cruise/28 top) were standard in the Pearson 34 (rather than gas engines). The now-standard 454-cid gas engines will probably cruise the Catalina 34 around 21 knots. ❏

SPECIFICATIONS

Length......................33'9"
Beam.......................13'0"
Draft ....3'4"
Weight ....19,000#
Clearance.................14'3"
Water...................70 Gals.
Fuel ....310 Gals.
Cockpit..............65 Sq. Ft.
Hull Type ....Deep-V
Designer........Hunt Assoc.

Production
1990–Current

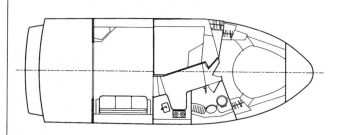

SABRELINE 34

An upright, slightly Downeast profile and an attractive interior characterize the Sabreline 34 Sedan, the most recent powerboat design from Sabre Yachts. She's built on the same hull (14° deadrise aft) used in the original Sabreline 36 model. This is a livable and versatile cruiser ideally suited for two. Like all Sabre boats (sail or power) there's no shortage of craftsmanship and attention to detail in the way she's put together. Her traditional teak interior is arranged with the galley forward in the salon opposite the lower helm and a walkaround island berth in the state-room. Everything is carefully arranged with an eye toward practicality and comfort. The large salon windows all open (so does the center windshield forward) and ventilation in this boat is exceptional. The 34 isn't a wide-beam boat so the interior dimensions are somewhat limited. Features include good storage, excellent engine access, stall shower with wet locker (nice touch), a roomy cockpit, and a quiet underwater exhaust system. Economical to operate and a good performer, the Sabreline 34 will cruise at 18 knots (1.3 mpg) with twin 210-hp Cummins diesels. ❏

SPECIFICATIONS

Length	34'0"
Beam	12'6"
Draft	3'3"
Weight	17,800#
Clearance	12'8"
Water	160 Gals.
Fuel	250 Gals.
Cockpit	70 Sq. Ft.
Hull Type	Modified-V
Designer	Sabre

Production
1991–Current

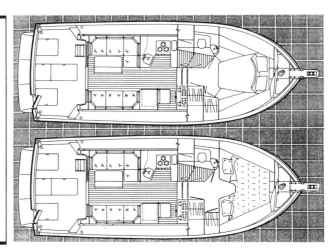

WILBUR 34 CRUISER

For those whose love of boats goes beyond the limitations of today's cooky-cutter production models, the Wilbur 34 is presented as an example of the nautical charm and grace inherent in a pure Downeast-style design. Built on a semi-custom basis by Lee S. Wilbur & Co. in Manset, Maine, the Wilbur 34 enjoys a reputation for excellent sea-keeping characteristics, and dependable, economical operation. Construction is solid fiberglass with balsa coring applied in the deck and superstructure. Like most classic New England designs, the Wilbur 34 has a keel-protected prop and running gear. The traditional interior layout is straightforward (unyielding to current designer trends) with the emphasis on comfort and practicality. The galley-up layout (pictured below) is just one of several custom interior floor-plans available. Outside, the cockpit is large enough for serious fishing. Aside from the Cruiser, the Wilbur 34 is available in three fishing models. A single 375-hp Caterpillar diesel will cruise around 19 knots with a top speed of 22 knots. Several smaller diesel engines are offered depending on speed requirements. ❑

SPECIFICATIONS

Length	34'4"
Length WL	32'3"
Beam	12'0"
Draft	3'8"
Weight	15,000#
Clearance	NA
Water	80 Gals.
Fuel	200 Gals.
Cockpit	NA
Hull Type	Semi-Disp.
Designer	Ralph Ellis

Production
1982–Current

NOTABLE DESIGNS

CABO 35 SPORTFISHERMAN

The new Cabo 35 SF is a stylish and well-built West Coast fisherman with excellent performance and one of the largest cockpits in her class. She's constructed on a modified-V hull, with vacuum-bagged Airex coring above the waterline, and 17° of transom deadrise. Her low-slung profile is the result of locating the motors aft in cockpit engine boxes, thus allowing the salon sole to be set low in the hull. Considering her oversized cockpit, the Cabo's interior is surprisingly open and spacious thanks to wraparound cabin windows and a wide beam. (There's a large storage area beneath the salon sole.) The appealing galley-up layout includes a long 8' settee (with hidden rod storage) in the salon, and an island berth in the stateroom, while the galley-down floorplan has a stall shower in the head compartment. Additional features include two in-deck fishboxes, transom door and gate, excellent engine access, single-lever helm controls ,and very wide sidedecks with sturdy rails. A good-running boat, optional 375-hp Cats will cruise the Cabo 35 efficiently at 27 knots (30 gph) and reach around 32 knots top. ❏

SPECIFICATIONS

Length	34'6"
Beam	13'0"
Draft	2'6"
Weight	20,000#
Clearance	11'3"
Water	80 Gals.
Fuel	425 Gals.
Cockpit	130 Sq. Ft.
Hull Type	Modified-V
Designer	Crealock

Production
1992–Current

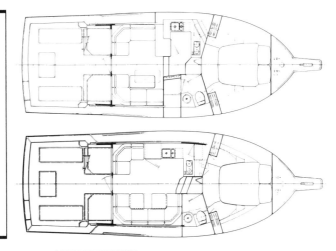

CONTENDER 35

The Contender 35 is a high performance, thoroughly modern tournament fishing boat designed for serious
offshore anglers. She's built on a narrow, deep-V hull (24° deadrise aft), with
Baltec coring from the waterline up and
a unique integral swim platform extension. A good-looking boat, the
Contender 35 is available with three
separate cockpit configurations, however the aft-console/L-shaped settee
layout (pictured above) is the most popular, according to the builder. (Twin
helm consoles can also be fitted aft or
the helm can be aft and midships.)

Regardless of the cockpit layout the
interior remains fixed. Fold-up bunks
provide sleeping for a party of four with
a stand-up head, high-low table, and
small galley. Notable features of the
Contender 35 include excellent engine
access (the whole center section of the
deck rises hydraulically), a well-
arranged helm console with tilt wheel,
40-gallon livewell, two removable fishboxes, and concealed rod storage below.
Available with inboard or outboard
power (most late models have had the
outboards), twin 250-hp Cummins
diesels will cruise at a fast 32 knots. ❏

SPECIFICATIONS

Length	35'0'
Beam	10'0"
Draft	2'0"
Weight w/o power	5,200#
Clearance	NA
Water	45 Gals.
Fuel	250 Gals.
Cockpit	NA
Hull Type	Deep-V
Designer	Contender

Production
1989–Current

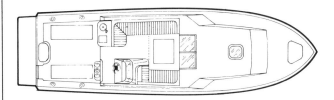

DORAL 350 BOCA GRANDE

For those who have an appreciation for quality and don't mind paying for it, the Doral 350 is an impressive mid-sized express cruiser. She's built in Canada and currently represents the largest offering in Doral's fleet. Expensive, yes, but well built. Features include a stylish curved windshield, molded pulpit, foredeck sunpad, a huge hydraulically-activated cockpit hatch for engine access, and an innovative power helm seat that can serve as a stand-up bolster when the seas pick up. The conventional mid-cabin floorplan of the Boca Grande is open and spacious, with a curtain providing limited privacy in the forward stateroom. The mid-cabin has pit-style lounge seating and an adjustable dinette table and the head has a separate shower stall. A good-looking cruiser with meticulous detailing and finish, Doral's decision to emply a conventional transom design rather than a Hollywood-glitz Euro-transom is slightly refreshing. Built on a fully cored hull and driven through V-drives, she'll cruise around 17–18 knots with standard 454-cid Mer-Cruisers gas engines and reach 28 knots wide open. ❏

SPECIFICATIONS

Length w/pulpit	35'8"
Beam	12'6"
Draft	3'0"
Weight	13,900#
Clearance	10'0"
Water	80 Gals.
Fuel	260 Gals.
Cockpit	NA
Hull Type	Modified-V
Designer	Doral

Production
1991-Current

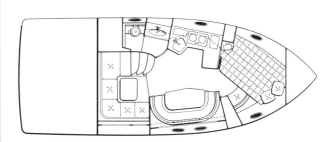

DUFFY 35 SPORT CRUISER

Designed with a greater emphasis on speed than most other Downeast-style boats of her type, the Duffy 35 is a well-built, semi-custom cruiser with distinctive lines and tremendous eye appeal. She's constructed on a solid fiberglass, modified-V hull with a fine entry, hard chines aft, and a full-length keel which provides protection for the underwater gear. Like most of the true Downeast designs, a fully equipped Duffy 35 is priced at the higher end of the market for boats in her size range. Aside from her obvious good looks and traditional charm, her great attractions are superb craftsmanship and lasting value. The Duffy is a versatile boat with a cockpit large enough for serious fishing, and an efficient interior layout well-suited for extended cruising. Features include a deckhouse galley, complete lower helm station, a large stall shower, and excellent access to the engine. A single Caterpillar 375-hp diesel will produce a surprisingly fast cruising speed of 25 knots and a top speed of nearly 30. Fast, seaworthy, and stable, the Duffy 35 is built on a limited production basis in Brooklin, Maine. ❑

SPECIFICATIONS

Length	35'1"
Length WL	33'4"
Beam	11'11"
Draft	3'3"
Weight	12,000#
Water	50 Gals.
Fuel, Std	100 Gals.
Fuel, Opt	200 Gals.
Cockpit	NA
Hull Type	Modified-V
Designer	S. Lincoln

Production
1983–Current

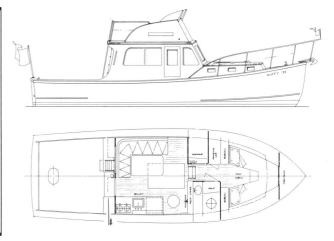

FORMULA 35 PC

Although Thunderbird Products (the builder of Formula boats) is best known for their line of high-performance speedboats and offshore racers, the company also builds a series of traditional express cruisers with the emphasis on attractive styling and good-quality construction. Built on a rugged deep-V hull (20° deadrise aft) with moderate beam and propeller pockets, the Formula 35 PC (Performance Cruiser) features side exhausts and colorful Imron-painted hull graphics. Her modern interior decor is an attractive blend of stylish fabrics and white Formica cabinetry and countertops. A pedestal island berth is forward, and the mid-cabin floorplan has facing lounge seats that convert into a double berth at night. Outside, a foldaway lounge at the transom, and L-shaped seating forward were standard, along with a radar arch and cockpit wet bar. Powered with 454-cid MerCruiser gas engines and driven through V-drives, the Formula 35 PC will cruise at 21–22 knots and reach a top speed of around 31 knots. This model was replaced in 1990 with the new Formula 36 PC. ❏

SPECIFICATIONS

Length......................35'0"
Beam.......................12'0"
Draft ....2'8"
Weight ....13,750#
Clearance ....10'2"
Water..................50 Gals.
Fuel ....275 Gals.
Cockpit.......................NA
Hull Type ....Deep-V
Designer............In-House

Production
1986–89

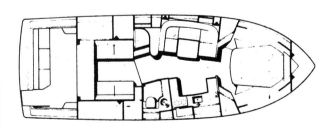

NAUSET 35 SPORT CRUISER

Nauset Marine is a New England builder of commercial workboats and custom cruisers from 12 to 42 feet. Among their more notable designs is the Nauset 35 Sport Cruiser, a boat the company has been building since 1984. The Nauset 35 is constructed on the old Bruno-Stillman 35 hull — an extremely popular design used in the production of some 350 boats from 1973 until 1984 when the company closed down. Nauset bought the molds and have since built nearly 40 Nauset 35s for private use. Construction is solid fiberglass with a single-piece inner liner, and a deep, prop-protecting keel. The interior has changed little from the original Bruno-Stillman layout, although the deckhouse profile is completely new. Features include a standard lower helm, wide sidedecks (well-protected with raised bulwarks and high railings), prominent bowsprit, and a very large cockpit with room for a mounted chair. Among several single- and twin-engine options, a single 375-hp Cat (17–18 knots cruise/24 top) has proven most popular. With her classic profile and seakindly hull, the Nauset 35 is an extremely appealing design. ❑

SPECIFICATIONS

Length	35'0"
Length WL	NA
Beam	12'0"
Draft	3'0"
Weight	17,000#
Clearance	NA
Water	40 Gals.
Fuel	150 Gals.
Hull Type	Semi-Disp.
Designer	R. Lowell

Production
1984–Current

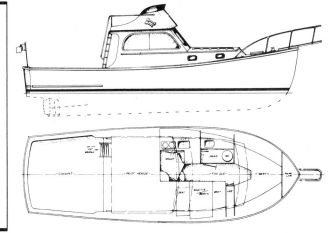

PT 35 SUNDECK

The PT 35 Sundeck will appeal to those seeking a compact double-cabin trawler without the teak decks and trim found on most of the Asian imports of her era. No lightweight at 20,000 lbs., she features a practical deck plan (for her size), and an efficient two-stateroom layout. Because of her limited LOA, the PT 35 is a bit small for a hard-top — without it, she has a fairly pleasing profile compared with most other small double-cabin models we've seen. The galley-up floorplan results in a large forward stateroom at the expense of a very small salon, while the galley down version seems more functional. Either way, a lower helm was standard, and there are convenient sliding deck access doors port *and* starboard in the salon. Just about everything below is built of teak, trimmed with it, or covered by it, and the quality of the joinerwork is good. There were several engine options available including both single- and twin-diesel applications. She may look like a trawler, but with a single 200-hp Perkins the PT 35 Sundeck can achieve a top speed of 12–13 knots. Twin-diesel models can reach about 20 knots. ❏

SPECIFICATIONS

Length	35'4"
Length WL	31'10"
Beam	12'6"
Draft	3'0"
Weight	20,000#
Clearance	NA
Water	100 Gals.
Fuel	300 Gals.
Hull Type	Semi-Disp.
Designer	J. Norek

Production
1984–90

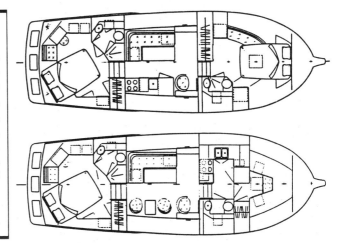

BLACK WATCH 36 SPORTFISHERMAN

Built on a semi-custom basis, the Black Watch 36 is a lightweight, high-tech flybridge fisherman with top-quality construction and superb offshore performance. Her hull — a narrow Hunt-designed deep-V with 18° of transom deadrise — is fully balsa cored, vacuum-bagged, and reinforced on the bottom with Kevlar. Aside from her graceful appearance and meticulous detailing, perhaps the most striking feature of the Black Watch 36 is her oversized fishing cockpit. Indeed, it's so big (and the beam so narrow) that the cabin layout is necessarily compact compared with other boats her size. With V-bunks, galley, dinette, and head, the Black Watch 36 provides accommodations for four with good headroom, overhead rod storage, and teak-and-holly sole. Note the absence of a stall shower in the head. The motors are easily accessed via engine boxes in the cockpit and the bridge is arranged with a wraparound helm console, Panish controls, and guest seating forward. A good-running boat with optional 291-hp Cummins diesels, she'll cruise at 24 knots (18–20 gph) and reach a top speed of 27–28 knots.   ❏

SPECIFICATIONS

Length	36'2"
Beam	11'4"
Draft	2'7"
Weight	13,900#
Clearance	11'0"
Cockpit	150 Sq. Ft.
Water	60 Gals.
Fuel	300 Gals.
Hull Type	Deep-V
Designer	Hunt Assoc.

Production
1991–Current

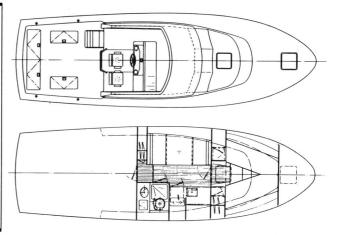

CAPE DORY 36 POWERYACHT

The distinctive Downeast appearance of the Cape Dory 36 Poweryacht is very much in keeping with her New England heritage. She was built on a modified-V hull with balsa coring above the waterline, a full-length keel, wide beam, and 15° of deadrise at the transom. The keel provides prop protection allowing an extra margin of error in shallow waters. The Cape Dory's interior shows the traditional workmanship identified with this builder. The two-stateroom layout is standard and a dinette option (replacing the guest cabin) is available. The roomy head compartment contains a man-sized stall shower. Designed with an eye toward the sportfishing market, the Cape Dory's 77 sq. ft. cockpit is big enough for a couple of light-tackle anglers and comes equipped with a standard transom door and teak covering boards. Twin 454-cid gas engines are standard and cruise at 20+ knots. Optional 250-hp GM 8.2 diesels cruise 19–20 knots with a top speed of 23 knots. No longer in production, the last Cape Dory 36 was built in 1990, when the company went out of business and the molds were sold. ❑

SPECIFICATIONS

Length	35'9"
Length WL	31'7"
Beam	13'6"
Draft	3'6"
Weight	18,000#
Clearance	13'0"
Water	100 Gals.
Fuel	350 Gals.
Cockpit	77 Sq. Ft.
Hull Type	Modified-V
Designer	Clive Dent

Production
1988–90

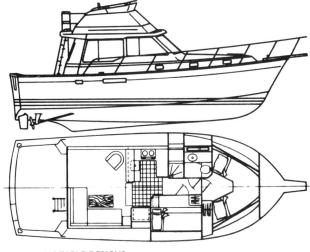

DELTA 36 SFX

Delta boats are well known in the charterboat trade for their strictly business approach to the basics. The hulls are generally Coast Guard approved and the construction is rugged with the emphasis on reliability. In the Delta 36 SFX, however, there's more than just a tough deep-V hull and a big fishing cockpit. This is truly an innovative and practical boat with an outright aggressive appearance. What sets her apart from most other sportfishers in the mid-range market is her unique raised command bridge — a spacious platform that splits the difference between a true flybridge and the raised bridgedeck used in open express boats. Positioned about three feet above the cockpit level, this sensible concept provides a stand-up engine room (virtually unheard of in a small fisherman), with direct cockpit access and extraordinary headroom below. Inside, the layout is modern and very attractive with a circular pit-style dinette, linear galley, and double berth forward. The head does not include a stall shower. A good seaboat, she'll cruise around 26 knots with the optional 425-hp Cat diesels. ❏

SPECIFICATIONS

Length	36'3"
Beam	12'2"
Draft	3'0"
Weight	17,200#
Clearance	NA
Water	50 Gals.
Fuel	400 Gals.
Cockpit	98 Sq. Ft.
Hull Type	Deep-V
Designer	Delta

Production
1987–Current

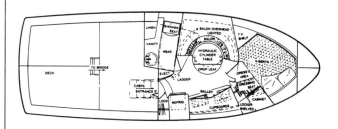

FORMULA 36 PC

Built to the high Formula production standards, the 36 PC (and her sistership, the 36 Express) is a good-looking Eurostyle cruiser designed to replace the earlier Formula 35 PC model (1985–89). She's built on a wide-beam modified-V hull (18° deadrise aft) with prop pockets, and features an integral swim platform and bow pulpit in addition to her curved windshield and striking Imron graphics. Below, the mid-cabin floorplan of the 36 PC provides berths for six with a compact galley, double-entry head, built-in overhead entertainment center, and a complete absence of teak trim. (The Express version omits the mid-cabin stateroom in favor of a huge storage area forward of the engines, and increased cockpit dimensions.) The interior is among the best to be found in this type of boat and the finish work is above average. In the cockpit, a hydraulically operated hatch in the sole provides outstanding access to the engines. Unlike most mid-cabin designs, the PC does not have V-drives. Standard 454-cid gas engines will cruise at 17 knots and reach 26–27 knots top. GM 300-hp 8.2 diesels are optional. ❏

SPECIFICATIONS

Length	34'0"
Length WL	NA
Beam	13'3"
Draft	2'8"
Weight	15,000#
Clearance	10'9"
Water	60 Gals.
Fuel	300 Gals.
Hull Type	Modified-V
Designer	J. Adams

Production
1990–Current

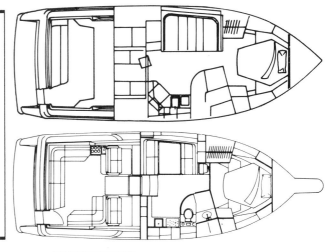

NOTABLE DESIGNS

FOUR WINNS 365 EXPRESS

The Four Winns 365 is another of the good-looking mid-cabin express cruisers increasingly popular in today's sportboat market. Indeed, it's becoming difficult to distinguish one from another, but the 365 does have something none of the others can claim — an optional Jacuzzi spa hidden below the island berth in the forward stateroom (thereby giving new meaning to the term "sportboat"). She's built on a modified-V hull with cored hullsides and prop pockets aft. Note the long, sweeping foredeck of the 365 — the helm is well aft in this boat, thus reducing cockpit space in favor of an unusually spacious, wide-open interior. Notable features include hidden foredeck lockers, postless fold-away dinette table, excellent access to the engines and generator, tilt steering wheel, side exhausts, good sidedecks, and a unique air induction system designed to lower the risk of cockpit fumes. No racehorse, the 365's sedate performance stands in contrast to her aggressive appearance. Standard 454-cid Crusaders (V-drives) will cruise at 16 knots (26 top) and optional 502s will cruise at 18–19 knots (28 knots top). ❏

SPECIFICATIONS

Length w/pulpit ....36'0"
Beam.........................13'2"
Draft ....3'2"
Weight ....18,600#
Clearance ....10'4"
Water....................98 Gals.
Fuel ....315 Gals.
Cockpit ....NA
Hull Type.........Modified-V
Designer ....Blackwell

Production
1991-Current

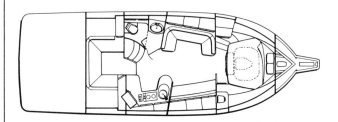

LITTLE HARBOR 36

For those who can afford the cost of a custom yacht, the Little Harbor 36 is a high-tech masterpiece of classic American styling. Featuring a traditional trunk cabin foredeck, she's built on a conservative 11' beam with Kevlar and S-glass laminates. and a vacuum-bagged balsa core. The hull is a deep-V although deadrise at the transom is only 16°. Simply put, the Little Harbor 36 is built to the highest standards, which is why a new one will exceed $350,000. Because these are custom yachts, there's a variety of layouts an owner might choose from to personalize his boat. In any case, expect to see plenty of varnished teak cabinetry belowdeck, as well as Corian countertops in the head, and other quality furnishings throughout. The bi-level cockpit is arranged with a dinette to port. Lift-up helm and companion sections provide excellent access to the engine room. A handsome boat by any standard (note the teak-framed windshield), the cockpit can be adapted to serious sportfishing pursuits. Several diesel options are offered. Typically, 300-hp Cummins diesels will cruise the Little Harbor 36 at 24–25 knots. ❏

SPECIFICATIONS

Length	36'2"
Length WL	29'7"
Beam	11'0"
Draft	3'1"
Weight	16,000#
Clearance	8'0"
Water	120 Gals.
Fuel	300 Gals.
Hull Type	Deep-V
Designer	Hunt

Production
1990–Current

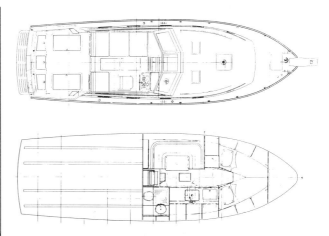

MANATEE 36

The Manatee 36 is a particularly well named boat — she's fat and slow (just like a real manatee) and she's certainly no award-winner when it comes to looks. Built in Taiwan, she's constructed on a cored, full-displacement hull with a fairly wide beam, a deep keel, and rounded bilges aft. Perhaps the most notable feature of the Manatee 36 is the amount of usable living space packed inside this boat. The spacious salon uses the hull's full width (no side-decks outside) and the beam is carried well forward resulting in an unusually large master stateroom. The entire lay-out is conveniently arranged on a single level and the interior is completely finished with traditional teak cabinetry and woodwork. Topside, the semi-enclosed flybridge is arranged with wraparound lounge seating for guests, and an extended cockpit overhang provides space for a dinghy. Note the rounded transom and weather-protected aft deck. A single 100-hp Volvo diesel will cruise the Manatee 36 for 1,100 miles at a leisurely 6–7 knot speed. Over 90 have been delivered, making the Manatee 36 a very popular model. ❏

SPECIFICATIONS

Length	36'4"
Length WL	34'0"
Beam	13'8"
Draft	3'2"
Weight	23,000#
Clearance	14'0"
Water	300 Gals.
Fuel	280 Gals.
Hull Type	Displacement
Designer	Jim Krogen

Production
1984–Current

MONK 36 TRAWLER

Also marketed as the Miracle 36 and Enterprise 36 (among other names), this sturdy Taiwan import gained popularity in the mid-1980s as an affordable family cruiser with a traditional teak interior and classic trawler profile. Her simulated planked hull is solid fiberglass and features a full-length skeg keel and a protected prop. Early models came with plenty of exterior teak — decks, window frames, hatches, rails, etc. — while later models eliminated most of it while still retaining the full teak interior. (The joinerwork found throughout the Monk 36 is impressive.) All had sliding deck doors port and starboard in the salon as well as a lower helm. Several stateroom configurations were offered over the years, but the galley location (aft and to starboard in the salon) remained the same. Removable (and heavy) teak hatches in the salon sole provide excellent access to the engine room. Outside, the full walkaround sidedecks are protected by raised bulwarks and a high rail. A single 135-hp Ford Lehman diesel was standard in the Monk 36 and she'll cruise economically at 7–8 knots with a range of close to 700 miles. ❑

SPECIFICATIONS

Length	36'0"
Length WL	NA
Beam	13'0"
Draft	4'0"
Weight	18,000#
Clearance	NA
Water	120 Gals.
Fuel	320 Gals.
Hull Type	Semi-Disp.
Designer	Ed Monk

Production
1982–?

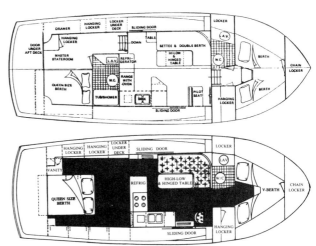

ORCA 36

Innovation is a term dear to the hearts of many boatbuilders but with few exceptions the word has mostly become a marketing tool. Enter the Orca 36, a West Coast stand-up fisherman with an unconventional profile and plenty of space-age engineering. The Orca's deep-V hull (23° deadrise aft) is fully cored with Airex, reinforced with Kevlar and carbon fiber, and vacuum bagged with vinylester resins. Her unique, aerodynamically shaped marlin tower permits true 360° walkaround fishing access, and the hardtop is canted down 4° to match the boat's running angle for reduced windage. The Orca's bottom is also clean — no thru-hulls, just a sea chest in the engine room fed from the transom. There are two fish-boxes in the cockpit sole, and the helm seat module rolls aft to expose the engine compartment. The interior is one of the more spacious found in a boat of this type with good headroom, over-sized head, and berths for four. A superb performer, 300-hp Cummins diesels deliver a top speed of 34 knots — hard to believe in a 36' boat. At a steady 25 knot cruise (16 gph) the Orca's range is around 700 miles! ❏

SPECIFICATIONS

Length	36'0"
Beam	13'0"
Draft	3'0"
Weight	15,000#
Clearance	17'3"
Water	50 Gals.
Fuel	500 Gals.
Cockpit	NA
Hull Type	Deep-V
Designer	C. Jannace

Production
1990–Current

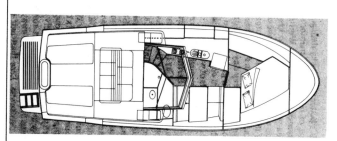

PACE 36 SPORTFISHERMAN

The classic Egg Harbor 36 Sedan has been reborn in the Pace 36 Sportfisherman. Built in Taiwan using the Egg Harbor molds, hull construction is solid fiberglass (as per the original specs), and the hull form is a modified-V with nearly flat aftersections for quick planing and speed. This hull was first used some years ago in the Pacemaker 36 (and later for the Egg Harbor 36), and while the ride can be a little harsh in a chop, she can be expected to provide good handling characteristics in most sea conditions. The Pace 36 is a good-looking boat with a traditional Jersey-style profile. The black mask around the deckhouse distinguishes her from the earlier Egg Harbor 36 models. Inside, the revised teak interior layout offers a choice of single or twin staterooms with a double berth in the master. In keeping with her Egg Harbor heritage, the Pace 36 features a teak cockpit sole, as well as teak covering boards and toerail. Crusader 454-cid gas engines are standard and will cruise the Pace 36 at 18 knots with 27 knots top. The optional 320-hp Cat diesels will cruise around 22 knots and turn 26 knots wide open. ❑

SPECIFICATIONS

Length	36'0"
Beam	13'3"
Draft	2'9"
Weight	20,000#
Clearance	12'2"
Water	75 Gals.
Fuel	400 Gals.
Cockpit	NA
Hull Type	Modified-V
Designer	Egg Harbor

Production
1988–Current

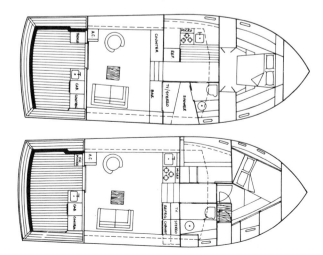

NOTABLE DESIGNS

PACIFICA 36 SF

A handsome boat with a distinctive profile and aggressive styling, the Pacifica 36 is a limited-production sportfisherman (about 25 have been built since 1974) designed for serious anglers. She's constructed on a modified-V hull form with a relatively deep keel for stability and generous flare at the bow. The Pacifica 36 is primarily aimed at the West Coast market and features wide sidedecks and a forward helm console on the flybridge (an East Coast, tournament-style flybridge is available). The uncluttered cockpit — with just over 80 sq. ft. of usable space — is not large compared to others in her class but suitable for most anglers. Inside, the Pacifica 36 can sleep six with the salon dinette and settee converted. V-berths are located in the stateroom and the split head features a huge shower to starboard. A lower helm is standard, and the interior is finished with high-pressure laminate countertops with teak trim. At only 16,000 lbs., the Pacifica 36 SF is a light boat and her performance with 375-hp Cat diesels (26 knots cruise/30 knots top) is impressive. Pacifica also offers a 36' express model on this same hull. ❏

SPECIFICATIONS

Length......................36'0"
Beam........................13'0"
Draft ....3'4"
Weight ....16,000#
Clearance ....NA
Water...................90 Gals.
Fuel ....300 Gals.
Cockpit..............83 Sq. Ft.
Hull Type.........Modified-V
Designer ....John Norek

Production
1974–Current

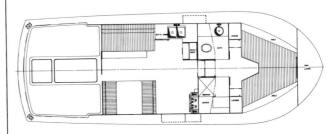

REGAL 360 COMMODORE

Regal has long been known as a quality builder of small boats, and when the inboard-powered 360 Commodore was introduced in 1985, expectations were high. Built on a modified-V hull with a steep 17° of deadrise at the transom, the styling of the 360 is crisp in spite of a relatively high foredeck profile. A curved wraparound windshield and elliptical ports add a distinct Continental flair to her appearance, and the exterior glasswork and hardware are above average throughout. Below, the luxurious salon is dominated by a huge circular lounge with a hinged walnut table in the center — an excellent entertaining arrangement that converts into a very large double berth at night. A private mid-cabin is tucked away under the bridgedeck with partial standing headroom, and an offset double berth is fitted in the forward stateroom. There's seating for eight in the roomy cockpit, and access to the engines and V-drives is via two large hatches in the sole. A good-running boat, the Regal 360 Commodore will cruise around 20 knots and reach 29–30 knots with twin 454-cid gas engines. ❏

SPECIFICATIONS

Length	36'1"
Beam	13'1"
Draft	2'10"
Weight	17,000#
Clearance	9'7"
Water	125 Gals.
Fuel	280 Gals.
Cockpit	120 Sq. Ft.
Hull Type	Modified-V
Designer	Jim Ginter

Production
1985–90

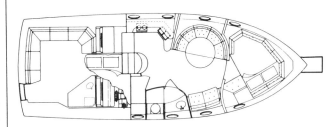

SABRELINE 36

Growing numbers of leading sailboat manufacturers are turning to powerboat designs in an effort to retain past customers making the glorious transition from sail to power. Such a boat is the new Sabreline 36, a conservative trawler-style cruiser built on a fully cored, modified-V hull with hard chines aft and 14° of deadrise at the transom. With her wide sidedecks and moderate beam, the Sabreline 36 is not a notably roomy boat inside, although her traditional teak trim and cabinetry, white Formica counters, and large cabin windows give the interior a wide open

and very inviting character. The galley and a lower helm are in the salon along with facing settees, and port and starboard sliding doors provide convenient access to the decks. The standard layout has twin berths in the aft cabin and a double berth is optional. Each stateroom has its own head, and the aft cabin has a stall shower as well as a direct passageway to the aft deck. A comfortable and good-running boat, standard 250-hp 8.2 GM diesels will cruise the Sabreline 36 a very respectable 17–18 knots and turn 22+ knots wide open. ❑

SPECIFICATIONS

Length	36'0"
Length WL	32'4"
Beam	12'6"
Draft	4'3"
Weight	20,000#
Clearance	12'6"
Water	225 Gals.
Fuel	250 Gals.
Cockpit	NA
Hull Type	Modified-V
Designer	Sabre

Production
1989–Current

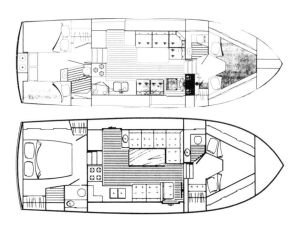

STAMAS 360 EXPRESS

At first glance, the Stamas 360 appears to be yet another mid-cabin family express with modern styling and a big cockpit. But Stamas has built their reputation on fishing boats, and the new 360 is more than just a good looking express. Like the Tiara 36, she's designed to serve as a stable offshore fishing platform as well as a comfortable day cruiser. Hull construction is solid fiberglass with a steep 18° of deadrise at the transom. Like many other manufacturers, the 360 uses prop pockets to reduce shaft angles and improve running efficiency.

Note that she has a long keel below to protect the running gear in the event of grounding. In a departure from most of today's mid cabin designs, the Stamas 360 has a single-level cockpit instead of a raised bridgedeck. Her belowdecks accommodations are attractive and very comfortable, however the stateroom lacks a privacy door. Cockpit features include flush-mounted rod holders, insulated fishwell, baitwell, and transom storage. An competent performer with 454-cid gas engines, she'll cruise around 18–19 knots and reach 27 knots wide open. ❑

SPECIFICATIONS

Length w/Pulpit	36'6"
Beam	13'2"
Draft	2'4"
Weight	16,975#
Clearance	8'3"
Water	90 Gals.
Fuel	372 Gals.
Cockpit	155 Sq. Ft.
Hull Type	Modified-V
Designer	Jim Wynn

Production
1992–Current

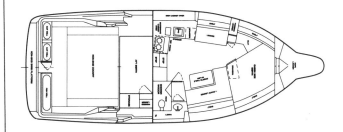

SHANNON VOYAGER 36

Trawler-style boats with un-trawler-like performance aren't necessarily new (they've been coming in from Taiwan for years), but the hint of Downeast character and the modern planing hull design of the Voyager 36 are distinctive. The Voyager is built to high standards by the Shannon Boat Co. — a firm whose reputation derives principally from the upper end of the sailboat market. The hull is cored from the waterline up with a sharp entry and a modest keel. With her upright superstructure, the Voyager would look topheavy if it weren't for her graceful sheer. The practical sedan layout is ideal for extended cruising where the utility of a cockpit is most appreciated. Her galley-up floorplan includes two staterooms, a head with tub/shower, and a lower helm with deck access door. Other features include very secure sidedecks, radar mast, and a spacious flybridge with L-shaped guest seating. The engines are placed quite close together in the Voyager's large engine room. A good performer with just 250-hp GM 8.2 diesels, she'll cruise economically at 18–19 knots burning just 20 gph. ❏

SPECIFICATIONS

Length	35'7"
Beam	13'3"
Draft	3'0"
Weight	17,500#
Clearance	12'6"
Water	150 Gals.
Fuel	325 Gals.
Cockpit	75 Sq. Ft.
Hull Type	Modified-V
Designer	W. Schultz

Production
1991–Current

LORD NELSON VICTORY 37 TUG

Based on a traditional New England workboat hull, the Lord Nelson Victory 37 Tug is a long-range cruiser with a yacht-like interior to go with her salty profile. She's built in Taiwan on a solid fiberglass displacement hull with a plumb bow, full-length (ballasted) keel, and a rounded transom. High bulwarks surround the entire deck for safety. The raised pilothouse (focal point of any tug design) is completely enclosed and gives the helmsman a full 360° view. The original floorplan was updated in 1990, relocating the galley to starboard and opening up the stateroom considerably. Companionway steps lead aft into the comfortable salon, and a pantry door in the galley opens to the spacious engine room below. Forward, the stateroom features a double berth, and head with stall shower. The original teak decks were also updated in 1990 to a low-maintanance fiberglass nonskid surface, and the teak handrails were replaced with stainless steel. A popular model with nearly 80 delivered to date, the Victory 37 has an honest cruising range of about a thousand miles with a single 150-hp Cummins diesel. ❏

SPECIFICATIONS

Length	36'11"
Length WL	33'4"
Beam	13'2"
Draft	3'6"
Weight	20,500#
Clearance	12'6"
Water	185 Gals.
Fuel	250 Gals.
Hull Type	Displacement
Designer	Jim Bachus

Production
1984–Current

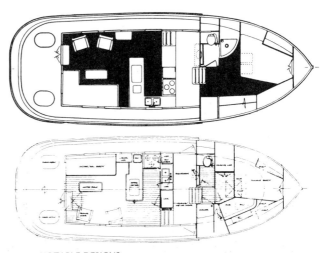

MARINETTE 37 MOTOR YACHT

The Marinette 37 MY (basically a downsized version of the larger Marinette 41 Motor Yacht) is a good-looking design constructed of lightweight, welded marine aluminum. Aside from her attractive profile, the Marinette 37 is somewhat unique for her size in that she features walkaround double berths in both staterooms as well as stall showers fore and aft — the kind of accommodations seldom found in boats under 40 feet. The price for this luxury is seen in the relatively compact main salon dimensions. A lower helm was standard (to port, which is a little

unusual and takes some getting used to), and the spacious galley is located forward a few steps down from the salon level. The interior is finished with teak trim and cabinetry throughout, and the tinted wraparound cabin windows provide a good deal of natural lighting. The 37's full-width aft deck offers a sizable open-air entertainment platform with room for several chairs. A light boat for her size and a good performer, the Marinette 37 Motor Yacht with the standard 454-cid Crusader gas engines will cruise around 19 knots and reach a top speed of 27–28 knots. ❏

SPECIFICATIONS

Length	37'0"
Beam	13'8"
Draft	3'0"
Weight	16,000#
Clearance	12'0"
Water	120 Gals.
Fuel	300 Gals.
Hull Type	Modified-V
Construction	Aluminum
Designer	Marinette

Production
1988–91

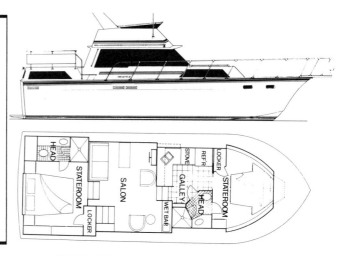

ROUGHWATER 37

The Roughwater 37 is an improved version of the original Roughwater 36 that began production in Taiwan in 1969. These boats have earned a reputation over the years for dependable, seaworthy operation, and several have been used in commercial service. Built on a fiberglass semi-displacement hull with a full-length keel, the Roughwater 37 was completely retooled in 1983. Hard chines replaced the original soft chines aft, and the engine room was enlarged, allowing for the installation of twin diesels. Her fine entry and relatively narrow beam pro-duce an efficient and easily driven hull with a good turn of speed. Inside, the galley and dinette are forward of the pilothouse/salon and separated by a privacy door. While the 37's interior isn't spacious by today's standards, it's still comfortable with an attractive mix of teak woodwork and off-white Formica surfaces throughout. Roughwater 37s are offered in single- and twin-screw versions. With a single 250-hp GM 8.2 diesel, she'll cruise around 13 knots, and with twin 8.2s she's capable of a steady 19-knot cruising speed. ❏

SPECIFICATIONS

Length......................37'0"
Length WL ....33'0"
Beam.......................11'7"
Draft ....4'0"
Weight ....17,900#
Clearance ....13'6"
Water.................100 Gals.
Fuel............230/300 Gals.
Cockpit........................NA
Hull Type ....Semi-Disp.
Designer ....Ed Monk, Jr.

Production
1981–Current

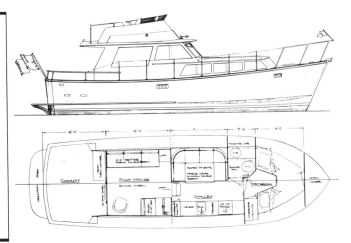

CHASE 38 SPORTFISHERMAN

Those with a taste for the unusual will find the Chase 38 an interesting design. She's built in Costa Rica with modern Airex-cored construction, a distinctive raised deck profile and plenty of exterior and interior teak. The Chase 38 has a huge bridgedeck platform with wraparound seating for a crowd — a superb entertaining area several steps above the cockpit with a walk-thru to the foredeck. The cockpit is large enough for a full-size chair and features a unique fold-up swim platform. The cabin is entered from a companionway ladder located next to the helm on the bridgedeck. It's a few steps down, too, and one is immediately confronted with an abundance of beautiful varnished teak woodwork and brass accessories more common to a sailboat than a sportfisherman. The belowdecks layout isn't notably spacious but includes a stall shower in the head and an island berth forward. Access to the large engine room is from the cockpit. Cat diesels are standard and GM 6-71s and 6V92s are optional. No lightweight, 375-hp Cats will cruise a loaded Chase 38 around 23 knots while the larger 550-hp 6V92s will cruise about 30 knots. ❏

SPECIFICATIONS

Length ....38'0"
Beam.......................13'9"
Draft ....4'9"
Weight ....28,000#
Clearance ....NA
Water.................130 Gals.
Fuel ....500 Gals.
Cockpit............108 Sq. Ft.
Hull Type ....Deep V
Designer.....Hunt & Assoc.

Production
1988–Current

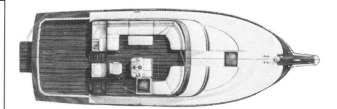

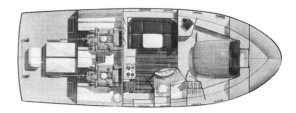

DAWSON 38 SPORTFISHERMAN

The Dawson 38 is a limited produc-tion, semi-custom fisherman de-signed to appeal to the tournament-level angler. The hull is not a new design; it was first developed back in 1975 in Pensacola, and has since been used for commercial and charter service. The hulls are purchased and shipped to New Jersey where the Dawson 38 is fin-ished out at the old Pacemaker yard. With a steep 24° of deadrise aft, the Dawson has more "V" than any other boat of her type currently available on the market. An attractive design, her styling is on the conservative side and most will view the Dawson as a strictly business sportfisherman in spite of her comfortable interior. The two-stateroom floorplan includes a centerline double bed forward and conventional bunk berths in the guest cabin. The galley is in the salon, and the extensive use of solid teak cabinetry and top-quality fixtures is impressive. Standard 375-hp Cats will cruise the Dawson 38 around 26 knots (30 knots top), and optional 485-hp 6-71s cruise at a fast 31 knots (33–34 knots wide open). About 20 have been sold and an express model became available in 1991. ❏

SPECIFICATIONS

Length	38'0"
Beam	13'8"
Draft	3'6"
Weight	28,000#
Clearance	NA
Water	90 Gals.
Fuel	400 Gals.
Cockpit	100 Sq. Ft.
Hull Type	Deep-V
Designer	Tom Dawson

Production
1987-Current

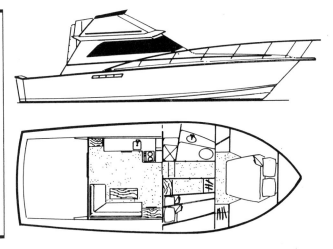

NOTABLE DESIGNS

DELTA 38 SPORTFISHERMAN

The first Delta 38s were commercial dive and charter boats, where they earned a reputation for dependability and offshore stability. A semi-custom model, about 70 have been built (most to USCG specifications), and while the majority are used commercially there are many that are privately owned as well. Her modified-V hull is narrow with 13° of deadrise aft and a sprayrail forward — a no-nonsense fishing platform with solid fiberglass construction and proven offshore performance. The cockpit in this boat is huge with low freeboard, a useful bridge overhang, and plenty of space for tackle centers and a full-size chair. The interior dimensions are limited due to the over-size cockpit and the unique 4' collission bulkhead forward (a watertight compartment required by the CG in certified boats). A lower helm is standard and V-berths are below with a galley and small head. The Delta 38 has been offered with a wide variety of power options including GM, Cat, Volvo, and Cummins diesels to 425-hp. A good-running boat, she'll appeal to anglers seeking simplicity and old fashioned durability. ❏

SPECIFICATIONS

Length ....38'0"
Length WL ....34'8"
Beam........................12'5"
Draft ....3'0"
Weight ....19,500#
Clearance ....NA
Water...................50 Gals.
Fuel ....300 Gals.
Cockpit............120 Sq. Ft.
Hull Type.........Modified-V
Designer ....Delta

Production
1984–Current

INTREPID 38

With her high-tech materials and state-of-the-art construction, the Intrepid 38 is a very specialized boat with a price tag to match. She built on a stepped, deep-V hull similar to that used by racing boats. The beam is moderate and the styling is crisp and aggressive. Her primary purpose is offshore fishing and she's the largest production inboard *center console* dayboat on the market. The walkaround deck layout will appeal to most light-tackle and stand-up anglers. The cockpit will easily handle a full-size chair, and there are molded steps in the corners. The helm is set well aft on the bridgedeck with seating forward — innovative but windy with no screen. The compact helm console provides space for flush mounting most electronics and a hydraulically operated hatch provides excellent access to the motors below. Inside, the accommodations are basic with a small galley, kingsize V-berths, a stand-up head, and a unique double berth tucked below the helm. To date, all Intrepid 38s have been powered with 400-hp Merlin diesels which will cruise at 28–29 knots and reach 35 knots top. Cats are optional. ❏

SPECIFICATIONS

Length	37'6"
Beam	12'0"
Draft	2'6"
Weight	14,000#
Clearance	NA
Water	52 Gals.
Fuel	300 Gals.
Cockpit	108 Sq. Ft.
Hull Type	Deep-V
Designer	M. Peters

Production
1991–Current

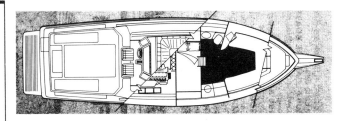

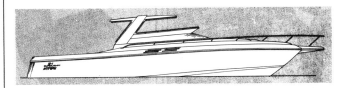

MEDITERRANEAN 38 CONVERTIBLE

The Mediterranean 38 is a sturdy West Coast fisherman with a good deal of value packed into her low factory-direct price. She's built on a balsa-cored deep-V hull (18° deadrise) and the construction involves some 65 individual molds, resulting in a finished, gelcoated surface everywhere you look. Two interior layouts are offered with the single-stateroom floorplan being more popular. An overhead compartment in the salon can store six rods and reels. The interior is comprised of laminated teak cabinets and decorator fabrics. Outside, the sidedecks are very wide, and a tackle center and fish box are standard in the cockpit. (Some anglers may not like the inward-opening transom door.) The "step" in the sheer was eliminated in 1987, and in 1988 the cockpit was rearranged and the fuel increased to 450 gallons. The flybridge can be ordered with the helm console forward for the West Coast, or aft for warm-weather anglers. Cummins 300-hp diesels will cruise at an economical 24 knots and reach 28 knots top. A popular boat (but no award-winner when it comes to styling), over 100 have been built. ❑

SPECIFICATIONS

Length	38'4"
Length WL	32'7"
Beam	12'6"
Draft	3'2"
Weight	21,000#
Clearance	11'6"
Water	100 Gals.
Fuel	300/450 Gals.
Cockpit	NA
Hull Type	Deep-V
Designer	Dick Valdes

Production
1985–Current

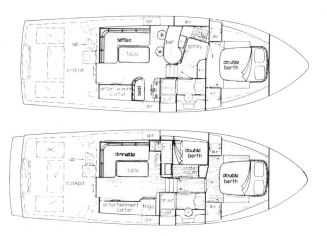

PEARSON 38 CONVERTIBLE

Pearson Yachts developed several powerboat designs in the past, and in the early 1960s the Pearson name was no stranger to the powerboat industry. With the downturn of the sailboat market in recent years, Pearson once again decided to build powerboats. The first, the 38 Convertible, was introduced in 1987. She's designed by Hunt Associates and features their famous deep-V hull (19° deadrise aft) with a practical two-stateroom floorplan. This is a high-quality family cruiser/sportfisherman with a soft ride and very upscale accommodations. Those who have seen and inspected the Pearson 38 have been impressed, especially with the attractive oak-trimmed Formica interior decor. Topside, the tournament-style bridge is well designed. Construction, mechanical systems, and detailing are above average and the engine room is quite large. Standard 375-hp Caterpillar diesels will cruise the Pearson 38 at 22–23 knots with a top speed of about 26 knots. Note that a double-cabin version of the Pearson 38 was introduced in 1988. Pearson went bankrupt in 1991, thus ending the production of this model. ❏

SPECIFICATIONS

Length	37'6"
Beam	13'10"
Draft	3'9"
Weight	24,000#
Clearance	NA
Water	120 Gals.
Fuel	410 Gals.
Cockpit	NA
Hull Type	Deep-V
Designer	Hunt Assoc.

Production
1987–9

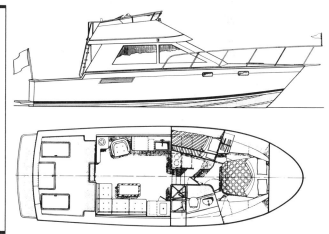

PEARSON 38 DOUBLE CABIN

The Pearson 38 Double Cabin (introduced in 1988) followed by a year the debut of the well-received Pearson 38 Convertible. She was built on the same deep-V (19° deadrise) hull used in the convertible with a solid fiberglass bottom and balsa coring in the hullsides and decks. Unlike many mid-sized double-cabin designs (usually convertibles with aft staterooms rather than cockpits), the lines of the Pearson 38 are graceful and flowing — not exactly beautiful, but there are no beautiful double cabins under 40 feet. Aside from her offshore hull construction and quality workmanship, the principal characteristics of the 38 are found below in the comfortable two-stateroom, galley-down accommodation plan. Both heads are equipped with stall showers, the U-shaped galley is suitably large, the salon dimensions are livable, and walkaround double berths are located in each of the staterooms. The aft deck, however, is small. Twin 320-hp gas engines were standard (16 knots cruise/24–25 top), and 320-hp Cat diesels are optional (20-knot cruise/24 knots top). ❑

SPECIFICATIONS

Length	37'9"
Length WL	31'11"
Beam	13'10"
Draft	3'9"
Weight	25,000#
Clearance	13'0"
Water	100 Gals.
Fuel	300 Gals.
Hull Type	Deep-V
Designer	Hunt Assoc.

Production
1988–91

NOTABLE DESIGNS

REGAL 380 COMMODORE

Flagship of the Regal line, the 380 Commodore is an upscale family cruiser with plenty of eye appeal and several attractive features. She incorporates the popular mid-cabin floorplan to provide two private staterooms below and concentrates a lot of attention in the cockpit where a stylish Eurostyle white helm console steals the show. The 380 is built on a modified-V hull (17° deadrise aft), with cored hullsides and prop pockets. Her large bi-level cockpit comes with sculptured L-shaped lounge seating, good engine access (for an express), and recessed fender storage in the transom.

Note the foredeck sunpads. Below, the starboard salon settee can be pulled up to the dinette table for extra seating — a practical innovation. Retaining traditional teakwood for doors and trim, the interior is comprised of quality fabrics and durable hardware throughout. The mid-cabin is nearly large enough to be called a true stateroom with standing headroom and a small settee. We like the *circular* shower stall. A relatively light boat for her size, standard 454-cid MerCruiser gas engines (with V-drives) will cruise the 380 Commodore around 18–19 knots and provide a top speed of 28 knots. ❑

SPECIFICATIONS

Length	39'5"
Beam	13'1"
Draft	3'0"
Weight	18,000#
Clearance	9'5"
Water	125 Gals.
Fuel	280 Gals.
Cockpit	110 Sq. Ft.
Hull Type	Modified-V
Designer	Regal

Production
1991–Current

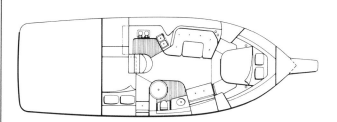

RONIN 38 CONVERTIBLE

Looking a lot like a Hatteras, the Ronin 38 Convertible is built in Taiwan by Ta Chiao. She's constructed on a modified-V hull (15° deadrise aft) with a wide beam and balsa coring in the hullsides. Just three separate molds are required — the hull, superstructure, and flybridge — and there are no seams in the cockpit or screws on the bridge. A good-looking boat with a solid front windshield and handsome sportfish lines, the Ronin 38 is available with a galley-down, single-stateroom layout, or with the galley in the salon and two staterooms forward. The interior is finished in solid teak or light oak woodwork, and good craftsmanship is clearly evident throughout. A hatch in the salon sole reveals a well-organized engine room with good access to motors and generator. Outside, the large cockpit is set up for serious fishing and includes a transom door and gate, livewell, freezer, and freshwater washdown. Standard Cat 375-hp diesels cruise the Ronin 38 at 22–23 knots and reach a top speed of 27. The optional 485-hp 6-71s will provide a cruising speed of 25–26 knots and a top speed of 29 knots. ❏

SPECIFICATIONS

Length	38'3"
Beam	13'11"
Draft	3'6"
Weight	26,000#
Clearance	12'8"
Water	100 Gals.
Fuel	370 Gals.
Cockpit	108 Sq. Ft.
Hull Type	Modified-V
Designer	Unknown

Production
1986–Current

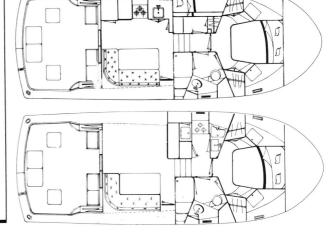

WILBUR 38 CRUISER

The Wilbur 38 is a traditional Down-east-style cruiser built in Maine. Her distinctive lobsterboat heritage is reflected in the timeless beauty of her classic New England styling and the flexibility of her rugged, semi-displacement hull design. While not inexpensive, the Lee Wilbur yard is well known for its commitment to top-quality engineering and above-average production standards. Each Wilbur 38 is built on a semi-custom basis, and the result is a yacht in which the elements of traditional styling are intimately matched with the interior priorities of her owner. There are four basic versions of the Wilbur 38 available— three cruising models (one with an extended hardtop) with two staterooms and a deckhouse galley, and a flybridge fisherman with an enlarged cockpit, a slightly smaller salon, and a single stateroom forward. All feature truly elegant teak interior joinerwork and cabinetry, and virtually everything is created in-house at the Wilbur yard. A Wilbur 38 equipped with twin 375-hp Caterpillar diesels can be expected to cruise at a respectable 22 knots and reach 26 knots wide open. ❏

SPECIFICATIONS

Length	38'0"
Length WL	35'7"
Beam	13'0"
Draft	4'0"
Weight	22,500#
Clearance	NA
Water	150 Gals.
Fuel	500 Gals.
Cockpit	NA
Hull Type	Semi-Disp.
Designer	Ralph Ellis

Production
1980–Current

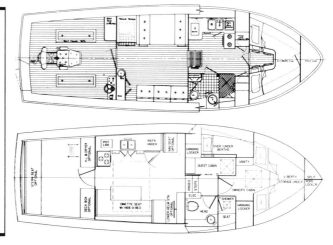

CAPE DORY 40 EXPLORER

With her distinctive trawler profile and upright deckhouse, the 40 Explorer is the latest in the Cape Dory series of well-built Downeast family cruisers. She's constructed on a modified-V hull (14° of transom deadrise) with cored hullsides, a deep forefoot, and a long keel that protects the running gear. A good-looking design, the interior of the Cape Dory is quite spacious for a 40' sedan, although the cockpit is on the small side. The deckhouse galley is open to the salon, and large wraparound cabin windows only add to the impression of interior space.

There are two portside heads (one with a stall shower), and the interior is completely finished with teak cabinetry and teak and holly flooring. There's a deck door at the lower helm, and the wide sidedecks are protected with raised bulwarks. The flybridge is very roomy (note the offset cockpit ladder) with guest seating aft of the helm. Additional features include underwater exhausts, teak cockpit sole, and transom door. Standard 291-hp 3116 Cats will cruise the Cape Dory 40 efficiently at 18 knots (only 20 gph) and reach a top speed of 23–24 knots. ❏

SPECIFICATIONS

Length	40'0"
Length WL	36'5"
Beam	13'10"
Draft	3'9"
Weight	25,000#
Clearance	13'3"
Water	170 Gals.
Fuel	400 Gals.
Cockpit	NA
Hull Type	Modified-V
Designer	Clive Dent

Production
1992–Current

NOTABLE DESIGNS

HERITAGE 40 SUNDECK MY

With her upright profile and trawler-style appearance, the Heritage 40 is one of the better-looking sundeck yachts in her class. She was built in Taiwan by Nova Marine on a solid fiberglass, modified-V hull with moderate beam, simulated lapstrake hullsides, and considerable flare at the bow. An affordably priced boat, it's notable that her actual length is less than 39'. The all-teak interior of the Heritage 40 is very inviting and her efficient galley/dinette-down floorplan is practical and well arranged. There's a deck access door in the salon (a lower helm was optional) and the forward stateroom is best described as a tight fit. The salon dimensions are about average, but the aft stateroom is quite roomy for a 39-footer. The Oriental teak carving on bulkhead doors is impressive and all of the woodwork is well crafted. Outside, the sidedecks are reasonably wide, and the aft deck comes with a wet bar and wing doors. Several diesel options were offered in the Heritage 40. The 135-hp Lehmans will cruise around 9 knots, and the popular 200-hp Volvos cruise at 13–14 knots and reach about 17 knots wide open. ❑

SPECIFICATIONS

Length	38'9"
Length WL	34'7"
Beam	13'6"
Draft	3'7"
Weight	25,000#
Clearance	NA
Water	200 Gals.
Fuel	400 Gals.
Hull Type	Modified-V
Designer	Nova Yachts

Production
1984–90

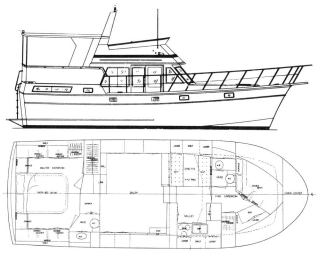

NOTABLE DESIGNS

KHA SHING 40 SUNDECK MY

Certainly one of the more popular Taiwan imports, the Kha Shing 40 is better known as the Spindrift 40 MY on the West Coast and the Vista or Southern Star 40 MY on the East Coast. She's a competent semi-displacement sundeck trawler with a solid fiberglass hull, shallow keel, and an unusually modern profile. Over 120 of these boats have been sold into the U.S. market and most have been delivered with a two-stateroom layout with the galley down and a lower helm in the salon. The interior is teak and the cabinetry and joinerwork are impressive. With her wrap-around cabin windows and excellent headroom, the salon of the Kha Shing 40 is quite open in spite of all the teak. Notable features include deck access doors, secure sidedecks, teak handrails, and a roomy master stateroom whose dimensions are impressive for a 40-footer. Outside, the aft deck is fairly spacious with room for several chairs. Economical and capable of greater than trawler speeds, many (if not most) Kha Shing 40s are powered with 165-hp or 200-hp Volvo diesels. Cruising speeds are about 11–13 knots and top speed is around 15–16 knots. ❏

SPECIFICATIONS

Length	39'6"
Length WL	34'0"
Beam	14'0"
Draft	3'7"
Weight	22,800#
Clearance	15'1"
Water	200 Gals.
Fuel	300/340 Gals.
Hull Type	Semi-Disp.
Designer	Kha Shing

Production
1980–Current

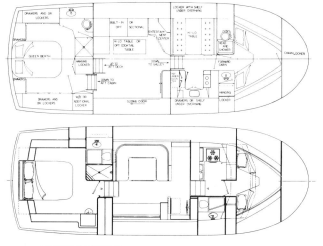

NOTABLE DESIGNS

MIDNIGHT LACE 40 EXPRESS

The first new Midnight Lace model in a decade, the 40 Express is a more modern design than her narrow-beamed, commuter-styled predecessors with greater belowdeck space. Retained, however, is the aggressive jet-black hull with red boot stripe, teak transom and unique foredeck cockpit — distinctive features of previous Midnight Lace 44 and 52 models. Built in the U.S., the 40 Express is constructed on a cored hull with a fine entry and a moderate 14° of deadrise at the transom. V-drives are used to move the engines aft and thus free up additional cabin volume while keeping the overall profile down. The basic two-stateroom, galley-up white ash interior is modern and well arranged. The cockpit is raised two steps from the salon level, and while not intended for any serious fishing, it is large enough to satisfy weekend anglers. Additional features include excellent engine room access, side exhausts, and a stylish helm console with room to flush mount most electronics. A good performer with 300-hp Cummins diesels, she'll cruise efficiently at 23 knots burning only 1 gpm. Top speed is about 27–28 knots. ❏

SPECIFICATIONS

Length	40'3"
Length WL	35'4"
Beam	13'6"
Draft	3'8"
Weight	22,900#
Clearance	16'0"
Water	100 Gals.
Fuel	400 Gals.
Hull Type	Modified-V
Designer	Tom Fexas

Production
1991–Current

PACE 40 SPORTFISHERMAN

The Pace 40 Sportfisherman is a re-creation of the earlier Egg Harbor 40 Sedan built from 1975 until early 1986. (The molds for five Egg Harbor designs were purchased and sent to Taiwan, where the Pace series of boats is currently being constructed by Nautique Yachts in Kaohsiung.) Aside from her solid front windshield and bold deckhouse mask, the Pace 40's styling remains very close to the original Egg Harbor 40 Sedan. The interior arrangement is also similar to that used in (later-model) Egg 40s with a mid-level galley, two staterooms below, and a single head compartment. The breakfast bar found in the original Egg 40 is eliminated in the Pace, thereby opening up the salon considerably. A generous amount of well-crafted teak cabinetry and paneling is applied throughout. The cockpit features a teak sole and covering boards, bait-prep center, and a transom door. Caterpillar 375-hp diesels will cruise the Pace 40 SF around 22 knots, and the larger 485-hp GM 6-71s cruise about 25 knots. A handsome boat, the Pace 40 is a good reproduction of a classic David Martin, Jersey-style sportfisherman. ❏

SPECIFICATIONS

Length......................40'0"
Beam.........................14'0"
Draft ....2'9"
Weight ....28,000#
Clearance ....NA
Water.................100 Gals.
Fuel ....450 Gals.
Cockpit..............95 Sq. Ft.
Hull Type.........Modified-V
Designer ....D. Martin

Production
1988–Current

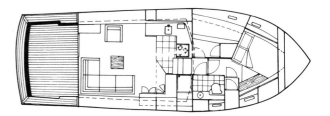

PILGRIM 40

With her tugboat profile, fake smokestack, and trolly-car windows the Pilgrim 40 is a real eye-catcher in a sea of boring designs. Over fifty were built at Pilgrim Marine in Ontario during her production run, and today a used Pilgrim 40 will attract attention on the brokerage market. She's built on a full keel, full displacement hull with a plumb bow and rounded bilges. Balsa coring is used above the waterline as well as in the deck and superstructure. A bow thruster was standard, and the prop is fully protected by the rudder and skeg. Inside, the pilothouse is raised three steps from the salon and galley. This separate wheelhouse is particularly well arranged with excellent visability ahead and sliding access doors port and starboard. There's a huge storage area beneath the galley sole. The protected cockpit is large enough for a few deck chairs, and 30" raised bulwarks provide added security all around the decks. An economical and completely practical liveaboard cruiser, most Pilgrim 40s were fitted with a 100-hp Westerbeke diesel which provides a steady 8-knot cruising speed at 3 gph. Note that a flybridge was optional. ❏

SPECIFICATIONS

Length......................40'0"
Beam........................14'0"
Draft ....3'6"
Weight ....25,000#
Clearance ....22'0"
Water.................240 Gals.
Fuel ....142 Gals.
Cockpit........................NA
Hull Type.....Displacement
Designer.......Ted Gozzard

Production
1984-91

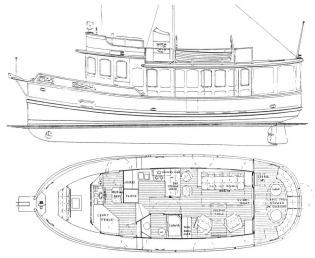

NOTABLE DESIGNS

W.C. HYATT 40 SUNDECK

The W.C. Hyatt 40 Sundeck is a good-looking Taiwan import with a clean profile and a practical two-stateroom interior layout. Aimed at the affordable end of the family cruising market, she's constructed on a modified-V hull with balsa-cored hullsides, moderate transom deadrise, and a fairly deep keel below. Two floorplans are offered in the Hyatt — one has an offset double berth in the guest stateroom and a split forward head, and the alternate layout has stacked single berths forward and a single head compartment. Either way, the galley and dinette are down and a lower helm is standard. While the salon dimensions are moderate compared with other boats her size, the master stateroom is quite spacious and includes a huge hanging locker to port. The sundeck is also roomy and may be enclosed with wing doors and hard enclosure panels. Additional features include a full teak interior, wide sidedecks, comfortable bridge, and a well-arranged engine room with fairly good access to the motors. Optional 300-hp Cummins diesels cruise the Hyatt 40 around 15–16 knots, and 375-hp Cats cruise at 22 knots. ❑

SPECIFICATIONS

Length	39'9"
Length WL	NA
Beam	14'5"
Draft	2'10"
Weight	26,000#
Clearance	16'1"
Water	180 Gals.
Fuel	350 Gals.
Hull Type	Modified-V
Designer	Hyatt

Production
1988–Current

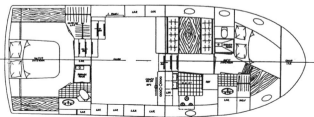

WILLARD 40 TRAWLER

The Willard 40 is a full-displacement, ballasted trawler designed for extended offshore cruising. Built on a semi-custom basis in Anaheim, California, she is highly regarded for her seakindly hull and quality construction. The mere fact that the Willard 40 is a real (i.e., displacement) trawler nearly puts her in a class by herself in today's market. Her sedan layout includes two staterooms below with the owner's stateroom and private head to port and V-berths forward. A second head with stall shower is opposite the master stateroom. The salon and galley are on the deckhouse level, and the interior is tastefully finished in teak and rattan woodwork and vinyl wallcoverings — not a plush interior, but eminently practical for serious cruising. The flybridge features unique drop-down steps to the foredeck — a good idea since the sidedecks are somewhat narrow. The mast (for a steadying sail) is functional rather than cosmetic. With the standard 130-hp Perkins diesel, the Willard 40 will cruise at 8 knots burning 3 gph for a range of 1,500+ miles. Willard also builds a pilothouse model on this hull. ❑

SPECIFICATIONS

Length	39'9"
Length WL	36'1"
Beam	13'8"
Draft	4'3"
Weight	33,000#
Clearance	12'0"
Water	260 Gals.
Fuel	600 Gals.
Cockpit	79 Sq. Ft.
Hull Type	Displacement
Designer	Willard

Production
1973–Current

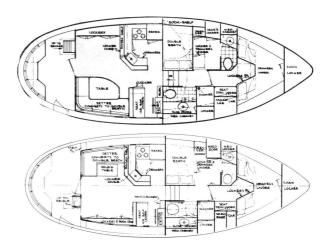

NOTABLE DESIGNS

AQUARIUS 41 MOTOR YACHT

With her excessively outlined salon windows and prominent reverse arch, the styling of the Aquarius 41 MY is distinctive, to say the least. The Aquarius is built in Taiwan on a solid fiberglass hull with a wide beam and a long keel below. Her two-stateroom, galley-down floorplan features an expansive salon comparable in size to what might be expected in a somewhat larger boat. A dinette is opposite the galley and a built-in entertainment center is to port in the salon. Teak woodwork is applied extensively throughout the boat. The generous salon dimen-sions come at a price however, and both staterooms in the Aquarius 41 are a lit-tle tight — especially the forward cabin which is more useful for storage than adult sleeping quarters. Outside, the aft deck is small with limited entertain-ment capabilities. The flybridge, on the other hand, is downright expansive with wraparound bench seating aft of the helm and room for a crowd. The Perkins 200-hp, or the now-standard Cummins 210-hp diesels will cruise the Aquarius economically at 12–13 knots. Optional 375-hp Cats will cruise around 21 knots. ❏

SPECIFICATIONS

Length	40'6"
Length WL	37'0"
Beam	14'10"
Draft	3'0"
Weight	26,000#
Clearance	NA
Water	200 Gals.
Fuel	400 Gals.
Hull Type	Modified-V
Designer	Unknown

Production
1987–Current

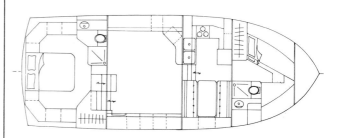

MARINETTE 41 MOTOR YACHT

The Marinette 41 is the largest motor yacht built by Aluminum Cruisers (which has recently been purchased by Harbor Master). After some 30 years of manufacturing the only series of small and mid-size aluminum yachts in the U.S., this Tennessee builder has long since proven the durability of their designs. The 41 Motor Yacht is a handsome boat with clean, well-balanced lines and an attractive dockside profile. Below, her two-stateroom interior is arranged with both the galley and dinette down, allowing for an open and relatively uncluttered salon. Walk-around double berths are located in each of the private staterooms. In an interesting departure from the norm, the forward head in the Marinette 41 is larger than the one adjoining the owner's stateroom aft — a practical feature considering that the forward head often gets the most use. A revised layout with the galley and head to starboard was introduced in 1990. The Marinette 41 MY performs quite well (19 knots cruise/27 knots top) with the standard 454-cid Crusader gas engines. Note that the less popular Marinette 41 Convertible is built on this same hull design. ❏

SPECIFICATIONS

Length......................41'0"
Beam........................14'0"
Draft ....3'0"
Weight ....18,000#
Clearance ....12'0"
Water.................150 Gals.
Fuel ....350 Gals.
Hull Type.........Modified-V
Construction ....Aluminum
Designer............Marinette

Production
1987–Current

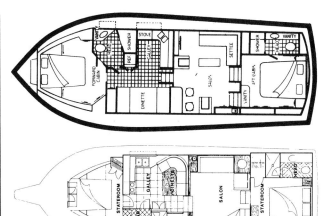

NOTABLE DESIGNS

PRESIDENT 41 DOUBLE CABIN

The President 41 was one of the more popular Asian imports during the 1980s due to her moderate price tag and roomy accommodation plan. While she displays a distinct trawler-like profile, the 41 is nonetheless built on a conventional modified-V hull with a deep forefoot, a prop-protecting 18" keel, and 14° of deadrise at the transom. The hull is solid fiberglass, and the decks and house are cored with balsa. The two-stateroom interior of the President 41 is unusually open and spacious and completely finished with grain-matched teak paneling and cabinetry throughout. A lower station was standard, and the galley and dinette are down from the salon level. A double berth is fitted in the forward stateroom, and twin singles (or a walkaround queen berth) were offered in the aft cabin– a somewhat unusual layout. Topside, the helm console is set well forward on the bridge with guest seating for five. Most President 41s were sold with the 120/135-hp Lehman diesels which provide an economical 8–9 knot cruising speed. The larger 225-hp Lehmans will cruise at around 13 knots and reach a top speed of 15–16 knots.   ❏

SPECIFICATIONS

Length	40'6"
Length WL	35'10"
Beam	13'5"
Draft	2'10"
Weight	22,500#
Clearance	NA
Water	120 Gals.
Fuel, Std	420 Gals.
Hull Type	Modified-V
Designer	G. Stadel

Production
1982–88

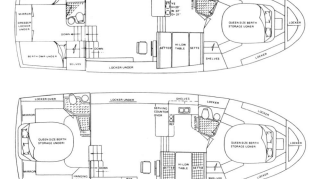

NOTABLE DESIGNS

CHB 42 SUNDECK MOTOR YACHT

Chung Hwa is generally regarded as one of the more experienced Taiwan builders with a string of successful models sold into the U.S. market. The CHB 42 (also known as the Present 42) is an affordable double cabin sundeck design with a trawler-style profile, conventional semi-displacement hull, full teak interior, and simulated lapstrake hullsides. Aside from the traditional interior woodwork and practical two-stateroom dinette layout, the CHB 42 features a fairly large salon separated from the galley with a convenient breakfast bar. A lower sta-

tion was standard along with a convenient deck access door, and the aft head contains the only stall shower. CHB offered a range of diesel options for the 42 Sundeck, but most came with twin 135-hp or 225-hp Lehmans or twin 200-hp Perkins. Economical to operate, the larger engine options will provide cruising speeds in the 12–14 knot range while the less powerful Lehmans reduce the CHB 42 Sundeck to trawler speeds. At hull speeds, the cruising range exceeds 600 miles. (The factory weight of only 20,000 lbs. seems low for a boat this size.) ❑

SPECIFICATIONS

Length	41'10"
Length WL	38'0"
Beam	13'8"
Draft	3'6"
Weight	20,000#
Clearance	NA
Water	200 Gals.
Fuel	450 Gals.
Hull Type	Semi-Disp.
Designer	Unknown

Production
1983–87

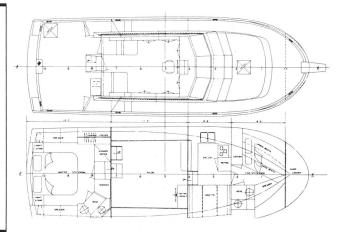

DUFFY 42 FLYBRIDGE CRUISER

An enduring lobsterboat profile and a high level of craftsmanship have made the Duffy 42 one of the more popular Downeast cruisers currently on the market. These are rugged, semi-custom boats with cored hulls and a full length keel below — seaworthy designs with beautiful sheers, protected running gear, and generous cockpits. There are several versions of the Duffy 42, and each is finished out to a buyer's individual specifications. The two-stateroom, galley-up floorplan of the FB Cruiser features an island berth forward and over/under berths in the guest cabin. A lower helm is standard, and the conservative decor of white Formica cabinetry and teak trim is attractive and straightforward. Hardware, appliances, and systems are first class. The engine room access is good, and a transom door and swim platform are standard. Most of the Duffy 42s built for private use (many are used commercially) have been powered with a single 375-hp Cat which delivers a 14–15 knot cruising speed around 18 knots wide open. Cruising range is an impressive 500+ miles. A class act, used Duffy 42s often are hard to find. ❏

SPECIFICATIONS

Length	42'0"
Length WL	39'8"
Beam	14'6"
Draft	4'6"
Weight	24,000#
Clearance	NA
Water	100 Gals.
Fuel	500 Gals.
Hull Type	Semi-Disp.
Designer	S. Lincoln

Production
1985–Current

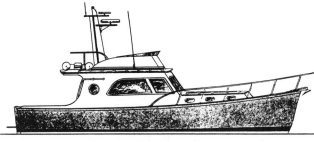

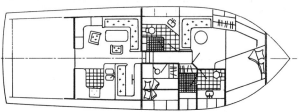

FEXAS 42 SPORT SEDAN

Imported as the Ultimate 42 and (currently) the Mikelson 42, this good-looking cruiser is perhaps best known as the Fexas 42 Sport Sedan. She's built by Bluewater in Taiwan on a soft-chined hull with a somewhat narrow beam, with a fine entry and shallow keel. The hull itself is fully Airex-cored and she weighs in at an efficient 24,000 lbs. What sets the Fexas 42 apart from the mass of other mid-size sedan models is her superb styling. Note the rakish fore and aft bridge overhangs and distinctive stepped salon windows. While several floorplans have been offered over the years, most 42s have been delivered with a two-stateroom teak interior with a lower helm and single head. The salon dimensions — while certainly adequate — are limited by her relatively narrow beam and generous sidedecks. The flybridge is arranged with the helm forward and facing settees fore and aft. A good performer with now-standard 300-hp Cat 3116 diesels, the Fexas 42 will cruise very efficiently at 21 knots and deliver a top speed of around 24–25 knots. Early models powered with 260-hp GM 8.2s are a knot or two slower. ❏

SPECIFICATIONS

Length	41'9"
Length WL	37'9"
Beam	13'0"
Draft	3'0"
Weight	24,000#
Clearance	10'4"
Water	200 Gals.
Fuel	400 Gals.
Hull Type	Semi-Disp.
Designer	Tom Fexas

Production
1984–Current

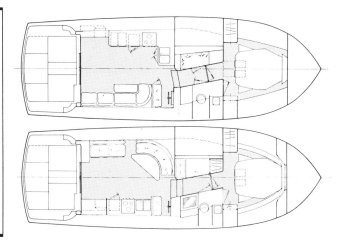

KROGEN 42 TRAWLER

The Krogen 42 is one of the very few trawler-style boats actually built on a full displacement hull. As such, she displays all of the characteristics normally associated with such long-range designs, including a comfortable ride, excellent seaworthiness, and the easy rolling motion typical of any soft-chined boat. The Krogen is a particularly salty-looking vessel with a distinctive profile and an upright bow. Inside, the focal point of the boat is the functional pilothouse with watch berth, located a few steps up from the salon level. Until hull #65 (1985), the Krogen

42s were built with glass-over-plywood decks with a fiberglass hull and superstructure. Beginning with hull #66 construction became all fiberglass. A single Lehman diesel is standard and a unique "get home" feature allows the generator to be used as an emergency back-up engine. At her 8-knot hull speed, the Krogen 42 has a range of 2,000+ miles. Over 150 have been sold to date. Note that a Krogen 42 Wide Body with a full-width salon was introduced in 1989. Originally built by Chien Hwa, the 42 is currently constructed at the Asia Boat Co. in Taiwan. ❏

SPECIFICATIONS

Length	42'4"
Length WL	39'6"
Beam	15'0"
Draft	4'7"
Weight	39,500#
Clearance	NA
Water	360 Gals.
Fuel	700 Gals.
Hull Type	Displacement
Designer	Jim Krogen

Production
1979–Current

PT 42 COCKPIT MOTOR YACHT

The PT 42 Cockpit MY was a fairly popular Asian import with a good deal of value built into her affordable price tag. Built by Cheer Men in Taiwan, the 42 is basically a PT 38 Sundeck MY with a 4' cockpit extension. She was constructed on a solid fiberglass, modified-V hull with moderate beam and an extended keel below for directional stability. The overall quality of the PT 42 is about average and she has a modern, clean-cut deckhouse profile. Inside, the all-teak layout is arranged in the conventional manner with a walkaround double berth in the aft stateroom and V-berths forward. The galley in the PT 42 is down and almost hidden from salon view so the layout isn't as open as some. Deck access doors are port and starboard in the salon, and a lower helm was standard. In addition to the versatile cockpit, she has a roomy aft deck entertaining platform and additional space for six on the flybridge. With twin 225-hp Lehman diesels, the PT 42 Cockpit MY will cruise economically around 14 knots and reach a top speed of 17 knots. Larger 250-hp Cummins diesels will add 1 to 2 knots to those speeds. ❏

SPECIFICATIONS

Length	42'0"
Length WL	38'3"
Beam	13'6"
Draft	3'6"
Weight	25,000#
Clearance	NA
Water	150 Gals.
Fuel	300 Gals.
Cockpit	NA
Hull Type	Semi-Disp.
Designer	John Norek

Production
1984–90

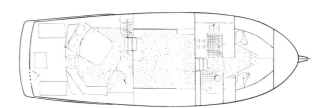

ROUGHWATER 42

Because there are many experienced cruisers who still value practical design above Eurostyle glitz, capable boats like the Roughwater 42 will probably always have a secure nitch in the marketplace. She's Taiwan-built on a solid fiberglass, semi-displacement hull with a full-length keel and hard chines — an efficient and easily driven hull form with above-average seakeeping characteristics. First introduced as the Roughwater 41 in 1973, the original soft-chined hull was completely retooled in 1983 and lengthened to 42 feet (although the 41 remained avail-

able through 1985). The Roughwater 42 is a notably larger boat than her predecessor, with a bigger pilothouse and a queen berth in the aft stateroom. The galley is aft in the salon, the dinette is forward, and a sliding deck access door is to starboard. Note the large wraparound deckhouse windows. Topside, the small enclosed wheelhouse provides good helm visibility while leaving enough room aft for a sun deck. Economical 250-hp GM 8.2 diesels will cruise the Roughwater 42 around 16 knots and reach a top speed of 21 knots.   ❑

SPECIFICATIONS

Length	42'0"
Length WL	37'0"
Beam	13'0"
Draft	4'0"
Weight	22,000#
Clearance	NA
Water	150 Gals.
Fuel	250 Gals.
Hull Type	Semi-Disp.
Designer	Ed Monk, Jr.

Production
1983–Current

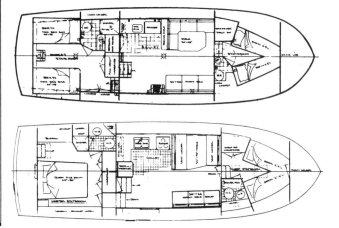

SILHOUETTE 42

For those who appreciate fresh and innovative thinking, the Silhouette 42 is truly an exceptional design. If her profile is unusual, the Silhouette manages to offer a unique interior layout with more room than might be expected. She's built in Taiwan by Chien Hwa on a PVC-cored, modified-V hull form. While there are several unusual features in the Silhouette 42, it's the semi-enclosed pilothouse/sundeck and the wide-open aft stateroom (with its sliding glass door and private cockpit) that attract the most attention. A real surprise is the hydraulically operated stern gate which drops to create a practically wide-open transom and swim platform. Inside, a breakfast bar separates the spacious main salon from the galley below, and both staterooms feature double berths and stall showers. The interior is finished with light ash (or teak) woodwork and mica veneers. With standard Caterpillar 375-hp diesels, the Silhouette 42 will cruise around 21 knots and reach a top speed of 25–26 knots. Note that the larger Silhouette 44 Sport Cruiser is the same boat with a Eurostyle profile, revised interior, and larger cockpit. ❑

SPECIFICATIONS

Length	41'10"
Length WL	37'6"
Beam	14'6"
Draft	3'2"
Weight	28,000#
Clearance	NA
Water	150 Gals.
Fuel	400 Gals.
Cockpit	NA
Hull Type	Modified-V
Designer	J. Krogen

Production
1987–Current

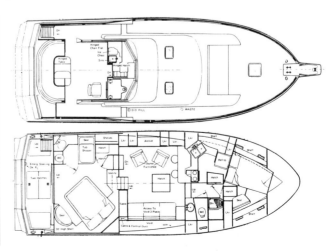

PRESIDENT 43 DOUBLE CABIN

A good-looking boat with a trawler-style profile and set-back house, the President 43 MY achieved a good deal of popularity with those seeking a roomy and affordable family cruising yacht. She was constructed on a solid fiberglass hull with moderate beam and a shallow, full-length keel below. At just 28,000 lbs., the President is a fairly lightweight boat for her size. Her two-stateroom, galley-down floorplan was available with queen berths in both staterooms (an alternate layout has stacked single berths forward and the convenience of a second stall shower in the guest head), and the interior is fully finished with teak woodwork and cabinetry. Either way, the staterooms are quite large while the salon dimensions are about average. Note that a lower helm station was optional. Additional features include a spacious aft deck platform, secure sidedecks, a fairly small flybridge, and a standard factory hardtop. Several diesel options were offered in the President 43 including Lehmans, 8.2 GMs, and Cummins. The popular 275-hp Lehmans will cruise the President 43 MY at 14 knots and reach about 17 knots top. ❏

SPECIFICATIONS

Length	42'6"
Length WL	37'10"
Beam	13'10"
Draft	3'2"
Weight	28,000#
Clearance	12'4"
Water	120 Gals.
Fuel	420 Gals.
Hull Type	Semi-Disp.
Designer	G. Stadel

Production
1984–90

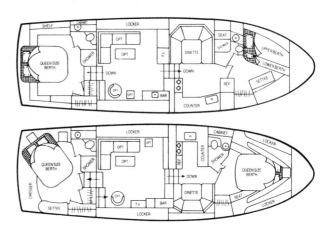

DAVIS 44 SPORTFISHERMAN

Designed as an affordable alternative to the successful Davis 47, the new 44 SF offers an incredibly well-proportioned profile, a smooth ride, and good offshore performance. Her hull features a very fine entry and greatly flared bow, and has a solid fiberglass bottom with cored hullsides. Three floorplans are offered: a single-stateroom/dinette arrangement, a two-stateroom/two-head model, and a two-stateroom/single-head design with built-in washer/dryer. All offer a mid-level galley and a spacious salon with traditional teak cabinetry and woodwork. Not surprisingly, the cockpit is set up for tournament-level anglers with plenty of workspace, engine room access door, a huge in-deck fishbox, and modular tackle centers. The flybridge has an extended cockpit overhang, and the custom-style helm console features Panish controls and a pop-up instrument pod. Standard engines in the Davis 44 SF are 485-hp 6-71s which cruise at 23 knots and reach 26–27 knots wide open. Optional 550-hp 6V92s cruise at 27 knots (30 knots top), and 645 MANs will cruise around 29 knots and deliver 33+ wide open. ❑

SPECIFICATIONS

Length	44'5"
Beam	15'3"
Draft	4'0"
Weight	35,000#
Clearance	NA
Water	135 Gals.
Fuel	650 Gals.
Cockpit	NA
Hull Type	Modified-V
Designer	Davis

Production
1991–Current

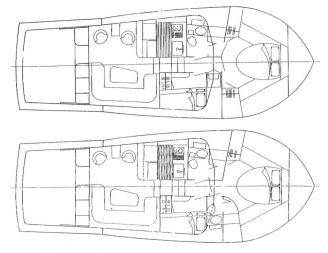

DAVIS 44 EXPRESS SF

Following the introduction of the 44 Flybridge SF by just one year, the 44 Express is built on the same easy-riding modified-V hull with greatly flared bow sections and moderate deadrise at the transom. As tournament-style day-boats go, the Davis 44 Express is the next best thing to custom-built, and her graceful lines can't be denied. The emphasis here is clearly on fishability: the cockpit (three steps below the bridgedeck level) is designed with low-freeboard gunnels and features a complete set of molded tackle centers, livewell, offset transom door, and direct access to the engine room. Davis is offering a choice of bridgedeck lay-outs for the 44 Express — one with a centerline helm, and the other with the helm forward. There are also two interior floorplans, and both include an island berth forward, small galley, and separate stall shower in the head. Standard engines are 485-hp 6-71s which cruise at 23 knots and reach 26–27 knots wide open (with a full tower). Optional 550-hp 6V92s cruise at 27 knots (30 knots top) and 645 MANs will cruise around 29 knots and deliver 33+ knots top. ❑

SPECIFICATIONS

Length	44'5"
Beam	15'3"
Draft	4'0"
Weight	35,000#
Clearance	NA
Water	135 Gals.
Fuel	500 Gals.
Cockpit	NA
Hull Type	Modified-V
Designer	Davis

Production
1992–Current

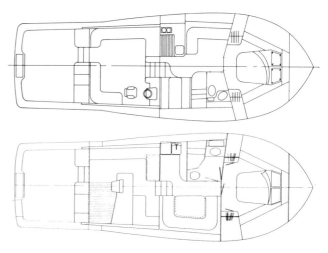

EMBASSY 444 SUNDECK MY

Built by Nova Marine in Taiwan, the Embassy 444 is constructed on a modern hull form with moderate beam, balsa coring above the waterline, and a shallow keel below. Her steep 18° of transom deadrise is notable — it's about as close to a deep-V hull as you're likely to see on a cruising yacht which adds considerably to her stability at cruising speeds. The two-stateroom layout of the Embassy 444 is ideal for cruising with an extra couple since both heads are fitted with stall showers and both staterooms have walkaround double berths. (The forward head is as large as that found in the master stateroom, which makes this floorplan a little unusual.) Most 444s have been delivered with teak interiors, however light ash or oak woodwork is also available. The side-decks are quite wide, and the raised afterdeck is roomy enough for the requisite deck furnishings. The (boxy) helm console provides space for flush mounting of electronics and there's plenty of guest seating on the flybridge. With the popular 375-hp Cats, the Embassy 444 will cruise economically at 22 knots and reach a top speed of around 26 knots. ❏

SPECIFICATIONS

Length	44'4"
Length WL	NA
Beam	15'0"
Draft	3'6"
Weight	26,000#
Clearance	NA
Water	200 Gals.
Fuel	500 Gals.
Hull Type	Modified-V
Designer	Nova

Production
1987–Current

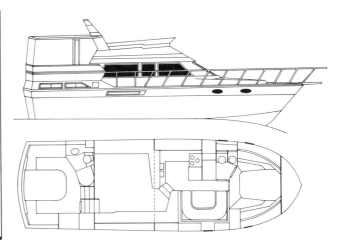

NOTABLE DESIGNS

HERITAGE 44 SUNDECK MY

The Heritage 44 was constructed on the same all-glass hull used in the construction of the smaller Heritage 40 Sundeck, with the extra length committed to an enlarged galley and dinette area and a more spacious salon and master stateroom. Built in Taiwan by Nova Marine, the Heritage 44 is an affordable trawler-style family cruiser, and her simulated lapstrake hull adds much to her traditional appeal. Her floorplan features a large galley and dinette down from the salon level and over/under single berths in the guest stateroom. This is a fairly straightfor-ward and practical layout for a cruising boat, although the lack of a stall shower in the forward head is unfortunate. The teak woodwork — some of which is carved — is first-rate throughout. There's a deck access door in the salon (the lower helm was optional) and both the master stateroom and sundeck above are quite roomy. Standard engines were 135-hp Perkins or Lehman diesels (about 8–9 knots cruise), and 200-hp Perkins were a popular option (14 knot cruise/16–17 knots wide open) among several other choices. ❑

SPECIFICATIONS

Length	43'5"
Length WL	39'5"
Beam	13'8"
Draft	3'10"
Weight	27,100#
Clearance	NA
Water	300 Gals.
Fuel	500 Gals.
Hull Type	Modified-V
Designer	Nova Marine

Production
1985–90

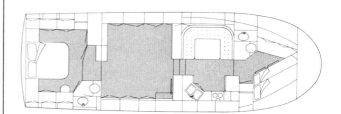

W.C. HYATT 44 MOTOR YACHT

As Taiwan motor yachts go, the W.C. Hyatt 44 is a better-looking boat than most double cabin designs in her size range. Her lines are clean and modern, and her rakish appearance makes her easy to pick out in a crowd. She's built on a modified-V hull (12° transom deadrise) with a fairly narrow beam and balsa coring in the hullsides — the same hull mold used in the production of the Hyatt 40 MY. Her conventional two-stateroom, galley-down interior is attractively finished with traditional teak woodwork and trim throughout, and there are queen berths fore and aft. The layout includes separate stall showers in both head compartments, and a lower helm is optional. (A three-stateroom layout with a deckhouse galley and a smaller salon is also available.) The aft deck is about average in size and comes with molded bridge steps and a built-in wet bar. The flybridge is arranged with the helm forward, and guest seating for a crowd. Several diesel engine choices are available. The largest — 375-hp Caterpillars — provide a cruising speed of 22–23 knots and a top speed of about 26 knots. ❏

SPECIFICATIONS

Length	44'0"
Length WL	NA
Beam	14'5"
Draft	3'0"
Weight	33,500#
Clearance	18'5"
Water	165 Gals.
Fuel	450 Gals.
Hull Type	Modified-V
Designer	G. Chin

Production
1988–Current

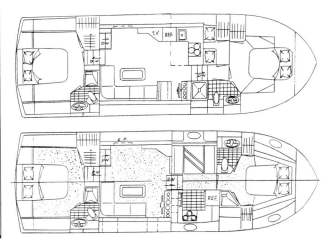

MIDNIGHT LACE 44 EXPRESS CRUISER

The Midnight Lace 44 is the boat that put Tom Fexas on the map. The prototype was built in Stuart, Florida and introduced at the Ft. Lauderdale Boat Show in 1978 where she literally stole the show. Based on the elegant commuter-style boats of the 1920s, the Midnight Lace 44 is a completely modern blend of lightweight cored construction and a highly efficient "penetrating" hull form. She features a very narrow beam with a fine entry, flared bow, and tightly rounded bilges. The Midnight Laces were built in Hong Kong at Golden Wave Shipyard, and

were offered with a choice of floorplans (single- or two-stateroom layouts). Orignally offered as an express, a flybridge became available in 1979, although most 44s were sold without it. Note the unique forward cockpit (accessed from the forward stateroom) and the beautiful brightwork of the house. A remarkably classy and efficient boat, standard 220-hp GM 8.2 diesels (driven through V-drives) will cruise the Midnight Lace 44 at 21 knots burning only 14 gph! Top speed is around 25 knots. Larger 260-hp GM 8.2s were optional. ❏

SPECIFICATIONS

Length	44'0"
Length WL	39'6"
Beam	11'0"
Draft	2'10"
Weight	15,900#
Clearance	16'0"
Water	130 Gals.
Fuel	250 Gals.
Hull Type	Semi-Disp.
Designer	Tom Fexas

Production
1978–89

PACIFICA 44 SPORTFISHERMAN

The Pacifica 44 SF has been in production for two decades without undergoing any significant design changes — a remarkable testament to her enduring popularity among serious West Coast sportfishermen. She's never been a high-production model (about 65 have been sold to date), but the 44 remains Pacifica's most popular boat ever. Built on a modified-V hull with 11° of deadrise aft and considerable flare at the bow, the 44 is notable for her huge fishing cockpit and rugged construction. Her interior consists of two full staterooms (each with a double bed), two heads, and a handy midships lounge in the companionway that converts to over/under berths. The salon is arranged with the galley to port, and the original standard lower helm has become an option. As is the case with many West Coast sportfishermen, the 44's wide sidedecks result in a salon of limited (but adequate) dimensions. A good performer, many were equipped with the 435-hp GM 8V71 diesels which cruise at 22–23 knots and reach 26 knots top. The larger 550-hp GM 6V92s will cruise around 26–27 knots and turn 30 wide open. ❑

SPECIFICATIONS

Length......................44'0"
Beam........................15'0"
Draft ....4'2"
Weight ....33,000#
Clearance ....NA
Water.................120 Gals.
Fuel............650/750 Gals.
Cockpit............148 Sq. Ft.
Hull Type.........Modified-V
Designer ....John Norek

Production
1970–Current

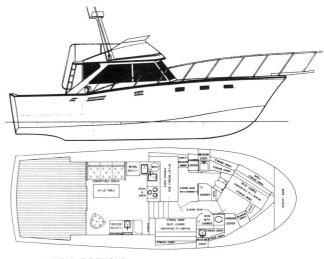

SOUTHERN CROSS 44 SF

A great-looking design from Tom Fexas, the Southern Cross 44 Sportfisherman is an Australian import with a number of innovative and practical design features. Beginning with a fully cored hull, her unique chamfered transom allows the 44 to back down hard with less tendency to flood the cockpit. The air intakes are hidden in the after edge of the house, and underwater exhausts run through the stringers. At 28,000 lbs., the Southern Cross is a relatively light boat for her size, and those who have run her agree that her seakeeping characteristics are above-average. The cockpit is equipped with controls, bait prep station, transom door with gate, and a livewell. Direct access to the spacious engine room is provided via a cockpit door. Four steps up from the cockpit (quite unusual), the salon features silver ash woodwork and stylish fabrics to create an especially attractive interior. A centerline queen berth is fitted in the forward stateroom, and stacked bunks are found in the guest cabin. A good-running boat, 540-hp 6V92s will cruise the Southern Cross 44 around 27–28 knots and the top speed is 31 knots. ❑

SPECIFICATIONS

Length......................44'2"
Beam........................14'6"
Draft ....3'0"
Weight ....28,000#
Clearance ....12'6"
Water.................100 Gals.
Fuel ....550 Gals.
Cockpit............110 Sq. Ft.
Hull Type.........Modified-V
Designer..........Tom Fexas

Production
1987–90

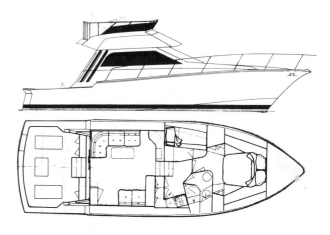

INDEPENDENCE 45 TRAWLER

The Independence 45 is an upscale luxury trawler with genuine live-aboard accommodations designed for extended cruising. This is basically a displacement yacht with a long, deep keel and protected prop, but with hard chines aft (rather than rounded bilges) to reduce roll. Originally called the Positive 42, she's built in Taiwan to a high standard of workmanship and finish. The two-stateroom teak interior of the Independence 45 is arranged with the galley to port in the (full-width) salon, and with two heads with stall showers on the lower level. The after-deck, with its teak sole and transom door, is partially weather protected with a bridge overhang. The raised pilothouse, which provides a full 360° view around the boat, can be reached directly from the salon or from the outside through port and starboard deck doors. An upperdeck helm is optional. There are molded steps on both sides of the house to the flybridge where there's adequate space for dinghy storage. A single 135-hp Lehman (or Lugger) diesel is standard. She'll cruise economically at 7–8 knots with a range of over 1,000 miles. ❏

SPECIFICATIONS

Length ....44'6"
Length WL ....40'9"
Beam.......................14'6"
Draft ....4'6"
Weight ....36,000#
Clearance ....13'6"
Water................300 Gals.
Fuel ....600 Gals.
Hull ....Displacement
Designer............J. Backus

Production
1987–Current

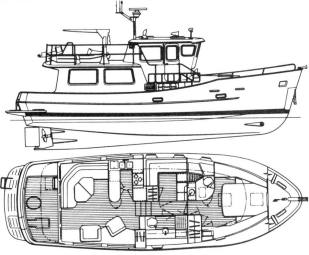

WEST BAY 4500 PILOTHOUSE

For those more interested in seaworthy construction than glitz, the West Bay 4500 PH is a reminder of why many boating enthusiasts favor boats from the Pacific Northwest. The West Bay 4500 was built in British Columbia on a commercial hull originally designed for RCMP and Canadian Coast Guard search-and-rescue purposes. Constructed with a watertight bulkhead forward and a watertight engine room, her solid glass hull features a flared bow, moderate beam, and a modified-V bottom. Inside, the layout is arranged with access to the lower-level staterooms via a salon companionway rather than from the pilothouse. The galley is forward in the salon, and there are three staterooms and two full heads in the standard floorplan. (A two-stateroom layout with an enlarged master was optional.) Additional features include a spacious cockpit with engine room access, walka-round sidedecks, and oak cabinetry and trim throughout. Among several engine options, 300-hp Cummins or 320-hp Cats will cruise around 19–20 knots, and 375-hp/425-hp Cats cruise at 22 and 24 knots respectively. A total of 15 West Bay 4500s were built. ❑

SPECIFICATIONS

Length	45'0"
Length WL	NA
Beam	14'10"
Draft	3'0"
Weight	32,000#
Clearance	NA
Water	206 Gals.
Fuel	540 Gals.
Hull Type	Modified-V
Designer	B. Vermeulen

Production
1985–91

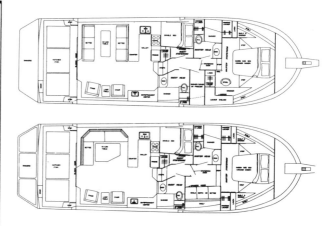

NORDHAVN 46

The Nordhavn 46 is one of the best-quality Taiwan import the authors have encountered on the powerboat market. Imported by Pacific Asian Enterprises, the Nordhavn is a highly practical pilothouse design with a ballasted displacement hull and the distinctive profile of a North Sea workboat. The layout of this unusual little ship is practical and quite innovative. The pilothouse is amidships with full 360° visibility. The windshield is canted, and a stout bridge coaming protects the house from breaking seas. Below, a companionway from the salon leads down to the midships owner's stateroom, while the forward guest stateroom is reached separately from the pilothouse. The glasswork and teak joinery — and the quality hardware and fixtures used throughout — are quite exceptional. Additional features include a dry exhaust system, keel-cooler (for engine cooling), a single sidedeck (the salon extends to the portside rail), and functional mast and boom. Powered with a single 143-hp Lugger diesel, the Nordhavn will cruise at 8 knots at 3–4 gph for a cruising range of some 1,500+ miles. Definitely a piece of work.   ❏

SPECIFICATIONS

Length	45'9"
Length WL	38'4"
Beam	15'5"
Draft	5'0"
Weight	48,320#
Clearance	26'0"
Water	290 Gals.
Fuel	830 Gals.
Hull Type	Displacement
Designer	J. Leishman

Production
1989–Current

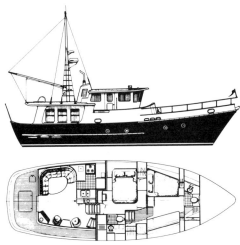

VISTA 46 MOTOR YACHT

A good-looking boat with a low-profile deckhouse and rakish flybridge, the Vista 46 MY has been a fairly popular design since her introduction in 1985. Built in Taiwan by Kha Shing, she's also been known as the Spindrift 46 and Southern Star 46 —basically the same boats but with different deckhouse molds and revised interior floorplans. She's constructed on a solid fiberglass, modified-V hull with a well-flared bow and a shallow, full-length keel below. Two floorplans are available in the Vista 46 and both are arranged with the galley and dinette down from the salon level. A lower helm is optional (the deck access door is standard) and the master stateroom dimensions are very generous. The interior is finished with an abundance of well-crafted teak (or oak) woodwork. Outside, the aft deck is large enough for several deck chairs and there's guest seating aft of the helm on the bridge. Many were sold with optional teak decks. Several diesel engines have been offered in the Vista 46 MY over the years. The popular 375-hp Cats will cruise at 17–18 knots and reach a top speed of around 20 knots. ❏

SPECIFICATIONS

Length	46'6"
Length WL	41'6"
Beam	15'0"
Draft	3'8"
Weight	36,000#
Clearance	15'9"
Water	160 Gals.
Fuel	500 Gals.
Hull Type	Modified-V
Designer	Kha Shing

Production
1985–Current

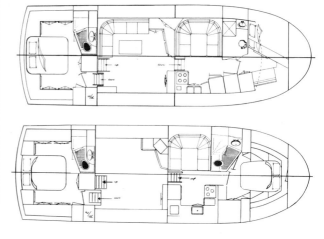

DAVIS 47 SPORTFISHERMAN

Davis boats are highly regarded for their excellent seakeeping characteristics and superb Carolina styling and craftsmanship. The Davis 47 SF has the distinctive appearance of a custom design but without the associated expenses and maintenance costs. She's built on a modified-V hull with Divinyell coring used in the hullsides from the waterline up. (Early models were built with fully cored hulls.) After experimenting with several different floorplans since 1986, Davis in 1990 introduced two layouts (see below) that remain standard today. The more popular galley-down version features a huge salon, and the galley-up floorplan has three staterooms. Access to the engine room is through a door in the cockpit. A custom-style, teak helm console with single-lever controls dominates the flybridge. Her fully equipped cockpit features a molded tackle center with freezer, teak covering boards, transom door, and two in-deck storage boxes. Standard 735-hp 8V92s will cruise around 25 knots (29 knots top), and optional 820-hp MANs cruise around 29 knots (33 top). Fuel was increased for 1990. Over 90 have been built to date. ❑

SPECIFICATIONS

Length	47'0"
Beam	16'0"
Draft	4'0"
Weight	45,000#
Clearance	12'10"
Water	150 Gals.
Fuel	750/840 Gals.
Cockpit	NA
Hull Type	Modified-V
Designer	Davis

Production
1986–Current

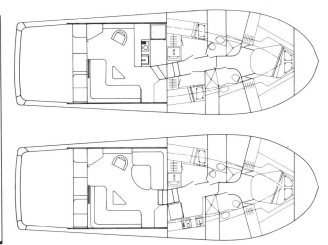

HYLAS 47 CONVERTIBLE

Built in Taiwan by Queen Long Marine, the Hylas 47 is a rakish convertible design with an aggressive, Eurostyle profile and an notably wide beam. The hull was drawn by Jim Wynn and features balsa-cored hull-sides, prop pockets aft, and plenty of freeboard all around. The interior layout is incredibly expansive thanks to the super-wide beam, and the Hylas is the only boat in this size range to feature walkaround queen berths in *both* staterooms. (A three-stateroom layout with the galley up is optional.) The front windows are real, not glassed-over. Both head compartments have separate stall showers. The deep cockpit is large enough for a fighting chair, but the gunnels are abnormally high and not well-suited to fishing. Note the cockpit engine room access door. On balance, the main features of the Hylas are centered around her spacious acco-modations and glitzy appearance, and while she looks like a competent fisher-man, she's really more suited to family cruising. Twin 450-hp 6-71 diesels will cruise at 22-23 knots (26 top), and optional 550-hp 6V92s cruise about 24 knots and reach 27 knots top. ❏

SPECIFICATIONS

Length	46'6"
Length WL	40'5"
Beam	16'9"
Draft	3'10"
Weight	38,000#
Clearance	13'4"
Water	160 Gals.
Fuel	600 Gals.
Cockpit	NA
Hull Type	Modified-V
Designer	Jim Wynne

Production
1987–Current

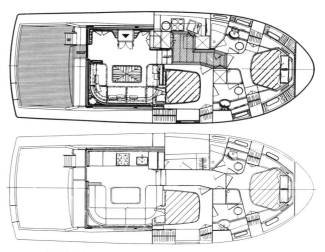

CAMARGUE 48 YACHTFISHER

The Camargue 48 YF stands out among Asian imports for her modern profile, excellent glasswork, and above average fit and finish. Introduced in 1987, she's basically a Camargue 42 Sundeck with a cockpit extension. Both boats are still in production and just under fifty of the 48s have been built to date. The hull is a modified-V affair with moderate beam and relatively flat aftersections. Hullsides are Airex-cored above the waterline. Although she has a very practical two-stateroom floorplan, the 48 YF skimps a little in guest stateroom dimensions in exchange for a longer, more open and comfortable salon. The portside lower helm is cleverly concealed within an exquisite roll-top console — very nice. The teak interior woodwork is very impressive. The extra-wide sidedecks are worth noting, as is the well-organized engine room and comfortable bridge. A handsome yacht with a low profile and clean lines, standard 375-hp Caterpillar diesels will cruise the Camargue 48 YF around 18–19 knots, and the optional 485-hp 6-71s will provide a brisk 22–23 knots at cruise and 27 knots wide open. ❑

SPECIFICATIONS

Length	48'0"
Length WL	NA
Beam	15'5"
Draft	3'3"
Weight	38,000#
Clearance	NA
Water	210 Gals.
Fuel	600 Gals.
Hull Type	Modified-V
Designer	Camargue

Production
1987–Current

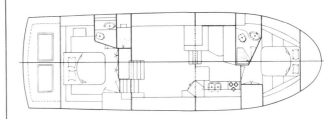

CHB 48 MOTOR YACHT

Marketed under the names of Seamaster, Ponderosa, and Embassy (among others), the CHB 48 has been a popular Taiwan import for a number of years. Built by Chung Hwa, she bears a striking (and probably not accidental) similarity to the original Hatteras 48 MY (1981-84). Her solid fiberglass hull is a modified-V design with moderate beam and a shallow keel. The three-stateroom, three-head floorplan (with only a single stall shower) is virtually identical to the Hatteras 48, and teak cabinetry and woodwork are liberally applied thoughout. A lower helm was optional, and there's a work bench in the stand-up engine room. The CHB 48 features a truly spacious afterdeck with wet bar and wing doors, and there's seating for eight on the large bridge. The sidedecks on this boat are very wide. At 39,000 lbs., the CHB is slightly lighter than the Hatteras she imitates, and nearly all were brought in with 375-hp Cat diesels. The cruising speed is a conservative 13–14 knots, and the top speed is about 17–18 knots. Like Hatteras, Chung Hwa also offered the 48 in a two-stateroom cockpit model. ❑

SPECIFICATIONS

Length	47'8"
Length WL	43'6"
Beam	15'4"
Draft	3'10"
Weight	39,000#
Clearance	16'10"
Water	200 Gals.
Fuel	520 Gals.
Hull Type	Modified-V
Designer	NA

Production
1983–Current

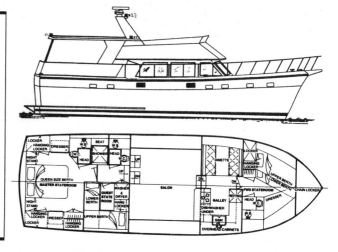

MIKELSON 48 SEDAN SF

The Mikelson 48 is a completely radical sedan sportfisherman whose innovations go quite beyond her unusual exterior profile. Designed by Tom Fexas and built by Bluewater in Taiwan, the 48 is constructed on a beamy, fully cored hull with rounded bilges and a reverse transom. The result is a surprisingly fast boat (23-knot cruise) with just 425-hp Cat diesels and V-drives. (The V-drives are used to get the engines aft where they're accessed from the cockpit — a very unusual application in a boat this size.) The Mikelson comes with a spacious two-stateroom, galley-down teak interior with two built-in settees in the salon, and stall showers in both heads. A three-stateroom floorplan is also available. The cockpit isn't deep, but it's still big and there's a swim platform recessed into the reverse transom. (The Mikelson 50 SF — basically the same boat — eliminates this reverse transom and adds size to the cockpit.) The flybridge is huge with two helm stations and a circular dinette aft of the helm. A good-selling yacht with excellent range, the Mikelson 48 is an extremely innovative sedan with a very pleasing profile. ❏

SPECIFICATIONS

Length .... 48'6"
Beam .... 16'8"
Draft .... 3'6"
Weight .... 35,000#
Clearance .... NA
Water .... 300 Gals.
Fuel .... 1,000 Gals.
Cockpit .... NA
Hull Type .... Modified-V
Designer .... Tom Fexas

Production
1990–Current

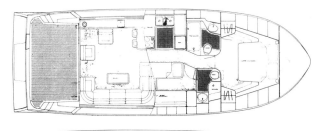

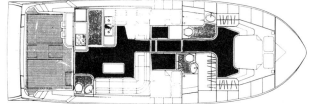

NORDIC 480 MOTOR YACHT

The Nordic 480 is a handsome pilot-house design built in Bellingham, Washington on a semi-custom basis. Nordic Yachts wasn't a high-volume builder, but the yard (no longer in business) was known for good-quality construction standards. The 480 rides on a relatively wide modified-V hull with balsa coring from the waterline up and a long keel for increased directional stability. While the interior floorplans were often modified to suit the requirements of the buyer, most 480s are two-stateroom arrangements with a queen berth in the master. The salon's width is somewhat limited by the wide walka-round sidedecks, but the dimensions are more than adequate. The grain-matched teak cabinetry and joinerwork are superb. The pilothouse features a sliding deck door and provides direct access to the bridge via a beautiful teak stairway abaft the helm. The larger Nordic 520 has the same interior layout as the 480, but with a larger cockpit. Most Nordic 480s were equipped with optional 375-hp Caterpillar diesels which provide a cruising speed of 17–18 knots and a top speed of around 21 knots. ❏

SPECIFICATIONS

Length	48'0"
Beam	15'8"
Draft	3'11"
Weight	39,500#
Clearance	13'1"
Water	200 Gals.
Fuel	600 Gals.
Cockpit	NA
Hull Type	Modified-V
Designer	A. Nordtvedt

Production
1985–91

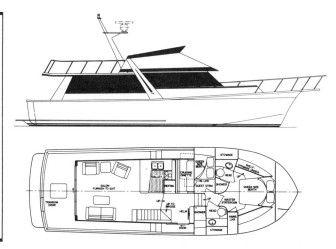

PACE 48 SPORTFISHERMAN

Purists will recognize the familiar lines of the Pace 48 SF as those of the old Egg Harbor 48 — the original "Golden Egg." Indeed, this is the same boat right down to the foredeck storage box and the teak cockpit, but with a new wraparound black mask and solid front windshield panels. Now built in Taiwan, the original Egg Harbor molds were reworked for the new production run. Construction is identical to the earlier specifications with a solid fiberglass hull and balsa coring in the decks and superstructure. This is a narrow hull design with a fine entry and a flat 2° of deadrise at the transom. Where the original Eggs had plenty of exterior teak, so too does the Pace. Teak is used inside as well — lots of it — and those who enjoy the ambience of a traditional interior will will like the feel of the Pace 48's salon. The two-stateroom, two-head layout is similar to the later-model Eggs with a dinette added opposite the step-down galley. Power is 735-hp 8V92 diesels, which fit nicely in the large engine room. A good-running boat, her cruising speed is 26–27 knots and the Pace 48 has a top speed of around 29 knots. ❏

SPECIFICATIONS

Length	48'2"
Beam	15'0"
Draft	4'4"
Weight	40,000#
Clearance	NA
Water	200 Gals.
Fuel	720 Gals.
Cockpit	NA
Hull Type	Modified-V
Designer	D. Martin

Production
1987–Current

RONIN 48 CONVERTIBLE

To date, Ronin is one of the *very* few Taiwan sportfishermen to have at least cracked the long-standing resistance to Asian imports among hardcore anglers. Like the smaller Ronin 38, the 48 Convertible is by Ta Chiao, a well-established builder of both power- and sailboats. She's constructed on a conventional modified-V hull with generous flare at the bow and 15° of deadrise at the transom. The hullsides are cored with end-grain balsa, and the boat is assembled with only three separate molds, which adds strength and rigidity while reducing seals and leaks.

In appearance, the Ronin 48 Convertible has a strong resemblance to Brand H (as in Hatteras). The styling is very contemporary and completely in line with popular sportfish trends. Inside, the 48 offers a choice of two or three staterooms with the galley up or down. The teak (or light oak) interior woodwork is very attractive, and the large engine room is arranged with good access to the motors. With optional 735-hp 8V92s, the Ronin 48 will cruise around 27 knots and reach 30+ knots wide open. Twin 840-hp MAN diesels became optional in 1990. ❏

SPECIFICATIONS

Length	48'8"
Beam	15'10"
Draft	4'0"
Weight	46,000#
Clearance	14'3"
Water	200 Gals.
Fuel	850 Gals.
Cockpit	NA
Hull Type	Modified-V
Designer	Unknown

Production
1987–Current

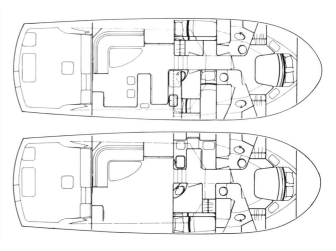

TUNG HWA 48 MOTOR YACHT

Marketed in the U.S. as the Offshore or Hartmann-Palmer 48, the Tung Hwa 48 is an attractive and practical sedan model with several features of interest to experienced cruisers. While she's not designed with the mega-volume interior found in many other yachts of her size, the Tung Hwa does places a priority on outdoor recreation as her generous deck areas suggest. Not only are the walkaround sidedecks wide and the cockpit spacious, but the flybridge dimensions are huge for a boat of this size. Constructed on a modified-V hull with balsa coring from the waterline up, the interior is arranged with the salon and galley on the same level. A stairway abaft the lower helm leads up to the bridge, and two double staterooms and two heads are forward. Varnished teak woodwork and cabinetry are used throughout, and 360° windows make the salon seem a bit more expansive than it really is. Bridge overhangs provide weather protection for the cockpit and walkways. Among several diesel options, the popular 375-hp Cats will cruise the Tung Hwa 48 MY at 16–17 knots and reach a top speed of about 20 knots top.   ❏

SPECIFICATIONS

Length	48'6"
Length WL	43'0"
Beam	15'6"
Draft	3'6"
Weight	38,000#
Clearance	15'2"
Water	325 Gals.
Fuel	600 Gals.
Hull Type	Modified-V
Designer	Wm. Crealock

Production
1987–Current

NOTABLE DESIGNS

TUNG HWA 48 YACHTFISHER

The Tung Hwa 48 Yachtfish (built in Taiwan and previously marketed in the U.S. as the Offshore or Hartmann-Palmer 48 YF) features a conventional double-cabin interior with a raised aft deck, together with the versatility and convenience of a small cockpit. (Since the cockpit dimensions are too small for any serious fishing, the "Yachtfish" designation is somewhat misleading.) Like the Tung Hwa 48 MY, the hull of the 48 Yachtfish is cored from the waterline up and her generous bow flare and sharp entry insure a dry and comfortable ride. Inside, the 48's prac-

tical two-stateroom floorplan is available with or without a dinette. Features include a full teak interior, lower helm position, sliding deck access doors port and starboard, and a tub/shower in the aft head. A door in the aft stateroom bulkhead leads directly into the cockpit — a very convenient feature. The walkaround sidedecks are quite wide and protected with raised bulwarks. A good-looking boat with a easy ride, the Tung Hwa 48 YF will cruise at 16–17 knots with 375-hp Cat diesels and reach a top speed of around 20 knots. ❏

SPECIFICATIONS

Length	48'3"
Length WL	43'0"
Beam	15'6"
Draft	3'6"
Weight	38,000#
Clearance	15'2"
Water	325 Gals.
Fuel	600 Gals.
Hull Type	Modified-V
Designer	Wm. Crealock

Production
1985–Current

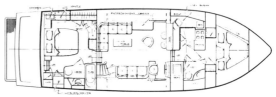

VISTA 48/50 SPORTFISHERMAN

The Vista 48 and 50 SF are basically the same boat with the 50 having a slightly larger salon. Built on a fully cored and beamy modified-V hull, the Vista weighs in at only 36,000 lbs. — light for a 48-footer and typical of most Fexas-designed boats. Note the raked flybridge and distinctive foredeck "arms" extending from both sides of the deckhouse. The accommodations of the Vista 48 are spacious and very open. The standard two-stateroom layout includes two heads with stall showers, and the alternate three-stateroom floorplan moves the galley up into the salon.

Teak paneling and trim are used throughout the interior, and light oak woodwork is available. A sliding door opens into the huge and unobstructed fishing cockpit which is down two steps from the salon level. A molded tackle center is standard along with cockpit controls, transom door, fishbox, etc, and there's direct cockpit access to the Vista's enormous engine room. Engine options include 375-hp Cats, 550-hp 6V92s, and 735-hp 8V92s. The popular 6V92s will cruise the Vista 48/50 at an honest 24 knots and deliver a top speed of around 28 knots. ❏

SPECIFICATIONS

Length	48'0"
Beam	16'0"
Draft	3'1"
Weight	36,000#
Clearance	13'10"
Water	180 Gals.
Fuel	700 Gals.
Cockpit	NA
Hull Type	Modified-V
Designer	Tom Fexas

Production
1986–Current

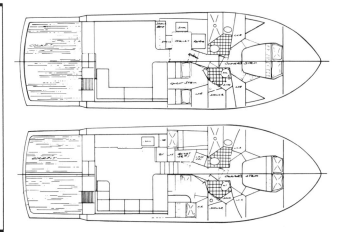

HYUNDAI 49 MOTOR YACHT

The introduction of the Hyundai 49 MY (marketed in the U.S. as the Elegant 49 or the Sonata 5300) in early 1988 was greeted by skepticism within the yachting community. The first yacht ever produced by Hyundai in Korea, the price was low but the quality and attention to detail failed to meet expectations. (The detailing has improved considerably since the early deliveries.) To most observers, the styling of the Elegant 49 is different (to say the least), and the boat has a distinctively awkward appearance at dockside. She's built on a fully-cored hull with 14° of transom deadrise. Inside, the two-stateroom, galley-down interior features a dinette, spacious salon, traditional teak paneling and attractive off-white laminates — a modern and appealing decor for an Asian boat. The forward stateroom is small but the salon is big. Features include a lower helm (with deck door), wide sidedecks, and a Jacuzzi in the aft head. Note the absence of a stall shower in the forward head. Speeds with optional 375-hp Cats (300-hp GM 8.2s are standard) are 15 knots at cruise and about 19–20 knots top. ❑

SPECIFICATIONS

Length	48'6"
Length WL	NA
Beam	15'8"
Draft	3'6"
Weight	40,000#
Clearance	NA
Water	300 Gals.
Fuel	700 Gals.
Hull Type	Modified-V
Designer	S. Turner

Production
1988–Current

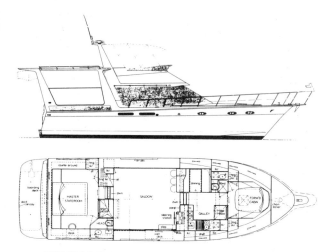

NOTABLE DESIGNS

FEXAS 50 MY/56 YF

Originally imported as the Ultimate 50, a cockpit was added the following year and Mikelson Yachts distributed her as the Fexas 56 Yachtfisher. (She's currently marketed as the Mikelson 56 YF.) Built in Taiwan on a beamy, fully cored hull with a shallow keel, and flat aftersections, an innovative floorplan is the most notable feature of the Fexas 56. While this layout can be semi-customized to meet an owner's taste, the galley companionway is offset completely to starboard (rather than near the centerline) giving the salon a wide open and incredibly spa-cious appearance. The interior is finished with teak woodwork and Formica, and the decor is decidedly modern and upscale. Additional features include a roomy and well-detailed engine room, cockpit transom door, salon entertainment center, radar mast, and a modern flybridge helm arrangement with generous guest seating. Several engine options have been offered. Now-standard 550-hp 6V92s cruise around 22 knots (25 knots top), and the popular 735-hp 8V92s will deliver a fast 25 knots at cruise and reach a top speed of 28–29 knots. ❏

SPECIFICATIONS

Length	56'2"
Length WL	48'4"
Beam	17'0"
Draft	3'6"
Weight	49,000#
Clearance	NA
Water	200 Gals.
Fuel	700 Gals.
Hull Type	Modified-V
Designer	Tom Fexas

Production
1986–Current

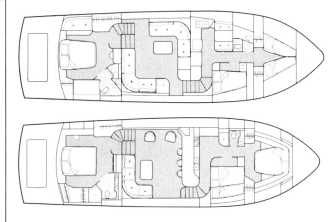

HIGH-TECH 50/55 EURO MY

For those looking for something different from the traditional Asian import, the Hi-Tech 50 and 55 (pictured above) project the kind of streamlined European styling and impressive performance increasingly popular with U.S. buyers. Built in Taiwan by Johnson Yachts, the High-Tech 50 has a conventional transom, while the newer 55 (introduced in 1990) has a stylish reverse transom and integral swim platform. The hull is a deep modified-V design with a wide beam and balsa coring in the hullsides. Inside, the three-stateroom, three-head floorplan of the High-Tech 50/55 is a modern blend of light-colored woodwork and cabinetry (oak, ash, or cherry), rounded corners, and decorator fabrics. The standard layout has a queen berth in the forward stateroom, stall showers in each head, and a classy lower helm station. (An alternate arrangement has twin staterooms forward.) A canted stainless-and-glass sliding door opens to the aft deck with its teak sole, extended bridge overhang, and molded bridge steps. Standard 735-hp 8-92s will cruise either model at a fast 24–25 knots and reach a top speed of around 28 knots. ❑

SPECIFICATIONS

Length	50'0"/55'0"
Length WL	NA
Beam	16'0"
Draft	4'0"
Weight	40,000#
Clearance	NA
Water	200 Gals.
Fuel	550 Gals.
Hull Type	Modified-V
Designer	Bill Dixon

Production
1988–Current

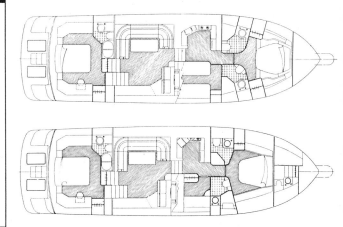

NORDIC 500 MOTOR YACHT

Traditional pilothouse cruising yachts have long been popular in Pacific Northwest waters, where adverse weather conditions often stress the importance of a secure inside helm position. A handsome boat, the Nordic 500 Motor Yacht is a true raised pilothouse design with goo all-around cruising capabilities. Because these boats were built on a semi-custom basis, each Nordic 500 is to some extent a personalized yacht reflecting the tastes and priorities of her owner. The standard interior layout called for three staterooms and two heads forward (both with stall showers) with the pilothouse raised five steps up from the salon level. Inside and out, the level of finish in the Nordic 500 is well above average. A practical and versatile yacht, a few of the more notable features found aboard the 500 include wide, protected sidedecks, a very large cockpit with a transom door, flybridge storage for a Whaler, and an efficient and notably seaworthy hull. With the optional 450-hp 6-71 diesels, the cruising speed of the Nordic 500 MY is a respectable 20 knots and the top speed is 23–24 knots. ❏

SPECIFICATIONS

Length	50'0"
Beam	15'8"
Draft	3'11"
Weight	39,500#
Clearance	13'1"
Water	200 Gals.
Fuel	600 Gals.
Cockpit	NA
Hull Type	Modified-V
Designer	A. Nordtvedt

Production
1988–90

NOTABLE DESIGNS

KHA SHING 52 MOTOR YACHT

A distinctive boat with her low-slung profile and rakish appearance, the Kha Shing 52 enjoyed popularity on both the East Coast, where she was marketed as the Southern Star (or Vista), and the West Coast, where she's best-known as the Spindrift 52. Her narrow-beam hull is solid fiberglass with considerable flare at the bow and a shallow keel below. Kha Shing offered a variety of interior layouts for the 52 over the years, however the three-stateroom floorplan pictured below was probably the most popular. The fore and aft staterooms are both quite spacious and fitted with double berths, while the guest cabin can easily serve as an office or study. A lower helm and deck access door were standard and the salon dimensions are generous in spite of the narrow beam. The aft deck is huge — among the largest to be found on any boat this size. Additional features include wide sidedecks, full teak interior, and three heads (but only one stall shower). Several engines were offered in the Kha Shing 52 including Volvo and Cat diesels. The 375-hp Cats cruise around 15–16 knots and reach about 18 knots top. ❏

SPECIFICATIONS

Length	52'2"
Length WL	47'6"
Beam	15'0"
Draft	3'10"
Weight	60,000#
Clearance	NA
Water	300 Gals.
Fuel	600 Gals.
Hull Type	Modified-V
Designer	Kha Shing

Production
1984–90

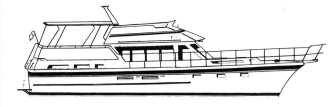

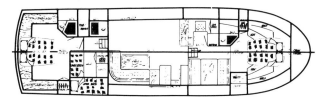

MIDNIGHT LACE 52 EXPRESS CRUISER

Based upon the successful Midnight Lace 44, the Midnight Lace 52 has the same low-profile, commuter-style lines but with a wider beam and a more modern interior arrangement. Hull and superstructure are of Airex-cored fiberglass, and the factory weight of only 19,850 lbs. is extraordinary in a 52' yacht. The easily driven hull (the beam is only 13') features a heavily flared and raked bow, reverse transom, rounded bilges, and 8° of transom deadrise. Although the interior dimensions are not large, the accommodations are comfortable and finished with tradi-tional teak woodwork and cabinetry. The floorplan has the owner's state-room forward at the end of the S-shaped passageway with a small guest cabin to starboard. The engines (with V-drives) are located well aft, below the cockpit. The helm position is eleva-ted, and the classy foredeck cockpit of the original Lace 44 remains in the 52. The flybridge was a popular option, and all but two (of the 16 built) were so equipped. Twin 260-hp 8.2 diesels cruise the Lace 52 very efficiently at 21 knots (22 gph) and reach a top speed of 24 knots. ❑

SPECIFICATIONS

Length	52'6"
Length WL	47'6"
Beam	13'0"
Draft	3'0"
Weight	19,850#
Clearance	20'0"
Water	230 Gals.
Fuel	480 Gals.
Hull Type	Modified-V
Designer	Tom Fexas

Production
1982–89

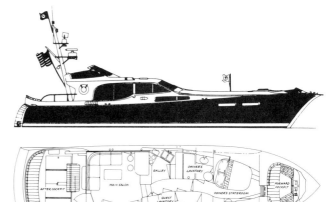

OFFSHORE 52 SEDAN MY

Sedan-style yachts may lack the mega-volume interior dimensions of their motor yacht counterparts, but they're nearly always better-looking boats. The low-profile deckhouse and modern styling of the Offshore 52 give her a distinctive and altogether pleasing appearance and most will agree that she is indeed a handsome yacht. Built by Camargue in Taiwan, her modified-V hull (12° of deadrise aft) incorporates a wide beam with a cutaway keel and generous flare at the bow. Inside, her three-stateroom floorplan is arranged with the galley open to the salon and stall showers in both heads. Access to the spacious bridge is via a staircase in the salon and a lower helm (with P&S deck doors) is standard. The interior is finished with plenty of traditional teak woodwork and cabinetry with teak and holly flooring throughout. Additional features include a good-size cockpit with transom door and storage bins, very wide sidedecks with bulwarks, large wraparound salon windows, and a spacious flybridge with room for a dinghy. Standard 485-hp 6-71s will cruise at 17 knots and reach about 20 knots top. ❑

SPECIFICATIONS

Length ....52'0"
Beam......................16'10"
Draft ....4'4"
Weight ....52,000#
Clearance ....NA
Water.................400 Gals.
Fuel ....750 Gals.
Cockpit.........................NA
Hull Type.........Modified-V
Designer ....Crealock

Production
1991–Current

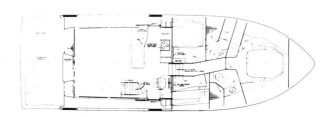

PT 52 COCKPIT MOTOR YACHT

The PT 52 was a straightforward Taiwan import with a moderate price tag, average quality, and expansive interior accommodations. Built by Cheer Men in Taiwan on a solid fiberglass hull with moderate beam, the PT 52 Cockpit MY is actually a PT 46 Sundeck with a cockpit extension. She presents a modern profile and features a lot of outside deck space and a practical interior layout. Two floorplans were offered: the standard two-stateroom layout has a full dinette opposite the down galley, and the three-stateroom version eliminates the dinette in favor of a large guest cabin with a double berth. Stall showers are fitted in both heads, and an access door in the master stateroom opens directly into the cockpit — a useful feature in any cockpit MY. The main salon is especially open and expansive with wraparound cabin windows and teak paneling. Outside, the covered aft deck and flybridge are equally spacious with plenty of entertaining space. With a pair of relatively small 270-hp Cummins VT-555 diesels (one of several engine options), she'll cruise at a respectable 17–18 knots and reach a top speed of around 22 knots. ❏

SPECIFICATIONS

Length	52'4"
Length WL	46'4"
Beam	15'9"
Draft	3'0"
Weight	32,500#
Clearance	NA
Water	200 Gals.
Fuel	600 Gals.
Cockpit	NA
Hull Type	Modified-V
Designer	John Norek

Production
1986–90

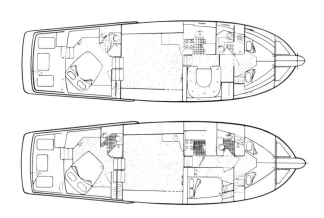

SOUTHERN CROSS 52 SF

Southern Cross *was* the Australian builder who ran those full-page ads a few years ago promising to introduce a sportfisherman destined to "blow Bertram and Hatteras out of the bloody water." They were talking about the Southern Cross 52, a sleek Fexas design with plenty of high tech construction and not a lot of weight. She never really caught on with serious anglers (her eagerly awaited introduction at the '85 Lauderdale boat show was a bust) and only seven were sold in the U.S. before Southern Cross closed down in 1991. In some ways the 52 was ahead of her time — lightweight, fully-cored construction and ash interiors have since become more popular within the sportfishing community. Several floorplans were offered (early models had the galley aft in the salon) with the three-stateroom, galley-up layout being preferred. Narrow in the beam and with a very low cockpit, the 52 SF never attained the promised 37-knot performance. Instead she turned a still-fast 34 knots wide open with just 740-hp 8V92s (which isn't bad — a late model Hatteras 52 barely manages 27 knots top with the same motors).   ❑

SPECIFICATIONS

Length	52'0"
Beam	15'6"
Draft	3'6"
Weight	38,000#
Clearance	NA
Water	150 Gals.
Fuel	1,000 Gals.
Cockpit	144 Sq. Ft.
Hull Type	Modified-V
Designer	Tom Fexas

Production
1986-1990

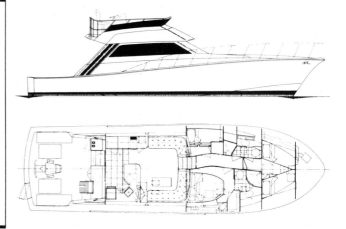

DYNA 53 COCKPIT MY

Equally well known in marine circles as the Vantare 53, the Dyna 53 Cockpit MY is a modern, low-profile yacht with a streamlined appearance, moderate beam, and an unusually large cockpit. The hullsides are cored from the chines up, and there's a shallow keel below for stability. Designed as a two-stateroom yacht, a lower helm is optional and the galley and dinette are down in the conventional manner. Note that both heads have shower stalls — definitely a plus — and both staterooms have walkaround double berths. Like most Taiwan imports, the salon furnish-ing are "built-ins" — *not* a plus but that's the way they come. The interiors in early models were teak, but most now have the more contemporary light oak woodwork. The Dyna is a well-finished yacht and much of the detailing is excellent. Additional features include wing doors, dinghy storage on the hardtop, side exhausts, and wide side-decks around the house. The engine room is a tight fit. The most popular engine option (among many) for the Dyna 53 CMY is the 485-hp GM 6-71s which will cruise at 18–19 knots and turn 22 knots wide open.   ❏

SPECIFICATIONS

Length .... 52'6"
Beam .... 15'6"
Draft .... 3'6"
Weight .... 38,000#
Clearance .... 15'6"
Water .... 250 Gals.
Fuel .... 650/750 Gals.
Cockpit .... 78 Sq. Ft.
Hull Type .... Modified-V
Designer .... Terry Yen

Production
1990–Current

FLEMING 53/55 MOTOR YACHT

The Fleming 50, 53 (pictured above), and 55 MYs differ only in the size of their cockpits. A handsome trawler-style design, the Fleming is a modern-day version of the old Alaskan 49 Pilothouse (one of a series of wood trawlers built by Grand Banks in the 1960s). The beam is wider for added stability and interior volume, and the enlarged flybridge has more lounge seating, but otherwise the lines are nearly identical. Flemings are built by Tung Hwa in Taiwan on an all-new, easily driven semi-displacement hull with simulated lapstrake hullsides and a deep, prop-protecting keel. Inside, the look is total teak and the joinery is flawless. The standard two-stateroom floorplan has the galley in the salon and a large dinette on the pilothouse level opposite the superb lower helm. The master stateroom is huge and both heads are fitted with stall showers. (A three-stateroom floorplan is optional.) The engine room is tight but lazerette storage is excellent. A very impressive boat, Cat 210-hp diesels produce a cruising speed of 10 knots (about 12 knots top), and the 425-hp Cats cruise at 14 knots and reach 17–18 knots top. ❏

SPECIFICATIONS

Length	50'9"
Length WL	45'10"
Beam	16'0"
Draft	5'0"
Weight	60,000#
Clearance	NA
Water	300 Gals.
Fuel	1,000 Gals.
Hull Type	Semi-Disp.
Designer	L. Drake

Production
1987–Current

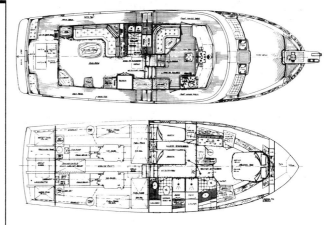

SOUTHERN CROSS 53 COCKPIT MY

The Australian-built Southern Cross 53 is a traditional flush-deck motor-yacht with a practical cruising layout and comfortable accommodations. Cockpits add great versatility to any motor yacht, and the spacious open-air aft deck and wide walkaround side-decks of the Southern Cross only add to her appeal. The double-deck layout is arranged with the galley completely open to the salon and there are P&S deck access doors in the wheelhouse. Most interiors were finished out on a semi-custom basis (nine were sold in the U.S.). The comfortable aft deck with its protective bridge overhang is a superb outdoor entertaining area. Note that the engine room is aft in the Southern Cross 53 and all three state-rooms on the lower level have private heads with stall showers. Additional features include teak decks, exceptional lower helm visability, underwater exhausts, and an attractive silver ash interior. With just 435-hp 6V71 diesels (certainly not among GMs most popular engines), the cruising speed is 15–16 knots and the top speed is around 19 knots. Optional 540-hp 6V92s will cruise at 18–19 knots. ❑

SPECIFICATIONS

Length	53'0"
Length WL	NA
Beam	16'0"
Draft	3'10"
Weight	50,000#
Clearance	19'5"
Water	400 Gals.
Fuel	800 Gals.
Hull Type	Modified-V
Designer	Tom Fexas

Production
1987–90

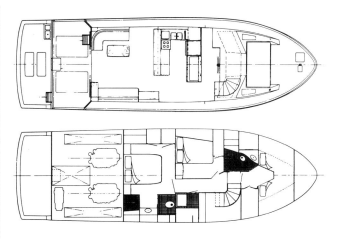

KHA SHING 55 MONTE FINO

The Kha Shing 55 Monte Fino was one of the first of the truly Eurostyle Taiwan imports when she was introduced in 1986. (Close to forty have been sold to date.) Italian in profile, she's constructed on a modified-V hull with a shallow keel and cored hullsides. The interior layout of the Monte Fino is somewhat unusual in that the galley is *up* in the pilothouse rather than *down* in the salon as it generally is in a raised pilothouse yacht. Too, the roomy salon is "sunken" a step below the aft deck level which adds to the impression of spaciousness. There's also an unusual small crew berth aft of the engine room. The contemporary interior is lavishly styled in modern off-white laminates, Corian countertops, and Ultrasuede wall coverings. The 55 Monte Fino has full walkaround sidedecks (a widebody model is available), a large flybridge with a long overhang, and a comfortable aft deck. (Unless you want to store the dinghy on the foredeck, you'll need a pair of transom davits.) A decent performer with the optional 760-hp 8V92s, she'll cruise around 18–19 knots and deliver a top speed of 22 knots. ❑

SPECIFICATIONS

Length	54'6"
Length WL	NA
Beam	16'10"
Draft	4'9"
Weight	53,750#
Clearance	23'3"
Water	300 Gals.
Fuel	800 Gals.
Hull Type	Modified-V
Designer	J. Antrim

Production
1986–Current

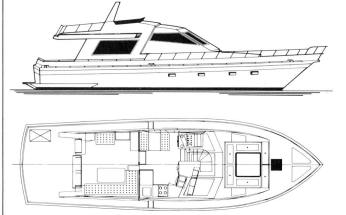

OFFSHORE 55 PILOTHOUSE

Pilothouse yachts have a strong following in the Northwest, where the advantages of a raised indoor helm can be appreciated year-round. Built by one of the better Taiwan yards (Camargue) on a modified-V hull with 12° deadrise aft and cored hullsides, the Offshore 55 is a particularly good-looking yacht with plenty of beam and interior volume. Her three-stateroom layout is arranged with the galley in the salon and the master stateroom beneath the pilothouse. (Note the private salon staircase to the master stateroom.) Both heads have shower stalls and the forward VIP stateroom has a centerline island berth. The pilothouse features sliding deck doors, dinette, pass-thru to the galley, and a circular staircase to the bridge, and the interior is finished with traditional teak paneling and cabinetry. Having the cockpit on the salon level makes the entire area into a vast entertainment platform at water's edge. The engine room is large for a sedan-style boat and the bridge has plenty of guest seating plus a wet bar and space for a dinghy. Standard 485-hp 6-71s cruise at 16–17 knots and optional 550-hp 6V92s cruise around 18 knots. ❑

SPECIFICATIONS

Length	55'0"
Beam	16'10"
Draft	4'4"
Weight	52,000#
Clearance	NA
Water	400 Gals.
Fuel	700 Gals.
Cockpit	NA
Hull Type	Modified-V
Designer	Crealock

Production
1990–Current

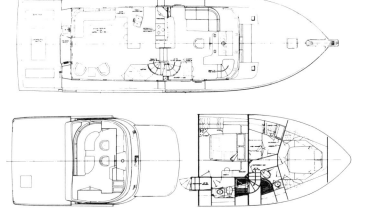

NOTABLE DESIGNS

HARTMANN-PALMER 56 MY

Built by Lien Hwa in Taiwan, the Hartmann-Palmer 56 MY bears a strong resemblance (in profile, at least) to the Hatteras 53 MY. Her popularity during the mid-1980s had much to do with an affordable price and a spacious teak-paneled interior. She was constructed with cored hullsides and features a wide beam and underwater exhausts. The traditional double-deck layout places the galley and dinette down from the salon level. The generous 12' x 14' salon dimensions are more than adequate and the afterdeck is even larger. A curved staircase aft in the salon leads down to a spacious master stateroom with a tub/shower. A walk-in engine room separates the master from the guest cabins forward. Outside of the engine room, just about everything you see inside the Hartmann-Palmer 56 is either made out of teak, covered by it, or trimmed with it. No lightweight, the standard 450-hp GM 6-71s deliver an anemic 13–14 knot cruising speed when fully loaded and 17 knots flat out. The optional 600-hp 8V92TIs provide 16–17 knots cruise and 19 knots top. Note the generous fuel capacity. ❑

SPECIFICATIONS

Length	56'1"
Length WL	51'0"
Beam	17'1"
Draft	4'2"
Weight	57,350#
Clearance	21'1"
Water	600 Gals.
Fuel	1,400 Gals.
Hull Type	Modified-V
Designer	Seaton/Neville

Production
1984–87

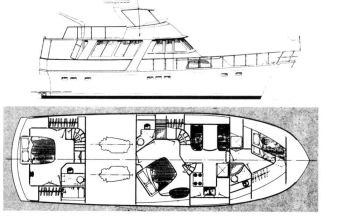

STEVENS 59/67 COCKPIT MY

The Stevens 59 MY (pictured above) and 67 CMY incorporate more innovative design concepts than most other motor yachts their size. Granted, the profile of the 59 is less than graceful, but the unique raised pilothouse layout, expansive full-width deckhouse, and four-stateroom floorplan provide the comforts one might expect on a larger boat. Built by Grand Harbour Yachts in Taiwan, the Stevens rides on a modified-V hull with a deep keel and 10° transom deadrise. The 59 uses V-drives to apply the power — unusual in a boat this size — while the 67 has a conventional straight-dive installation. Note that the 59 MY and 67 CMY have completely different floorplans. In the 59, crew quarters are forward (with foredeck access), while the 67 has a more conventional layout with the forward stateroom accessed from the lower level. The central pilothouse configuration allows for the addition of a formal dining area forward on the deckhouse level, and the big 100 sq. ft. cockpit of the 67 smooths out the 59's uneven profile. The Stevens 59 will cruise at a respectable 19 knots with optional 735-hp 8V92 diesels. ❏

SPECIFICATIONS

Length	58'10"/66'10"
Length WL	NA
Beam	17'10"
Draft	4'9"
Weight	70/75,000#
Clearance	17'1"
Water	300 Gals.
Fuel	1,000/1,200 Gals.
Hull Type	Modified-V
Designer	S&S

Production
1989–Current

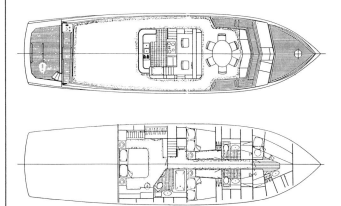

INTERCONTINENTAL 60 MY

Built in Taiwan, the Intercontinental 60 is available with a variety of accommodation plans including aft or mid engine rooms, full-beam or walkaround deckhouse, and three or four staterooms on the lower level. She's constructed on a semi-displacement hull with Knytex glass and Divinycell coring, and an Awlgrip paint job is applied to the exterior. With an 18' beam, the Intercontinental is a roomy boat inside. The standard three-stateroom floorplan has the galley on the deckhouse level, separated from the salon by a pass-thru serving counter. A convenient day head is opposite the galley, and a salon stairwell provides access to the spacious master stateroom. The interior is finished with light-grain teak throughout. Additional features include a large aft deck with built-in lounge seating, roomy VIP guest cabin, sliding deck access doors in the wheelhouse (the wraparound lower helm setup is unique), and an extended flybridge with plenty of guest seating. Standard 550-hp 6V92s will cruise around 13 knots, and optional 735-hp 8V92s will cruise at 18 knots. ❏

SPECIFICATIONS

Length	60'0"
Length WL	52'1"
Beam	18'0"
Draft	5'0"
Weight	66,000#
Clearance	NA
Water	400 Gals.
Fuel	1,200 Gals.
Hull Type	Semi-Disp.
Designer	Sharp

Production
1990–Current

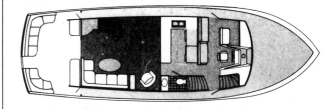

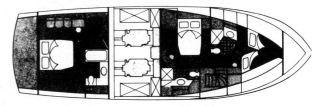

TANGO 60 MOTOR YACHT

The Tango 60 is one of just a few Argentine boats imported into the U.S. market. Built on a solid fiberglass hull and styled along the lines of a European yacht, the Tango is offered in the standard open aft deck version (pictured above) with walkaround sidedecks, or a widebody configuration with no aft deck and a huge salon. Both models have the same flybridge and lower-level layouts. Inside, the light oak interior is arranged with the galley and dinette up. The U-shaped galley is efficient (if somewhat small), and there's a convenient stairway (instead of a ladder) in the salon leading up to the bridge. A staircase aft in the salon provides access to a *huge* master stateroom with it's own Jacuzzi. A full-width engine room separates the master stateroom from three forward staterooms, each with a private head. The Tango's flybridge — set well aft over the house — is large enough for entertaining but there's no space for dinghy storage. Additional features include a workbench in the engine room and deck access doors in the wheelhouse. Standard 735-hp 8V92s will cruise at 18 knots with a top speed of about 21 knots. ❏

SPECIFICATIONS

Length	60'0"
Length WL	NA
Beam	17'6"
Draft	4'0"
Weight	78,400#
Clearance	16'8"
Water	400 Gals.
Fuel	1,075 Gals.
Hull Type	Modified-V
Designer	Napier

Production
1989–Current

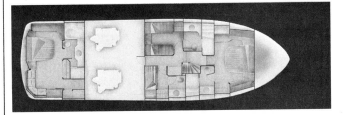

TEMPEST 60 SPORT YACHT

Built by Tempest Yachts in Miami, the 60 Sport Yacht is a limited production high-performance sportboat with a thoroughly European profile. Fully half of the boat's LOA is given over to a *huge* bi-level cockpit which includes a collapsible sun lounge, fore and aft bench seating, and wet bar. Her space-age helm console — with retractable electronics pod, single-lever controls, and a tilt wheel — is most impressive. The high-style interior of the Tempest is a striking — blend of mirrored walls, lacquered cabinetry, indirect lighting and suede wall coverings. While the interior dimensions are modest for a 60-footer, the master stateroom (aft, under the bridgedeck) is large and features a bathtub in the head. The guest stateroom is forward, and there's a third sleeping area in a small compartment abaft the engine room. With Tempest's unique "T-Torque" drive system, the shafts (fixed an at 8° down-angle) extend through the transom. The Tempest 60 performs well at speed (when the props are partially exposed) and in shallow water. Standard 1,050-hp Cats provide an exhilarating 35-knot cruising speed and 40+ knots top. ❑

SPECIFICATIONS

Length	60'0"
Length WL	NA
Beam	15'9"
Draft	3'6"
Weight	50,000#
Clearance	NA
Water	250 Gals.
Fuel	1,000 Gals.
Hull Type	Modified-V
Designer	P. Scanu

Production
1988–Current

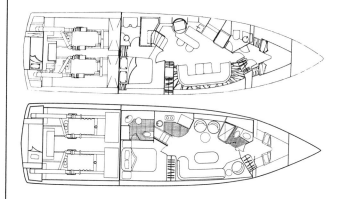

DAVIS 61 SPORTFISHERMAN

The Davis 61 SF is one of the most seductively beautiful yachts ever to roll out of a production yard. Yet behind that classic sportfish profile and aggressive styling lurks the heart of a proven big-game tournament-winner with truly outstanding performance capabilities. Indeed, it's been said many times that her ability to run into a head sea is better than any other boat in her class. In the Davis 61, a buyer can get the look and feel of a very expensive custom boat for the price of a high-quality production model. The result is a luxury sportfisherman with an elegant teak interior, four state-rooms (two with double berths), and a huge fishing cockpit with a teak sole and covering boards. Other features include cockpit access to the engine room, a stunning custom teak helm console on the flybridge with Panish controls and pop-up electronics display, and the availability of huge 1,400-hp 16V92s for an honest 31-knot cruising speed. Standard 1,040-hp 12V92s cruise at 27 knots (with a tower and full fuel) and reach a top speed of 31 knots. A good-selling boat, nearly 50 have been built. ❏

SPECIFICATIONS

Length	61'0"
Beam	17'6"
Draft	5'8"
Weight	80,000#
Clearance	18'0"
Water	250 Gals.
Fuel	1,550 Gals.
Cockpit	185 Sq. Ft.
Hull Type	Modified-V
Designer	G. Van Tassel

Production
1987–Current

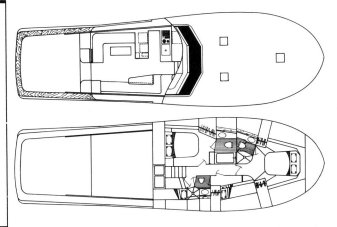

HIGH-TECH 63 EURO MY

The High-Tech 63 is among only a handful of truly distinctive production yachts now being imported from Taiwan. Built by Johnson Yachts and styled with the pure Italian profile of an Azimut or Posillipo, she's constructed on a modified-V hull with cored hullsides and a fairly deep 16° of deadrise at the transom. The 19' beam is quite wide for a hull of this length, and the interior accommodations are as spacious as they are lush. The four-stateroom layout is totally European in execution and it's going to take a second look to tell this from a real Italian yacht. The galley and dinette are on the pilothouse level, resulting in a completely expansive and uncluttered salon with a huge wraparound settee and full view of the cockpit. The master stateroom is aft with private access via a curved salon staircase. Additional features include a stainless-and-glass salon bulhead, roomy aft deck with protective bridge overhang, and a very big flybridge. An all-around stylish package, the Johnson/High-Tech 63 will cruise at 17–18 knots with standard 735-hp 8V92s and reach a top speed of around 22 knots. ❑

SPECIFICATIONS

Length	63'0"
Length WL	55'11"
Beam	19'0"
Draft	4'5"
Weight	56,000#
Clearance	NA
Water	400 Gals.
Fuel	1,000 Gals.
Hull Type	Modified-V
Designer	Bill Dixon

Production
1990–Current

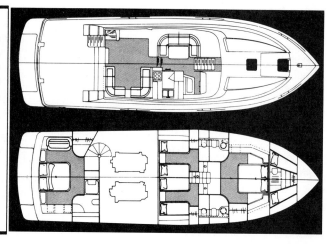

VANTARE 58/64 COCKPIT MY

With her short foredeck and some-what bulky profile, the Vantare 58 and 64 CMY (pictured above) may not have the most graceful profiles in the marina but both have the interior volume of larger boats. (The difference between the two is the cockpit of the 64.) They're built by CHB in Taiwan using a fully cored modified-V hull (10° transom deadrise) and modern high-tech glass laminates. The standard four-stateroom layout is fairly conventional with two exceptions: one of the guest staterooms serves as an office with a built-in desk and bookshelves, and the

Vantare's pilothouse is particularly large. The full-width salon is open to the galley and sliding glass doors lead to the semi-enclosed afterdeck. Light oak or traditional teak cabinetry and wood-work are used throughout the interior. (Note that many have been delivered with semi-custom layouts, and that the 64 CMY is offered with the engine room aft (with V-drives) and a more spacious lower-level floorplan.) Cat 375-hp diesels are standard (13–14 knots cruise). Optional 550-hp 6V92s cruise around 15 knots and 735-hp 8V92s cruise at a respectable 18–19 knots.   ❏

SPECIFICATIONS

Length	64'0"
Length WL	57'9"
Beam	17'6"
Draft	3'7"
Weight	70,000#
Clearance	19'6"
Water	390 Gals.
Fuel	1,300 Gals.
Hull Type	Modified-V
Designer	Jack Sarin

Production
1987–Current

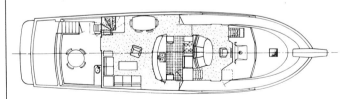

DONZI 65 SPORTFISHERMAN

Currently built on a semi-custom basis by Roscioli International, the Donzi 65 is a truly magnificent display of big-time sportfishing elegance. The beauty is more than skin deep: construction of the Donzi 65 is state-of-the-art with Divinycell hull coring and a long list of exotic materials used to create a strong and relatively lightweight structure. The hull is a modified-V design with a sharp entry forward and 12° of deadrise at the transom. The Donzi's cockpit is huge and her full-width flybridge is massive with room for a dozen people. Several three- and four-stateroom layouts are offered, and all feature a huge deckhouse with the galley forward to port. Beneath the salon sole is an extravagant stand-up engine room that runs about a third of the boat's LOA. Access is via the cockpit or through a bulkhead door next to the crew quarters. The teak or ash interior woodwork and decor appointments are all opulent in the extreme. GM 12V92s are standard, but the engines of choice have been the massive 1,440-hp 16V92s which will cruise the Donzi 65 at a fast 28 knots and reach 32 knots wide open. ❑

SPECIFICATIONS

Length	65'0"
Beam	18'8"
Draft	5'2"
Weight	72,000#
Clearance	14'4"
Water	350 Gals.
Fuel	2000 Gals.
Cockpit	NA
Hull Type	Modified-V
Designer	John Garland

Production
1987–Current

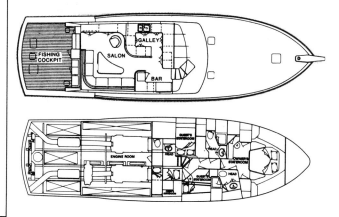

ADDRESSES

The following addresses and phone numbers are provided for manufacturers or importers whose boats are listed in the Notable Designs chapter. (Note that several manufacturers whose products are listed in this chapter are now out of business.)

Albemarle Boats
PO Box 349
Edenton, NC 27932
(919) 482-7423

Aquarius Marine
29-1 Hsin Lung Rd.
Ping Chen Chun, Taiwan
(03) 469-5066

Astilleros KB, S.A.
Ayacucho 344
S. Fernando (1646), Argentina
(541) 745-0305

Bimini Marine
Foot of Bay Avenue
Point Pleasant, NJ 08742
(908) 899-1801

Black Watch
Little Harbor Landing
Portsmouth, RI 02871
(401) 683-5777

Boating Corp. of America
PO Box 8126
Gallatin, TN 37066
(615) 452-4343

Boston Whaler
1149 Hingham St.
Rockland, MA 02370
(617) 871-1400

Brendan 32 (see Shannon Boat Co.)

Cabo 35 (see Cat Harbor Boats)

Cabo Rico Yachts
2258 SE 17th St.
Ft. Lauderdale, FL 33316
(305) 462-6699

Cape Dory (see Newport Shipyards)

Carmargue Yachts
29 Hsin Yeh Rd.
Ta Fa Ind. Dist.
Kaohsiung, Taiwan
(07) 782-2867

Cat Harbor Boats
9780 Rancho Rd.
Adelanto, CA 92301
(619) 246-8917

Chase 38 (see Cabo Rico)

Contender Boats
395 NE 59th St.
Miami, FL 33137
(305) 759-0690

Davis Yachts
PO Box 609
Wanchese, NC 27981
(919) 473-1111

Dawson Yachts
River Rd.
Lower Bank, NJ 08215
(609) 965-5757

Delta Boats
770 Mullet Rd.
Cape Canaveral, FL 32920
(407) 783-3536

Donzi 65 (see Roscioli)

Doral Boats
PO Box 667
Grand-Mere, Quebec G9T 5L4
(819) 533-5735

Duffy & Duffy Boats
Brooklin, ME 04616
(207) 359-4600

Dyer Boats (see The Anchorage)

Eagle 32 (see Transpac Marine)

Ellis Boat Co.
Seawall Road
Manset, ME 04656
(207) 244-9222

Embassy Yachts
Stutson Street Extension
Rochester, NY 14612
(716) 342-5150

Falmouth Yachts
510 31st St.
Newport Beach, CA 92663
(714) 723-4225

Fleming 53 (see Falmouth Yachts)

Formula (See Thunderbird Products)

Four Winns
925 Frisbie St.
Cadillac, MI 49601
(616) 775-1351

Hans Christian
7078 Bembe Beach Rd.
Annapolis, MD 21403
(301) 268-4213

High-Tech
1535 17th Street Quay
Ft. Lauderdale, FL 33316
(305) 524-6911

Hinckley Co.
Shore Rd.
Southwest Harbor, ME 04679
(207) 244-5531

Hylas 47 (see Queen Long)

Independence 45 (see Hans Christian)

Innovator Boats
2507 West Coast Hwy., #201
Newport Beach, CA 92663
(714) 645-8020

Intercontinental Yachts
2509 NASA Rd. 1
Seabrook, TX 77586
(714) 474-4101

Intrepid Powerboats
6101 45th St.
St. Petersburg, FL 33714
(813) 528-1086

Kadey-Krogen Yachts
1310 NW 18th Ave.
Miami, FL 33125
(305) 326-0266

Kha Sing
10 Kuang Yang St.
Hsiao Kang
Kaohsiung, Taiwan
(07) 802-0345

Krogen (see Kadey-Krogen)

Kong & Halvorsen
Box 79259
Mongkok Post Office
Kowloon, Hong Kong

Little Harbor
One Little Harbor Landing
Portsmouth, RI 02871
(401) 683-5600

Lord Nelson Yachts
927 N. Northlake Way
Seattle, WA 98103
(206) 548-1017

Luhrs
255 Diesel Rd.
St. Augustine, FL 32086
(904) 829-0500

Mainship
255 Diesel Rd.
St. Augustine, FL 32086
(904) 829-0500

Marinette
(see Boating Corp. of America)

Mediterranean Yachts
2500 S. Susan St.
Santa Ana, CA 92704
(714) 556-8920

Midnight Lace (see Rex Meyer Yachts)

Mikelson Yachts
2330 Shelter Island Dr., #202
San Diego, CA 92106
(619) 222-5007

Nauset Marine
Route 6A
Orleans, MA, 02653
(508) 255-0777

Nautique Yachts
100 Central 2nd St.
Kaohsiung 811, Taiwan
(07) 363-1201

Newport Shipyards
97 Broad Common Rd.
Bristol, RI 02809
(401) 253-4343

Nordhavn (see Pacific-Asian Ent.)

Nordic Tugs
1197 Westar Lane
Burlington, WA 98233
(206) 757-8847

Nova Marine
6/F-8, 375, Hsin Yi Rd., Sec. 4
Taipei, Taiwan
(02) 701-5254

Offshore Yachts
3404 Via Oporto, #201
Newport Beach, CA 92663
(714) 673-5401

Orca Yachts
515 Seabreeze Blvd.
Ft. Lauderdale, FL 33316
(305) 522-4535

Pace Yachts (see Nautique Yachts)

Pacific Asian Ent.
Dana Point, CA 92629
(714) 496-4848

Pacifica Yachts
928 W. 17th St.
Costa Mesa, CA 92627
(714) 645-5570

Performer Yachts
2510 Professional Dr.
Richmond, VA 23235
(804) 320-2777

Pilgrim Yachts
100 Rosedale Valley Rd.
Toronto, Ontario, M4W 1P7
(416) 920-6059

Portsmouth Boat Co.
22 Strad Rd., Box 457
Seabrook, NH 03874
(603) 929-1088

Queen Long Marine
#4 Tung Ya Rd.
Kaohsiung, Taiwan
(07) 831-5216

Regal Marine
2300 Jet Port Dr.
Orlando, FL 32809
(407) 851-4360

Rex Meyer Yachts
1470 Dolger Place
Sanford, FL 32771
(800) 323-6108

Ronin (see Ta Chiao)

Roscioli Int'l
3201 State Rd. 84.
Ft. Lauderdale, FL 33312
(305) 581-9200

Sabre Yachts
PO Box 10
South Casco, ME 04077
(207) 655-3831

Sabreline (see Sabre Yachts)

Shamrock Marine
PO Box 150189
Cape Coral, FL 33915
(813) 574-4612

Shannon Boat Co.
Box 388, 19 Broad Common Rd.
Bristol, RI 02809
(401) 253-2441

Silverton
255 Diesel Rd.
St. Augustine, FL 32086
(904) 829-0500

Stamas Yachts
300 Pampas Ave.
Tarpon Springs, FL 34689
(813) 937-4118

Stevens Motor Yachts
PO Box 4
Stevensville, MD 21666
(301) 643-7569

Ta Chiao
12-1 Su Toe
Pali Shiang, Taipei Hsien
Taiwan, (02) 618-3611

Tango (see Astilleros KB)

Tempest Yachts
3333 NE 188th St.
North Miami Beach, FL 33180
(305) 937-4400

The Anchorage
57 Miller St.
Warren, RI 02885
(401) 245-3300

Thunderbird Products
PO Box 501
Decatur, IN 46733
(219) 724-9111

Transpac Marine
Wu Ku PO Box 15
Taipei, Taiwan 24899
(02) 618-3621

Tung Hwa Ind.
#205 Wan-Tan Rd.
Ping-Tong Hsien, Taiwan
(08) 777-2333

Vantare, Int'l.
809 Fairview Place North
Seattle, WA 98108
(206) 624-9199

W.C. Hyatt
400 Utica Pike
Jeffersonville, IN 47130
(812) 282-3569

West Bay Boat Builders
8295 River Rd.
Delta, B.C. (Canada) V4G 1B4
(604) 946-6224

Wilbur
Lee S. Wilbur, Inc.
Seawall Rd.
Manset, ME 04656
(207) 244-5000

Willard Marine
1250 N. Grove St.
Anaheim, CA 92806
(714) 666-2150

Yacht Style
Design and Decor Ideas from the World's Finest Yachts
by Dan Spurr

*"This is no mere coffee-table book. Frequent checklists and pithy sidebar 'Interviews' of
top designers address various design attributes."* —Cruising World

*"Spurr's text, including yacht profiles, interviews, and straight-ahead practical informa-
tion, would be valuable enough to attract the sailor's hand even with ut the lavish photos
of gleaming brightwork and stainless, polished brass and glowing dials."*
—Sailing World

*"An exciting book . . . both beautiful and useful . . . Spurr gives you intelligent, objective
discussions of what you're looking at in the spectacular photographs."* —WoodenBoat

With this book you can transform your boat into a yacht, and have fun doing it. Printed
in full color throughout, *Yacht Style*'s 500 stunning photographs offer a wealth of innovative solutions to questions of light, space, color, materials, access, and stowage in boats
from small cruisers to megayachts, both power and sail. Dan Spurr's lively and often
opinionated text is further enhanced by a dozen profiles of individual boats plus 16
interviews with such luminaries as powerboat designer Tom Fexas, cruising sailboat
designer Robert Perry, and yacht interior designer Blanche Bloomfield. This is the boat
owner's ultimate idea book, with hundreds of suggestions for improving your boat. 350
pages, 550 illus. (including 523 color photos). $49.95 hardcover. Book No. 60130.

Boatowner's Mechanical and Electrical Manual
How to Maintain, Repair, and Improve Your Boat's Essential Systems
by Nigel Calder

*"An impressive compilation of advice on boat equipment and systems—one of the best
we've seen. The drawings are excellent and the text will aid the average boat owner in
performing most maintenance and repair jobs. Much of the information cannot be found
anywhere else."* —Practical Sailor

"This book should come as standard equipment with every boat." —SAIL

"Possibly the most thorough volume on boat maintenance ever produced." —Better Boat

*"A major achievement for both author and publisher. It would be hard to imagine any-
thing going wrong on a boat that couldn't be figured out with this book at hand; the price
is a bargain."* —Sailing World

"Well worth the price." —Powerboat Reports

Calder walks the reader through the repair, maintenance, and setting up of the boat's primary systems, including the electrical system, electronics equipment, generator sets, solar
panels, wind and water generators, the engine, transmission, refrigeration and air conditioning, waste disposal systems, pumps, steering, stoves, heaters, lanterns, spars, standing and running rigging, and furling systems—all the areas on any boat—sail or power—
most prone to problems. Destined to be a highly trusted, grease-encrusted companion
aboard boats of all types. 544 pages, 300 photos. $39.95 hardcover. Book No. 60128.

Brightwork
The Art of Finishing Wood
by Rebecca Wittman

"Packed with useful information for both amateur and professional refinishers alike . . . . a first class and highly readable text that should be mandatory reading for anyone who owns or is contemplating owning a wood-trimmed vessel . . . . the book's only drawback is that it's so beautifully illustrated that you'll need to buy a second copy to replace the one assigned to your coffee table." —Sailing

"There's no doubt Wittman is a wood finishing pro." —The Ensign

A rarity among boating and boat maintenance books: a *beautiful* how-to book, with 59 lush four-color photographs that celebrate the incomparable look and texture of oiled, varnished, and bare wood surfaces on boats. Rebecca Wittman's meticulously thorough yet graceful and entertaining text details in 17 chapters how to achieve stunning results. Two excerpts from the book, which appeared in *WoodenBoat* in 1988, elicited more favorable letters from readers than anything else the magazine has published in recent years. Brightwork in any guise is the crowning touch that elevates one boat in an anchorage above the rest. 182 pages, 59 four-color photos. $34.95 hardcover. Book No. 60129.

The Fiberglass Boat Repair Manual
by Allan H. Vaitses

"The aroma of resin wafting out of this manual is refreshing. This book will save you money and grief before you can say woven roving." —Sailing

"Represents the distillation of half a lifetime of experience . . . . filled with excellent drawings that serve as almost infallible guides . . . ." —SAIL

". . . a valuable addition to the library of any boater who is seriously interested in doing his own repairs, as well as intercepting minor problems before they become major projects. The section on recognizing and repairing saturated cores would, by itself, justify the price of this book for most conscientious boat owners." —Better Boat

"Whether it's a deteriorated gel coat, a hole, a delaminated deck, or the need to add heavier hardware, [Vaitses] can tell you how to fix it." —The Ensign

This is the definitive book on the subject, covering not just cosmetic dings and scratches, but also major repairs of structural damage to hull and decks—delamination, refinishing, blistering, etc. A manual for the owner of a sail or power boat, large or small, who desires an encyclopedic source for the care of his or her boat. Also invaluable for anyone seeking to buy and restore an old and perhaps damaged boat. 192 pages, 200 illus. $29.95 hardcover. Book No. 60530.

The International Marine Boat Manager
Your Vessel's Custom Handbook of Operating and Service Procedures
by Bob Payne & Nick Ellison

This unique handbook is an onboard fingertip reference covering step-by-step responses to any emergency, pre- and post-voyage checklists, mechanical and electrical troubleshooting, and other vital topics. It is also (and herein lies its uniqueness) a fill-in-the-blanks prompter. It asks you to look at your boat system by system—engine, electronics, steering, etc.—and record each detail of information about each piece of equipment on board. This creates a guided tour, in writing, of your boat, and provides instant access to model numbers, maintenance histories, and manufacturer and dealer information. The result is invaluable when you need to order replacements, buy insurance, or charter or sell your boat. The *Boat Manager* could mean the difference between a day on the water and a day on the telephone; it may even mean the difference between a disaster and a crisis overcome. Liberally sprinkled throughout with synopses of operating and emergency procedures, it is an instant reference for those times when information is needed *fast*. Spiralbound, 310 pages. $24.95 spiralbound. Book No. 60284.

Runabout Renovation
How to Find and Fix Up an Old Fiberglass Speedboat
by Jim Anderson

"If you're planning to buy a used boat, Anderson's book will help you during inspection, surveying and making a sound offer."　　　　　　　　　　　　—The Ensign

Here is a complete guide to turning a rundown fiberglass runabout into a real showpiece. Author Jim Anderson, a professional runabout renovator, leads you through the whole process—choosing and surveying a boat, replacing the floor, building a new transom, cosmetic repairs and repainting, reupholstering and adding new carpet to the interior, upgrading the electrical and mechanical systems, and more. There's even a section on how to repair aluminum boats. You'll find everything you need to know to own a better boat than you can buy new, for half the price or less. And rejuvenated runabouts have more class. 152 pages, 75 illus. $14.95 paperbound. Book No. 60271.

Getting Started in Powerboating
The Guide to Selection and Seamanship
by Captain Bob Armstrong

" . . . tells how to read between the lines of magazine boat reviews and tests."
　　　　　　　　　　　　—Soundings

The first single-source reference guide for powerboaters. Covers how to choose a boat, boat handling, displacement, planing, and semidisplacement hull characteristics, engines and drive trains, and more. Includes invaluable discussions on docking, spring lines, and heavy weather. A delivery skipper, private yacht captain, and boat reviewer, Bob Armstrong is well known to readers of *Power and Motoryacht*, *Boating*, and *Motorboat* magazines. 224 pages, 175 illus. $17.95 paperbound. Book No. 60214.

Marine Diesel Engines
Maintenance, Troubleshooting, and Repair
Second Edition
by Nigel Calder

"Many boatmen less adept in the wrench arts might be intimidated by things Nigel Calder can do in his sleep. However, if you're drifting around offshore you'll try things that you'd never dream of back in the marina, and if Marine Diesel Engines *saves you a tow it's paid for itself 20 times over."*　　　　　　　—Power and Motoryacht

"Particularly valuable are the chapters on troubleshooting, gearboxes, and engine installation."　　　　　　　　　　　　—Better Boat

Since its publication in 1987, Nigel Calder's *Marine Diesel Engines* has been the most respected—and best-selling—book ever written to guide the owners of marine diesels through the labyrinth of maintenance and repair. Now completely revised and expanded to cover the larger turbocharged diesels found aboard cruisers and sportfishing boats, the second edition is even more comprehensive and easier to understand, with all-new troubleshooting and maintenance charts, and 50 new illustrations. 224 pages, 246 illus. $24.95 hardcover. Book No. 60295.

Look for These and Other International Marine Books at Your Local Bookstore

To Order Call Toll Free 1-800-822-8158

(outside the U.S., call 717-794-2191)

or write to International Marine, A Division of TAB Books,
Blue Ridge Summit, PA 17294-0840.

Title	Product No.	Quantity	Price

☐ Check or money order made payable to TAB Books

Charge my
☐ VISA ☐ Mastercard ☐ American Express

Acct. No. _____ Exp. _____

Signature _____

Name _____

Address _____

City _____

State _____ Zip _____

Subtotal: _____

Postage and Handling: _____
($3.00 in U.S., $5.00 outside U.S.):

Add applicable state and local sales tax:: _____

TOTAL _____

International Marine catalog free with purchase; otherwise send $1.00 in check or money order and receive $1.00 credit on your next purchase.

Orders outside U.S. must pay with international money order in U.S. dollars.

If for any reason you are not satisfied with the book(s) you order, simply return it (them) within 15 days and receive a full refund.